D1505405

Energy
Consumption in
Manufacturing

A Report to the Energy Policy Project of the Ford Foundation

Energy Consumption in Manufacturing

John G. Myers   Bernard A. Gelb   Leonard Nakamura

Noreen Preston   Elisabeth K. Rabitsch

Paul A. Parker   M.F. Elliott–Jones

Mark Wehle   Hirohiko Chiba

Saul Levmore   Anthony D. Apostolides

Barry Kolatch   Nancy Garvey

of

The Conference Board

This study was supported by the Research Applied to National Needs division of The National Science Foundation, the Energy Policy Project of the Ford Foundation, and the Energy Information Center of The Conference Board

Ballinger Publishing Company ● Cambridge, Mass.
A Subsidiary of J.B. Lippincott Company

Published in the United States of America by Ballinger Publishing Company, Cambridge, Mass.

First Printing, 1974

Library of Congress Catalog Card Number: 74–8111

International Standard Book Number: 0–88410–307–2
                                    0–88410–323–4 (pbk.)

Printed in the United States of America

Library of Congress Cataloging in Publication Data

Conference Board.
        Energy consumption in manufacturing.
        Includes bibliographies.
        1. Energy policy—United States. 2. United States—Industries.
I. Myers, John G. Joint Author II. Title.
HD9502.U52C66 1974   338.4   74–8111
ISBN 0–88410–307–2
ISBN 0–88410–323–4 (pbk.)

Contents

v

Chapter Seven
Bread, Cake, and Related Products—SIC 2051   153
Saul Levmore

Part Two
Paper Industries (see also Chapter 32)

Chapter Eight
Corrugated and Solid Fiber Boxes—SIC 2653   161
Paul A. Parker

List of Figures

List of Charts

List of Tables

Note

This volume is a report on a study begun in 1972 to determine trends in energy use in manufacturing, to explain these trends in terms of production processes and technology in selected manufacturing industries, and to project energy use in manufacturing to 1980. Six groups of industries in manufacturing were selected for intensive study by reason of their predominant position as heavy energy users. These groups are food industries, paper industries, chemicals industries, petroleum and coal products industries, stone, clay, and glass industries, and primary metal industries. Together they account for nearly four-fifths of all energy use in manufacturing.

Our study was prepared in fulfillment of research contracts with The Energy Policy Project of the Ford Foundation and the Research Applied to National Needs Division of the National Science Foundation. We are grateful to them not only for their financial support but also for encouraging The Conference Board's research interest in an important field.

Acknowledgments

We wish to acknowledge our substantial debts.

The first is to the hundreds of companies who responded to our surveys. They devoted large amounts of time to fill out mail questionnaires, to participate in personal interviews, and to carry on lengthy telephone calls. Valuable information, advice, and criticism resulted from these contacts. The majority of the companies are Associates of The Conference Board.

The second large debt is to employees of the U.S. Census Bureau and other government agencies who provided data, technical advice and assistance, and guidance. These were furnished, often at very short notice, in a most cooperative spirit.

Thanks are also due to the large number of consultants and experts in trade associations and other groups who gave generously of their time and effort.

This report is based on the joint work of a large number of persons, including the authors of the several chapters as well as a large segment of the staff of The Conference Board who devoted many long hours of hard work to the production of this volume.

Professor Clopper Almon, Jr., and his staff of the Maryland Interindustry Forecasting Project contributed valuable advice and produced at short notice the data that underlie most of the projections.

We received from many persons valuable criticism of an early version of this report. Their comments helped us to improve the quality of the report and to avoid some serious errors.

Our thanks to one and all.

The Authors

Chapter One

Summary Report

John G. Myers

SECTION I. INTRODUCTION AND PRINCIPAL FINDINGS

The industrial sector of the economy absorbs about 40% of all fuels and electricity consumed in the U.S. Most of that figure represents energy used in manufacturing for heat and power. Future energy use by manufacturing is therefore a very important factor in determining how the nation will cope with its energy problems now and during the rest of the 1970s.

In the preparation of projections of future demand and supply of energy for the economy, industrial use and, frequently, other uses are often projected in simplistic fashion, assuming either that the present relationship between energy use and physical output will continue into the future or, somewhat better, that the overall trend of the past will continue. The study described here is based on the premise that much more accurate projections of energy use could be made by studying in detail the heaviest energy users among manufacturing industries.

A major portion of the study is devoted to examining and understanding past developments in energy use, in terms of changes in production processes and technology. A second goal is to identify, insofar as possible, changes in processes and technology that are likely to be introduced within the next seven years and that will have a significant effect on energy use. With the aid of this information, considerably more accurate guides to future energy demand by the manufacturing sector can be prepared. An additional objective of the study is to identify industries that have or are likely to have serious problems in energy use; this information would be useful to firms, industry associations, and government in framing policies to solve such problems.

1

Principal Findings

1. Significant savings in energy use have been realized by the manufacturing sector in the past. Energy use per unit of product declined at a 1.6% average annual rate from 1954 to 1967[a]. As a result, while total manufacturing output rose 87%, total energy use rose only 53%. This was achieved in a period of stable or declining relative prices of energy.

2. There was a shift within manufacturing away from the energy-intensive industries, as a group, and toward the less-energy-intensive industries. The former are mainly basic materials producers, so this shift is part of the long-term historical development toward higher degrees of fabrication. This contributed to the decline in the energy-output ratio for all manufacturing.

3. The principal method by which energy use per unit of output was reduced was a substitution of capital embodying new technology for energy. There was also some substitution of management for energy. In the past, these developments were largely incidental to innovations designed primarily to increase productivity.

4. Capital that is substituted for energy use can be classified into two categories, housekeeping additions and those that are related to changes in production processes. Housekeeping changes are mainly directed toward preventing energy waste and can generally be introduced more quickly than capital related to process changes, but both types go on simultaneously.

5. Recent sharp increases in energy prices, together with present and expected interruptions in supplies of energy, will result in an acceleration in energy savings in manufacturing. The projections presented in this report indicate that energy use per unit of output will decline at an average rate of 2.0% from 1967 to 1980.

6. The projected rate of decline is based on the most likely changes that will take place, in the judgments of the authors of the industry essays. The existing stock of productive equipment and likely rate of replacement in the industries studied were taken into account, together with known technology. Because of this, the projections represent economically probable developments, rather than technically possible optimums.

7. The large energy users in manufacturing are: primary metal industries; chemicals industries; petroleum and coal products industries; stone, clay, and glass industries; paper industries; and food industries. In 1967, these accounted for 77% of all purchased energy used in manufacturing (excluding captive energy produced within an industry). These groups reduced their energy use per unit of output in the period from 1954 to 1967 at a rapid (1.4%) rate,[b]

---

[a]Gross energy consumed, including "captive consumption" of the petroleum refining and the blast furnaces and steel mills industries. See Table 1-5. Captive consumption is described in "5. Energy data" in Section II of this chapter.

[b]Including "captive consumption" of the petroleum refining and blast furnaces and steel mills industries. See Table 1-5.

and they are projected to accelerate their energy saving per unit of output in the future, particularly from 1975 to 1980.

8. In addition, the shift from the energy-intensive to the less energy-intensive industries observed in the past should accelerate. This is a further response to the relative rise in energy prices, which favors the less-energy-intensive industries as compared with the energy-intensive industries.

9. Improved management practices can result in substantial energy savings in the very short run but do not have the potential for long-term energy savings that capital substitution does.

10. There is an increasing use of BTU accounting in manufacturing. In this system careful track is kept of all energy-bearing materials that enter a plant in order to determine where energy is used. This approach permits the detection of problem areas where energy savings can be instituted. Wider application of BTU accounting holds promise for further reducing energy use in manufacturing.

11. There is little knowledge of the amount of past savings in energy use within industry. This is particularly true at the plant level but extends throughout all levels in many manufacturing industries. One result of this is that individual plants or firms prepare poor projections of their energy use because they do not know past trends.

12. Data on energy use in manufacturing are difficult to obtain. Historical records for plants are generally not studied in detail within the company; frequently they are not retained. Moreover, Census data at the 4-digit level often mask trends in the industry subgroup within which an individual plant or corporation may operate. And total use of energy resources is frequently understated by the Census definition of purchased fuels and energy for heat and power. This omits captive consumption of fuels in many industries. It also omits energy derived from fuels used as raw materials (feedstocks). These data problems stem from, and contribute to, an inadequate degree of attention to the energy problem.

13. Our preliminary findings indicate a heavy use of fuels drawn from sources outside the customary energy base. An example of this is the use of wood wastes in paper production. Little statistical information is available on this point, but it deserves further attention.

14. An important factor in determining energy use per unit of output within an industry, or firm, is the product mix. This is an application of the same principle that underlies the shift from energy-intensive to other manufacturing industries. Within the range of products of a single plant, energy use per unit (for the entire plant) can rise or fall according to whether energy-intensive products become more or less important in the product mix. Rising energy prices will often, but not always lead to a change in product mix toward less-energy-intensive products.

15. There is a cyclical effect in energy use per unit of output. When

capacity utilization is low, energy use per unit is high. Similarly, when capacity utilization is very high, energy use per unit of output is often high. There is an optimum level where energy use per unit of output is minimized. When this cyclical pattern is ignored in making comparisons between energy use in two points of time, an erroneous conclusion may easily be drawn. In a similar fashion, errors can result if one ignores the effect of changes in the product mix.

16. Our study was confined to manufacturing operations, according to the Standard Industrial Classification. However, there is a substantial amount of shifting of energy use forward and back along the production process. Some of this results in apparent energy savings in manufacturing that are offset in part at least by increases in other sectors; for example, metal manufacturing industries may receive higher quality, pre-processed ore inputs, which require heavier energy use in mining. In some cases, energy use is shifted abroad, as is the case where smelting or petroleum refining is shifted outside the country and products are imported. Another example of misleading shifts is when new materials reduce energy use in one industry, but require increased energy use in other manufacturing industries — such as the change from glass to paper-and-plastic containers in the fluid milk industry and the increasing use of oxygen in the blast furnaces and steel works industry. Energy use per unit of output is thus reduced in the using industry, but energy use is increased elsewhere — in paper and plastics manufacture in the first instance, and in the manufacture of industrial gases in the second instance.

17. Energy-bearing products such as polythylene are possible sources of energy. Greater recognition of such energy resources by the consumer should be encouraged. Some energy-bearing materials, such as ethylene glycol used as anti-freeze, are very difficult to use as energy resources. In many cases these can be recycled. More important energy saving can be achieved by recycling of energy-intensive products. Obvious examples are steel, glass, paper, and aluminum. More extensive reuse of both types of materials should be encouraged.

18. The relations between control of air and water pollution and energy use are highly complex. In many cases, control of pollution, particularly in the short run, increases energy use per unit of output. In other cases, efforts to reduce air and water pollution have led to energy savings, for it has been found that the materials formerly discharged into the air or water contain energy-bearing materials or heat that can be captured.

Outline of Study

1. **Advisory group.** At the beginning of the study we decided to assemble an advisory group. The initial membership was designed to provide representation in the major industry groups: food; paper; chemicals; petroleum refining; stone, clay and glass; and primary metals. This group was of consider-

able aid to us in the early stages of our study, providing valuable advice on design of our mail survey of corporations. We soon learned, however, that we would need industry advice on a wider scale. In the several months of study, therefore, we assembled a large, informal group of advisers to supplement the initial panel. Both the formal and informal groups provided very valuable technical and critical assistance in many aspects of the study, particularly in preparation of the industry essays.

2. **Basic data and conversion factors.** An early effort in our study was to assemble a set of basic data on output and energy use in manufacturing. We determined that continuous data over several years were available for a set of 37 4-digit SIC (Standard Industrial Classification) industries; these were chosen on the bases of (1) size of total energy use and (2) affording representation within each of the six broad groups. The basic set of data was collected from the Bureau of the Census' *Census of Manufactures* from 1947 through 1967. For the 37 4-digit SIC industries, some grouping was made to provide continuity of definition for as much of the period as possible.

Data on energy, however, are reported by type of fuel. To be useful for our analysis, it was necessary to prepare a set of conversion factors in order to express the different types of fuel or energy in a common unit, the British Thermal Unit (BTU).

3. **Company survey.** A survey of companies in the six 2-digit groups was undertaken to obtain current data that would bear on a number of questions relevant to our study. The main elements of the survey, which was carried out by means of a mail questionnaire with mail and telephone follow-ups, were: (1) to determine the extent of the company perception of the current energy situation in the nation, (2) to learn the extent to which and the ways in which companies were responding to their perceptions of energy problems, (3) to collect current data on energy used by these companies, and (4) to collect data on plans for energy use to 1980.

The survey was sent to 211 companies, of which more than one-half responded with one or more questionnaires. Several of the larger companies had production facilities in more than one of the six 2-digit groups and responded for each group.

4. **Methodology and pilot studies.** The original request that led to The Conference Board study sought information on explanations of past trends and likely future developments in terms of production processes and technology in the 4-digit industries included in the six 2-digit groups. We learned that there were about 140 such 4-digit industries and that an undertaking of this magnitude was impractical. Both the size of our research staff and the limited time available prohibited us from attempting such an extensive study. Instead, we decided to

take two simultaneous approaches. The first was to select a moderate number of large energy-using industries from among the 140 in the six groups, and to prepare an essay—based mainly on published sources—for each. The second was to develop a methodology for very intensive study of energy use and to test the methodology through pilot studies. The 28 industry essays are presented in Chapters Two through Twenty-Nine, covering 32 industries at the 4-digit level. The methodology and pilot studies are presented in Chapters Thirty through Thirty-Two; the pilot studies are on aluminum, and on pulp, paper, and paperboard mills. Highlights of these 31 chapters may be found in Section III of this chapter.

5. Industry essays. The general procedure followed in preparing the industry essays was as follows:

(a) The statistics assembled from the *Census of Manufactures* were analyzed and, where possible, compared with alternative sources such as trade association or other government agency data. Examples of the latter are data from the U.S. Bureau of Mines and the U.S. Tariff Commission. Such comparisons permitted verification or correction of the basic data for some industries. In a few cases, it was decided to use the alternative source, rather than the Census statistics, as the primary body of data for the industry.

(b) The second stage was to undertake a survey of the literature on the industry. Monographs and journals were consulted to aid in understanding the products, inputs, and production processes employed, and to aid in interpreting changes in the ratio of energy use to output for the 20-year period from 1947 to 1967. An additional purpose of the literature survey was to learn of new developments and of current "best usage" that would provide clues to likely future developments in the industry, and to the potential for such developments.

(c) The author of each industry essay had access to the questionnaires obtained from the company survey. In many cases these provided useful information on specific industries, aided in providing a framework of data within which the specific industry activity or development could be studied, and perhaps most important, provided the researchers with the names of persons who could be contacted for technical information.

(d) For each industry essay, industry experts were consulted. These were drawn from the advisory group, the respondents to the company questionnaires, experts drawn from the academic world or the consulting community, and Associates of The Conference Board. When time permitted, we sent preliminary drafts of the industry essays to such persons for comment and criticism. In most cases, however, we had informal contacts, by telephone or visit, with industry representatives to obtain technical advice. Such contacts were particularly helpful in learning about past and prospective changes in production processes and technology. In all cases, we sent drafts of this report to as wide an audience as possible in order to obtain criticisms of our analysis and approach.

6. Projections of output. A variety of sources was used to obtain projections of output for the individual industries studied. The basic source, however, was obtained from the Maryland Interindustry Forecasting Model (MIFM), using projections for 1975 and 1980 prepared by the author.[1] These projections are on a "full employment" basis, set at 4.5% unemployment. The long-term rate of growth of productivity (GNP in constant dollars per man-hour) in the private sector is set at 3.0% per year. The implied rate of growth of GNP (in constant dollars) from 1971 to 1975 is 6.3% per year, and from 1975 to 1980, 4.3% per year. The reason for the more rapid rise in the earlier period is a combination of (1) recovery from the depressed level of 1971 to full employment in 1975, (2) a cyclical recovery in productivity change, and (3) a more rapid rate of growth of the labor force in the earlier part of the decade than in the latter.

The MIFM output projections, based on Conference Board assumptions as to growth of GNP and of the labor force, were prepared on a constant dollar value of production basis for all manufacturing and for 2- or 3-digit SIC groupings; for 4-digit industries, the measure obtained from the model is constant dollar sales for domestic use, defined as domestic production plus imports minus exports. The writers of the individual essays examined the MIFM projections and decided whether or not to adopt them. This was done on the basis of the importance of imports and exports in the products of the industry, and on the availability of alternative projections that seemed superior in the judgment of the individual analysts. Many alternative projections came from industry or other sources; a few were prepared by the authors of the industry essays.

In the case of the projections for all manufacturing and for 2-digit groups presented in this summary, the output forecasts of the MIFM were employed. Where the analysts had modified individual industry projections, the MIFM 2-digit group forecasts were similarly changed.

7. Projections of energy-output ratios. Two different measures of energy use have been used in this study. Both are of heat value in British Thermal Units (BTUs) and differ only in the treatment of purchased electricity. "Useful energy" (UE) measures purchased electricity in terms of its theoretical heating power (3,412 BTUs), a constant amount. "Gross energy consumed" (GEC) measures purchased electricity in terms of the average amount of fossil fuel required to make a kilowatt hour of electricity by public utilities; this quantity varies over time. Other conversion and transmission losses were not taken into account, nor energy used in producing raw materials and capital equipment. Energy-output ratios were projected on both bases: gross energy consumed per unit of output, and useful energy per unit of output. The two differ in level according to the importance of purchased electricity in the industry or group; they differ in trend because of changes in the relative importance of purchased electricity as a source of power, and because of the changing efficiency of utility plants over time, which is reflected in the GEC conversion factors.

Gross energy consumed is the relevant measure from the point of view of the economy, for it reveals the demand of the industry on the energy resource base.[c] For that reason, GEC and GEC per unit of output are the measures used in this chapter. Unless otherwise specified, "energy use" refers to gross energy consumed.

It is important to recognize that "efficiency" of production does not necessarily mean minimizing the energy-output ratio. It is, in economic terms, "efficient" to produce at the lowest possible total cost per unit. This may well mean, in some circumstances, raising the energy-output ratio (see the discussion in Section II of this chapter).

The ratios were projected on the basis of past trends, knowledge of likely changes in production processes and technology, and new capital equipment. Such knowledge was obtained from reading the literature and from discussions with experts on the individual industries.

8. Projection of total energy use. There is a simple relationship between the level of output, discussed in (6), the energy-output ratio, discussed in (7), and total energy; total energy is simply the product of the level of output and the energy-output ratio. Errors in the projections of either total shipments or the energy-output ratio will, of course, cause errors in the projections of total energy. The results summarized in this volume are subject to errors from both sources, but they have been prepared as carefully as was feasible by the authors of the several chapters and were compared and analyzed for consistency.

SECTION II.   APPROACH, HISTORY, AND PROJECTIONS

Conceptual Questions and Data Sources

1. Derived demand. The demand for energy in manufacturing stems from the demand for the product the energy is used to produce; in technical economics the manufacturing demand for energy is a derived demand. Several characteristics of the demand for energy can be deduced from this definition. The first is that the response of a manufacturer's demand for energy depends on

---

[c]Further discussion may be found in Section II of this chapter, under "5. Energy Data," and in Chapter Thirty, on methodology.

how responsive sales of his product are to price changes. If the price of energy rises substantially, he will decrease his total energy use according to how far his sales will decline when he passes on the energy cost increase to his buyers. The rise in the price of energy, therefore, will have differing effects from industry to industry according to how much sales fall off when the energy price increase is incorporated in the price of the product produced.

The second consequence is that a rise in the price of energy will reduce a manufacturer's demand for energy further the more easily he can substitute other productive resources, such as capital equipment or labor, for energy. If only one production process is known, for example, the ratio of energy to output may be comparatively stable. On the other hand, in many manufacturing processes it is possible to recover waste heat, or to reuse wastes to produce energy. Such operations often require capital investment, which is, in fact, a substitution of capital for energy.

The third important factor depends on the availability of other factors, and on the response of their prices to increases in demand. If there were a rush toward purchase of heat-recovery equipment over a short period of time the price of such equipment might be raised sharply, which would lead to less energy saving in the short run, because it would be uneconomical to make a substitution of capital for energy.

In this study, we have examined a broad range of industries in terms of their energy use over time, and have attempted to explain changes in energy use in terms of production processes, product mix, and other aspects of operations within the industries. We have not examined the other two factors mentioned above, namely, the demand response to price changes in each industry's products, and the price response of capital goods that could be substituted for energy in manufacturing. These two considerations are important qualifications of the possibilities of increasing energy savings beyond the rates that we have projected. Although production processes may exist that would lead to more energy savings than projected, these may be too costly to be economical to manufacturers.

The ways energy can be saved may be classified into two broad groups: "housekeeping" changes, such as the capture of process heat and the conversion of "wastes" to sources of energy; and changes in production processes to those that use less energy per unit of output. Both usually require capital investment. The former most often entail capital additions, which represent the substitution of capital for purchased energy. There are also some housekeeping changes, such as control over electricity and gasoline use, that require only more careful management. Process changes usually require capital replacement, for the equipment associated with an old process is often unusable with the new. A few housekeeping changes require capital replacement as well, such as the replacement of smoke stacks, distilling towers, furnaces, and steam pipes.

Both capital additions and capital replacement depend on a number of factors, including the age structure of existing plants, the rate of construction of new capital equipment, capital goods prices, interest rates (for borrowing or alternative investment), and the difference in energy intensity between the existing plant and that proposed (new or modified).

Recently constructed plants that have several years of useful life remaining are more likely to have capital added on to save energy. Older plants are, obviously, more likely to be replaced. Capital additions do not usually achieve as much energy saving as new plants designed with energy saving in mind, yet can achieve important results.

In the short run, therefore, capital additions are likely to predominate. But the replacement of old capital by more energy-saving plant and equipment will go on continually so long as energy prices remain above past expectations.

2. Efficiency and energy use. We consider efficiency to be an economic concept related to profit maximization. If the use of a given input, such as fuel or electric energy, results in higher profits, it is "efficient" to use it. It becomes "inefficient" to use it when it is no longer profitable to do so. An example is provided by the ready-mixed concrete industry: here, capital and energy are substituted for labor, lowering total costs and increasing profits, but raising the energy-output ratio continually over time.

This apparently simple concept is somewhat ambiguous, however, since profit maximization over time usually entails additional capital investment. In this case, what is being maximized is expected future receipts less expected future costs per dollar invested, and such expectations are based on imperfect knowledge about the future. Expectations about future prices of energy, such as those collected in our surveys of manufacturing companies, suggest conceptions of the relation of energy prices to other prices that have been sharply revised since the time when much of the present capital stock in manufacturing was put into place. When energy prices were constant or falling relative to the general price level, and that pattern was expected to continue into the future, machinery was purchased and plants built in order to utilize processes that now may be inappropriate.

What is efficient in the economic sense today, therefore, is usually energy-saving, which was not necessarily the case in the past. For an existing set of capital equipment, the most efficient use is often much different from that for a new plant, which can be designed on the basis of today's conditions. Past behavior, however, that led to more energy use per unit of output, or to the use of fuels such as natural gas that later became in short supply, was not inefficient if it appeared likely to yield larger profits. The term "efficient energy utilization," or similar terms, may be misleading in discussing historical developments. For this reason, we have attempted to avoid them in this report.

An example is afforded by different methods of projecting energy use. Our projections take into account the existing stocks of production facilities and the proportion that will likely be replaced by 1975 and 1980—on the basis of expected changes in energy prices, among other things. An alternative method would be to assume that all productive facilities in 1980 would embody the (known) technology that would use least energy. The latter assumes that (1) all existing capital that does not embody, or is inconsistent with, the new technology is replaced by 1980, and that (2) energy cost is the only consideration. We do not consider this to be a realistic method. It is certainly not "efficient" in the sense stated above, for it would undoubtedly cause substantial losses to manufacturing companies if they were to scrap valuable, profit-making capital equipment. In addition, it would probably be impossible to replace all the capital stock in manufacturing by 1980.

3. **Cyclical effects.** There is often a cyclical effect in the amount of energy used per unit of output. This can be clearly seen in the behavior of the energy-output ratio for steel. In 1969, energy input per short ton of raw steel was low compared with the trend. In 1958 and 1971, energy input was high compared with the trend. Steel output was quite high, relative to capacity, in 1969, but very low in 1958 and 1971. Energy use appears to have a component similar to fixed cost, resulting in high use per unit when the level of production is low. Thus, energy is "wasted" in years when output is low relative to available capacity. One reason for this is simply the avoidance, at high levels of output, of reheating furnaces or boilers that are allowed to cool during slack periods. This problem is important in preparing projections of energy use, both per unit of output and in total. Since our projections for 1975 and 1980 are for an economy operating near full capacity, a projection from a year when output was also near capacity level is appropriate.

In some industries, another consideration emerges. As capacity limits are approached in chemicals and petroleum refining, for example, energy use per unit may increase in order to raise output. That is, as capacity becomes a limiting factor, energy-using and capital-saving methods are possible, and hence used. The main technique in these industries is to increase the number of runs per unit of time; this lowers the yield per run but increases the total yield per period of time. For example, if a given chemical process produces a product at a decreasing rate per unit of time, each processing run can be aborted earlier, when capacity is limited, to produce more output. Energy use, which is related to the run rather than to the yield per run, will then rise per unit of output. The cyclical effect is still there, but it is somewhat more complex. In periods of very high demand, when the manufacturing sector is straining to produce all that is asked of it, energy use per unit will be higher than at a point when production is near its most economically efficient rate.

This illustrates that the energy-output ratio is similar to the labor-output ratio (the reciprocal of labor productivity). The labor-output ratio declines as output expands until the most "efficient" operating rate is found (this is at the bottom of the average total cost curve); beyond that point, labor use per unit begins to rise.

4. Measurement of output. The basic source for our production measure is the Census output indexes. These are indexes of physical quantities produced computed by the Census Bureau between pairs of Census years. They thus cover the periods 1947-1954, 1954-1958, 1958-1963, and 1963-1967. The version we chose, of the three versions available, is the "cross-weighted" index. In this version, each commodity is weighted by the average unit value in the two Census years. For example, the index for blast furnaces and steel mills (SIC 3312) from 1947 to 1954 measures the change in production between those years. The number of tons of pig iron shipped in 1947, weighted by the average unit value in 1947 and 1954, is in the base of the index; the numerator includes the number of tons of pig iron produced in 1954, also weighted by the average unit value in 1947 and 1954.

To obtain an output index for an industry group (2-digit SIC level), the indexes for the 4-digit industries in the group are combined using value-added weights. Similarly, the output index for all manufacturing is obtained by combining the value-added-weighted indexes of all the 2-digit groups in manufacturing. (See Appendix 2 to this chapter for a thorough discussion.)

One complicating factor arose from the fact that fuel statistics associated with the 1963 Census of Manufactures were collected for the year 1962. In order to have an output measure for the same time period as the fuel statistics, we adjusted the output index for each industry or industry group we studied by extrapolating with the Federal Reserve Board Industrial Production Index, from 1963 (back) to 1962, for the most comparable industrial group. These computations were to provide a set of four production indexes for each industry we studied. These were linked together to form a continuous index with a base of 1967 = 100. The output index combined with a measure of energy use permits us to determine whether output or energy grew more rapidly in the past, i.e., whether the ratio of energy to output was rising or falling. A further dimension can be added to this important comparison, however, by putting both measures, energy and output, in absolute terms. Then comparisons can be made between the "energy intensity" of industries; that is, the number of energy units measured in BTUs per unit of output measured in dollars of constant purchasing power. Based on our own analysis and discussions with other analysts well versed in this topic, we decided to use the value of shipments in 1967 as the basic output level of the narrowly defined industry groups (generally 4-digit SIC). For 2-digit industry groups and all manufacturing, we decided to use value added in 1967 for the level of output.

The value of shipments is shorthand for the "total value of shipments and other receipts" shown in Census statistics. It embraces the total value of products shipped by each establishment in the industry, including shipments to other plants owned by the same company, and "miscellaneous receipts," including resales and contract work. Value added is derived by subtracting the total costs of materials (including materials, supplies, fuel, electric energy, cost of resales, and miscellaneous receipts) from the value of shipments and other receipts, and by adjusting the resulting amount by the net change in the finished products and work-in-process inventories between the beginning and end of the year.[2]

The value-added measure is more appropriate for broad industry groups or sectors because it eliminates most double counting. Products produced by one 4-digit industry, for example, are frequently shipped to another 4-digit industry within the same 2-digit group, and even more frequently among 2-digit groups. The value of shipments measure is therefore inappropriate for comparing these broader groups or sectors. For the more narrowly defined industries, product as measured by shipments contains some double counting, but the problem is less serious, and major distortions appear only in a few cases. The cost of materials relative to shipments varies widely among manufacturing industries. In food and petroleum refining, for example, the ratio is quite high; in paper, and in stone, clay, and glass, it is relatively low.

In a few cases, other measures of output are available for a given industry. Examples are trade association statistics and data from the Bureau of Mines, and Tariff Commission. Such data were used to supplement or expand the analysis and were sometimes sufficient for the preparation of annual estimates, which in turn could be used to examine cyclical effects on energy use.

For the narrowly defined industries, the 1967 value of shipments was multiplied by the production index described above. The result was a measure of output in constant 1967 dollars set at the level of total shipments by the industry. For industry groups and all manufacturing, the measures represent constant dollar estimates of output set at the level of value added by the group or sector.

Finally, the output measures for 4-digit industries were extended by projections prepared or obtained by the industry analyst, or taken from the MIFM. For 2-digit manufacturing groups and for all manufacturing, the MIFM projections were used in all cases. Where changes in the MIFM projection were made at the 4-digit level, the parent 2-digit group was adjusted to the same extent, but not total manufacturing. The assumption is that the "slack" is taken up by other, less-energy-intensive manufacturing groups.

5. Energy data. The basic source of our energy information is the *U.S. Census of Manufactures* for 1947, 1954, 1958, and 1967. Energy data were collected for the same years as output and other data. For the 1963 and 1972 Censuses, energy information was collected during the annual survey of manufactures for the preceding year, and refers to the preceding year, that is 1962 and 1971.[c] As mentioned above (measurement of output), the output measure for 1963 was shifted back to 1962 by use of the FRB *Industrial Production Index.*

For all industries, except petroleum refining (SIC 2911) and blast furnaces and steel mills (SIC 3312), the Census data refer to purchased fuels and electric energy. For each fuel and for purchased electric energy, both the physical quantities and the total value are available in the Census statistics. The physical quantity figures were converted to British Thermal Units (BTUs) by means of the conversion factors shown in Appendix 3 to this chapter. These factors were chosen after a careful review of available information from several sources, including the Bureau of the Census, the Bureau of Mines, and the Federal Power Commission, and from a number of trade organizations and industry experts with whom we consulted. The factors chosen differ somewhat from those of the Census Bureau but are the most accurate insofar as we were able to determine.

As stated in Section I of this chapter, two measures of energy use were employed in this report. The first, termed "useful energy," represents the direct theoretical heat value of the fuels and purchased electricity used in manufacturing. "Gross energy" differs only in that it includes the heat losses incurred by electric utilities in the process of generating the power. These losses have amounted to about two-thirds of the total BTU input at electric utilities in recent years (see Appendix 3 to this chapter). The gross measure takes into account both the direct and the indirect calls upon energy resources by manufacturing, at least insofar as electricity is concerned. A more complete measure of gross energy demanded would have taken into account other conversion and transmission losses; one of the most important of these is the transmission loss in natural gas. Lack of time prevented us from taking other indirect energy demands into account.

For an individual industry, the gross energy use measure is incomplete in another sense, for it does not include the energy used in producing the raw materials absorbed by that industry, nor the energy used in producing the capital equipment employed by that industry. In constructing our gross energy measure we have attempted merely to carry energy use back to the power plant, but not beyond. The entire manufacturing sector, on the other hand, includes most of the production of capital equipment and raw materials, so aggregate energy for all manufacturing covers much of that expended in their production. An obvious exception is the omission of energy used in other sectors (transportation, mining, agriculture, etc.) while producing raw materials for manufacturing. Conceptually, the direct and indirect energy use for a given product

[c]Comprehensive data from the 1972 Census are not yet available (March 1974). Neither the output indexes nor detailed electricity information, at the 4-digit level have been issued. For this reason, we have not attempted to extend our historical analysis of most individual industries beyond 1967.

could be derived by means of input-output analysis, but an input-output table with the necessary detail on energy use does not exist.

While the gross energy measure is helpful in indicating the impact of an industry on total energy use, it is not a good indicator of the effects on energy use brought about by changes within the industry: this is because changes in generating efficiency of electric utilities are incorporated into the energy use totals of the manufacturing industry. As shown in Appendix 3, the average thermal efficiency of public utilities fell nearly one-third from 1947 to 1967, and then rose slightly from 1967 to 1971.

The useful energy measure, on the other hand, does not suffer from that problem and more accurately reflects technological developments as well as changes in production process and product mix on energy use over time. Yet it (UE) creates distortions if the industry generates part of its electricity internally ("captive" power plants) and the proportion changes over time. Such a development can affect the useful energy measure to a significant degree.

In the cases of petroleum refining, and blast furnaces and steel mills, the Census data provide information on "captive consumption" of energy. This concept refers to the use of raw materials—crude petroleum in the case of petroleum refining, and coal in the case of blast furnaces and steel mills—that are converted to other products and subsequently used to provide heat and power. In these industries, captive consumption often amounts to a total number of BTUs as large as those available from *purchased* fuels and electric energy. Captive consumption is important in several other industries, notably in chemicals and paper production, but is not collected in the Census surveys. In the industry reports on the chemicals and the pulp and paper industries, some estimates are presented of the quantity of captive consumption for a recent year, but these estimates are not incorporated in the statistics presented in the tables in this chapter.

Alternative conceptual schemes are possible for measuring energy use in manufacturing that would be more comprehensive and provide deeper insights. One that is particularly appealing is to measure the absorption of all energy-bearing materials by manufacturing, and to subtract from it the energy contained in all products shipped from manufacturing. In this way, the difficult problems associated with the use of energy materials both for fuels and for raw materials (of which the largest category is for feedstocks in chemicals and petroleum refining) would be appropriately taken into account, and the total demand on the energy resources base of the nation by manufacturing would be correctly measured. There are many instances where the raw materials use is not fully taken into account in the framework within which the Census data are collected. One complication with this problem is the use of materials that are not ordinarily considered to be sources of energy. Examples are the use of wastes, as in paper manufacturing.

A more instructive scheme would be to divide the measure of

absorption of energy-bearing materials by manufacturing into two groups, those normally considered as energy materials (mainly fossil fuels such as coal, natural gas, and petroleum), and other materials that are used to provide energy, such as wood. A similar division could be made of the energy content of shipments out of the manufacturing sector, for many of these eventually are used to provide energy to the nation, and undoubtedly more will be in the future. Obvious examples of these are wood, paper products, and plastics.

Sketch of Energy Use in Manufacturing

In 1967, the most recent year for which comprehensive statistics are available, the six 2-digit industry groups discussed in this report consumed 77% of all energy purchased by the manufacturing sector in the form of fuels and electricity for heat and power, figured on a gross energy consumed basis (Table 1-1). The largest energy users among the six 2-digit groups are primary metal industries (SIC 33), which used 22% of the manufacturing total, and chemicals industries (SIC 28), which also used 22%. As shown in Table 1-4, on a value of shipments basis the energy-output ratio was highest for stone, clay and glass, followed by chemicals, primary metals, and petroleum and coal products. When related (more correctly) to value added, it is seen that the most "energy-intensive" group is petroleum and coal products, followed by: primary metals; stone, clay and glass; and paper. The reason for using energy per unit of value added, as discussed earlier, is to eliminate two effects — double counting in the shipments data among establishments in the same 2-digit group and, in particular, the related problem of combining establishments that represent two stages in the production process: primary and secondary production. If two industries used the same quantity of energy per unit of value added, and the inputs to the second were the shipments of the first, the first (or primary) industry would have a much higher energy-shipments ratio than the second, merely because the shipments of the second, or fabricating industry, would include the costs of buying the shipments of the primary industry, greatly increasing the denominator of the energy-shipments ratio.

Turning to the 37 detailed industries that we have studied, a tabulation of all purchased energy in 1967 reveals that they account for 64% of the total for all manufacturing (Table 1-4). Individual large users of energy are blast furnaces and steel mills (SIC 3312), accounting for 12% of all manufacturing; petroleum refining (SIC 2911), 9%; industrial inorganic chemicals, n.e.c. (SIC 2819), 6%; and industrial organic chemicals, n.e.c. (SIC 2818), 6%. These four account for one-third of all purchased energy used in total manufacturing. The essays devoted to these industries reflect their importance as energy users. At the other extreme, frozen fruits and vegetables (SIC 2037), and nonferrous wire drawing, insulating (SIC 3357), each use only 0.2% of the manufacturing total, and the essays devoted to these two industries are correspondingly brief.

If we measure "energy intensity" as the number of BTUs per dollar of output, we find that the most energy-intensive industries are not necessarily the largest users. The manufacture of lime (SIC 3274) is by far the most energy intensive, whether measured on the basis of energy per dollar of shipments or of value added, yet it accounts for only 0.5% of energy use in manufacturing. Other highly energy-intensive industries are hydraulic cement (SIC 3241), alkalies and chlorine (SIC 2812), primary aluminum (SIC 3334), and electrometallurgical products (SIC 3313). The rankings differ between energy per dollar of shipments and energy per dollar of value added, but these industries are highly energy-intensive on either basis. They consume 3.3%, 1.7%, 3.8%, and 0.8%, respectively, of the manufacturing total, so only the cement and aluminum industries might be considered heavy aggregate users of energy.

In the 13-year period from 1954 to 1967, the energy-output ratio for all manufacturing fell substantially (Table 1-5). When only purchased energy is included, the ratio declines at a 1.3% annual rate. When the captive consumption of petroleum refining and steel making is included, the rate of decline is 1.6% per year. The most rapidly declining industries were chemicals, which fell at more than twice the overall rate, followed by food, and stone, clay and glass. The other industries showed more modest rates of decline. Petroleum and coal products increased their purchased energy per unit, but their energy per unit dropped when captive consumption is included. The explanation for this is the substitution of purchased energy, largely from natural gas, for captive energy, largely from petroleum products, in petroleum refining; substantial net savings were found for the combination of purchased and captive energy, per unit of output (Chart 1-4). Other manufacturing, the 15 2-digit groups that are not highly energy-intensive groups, showed slower energy saving per unit than the average of the 6 energy-intensive groups.

The fact that purchased energy per unit in all manufacturing showed a more rapid decline (1.3%) than either (1) the average of the six energy-intensive groups (1.2%), or (2) the average of other manufacturing (1.0%), reveals a shift in weight away from the energy-intensive industries and toward the less energy-intensive. The large energy-using industries, which are principally primary producers, that is, in early stages of the manufacturing process, are declining in relative importance in manufacturing. This reflects the trend toward a greater degree of fabrication in manufacturing, a trend that has its origins in the earliest stages of industrial development, or even before.

The Energy Problem in Manufacturing

The years since 1967 have shown rapid change in energy supply conditions. All sectors of the economy have been affected by a mounting wave of higher prices and supply difficulties. The reasons for this are complex and will not be gone into here. In the last year, shortages and rapidly increasing energy

Table 1-1   Gross Energy Consumed by High-Energy-Using Manufacturing Groups, Selected Years 1947-1980
(trillion BTUs)

	1947	1954	1958	1962	1967	1971	1975	1980
Purchased by all manufacturing plus energy produced and consumed in the same establishment ("captive consumption") by SICs 2911 and 3312	10,535	11,934	13,057	14,941	18,264	19,864	24,167	27,763
Purchased by all manufacturing	8,738	9,766	10,696	12,485	15,463	17,060	20,919	24,383
By six high-energy-using 2-digit groups								
Food and kindred products (SIC 20)	857	883	951	992	1,098	1,286	1,284	1,453
Paper and allied products (SIC 26)	635	801	932	1,068	1,367	1,560	1,725	1,771
Chemicals and allied products (SIC 28)	1,023	1,753	2,282	2,592	3,257	3,473	4,997	6,020
Petroleum and coal products (SIC 29)	550	695	1,018	1,252	1,543	1,820	2,083	2,302
Stone, clay, and glass products (SIC 32)	929	1,032	1,058	1,178	1,341	1,444	1,617	1,864
Primary metal industries (SIC 33)	2,547	2,499	2,182	2,833	3,340	3,364	4,031	4,655
Sum of six groups	6,541	7,663	8,423	9,915	11,946	12,947	15,737	18,065
By all other manufacturing	2,197	2,103	2,273	2,570	3,517	4,113	5,182	6,318
Captive consumption								
By petroleum refining (SIC 2911)	724	1,115	1,081	1,159	1,144	1,223	1,268	1,287
By blast furnaces and steel mills (SIC 3312)	1,073	1,053	1,280	1,297	1,657	1,581	1,980	2,093

Notes

1. Captive consumption excludes all but that within petroleum refining (SIC 2911) and blast furnaces and steel mills (SIC 3312).

2. Fuels exclude feedstocks (chiefly petroleum derivatives used as raw materials for organic chemicals and plastics materials manufacture).

3. Fuels and electricity consumption is mostly based on Bureau of the Census data, which do not necessarily agree with those of the Bureau of Mines.

4. Purchased for primary metals and all manufacturing may be too high and captive for primary metals too low in 1947 and 1954. Interplant transfers of coke, coke-oven gas, coal, tar, and blast furnace gas that were included in fuel purchases in 1954 but would be excluded on the classification scheme of later years is estimated at $599 million (out of $1.8 and $4.9 billion of energy purchased by primary metals and all manufacturing). U.S. Bureau of the Census, *Census of Manufactures, 1967*, Special Series, *Fuels and Electric Energy Consumed* MC67(S)-4, (U.S. Govt. Printing Office, 1971), p. SR 4-8, note 1, and p. SR 4-12. But the transfers for coke alone of these must have been $868 million (the $618

million on p. SR 4-9 minus the \$250 million in the note). The \$599 million therefore seems too low. 1947 is affected because for primary metals the 1954 ratio of purchased to total energy is used to estimate purchased.

Sources. Purchased. All manufacturing: 1947—fuel and electricity purchases were obtained from U.S. Bureau of the Census, *Census of Manufactures, 1947* (U.S. Govt. Printing Office, 1950), p. 203. A typographical error was corrected in gas. Consumption was multiplied by the energy conversion factors listed for general use in Appendix 3 to this chapter, using for electricity the electric-plant heat rate of each year, to get what will be called "reported" energy (since it is calculated from census consumption without adjustment, except for the correction of a typographical error). To this were added the differences between the "reported" energies of food (SIC 20), stone, clay, and glass (SIC 32), and primary metals (SIC 33) and the BTU totals finally used for these industries. 1954-67—fuel and electricity purchases were obtained from U.S. Bureau of the Census, *Census of Manufactures, 1967*, Special Series, *Fuels and Electricity Consumed*, table 3. Coke purchased in 1954 was reduced to 15,748 thousand tons (*ibid.*, table 2, note 1). Reported energy was reduced by the difference between the reported and finally-used energies of stone, clay, and glass (SIC 32). 1971—"Reported" energy was used, obtained as follows from a preprint of the fuels and electric energy portion of the 1971 Annual Survey of Manufactures made available by the Bureau of the Census. Purchases were multiplied by conversion factors and the BTUs summed for 1971 and 1967 and divided by their aggregate costs in the two years. The quotients were applied to the 1967 conversion factors for other fuels and fuels n.s.k., lowering them to allow for the 1967-71 inflation. Otherwise the procedure and fuel conversion factors were the same as for 1947-67. 1975 and 1980—by addition. Food (SIC 20): 1947—reported energy with fluid milk was extrapolated back in proportion to that excluding fluid milk. 1954-71—reported energy. 1975 and 1980—for each past year the energy consumption of the 2-digit group was divided by the sum of the energy consumptions of those of its 4-digit industries that are included in this study. The ratio was extrapolated and multiplied by the sum of the projected energy consumptions of those 4-digit industries. Paper (SIC 26) and Chemicals (SIC 28): 1947-71—reported energy. 1975 and 1980—like food (high projection used for alkalies and chlorine, SIC 2812). Petroleum (SIC 29): 1947—from reported energy was subtracted that for by-product coke ovens (old SIC 2932) in *Census, 1947*, pp. 210-211. 1954-80—like food (MIFM projection was used for petroleum refining, SIC 2911). Stone, clay, and glass (SIC 32): 1947 and 1954—the energy finally used for 1958 was extrapolated back in proportion to reported energy excluding ready-mixed concrete (SIC 3273). 1958-71—reported energy less the difference for ready-mixed concrete between its reported energy and the figures of Table 22.1. 1975 and 1980—like food. Primary metals (SIC 33): 1947—the 1958 total energy for blast furnaces and steel mills (SIC 3312) from Table 24A-3 was extrapolated back by energy totals derived from data of the American Iron and Steel Institute (Table 24A-5). To this was added the reported energy for primary metals (SIC 33) less the energies for blast furnaces (SIC 3311) and steel works and rolling mills (SIC 3312), from 1947 *Census*, pp. 212-213. The sum was multiplied by the 1954 ratio of purchased energy to purchased plus captive (perhaps too high—see *Note*, above). 1954—coke was cut 38,624 thousand tons (as for all manufacturing, above) before computing reported energy (perhaps too high—see *Note*, above). 1958-80—like food (high projection was used for blast furnaces and steel mills, SIC 3312).

Captive. Petroleum refining (SIC 2911): 1947-71—purchased energy was subtracted from the total energy calculated from the Bureau of Mines data of Table 18.10. 1975 and 1980—the ratio of purchased to total gross energy was projected at 0.61 in 1975 and 0.63 in 1980 and applied to the MIFM total of Table 18.6. Blast furnaces and steel mills (SIC 3312): 1947—the 1958 ratio of total energy calculated from the *Census* to total energy calculated from American Iron and Steel Institute data was applied to the AISI total energy for 1947 (Tables 24A-3 and 24A-5). The purchased energy of SIC 33 less SIC 3312 was calculated from the 1947 *Census*, pp. 212-213, and added in to get total energy for SIC 33, and this was multiplied by one minus SIC 33's 1954 ratio of purchased to total energy. 1954—total energy was calculated as for 1947 and purchased was subtracted (purchased may be too high—see *Note*, above). 1958-67—Table 24A-3. 1971—the 1967 ratio of total energy from the *Census* to total energy from the AISI was applied to the latter's total energy for 1971, and purchased was subtracted (Tables 24A-5 and 24A-3). 1975 and 1980—the ratio of captive to total energy was projected at 0.50 in 1975 and 1980 and applied to the high total energy projection of Table 24A-5.

Table 1-2. Value Added by Manufacture, High-Energy-Using Manufacturing Groups, 1947–1980
(billion 1967 $)

Industry	1947	1954	1958	1962	1967	1971	1975	1980
All manufacturing · · · · · · · · · · · · · · · · · · ·	109.22	139.80	153.29	192.03	261.98	301.56	400.84	519.49
Six high energy-using groups								
Food and kindred products (SIC 20) · · · · · · · · ·	15.56	16.96	19.66	22.44	26.62	28.77	33.44	38.83
Paper and allied products (SIC 26) · · · · · · · ·	3.92	5.14	6.03	7.46	9.76	10.80	13.89	16.98
Chemicals and allied products (SIC 28) · · · · ·	5.16	8.47	11.30	15.78	23.55	29.08	42.98	59.23
Petroleum and coal products (SIC 29) · · · · · · ·	2.43	3.19	3.71	4.44	5.42	6.23	7.85	10.03
Stone, clay, and glass products (SIC 32) · · · · ·	4.14	5.13	5.89	6.94	8.33	8.78	10.61	12.96
Primary metal industries (SIC 33) · · · · · · · ·	12.40	12.77	12.44	15.22	19.98	18.95	26.73	31.87
Sum of six groups · · · · · · · · · · · · · · ·	43.61	51.66	59.03	72.28	93.66	101.91	134.56	169.24
All other manufacturing	65.61	88.14	94.26	119.75	168.32	199.05	266.28	350.23

Source: *All manufacturing:* 1947-62–1967 value added was multiplied by the chained Census production index on base 1967 = 100, and the 1963 figure so obtained was adjusted to 1962 (see Appendix 2 of this chapter). 1967–U.S. Bureau of the Census, *Census of Manufactures, 1967,* Volume II, part 1, table 3. 1971–extrapolated from 1967 by shipments in 1971 dollars obtained from the Maryland Interindustry Forecasting Model (MIFM). 1975 and 1980–projected by the MIFM. *Six two-digit groups:* 1947-71–like all manufacturing. 1975-80–for each covered year 1958-67, shipments were summed for the 4-digit industries within the 2-digit group and the sum divided into value added in the 2-digit group. The ratios of 4-digit sum to group were projected and multiplied by the sums of the projections of shipments by the 4-digit industries. The resulting shipments projections were multiplied again by projections of each group's 1958-67 ratios of value added to shipments. *All other manufacturing:* by subtraction.

Table 1-3. Gross Energy Consumed per 1967 Dollar of Value Added, High-Energy-Using Manufacturing Groups, 1947–1980

(1,000 BTUs/1967 $)

	1947	1954	1958	1962	1967	1971	1975	1980
Purchased by all manufacturing plus energy produced and consumed in the same establishment ("captive consumption") by SICs 2911 and 3312[a]	96.5	85.4	85.2	77.8	69.7	65.9	60.3	53.4
Purchased by all manufacturing	80.0	69.9	69.8	65.0	59.0	56.6	52.2	46.9
By six high-energy-using 2-digit groups								
Food and kindred products (SIC 20)	55.1	52.0	48.4	44.2	41.2	44.7	38.4	37.4
Paper and allied products (SIC 26)	161.9	155.9	154.6	143.2	140.1	144.4	133.2	108.5
Chemicals and allied products (SIC 28)	198.2	207.0	201.8	164.3	138.3	119.4	116.3	101.6
Petroleum and coal products (SIC 29)	225.9	217.8	274.3	281.9	284.4	292.1	265.4	229.5
Stone, clay, and glass products (SIC 32)	224.4	201.1	179.5	169.7	160.9	164.3	152.4	143.8
Primary metal industries (SIC 33)	205.4	195.7	175.3	186.2	167.2	177.5	150.8	146.1
Average of six groups	150.0	148.3	142.7	137.2	127.5	127.0	117.0	106.7
By all other manufacturing	33.5	23.9	24.1	21.5	20.9	20.7	19.5	18.0
Captive consumption								
By petroleum refining (SIC 2911)[b]	297.0	349.4	291.4	261.1	210.8	196.2	161.4	128.3
By blast furnaces and steel mills (SIC 3312)[b]	86.5	82.5	102.9	85.2	82.9	83.4	74.1	65.7

[a]Same line in Table 1-1 was divided by all manufacturing in Table 1-2.

[b]Same lines in Table 1-1 were divided by the corresponding 2-digit groups in Table 1-2.

Note: See the chapters on paper and chemicals for more material on captive consumption. See *Note* to Table 1-1 about 1947 and 1954 figures for primary metals.

Sources: *All other manufacturing, 1975 and 1980:* a 1.5% per year decline was forecast from the 1971 figure.
All other manufacturing for 1947–71 and the remaining lines for all years: Table 1-1 was divided by Table 1-2 using unrounded figures.

Table 1-4. Gross Energy Purchased Compared with Shipments and Value Added, High-Energy-Using Manufacturing Industries, 1967

	Gross energy (trillion BTUs)	Shipments (million 1967 $)	Ratio gross energy to shipments (1)/(2) (1,000 BTUs/ 1967 $)	Value added (million 1967 $)	Ratio gross energy to value added (1)/(4) (1,000 BTUs/ 1967 $)
	(1)	(2)	(3)	(4)	(5)
All manufacturing	15,463.3	557,398	27.74	261,984	59.02
20 Food and kindred products	1,097.7	83,972	13.07	26,620	41.24
2011 Meatpacking plants	101.6	15,576	6.52	2,220	45.75
2026 Fluid milk	81.5	7,826	10.41	2,351	34.67
2033 Canned fruits and vegetables	54.3	3,468	15.65	1,413	38.42
2037 Frozen fruits and vegetables	36.4	2,082	17.50	764	47.66
2042 Prepared feeds	59.7	4,797	12.44	1,227	48.66
2051 Bread, cake, and related products . .	59.1	5,103	11.59	2,753	21.47
26 Paper and allied products	1,367.0	20,970	65.19	9,756	140.11
2611 Pulp mills	98.0	730	134.27	334	293.68
2621 Paper mills except building paper . .	603.2	4,844	124.52	2,356	255.99
2631 Paperboard mills	476.9	2,907	164.05	1,509	316.08
2653 Corrugated and solid fiber boxes . .	36.3	2,960	12.28	1,130	32.12
2661 Building paper and board mills . . .	49.9	341	146.32	184	271.64
28 Chemicals and allied products	3,257.1	42,148	77.28	23,550	138.31
2812 Alkalies and chlorine	266.9	720	370.76	419	636.69
2813 Industrial gases	112.3	589	190.61	401	280.12
2815 Cyclic intermediates and crudes . . .	149.8	1,597	93.79	730	205.35
2818 Industrial organic chemicals, n.e.c. . .	952.1	6,378	149.27	3,575	266.30
2819 Industrial inorganic chemicals, n.e.c. .	971.3	4,248	228.64	2,295	423.15
2821 Plastics materials and resins	160.0	3,474	46.04	1,635	97.85

SIC	Industry				
2822	Synthetic rubber	71.6	927	77.19	405	176.83
2823	Cellulosic man-made fibers	100.8	903	111.64	507	198.90
2824	Organic fibers, noncellulosic	107.4	2,033	52.83	1,252	85.80
29	Petroleum and coal products	1,543.0	22,043	70.00	5,426	284.38
2911	Petroleum refining	1,459.2	20,294	71.90	4,745	307.52
32	Stone, clay, and glass products	1,341.0	14,449	92.81	8,333	160.93
3211	Flat glass	60.5	611	99.10	423	143.06
3221	Glass containers	135.5	1,352	100.21	842	160.89
3229	Pressed and blown glass, n.e.c.	74.1	886	83.62	659	112.46
3241	Hydraulic cement	515.2	1,246	413.45	812	634.25
3251	Brick and structural clay tile	101.6	362	280.72	251	404.62
3273	Ready-mixed concrete	41.3	2,684	15.39	1,156	35.73
3274	Lime	81.9	176	465.44	100	818.18
33	Primary metal industries	3,339.9	46,731	71.47	19,978	167.18
3312	Blast furnaces and steel mills	1,810.6	19,621	92.28	8,910	203.21
3313	Electrometallurgical products	131.0	468	280.02	193	678.05
3321	Gray iron foundries	118.8	2,638	45.03	1,543	76.99
3323	Steel foundries	55.5	1,213	45.78	791	70.12
3334	Primary aluminum	589.4	1,609	366.31	812	726.04
3351	Copper rolling and drawing	43.7	2,391	18.28	704	62.04
3352	Aluminum rolling and drawing	96.0	2,959	32.45	939	102.27
3357	Nonferrous wire-drawing, insulating	37.9	3,591	10.56	1,330	28.49
3391	Iron and steel forgings	58.7	1,262	46.53	607	96.64

Sources: *Energy:* Ready-mixed concrete (SIC 3273)—Table 22.1. All other industries—like "reported energy" in Table 1.1 (with correction of a typographical error in fuel oil purchases by iron and steel forgings, SIC 3391). *Shipments and value added:* U.S. Bureau of the Census, *Census of Manufactures, 1967,* Volume II, part 1, table 3.

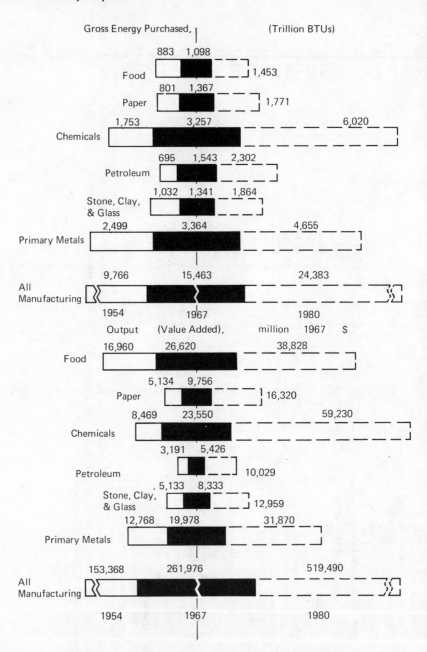

Chart 1-1. Gross Energy Purchased and Value Added, High-energy-using Manufacturing Groups, 1954, 1967, and 1980.

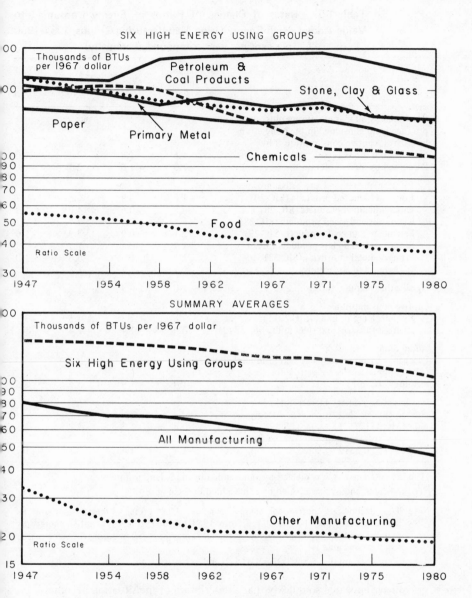

Chart 1-2. Gross Energy Purchased per 1967 Dollar of Value Added, High-energy-using Manufacturing Groups, 1947 to 1980.

Table 1-5.   Rates of Change of Ratios of Energy Consumed to
Value Added, High-Energy-Using Manufacturing Groups, 1954-1980
(per cent per year compounded annually)

	1954 to 1967	1967 to 1975	1975 to 1980	1967 to 1980
Purchased by all manufacturing plus energy produced and consumed in the same establishment ("captive consumption") by SICs 2911 and 3312	−1.6	−1.8	−2.4	−2.0
Purchased by all manufacturing	−1.3	−1.5	−2.1	−1.8
By six high-energy-using 2-digit groups				
Food and kindred products (SIC 20)	−1.8	−0.9	−0.5	−0.7
Paper and allied products (SIC 26)	−0.8	−0.6	−4.0	−1.9
Chemicals and allied products (SIC 28)	−3.1	−2.1	−2.7	−2.3
Petroleum and coal products (SIC 29)	+2.1	−0.9	−2.9	−1.6
Stone, clay, and glass products (SIC 32)	−1.7	−0.7	−1.2	−0.9
Primary metal industries (SIC 33)	−1.2	−1.3	−0.6	−1.0
Average of six groups	−1.2	−1.1	−1.8	−1.4
By all other manufacturing	−1.0	−0.9	−1.6	−1.1
Captive consumption				
By petroleum refining (SIC 2911)[a]	−3.8	−3.3	−4.5	−3.7
By blast furnaces and steel mills (SIC 3312)[a]	0.0	−1.4	−2.4	−1.8
Addendum Purchased by petroleum and coal products (SIC 29) plus captive by petroleum refining (SIC 2911)[a]	−1.0	−1.9	−3.5	−2.5
Purchased by primary metals (SIC 33) plus captive by blast furnaces and steel mills (SIC 3312)[a]	−0.8	−1.3	−1.2	−1.3
Purchased by six groups plus captive by SICs 2911 and 3312[b]	−1.4	−1.4	−2.1	−1.7

[a]The indicated energy was divided by value added in the 2-digit group.
[b]The indicated energy was divided by value added in the 6 groups.

Note: The decline of purchased energy per unit for primary metals and for all manufacturing may be overstated from 1954 to 1967; similarly, captive energy per unit for primary metals, shown as unchanged, may have fallen during the same period; see *Note* to Table 1-1.

Source: computed from Tables 1-1, 1-2, and 1-3.

prices have appeared so quickly that a description of the situation becomes promptly outdated. During the summer of 1973, plants were being shut down intermittently because of shortages of electricity, natural gas, and light fuel oils.

On March 8, 1973, we sent questionnaires to 211 large companies in the large energy-using groups; one purpose of the survey was to determine the extent of awareness of the energy problem. Many of the returns, which were completed in April 1973, showed only modest concern with energy supply

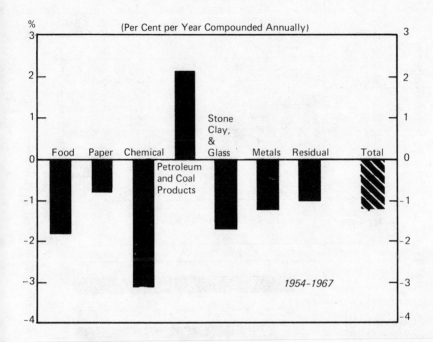

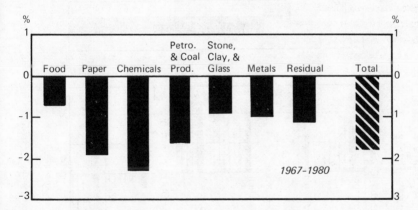

Chart 1-3. Rates of Change in the Ratio of Purchased Energy to Value Added, High-energy-using Manufacturing Groups, 1954 to 1980.

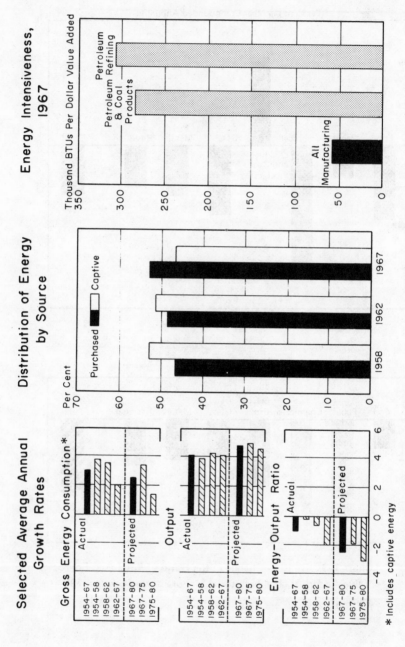

Chart 1-4.   Petroleum Refining. Sources: Department of Commerce; The Conference Board.

difficulties. We had occasion to speak with several of the respondents three or four months after they had completed their questionnaires, and the consensus of these discussions was that all companies had found the problems to have become much more serious by mid-summer. (The responses to the company survey of future energy demand are summarized and analyzed in Appendix 1 to this chapter.) It is safe to say that: (1) the degree of awareness has heightened considerably; (2) the assignment of high-level personnel to explore ways of dealing with the problems occasioned by rapidly rising energy prices and supply restrictions has accelerated; and (3) more funds have been allocated for new capital equipment and research into ways of economizing on energy use and using alternative sources of energy, often outside the normal fuel categories.

As of April 1973, the surveyed companies were anticipating very rapid increases in energy prices for the period from 1971 to 1980 in all fuel and energy categories. Energy prices were expected to rise at rates of 5% to 10% per year in absolute terms. Compared with expected increases in the general price level, energy prices were expected to rise at rates from one-fourth higher to double the overall rate of inflation.

Supply restrictions are, of course, closely related to environmental regulations. While it is not appropriate to go into the entire question of environmental regulations at this point, it should be noted that many industries have capital equipment that is geared to use only natural gas in some cases, light fuel oils in other cases, and electricity in yet others. When the supply of a specific energy source is interrupted, production may be halted in the short run. For manufacturing processes that permit use of alternative sources of energy, the alternatives may oe unfeasible to use because of emission problems. Finally, restrictions on air and water pollution have forced many industries to introduce expensive control equipment requiring large amounts of energy. To sum up, many manufacturers find themselves in a double bind: to reduce their own air and water pollution, they are required to use fuels in limited supply; or they are required to introduce processes using more energy in total. And these developments coincide with rapidly rising prices of energy and interruptions in supplies of fuels and electricity.

An example of the effects of control of air and water pollution on energy use may be drawn from Chapter Twenty-Three, Lime (SIC 3274). From 1958 to 1967, there was a rapid increase in the use of lime within the industry to purify water formerly discharged with wastes and to absorb air emissions (Chart 1-5). This resulted in a rapid increase in the energy-output ratio, which wiped out most of the energy saving that had taken place in the previous fifteen years.

Contrasting examples may be found in the petroleum refining and chemicals industries, where waste water flows such as cooling water can no longer be vented due to pollution restrictions. This requires that the water be pumped and recycled, which uses some additional energy for purification, but

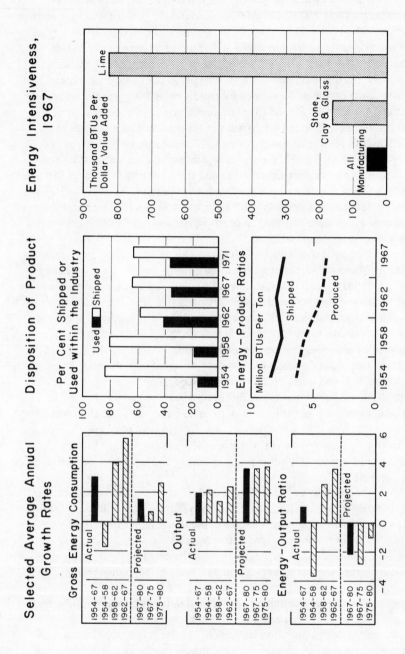

Chart 1-5. Lime. Sources: Department of Commerce; The Conference Board.

often saves much more energy (in the form of heat) than it uses. In many cases, the capital costs of pollution-control equipment are paid for by the energy savings. There are journal articles to this effect.[3]

Research and development to reduce energy use in manufacturing and to develop new sources of supply for manufacturing industries is one way companies are responding to the energy problem. Our survey indicated that a majority of large companies in the energy-intensive industries have undertaken R&D activity in the last five years to find ways of reducing energy use per unit of output and to develop new sources of supply. The proportion that has undertaken such activities is greater for the more energy-intensive industry groups (such as petroleum and coal products) than for those that are less energy-intensive (such as food industries).

Further, there is a definite relationship between size of company, on the one hand, and past and planned future expenditure on R&D directed toward energy use and sources—the larger the company, the more likely is such expenditure.[4] R&D is more commonly undertaken to seek methods of reducing energy use within the industry than to seek new supply sources. In almost all cases, the companies surveyed indicated that they plan to spend more on R&D in the rest of the decade than they did in the last five years.

Projections of Energy Use to 1980

The starting point was a long-term projection for the U.S. economy, to 1980, prepared at The Conference Board.[5] The main characteristics of this projection are the achievement of a 4.5% unemployment rate in 1975 and 1980, and a long-term labor productivity growth rate—beginning in 1965—of 3.0% for the private sector of the economy. Estimates of the total labor force, prepared by the author, take into account developments through mid-1972. This projection, prepared in August 1972, accords reasonably well with the level of the economy in 1973. The basic variables of the projection of GNP, namely, the unemployment rate, total labor force, and level of GNP in constant dollars for 1975 and 1980, were introduced into the MIFM INFORUM model to produce projections for all manufacturing, its 2-digit groups, and the 37 4-digit industries we studied. As noted in Section I, the individual analysts sometimes used other projections for individual industries, when in their judgment a superior projection was available.

The technique for obtaining the projections for all manufacturing, the six 2-digit energy-intensive groups, and for the "Residue" (the other 15 manufacturing groups), is as follows:

1. Take the sum of the 4-digit shipments projections by 2-digit group (converted to value added at the 1967 ratio of value added to shipments).

2. Adjust the INFORUM projection of shipments at the 2-digit level (also converted to value added by the 1967 ratio) to the long-term trend between the sum of the 4-digit industries (step 1) and the 2-digit group.

3. The INFORUM projection of total GNP originating in manufacturing was *not* adjusted.

4. Take the sum of the projected energy use of the 4-digit industries in each of the six energy-intensive 2-digit groups. Inflate to the 2-digit level by the long-term trend between the 4-digit sum and the 2-digit level.

5. For the Residue (the fifteen 2-digit groups not studied in detail), the decline in the energy-output ratio was projected at a 1.5% average annual rate, from 1971 to 1980.

The results of these operations yield the results shown in Tables 1-1 to 1-3. Briefly, value added for all manufacturing is projected to grow at a 5.4% rate from 1967 to 1980 (Table 1-2). The energy-output ratio is projected to decline at a 1.8% rate on a purchased energy basis and at a 2.0% rate when captive consumption in petroleum refining and steel making is included (Table 1-3).

A rise of 58% in purchased energy by the manufacturing sector is projected for the 13-year period from 1967 to 1980, or 43% from 1971, the most recent year for which information is available at this writing. When captive consumption in petroleum refining and steel making is included, the percentage rise is smaller, 52% from 1967, or 40% from 1971. These figures reflect the substantial savings projected in energy use per unit of output. If these savings did not occur, and energy use rose in proportion to value added from 1971 to 1980 (assuming this were possible), 5.0 quadrillion BTUs more in purchased energy (or 6.5 quadrillion BTUs more including captive) would be absorbed by the manufacturing sector in 1980 alone. That is, without the estimated saving, energy absorbed (including captive) would exceed the projected amount by 23%. This is the equivalent of 1.1 billion barrels of crude oil, or nearly twice the amount of crude imported by the nation in 1971 (0.6 billion barrels).

The rate of decline in the energy-output ratio is projected to be faster in the 1967 to 1980 period than it was in the preceding 13 years. This reflects an acceleration in the last five years of the projected period and is our best judgment about the long-term trend in manufacturing. It is noteworthy that the difference between the rates of decline for purchased plus captive energy, and for purchased energy, is greater in the forecast period than in the preceding 13 years. This indicates substantial economies in the use of feedstocks and raw materials in petroleum refining and steel making. We expect that these industries will reduce substantially their demands per unit of output on the nation's energy resources.

The decline in the relative importance of the high energy-using industries continues in the projection period. This is revealed by the fact that the energy-output ratio for all manufacturing declines much more rapidly than either the average of the six energy-intensive industries or the average of other manufacturing. The percentage of value added accounted for by the six energy-intensive groups is projected to decline from 35.8% in 1967 to 32.4% in 1980.

Among the six groups, those with the most rapid rates of decline in energy use per unit of output are chemicals, paper, and petroleum and coal products. For the last, the decline is accentuated when captive consumption is included.

The projected decline in energy use per unit of output is much more rapid from 1975 to 1980 than from 1967 to 1975. The eight years from 1967 to 1975 are unusual from the point of view of the trend of energy use. A great deal of capital expenditure is going into pollution-control equipment, leaving comparatively little funds for energy saving; in some cases, the equipment increases energy use. Also, the 1969-1970 recession and the lack of vigor in the first year of recovery (from the fourth quarter of 1970 to the fourth quarter of 1971) resulted in a high degree of over-capacity in manufacturing, low profits, and comparatively little capital replacement.

This situation changed abruptly with the rapid recovery in 1972, which yielded high profits and a reduced incentive to tend to energy saving, particularly in those industries where energy intensity and therefore energy costs per unit, are relatively low. The recent emergence of the energy problem has changed the outlook significantly, as outlined in the preceding section. But the time lag between perception of the problem and capital investment to save energy means that most of the 1967 to 1975 period will reveal behavior below trend in terms of energy saving. Pollution control and over-capacity are the primary causes.

From 1975 to 1980, response to the energy problem is expected to result in substantial gains in energy saving, and this period is therefore a better indicator of the long-term trend than are the preceding eight years. This is true especially because the figures undoubtedly understate the real possibilities for energy saving. The principal reasons for this understatement, in our opinion, are:

(1) Many of our projections of energy savings are based on the opinions of persons in the industries we studied, and there is a conservative bias in these responses.

(2) This bias is caused in part by a lack of knowledge among personnel in the industries regarding past achievements in energy saving and about opportunities for further gains.

(3) It is fairly certain that a higher rate of technological progress affecting energy saving will take place in the 1975 to 1980 period, but the parameters are impossible to foretell.

(4) The responses to our questionnaires and the information obtained from industry personnel referred almost entirely to known, proven technology.

(5) The energy-saving in our projections is in large part the accretion of small (from the point of view of the economy) improvements in housekeeping and process changes. Major new developments can alter the entire outlook for energy use and thus make our projections understate the situation in 1980.

SECTION III.   HIGHLIGHTS OF INDUSTRY ESSAYS AND PILOT STUDIES

Food Industries

Meatpacking plants (SIC 2011), Chapter Two. Output in this industry grew at a modest rate from 1947 to 1967 (1.9% per year), but gross energy consumption rose much more slowly (0.5% per year). As a result, the energy-output ratio fell at an average rate of 1.5% per year.

The principal change reducing energy use was the movement toward larger animal weights. This took two forms: beef accounted for an increasing share of total output; and each type of animal except hogs rose in average size. Since energy use in many of the slaughtering operations is not closely related to the size of the animal, a similar amount of energy is expended for large animals and for small. Energy requirements per pound of product, and even more per dollar of output (in constant prices), fell for this reason. There was a trend toward decentralization of the industry over the period and a related movement away from on-site generation of power to purchased gas and electricity; as a result, coal use declined sharply.

There were several factors that operated to raise energy consumption per unit in this industry: meat packing became more mechanized, the product was processed more extensively, and sanitary requirements were increased (especially rapid cooling and refrigeration). But these factors were more than offset by a change in the composition of the product, which served to lower the energy-output ratio substantially.

From 1967 to 1980, output is expected to rise more rapidly than before at a 2.8% rate. The energy-output ratio should continue to decline (at a 1.3% rate), but not as rapidly as in the past. The trend toward larger animals should continue, and the more recent trend toward larger (and fewer) plants, which use less energy per unit of output, should continue through the 1970s. Both these factors should reduce the per unit use of energy. But the trends toward more processing and toward more stringent sanitary requirements, both of which use more energy per unit, serve to offset part of the energy savings stemming from product composition and plant size. As a result, total energy use should rise at a 1.4% rate in this industry.

Fluid milk (SIC 2026), Chapter Three. This industry grew at an average rate of 2.4% from 1954 to 1967, while total energy consumption fell at a 4% rate (Chart 1-6). As a result, the energy-output ratio declined at a substantial 6.3% rate. The main developments in milk production were the rapid movement toward bulk receipt of milk in large containers, and to retail sales of milk in plastic-lined cartons. Both these developments resulted in substantial savings in energy formerly expended on sterilizing and washing milk cans and bottles.

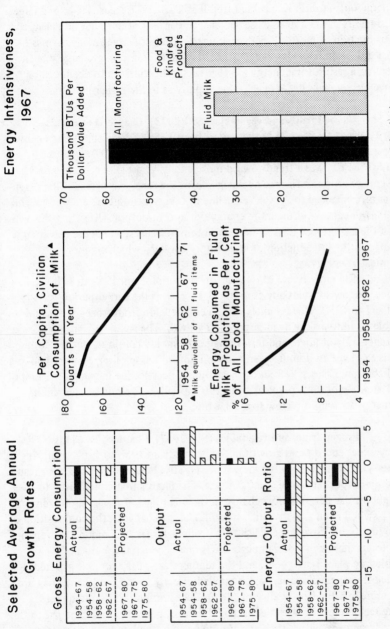

Chart 1-6. Fluid Milk. Sources: Department of Commerce; Department of Agriculture; The Conference Board.

In the 1967 to 1980 period, output is expected to slow substantially. The energy-output ratio is expected to fall at a 3% rate because fewer and larger establishments in the industry use less energy per unit of output, and because of the introduction of more efficient machinery. The very large energy savings of the past due to bulk receipt and changes in retail containers have largely been realized. As a result, total energy use is expected to continue to decline, at a 2.3% average annual rate, though not as rapidly as in the earlier period.

Canned fruits and vegetables (SIC 2033), Chapter Four. This industry grew at a 3.3% rate in the period from 1958 to 1967, but gross energy use grew faster. As a result, the energy-output ratio rose at a 0.4% rate. One reason for the rise was a trend toward more extensive use of electricity, for the useful energy-output ratio was unchanged over the nine-year period. Changes in product mix balanced to prevent a decline in energy per unit. There was a trend toward larger cans requiring more energy per unit of output. Offsetting this was a rise in the importance of fruit juices and tomato sauces, which use less energy per unit, and the introduction of large rotary cookers, which are more economical of energy.

The growth rate of output for the period from 1967 to 1980 is expected to slow substantially from the 3.3% rate of the earlier period to 1.5% from 1967 to 1980. This is largely due to competition from frozen fruits and vegetables, and to a slowing in population growth. The trends toward increasing importance of fruit juices and fewer small cans should continue, but the former factor is expected to dominate. In addition, introduction of large rotary cookers should continue. The net effect of these should be a decline in energy per unit of output at a rate of 0.4% per year from 1967 to 1980. The rate of increase in total energy use will thus slow to a 1.1% rate.

Frozen fruits and vegetables (SIC 2037), Chapter Five. This industry experienced rapid growth in the period from 1958 to 1967, averaging 7.8% per year. Total energy use grew more rapidly, however, at 8.5%. As a result, the energy-output ratio rose at a 0.7% rate. The factors that contributed to the rise in energy use per unit are a change in the technique of preparing frozen foods (a switch from slow to quick freezing), and a change in the composition of the product (more frozen specialities are produced). The technique for preparing frozen foods that declined in importance is one in which the fruits and vegetables are placed in a room, and the temperature of the room is lowered. In the quick-freezing technique, cold is applied directly to the foods, and they are frozen more rapidly. The quality of the product is improved by the quick-freezing technique, but it uses considerably more energy per unit. The rise in the share of frozen specialties, such as TV dinners and other ready-to-eat products, requires more energy because of the nature of the product—frozen specialties must be packaged before freezing and the packaging acts as an insulation, which slows freezing. Other products can be frozen before packaging.

In the future, output is expected to rise even more rapidly, at an 8.7% annual rate, from 1967 to 1980. This growth will be in part at the expense of canned foods. The energy-output ratio is expected to decline slightly in the 1970s, at a 0.1% rate, as the effects of change in product mix and freezing technique have largely been incorporated in the industry. Energy use is therefore projected to rise at an 8.6% rate.

There is a possibility of a reduction in direct energy use by the industry, a possibility stemming from the new technique of cryogenic freezing: in this method, liquid nitrogen is applied directly to the foods. At present, the technique is too expensive for wide adoption because of the cost of liquid nitrogen. The prospect for a substantial decline in the price of liquid nitrogen is not bright, however, since its production is very energy-intensive (see Chapter Eleven, Industrial Gases, SIC 2813). But it is possible that methods of recycling nitrogen may be developed and thus reduce energy needs.

Prepared feeds (SIC 2042), Chapter Six. In the 20-year period from 1947 to 1967, this industry grew rapidly, at a 4.5% rate. Total energy use grew even more, however, and the energy-output ratio rose at a 0.7% rate. The industry, which produces processed feeds for animals, fowls, and pets, has moved toward more intensive processing, in the form of pelletizing, crimping, and flaking of the final feed ration. More processing of feeds and the rapid rise in the share of pet food require more energy use per unit of output.

In the future, output is expected to rise somewhat more slowly, at a 3.7% rate from 1967 to 1980. The trends toward greater variety in products and more mixing and processing of products will lead to greater energy use per unit. As a result, the energy-output ratio is expected to rise, as before, at a 0.7% rate. Total energy use should accelerate to a 4.4% rate.

Bread, cake, and related products (SIC 2051), Chapter Seven. From 1947 to 1967 this industry grew at a slow 1.2% average rate and used almost the same amount of total energy at the beginning as at the end of the period. As a result, the energy-output ratio fell at a 1.1% rate.

There was a shift in composition of output that aided the decline of energy use per unit: bread rose in importance, compared with other baked goods; soft breads rose relative to hard-crust bread; and the baking of bread and other products was increasingly concentrated in large bakeries. All these changes acted to conserve energy per unit of output. A change in technique was probably the most important factor, however: large gas ovens that employ air agitation (convection) became common in large bakeries; these cut baking time by at least one-third. The combination of gas use and air agitation permits a higher quality product to be produced at lower temperatures in less time, thus reducing energy use significantly. There was probably some slight economy in energy through the introduction of continuous baking.

In the 1967 to 1980 period, the industry should realize slightly faster growth, at a 1.4% rate, and a more rapid rate of decline in the energy-output ratio, at a 2.1% rate. The principal reason for the saving in energy will be the continuing spread of new large gas ovens using air agitation throughout the industry. Total energy use should decline absolutely, at a 0.8% rate.

Paper Industries[d]

Corrugated and solid fiber boxes (SIC 2653), Chapter Eight. From 1958 to 1967, output in this industry rose at a 6.8% rate, while total energy use rose less rapidly, at a 5.8% rate, so the energy-output ratio declined at a 0.9% rate. The products of this industry are in very wide and expanding use throughout the economy. A substantial amount of the industry's energy is furnished by natural gas, and many plants are experiencing problems with interruptions of gas supply and electric power supply. The energy-output ratio fell at a rapid 2.1% rate from 1962 to 1967, reflecting improved production efficiency through increased operating speeds and greater width of processing sheets.

In the period from1967 to 1980, output is projected to rise at a 5.5% rate, while the energy-output ratio is expected to decline at only a 0.1% rate, resulting in a 5.5% rate of increase in total energy use. Energy savings from improvements in production efficiency appear to have largely been realized, thus limiting further decline in the energy-output ratio.

Building paper and board mills (SIC 2661), Chapter Nine. Output of this industry rose at a 2.1% average annual rate from 1954 to 1970 (Chart 1-7). Fuel and energy use figures for this industry are of uncertain value and must be treated with care. The energy-output ratio, computed from published Census data, fluctuates widely. The industry is highly variable in the rate of output, since it depends strongly on the rate of construction activity.

The energy-output ratio apparently rose sharply from 1954 to 1962 as a result of the upgrading of tar papers and shingles, which require more heat to produce. Subsequently, there was a change to a new, continuous-flow, tube heater process for the heating of asphalt and tar; this innovation, which began to affect the industry-wide statistics after 1962, resulted in energy saving.

From 1967 to 1980, output is projected to rise at a 3.9% rate. The industry is experiencing much difficulty in meeting the requirements of environmental regulations, which serve to increase fuel use and other operating costs. A change in product mix away from asphalt and crude petroleum saturated products is likely to reduce air pollution. And operating techniques that were previously too expensive have now become economically feasible to introduce because of high energy prices. Both are energy-saving, but are not expected to offset the requirements of air-pollution regulations, so the energy-output ratio is projected to rise at a 2.0% annual rate, resulting in a rise in total energy use at a 6.0% rate from 1967 to 1980.

[d]See also highlights of Chapter 32.

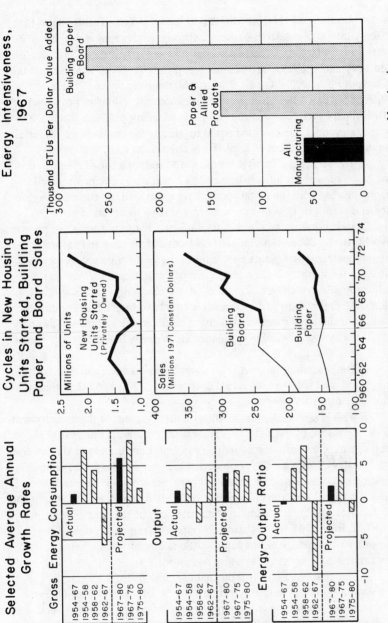

Chart 1-7. Building Paper and Board Mills. Sources: Department of Commerce; Maryland interindustry Forecasting Model; The Conference Board.

Chemicals Industries

Alkalies and chlorine (SIC 2812), Chapter Ten. This is one of the most energy-intensive industries in manufacturing. It uses a great deal of electricity—1%, in fact, of the nation's total. The industry grew 4.9% a year between 1947 and 1967. Energy use rose less rapidly (3.1%), and as a result the energy-output ratio declined at a 1.7% rate. All three segments of the industry saved energy per unit: the chlorine-caustic and soda ash subindustries (which make the primary products) and the group of secondary products (these are mostly in the product classes of industrial organic or inorganic chemicals n.e.c. and use the primary products of alkalies and chlorine as starting materials).

The electricity and steam needed to produce a ton of electrolytic chlorine have fallen about a twelfth since 1947, while improvements in cell design, culminating with the metal anode, have multiplied the current-carrying capacity of electrolytic cells by ten or more, reducing overhead expense.

Soda ash manufacture has shown little change in energy use per ton since World War II. Because of competition from caustic soda and natural sodium carbonate, no new plants were built in the postwar period. A recent innovation in the industry is the replacement of flame heat by steam heat in baking bicarbonate, which saves 2% to 3% of overall energy in the subindustry. Pollution control problems in disposing of wastes have forced many soda ash plants to close, and since these were likely to be the inefficient plants, this may have raised the average level of performance and thereby lowered energy use per unit.

The secondary products also probably saved energy substantially over the period, and their output grew faster from 1947 to 1967 than that of either branch of primary products.

With regard to the future, the growth of output of the industry will depend on the spread of the Kel-Chlor process among chlorine users in the industrial organic chemicals, n.e.c., industry (a major market of the alkalies and chlorine industry). If the Kel-Chlor process, which produces chlorine from by-product hydrochloric acid, is widely adopted, the growth in demand for chlorine from the alkalies and chlorine industry will be much smaller than if the process does not gain great popularity. Our estimates of the growth of output for the period from 1967 to 1980 are 2.5% rate with rapid adoption of the process, and a 3.9% rate for slow adoption. (Soda ash output, included in the industry total, is not expected to change significantly.)

Energy use per unit is projected to rise slightly (0.1% rate) in the event of slower growth of output, yielding a rise in total energy use at a 2.6% rate. For rapid output growth, the energy-output ratio is projected to decline at a 0.3% rate, yielding a rise in total energy use of 3.6% per year.

Industrial gases (SIC 2813), Chapter Eleven. This industry experienced rapid growth, at a rate of 9.7%, from 1947 to 1967. Energy use grew slightly less rapidly, at 9.1%, so the energy-output ratio fell at a rate of 0.5% per year. There was a broad range of advances in technology in the industry, including the introduction of several new types of capital equipment, most of which were related to changes in processes.

One such change is a slow rise in the use of the partial oxidation process in hydrogen production, replacing the process of steam reforming of natural gas. Fuel requirements for heat and power decline from 210 BTUs per cubic foot to 35 in this process change. This development brings up the related problem of feedstock usage, which we have noted throughout these volumes but have not been able to study in the detail the problem deserves. In this example, when the feedstock requirement of 240 BTUs per cubic foot from natural gas in the older process and 350 BTUs from fuel oil in the newer process are added, the sum of the requirements is 450 for the older process and 385 for the newer, still an impressive decline in energy use. Another substantial change is in liquefaction. In producing liquid hydrogen, a change from the Joule-Thompson process to the expander cycle process lowered kwh per pound of hydrogen from 16, or 14, to 5, even more significant improvement.

Impressive gains of this sort were offset by a shift in the composition of the product from compound gases, such as carbon dioxide and acetylene, to elemental gases, such as nitrogen, helium, argon, and oxygen. While there was apparently a decline in energy requirements per unit for each gas over the historical period, the elemental gases use much more energy per unit, so the shift in composition in product of the industry raised energy substantially. The net effect was a slow rate of decline in the energy-output ratio.

In the future, output is projected to increase at a 7.8% rate from 1967 through 1980. For the entire period (1967 to 1980), the energy-output ratio is expected to decline at a 1.3% rate, resulting in a rise in total energy use at a 6.5% rate.

The continuing rapid rise in demand for industrial gases is tied to the expansion of their use in a number of larger industries. An example of this is oxygen use in steel making, a major market. The fast growing gases throughout the 1970s are nitrogen, argon, and oxygen.

The compound gases are expected to continue to decline as a share of the industry total, but they are now of little importance in the industry, so only a small effect on the energy-output ratio will result from that factor. There is now some overcapacity in the industry, and many plants are of recent vintage and employ technically efficient processes, so little capital equipment retirement is likely in the rest of the decade. The projected decline in the energy-output is based on an expected movement toward 1967 state-of-the-art production processes, due to new plant construction.

Cyclic intermediates and crudes (SIC 2815), Chapter Twelve. From 1954 to 1967, output of this industry rose at an average annual rate of 6.9%. The industry produces many different products, mainly cyclic organic intermediates, made principally from petrochemical feedstocks. Over the 13-year period, there was a shift from coal to petroleum as a raw material. For many products of this industry, there are a variety of chemical processes available. With time, shifts are made to less-energy-using processes as part of a general move toward lowering production costs. Product mix has had little effect on energy use per unit of output; process improvements have been much more important.

In the production of three of the industry's most important products, rapid decreases in energy needs can be documented. For example, in the production of cyclohexane, a large scale plant achieved the following changes in energy use: electricity fell 59%, steam fell 29%, and natural gas remained unchanged. Similiar improvements were noted for phenol and styrene production. As a result, total energy use rose at a much smaller rate than output, 4.1% as compared with 6.9%, and the energy-output ratio declined at a 2.8% rate.

The industry is projected to grow at a 6.3% rate from 1967 to 1980, while the energy-output ratio is projected to decline at a 2.7% rate. As a result, total energy use is expected to rise at only a 3.5% rate. The demand for the products of this industry stems from many sources, of which two of the fastest growing are plastics and man-made fibers. There are two movements occurring to reduce energy use per unit of output: one is toward the introduction of energy-saving techniques and devices in existing plants; the other is the construction of new plants incorporating energy conservation features. The expected rapid growth of the industry should make the latter the more significant factor, as capacity expands to meet rising demand for output.

Industrial organic chemicals, n.e.c. (SIC 2818), Chapter Thirteen. This industry, one of the largest energy users in manufacturing, is a catch-all industry. The great bulk of the products consist of acyclic hydrocarbons made from derivatives of petroleum and natural gas, frequently referred to as petrochemicals. Most of the products are sold to other industries for further processing. Important markets are plastics, synthetic fibers and synthetic rubber, fertilizers, pesticides, detergents, solvents, and gasoline additives. From 1954 to 1967, the industry experienced rapid growth, with output rising at an average annual rate of 10.0% (Chart 1–8). Energy use grew somewhat less rapidly, and the energy-output ratio therefore declined at a 0.7% annual rate.

The industry uses fuels and electricity for heat and power but also, as mentioned above, employs petroleum and natural gas for raw materials or feedstocks. Available data suggest that the use of feedstocks per unit of output did not fall as rapidly as energy use for heat and power over the 13-year period, but did indeed decline. Total absorption of energy-bearing materials therefore grew less rapidly than output. In other words, there was a saving of energy resources per unit of product by the industry.

There are three trends in production that affect energy use in the industry: economies of scale, which permit energy saving per unit of output; a movement toward more direct routes to products (such as the direct reduction of ethylene to ethyl alcohol as compared with the indirect route via ethyl sulfate), which saves energy by improving yields and permitting more capture of process heat; and the shift away from acetylene to ethylene and propylene as basic materials, which use more energy and feedstocks.

Strong demand from plastics, noncellulosic fibers, and a number of other chemical products is projected to result in a rapid rate of growth in output of this industry from 1967 to 1980. The trend toward low-lead and lead-free gasolines will probably lead to a substantial decline in the production of tetra ethyl lead and ethyl chloride, but these are not sufficiently important to reduce the overall rate of growth significantly.

The energy-output ratio is expected to fall at a 2.2% rate from 1967 to 1980, partly due to the continuing introduction of new processes into newly constructed plants, and also in response to rising relative prices of energy. The latter will lead to the adoption of chemical processes such as those used in Europe and Japan, where energy prices have long been relatively higher than in the U.S.; these processes consume less energy and also use less feedstocks.

Another source of energy will be through more use of, and more efficient, heat recovery. The recapture of process heat, usually confined to the most heat-yielding (exothermic) processes, will be extended to many others. Also, more research will be put into the development of machinery that captures process heat, which should result in more efficient heat recovery. Both these movements require more capital investment; the heat recovery aspect involves capital addition, while changes in processes require capital replacement. During the rest of the 1970s, expansion of process heat recovery will be a greater source of energy saving than changes in process.

Industrial inorganic chemicals, n.e.c. (SIC 2819), Chapter Fourteen. This is another large energy user, and another catch-all industry. As the title indicates, raw materials are not generally drawn from fossil fuels. The industry is highly energy-intensive. In the 1954 to 1967 period, output grew at an average annual rate of 6.1% and total energy at a 2.6% rate; the energy-output ratio declined at a 3.3% rate. The industry energy statistics are dominated by the presence of three large atomic energy plants that produce enriched uranium, mainly for Defense Department use. These plants use vast amounts of electricity, and the construction of two of them between 1954 and 1958 produced a surge

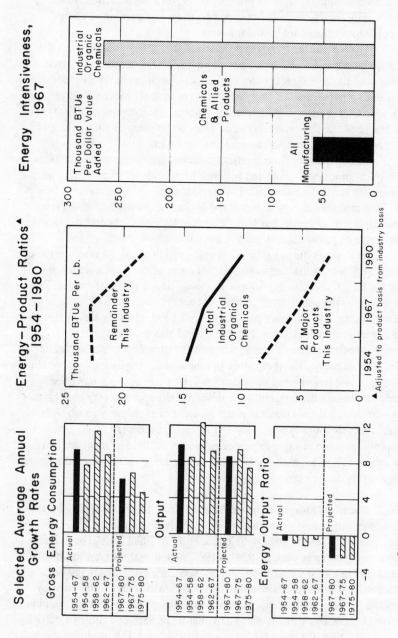

Chart 1-8.   Industrial Organic Chemicals, n.e.c. Sources: Department of Commerce; The Conference Board.

in energy use by the industry. Since that time, the level of their operation has declined. Total energy use by these plants swung the industry's energy-output ratio up and then down.

Information on production of other products indicates that substantial gains in energy saving were realized during the period. One example is the change in the production of phosphoric acid from the use of electric furnaces to the "wet process"; the latter uses much less energy. Another is the introduction of high efficiency turbine expanders to replace reciprocal expanders in the production of nitric acid; this leads to a 95% reduction in electricity use. A third example is the change from electric drive to air cooling and gas engine drives in ammonia production, as well as the introduction of new centrifugal compressors. These also result in very substantial reductions in energy use.

From 1967 to 1980, growth is expected to slow to a 5.5% rate. A shift to less energy-intensive chemicals is projected as a result of rising prices of energy and related rises in prices of feedstocks, as in ammonia production. Imports or substitute chemicals will probably replace, or satisfy, the growth in demand for many energy-intensive chemicals. Substantial changes in processes will also occur, where possible, to reduce energy use. There are also programs afoot in the production of enriched uranium that should reduce energy demand per unit in this sector of the industry.

These savings will be partially offset by an expected rise in the production of enriched uranium. The upshot is a decrease in the energy-output ratio at a 1.7% rate. This, combined with projected growth of output at 5.5% yields a rise in total energy use at a 3.7% rate.

Plastics materials and resins (SIC 2821), Chapter Fifteen. The products of this industry have very wide use in construction, transportation, consumer goods, and agriculture; further, their uses are spreading, resulting in very rapid growth at a 12.8% average annual rate from 1947 to 1967. This growth was aided by improvements in product quality, and by falling prices that were the result of large productivity gains. The industry uses oil and gas for both energy and feedstocks. Total energy use for heat and power rose less rapidly than output over the two decades, and as a result the energy-output ratio declined at a sharp 3.5% rate. There were large improvements in process technology that caused this decline.

The industry is projected to grow at an 8.9% average annual rate from 1967 to 1980. The products of the industry should continue to grow in use and to find new markets. Difficulties in obtaining supplies of feedstocks are likely to limit this growth, however. The energy-output ratio is projected to decline at a 4.2% rate as a result of the introduction of new energy-saving techniques. Examples are the application of radiation-induced polymerization in the production of both low-density and high-density polyethylene, and in polyvinyl chloride. The rapid growth in output, combined with the substantial rate of decline of energy per unit, yields an increase in total energy at a 6.2% rate.

Synthetic rubber (SIC 2822), Chapter Sixteen. In the 20-year period from 1947 to 1967, this industry grew rapidly, at a 6.7% average annual rate. The growth was partly at the expense of natural rubber—synthetic rubber increased its share of all new rubber from one-half to three-fourths in the two decades. Total energy use grew at an 8.2% rate, yielding a rise in the energy-output ratio at a 1.4% rate. The ratio was practically unchanged from 1947 to 1962, but grew substantially from 1962 to 1967. This development resulted from a change in the product mix, largely the result of the introduction of energy-intensive stereo elastomers.

From 1967 to 1980, output is projected to rise at a 5.7% rate and the energy-output ratio to continue to rise at a 1.3% rate. As a result, total energy use should rise at a 7.1% rate. Increasing attention to the recovery of "waste" heat and to the use of heat exchangers to recover waste streams is not expected to be adequate to offset the continuing change in product mix toward the more energy-intensive stereo elastomers.

Man-made fibers (SIC 2823, 2824), Chapter Seventeen. Over the period from 1958 to 1967, the production of cellulosic man-made fibers (largely rayon and acetate) rose at a 3.9% rate, while total energy use rose at only a 0.8% rate. As a result, the energy-output ratio fell at a substantial 3.0% rate. The newer industry, synthetic organic fibers, except cellulosic (largely nylon, acrylic, and polyesters), rose at a much more rapid rate of 18.7%. Total energy use in this industry did not keep pace, so the energy-output ratio declined at a 2.4% rate. In both the older and the newer industries, substantial advances in product technology and economies of large-scale production aided the rapid rates of energy saving. In the case of cellulosic fibers, integration (backwards) with cyclic intermediates also saved energy.

Growth of both industries is projected to be slower in the 1967 to 1980 period, with cellulosic fibers growing at a 3.2% rate and noncellulosic fibers at an 11.1% rate. The energy-output ratios are expected to decline in each industry more rapidly than in the historical period, at a 3.6% rate for cellulosic and at a 2.9% rate for noncellulosic, reflecting continued advances in production technology, larger-scale (energy-saving) operations, and adoption of energy-conservation measures in response to increasing energy prices. As a result, total energy use is expected to fall at a 0.5% rate for cellulosic fibers, and to rise at an 8.0% rate for noncellulosic fibers.

Petroleum Refining

Petroleum refining (SIC 2911), Chapter Eighteen. This is the second largest energy user in manufacturing, accounting for 9.4% of total energy purchased by manufacturing. It is also highly energy-intensive, in terms of value added. From 1947 to 1967, output grew at an average annual rate of 4.4% and total energy use (including captive) at a 3.8% rate. As a result, the energy-output ratio fell at a 0.7% rate for the entire period. There was an acceleration in the decline of the energy-output ratio, which fell at a 1.7% rate from 1962 to 1971 compared with a 0.4% rate of decline in the 1954 to 1962 period. The energy measure of this industry includes captive consumption of fuels and energy from process by-products. Purchased fuels and energy grew at a more rapid rate than total output from 1947 to 1967, reflecting a relative decline in the use of industry products to generate heat and power; it was found to be economical to sell more products and to purchase energy from less costly sources over the 20-year period.

Feedstocks are very important to the industry. A more complete measure of the effect of the industry on energy resources of the domestic economy would be made by comparing the BTU content of all feedstocks and purchased fuels and energy to the BTU content of produced fuels and feedstocks. Such a complete accounting would require a major research project, however, and has not been attempted here. But it should be noted that crude oil consumption per constant dollar of output has declined more rapidly than energy for heat and power over the period from 1954 to 1971.

Process changes that have reduced the energy-output ratio are catalytic cracking, catalytic reforming, and hydrogen processing. These technological changes, as well as changes in capital stock, have offset increases in processing (especially to raise the octane level of gasoline), which acted to raise energy use per unit of output. The switch from aviation gasoline to jet fuel lowered energy requirements, as did the early rise in the importance of diesel fuel (which has had a stable share of the industry's output since 1954). The decline in the relative importance of residual fuel oil (from 23% to 7% over 20 years) illustrates the effect of increased processing.

Output in the future depends largely on developments in automobile engines. Legal requirements to reduce air pollution by automobiles will have uncertain effects on the type of engines that will be produced in the second half of the Seventies. The effects on gasoline sales of higher gas prices are also very uncertain. A rate of growth of 5.0% is projected for the period from 1971 to 1980, with a slower rate from 1975 on. The recent, more rapid rate of decline in the energy-output ratio is expected to accelerate to 2.9%.

This is expected for two principal reasons. First, greater attention to maintenance and repair, a more systematic review of operating practices, and a higher rate of innovation should boost the trend rate of decline in the energy-output ratio to 2.0%. Second, the introduction of capital improvements, such as more extensive capture of heat from waste streams and production process, should lead to lump-sum improvements that will reduce the energy-output ratio by 7.0% by 1980. New refineries, built to cope with growing demand, will incorporate much greater energy conservation. Total use of energy for heat and power by the industry is therefore projected to rise at a 1.8% rate over the 1971 to 1980 period.

Stone, Clay, and Glass Industries

Basic glass (SIC 3211, 3221, 3229), Chapter Nineteen. We have combined three SIC industries, flat glass, glass containers, and pressed and blown glass, n.e.c., because of the similarity of the production operation that consumes a major portion—about 70%—of total energy used. The annealing process—also common to almost all production of glass products—accounts for a substantial part of the remaining energy consumption. Historical data for these industries are available from 1947 to 1971.

The combined industries use a large fraction of all energy in manufacturing, 1.7%. Basic glass has grown more slowly than GNP over the historical period because the major markets—autos, construction, food, and housewares—also grew less rapidly than the entire economy. The industries are also affected by imports and by competition from substitute materials. Over the 24-year period, output grew at a 3.3% rate, while total energy use grew at a 2.4% rate. As a result, the energy-output ratio declined at a 0.8% rate.

A number of technological and marketing developments can be credited for these movements in aggregate and per unit energy consumption. Increases in energy saving have come about mainly through (1) economies from the use of increasingly larger furnaces, (2) growing reuse of waste heat, (3) the introduction of an auxiliary heating unit inside the body of molten glass in the furnace, and (4) a shift to lighter weight bottles by the glass container industry. Increases in energy consumption by pollution-control equipment and increased mechanization have partially offset the savings won.

There was a sharp drop in the use of coal and oil by the industry in the 24-year period; this was offset by a large increase in the use of natural gas and a smaller increase in electricity use.

From 1971 to 1980, output is projected to rise more rapidly, partly as a result of the recovery from the depressed level of 1971. The rate of growth is still below that of GNP, because markets are projected to continue to face competition from imports and substitutes.

The energy-output ratio is projected to be practically unchanged, declining at a 0.1% rate. As a whole, there does not appear to be any ongoing technological shift or new development on the horizon that will drastically affect energy use per unit of output between now and 1980. Average furnace size may increase further, but there are limitations to major change in this period. The use of electric boosters probably will become more widespread. Prospects for energy savings seem to be best in the flat glass industry, through further conversion to the float process of making plate glass. An increase in recycling of used glass should help, for glass melts more rapidly than its raw materials—this is a good prospect for energy saving.

Hydraulic cement (SIC 3241), Chapter Twenty. This industry is a large user of energy, accounting for 3.3% of total purchased manufacturing energy. It is also very energy-intensive. The principal product of the industry is portland cement. In the 1947 to 1967 period, output grew at a rate of 3.0%, slower than GNP, mainly because of the slower growth of construction activity. In this period, the nation switched from being a net exporter to a net importer of cement, which also served to slow growth.

Total energy use grew at a 2.1% rate during the 20 years under review, resulting in a decline in the energy-output ratio at a 1.0% rate. Energy savings have come about mainly through (1) the growing reuse of waste heat, (2) economies of scale won through the use of increasingly larger plants, and (3) advances in mechanization. These developments have been partly countered by the greater per unit energy requirements of increased mechanization and of pollution-control equipment.

There was a rise in the relative use of natural gas by the industry from 1947 to 1967, mainly at the expense of coal.

Since 1967, there has been a surge in imports, which is expected to continue. As a result, output is projected to grow at a slower rate (2.7%) from 1967 to 1980. The energy-output ratio is projected to decline at a more rapid rate of 1.6% yielding an increase in total energy at a 1.1% rate. The basic change expected to affect the energy-output ratio is a shift from the wet process to the less energy-intensive dry process of manufacture. In addition, the three items enumerated above are expected to continue. Coal is expected to rise substantially in importance as fuel for the industry, at the expense of natural gas; this is a reversal of the shift that took place in the 1947 to 1967 period.

Brick and structural clay tile (SIC 3251), Chapter Twenty-One. This industry is quite energy-intensive, as are most of the industries studied in the stone, clay, and glass group. It experienced a slow growth in output from 1947 to 1967 at an average annual rate of 1.7%, while total energy use rose at a 0.8% rate. The cement industry has expanded largely at the expense of the brick industry. Bricks have suffered from competition with other building materials such as concrete blocks and cheap steel.

There have been uneven changes in the energy-output ratio over the 20-year period. Improvements in drying and firing yielded energy savings from 1947 to 1958. An increase in the share of product accounted for by bricks, which are more energy-intensive, and the introduction of automation processes, raised the energy-output ratio from 1958 to 1962. The introduction of tunnel kilns, which are less energy using per unit of output than periodic kilns, lowered the rate from 1962 to 1967. For the entire 20 years, the energy-output ratio declined at a 0.9% rate.

From 1967 to 1980, output is projected to rise at a 2.0% rate, largely as a result of greater construction activity. The energy-output ratio is projected to decline more slowly than before, at a 0.3% rate. The effects of the shift in product mix to brick, which raises energy use per unit, and the spread of tunnel kilns, which lowers it, have been largely expended. The most likely outcome in the 1970s is a return to the 1958 level of energy use per unit, expected to be achieved through energy-control programs in the industry. The output and the energy-output ratio projections, taken together, yield a rise in total energy at a 1.7% rate from 1967 to 1980.

Ready-mixed concrete (SIC 3273), Chapter Twenty-Two. This is a relatively new industry which has grown rapidly, at a 4.9% average annual rate from 1958 to 1967. The growth is the result of a shift to mixing of concrete by suppliers, as opposed to on-site mixing builders. The industry has been characterized by a rapid increase in mechanization, which raised energy use at a 10.2% average annual rate—even faster than output. As a consquence, the energy-output ratio rose at a 5.0% rate.

The industry is projected to grow at a 3.4% rate from 1967 to 1980, reflecting an increase in its share of total concrete preparation and a greater total use of concrete in the economy. The energy-output ratio is projected to continue to rise, though not as rapidly as before, at a 3.8% rate. This expec-tation is based on the definite trend toward continued mechanization, substituting capital (and energy) for labor, as well as on an increase in the pro-vision of the product in cold weather, which requires more energy to maintain the heat of the concrete.

Lime (SIC 3274), Chapter Twenty-Three. This is the most energy-intensive industry in manufacturing, although it consumes a relatively small fraction of the manufacturing energy total. Lime produced and shipped by the industry rose at a 2% average annual rate from 1947 to 1967. This was produced with total energy that grew at a 1.8% rate, resulting in an energy-shipments ratio that declined at a 0.1% rate. A large and increasing share of lime is consumed within the industry; this development is mainly due to control of air and water pollution by the industry, and has resulted in a rapid increase in the energy-shipments ratio from 1958 to 1967, which wiped out most of the energy saving that had taken place in the previous 15 years.

When energy is related to total production of lime, including that produced and consumed within the industry, energy per unit is seen to have fallen at a rapid 3.5%; this illustrates the significant effect of pollution control on the industry's energy use. Process data document the substantial savings realized in production, such as the gains made in baking by both rotary and vertical kilns. Also, newly developed processes such as the fluid-bed kiln use much less energy than was prevalent in the 1950s.

In the future, shipments are projected to increase at a 6.2% rate, paralleling the growth of total production (including captive consumption of lime) in the industry. The energy-output ratio is projected to decline at a rapid 4.5% rate. The pollution-control equipment is largely installed, and many old plants have been closed. The rise in the share of production for use in the industry should largely cease and the new energy-saving processes act with nearly full force. As a result of the projected rapid decline in the energy-output ratio, total energy is projected to rise more slowly than in the 1947 to 1967 period, at a 1.4% rate, despite the accelerated rate of shipments of the industry.

Primary Metal Industries[e]

Blast furnaces and steel mills (SIC 3312), Chapter Twenty-Four. This industry is the largest energy user in manufacturing, accounting for 11.7% of total dollars spent on purchased energy. The industry covers four principal manufacturing operations: coke ovens, blast furnaces, steel works, and rolling mills. The large, vertically integrated iron and steel mills in the United States combine all of these operations. Smaller steel mills often specialize in one or more of the basic steel-making processes.

Coal purchased for the use by the industry is treated as a raw material, since it is processed by coke ovens to produce coke, breeze, gas, and other by-products. The coke, breeze, and gas, in turn, are used in later stages in the industry's operations. The industry therefore consumes much "captive" energy, from these sources and from blast furnace gas. The total captive consumption of energy nearly equalled purchased energy in 1967 (1.7 quadrillion BTUs vs. 1.8 quadrillion).

The industry is highly cyclical, so the average growth rate from 1947 to 1972 of nearly 2% masks substantial fluctuations from year to year both in output and in energy use per unit of output. Total energy use (including captive consumption) grew more slowly than output over the 25 years, so the energy-output ratio fell about 1% per year (Chart 1-9).

Important energy-saving improvements occured in the following processes: (1) better charge preparation and fuel injection for blast furnaces, (2) development of the top-oxygen blown converter process, and (3) development of continuous processes for casting, rolling, and finishing of steel.

The industry is projected to achieve a faster growth rate from 1972 to 1980 of 3.5%, producing 175 million short tons of raw steel in 1980. Energy use per unit of output is projected to decline at a 1.1% rate over the 8-year period; this decline is predicated on a more than 8% total drop from 1972 to 1980 in energy use (including captive) per ton of raw steel. The drop in

[e]See also highlights of Chapter 31.

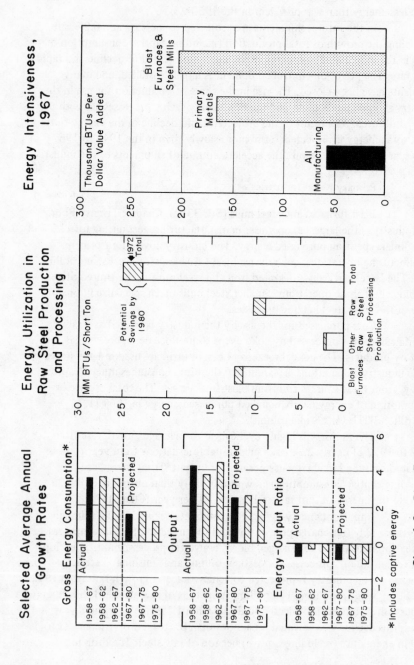

Chart 1-9. Blast Furnaces and Steel Mills. Sources: Department of Commerce; The Conference Board.

requirements stems from the following expected developments: (1) a 5% to 6% decline in per unit energy use in blast furnace operations through pre-reduction of iron ores, the use of high-quality pellets and self-fluxing sinter, and the use of hydrocarbon injection into the furnace; (2) a 10% drop in per unit energy use in raw steel processing through the spread of continuous casting operations; and (3) a 5 to 10% drop in per unit energy use in steel melting operations through the continuing spread of the basic oxygen process and the use of oxygen in the open-hearth furnace (reducing process time).

Electrometallurgical products (SIC 3313), Chapter Twenty-Five. This is a highly energy-intensive industry that produces (mainly) ferroalloys for use in steel making. The industry grew relatively slowly in the 1947-67 period at an average annual rate of 1.6%. Production fluctuated widely in intervening years owing to the heavy dependence on the steel industry as a market.

Total energy use grew more rapidly over the same period at a 2.2% rate. This was the result, in large part, of changes in the product mix toward more energy-intensive ferroalloys and, more recently, of the installation of air-pollution-control equipment. As a result, the energy-output ratio rose at a 0.6% rate.

A net decline in output is projected for the 1967 to 1980 period as a result of increases in imports. The energy-output ratio is expected to continue to rise at a 1.0% rate; energy saving from the use of large furnaces and automated mixing and charging operations is expected to be more than offset by a continuing shift to a more energy-intensive product mix and to further installation of pollution-control equipment. Total energy use, however, should decline slightly, at a 0.2% rate, because of the projected drop in output.

Gray iron and steel foundries (SIC 3321, 3323), Chapter Twenty-Six. Both industries experienced slow growth from 1947 to 1967. Output grew more rapidly in the latter part of the period, as the major buying sectors (motor vehicles, farm machinery and equipment, railroad equipment, and construction equipment) picked up in the 1960s. No definite trends are discernible in the energy-output ratios of foundries. Changes that saved energy within the industries, such as a rise in average plant size, were offset by changing demands of buyers, who required products that were more energy-intensive.

There are many uncertainties in the growth prospects for the industries; these are mainly related to the auto market, which is the most important for foundry products. Installation of air-pollution control devices is expected to offset, in whole or part, any energy savings. A small rate of decline is therefore projected for the energy-output ratio of gray iron foundries, at 0.2%; a slight rise, at 0.4%, is projected for steel foundries. Assuming that housings for rotors of Wankel engines will be made of aluminum, output is projected at a 4.8% rate for gray iron foundries; this, combined with the projected rate of decline in the energy-output ratio, yields a rise in total energy at a 4.6% rate. For steel foundries, a 3.8% growth rate is projected, which together with the expected rise in the energy-output ratio yields a 4.3% growth rate for total energy in this industry.

Copper rolling and drawing (SIC 3351), Chapter Twenty-Seven. In the period from 1947 to 1967, the output of this industry rose at a modest 1.0% rate. Production in 1967 was depressed by a strike in copper mining and smelting, so the true long-term growth rate is slightly understated. The data on energy use for this industry are of uncertain precision, owing to changing industrial coverage.

The energy-output ratio fluctuated in a narrow range over the two decades. The major technological change was in the rolling sector of the industry, where semi-continuous production was introduced in the period from 1958 to 1962, thus eliminating several reducing runs, which resulted in energy savings. Total energy use rose at a 0.7% rate for the 20-year period, and as a consequence the energy-output ratio fell at a 0.3% rate.

For the period from 1967 to 1980, output is projected to rise at a 2.0% rate. An innovation is expected to be introduced in the extrusion die wiremaking process, which requires only one run rather than several and should lead to considerable energy saving. The energy-output ratio is expected to continue to decline at a 0.3% rate as a result of the introduction of this process and from other similar improvements. As a consequence, total energy is projected to rise at a 1.7% rate.

Nonferrous wiredrawing, insulating (SIC 3357), Chapter Twenty-Eight. In the period from 1958 to 1967, output grew at a rapid 7.4% rate, while total energy use rose at only a 4.5% rate. As a result, the energy-output ratio declined at a rapid 2.6% rate. A new generation of wiredrawing machinery, introduced since 1958, resulted in substantial energy saving in this industry.

In the 1967 to 1980 period, output is projected to rise at a 4.2% rate. New continuous-process machinery will continue to spread through the industry, producing energy savings. But pollution-control measures to purify wastes and a new wirecoating process that uses more energy will act to offset the gains. On balance, the energy-output ratio is projected to decline at a 0.8% rate, slower than in the past. Consequently, total energy use is expected to rise at a 3.4% rate.

Iron and steel forgings (SIC 3391), Chapter Twenty-Nine. Output rose at a 2.6% rate for this industry from 1947 to 1967. The energy-output ratio was nearly constant from 1947 to 1962, then dropped sharply. Since the most widely used furnaces, those fueled by oil or gas, must be operated on a continuous basis regardless of the volume of throughput, energy per unit depends strongly on the rate of utilization of capacity. The latter rose substantially from 1962 to 1967, lowering the energy-output ratio in those five years. Also, newer electric furnaces, first used in the mid-1960s, are less wasteful of energy, since they can be turned off when not needed. For the 20-year period, total energy use rose at a 1.3% rate, yielding a decline in the energy-output ratio at a 1.3% rate.

Output is projected to rise at a 3.9% rate from 1967 to 1980, provided that limitations of skilled manpower and productive capacity can be overcome. The energy saving factors of full-capacity utilization and introduction of electric furnaces will continue to provide energy savings; but since both factors have already had their major impact, a slowing of the decline in the energy-output ratio is projected, to a 0.9% rate. Consequently, total energy should rise at a 2.9% rate.

Methodology and Pilot Studies

Methodology, Chapter Thirty. In the industry essays just reviewed, the authors had two principal goals: For the historical period, to identify the changes in technology, production processes, and output mix that would explain changes in the energy-output ratio; for the future, to infer the effects of likely changes in these three factors on the energy-output ratio. The inferences about the past and the future are usually not based on quantified information, owing to the lack of availability of such information. In the methodology study, a technique is proposed for quantifying these factors; it is then employed in two pilot studies.

Essentially, the technique is to construct, for an industry, a series of matrixes, one for each year studied. The rows are energy sources, the columns are energy-using processes, and the data in the cells are quantities of output. Changes between matrixes representing different years permit precise measures of the effects of energy saving within processes, and those that result from process change. By constructing a table for each type of output, the effect of changes in product composition can also be measured.

Detailed data are required for the preparation of each matrix, and such data must ordinarily be obtained from companies or establishments in the industry studied.

Aluminum (SIC 3334, 3352), Chapter Thirty-One. Aluminum is a major energy user and energy is a substantial fraction of the total cost of production of this metal. Total output grew at a rapid 8.6% rate from 1947 to 1972 and is projected to grow between 5% and 6% per year from 1972 to 1980.

Adequate data are not available for computing precise measures of historical energy use in the industry. Future energy use depends in large part on the location of expansions in alumina capacity: if expansions in capacity are located in the United States, energy use per pound of aluminum ingot (from virgin materials) is projected to decline by 0.9% a year from 1971 to 1980; if increases in alumina production take place abroad in ore-producing countries, energy per pound of ingot will decline more rapidly.

The major source of energy for the industry is electricity, followed by natural gas and oil. Use of natural gas is expected to decline substantially by 1980, from 30% to 17% of total energy inputs. Electricity use per unit of product has not changed appreciably in the past, but rapid increases in electricity prices are expected to lead to significant reductions in the future. Such changes will require substantial rebuilding of present plants or construction of new plants and are not projected to have important impacts on energy use during the remainder of this decade. Introduction of the chloride process promises significant economies in the future.

Pulp, paper, and paperboard mills (SIC 2611, 2621, 2631), Chapter Thirty-Two. These industries are major energy users. In 1971, together they absorbed 7.7% of all energy purchased by the manufacturing sector. The analysis of these industries is based on a survey of mills from which questionnaires were obtained. Survey respondents accounted for one-fourth of all production in 1971 and provided much detailed data; historical information for years prior to 1971 was obtained from only a small number of respondents and is inadequate to permit analysis.

In 1971 nearly 39% of total energy was obtained from waste and by-product sources (primarily "black liquors"). The importance of such "captive consumption" has apparently risen significantly in recent years, partly because of pollution-control regulations. Use of wastes is expected to continue to expand, as water-pollution controls tighten and purchased energy prices rise.

Output is projected to grow at a 4.2% rate from 1971 to 1980. The energy-output ratio, including captive consumption, is expected to decline at a 2% rate from 1971 to 1975 as a result of renovation of existing plant and replacement of obsolete plant, both serving to spread energy-saving techniques throughout industry. During the period from 1975 to 1980, totally new plants will begin operation and be designed to take full advantage of energy-saving technology such as recycling process steam and incorporating further use of waste products for energy. As a result, the energy-output ratio is projected to decline at a rapid 4% rate in the latter period. Total energy use, from 1971 to 1980, is projected to rise at only a 1.1% rate, despite the rapid growth anticipated for output.

Notes

[1] The Maryland Interindustry Forecasting Model was developed at the University of Maryland under the direction of Professor Clopper Almon, Jr.

Development of the model is supported by a number of organizations. The Conference Board is a member of the sponsoring group. Formally named INFORUM, the model is referred to as MIFM or INFORUM throughout this report.

[2] *1967 Census of Manufactures,* Volume I, page 19.

[3] For example, see "New Burner Saves Fuel, Lowers Pollution," *Oil and Gas Journal,* February 22, 1971, p. 95.

[4] This relationship between size and R&D on energy is similar to that between size and R&D in general: larger companies spend more on R&D than the smaller ones.

[5] John G. Myers, "Some Basic Factors in Long Range Economic Projections," 1972 *Proceedings*, Business and Economic Statistics Section, American Statistical Association, pp. 170-174.

SECTION IV.   APPENDIXES

1. Company Survey of Future Energy Demand
Bernard A. Gelb

Purpose

A general mail survey of future energy demand in U.S. manufacturing was conducted as an element of and a major input to the overall study of energy use by the manufacturing sector. Briefly, its objective was to survey company perceptions of the "energy crisis," and the extent and character of plans for future energy use. It should be emphasized that the survey was conducted in the spring of 1973.

The general survey (as distinguished from the mailing to paper industry establishments discussed in Chapter Thirty-Two) was conceived as and designed to be an essential source of information that would complement the quantitative and nonquantitative data from published sources and interviews. It had two general objectives: (1) to obtain estimates of anticipated trends in energy use by the six 2-digit industry groups, and to get an idea of the manufacturing processes in which changes in energy use per unit of output are expected to take place; (2) to obtain information on company perceptions of the energy situation—specifically the aspects of price, supply availability, and environmental regulations—and information on the nature of the steps that manufacturers have taken and expect to take as regards energy use.

More specifically, the questionnaire (attached) was designed to develop information on the following: (1) the mix of fuels or energy forms used by the firms and industries under study; (2) anticipated changes in energy use— regarding mix and regarding relationship to output—between 1971 and 1980; (3) plans to change technology, operations, or facilities that are expected to have a measurable effect on fuel or energy use per unit of output; (4) the effects on energy use of changes in prices and availability of energy supplies, and of environmental restrictions; (5) the extent to which firms are giving and plan to give attention to the question of possible energy shortages and to the obtaining and use of energy, including research and development programs.

This plan was chosen on the basis of internal analysis and on the basis of reactions by representatives of industry to early drafts of the questionnaire. Largely because our industry advisory panel believed that the questionnaire was at first much too long, we scrapped our original plans to try to get historical information on energy use and on the factors affecting energy use.

Procedures and Volume of Response

To obtain the desired data, a sample of 212 companies in the six 2-digit industry groups under study was chosen from the membership of The Conference Board. We selected the largest 35 to 40 firms, plus a sprinkling of medium-sized and small firms, in each of the groups except paper (SIC 26). For the latter, only ten firms were chosen because of overlapping problems with the sample for the pilot study on paper and paperboard mills. In early February, a letter from the president of The Conference Board was sent to the chief executive officer of each of the 212 companies briefly informing them of the nature of our objectives and requesting them to indicate on a postcard to whom we should send the questionnaire that was to come shortly. Nearly three-quarters—154—responded as requested.

Questionnaires were sent on March 8, 1973 with an explanatory cover letter from the Director of the Division of Economic Research to all companies except the one that refused. Five weeks later, we sent a brief follow-up letter with another copy of the questionnaire to those firms that had not returned questionnaires; and three weeks after that we telephoned most of the companies that still had not responded. These follow-ups proved to be effective as prodders or reminders. About half of those who were followed up subsequently completed and returned their questionnaires; some asked for another copy of the questionnaire because theirs had been misplaced.

Mainly large companies were chosen because these were believed to be best informed about the energy situation. While the response may not be strictly representative, the purposes of the survey probably have been served.

Altogether, we received 150 completed questionnaires from 120 responding companies. A number of firms completed one or more additional questionnaires to cover operations that were in another 2-digit industry; a few reported divisions or subsidiaries in the same industry on separate questionnaires. In addition to the one refusal by postcard, fifteen or so other companies indicated by letter or phone that they were unable to or would not participate in the survey.

In relative terms the responses covered the industry groups fairly evenly; and the proportions of the industry groups that we covered are relatively high, except for food and paper. By matching the number of employees of the companies that responded to the survey against the total number of employees in the respective industry groups, we calculated that our coverage is 15% for food, 21% for paper, 37% for chemicals, 36% for petroleum and coal products, 27% for stone, clay, and glass, and 32% for primary metals (see Table 1A-1). In the case of food, we attribute the lower coverage to the very large number of companies in SIC 20. As regards paper, we started with a very small sample because we planned to supplement our responses with information obtained from the surveys of paper companies done in connection with the pilot study of pulp, paper, and paperboard mills. Because such information was obtained through different questionnaires and tabulating procedures, the survey data on SIC 26 included here is less comprehensive than that for the other industry groups. What is included here is mainly for broad comparisons between the 2-digit industry groups.

Quality of the Response

The quality of the written answers to the questions was, in general, fair to good; as to be expected, however, there were some extreme variations in apparent conscientiousness. Not surprisingly, those questions of a "multiple choice" or "yes-no" nature—items 6B, 7, and 8—were most thoroughly answered. Those that required the extraction of data, the calculation of percentages, and the reporting of projections—items 1, 3, and 6A—were most poorly answered. No more than one questionnaire in 20 was perfectly filled out. We believe, however, that we rectified nearly all of the cases of incorrect or incomplete response. This involved an intensive effort of telephoning, with telephone calls made to all but a handful of responding companies.

Table 1A-1. Coverage by Industry

Industry	Employment of Responding Companies	Total Industry Employment (1972)	Respondees as a Per Cent of Total	Number of Responding Companies
SIC 20 Food and kindred products	258,062	1,751,100	14.7	32
SIC 26 Paper and allied products	150,000	697,000	21.5	11*
SIC 28 Chemicals and allied products	371,027	1,002,200	37.0	35
SIC 29 Petroleum and coal products	67,546	189,600	35.6	16
SIC 32 Stone, clay, and glass products	177,287	660,000	26.9	21
SIC 33 Primary metal industries	394,941	1,234,800	32.0	40
Six industries combined . .	1,418,863	5,534,700	25.6	165*

*This includes respondents to the survey in connection with the paper industry pilot study.
Sources: The Conference Board; U.S. Bureau of Labor Statistics.

Summary of Findings

In general, manufacturing companies in the six 2-digit industries we covered anticipate that they will have to shift to relatively less use of natural gas—largely because of expected supply problems, partly because of price increases. While some supply and price problems for oil are anticipated, on the whole they do not seem to be regarded as seriously as those for gas. Only a few firms expect more than minor problems in getting a desired supply of electricity; there is relatively little expectation or *concern* about price increases of electricity. The impression we obtained is that coal would be used more if restrictions for environmental protection were eased.

In most cases, companies expect to reduce energy use per unit of output—largely through the achievement of a number of small efficiencies, rather than through some major technological or systems breakthrough. Where overall energy use per unit of output is expected to increase, it is usually due to a shift to a more energy-intensive product mix.

Research and development for reducing energy use per unit of output is much more prevalent than R&D for further developing corporate sources of energy, and more of both is expected to be done in the future than has been done in the past. A substantial minority of companies, however, have not done and do not expect to do any R&D for either purpose.

Nearly all companies indicated that they are concerned about an energy problem and that some action has been taken, or that responsibility for energy-related matters has been assigned to particular persons or company units.

Energy Use Per Unit of Output, and by Type

Judging by the survey, manufacturers in the industry groups (except SIC 26) covered in the study expect to continue to be able to reduce their energy use per unit of output, but at a slower rate than previously. Chemicals producers, for example, had achieved the most rapid decline in the energy-output ratio during the postwar period until 1967—2.2% a year, on average; but the surveyed companies reported expectations (weighted by employment) of an average drop of 1.7% between 1971 and 1980.

As noted elsewhere, however, experience gained in obtaining the survey data, in interviews with industry experts, and in analyses of industry statistics and technical data has led us to the opinion that many industry people tend to underestimate the extent of past declines in energy use per unit of output in their own industry and to underestimate the potential of energy saving for the future.

Replies from stone, clay, and glass firms indicate an average annual drop of 0.8% between 1971 and 1980, the same rate of decline as that experienced by the 2-digit SIC group between 1947 and 1967. Petroleum and coal products companies project, on average, an annual decline of 0.5%,

Table 1A-2. Projections of Energy Use per Unit of Output
(responses to item #6A)

Industry	Industry Average[1] 1975 (1971 = 100)	Industry Average[1] 1980 (1971 = 100)	Average Annual Per Cent Change 1971-1980	Total Number of Companies Reporting	Companies Reporting No Change	Average Annual Per Cent Changes 1947-1967[2]	BTU Per $ of Value Added[3]
SIC 20 Food and kindred products	99.27	99.20	-0.1	30	10	-2.2	41,200
SIC 26 Paper and allied products	(s)	(s)	(s)	(s)	(s)	-0.8	140,100
SIC 28 Chemicals and allied products	99.59	86.31	-1.7	33	7	-2.2	138,300
SIC 29 Petroleum and coal products	97.35	95.94	-0.5	16	3	-1.4	284,400
SIC 32 Stone, clay, and glass products	96.05	92.87	-0.8	21	6	-0.8	160,900
SIC 33 Primary metal industries	96.33	93.77	-0.7	37	7	-1.6	167,200

[1] Weighted by number of employees of responding companies.
[2] Observed for the entire industry groups from Census Bureau data.
[3] 1967 data excludes consumption of energy from captive sources.
(s) Number of reporting companies too small to show data
Sources: Table 1-3; The Conference Board.

compared with a 1.4% rate for the entire SIC 29 group from 1947 to 1967. Producers of primary metals expect to reduce energy use per unit of output by 0.7% a year, as against 1.6% the average annual rate during the 1947-1967 period. Expectations of an 0.1% yearly rate of decline are reported by food manufacturers but, as is discussed in the section on the food group below, we believe that this is not a true figure.

As regards energy use by type of fuel, or electricity, a strong shift away from gas is expected by firms in all five industry groups for which we could compile data. In terms of the proportion of their total energy use (in BTUs), chemical makers foresee a drop in gas from 51% in 1971 to 28% in 1980; petroleum firms report an anticipated decline from 71% to 41%; stone, clay, and glass people, from 63% to 35%; food producers, from 55% to 43%; and primary metal companies, from 22% to 13%. Manufacturers in these industries expect to make up the difference, partly with greater use of fuel oils (mostly heavy) and partly with greater use of electricity (see Table 1A-3).

In obtaining these data on energy use by type, by asking for the per cent of total energy use accounted for by each firm's three main fuel or energy forms, we found that industry's specialization of fuel use is rather high. In none of the five industry groups does the energy accounted for by the fourth- or lower-ranking fuels or energy forms represent more than 8.3%; and in three groups it represented less than 5%.

Price Expectations

In all five industry groups for which the survey produced sufficient data, companies expect real prices of fuels and electricity to increase between 1971 and 1980. And in all five industry groups, the real price of gas is antici-pated to rise faster than that of other energy sources.

Although their expectations of nominal price rises in fuels and electricity are about average for the five industry groups, companies in the chemicals industry group (SIC 28) anticipate the highest rate of increase in real prices of energy. When weighted by size of firm (number of employees), chemicals company expectations are that the real price of gas will rise an average of 2.5% a year between 1971 and 1980; electricity, 1.7% a year; and fuel oils, 1.6% a year. SIC 28 uses more BTUs than any other 2-digit manufac-turing industry group. Price change expectations for the 2-digit industry groups are shown in detail in Table 1A-4.

Energy Use Difficulties

Anticipations that relatively less gas will be used in 1980 than in 1971 are, apparently, at least partly founded on the belief that gas will be harder to get in relation to their projected needs than it is now in relation to present needs. Roughly two-thirds of gas-using companies (weighted by approxi-mate volume of gas consumed) in each of the chemicals, petroleum, and primary

Table 1A-3. Main Fuels or Energy Forms
(responses to item #1)

	Coal	Coke	Light Fuel Oils	Heavy Fuel Oils	Gas	Purchased Electricity	Other	Total
SIC 20 Food								
Weighted %								
1971	2.6	0	4.6	14.3	55.2	18.6	0.2	95.5
1975	2.0	0	6.0	16.4	50.5	19.1	0.2	94.2
1980	2.1	0	9.9	18.8	43.0	19.8	0.2	93.8
Number of mentions								
1971	2	0	15	15	27	26	2	87
1975	2	0	14	16	26	24	2	84
1980	2	0	12	16	27	23	1	81
SIC 26 Paper	Number of reporting companies too small to show data.							
SIC 28 Chemicals								
Weighted %								
1971	18.1	0.3	1.5	10.8	50.9	8.1	2.0	91.7
1975	16.4	0.3	3.2	20.4	40.7	7.0	1.8	89.8
1980	13.0	0.3	3.3	30.5	28.1	11.4	1.9	88.5
Number of mentions								
1971	11	1	6	11	31	28	5	93
1975	10	1	8	15	32	26	6	98
1980	11	1	10	18	27	24	5	96
SIC 29 Petroleum								
Weighted %								
1971	1.9	2.4	0	11.5	70.8	6.0	1.3	93.9
1975	0.9	1.4	0.9	17.6	63.9	8.0	0.3	93.0
1980	0.9	1.4	11.7	26.3	40.7	11.3	0.2	92.5
Number of mentions								
1971	2	2	0	11	16	12	2	45
1975	1	1	1	13	15	11	1	43
1980	1	1	3	13	13	11	1	43
SIC 32 Stone, clay and glass								
Weighted %								
1971	1.7	5.1	3.5	5.0	62.5	17.5	0.1	95.4
1975	2.6	5.0	8.7	7.3	49.2	21.1	0.1	94.0
1980	2.8	5.0	17.2	10.1	34.8	23.0	0.1	93.0
Number of mentions								
1971	6	1	8	11	19	15	1	61
1975	6	1	10	12	18	14	1	62
1980	5	1	12	11	17	13	1	60
SIC 33 Primary metals								
Weighted %								
1971	59.4	0.2	0.4	5.5	22.2	7.9	0	95.6
1975	56.8	0.2	1.3	10.2	16.9	9.2	0.5	95.1
1980	57.2	0.2	1.1	12.5	13.2	9.8	0.5	94.5
Number of mentions								
1971	13	4	10	15	37	30	0	109
1975	9	4	13	13	37	32	2	110
1980	9	4	12	15	34	33	2	109

Note: Percentages do not add to 100 because respondents were asked for their three main fuels only. Fuel use is weighted by number of employees of responding companies.

Source: The Conference Board.

Table 1A-4   Price Expectations
(responses to item #2)

Energy Form	Absolute Change			Relative Change*		
	1971-1975	*1975-1980*	*1971-1980*	*1971-1975*	*1975-1980*	*1971-1980*
	Average Annual Per Cent Increase (Weighted by Employment)					
20 Food						
Coal	8.2	6.5	7.2	1.7	1.3	1.5
Coke	–	–	–	–	–	–
Light fuel oils ...	11.0	12.2	11.6	2.2	2.5	2.3
Heavy fuel oils ...	10.2	10.5	10.4	2.1	2.2	2.1
Gas	11.0	11.8	11.4	2.2	2.4	2.3
Electricity	6.6	8.8	7.8	1.3	1.7	1.6
26 Paper						
Coal	5	6	5.5	1.1	1.7	1.5
Coke	–	–	–	–	–	–
Light fuel oils ...	8	6	6.9	1.8	1.7	1.8
Heavy fuel oils ...	9	8	8.4	2.0	2.3	2.2
Gas	12	11	11.4	2.7	3.1	2.9
Electricity	6	7	6.6	1.3	2.0	1.7
28 Chemicals						
Coal	4.9	4.9	4.9	1.3	1.4	1.3
Coke	2.4	4.9	5.3	0.6	1.5	1.6
Light fuel oils ...	7.5	7.0	7.2	1.6	1.6	1.6
Heavy fuel oils ...	8.1	6.0	7.1	1.6	1.5	1.6
Gas	11.0	8.0	9.2	2.9	2.1	2.5
Electricity	6.8	5.6	6.2	1.8	1.7	1.7
29 Petroleum						
Coal	7.2	4.7	5.8	1.6	1.1	1.3
Coke	–	–	–	–	–	–
Light fuel oils ...	8.4	6.4	7.3	2.0	1.6	1.8
Heavy fuel oils ...	9.1	6.5	7.6	2.3	1.8	2.0
Gas	11.7	8.2	9.4	3.0	2.1	2.5
Electricity	7.6	7.1	7.3	1.9	2.0	1.9
32 Stone, clay, glass						
Coal	8.0	4.7	6.1	1.7	1.0	1.4
Coke	4.4	4.4	4.4	1.0	1.1	1.1
Light fuel oils ...	8.9	5.9	7.3	1.7	1.2	1.4
Heavy fuel oils ...	6.6	6.0	6.2	1.5	1.3	1.4
Gas	9.2	8.3	8.7	1.8	1.7	1.8
Electricity	5.7	4.6	5.1	1.1	1.0	1.1

Table 1A-4 (continued)

Energy Form	Absolute Change			Relative Change*		
	1971-1975	1975-1980	1971-1980	1971-1975	1975-1980	1971-1980
	Average Annual Per Cent Increase (Weighted by Employment)					
33 Primary metals						
Coal	7.0	4.8	5.7	1.5	1.1	1.3
Coke	6.0	4.9	5.4	1.2	1.2	1.2
Light fuel oils ...	5.9	5.8	5.8	1.3	1.8	1.5
Heavy fuel oils ...	6.5	6.4	6.4	1.3	1.7	1.5
Gas	9.2	8.8	9.0	1.7	2.1	1.9
Electricity	6.3	6.0	6.1	1.3	1.3	1.3

*Absolute change expected divided by expected change in general price level. $(1 + R_a) \div (1 + R_g)$, where R_a = average annual per cent increase ÷ 100 in energy prices and R_g = average annual per cent increase ÷ 100 in the general price level.

Source: The Conference Board.

metals groups foresee either market unavailability or interruptible service conditions, or both, as obstacles preventing them from using the amount of gas they otherwise would use. In food and in stone, clay, and glass, about 45% and 55%, respectively, foresee such difficulties. Gas is the main source of energy for all of the 2-digit industry groups under study, except for primary metals, insofar as the surveyed firms are concerned.

Generally, anticipations of a greater degree of interruption of gas supply are more prevalent than expectations of specific and outright limitations on yearly supply. From what was gathered during interviews of the paper companies (done in connection with the paper industry pilot study) and what was collected from the general mail survey, this holds as much for SIC 26 as it does for the five other 2-digit industry groups.

Problems with coal run in a different vein. The main difficulties are, according to the survey responses, restrictions or regulations on their use for environmental purposes. For example, 80% of coal users (again weighted by approximate consumption) in stone, clay, and glass, 70% of users in food, and 50% of users in chemicals anticipate problems of this nature between now and 1980. Users of residual fuel oils expect some difficulties due to environmental regulations, and also a moderate outcropping of unavailability and interruptions.

Relatively little difficulty is foreseen in the obtaining and using of distillate fuel oils and of electricity. Table 1A-5 contains additional data on anticipations of non-price energy use problems.

Table 1A-5.   Non-price Difficulties
(Responses to Item #3)

	Not Affected	Market Unavailability	Interruptible Service	Stiffer Regulation Emissions Effluents	Other
	Per Cent of Normal Fuel or Energy Use				
20 Food					
Coal	29.6	0.5	0	69.8	0
Coke	–	–	–	–	–
Light fuel oils	66.0	24.7	5.5	3.0	0
Heavy fuel oils	60.4	6.7	4.9	28.0	0
Gas	56.2	11.0	32.1	0.7	0
Electricity	95.5	0.3	3.5	0.6	0.1
26 Paper	Number of reporting companies too small to show data				
28 Chemicals					
Coal	50.0	0	0	50.0	0
Coke	77.6	22.4	0	0	0
Light fuel oils	49.3	31.9	10.0	8.9	0
Heavy fuel oils	31.4	9.8	37.6	21.3	0
Gas	36.7	41.4	21.9	0	0
Electricity	88.7	2.0	9.3	0	0
29 Petroleum					
Coal	76.3	0	0	23.7	0
Coke	100.0	0	0	0	0
Light fuel oils	97.2	2.7	0.1	0	0
Heavy fuel oils	44.1	0.9	0	54.6	0.4
Gas	30.1	26.6	40.2	0	3.0
Electricity	72.5	2.3	23.3	2.0	0
32 Stone, clay and glass					
Coal	17.3	1.3	1.6	79.8	0
Coke	0	0	2.2	97.8	0
Light fuel oils	51.4	43.0	4.2	1.4	0
Heavy fuel oils	82.1	7.7	3.7	6.6	0
Gas	42.6	10.9	45.8	0.6	0.1
Electricity	95.0	3.8	1.3	0	0
33 Primary metals					
Coal	56.3	0	0	43.7	0
Coke	Number of reporting companies too small to show data				
Light fuel oils	78.5	15.7	0.1	4.0	1.7
Heavy fuel oils	62.0	10.9	15.2	8.9	3.1
Gas	37.9	30.7	31.5	0	0
Electricity	84.3	0.2	14.1	1.4	0

Source: The Conference Board.

Research and Development Activities

Before getting into the particulars of our findings on R&D activities, four simple general statements can be made: (1) More companies have done and more plan to do R&D for reducing energy use per unit of output than for developing corporate sources of supply. (2) Relatively more large companies do R&D than small companies. (3) The extent of intentions to engage in or to finance R&D in the future is greater than the extent to which companies actually did so during the past five years. (4) The relative prevalence of R&D on energy use and supply among the six industry groups is roughly correlated with the relative level of total R&D activity.

Not unexpectedly, the industry group with the highest ratio of energy use (in BTUs) per dollar of value added, petroleum and coal products (SIC 29), had the highest combined incidence of R&D activity over the past five years. Correspondingly, the industry group (among those The Conference Board studied) with the lowest ratio of energy use per dollar of value added, food and kindred products (SIC 20), showed the lowest incidence of R&D activity. It is plausible that businesses with relatively higher per-unit energy cost will spend more effort reducing those costs than businesses with relatively lower per-unit energy costs. Of the petroleum and coal products manufacturers (SIC 29) reporting, 69% said they had engaged in or financed R&D for the purpose of reducing energy use per unit of output, and 87% indicated R&D for the development of corporate sources of energy supply. On a weighted basis (by employment), the proportions become 87% and 95%, respectively, reflecting relatively greater R&D activity by larger companies. In SIC 20, 52% indicated R&D for cutting energy use per unit of output, and 26% for developing sources, on an unweighted basis; when size is taken into account, the proportions read 74% and 36%, respectively. (See Table 1A-6). The level of R&D incidence among other industry groups falls between these two groups; but among these, a correlation between the relative extent of R&D on energy and the relative ratio of energy use per dollar of value added is difficult to find.

Except for food and paper, this kind of correlation is difficult to find among the indications of energy R&D planned for the next seven or eight years. No overall increase in prevalence among petroleum and coal products manufacturers and food producers seems to be planned, but more primary metal makers foresee more widespread energy R&D for the next seven years. As a result, the weighted combined incidence of energy R&D among primary metal producers is the highest for the 1973-1980 period among the six industry groups. Food remains the lowest of the list; paper is next to last.

For all six industry groups as a whole, however the percentage of companies indicating performance or financing of energy R&D is higher for the period between now and 1980 than for the past five years. Interestingly, most of the rise occurs among smaller companies, a phenomenon that could be considered symptomatic of a "filtering down" process. In a certain sense, the

Table 1A-6.   Research and Development
(responses to item #7)

	Past Five Years				Between Now and 1980			
	To Reduce Energy-Output		To Develop Sources		To Reduce Energy-Output		To Develop Sources	
	Yes	No	Yes	No	Yes	No	Yes	No
Food								
Weighted %	74	26	36	64	68	32	37	63
Unweighted % . . .	52	48	26	74	65	35	32	68
(Number)	(16)	(15)	(7)	(20)	(20)	(11)	(9)	(19)
Paper								
Weighted %	60	40	61	39	87	13	68	32
(Number)	(7)	(3)	(6)	(5)	(8)	(2)	(6)	(4)
Chemicals								
Weighted %	96	4	82	18	98	2	83	17
Unweighted % . . .	79	21	68	32	88	12	74	26
(Number)	(27)	(7)	(23)	(11)	(30)	(4)	(25)	(9)
Petroleum								
Weighted %	87	13	95	5	90	10	91	9
Unweighted % . . .	69	31	87	13	75	25	87	13
(Number)	(11)	(5)	(14)	(2)	(12)	(4)	(14)	(2)
Stone, clay and glass								
Weighted %	91	9	84	16	94	6	86	14
Unweighted % . . .	62	38	48	52	70	30	58	42
(Number)	(13)	(8)	(10)	(11)	(14)	(6)	(11)	(8)
Primary metals								
Weighted %	86	14	88	12	97	3	90	10
Unweighted % . . .	50	50	31	69	76	24	43	57
(Number)	(20)	(20)	(11)	(25)	(29)	(9)	(15)	(20)

Source: The Conference Board.

planned increase and the nature of the increase are indications of a spread in and, perhaps, a heightening of industry's perception of an "energy problem."

Miscellaneous Comments, by Industry Group
Food (SIC 20). Coverage of the food group was 14.7%, as measured by employment. The food industry is the least energy-intensive of the six groups surveyed, in terms of BTUs used per dollar of value added. Of the six major groups, food companies project the smallest rate of decline in energy use per unit of output through 1980—0.1% a year. This group also indicates the lowest present and future incidence (per cent of companies reporting) of research and development for energy-use and energy-supply purposes. This low level of

Table 1A-7.   How Companies Have Responded to the Energy Problem
(responses to item #8)

SIC	Special Committee or Task Force	Encouragement of Trade Assoc. Activity	Designation of Primary Responsibility to Plant Mgrs.	High Priority Assignment to Corp. Planning Unit	Increased Consideration of Energy Use	Maintenance Program	Other	Concern Ratio* (and number of companies reporting)
20	10	7	11	11	14	19	6	2.4 (32)
26	5	6	3	6	8	6	0	3.1 (11)
28	23	10	11	15	20	20	12	3.2 (35)
29	9	10	12	7	14	12	3	4.2 (16)
32	10	3	5	5	11	9	4	2.2 (21)
33	12	10	22	12	24	19	3	2.6 (40)

*The "concern ratio" equals the total number of "checks" divided by the number of companies in each industry responding at all to this item. Respondents were permitted to check more than one "form of concern," if applicable.

Source: The Conference Board.

R&D is a logical result of the lesser importance of energy to food manufacturing.

For the above reason, it is also not unexpected that food companies, when responding to the question regarding the form taken by their concern for the energy problem, checked fewer actions, on the average, than companies in the other industry groups.

Responses by the food companies to the survey questions asking for quantitative data probably are less reliable than those from firms in other industry groups. Almost half of the respondents characterized all or part of their projections as an "educated guess," and we believe that several of the companies reported energy use—total, or by source—based on the dollar purchases rather than BTU equivalent of the physical units. Because electricity is so much more expensive per BTU, this distorts trends in "energy use" when the share of electricity is changing and it unduly raises the proportion of energy use attributable to purchased electricity.

Food manufacturers reported expectations of only a 0.1% decline per year. This may be low due to the relatively high number of respondents in the industry who, lacking data, made a guess that there would be no change. Since energy cost per dollar of value added is relatively low in this industry, firms in SIC 20 have the least incentive (among the six groups) to keep track of energy costs. Also, the products of food firms are more heterogeneous, discouraging efforts to compare energy use with output.

Chemicals (SIC 28). Coverage of this group, 37.0% of industry employment, is the highest of the six groups. When consumption of energy derived from fuels produced and consumed in the same establishment (including by-product fuels) is considered along with purchased energy, the chemicals group is one of the two most energy-intensive of the six covered.

The reporting chemicals companies expect energy use per unit of output to decline at an average rate of 1.7% a year between 1971 and 1980, not much slower than the average 2.2% drop experienced by *all* chemicals producers between 1947 and 1967. The decline anticipated by large firms (over 10,000 employees) is about the same as that for smaller companies. In general, the larger companies expect to grow more rapidly and to shift fuels more sharply.

In those cases where firms said they expect energy use per unit of output to increase, it was attributed to a projected shift in the product mix toward more energy-intensive products. About two-thirds of the companies reported that they expect process heat requirements per unit of output to drop. It is our belief that this may be too low; our detailed studies of industries in the chemicals group have revealed that industry technical experts for almost every chemical covered expect per unit energy needs for process heat to continue to decline.

Petroleum and Coal Products (SIC 29). The fact that petroleum companies are in the business of producing energy is probably why their concern with the energy problem appears to be greater than that of companies in the other industry groups. Use of energy sources for feedstocks at various stages of production is about ten times that consumed by process requirements in petroleum refining. Responding petroleum companies checked far more "actions," on average, than companies in other industry groups. Perhaps their energy-consciousness explains why petroleum companies reported the highest rates of expected real prices of energy of any of the five groups.

The projections by the firms surveyed of a 0.5% average annual decline of energy use per unit of output between 1971 and 1980 appear to us too slow, considering past trends and already existing technology that—when more widely used—has considerable energy-saving potential. (See report on Petroleum Refining in Chapter Eighteen.) However, the output measure used in the projections is barrels per day, which does not take quality improvements into account.

A major finding of the survey is that petroleum companies, which are large users of gas, plan to cut down substantially on their relative use of it—from 71% of total useful BTUs in 1971 to 41% in 1980. But since a considerable portion of their process energy comes from self-produced fuels and energy, the survey, which does not cover energy derived from self-produced fuels and by-products, tends to overstate the relative contribution of gas, the relative size of the shift, and—by implication—the relative impact of the shift on other purchased energy forms.

Stone, Clay, and Glass (SIC 32). The stone, clay, and glass group is represented in the survey by 21 companies, which account for 27% of that industry group's employment. Three-fourths of the responding firms are either glass or cement producers. This kind of representation does not especially distort the overall survey data for the SIC group, however, because cement and glass production together account for 56% of total energy consumption by SIC 32.

Although energy use by the stone, clay, and glass industry group is relatively high in relation to value added, the companies responding to the survey do not appear to have a high perception of any energy problem. Their expectations of real price increases are the lowest of the six industries; and their "concern" for the energy problem has evoked fewer forms of action (as defined by the questionnaire) than all the other industry groups. But the incidence of and plans for research and development for the purpose of reducing energy use per unit of output is moderate to high.

Below, there are summary data for respondents in the cement and glass industries, respectively:

Distribution of Energy Use by Source (Per Cent)

	Coal	Coke	Light Fuel Oils	Heavy Fuel Oils	Gas	Purchased Electricity	Energy Use Per Unit of Output (Index: 1971 = 100)
Cement							
1971 ...	16.5	–	–	13.9	51.1	11.2	100.0
1975 ...	29.3	–	–	20.1	30.6	16.9	97.5
1980 ...	48.0	–	–	20.7	10.8	18.3	95.5
Glass							
1971 ...	–	–	4.0	2.1	72.4	20.4	100.0
1975 ...	–	–	11.5	4.0	57.1	24.9	95.9
1980 ...	–	–	22.3	7.4	40.2	27.0	91.9

Source: The Conference Board.

Primary Metals (SIC 33). The primary metals group, with 40 responses, has the largest sample of the six industries surveyed. One quarter of the responding companies, however, are steel producers of much larger average size (by employment) than the other responding firms. This makes the SIC group "averages" unduly like those for steel companies alone. Thus, the weighted average of energy consumption shows coal to account for about 60% of total energy consumption and coke less than 1%, whereas the fuel purchase data from the 1967 *Census of Manufacturers* (close enough in time to be roughly comparable) show coal to account for 10% and coke to account for 13% of energy use by SIC 33. Projections of energy use per unit of output also are dominated by the steel company replies.

In addition to steel, copper refining is represented by a number of responses. Both subgroups are large enough to justify a separate tabulation. Summary data for the two groups are shown below:

Distribution of Energy Use by Source (Per Cent)

	Coal	Coke	Light Fuel Oils	Heavy Fuel Oils	Gas	Purchased Electricity	Energy Use Per Unit of Output (Index: 1971 = 100)
Steel							
1971	68.1%	2.7%	0	4.9%	16.2%	2.8%	100.0
1975	65.3	2.6	0	10.7	12.1	3.7	95.5
1980	65.7	2.6	0	12.6	8.9	4.3	93.4
Copper Refining							
1971	13.8%	–	3.0%	5.8%	71.4%	5.9%	100.0
1975	16.3	–	13.8	9.5	49.8	10.0	113.7
1980	16.2	–	13.8	15.5	43.7	10.1	109.7

Source: The Conference Board.

Survey of Future Energy Demand—U.S. Manufacturing

General instructions: This survey covers the six industry groups listed below. Please limit your answers to operations in one of these groups. If your company produces goods in more than one of the groups, please complete a separate questionnaire for each. (You may photocopy the form or request additional ones.) *Exclude operations outside the United States and all establishments that are pulp, paper, or paperboard mills (SIC codes 2611, 2621, 2631) or are primary producers, rollers, and drawers of aluminum (SIC codes 3334, 3352).*

All information is treated as strictly confidential. Completed forms remain the property of the Board and will not be made available to anyone, including government agencies. The information will be used only for statistical purposes.

Please complete and return this form as promptly as possible, *but no later than April 1, 1973.* Should you need clarification of any items or additional copies of the questionnaire, please call or write Bernard A. Gelb at The Conference Board. Feel free to use the extra space for additional data or comments on any or all of the topics.

Industry group covered by answers to this questionnaire (check one):

☐ Food and kindred products (SIC 20)
☐ Paper and allied products (SIC 26)
☐ Chemicals and allied products (SIC 28)

☐ Petroleum and coal products (SIC 29)
☐ Stone, clay, and glass products (SIC 32)
☐ Primary metals (SIC 33)

Total employees
at establishments
in the industry
checked:

Firm, or division _____

City or town,
State, Zip Code _____

(continued)

Corporate headquarters:
(if different from above)

City or town,
State, Zip Code

Number _____

As of _____
(date)

	Coal	Coke	Light Fuel Oils	Heavy Fuel Oils	Gas*	Purchased Electricity	Other (specify)

State Approximate Percent of Total Energy Use

*Piped natural or manufactured gas

(1) A. What were the *three main* fuel or energy forms used by your company in 1971?

B. Which three do you expect your company will use most

... in 1975?

... in 1980?

(2) What price changes do you expect between 1971 and 1980?

...for fuel or energy supplies you do not have under firm price contract? Include in energy price changes any increases (or decreases) in costs caused by fuel specifications that are imposed by law or regulatory authority. (Please also indicate your expectations of change in the general price level, to permit comparisons with expected fuel price increases.)

Fuel or Energy Source	Average Annual Percent Change in Price	
	1971-1975	1975-1980
Coal		
Coke		
Light fuel oils		
Heavy fuel oils		
Piped natural gas		
Electricity		
Other used by you:		
GENERAL PRICE LEVEL		

(3) If your company expects non-price difficulties between now and 1980 in obtaining or using fuels or energy forms you are now using, *state in the last four columns the approximate percentage of normal fuel or energy use expected to be affected.*

Fuel or Energy Source	Percentage of Use Not Affected by the Following	Market Unavailability	Interruptible Service or Supplies	Stiffer Regulation of Emissions & Effluents	Other (specify)
Coal					
Coke					
Light fuel oils					
Heavy fuel oils					
Gas (piped)					
Electricity					
Other (specify)					

(continued)

(4) Roughly, what proportion of planned output will be produced by . . .

	in 1975	in 1980
(A) Existing plant and equipment	%	%
(B) New plant and equipment, present site(s)	%	%
(C) New plant and equipment, new site(s)	%	%
Total =	100%	100%

(5) If your firm plans to introduce changes in technology, operations, facilities, or location between now and 1980 that are expected to have a measurable effect on fuel or energy use, please indicate by type of energy application.

Energy Application	Change in Mix* (√ where appropriate)	Effect on Fuel or Energy Use Per Unit of Output (check one column)						
		Decrease			None	Increase		
		Over 25%	11%-25%	1%-10%		1%-10%	11%-25%	Over 25%
Process heating								
Mechanical—in plant								
Electrolysis								
Transportation—outside plant								
Other (please specify)								
Total								

*Change in the shares of fuel and energy forms presently used, or change in the type(s) of fuel or energy form(s) used.

(6) A. What are your company's plans, projections, or anticipations of over-all fuel or energy use in 1975 and 1980? State them in whatever form you wish, but in order for them to be useful in our study they must be related to some

measure of output (in physical terms or in constant prices). Please identify the figures clearly and make sure that a 1971 base figure for your projections is shown. If any of the fuel or energy you use is from company-owned sources, please indicate total consumption rather than purchases.

	Item and Form	Unit of Measurement (specify and/or check)	1971	1975	1980
Fuel and Energy Use (check one)	☐ Total physical consumption	Thousands of ___ (specify unit)			
	☐ Total purchases in constant prices	Thousands of dollars Base year: ___			
	☐ Consumption per unit of output	Units of fuel ___ of output			
Output (check one)	☐ Production	Thousands of physical units Unit: ___			
	☐ Shipments				
	☐ Sales (including intra-company transactions at market value)	Thousands of constant dollars Base year: ___			

(6) B. What is the basis of these projections or anticipations for ....
(Check one for each year.)

1975?   1980?

(a) Complete and consistent company or division sales, budget, or economic projections   ___   ___

(b) Informal, but carefully prepared, forecasts by a departmental or other function unit   ___   ___

(c) An educated guess on the basis of expertise; our company does not project or forecast in this detail this far in advance   ___   ___

(d) Other (specify) ___

(continued)

	Yes	No

(7) A. In the past five years, have you engaged in or financed any research and development with the specific objective of . . .

   (a) reducing energy use per unit of output?
   (b) further developing corporate sources of energy

B. Do you plan to engage in or finance any research and development between now and 1980 with the specific objective of . . .

   (a) reducing energy use per unit of output
   (b) further developing corporate sources of energy

(8) What form has company concern for the energy problem taken? (check one or more)

☐ Special committee or task force   ☐ permanent
   to formulate energy policy: ☐ ad hoc
☐ Encouragement of trade association activity
☐ Designation of primary responsibility to plant managers
☐ High priority assignment to corporate planning unit
☐ Increased consideration of energy use in procurement of equipment and supplies
☐ Maintenance program with special attention to economizing on energy use
☐ Other (describe briefly) _____

(9) Last year, your establishments completed *Form MA-100* for the Bureau of the Census in connection with the *1971 Annual Survey of Manufactures*. The information on them concerning output and fuel use would be very useful to us for our

statistical analysis, but the Census Bureau, by law, cannot make those schedules available to anyone. Please, if possible, send us photocopies of your file copies of the 1971 MA-100's for those establishments in the industry group you have covered in this questionnaire.

☐ Photocopies of MA-100's enclosed   ☐ Photocopies of MA-100's not available

Name and title of person
completing this form: _____

Address (if different from
that shown in 1st page): _____

Telephone No.: _____

THE CONFERENCE BOARD · 845 THIRD AVENUE · NEW YORK, N.Y. 10022 · PL9-0900

2. Measurement of Output
Bernard A. Gelb

To determine the trend in the relation of fuel and other energy consumption to output in manufacturing industries, it is necessary, of course, to measure both energy consumption and output in constant prices. This appendix describes our methodology for estimating output in such terms; in doing so it amplifies the section on measurement of output in Section II of Chapter One.

This study has analyzed 37 manufacturing industries that have been defined as industries by the Census Bureau for purposes of statistical reporting at the 4-digit level of aggregation; and it has analyzed six groups of manufacturing industries at the 2-digit level (which include the 37 4-digit industries) as well as the manufacturing sector as a whole.

Basic inputs

Two main statistical inputs for each industry (or group) are required to obtain estimates of the level of "real" industry output and of its movement over time: A benchmark estimate of output in dollars for one Census year, and the relative movement during the period under study. Both types of input were obtained primarily from the several postwar *Censuses of Manufactures*.

For the six industry groups (aggregation at the 2-digit level) and for manufacturing as a whole, value added in 1967 was chosen as the benchmark estimate of output. Value added is a close approximation of an unduplicated measure of output, owing to the exclusion from it of the value of purchases of intermediate products from other industries or from firms in the same industry or group. Such exclusion is particularly important at these levels of aggregation.

For the 37 manufacturing industries at the 4-digit level, the value of shipments in 1967 was chosen as the benchmark measure of output. While it was recognized that a given magnitude of shipments includes duplication even at this level of aggregation, shipments were chosen because the concept and amounts are familiar to analysts of the individual industries and, therefore, any ratios of energy use to "output" that would be developed would be more meaningful to more people. Risk of "error" is minimized in two respects: The relative extent of duplication is much less at this level of aggregation than among 2-digit groups; and, because of our choice of methods for establishing output levels in earlier years (see below), the relative movement of "output" would be the same whether benchmarked on value added or on shipments.

Indexes of production developed by the Census Bureau (as a regular part of the Census program) were used at all levels of aggregation in this study to establish the movement in output of each industry and group during the period covered. These movements were then applied to the benchmark figures chosen for 1967 at each level of aggregation.

Benchmark figures

The Census and *Annual Surveys of Manufactures* give data on shipments and on value added—both possible measures of output—from the 4-digit level of aggregation up through the manufacturing sector as a whole.

Value added by manufacture has the virture of avoiding the double-counting that occurs in total shipments when one industry's finished product is part of another industry's materials consumed, appearing therefore twice in the value of shipments of the group (since the price of the final shipments must cover the cost of the intermediate shipments). Among the industry groups covered in this study, such double-counting is particularly prevalent within paper and allied products (SIC 26) and would swell the apparent importance of its output in comparison with other industries' output if shipments were used as the measure.

The following equality shows how the use of the value-added concept avoids double-counting:

Value added equals:
Value of shipments
Less: materials (including supplies), fuel, electric energy, cost of resales, and miscellaneous receipts.
Plus: increase in inventory of finished products and work in process over the past year.

The subtraction of materials and supplies eliminates much of the back-and-forth shipments of intermediate products that would otherwise exaggerate the importance of those industries that tend to interchange intermediate products. Energy to *value added* ratios should therefore be more directly comparable among industries than are energy to *shipments* ratios.

Value added, as measured by the Census Bureau, does, however, contain some of the value of product of other industries or sectors; for depreciation, property taxes, maintenance and repairs performed by outside contractors, rental payments, insurance, advertising, legal, and accounting services are not subtracted. To the extent that these items are used in an industry, value added exaggerates the value of the output originating in that industry.

Value added is used here as a measure of 1967 output of 2-digit groups and of all manufacturing, because it is believed that shipments of intermediate materials from company to company and industry to industry within a 2-digit group would be too large and too variable (between groups) a fraction of total group shipments for proper comparisons over time and between groups.

But adoption of value added as a benchmark—at the two-digit or four-digit level—introduces an unknown risk. Census Bureau indexes available to establish output for years prior to 1967 actually are indexes of shipments, corrected for inventory change and deflated to eliminate price change. Their use with value added is approximately like "adding apples and pears" if they do not experience the same relative movement; the difficulty or impossibility of deflating value added makes it difficult to say whether this is the case or not. In current dollars, their movements have not agreed in many cases.

The dollar value of shipments in 1967 was taken as the 1967 output—the output benchmark—of industries at the 4-digit level. This was done for a combination of three reasons: The value of shipments is more appropriate to use with the Census Bureau's indexes of production; the degree of double-counting is much less at this level of aggregation; and the shipments measure is more meaningful than value added to most industry analysts.

Relative movements

Production indexes computed by the Bureau of the Census, based on published and unpublished figures in the *Census of Manufactures,* were used at all levels of aggregation in this study to establish the relative movement of output during the period covered.

The Census output indexes are essentially physical shipments indexes corrected for inventory change. Basically, the Census Bureau's procedure is as follows: Within a 4-digit industry, shipments of product groups (at a 5-digit level) in dollar terms are deflated by appropriate price indexes; each group is weighted by the ratio of value added to shipments of that product group; and indexes are calculated from the sums of the products of the deflated shipments and ratios. To obtain indexes of output for higher levels of aggregation, 4-digit industry indexes are weighted by their respective ratios of value added to shipments, and so on.

It is important to note that the practice of weighting by the ratio of value added to shipments is done to give proper "weight" to the contribution to final value involved in the production of each product. Thus, production processes that involve high-cost materials but add relatively little value are not assigned more importance than processes that use low-cost materials but add relatively more value. There is more "duplication" in the former's value of shipments than in the latter's because the value of materials purchased is eventually reflected in value of shipments. This weighting procedure eliminates the possibility that the movement of an output index will be distorted by changes between Census years in the relative amount of duplication in an industry.

Census output indexes are calculated for only two Censuses (adjacent) at a time. A single index series for an industry (for example) covering several Censuses was constructed by The Conference Board by linking the several pairs of indexes, and then setting 1967 equal to 100 for the series, the indexes extend back to 1947 for each 2-digit group; the index for each industry was extended as far back as fuel and electricity data were fairly continuous.

There is also the question of which year's value-added weights should be used when calculating indexes over a pair of Census years. The Census Bureau computed indexes using base-year weights, index-year weights, and cross weights—the Marshall-Edgeworth formula; the last is an average of base-year and index-year weights. The Conference Board used the cross-weighted indexes in order to take account of the regimens of both periods and to avoid the inherent biases of base-year and index-year weights, which could be reinforced by the chaining procedure.

The year 1962 posed a minor problem: fuel and electricity data in the 1963 Census volumes are for 1962 rather than 1963, while the other basic data—shipments, value added, etc.,—are for 1963. To solve this, the 1963 output index numbers were multiplied by the ratio of 1962 to 1963 for the most relevant Federal Reserve *Index of Industrial Production*—often that for the 2-digit group that includes the industry. (In two cases, a more complicated method was used.) Indexes are from the Board of Governors of the Federal Reserve System, "Detailed Industrial Production Series, January 1954-March 1971, 1971 Revision."

These indexes—of gross output, weighted by value added—are, in general, valid measures of movements in net output. They will not be distorted by shifts to more or less processed product classes within an industry or by shifts from industries with high ratios of value added to those with low ratios (or vice versa). They will be improperly affected, however, by changes in the mix of products (in terms of value-added ratios) within product classes, by changes in the "efficiency" of materials use per unit of output, and by changes in the degree of vertical integration. Because these types of changes were considered in the individual industry analyses of trends in energy use per unit of output, it is not believed that such possible distortions in the indexes of output affected basic conclusions.

Sources of data

Both benchmark levels—value added and shipments—were taken from the summary table of the *1967 Census of Manufactures,* Volume I.

The Census output indexes, which are available only for years in which censuses were taken, were obtained for 1947, 1954, 1958, and 1963 from the *1963 Census of Manufactures,* Volume 4, "Indexes of Production," Table 3 and Appendix C; output indexes for 1967—"based" on 1963—were obtained directly from the Bureau of the Census.

3. Energy Conversion Factors

Fuel and Steam

Item	Units	Factor	General or Special*
Coal, anthracite	million BTUs/ton	25.4	AP
Coal, bituminous or mixed	million BTUs/ton	25.8	G
Coke	million BTUs/ton	26.0	G
Fuel oil, unspecified	million BTUs/barrel	5.8	G
Fuel oil, distillate	million BTUs/barrel	5.825	AP
Fuel oil, residual	million BTUs/barrel	6.287	AP

Item	1947-67	1971	General or Special*
Fuels, n.s.k. (not specified by kind)			
by industry	(million BTUs per current $ spent)		
All manufacturing	2.515	1.954	G
Food (SIC 20)	2.190	1.749	G
Paper (SIC 26)	2.777	1.956	G
Chemicals (SIC 28)	3.357	2.426	G
Petroleum (SIC 29)	4.050	3.417	G
Stone, clay, glass (SIC 32)	2.498	1.984	G
Primary metals (SIC 33)	2.262	1.750	G

Item	1947-67	1971	General or Special*
	(million BTUs per current $ spent)		
Fuels, other			
Petroleum (SIC 29)	3.112	2.626	G
All manufacturing and the other five two-digit industries	Same as Fuels, n.s.k.		G

*Abbreviations: G—general use; A—aluminum (Chapter 31); B—blast furnaces and steel mills (Chapter 24); P—pulp, paper, and paperboard mills (Chapter 32).

Note. Tons are short tons. Barrels are 42 gallons.

Sources: Anthracite, liq. petroleum gas, and petroleum coke: Bureau of Mines, *Mineral Industry Surveys: Crude Petroleum, Petroleum Products and Natural Gas Liquids,* December 1971, p. 36 ("*Mines Petroleum*"). Bit. coal, coke, tar: U.S. Bureau of the Census, *Census of Manufactures, 1967,* Special Series, *Fuels and Electric Energy Consumed,* MC 67 (S)-4 (U.S. Govt. Printing Office, 1971), p. 6, times 3,412 BTUs/kwh. ("*Census Fuels*"). Fuel oil; *Mines Petroleum* and *Census Fuels.* Fuels n.s.k.: 1947-67—U.S. Bureau of the Census, "Memorandum for the Staff," C-67-M-63, Supplement 1, November 20, 1969 ("Census memorandum"), table 5 col. 5, times 3,412 BTUs/kwh. 1971—the 1947-67 factors were adjusted for 1967-71 price change (see source notes to Table 1-1, all manufacturing, 1971). Fuels, other. Petroleum (SIC 29)—1947-67: "Census memorandum," table 6—total kwh equivalent of 1962 residual fuels and acid sludge consumption was divided by its cost and multiplied by 3,412. 1971: the 1947-67 factor was adjusted for 1967-71 price change as above. All other groups for all years: same factors as for fuels n.s.k. Gas, blast furnace: American Iron and Steel Institute, *Annual Statistical Report, 1971,* p. 59 (*Census Fuels* gives 92). Gas, coke oven: *Census Fuels* and U.S. Bureau of Mines, *Minerals Yearbook, 1972,* Vol. I, p. 442

	Units	Factor	General or Special*
Gas, blast furnace	BTUs/cu. ft.	95	B
Gas, coke oven	BTUs/cu. ft.	550	B
Gas, liquefied petroleum	million BTUs/barrel	4.0	B
Gas, natural, mixed, or unspecified	BTUs/cu. ft.	1,035	G
Gas, propane	1,000 BTUs/gal.	92	AP
Petroleum coke	million BTUs/barrel	6.024	AP
Steam, process—generation of ...	1,000 BTUs/lb.	1.35-1.40	G
Tar and pitch	million BTUs/barrel	6.0	B

PULP AND PAPER INDUSTRY WASTE

	Units	Factor	General or Special*
Bark	million BTUs/ton	10.5	P
Hogged wood fuel	million BTUs/ton	18.0	P
Spent pulping liquors	million BTUs/ton	13.4	P

ELECTRICITY GENERATION

Electricity, gross energy basis
Fossil-fueled steam-electric plants, national average annual heat rate, Federal Power Commission

1947	1954	1958	1962	1967	1971-80	General or special*
		(BTUs per kilowatt-hour)				
15,600	12,180	11,085	10,558	10,432	10,500	G

	Factor	General or special*
	(BTUs/kwh)	
Hydro and nuclear plants: heat equivalent	10,583	AP
Radial engine (gas)	10,100	A
Turbine, steam (oil or gas)	10,400	A
Electricity, useful energy basis	3,412	G

(AISI gives 500). Gas, natural, mixed or unspecified: *Mines Petroleum* for years through 1964; figure is identical with that given in *Census Fuels* (AISI gives 1,000). Gas, propane, and pulp and paper industry waste: courtesy of American Paper Institute. Steam: for saturated steam at 140-160 lbs. gauge, containing 1191 BTUs/cu. ft., with 85% to 88% boiler efficiency, from an engineer for an electric utility company. Electricity, fossil-fueled steam average: U.S. Dept. of the Interior, "U.S. Energy Use at New High in 1971," news release dated March 31, 1972. Electricity, steam turbine, aluminum industry: from interviews.

Part One

Food Industries

Chapter Two

Meatpacking Plants—SIC 2011

Noreen Preston

SECTION I.   SUMMARY AND CONCLUSIONS

The Bureau of the Census Standard Industrial Classification defines the
Meatpacking Plants industry, SIC 2011, as follows:

> Establishments primarily engaged in the slaughtering for their own
account or on a contract basis for the trade, of cattle, hogs, sheep, lambs, calves,
horses, and other animals except small game for meat to be sold or to be used on
the same premises in canning and curing, and in making sausage, lard, and other
products.

> Establishments primarily engaged in manufacturing sausages and
meat specialties from purchased meats are classified in Industry 2013; and
establishments primarily engaged in killing, dressing, packing, and canning
poultry, rabbits, and other small game are classified in Industry 2015.

Two major developments have occurred within the meatpacking
industry since 1947. These have been:

(1) Decentralization.
(2) A step-up in demand for red meat, especially beef.

After World War II, the industry began a period marked by expansion, decentralization, and specialization. Rapidly rising costs of labor and
transportation prompted the construction of new plants away from the central
cities and closer to the source of raw material. Technological changes in refrigeration and transportation allowed for the shipment of meat over long distances.
When new plants were constructed, new efficient equipment was installed. At
first, this led to a sharp increase in energy consumption. Most of the new, highly
automated plants were in operation by the mid-1950s. Total energy consumption
between 1947 and 1954 increased sharply. A substantial part of the increase was

89

due to a jump in the energy consumption in the processing of prepared meats—a segment of the industry that became highly automated. As output increased, unit overhead energy costs began to decline with the addition of more efficient equipment; more output was possible while total energy use remained at a relatively constant level.

Energy and fuel have not been major cost items in the industry. Gas, primarily natural gas, is the principal fuel consumed. The principal use of gas is for boiler fuel. Steam is used in the plants for rendering and other meat processing. Hot water from the steam cycles is utilized throughout plants for washing animal carcasses and for the constant cleaning processes.

Per capita consumption of meat has risen sharply. Most of the large increase is due to a heavy demand for beef. The industry has responded with large increases in output that are not only due to increases in the number of slaughters, but also to two other causes. First, the average animal weight has been increasing, with the largest gains for cattle. Second, waste has been reduced so that the ratio of meat output to total weight of animals slaughtered has increased.

Total meat output in pounds rose 81% between 1947 and 1971. Output is projected to rise 32% more between 1971 and 1980. Gains in output should be slightly faster in the 1971-75 period than in 1975 to 1980. In 1967, shipments of the industry were valued at $15,576 million; they should rise to $22,169 million by 1980 in 1967 prices.

Aside from fluctuations that may occur in the short run, the demand for beef and other meats should continue to increase requiring additional fuel and energy. But while the total amount of energy consumed will continue to increase, the energy-output ratio should decline. That is, less energy, either per pound of meat obtained as a result of slaughter or per pound of meat processed as a prepared meat, should be used. Total energy consumed rose between 1947 and 1954 as many firms within the industry switched over to more highly automated equipment. Between 1954 and 1958, and between 1958 and 1962, consumption of total energy declined, although output increased. A rise in energy use occurred between 1962 and 1967; however, this gain was not so large as the rise in total output.

The energy-output ratio has been declining steadily since 1954, and this trend should continue. In 1967, BTUs per constant dollar of shipments (on a useful energy basis[a]) were 5,392; unit energy use in 1980 should fall to approximately 4,000 BTUs. Concentration on processing larger animals accounts for part of the drop in unit energy consumption.

[a]See Chapter One, pages 14-15, for definitions of useful and gross energy.

Table 2-1. Historical Data and Projections

	1947	1954	1958	1962	1967	1971	1975	1980
Value of Shipments								
1967 $ (millions)	$10,626	$11,688	$12,176	$13,665	$15,576	$16,794	$19,123	$22,169
Current $ (millions)	8,970	10,265	11,972	12,491	15,576	–	–	–
Production (million lbs.)								
Meat (red)	17,850	20,603	20,707	24,913	29,102	32,288	36,765	42,621
Lard	1,819	1,979	2,114	2,295	1,932	1,758	1,576	1,374
Total BTUs consumed (trillions)								
Useful energy	80.4	99.1	87.6	81.5	84.0	85.2	88.4	91.7
Gross energy	92.7	113.0	100.9	96.2	101.6	105.9	112.7	121.3
1,000 BTUs/1967 $ of shipments								
Useful energy	7.6	8.4	7.2	6.0	5.4	5.1	4.6	4.1
Gross energy	8.7	9.7	8.3	7.0	6.5	6.3	5.9	5.5

Source: Bureau of the Census, *Census of Manufactures*; The Conference Board.

SECTION II. HISTORICAL DEVELOPMENTS

Demand for Meat

There has been a striking expansion in the amount of meat produced since the 1930s. Increased meat production has met the needs of an expanding population. Consumer demand has been accelerated by increased per capita consumption of meat, especially beef. In 1950, per capita consumption of meat was 144.6 pounds; by 1969, consumption grew to 182.0 pounds per capita. Per capita consumption of beef rose 71.3% between 1950 and 1972. Steadily rising disposable personal income has played a large part in increasing the per capita consumption of meat. Larger refrigerators and expanded use of freezers in the home, increased supermarket retailing, self-service displays, and better quality meat have aided the consumer by increasing the availability of the supply of meat.

Supply

Production, in terms of pounds of meat produced for consumption, has increased 81% since 1947. Between 1947 and 1971 there has been a rather large and rapid increase in beef production relative to other meats. In 1947, beef was 48% of the total pounds produced and in 1971 had grown to 56% of total meat output. A large part of the stepped-up output can be attributed to the growth in the average size of the animals slaughtered. This has been made possible by improved methods of selective breeding of animals and a steep uptrend in the production of feed. Currently, there is a growing preference for feeding animals on feedlots, where the efficient methods and the quality of feedstuffs are at an optimum level to prepare animals for slaughter. Efficient feeding practices have yielded more meat per animal and advances in technology have made more of each animal available for consumption.

Aside from improved quality, there have been few variations in the product sold. Changes have consisted mainly of different cuts, slicing, deboning, trimming, and curing. However, there have been increased amounts of meat used in soups, frozen dinners, and ready-to-serve items.

The merchandising of meat has become more standard with respect to cuts of meat. Growth of retail chain stores and also the increase in volume of meat going to hotels, restaurants, institutions, and fast-food franchises have focused on higher volumes of particular standard cuts. As of the mid-1960s two-thirds of meat sales were made in self-service meat departments. New mass methods of wholesaling and retailing have perhaps introduced certain economies of scale to the packer. With higher demand for standard cuts, output per hour might increase while certain overhead energy costs like refrigeration and conveyor belt operation remain fixed.

Technological Developments

Prior to the 1950s much of the slaughtering of animals was performed at the terminal markets such as Chicago and Omaha. Since that time, the industry has become very decentralized. Much of the activity at these terminal markets was concentrated in the hands of a few large firms. Currently, the market is dominated by a large number of intermediate-sized firms located near the areas where the animals are raised. Energy needs have changed over the years and slaughtering operations have become part of processing operations in what is now called the full-line or integrated plant.

Part of the electrical power used during the processing of animals at the old terminal markets had been generated internally. By the mid-1950s, most of the decentralization of plants had occurred, involving a switch to purchased power for nearly all of required energy. Also, at the time of decentralization, the new plants utilized a whole new array of mechanized equipment that significantly reduced labor requirements, but increased the total amount of energy used. Table 2-2 illustrates the jump in energy requirements between 1947 and 1954. Also, prior to 1960, much excess capacity existed in the industry, which represented certain overhead costs and prevented plants from operating at maximum efficiency levels.

The technology of slaughtering and processing changed dramatically during the 1950s and has greatly improved speed and efficiency. The meatpacking industry was the first major industry to develop mechanical and continuous line production. One major improvement has been the development of on-the-rail dressing of cattle. The animals are suspended from an overhead rail after felling (which is now done by either mechanical, electrical, or chemical

Table 2-2. Energy Inputs, 1947-1967
(trillion BTUs)

	1947	1954	1958	1962	1967
Coal	43.4	37.7	28.3	18.5	14.5
Coke and breeze	–	0.1	–	–	–
Total fuel oil	7.4	8.7	9.7	7.6	6.1
Gas	23.5	38.5	33.8	36.4	35.6
Other fuels	2.6	8.8	6.4	12.0	8.3
Fuels, n.s.k.	–	–	3.7	–	10.9
Electric energy*	3.5	5.4	5.9	7.0	8.5
Total	80.4	99.1	87.6	81.5	84.0

*Converted on useful energy basis.
n.s.k.–not specified by kind.
Sources: Bureau of the Census, *Census of Manufactures*; The Conference Board.

means). While the animals are suspended, they are bled, the heads are removed, the skins are removed by the use of mechanical hide-pullers, and the carcasses are split with a power saw and the viscera are removed. Animal parts to be processed are sawed and deboned and all meat is chilled. At all points during the slaughtering process there is continuous washing with pressure hoses. Government meat inspection regulations have focused heavily on sanitary conditions within the industry. Slaughterhouses have been forced to reduce temperatures throughout and are now moving towards air-conditioning slaughterhouse floors. Additional cooling capacity is necessary to remove body heat from animals quicker for sanitary reasons. Requirements for sterilization and cleanliness have added to the already high consumption of energy for cooling and refrigeration purposes. Operating expenses as a percentage of the industry sales dollar have increased substantially since 1947, while expenditures for raw materials (mainly livestock) have considerably declined.

Following is a list of post-war technological developments:

On-the-rail dressing of cattle.
Moving-top inspection tables.
More efficient refrigeration.
Electronic smoking of meats.
Mechanical boning knives, pneumatic powered boning knives.
High speed saws.
Low-temperature centrifugal separation of fats.
Continuous frankfurter machines.
Semi-automatic slicing, weighing, and packaging systems for packaging bacon.
Introduction of computer use.
Introduction in 1952 of first mechanically refrigerated rail car.
Introduction in 1956 of containerized shipments of meats. These containers are
    insulated, carry their own mechanical refrigeration equipment, and are of dual
    use for rail flat cars and flat trucks.
Development during the 1950s of on-line automatic scales using electronic
    controls.
Passage of Federal Humane Slaughter Act in 1958 requiring the use of high-speed
    mechanical, electrical, or chemical means of rendering animals.

Between 1947 and 1967, energy purchased in the food industry increased 50%. The energy inputs in the meatpacking industry (measured in BTUs) over the same 20-year period increased only 4.5%. The energy consumed by the meatpacking industry as a proportion of all food industries (SIC 2000) has dropped since 1947 as shown in Table 2-3.

In 1947, slightly more than half of the energy consumed in the meatpacking industry was generated by coal, with about a third generated by gas. By 1967, the proportion of coal used had dropped considerably. In 1967,

Table 2-3. Total Purchased Energy, Food and Meatpacking
(trillion BTUs)

	1947	1954	1958	1962	1967
Food (SIC 2000)	619.4	777.4	829.9	856.2	926.4
Meatpacking (SIC 2011) ...	80.4	99.1	87.6	81.5	84.0
Meatpacking as % of food ..	13.0%	12.7%	10.6%	9.5%	9.1%

gas was the major source of energy, but coal use, which had dropped substantially, was the second major source of energy. The amount of fuel oil used has shown a slow decline. In 1947, energy generated by electricity was 4% of the total and had grown to 10% in 1967 (see Table 2-4).

Table 2-4. Per Cent Distribution of Energy Consumed, by Source

	1947	1954	1958	1962	1967
Coal	54.0%	38.0%	32.3%	22.7%	17.3%
Total fuel oil	9.2	8.7	11.1	9.3	7.3
Gas	29.2	38.6	38.6	44.7	42.1
Other fuels	3.2	8.8	7.3	14.7	9.9
Fuels, n.s.k.			4.2		13.0
Electric energy* ...	4.4	5.4	6.7	8.6	10.1
Total BTUs	100%	100%	100%	100%	100%

*Converted to BTU on useful energy basis.

Energy-Output Ratio

Data obtained from the Bureau of the Census were used to calculate energy-output ratios. For the energy-input measure, all forms of consumed energy were converted to BTU equivalents. Output is measured by the value of shipments converted to a 1967 constant dollar basis.

The energy-output ratio has shown a steady decline since 1954. Energy consumed per constant dollar of output in the meatpacking industry has been approximately half of that in the total food industry. This is because the majority of shipments of the meatpacking industry is of unprocessed products. The average annual rate of growth of the energy output-ratio between 1947 and 1954 was 1.5%. Between 1954 and 1958, the ratio declined at an average annual rate of 3.9% and 4.1% between 1958 and 1962. These rates of decline are considerably larger than the food industry as a whole, as shown in Table 2-5.

Table 2-5.   BTUs Consumed per 1967 Dollar of Shipments

	1947	1954	1958	1962	1967
		1,000 BTUs/1967 Dollar of Shipments			
SIC 2000 Food	14.7	16.5	15.3	14.0	13.1
SIC 2011 Meatpacking . .	8.7	9.7	8.3	7.0	6.5
	1947-1954	*1954-1958*	*1958-1962*	*1962-1967*	
		Average annual rates of change (per cent)			
SIC 2000 Food	1.64%	−1.82%	−2.25%	−1.40%	
SIC 2011 Meatpacking . .	1.46	−3.87	−4.07	−1.52	

Output in Physical Units

Output data in physical units have been obtained from the Bureau of the Census and the U.S. Department of Agriculture, Livestock and Meat Statistics, and from the American Meat Institute. These data are in two forms:

1. Number of head of commercially slaughtered cattle, calves, hogs, sheep, and lambs for the years 1947, 1954, 1958, and 1967. Slaughters for 1962 and 1971 have been estimated from U.S.D.A. and American Meat Institute data.
2. Pounds of meat and lard obtained from commercial slaughter. Meat is measured in dressed weight, which refers to the meat removed from carcasses

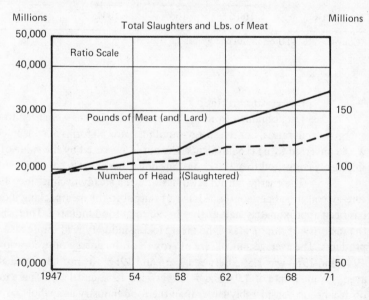

Chart 2-1.   Total Slaughters and Pounds of Meat.

Table 2-6.   Output—Head Slaughtered and Meat Produced

	1947	1954	1958	1962	1967	1971
Thousand head...	97,362	103,252	103,930	117,527	118,623	127,764
Million lbs, dressed weight (including lard)..	19,689	22,582	22,821	27,205	31,034	34,046

and classified as beef, veal, pork, lamb, and mutton. The total pounds were obtained by using the average animal weight for each type of animal in each year.

Since 1947, the number of animals slaughtered has shown a 31% increase. However, the total amount of pounds of meat produced has shown an 81% increase.

In 1947, cattle represented 19% of the slaughters and 48% of the meat output. Slaughter of cattle in 1971 was 23% of the total, yet the beef yield was 56% of total meat output.

Table 2-7 shows the number of animals slaughtered as well as the pounds of meat output by each species.

Table 2-7.   Commercial Slaughter

	1947	1954	1958	1962	1967	1971
			Thousand Head			
Cattle	18,260	21,607	20,413	22,692	28,253	29,678
Calves	10,170	9,254	6,682	5,396	4,230	2,638
Hogs	51,678	57,041	63,283	73,781	74,759	85,749
Sheep & lambs..	17,254	15,350	13,552	15,658	11,561	9,699
Total...	97,362	103,252	103,930	117,527	118,623	127,764
			Million lbs.			
Beef..........	8,600	10,911	10,656	13,025	16,726	18,133
Veal..........	1,170	1,129	795	675	537	369
Pork	7,338	7,872	8,606	10,477	11,261	13,291
Lamb & mutton	742	691	650	736	578	495
Lard	1,819	1,979	2,114	2,295	1,932	1,758
Total...	19,689	22,582	22,821	27,205	31,034	34,036
Total (excl. lard) ...	17,850	20,603	20,707	24,913	29,102	32,288

Meat Yield per Animal

Average meat yield per animal has shown a tremendous increase since 1947. This has been due largely to an abundance of feed supplies available at increasingly lower prices. The rapid expansion of the cattle feeding industry began less than two decades ago. Grain-fed animals made up only one-third of cattle slaughter in 1955, but in 1972 approximately 75% of the cattle slaughtered were finished in feedlots. Firms specializing in the custom feeding of cattle have grown in size and number. The proliferation of large-scale feedlots has affected the relationship between cattle numbers and meat production by reducing the time between weaning and slaughter and increasing the weight per animal. Most feedlots market their cattle by the age of fifteen months, compared with the two years or more formerly needed to get range animals to market size and condition. Shortening the feeding period removes animals from the inventory at an earlier age and thus results in larger beef supplies from a given inventory base. In addition to increasing efficiency, feeding improves the quality of meat in most instances. Many animals that would grade "good" on entering the feedlot have moved up to the level of "choice" when slaughtered. Larger animals for slaughter combined with better slaughtering techniques have meant more meat per animal available for consumption. Due to the high cost of the raw material to the meatpacking industry and a loss of approximately one-half of *live* animal weight during slaughtering, much effort is directed towards maximizing the extraction of edible or commercially useful parts of the animal from the carcass. Table 2-8 shows the average yield of dressed weight per head of livestock slaughtered.

Of the four classifications of meat output measured (beef, veal, pork, lamb and mutton), beef has shown the greatest increase in the 1947-1971 period. The number of calves, sheep, and lambs slaughtered has shown an almost steady decline since 1947. The slaughter of cattle has increased much faster since 1947 than the slaughter of hogs. The number of hogs slaughtered is much greater than that of cattle; and the large number of hogs slaughtered relative to other animals is due to their relatively young age at the time of slaughter. Hogs require only nine months to grow to slaughter weight, whereas cattle have averaged about two years—until the time that cattle feedlots were introduced. Also, the average hog weight has not grown as other average animal weights have because of the desirable quality of the meat yield from a lean hog. The large increase in number of head of cattle slaughtered, their large size relative to other species, and their growth in average size relative to other species since 1947 have helped to reduce the energy inputs per pound of meat output in the animal slaughtering process.

Use of a chemical substance called DES has helped increase live animal weight as well as reduce the time the animal spends in the feedlot. Live weight has also increased by reducing shrinkage (tissue shrinkage when animals were not fed on hauls to terminal markets).

While the average meat yield per animal slaughtered has shown large increases between 1947 and 1967, the average live weight for each different animal has also increased, although not quite as much as the average

Table 2-8. Average Yield per Head—Dressed Weight of Commercially Slaughtered Livestock, (pounds)

	Cattle	Calves	Hogs	Sheep & Lambs
1947	471	115	142	43
1954	505	122	138	45
1958	522	119	136	48
1962	574	125	142	47
1967	592	127	151	50
1971	611	140	155	51
Per cent change 1947-1971	29.7%	21.7%	9.2%	18.6%

Source: Department of Agriculture, *Livestock and Meat Statistics*.

Table 2-9. Average Live Weight vs. Average Dressed Weight (indexes, 1947 = 100)

	Cattle		Calves		Hogs		Sheep & Lambs	
	Live	Dressed	Live	Dressed	Live	Dressed	Live	Dressed
1947	100	100	100	100	100	100	100	100
1954	103	107	105	106	97	97	102	105
1958	110	111	101	103	95	96	105	112
1962	112	122	107	109	96	100	104	109
1967	114	126	110	110	97	106	109	116
1971	115	130	119	122	96	109	112	119

Table 2-10. Dressed Weight as Per Cent of Total Live Weight

	1947	1954	1958	1962	1967	1971
Cattle	52%	55%	53%	57%	58%	59%
Calves	55	55	56	56	56	56
Hogs	57	58	58	59	63	65
Sheep & lambs	46	47	49	48	50	49

dressed weight. The differences in live weight vs. dressed weight for the years observed indicate that certain applied processes must yield more of the animal available for consumption. This is especially true in the case of cattle and hogs. Hogs show a *decrease* of 4% in average live weight over the 20-year period, but an *increase* of 9% in average dressed weight. Table 2-10 shows the dressed weight (usable portion) by animal as a per cent of the average live weight before processing.

Small increases in dressing percentages add significantly to the total meat supply. This is especially true when considering the additional pounds added to the supply of beef.

If no increases in average animal weight had occurred since 1947, the actual pounds that would have been provided would have been significantly lower, as shown in Table 2-11.

In 1967, 77% of the *additional* pounds produced by an increase in animal weight were beef.

The effect of the increases in average animal weights on total output of meat is illustrated in Chart 2-2.

Table 2-12 shows the increase in average animal weight between 1947 and 1971 to be 24%. A rather large increase—8%—occurred between 1962 and 1967.

Table 2-11.   Pounds of Meat Produced Due to Gains in Animal Weight

(millions)

	1947 Average Weight	1954	1958	1962	1967	1971
Cattle.........	471	10,177	9,615	10,688	13,307	13,978
Calves	115	1,064	768	621	486	303
Hogs	142	8,100	8,986	10,477	10,590	12,176
Sheep & lambs ..	43	660	583	673	497	417
Total.......		20,001	19,952	22,459	24,880	26,874
Actual......		20,603	20,707	24,913	29,102	32,288

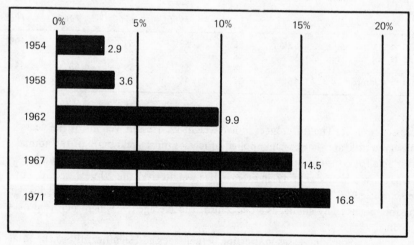

Chart 2-2. Portion of Total Output Due to Increases in Average Animal Weights Since 1947.

Table 2-12. Average Animal Weight

	1947	1954	1958	1962	1967	1971
Pounds	193	203	206	222	230	239
Index (1947 = 100)	(100)	(105)	(107)	(115)	(119)	(124)

Gains in average animal weight have undoubtedly contributed to lower energy input per pound of meat output. Essentially, the same slaughtering techniques must be applied to each animal; but the pound yield, due to higher weight per animal, is greater, especially in the case of cattle. If the number of animals slaughtered is held constant, the slaughtering processes (and thus energy consumed—given no technological changes to reduce energy inputs) remain constant, but output increases (due to larger yield per animal), and thus energy consumed per pound of output decreases. Therefore, certain energy economies must be realized when average animal weight increases.

Product Shifts

The series of indexes (1947 = 100) shown in Table 2-13 illustrate the changes in the number of slaughters and pounds of meat output since 1947.

Table 2-13. Meat Production Indexes, 1947 = 100

	1947	1954	1958	1962	1967	1971e
Cattle						
slaughters ..	100	118.3	111.8	124.3	154.7	162.5
lbs.	100	126.9	123.9	151.4	194.5	210.8
Calves						
slaughters ..	100	91.0	65.7	53.1	41.6	25.9
lbs.	100	96.5	67.9	57.7	45.9	31.5
Hogs						
slaughters ..	100	110.4	122.4	142.8	144.3	165.9
lbs.	100	107.3	117.3	142.8	153.5	181.1
Lambs & mutton						
slaughters ..	100	89.0	78.5	90.7	67.0	56.2
lbs.	100	93.1	87.6	99.2	77.9	66.7

e—estimated.

Table 2-14 shows the increases in output (pounds) under two hypothetical situations which illustrate:
(1) increases in output if the average weight of animals were held constant at their 1947 level;
(2) increases in output with weights constant *and* the mix of types of animals

slaughtered constant at the 1947 proportion (based on *actual* number of slaughters).

Table 2-14.   Meat Production and Product Mix
(index of pounds produced 1947 = 100)

	1947	1954	1958	1962	1967	1971e
Actual	100	115.4	116.0	139.6	163.0	180.9
Hypothetical Animal weights constant at 1947 level	100	112.0	111.8	125.8	139.4	150.6
Weights constant and mix constant at 1947 levels ..	100	105.9	106.6	120.5	121.6	131.0

e—estimated.

Each of the series in Table 2-14 is based on the actual number of slaughters that occurred, but shows how much the level of meat output is affected by average animal weight gains and by the changes in the mix of the types of animals slaughtered.

From Chart 2-3 it is apparent that changes in output since 1947 are not only due to more slaughters, but also to more pounds as a result of each slaughter *as well as* to shifts in the types of animals slaughtered. The importance of cattle becomes readily apparent. In 1967, beef accounted for 60% of the total value of shipments in the industry. The number of cattle slaughters increased 65% between 1947 and 1971. During that period, there was a shift in the types of meat produced—beef became a relatively more important product while the production of veal, lamb, and mutton fell off considerably.

The internal production shifts that have occurred since 1947 have affected the amount of energy consumed by the industry. Unit energy use per pound of output has declined faster than energy use per slaughter. In 1947, beef was the major product of the meat packing industry, and since that time has become dominant by a considerable margin. Changes in the number of cattle slaughtered (and, as a consequence larger pound yield) have led to corresponding changes in the total amount of energy consumed by the industry. While total energy use has been decreasing since 1954 in relation to increases in output, the magnitude and direction of these changes have followed a similar pattern to that of the increases in cattle slaughters.

Value of Shipments

Primary Products. The primary products of meatpacking plants represent almost all of their shipments. The specialization ratio measures the per cent of total output which is accounted for by primary products. The

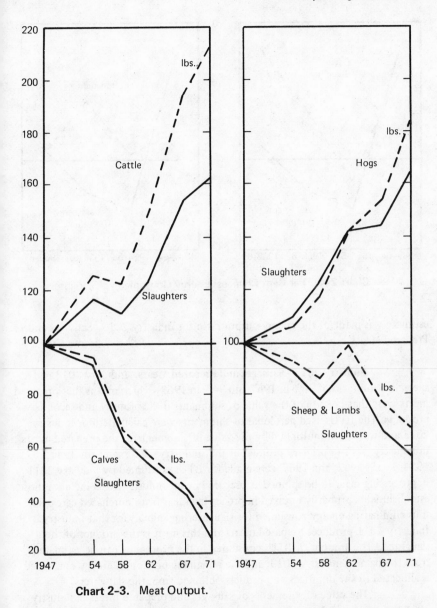

Chart 2-3. Meat Output.

specialization ratio for industry 2011 has been quite high—98% in 1954, 1958, 1963 and 1967. The primary products include beef, veal, lamb and mutton, pork, lard, skins, pelts and hides, processed or cured pork sausage and similar products, canned meats, and natural sausage casings. The primary products of industry 2011 have represented around 86% (in the Census years covered in this study) of these products shipped by all industries. In order to determine the amount of energy consumed for processing meat products by industry 2011, an

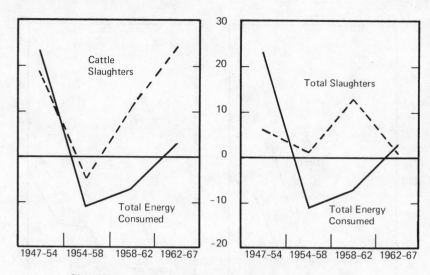

Chart 2-4. Per Cent Changes, Energy Consumed vs. Slaughters.

estimate was made of the energy-output ratio for industry 2013—Sausages and Prepared Meats.

Industry 2013—Sausages and Prepared Meats. Industry 2013 had a specialization ratio of 96% in 1967 and 94% in 1962—which means that prepared meats were that portion of the value of shipments of its primary and secondary products. The BTUs used per dollar of shipments were calculated for industry 2013 and were then multiplied by the value of shipments of the prepared meats in industry 2011 (a primary product of that industry). Estimates for 1947, 1954, 1958, 1962, and 1967 were made for BTUs consumed by industry 2011 in processing meat to be shipped as prepared meat. Industry 2013 includes those establishments primarily engaged in processing meat from purchased carcasses, thus eliminating energy consumed for slaughtering animals for that industry. Industry 2011 produces prepared meats and this meat is the product of their slaughters. The amount of BTUs consumed in the processing can be estimated from the data of industry 2013, and the remaining portion of energy consumed is allocated to the unprocessed products obtained from the slaughters.

The value of shipments of sausages and prepared meats in industry 2011 has represented a declining proportion of the total value of shipments of that industry. An even smaller proportion of the total energy consumed by industry 2011 was used for processing meat. Table 2-15 indicates those portions of energy consumed and value of shipments accounted for by prepared meat products.

Table 2-15.   Prepared Meats—Industry 2011

	1947	*1954*	*1958*	*1962*	*1967*
Sausages & prepared meats					
% of total value of shipments ..	23%	27%	22%	20%	18%
% of total energy used	15	21	19	14	19

The value of the shipments of industry 2013 for sausages and other prepared meats is quite close to the value of shipments of sausages and prepared meats in industry 2011.

Estimates were made of the energy consumed to process meat in industry 2011 by calculating the BTUs consumed per current dollar of shipments in industry 2013. These energy-output ratios were then applied to the current dollar value of shipments of sausages and prepared meats in industry 2011. These estimates appear in Table 2-16 along with the remaining portion of total energy consumed. It is *assumed* that the remaining BTUs used are for the remaining primary products obtained as a result of the slaughtering process (beef, veal, pork, lamb, mutton, skins, and lard). Since the specialization ratio for the industry is so high (98%), it is assumed that almost all of the energy consumed is for primary products.

When energy consumption is divided between BTUs required for meat processing (prepared meats) and for unprocessed products (beef, veal, pork, lamb, etc.), greater *fluctuations* in the amount of energy used are found for the processed than for the unprocessed products segment of the industry.

Table 2-16.   Energy Consumed—Industry 2013

	1947	*1954*	*1958*	*1962*	*1967*
Total BTUs (trillions)	12.1	20.7	16.3	11.8	16.2
1,000 BTUs/1967 $ of shipments ...	5.7	7.6	6.2	4.6	5.7

Table 2-17.   Energy Consumed—Prepared Meats and Unprocessed Products—Industry 2011

	1947	*1954*	*1958*	*1962*	*1967*
Total BTUs consumed (trillions) ...	80.4	99.1	87.6	81.5	84.0
BTUs for processing sausages and prepared meats (trillions) ..	12.1	20.7	16.3	11.7	16.2
Residual	68.3	78.4	71.3	69.8	67.8

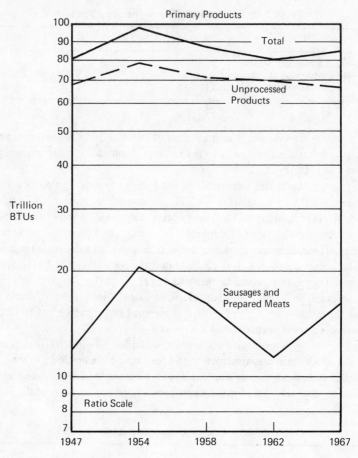

*Useful energy basis

Chart 2-5. Energy Consumed in Meatpacking Plants.

Between 1947 and 1954, there was an extremely large increase in the amount of energy consumed for processed products. In 1954, prepared meats accounted for an unusually large proportion—27%—of the total value of shipments of industry 2011. The steep rise in energy consumed by the total industry during that period can be at least partially explained by the large amount of meat processed at that time. Also, much of the mechanized equipment that is currently being used by the industry was introduced between 1947 and 1954.

Energy-Output Ratio—Physical Units

In calculating energy-input to product-output ratios, an output series in physical units rather than in value of shipments would eliminate certain shifts in product mix that are reflected in price. For example, changes in the volume of output of one animal species relative to another would create distortions in total output that is measured by value of shipments when one class of meat commands a higher market price. Average price will also fluctuate with different variations in the mix of grades of meat (for example: choice, prime, good, etc.) at different points in time. Value of shipments is not a true measure of volume of output and thus not of energy consumed.

For the portion of energy used on unprocessed products, two series have been created for energy used per unit of output. These are BTUs per pound (pounds of meat and lard obtained after slaughter) and BTUs per slaughter.

The amount of energy consumed per pound of output has declined approximately twice as fast as the amount of energy consumed per animal slaughtered. Much of the drop in energy use per unit can be explained by the internal production shift away from the slaughter of smaller animals. (It becomes apparent that as the meat produced per animal slaughtered increases, a savings in energy consumption occurs.)

Efficiencies in energy use can be determined by measuring total BTUs consumed each year for the same level of output as in 1947. For this series, BTUs are the total less those used for prepared meats. The 1947 level of production as a per cent of total output for each year is applied to the BTUs consumed in each year. The result shows the BTUs required for the same level of production as well as the efficiencies (or inefficiencies in the case of 1954) in energy use.

Table 2-18.   BTUs Consumed per Unit—Pounds and Slaughters

	1947	1954	1958	1962	1967
BTU/lb.	3,469	3,472	3,124	2,566	2,185
BTU/slaughter	701,506	759,307	686,039	592,906	571,559

Table 2-19.   Savings in Energy Consumption Since 1947

	1954	1958	1962	1967
1947 level of production as per cent of total	87.2%	86.3%	72.4%	63.4%
BTUs (trillions)	68.4	61.5	50.5	43.0
Energy savings for same level of production	(−0.1)	6.8	17.8	25.3

SECTION III.   FUTURE TRENDS

Raw Material

In the past, meat production has outpaced the increase in animal numbers. The boost that meat production received from the development and expansion of large-scale cattle feeding may be approaching the upper limits. However, further potential gains in meat production per animal still exist in the area of efficiency of feed conversion and average daily gain. Continued research and experimentation in breeding, nutritional requirements, and ration formulation could result in the production of a marketable animal in less than the fifteen months now required, but these gains will probably be very small and slow in coming. A continuation of the uptrend in average live weight seems likely, which means that meat production per animal will rise correspondingly. Another opportunity for increasing live weight lies in the new breeds of cattle being imported into the U.S. today. The crossbreeding of these with domestic breeds will be another step toward increasing meat production. Beef cattle should comprise a larger proportion of total slaughter in the future as the dairy herd continues to decline. Mature animals produce a higher proportion of usable meat than younger animals. The continuation of the trend away from calf slaughter will give an additional boost to the dressing percentage.

Energy

New plant construction will require more and more refrigeration capacity due to increasing markets for frozen and prepared foods. As refrigeration requirements go up in the meat packaging and processing plants, the possibility of greater electricity consumption will also increase. However, this trend could also favor gas if absorption air-conditioning systems and gas-engine-driven chillers are properly promoted.

The food and meat industries are highly regulated. Many of the regulations entail the consumption of large amounts of energy. Some meat industry specialists feel that regulations could be eased somewhat without introducing contamination or affecting the quality of the meat. The postponement of some newly proposed regulations is a likely course of action in an effort to curtail the rising energy needs of the industry.

Projections to 1980

Production projections have been made to 1980 by extrapolation of past trends. It has been assumed that the high demand for meat, especially for beef, will continue and that animal weight will also increase. Shipments should increase at a faster rate between 1971 and 1975 than between 1975 and 1980. Total output of red meats and lard should reach 38,341 million pounds by 1975 and almost 44,000 million pounds by 1980. Unit energy use has been declining since 1958 and is projected to continue to decline. Projections for

BTUs consumed per pound of output were combined with output projections to obtain estimates of total energy used for unprocessed meats. Estimates were then made of the energy used for the processing of prepared meats. The sum of the projections for processed and unprocessed meats yielded estimates for the entire industry. On a useful energy basis, total BTUs consumed in 1975 should be 89 trillion, and in 1980, 92 trillion. Separate projections of electricity on a gross consumption basis yielded totals of 113 trillion BTUs in 1975 and 121 trillion BTUs in 1980.

The energy-output ratio (on a useful energy basis) is expected to decline at an average annual rate of 2.3% between 1971 and 1975. Thereafter, the average annual rate of decline is 2.2%. Table 2-20 contains projections for 1971, 1975, and 1980 for output measures, energy-input measures, and energy-output ratios.

Table 2-20.　Projections to 1980

	1971	1975	1980
Value of shipments			
1967 $ (millions)	$16,794	$19,123	$22,169
Total BTUs consumed (trillions)			
Useful	85.8	89.1	92.4
Gross	106.7	113.4	122.0
1,000 BTUs/1967 $ of shipments			
Useful	5.1	4.7	4.2
Gross	6.3	5.9	5.5
Production (million lbs.)			
Meat	32,288	36,765	42,621
Lard	1,758	1,576	1,374
Total	34,036	38,341	43,995
Energy consumed (useful)			
Unprocessed meats (trillion BTUs)	68.6	71.3	73.9
Prepared meats (trillion BTUs)	17.2	17.8	18.5
Total useful energy			
(trillion BTUs)	85.8	89.1	92.4

SECTION IV.　BIBLIOGRAPHY

American Meat Institute. *Financial Facts about the Meat Packing Industry,* 1972.

———. *Meatfacts 73.*

Anglo-American Council on Productivity. *The Meat Processing Industry.*

De Graff, Herrell. *Beef Production and Distribution.* University of Oklahoma Press, Norman, Oklahoma, 1960.

Department of Agriculture..*Agricultural Statistics,* 1971.

——————. *Demand and Prices for Meat.* Technical Bulletin 1253.

——————. *The Food Marketing Industries, Recent and Prospective Structural Changes, 1966.*

——————. *Livestock and Meat Statistics,* Statistical Bulletin, 1970, 1969, 1965.

——————. *Livestock Slaughter,* Annual Summary, 1968-1972.

Department of Commerce. *Growth Pacesetters in American Industries* 1958-1968, October 1968.

Federal Reserve Bank of Kansas City. *Monthly Review,* April 1973.

Hall, Farrall, Rippen. *Encyclopedia of Food Engineering.* Westport, Connecticut: Avi Publishing Co., 1971.

Ives, J. Russell. *The Livestock and Meat Economy of the United States,* American Meat Institute.

Kirk-Othmer. *Encyclopedia of Chemical Technology,* Vol. 13, Second Edition, 1967.

National Commission on Food Marketing. *Organization and Competition in the Livestock and Meat Industry,* Technical Study No. 1, June 1966.

Chapter Three

Fluid Milk—SIC 2026

Noreen Preston

SECTION I.   INTRODUCTION AND SUMMARY

Description of the Industry

The Fluid Milk industry, SIC 2026, is defined as establishments primarily engaged in processing (pasteurizing, homogenizing, vitaminizing, bottling) and distributing fluid milk and cream, and related products.

Buttermilk, cultured
Cheese, cottage
Chocolate milk
Cottage cheese, including pot, bakers', and farmers' cheese
Cream, aerated
Cream, bottled
Cream, plastic
Cream, sour
Kumyss
Milk, acidophilus
Milk, bottled
Milk processing (pasteurizing, homogenizing, vitaminizing, bottling) and
    distribution: with or without manufacture of dairy products
Milk products made from fresh milk
Whipped cream
Yoghurt
Zoolak

The dairy industry is characterized by a large number of relatively small operations. Fluid milk producing establishments have been reduced in number by almost one-third since 1948. The trend towards fewer and larger plants has reduced unit costs. Because of the perishable nature of the product, plants were formerly located close to the source of milk. With improved packaging, refrigeration, and preservation technologies, there will be a trend to build new plants further away from the central cities and into areas of low labor and land costs. All of this will come about because spoilage is becoming of less concern in the fluid milk industry and because shipping costs are becoming relatively less important.

Cleanliness and sanitation are primary requirements in the dairy industry. Because of its cleanliness and flexibility, gas has become a major source of energy. Process heat is used principally for pasteurizing milk prior to further treatment and sterilization of dairy equipment and containers. Refrigeration is usually supplied by electrically-driven refrigeration equipment; however, gas-driven refrigeration may also be used. Additional fuel is required for pasteurizing since the adoption of the High-Temperature, Short-Time (HTST) technique. More rapid processing of dairy products has called for higher temperature steam and hot water for cleaning manufacturing utensils. However, at the same time, widespread introduction of plastic-lined packing materials has eliminated much of the extensive bottle washing and sanitizing facilities that were formerly required. For the most part, electrical requirements are quite small relative to thermal requirements.

Processes

Milk processing in commercial dairies is rigidly controlled by government agencies to assure the quality of the product and sanitation. There are five major processing steps in converting raw milk to the saleable product:

1. *Clarification.*   Milk is clarified in a centrifugal clarifier. This removes any sediment present. After this process, the butterfat is adjusted to a uniform percentage.

2. *Homogenization.*   The milk is forced under pressure through a system containing a metal plate with openings. In this process, the butterfat globules are greatly reduced in size. This prevents them from rising to the top of the milk and forming a layer of cream.

3. *Pasteurization.*   Pasteurization is accomplished by heating the milk to a specified temperature for a definite period of time. There are two methods of pasteurization. The old process is called the "holding method." Milk is heated in a jacketed vat to 145 degrees F., held at this temperature for 30 minutes, and then rapidly cooled. Because of the time involved with this method, it has for the most part been replaced by the HTST process. The High-Temperature, Short-Time method (or flash pasteurization) pumps raw milk into the pasteurizer and is heated to a temperature of 162 degrees F. and is held there for 16 seconds. The pasteurized milk is then cooled.

4. *Fortification.*   Milk is often enriched because it does not contain vitamin D. The process of fortification is most commonly accomplished by adding a concentrate of Vitamin D to the milk. Other practices include ultraviolet irradiation of milk and feeding cows irradiated yeast. Vitamin D fortified milk must contain at least 400 Vitamin D units per quart.

5. *Packaging.*   The cooled milk is packaged in glass bottles, wax-coated paper containers, cans or other material. The high degree of sanitation required necessitates well-controlled procedures for handling and cleaning the milk-treated utensils. To remove the milk solids, the utensils are rinsed and washed with an alkaline detergent solution at 125-130 degrees F., then rinsed with hot water, drained, dried, and sanitized. However, sanitization is more often done with chemicals than with heat.

Summary of Developments and Projections

The energy consumed by the fluid milk industry is a small proportion of the total energy used by all food industries. Energy consumption by food group (SIC 20) has increased 24% since 1954, while fluid milk (SIC 2026) has dropped 41%.

The basic steps in the milk processing system today include clarification, separation of some or all of the cream (depending on the ultimate product desired), pasteurization, and homogenization. There is much uniformity in major pieces of equipment in the industry, for example, in hot-water boilers, reciprocating engines and turbines, water pumps, clarifiers, pasteurizers, compressors, etc.

Gas has been the predominant source of energy within the industry. Substantial amounts of natural gas are used as well as gasoline and diesel fuel. The only type of energy that shows consistent and steady growth, however, is electricity.

The production of milk in fluid form has shown a slow but steady increase. Per capita consumption has been declining and will probably continue to do so. However, there should be an overall increase in output in response to the increase in demand from an expanding population.

Total energy consumed in 1954 was 126.3 trillion BTUs (this measures electricity on a useful energy basis). Between 1954 and 1958, there was a drop to 80.3 trillion BTUs. There are two explanations for this large drop, the first of which involves Census Bureau coverage. In 1954, the Census coverage was slightly smaller than that for 1958 and thereafter. Second, during this period most of the dairies handling fluid milk experienced a changeover from can receipt of milk to bulk receipt. When milk is delivered to the dairies in bulk form, it eliminates many of the energy-consuming activities necessary for handling milk cans, i.e., emptying, lifting, washing, sterilizing, etc. The amount of energy saved by receiving milk in bulk form is about two-thirds of the amount used for can receipt. With the decline in the number of dairies involved in the production of fluid milk, energy costs per unit of output have declined. With larger plants, output increases faster than energy inputs, and thus energy used per unit declines. When electricity is measured on a useful energy basis, the energy consumed per unit (BTUs per constant 1967 dollar of shipments) drops from 16.2 trillion in 1954 to 9.7 trillion in 1958. After 1958, there is a gradual decline, to 6.9 trillion BTUs in 1967.

The trend toward fewer establishments should continue, while output increases and operating machinery becomes more efficient. Output is projected to increase by almost 10½% between 1967 and 1980, and the total amount of energy consumed to drop from 64 trillion BTUs in 1967 to 45 trillion BTUs by 1980. This means a decline in the energy-output ratio from 8,200 BTUs to 5,200 BTUs per constant 1967 dollar of output. Table 3-1 contains historical data as well as projections for the industry.

Table 3-1.   Historical Data and Projections

	1954	*1958*	*1962*	*1967*	*1971*	*1975*	*1980*
Value of shipments							
1967 $ (millions) ...	$5,755	$7,123	$7,383	$7,826	$8,116	$8,322	$8,629
Current $ (millions) .	4,866	6,412	6,889	7,826	–	–	–
Total BTUs consumed (trillions)							
Useful energy[1]	126.3	80.2	70.9	63.8	57.6	51.6	44.9
Gross energy[1]	139.0	95.3	86.8	81.5	74.7	68.2	60.4
Total cost of fuel and electric energy							
Current $ (millions)	$60.1	$60.4	$66.9	$66.5	—	–	–
1,000 BTUs/1967 $ of shipments							
Useful energy	22.0	11.3	9.6	8.2	7.1	6.2	5.2
Gross energy	24.2	13.4	11.8	10.4	9.2	8.2	7.0

[1] See Chapter One, pages 14-15, for definitions of useful and gross energy.

SECTION II.   HISTORICAL DEVELOPMENTS

Energy Use

The energy consumed by the fluid milk industry was a declining proportion of the total energy used in the food industry as a whole between 1954 and 1967. The total BTUs (electricity measured on a gross energy consumed basis) used by the fluid milk industry in 1967 were only 7.4% of the total BTUs for all foods.

Table 3-2.   Total Energy Consumed in All Food Manufacturing and in Fluid Milk

(trillion BTUs*)

	1954	1958	1962	1967
All food manufacturing	882.7	951.0	992.3	1,097.7
Fluid milk...................	139.0	95.3	86.8	81.5
Milk as % of total............	15.7%	10.0%	8.7%	7.4%

*Gross energy consumed basis.

Table 3-3 shows BTUs consumed by the fluid milk industry, by type of fuel or power. Electricity has been measured on a useful energy basis.

Between 1954 and 1967, total energy consumed (measured in trillions of BTUs) declined by just about one-half. The largest drop occurred between 1954 and 1958, 36.5%. During this period, a change in operations radically affected the amount of energy required by the milk industry.

Prior to the mid-1950s, raw milk was delivered to a dairy in cans collected from the various dairy farms in the locality. Under this method of collection, a substantial amount of energy was required for lifting, moving, emptying, and especially for washing and sterilizing the cans. These processes have been eliminated by the introduction of bulk milk receipt. When milk is collected and transported in bulk form, milk cans are not utilized. Large stainless steel tanker trucks with capacities of 1,500 to 2,500 gallons are used to carry raw milk. These truck containers are filled by a hose from the dairy farm containers. By eliminating the use of cans, it was no longer necessary to operate the can conveyor, use the can receiving room, the can washer sterilizer, and other space and equipment. The conversion from can to bulk receipt led to an enormous savings in utility expenses. There is a large savings on steam because cans do not have to be washed. The total electricity and power consumption for the receiving operation is about two-thirds lower for bulk than for can receiving.

Between 1958 and 1967, total energy consumed declined at an average annual rate of 5.5%. Improved facilities for transporting milk have reduced the need for a large number of widely dispersed dairy plants. Equipment has improved but is costly. Hence, there has been a trend toward fewer and larger plants. The larger plants operate with expanded capacity, resulting in increased output with lower cost per unit of output.

Table 3-4 contains a distribution of types of energy consumed. The 1967 *Census of Manufactures* contains estimates of fuels consumed based on administrative records from the Internal Revenue Service and the Social Security Administration and not solely on establishment-reported forms. It is for this reason that much of the fuels consumed has been categorized as "not specified by kind."

Table 3-3. Total Energy Consumed in Fluid Milk Industry, by Source

(trillion BTUs)

	1954	1958	1962	1967
Coal	36.4	12.3	9.3	2.3
Total fuel oil	15.1	19.0	14.1	7.7
Gas	58.7	25.4	24.5	18.1
Other fuels	11.2	8.5	15.3	5.7
Fuels, n.s.k.	0	8.3	0	21.5
Electric energy*	4.9	6.7	7.6	8.6
Total energy consumed*	126.3	80.2	70.9	63.8

*Useful energy basis.

Table 3-4. Per Cent Distribution of Energy Consumption, by Type of Energy*

	1954	1958	1962	1967
Coal	28.8%	15.3%	13.1%	3.5%
Total fuel oil	11.9	23.7	19.9	12.0
Gas	46.5	31.7	34.6	28.4
Other fuels	8.9	10.6	21.7	8.9
Fuels, n.s.k.	0	10.3	0	33.7
Electric energy	3.9	8.4	10.7	13.5
Total	100%	100%	100%	100%

*Electricity converted on a useful energy basis.

An enormous drop in coal consumption occurred between 1954 and 1967. Sanitary standards within the industry are quite high; consequently, a shift to gas and other fuels is evident. Steam is the most economical and popular source of heat as well as the best sterilization medium for dairy plants. With fuel oil and electricity, a high degree of automatic operation is easily attained. These coal alternatives permit more uniform heating and reduce the cost of maintenance (the costs for cleaning within the industry run high). The efficiency of an oil-fired plant in a dairy is much higher than that of a hand-fired coal-burning plant.

Output

Output—measured in constant dollars of shipments—has increased at an average rate of 2.2% since 1954.

The growth in output between 1954 and 1958 is overstated due to changes in coverage in the Census years 1954 and 1958. An undetermined number of bottling and pasteurizing plants were classified in the *Census of*

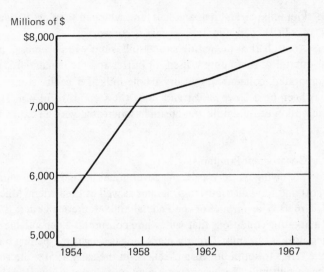

Chart 3-1. Value of Shipments.

Business in 1954 and attempts were made to reclassify them in 1958 in the *Census of Manufactures.* Hence, the value of shipments for 1954 is understated.

The specialization ratio (primary products as a per cent of primary plus secondary products) for the industry has been 90% in 1958, 1962 and 1967. Data for 1947 for fluid milk from the Bureau of the Census do not exist (see Appendix to this chapter).

With the high and consistent specialization rates for the industry, a per cent distribution of the value of shipments of primary products will present a fairly accurate picture of the product mix in the industry.

Packaged fluid milk and related products are the major portion of the primary products of the industry. Items in this category include packaged

Table 3-5.   Value of Shipments of Primary Products
(per cent distribution)

	1958	1963	1967
Bulk fluid milk and cream	11.8%	13.0%	11.1%
Packaged fluid milk and related products	76.3	73.7	69.8
Cottage cheese	3.3	3.1	3.3
Buttermilk, chocolate milk, etc.................	3.9	4.3 ⎫	15.8
Fluid milk and other products, n.s.k.*	4.7	5.9 ⎭	
Primary products	100%	100%	100%

*n.s.k. = not specified by kind.

fluid milk, skim milk, cream, half-and-half, and whipped topping. Between 1958 and 1967, very little change in product mix occurred.

About half of the nation's total milk supply has been used in fluid form. One-quarter of the supply is used for butter and the remainder is used for cheese, evaporated, condensed, and dry whole milk. Per capita consumption of milk has been on a downward trend since the second World War. However, total consumption of fluid milk and cream has increased with an expanding population.

Government Programs

Following World War II, the government has engaged in numerous price support and food distribution programs as well as the Federal Milk Marketing Orders. The purpose of the Federal Milk Marketing Orders is to maintain marketing conditions that will assure consumers a dependable supply of pure and wholesome milk. Orderly marketing is sought by spelling out in advance the terms for both buyers and sellers. In the early 1950s, the government was buying surplus milk. Rather than build up inventories, it diverted the surplus milk to charitable institutions and school milk programs. School milk programs have continued and expanded and helped sustain a high level of fluid milk consumption.

Energy-Output Ratio

Energy consumed per constant 1967 dollar of output declined 63% between 1954 and 1967. The sharpest decline occurred between 1954 and 1958, when energy per unit of output declined at an average annual rate of 16.7%. As previously mentioned, it was during this time that many dairy plants converted to bulk-receipt of milk from can receipt and thus reduced their fuel and power requirements.

In 1967, there were almost half as many fluid milk establishments in the industry as in 1954. Consolidation of operations has helped reduce overhead costs. After 1958, the average annual rate of decline in BTU per constant dollar of output was 3.5%. Chart 3-2 illustrates the decline in unit energy use.

BTUs per constant 1967 dollar of output are shown in Table 3-6 on both a gross energy consumed and useful energy basis.

The industry is a heavy user of gasoline for the transportation of fluid milk. With larger firms manufacturing a greater supply, more milk is transported from fewer locations, which leads to a saving of gasoline and diesel fuel per unit.

Efficiencies in fuel and power are realized in dairy plants as the size of the plant increases. Unit costs have been cut by a trend within the industry toward fewer and larger plants. Table 3-7 shows the decline in the number of plants since 1954.

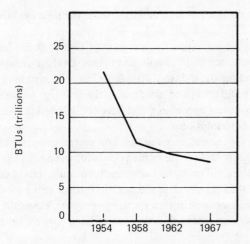

Chart 3-2. BTUs per 1967 Dollar of Shipments

Table 3-6.   BTUs per 1967 Dollar of Shipments

(trillions)

	Gross Energy Consumed Basis	Useful Energy Basis
1954	24.2	22.0
1958	13.4	11.3
1962	11.8	9.6
1967	10.4	8.2

Table 3-7.   Number of Establishments

1967	3,481
1963	4,619
1958	5,828
1954	6,669

SECTION III.   PROJECTIONS TO 1980

While the number of cattle on farms continues to increase in response to the stepped-up demand for beef, the size of the dairy herd has been declining. However, the milk obtained per cow has been increasing since 1955. According to figures published by the U.S. Department of Agriculture, the number of milk cows on farms has declined 41% since 1955, while the milk per cow has increased 61%.

Since 1955, the per capita consumption of fluid milk has been on a steady decline. The production of fluid milk and related products, however, has been increasing. Demand for the industry's products has been sustained by a rising population. The proliferation of products in the beverage industry and rise of consumer consciousness concerning diet have contributed to the fall-off in per capita fluid milk consumption.

Projections for the industry are based on several assumptions. It is reasonable to expect a fairly steady rise in the population even with the dropping off of the birth rate. Per capita consumption of milk should continue to decrease, although not as rapidly as in the past. In spite of rising food costs, there should be little product substitution for dairy products, especially for a staple such as milk. Rising incomes will defray the inflated cost of food products.

Energy consumed per unit of output should continue to decline, although not at the rate of decline since 1954. After 1958, the decline in unit energy used had been gradual due to greater efficiencies in operations. The decline in the number of fluid milk establishments should continue and thus bring about a corresponding drop in unit overhead costs.

Table 3-8 shows projections to 1980 for total energy requirements for the industry. Total BTUs (measuring electricity on a useful energy consumed basis) should drop to 45 trillion BTUs from 64 trillion BTUs in 1967. If electrical power is measured on a gross energy basis, the total number of BTUs required in 1980 should be 60 trillion, down from 81 trillion in 1967.

Table 3-8.   Projections to 1980

	1971	1975	1980
Total energy (trillion BTUs)			
Useful energy	57.6	51.6	44.9
Gross energy consumed	74.7	68.2	60.4
Output			
Constant 1967 $, (millions)	$8,116	$8,322	$8,629
1,000 BTUs/1967 $			
Useful energy	7.1	6.2	5.2
Gross energy consumed	9.2	8.2	7.0

SECTION IV.   APPENDIX: DATA LIMITATIONS

Census Bureau data for industry 2026 do not exist for 1947. Prior to 1954, the Standard Industrial Classification System did not consider plants that pasteurize or bottle fluid milk as manufacturing. In 1954, the specialization ratio (primary products as a per cent of primary plus secondary products) was only 82% in contrast with the 90% specialization ratio for the succeeding census years. The ratio was low because another industry (SIC 2027) was in existence as a separate classification of fluid milk and related products. For 1954, therefore, the value of shipments has been combined for SIC 2026 and 2027 in the report. It should also be noted that in 1954 a significant but undetermined number of plants were included in the *Census of Business* as retail trade establishments.

SECTION V.   SELECTED BIBLIOGRAPHY

Department of Agriculture. *Agricultural Statistics,* 1971.

————— . *Flexibility of Operation in Dairy Manufacturing Plants,* 1944-1961.

————— . *How Bulk Assembly Changes Marketing Costs,* Marketing Research Report #190, 1958.

————— . *Milk Production, Disposition and Income,* 1970-1972.

————— . Economic Research Service, *The Food Marketing Industries—Recent and Prospective Structural Changes,* May 1966.

Ferrall, A. W. *Engineering for Dairy and Food Products,* 1963.

Hinds, Max Kenyon. *Dairy Economics Handbook,* U.S. Department of Agriculture, 1958.

Kirk-Othmer. *Encyclopedia of Chemical Technology,* 2nd Edition, 1967.

Wilcox, George. *Milk, Cream and Butter Technology.* Park Ridge, New Jersey: Noyes Data Corporation, 1971.

Chapter Four

Canned Fruits and Vegetables—SIC 2033

Saul Levmore

SECTION I. INTRODUCTION AND SUMMARY

The Canned Fruits, Vegetables, Preserves, Jams, and Jellies industry, SIC 2033, hereafter referred to as Canned Fruits and Vegetables, includes establishments that process and package fruits, vegetables, and their juices; catsup and other tomato sauces; and jams, jellies, and preserves. It does not include seafood and soups.

Production in this industry has been growing at a decreasing rate. From 1954 to 1967 the annual rate of growth was approximately 4.1%; it fell to 2.1% for the period 1967 to 1971. The observations used were of appropriately weighted physical units.

Total energy consumed rose in different steps as gas began to replace steam in the early 1960s. Electricity consumption also rose with automation while oil and coal usage declined. The energy output ratio dropped slightly between 1958 to 1962 but then rose to about its former level by 1967.

It was shown that three major effects must be taken into consideration as we discuss the future of the industry. First, there is a definite trend within the industry toward the production of fruit juices. Second, there is a trend away from the smaller cans in all segments but the juices. Third, there is a growing reliance on large rotary cookers that operate more efficiently in terms of energy usage than do still retorts. It is thought that the second and third effects will balance each other, while the trend toward fruit juices will lower the energy-output ratio with time. The projections are for a 1% growth in output between 1971 and 1980 (led by the fruit juices) and in energy use between 1971 and 1975, followed by leveling off in energy demand.

If the costs of producing both canned and fresh foods continue to rise at high rates, then demand will decrease for the relatively more expensive fresh foods. In this case, a greater surplus for canning is created, tending to

123

increase the supply of canned foods and maintain their lower price. If this occurs, the demand for canned fruits and vegetables may exceed our projections.

SECTION II.   GENERAL FINDINGS

The Demand for Canned Fruits and Vegetables

The demand for canned fruits and vegetables over the past seventeen years has risen at a slow but steady rate. From 1954 to 1967 the value of shipments for the industry rose from $2,062 million to $3,468 million. This is equivalent to a rate of growth of approximately 4.1% a year. These figures are computed on a 1967 constant dollar basis by linking the *Census of Manufactures Industrial Production Index* to the 1967 value of shipments. For the period 1967 to 1971 shipments were estimated on the basis of National Canners Association data and data obtained from the *Annual Survey of Manufactures.* We arrive at a figure of $3,841 million for 1971, indicating a rate of growth in demand of about 3.7% a year from 1954 through 1971. Most significantly, if we isolate the 1967 to 1971 period, we have for these four years an annual growth rate of 2.1%.

Within the industry itself there has been little shift in composition. Table 4-2 summarizes the situation. In terms of updating this information, canned fruit juices have regained their rate of growth quite consistently and tomato sauce products have leveled off.

Table 4-1.   Shipments at 1967 Prices
(extrapolated with approximations for 1967-1971)

	1954	1958	1962	1967	1968	1969	1970	1971
Value in $ millions	$2,062	$2,597	$2,888	$3,468	$3,667	$3,747	$3,637	$3,841

Source: Bureau of the Census, *Annual Survey of Manufactures*; The Conference Board.

Table 4-2.   Share of Value of Production, by Product Classes

	1958	1963	1967
Canned fruits	29.2%	27.9%	25.2%
Canned vegetables	29.1	29.7	29.4
Canned hominy and mushrooms	1.6	1.5	1.6
Canned fruit juice	13.4	14.7	12.7
Canned vegetable juice	4.3	3.5	3.2
Catsup and other tomato sauces	11.2	11.5	15.6
Jams, jellies and preserves	9.0	8.8	7.5
Other	2.2	2.3	3.8

Note: Due to rounding, columns may not add to 100%.
Source: Bureau of the Census.

Energy Consumption

Energy usage in the Canned Fruits and Vegetables Industry increased at almost the same rate as the value of shipments. Energy use per unit of output (the energy-output ratio, which is measured in constant dollars as well) dropped somewhat from 1958 to 1962 and then rose to approximately its 1958 level by 1967.

Table 4-3 gives the total energy consumption of the Canned Fruits and Vegetables Industry. It says nothing of whether the energy-output ratio is rising or falling. For this we need a measure of the amount of energy used by the industry for a set amount of product. Table 4-4 gives this in terms of BTU per unit of output.

Table 4-3. Energy Utilization (trillion BTUs)

	1958	1962	1967
Useful energy[1]	36.5	38.5	48.2
Gross energy consumed[1]	39.0	42.5	54.3

[1] See Chapter One, pages 14-15, for definitions of useful and gross energy.
Sources: Bureau of the Census, *Census of Manufactures.*

Table 4-4. Energy Consumption per Unit Shipped (1,000 BTUs per 1967 $)

	1958	1962	1967
Useful energy	13.9	13.3	13.9
Gross energy consumed	15.0	14.7	15.6

Source: Bureau of the Census Data.

Demand Projections

Our projections are based on technological information and reports from within the industry itself. It is possible that our projections differ from those of the available model on account of anomalies in population growth projections.

We do have up-to-date statistics on output compiled by the canners themselves. In Table 4-5, Canned Vegetables includes mushrooms and tomato sauce products. It also includes tomato juice and therefore a substantial part of the vegetable juice subclassification. The difference between Table 4-5 and the industry as a whole is merely the subclassification of Jams, Jellies, and Preserves in addition to small amounts of vegetable juices.

Table 4-5.   Yearly Totals of Canned Vegetables, Fruits, and Fruit
Juices (1,000 cases)

	1962	1964	1966	1968	1970
Canned vegetable packs	283,203	268,390	290,760	296,676	219,620
Canned fruit packs	142,677	157,367	152,465	152,293	135,405
Canned fruit juice packs	45,703	47,558	61,279	56,915	69,725

Source: *Canned Food Pack Statistics*, National Canners Association.

Table 4-6.   Projected Shipments to 1980
(million 1967 $)

	1967	1971	1975	1980
Value of shipments	$3,468	$3,841	$3,995	$4,195

Fluctuations are not so much a result of oscillations in demand as in
supply. Canned food inventories are partially derived from the previous year's
surplus of fresh foods. While the demand for food is relatively constant,
inventories of canned foods are used when the current fresh food crop is insufficient. For the industry as a whole, demand has leveled off for quite some time
and the expected rate of growth is about that of the general population trend, or
about 1.5% a year. In terms of predicting energy demand for the industry,
however, we must consider trends in composition of the industry as well as
trends in the various processes.

The production of canned foods involves cooking food and sterilizing
the can as well as the food, either at the same time or in two separate processes.
In general, a product with high acidity can be sterilized before it is canned. This
is desirable from the point of view of costs, as the food requires far less energy
and time to be cooked and sterilized when the can does not surround it. For the
most part, juices and sauces are first cooked and then poured into containers.
From the perspective of the industry, the important property of these foods is
that they can be cooked very quickly. As a general rule, the faster a food can be
cooked, the better its quality.

The new competition that the canned food industry is facing comes
from frozen foods. Both stand to gain as the prices of fresh foods continue to
rise. This is because the labor costs of canned and frozen foods decrease relative
to those of fresh foods, which require more handling per unit of output.

Our projected rate of growth for the Canned Fruits and Vegetables
Industry is expected to match population growth, because frozen foods can be
expected to gain the market share lost by fresh foods, as frozen foods increase
in product quality and decrease in relative price. Canned foods are expected to
maintain their share of the market because of new processes that cut down on
cooking time and hence increase the quality of the product.

Energy Utilization Projections

While the industry is concerned with the quality of the product that results from very high temperatures for shorter time periods, the net result also includes a decrease in energy usage. This is because each $18°$ increase on the Fahrenheit scale produces a tenfold increase in organism destruction. Years ago, practically all the cooking was done by a process in which the cans were submerged and cooked either atmospherically (212 degrees F.) or through pressure cookers (approximately 275 degrees F.). In more recent years, large cookers, which are more efficient, have made substantial inroads in the market. Once again, they have caught on because the quality of their product is improved as a result of the diminished cooking time required. Nevertheless, they use less energy per unit output than their predecessors. Most of the new machines aid in convection by rotating the cans at high speeds, which has the effect of increasing the surface area that may be heated. As an example, creamed corn, which requires about 180 minutes of cooking in a still retort (no special aid to convection), is cooked for only 20 minutes in a high speed rotary cooker. Such high speed rotaries are used for at least one-fourth of the seasonal vegetables already.

Another major innovation has been the use of flame sterilizers. Rather than making use of steam, these machines use gas instead and heat the can with a flame of about 2,000 degrees Fahrenheit. Naturally, there are severe limitations; some foods cannot absorb such intense heat for even a very short period. The cooking portion of the entire process for the same can of creamed corn discussed above would require about seven minutes by the flame sterilization method.

What is important to extract from this discussion is that the trend in the industry is most definitely away from batch retorts and toward quicker cookers. The flame method, limited as its use may be, requires more energy per unit output than the large rotary cookers, but not more than the retorts.

What may be even more important than this is the information in Table 4-5. There is a trend toward more fruit juices, and it is unclear whether the diminishing share of vegetables and fruits will continue. It may be that as the quality of frozen foods improves, consumers buy frozen vegetables and other such products. On the other hand, juices that can be cooked prior to canning have a quality hard to match in frozen concentrates. The relative level of convenience between the two kinds of juices is difficult to weigh.

There is an offsetting effect to the shift in composition toward juices and to the shift in processes away from still retorts. This is the shift to larger cans. It should be obvious that two 8-ounce cans require far less energy for cooking than one 16-ounce can. Clearly, this is due to the far greater surface area entailed in the extra can. (As a matter of fact, within one can size there is an optimal shape as well, but as far as we can determine there has been no significant shift in this respect.) It happens that the trend in fruit juices is toward smaller cans; however, since the juices are cooked before they are poured into cans, this aspect is irrelevant for our purposes. Table 4-7 below also ignores tomato sauces for the same reason. The products listed are those with more than a 5% share of their respective classifications.

Table 4-7.   Vegetables: Relative Importance of Small Cans among Leading Industry Products

| | Per Cent of Cans Less Than 8 ozs. | | | Share of All Canned Vegetables (per cent) |
	1962	1967	1971	
Corn	8.2%	7.9%	6.4%	20.6%
Green Beans	6.9	5.5	5.5	17.2
Peas	14.5	13.3	11.7	12.1
Beets	10.3	9.3	7.4*	5.0

*1970 figure.

Table 4-8.   Fruits: Relative Importance of Small Cans among Leading Industry Products

| | Per Cent of Cans Less Than 8 ozs. | | | Share of All Canned Fruits (per cent) |
	1962	1967	1971	
Peaches	4.3%	5.6%	5.3%	24.4%
Pineapple	14.3	12.1	10.5*	19.2
Apple Sauce	2.9	4.1	2.7*	17.5
Fruit Cocktail	9.2	9.1	7.4	13.5
Pears	7.5	9.4	6.5	8.1
Cranberries	11.3	10.9	10.2	5.5

*1970 figure.
Source: National Canners Association; Appropriate conversion factors.

It is clear that there is a trend away from smaller cans in the Canned Vegetables subgrouping. The same is probably true although less obvious for fruits. What this means is that as the years go by the same total output will require more energy because larger cans are occupying an increasing part of the output of the total industry.

Thus within the industry it is difficult to project the future demand for energy. The shift to larger cans does indicate a greater energy-output ratio. On the other hand, we have the quickly growing trend toward rotary cookers, which have precisely the opposite effect as they turn the food while it is being cooked. In the final analysis, it does seem that the energy-output ratio will decline inasmuch as the growth in output within the industry will probably come from the fruit juice subgroup, where sterilizing requires the least energy of all. It would be quite reasonable to expect a leveling off of energy demand by 1975.

Table 4-9.   Projected Energy Demand to 1980
             (trillion BTUs)

	1967	*1971*	*1975*	*1980*
Useful energy	48.2	53.4	55.5	55.5
Gross energy consumed	54.3	60.2	62.6	62.6

These projections are for total energy demand. Within these projections we can expect the share pertaining to gas to increase. For the most part, gas is taking the place of coal as firms buy new machinery in anticipation of government-imposed environmental standards. It is cheaper than the low-sulphur coals. Industry spokesmen maintain that as gas shortages mount they will be forced to raise the prices to consumers considerably unless the environmental regulations are somewhat relaxed. The growth in usage of electric energy corresponds to the automation of the processes. It, too, can be expected to capture a continually increasing share through 1980.

SECTION III.   SELECTED BIBLIOGRAPHY

Department of Agriculture. Economic Report No. 81, *Convenience Foods.*

National Canners Association. *Canned Food Pack Statistics,* 1966, 1971-2.

——————. *Seasonal Patterns in Retail Sales of Canned Foods.*

—————— . *The Canning Industry,* 1959.

United Fresh Fruit and Vegetable Association. *Fruit and Vegetable Facts and Pointers,* 1965.

Chapter Five

Frozen Fruits and Vegetables—SIC 2037

Saul Levmore

SECTION I. INTRODUCTION AND SUMMARY

The Frozen Foods industry, SIC 2037, includes almost all frozen foods other than seafoods and dehydrated products (commonly known as freeze-dried). Some common products included in SIC 2037 are: frozen juices, dinners, fruits, vegetables, pies, pizzas, spaghetti with meatballs, and waffles.

Production in this industry has been growing at an increasing rate. During the period covered, production has grown at an annual rate of 3% for 1954-1958, 7.5% for 1958-1962, 7.9% for 1962-1967 and 8.4% for 1967-1971.

Total energy consumed rose at about the same annual rate. Gas and electricity were the primary movers as coal usage decreased and oil consumption fluctuated. The ratio of energy used per unit of output declined for the period ending in1962, but then increased at least to its former level by 1967.

The industry has been marked by seemingly daily technological innovations. The production processes are as varied as the number of establishments themselves. Some of these innovations required more energy than did the processes they were replacing; improvement of the quality of the final product has been the primary motivation.

In very recent times there have been some innovations which, if widely used, would cause a subtantial decrease in the usage of energy, but they have been prohibitively expensive for all but the most exotic delicacies.

The outlook for the next five to eight years is for continued increases in both output and energy demand. The forecast calls for an 8.75% annual growth rate through 1975 and close to a 9% rate for the five years between 1975 and 1980. Energy usage is expected to climb at only a slightly lower rate. It is very unlikely that the energy-output ratio could rise again, as the quality of the product seems to have reached a plateau. On the other hand, if the cost of liquid nitrogen were to fall dramatically there would be a decrease in the energy-output ratio.

131

SECTION II.   GENERAL FINDINGS

The Component Products

The three major subclasses of SIC 2037 in descending order of importance are: frozen specialties; frozen vegetables; and frozen fruits, juices, and ades. Specialties include such products as pies, nationality foods, baked goods, and dinners. In all cases, the products within SIC 2037 are subject to quality specifications. The competitive items are not homogeneous. Freezing methods are chosen not only for their relative costs but also for the quality products which they produce. The specialization and coverage ratios are 92% and 90% respectively.

The Demand for Frozen Fruits and Vegetables

Over the last seventeen years the frozen foods industry has grown substantially. From 1954 to 1967 the value of shipments for the industry rose from $961 million to $2,082 million. This is equivalent to a rate of growth of just under 6% a year. These figures are computed on a 1967 constant dollar basis by linking the *Census of Manufactures Industrial Production Index* to the 1967 value of shipments. In order to obtain figures for the years after 1967 we must extrapolate onto the values obtained from the *Annual Survey of Manufacturers,* both because of the need for constant dollar figures and because the Annual Survey and the Census do not cover precisely the same shipments. We have, then, a value of $2,877 million for 1971, or about a threefold increase from 1954. This indicates an increasing growth rate for the industry as well.

Within the industry itself there has been a large shift in composition. The industry grew as the demand for various specialties did. Frozen vegetables consistently occupy about one-fourth of the industry, but with time the share going to the specialties has increased while the portion associated with frozen fruits and juices has decreased dramatically. Although this is information essential to understanding the growth in value of shipments, it has little relation to the demand for energy. In general, it is not so much the products being frozen that determine energy usage, but rather it is the method of freezing and the volume of the products that matter. There is one exception that will be dealt with in the section on product analysis.

Table 5-1.   Shipments at 1967 Prices*

	1954	1958	1962	1967	1968	1969	1970	1971
Value in $ millions	961	1,060	1,421	2,082	2,289	2,564	2,708	2,877

*Extrapolated with approximations for the years 1967-1971 for purposes of conformity.
Source: Bureau of the Census; *Annual Survey of Manufactures.*

Table 5-2. Share of Value of Production, by Product Classes

	1958	1963	1967
Frozen fruits, juices and ades	39%	30%	21%
Frozen vegetables	25	27	29
Frozen specialties	35	42	44
Other (n.s.k.)	1	1	6

n.s.k.—not specified by kind.
Source: Bureau of the Census, *Annual Survey of Manufactures.*

Energy Consumption

Energy usage in the frozen foods industry increased at about the same pace as the value of shipments. Energy use per unit of output (measured in constant dollars once again) dropped slightly from 1958 to 1962 and then increased about as much as it had dropped by 1967.

Table 5-3 measures the total energy consumption of the industry. Data on BTUs per unit of output are shown in Table 5-4.

Table 5-3. Energy Utilization
(trillion BTUs)

	1958	1962	1967
Useful energy[1]	13.7	16.8	26.7
Gross energy[1] consumed	17.5	22.0	36.4

[1] See Chapter One, pages 14-15, for definitions of useful and gross energy.
Source: Bureau of Census, *Census of Manufactures.*

Table 5-4. Energy Consumption per Unit Shipped
(1,000 BTUs/1967 $)

	1958	1962	1967
Useful energy	12.9	11.9	12.8
Gross energy consumed	16.5	15.5	17.5

Source: Bureau of the Census data.

Demand Projections

The projection presented in this study is for an annual growth rate of 8.75% for the years 1971 to 1975; and then a slightly higher rate, perhaps even 9%, for the years 1976 to 1980. These demand projections are based on extrapolating trends while taking into account changes in technology,

competitive products, and other parameters. The Maryland Interindustry
Forecasting Model has an almost identical rate of growth for SIC 2037.

Table 5-5.   Projected Shipments to 1980
($ millions)

	1967	1971	1975	1980
Value of shipments (1967 dollars)	$2,082	$2,877	$4,025	$6,160

Table 5-6.   Energy Demand Projections to 1980

	1967	1975	1980
Useful energy (trillion BTUs)	26.7	50.7	77.6
Gross energy consumed (trillion BTUs)	36.4	69.2	105.9

Energy Utilization Projections

There is no reason to expect a substantial change in the energy
demanded per unit of output. Although there are a number of reasons why we
might expect a decrease, there are also considerations regarding lawful
emission standards that cause an increase in this ratio. We project a rate slightly
lower than that for the value of shipments, because there may be a trend toward
expensive but energy saving methods of freezing. The trend in the Frozen Food
industry has been away from such freezing methods as "sharp-freezing," which
involves the lowering of room temperature to freeze the product, and toward
"quick-freezing," in which the product is frozen in a few minutes either
individually (IQF, or Individually Quick Frozen) or prepackaged. It is when
quick-freezing is employed that the product can be expected to retain its
original quality, color, and shape most effectively.

There are various methods of quick-freezing. In general, it can be said
that each firm determines the method most suited to its plant and product and
that few standards exist. The more common techniques include direct immersion
(product dipped in refrigerant), indirect immersion (metal conductor added),
plate freezing (refrigerant passes through layers of metal plates), and double-belt
freezing in which foods are sprayed as they pass a given point.

From the point of view of energy demand the overwhelming switch
to quick-freezing has meant sharply increasing demands for energy in order to
operate fans and other required equipment. Multiple-plate freezers (known by

the name of their developer, Birdseye) were widely introduced and used relatively little energy while quick-freezing the product adequately. However, they were never able to dominate the industry because of the large labor costs associated with loading and unloading the many shelves. Some frozen foods are adaptable to the Birdseye-type "batch freezing by indirect contact" efficiently because they are of uniform package size and allow automated handling. Once again, air-blast techniques are the most versatile method, but are heavy energy users.

The latest widespread innovation has been the use of cryogenic freezing with liquid nitrogen or other low temperature refrigerants. In terms of food quality, this is the best method to date but costs are prohibitive. The cost of the nitrogen alone for one year is often the equal of the entire investment in freezing equipment of some other sort. Of course, the use of nitrogen eliminates the need for a remarkable proportion of the energy previously used. (No firm numbers are available yet, since the use of nitrogen has been limited.) If the cost of liquid nitrogen should for some reason drop substantially, we might expect dramatic decreases in the industry's demand for fuels.

Trends in Product Mix

We have noted a marked shift in the industry's consumption toward frozen specialties. It is our opinion, although industry statistics are unavailable, that this trend might account for the small rise in the energy used per unit output ratio. These specialities, for the most part, must be packaged for freezing. This acts as insulation which retards freezing and requires more energy for the task. In the case of frozen vegetables, on the other hand, the vegetables can be frozen as they pass along a belt before packaging. It is difficult to say how far the shift to specialties will go. It is certainly more convenient to freeze prepackaged foods and, above all, the packaging cuts down on evaporation, which must be a primary consideration with regard to the more expensive foods. As real prices of foods continue to increase, there is every reason to expect the trend towards prepackaging to continue, as evaporation becomes even more of a consideration. Even if increased prices mean a consumer shift to cheaper foods, we can still expect these foods too, to be prepackaged. In that case, any increase in plant efficiency would be more than offset by the need for more BTUs per unit frozen.

There is another factor which may be the cause of the fluctuating energy-output ratio. Capital expenditures for the frozen food industry have normally been increased each year at least 25% over the previous year. However, the early 1960s were years of particularly poor orange crops, and it appears that the rate of spending on capital expenditures was slowed. Thus, the existing machinery may have been used to greater capacity, which would lower the ratio under discussion (See Table 5-7 for these and related figures).

As far as the various fuels themselves are concerned, there is little to

Table 5-7.   Summary Statistics for the Industry, 1958 to 1967
($ millions)

	Value Added by Manufacture	Cost of Materials	Value of Production[1]	Capital Expenditures (new)
1967 Census	$759.3	$1,306.5	$2,066.8	$75.1
1966	679.0	1,207.5	1,884.8	81.9
1965	627.0	1,186.9	1,816.0	62.9
1964	560.5	1,095.8	1,651.6	50.0
1963 Census	550.2	999.5	1,548.7	44.6
1962	428.8	897.9	1,323.7	40.1
1961	403.0	879.4	1,274.6	28.4
1960	402.0	801.9	1,206.6	28.7
1959	346.0	763.0	1,111.8	23.1
1958 Census	323.8	702.9	1,025.9	21.0

Note: Non-census year figures are based on a representative sample from the Bureau of the Census, *Annual Survey of Manufactures.*

[1] Only work-in-process inventories are used in the calculation for the value of production.

be learned. Oil is used primarily for heating, and since the industry is a relatively new one, coal has never played a major role. Gas and electric energy are the primary sources of energy for the production processes. In the future, a small but steady increase is expected in the amount of electric energy generated by the industry itself for internal consumption.

SECTION III.   SELECTED BIBLIOGRAPHY

American Society of Heating, Refrigerating and Air Conditioning Engineers. *ASHRAE, 1971 Guide and Data Book, Applications.*

Bitting, Herbert W. *New Developments in the Frozen Food Industry.*

Derosier, Norman W. *The Technology of Food Preservation.* Avi Publishing Co., 1970.

Farrall, Arthur W. *Engineering for Dairy and Food Products.* John Wiley and Sons, New York, 1963.

Rasmussen, Clyde L. "Economics of Present and Future Freezing Methods." *ASHRAE,* June 1967.

Tressler, Donald. *The Freezing Preparation of Foods.* Avi Publishing Co., 1970.

Serials:
ASHRAE Journal
ASHRAE Transactions
Food Engineering
Food Technology

Chapter Six

Prepared Feeds—SIC 2042

Noreen Preston

SECTION I. SUMMARY AND CONCLUSIONS

Brief Description of the Industry

The Standard Industrial Classification definition of the Prepared Feeds for Animals and Fowls industry, SIC 2042, is as follows: Establishments primarily engaged in manufacturing prepared feeds for animals and fowls. Prepared feeds include poultry feed, livestock feed, dog food, and other pet foods (canned, frozen, and dry). This industry also includes establishments primarily engaged in manufacturing certain feed ingredients and adjuncts, such as alfalfa meal, feed supplements, and concentrates.

The specialization ratio in the prepared foods industry (primary products as a per cent of primary and secondary products) has been quite high—95%, 97%, 96%, and 97% in 1954, 1958, 1963 and 1967, respectively. The coverage ratio (the industry's production of its primary product related to total U.S. output of that product) was 90% in 1954, 91% in 1958, 93% in 1963, and 94% in 1967. If total output of feeds for animals and fowls by all industries is examined, it is safe to assume that a fairly accurate portrayal of industry 2042 will be obtained.

Summary of Developments and Projections

The animal feed industry has become one of the largest industries serving agriculture. The tremendous growth in the amount of meat produced and the gain in meat yield per animal are due largely to advances in the quality and quantity of commercial feeds. The expansion in numbers of livestock and fowls has raised the demand for more feeds. The general upward trend in consumption of meat, dairy products, poultry, and eggs has led to an increase in grain requirements.

Four major changes within the industry that have affected the amount of energy consumed per unit of output have been:

1. Increase in variety of feeds.
2. Shaping and standardization of feed shapes.
3. Change in product mix.
4. Acceleration in consumption of pet foods.

Product Developments

Since 1947, there has been virtually constant change in the variety of feeds produced. The mix of grains used for different feeds changes as newer and higher quality combinations are discovered. Also, the additives used are frequently changed, which affects the nutrient level for different types of animals. Drugs are added to the feeds, and switches from one type to another are frequent. Scientific discoveries as well as dictates from the Food and Drug Administration lead to alterations in "premixes" and "additives." Small variations in the processing affect the level of energy consumed.

Finished feeds are increasingly produced in standard shapes in order to ease handling and eliminate waste. This additional processing (such as pelletizing, crimping, or flaking) requires more manufacturing and hence consumes more energy than direct bagging of feeds.

Since the mid-1950s, the industry has experienced growth in demand for supplements and concentrates. This market has grown at a faster rate than that for complete feeds (see Appendix to this Chapter). Supplements and concentrates contain a greater variety of additives, but in smaller quantities. Thus, more processing is involved per unit of output.

The large increase in the number of pets per household has generated a high demand for dog and cat foods. This has increased the total amount of energy consumed by the prepared feeds industry.

Total useful energy[a] (measured in BTUs) consumed by the industry has risen from 15.6 trillion BTUs in 1947 to 48.7 trillion in 1967—an average annual growth rate of 5.9%. The general level of energy demand is expected to continue to increase, and by 1980 total useful energy consumed is projected to rise to 92.5 trillion BTUs. No major technological changes are expected within the industry. However, product mix should continue to change as improvements are made in additives (proteins, minerals, etc.) and ingredients used in various rations are improved. Also, the trend toward pelletizing, flaking, and crimping should become more widespread.

Measured on a gross energy consumed basis, 21.3 trillion BTUs were used in 1947; by 1980, gross energy consumed is projected to rise to 105 trillion BTUs. The value of shipments in constant 1967 dollars is expected to rise at an

[a]See Chapter One, pages 14-15, for definitions of useful and gross energy.

Table 6-1. Summary Table—Historical Data and Projections

	1947	1954	1958	1962	1967	1971	1975	1980
Value of shipments								
1967 $ (millions)	$1,981	$2,595	$3,045	$3,786	$4,797	$5,760	$6,383	$7,692
Current $ (millions)	2,112	2,981	3,238	3,652	4,797	—	—	—
Total BTUs consumed (trillions)								
Useful energy	15.6	23.1	22.3	33.0	48.7	61.6	71.5	92.5
Gross energy	21.3	29.7	30.1	42.0	59.7	73.7	84.3	104.6
Total cost of fuel and electric energy								
Current $ (millions)	$11.7	$18.8	$22.6	$32.8	$40.7	—	—	—
1,000 BTUs/constant 1967 $ of shipments								
Useful energy	7.9	8.9	7.3	8.7	10.2	10.7	11.2	12.0
Gross energy	10.8	11.4	9.9	11.1	12.4	12.8	13.1	13.6

Sources: Bureau of Census, *Census of Manufactures*; The Conference Board.

average annual rate of 3.3% between 1971 and 1980; current dollar value of shipments was $4,797 million in 1967, and 1980 shipments valued in 1967 dollars should reach $7,692 million. The energy-output ratio has been rising since 1958 and is projected to continue to increase. On a useful energy basis, the energy-output ratio rose from 7.9 (thousand BTUs per 1967 dollar of output) in 1947 to 10.2 in 1967 and is projected to reach 12.0 in 1980. Table 6-1 summarizes historical data and projections of energy and output for the prepared feeds industry.

SECTION II.   HISTORICAL DEVELOPMENTS

Output

Prepared feeds for poultry and livestock have accounted for approximately 85% of the primary products of the industry, while dog and cat food and feed materials have accounted for the remaining 14% of output between 1947 and 1967. Feeds for livestock and pet foods have shown phenomenal growth since 1947. Table 6-2 shows quantities shipped of prepared feeds products by all industries (including SIC 2042).

The growth in output of dog food and cat food has been very rapid. Annual sales of these products have increased 80% between 1965 and 1970 (more than 12% per year) due to the large number of families or households acquiring one or more pets. In 1970, 25.7% of all families owned one or more dogs, 10.4% owned at least one dog and one cat, and 9.1% owned one or more cats. In 1967, 15.5% of the value of shipments of the primary products of the prepared foods industry represented sales of dog and cat food.

Growth in output has also been substantial for poultry and livestock feeds. Since 1947, feeds, supplements, and concentrates for poultry have increased 59%; and the increase has been 129% for livestock. Output of the prepared feeds industry closely parallels the growth in output for the meat and poultry industries. Table 6-3 shows the growth in output of specific feeds products since 1947 in index form.

There have been two trends within the livestock (red meat) industry that have either effected or been affected by changes in the prepared feeds industry:

1. The large and rapid increase in the number of animals slaughtered, especially cattle.
2. The rapid increase in pounds of meat that each slaughter yields.

The number of livestock slaughtered has shown an increase of 31% between 1947 and 1971. The increase in the number of animals being prepared for slaughter has stepped up the demand for prepared foods. Accompanying this

Table 6-2. **Quantity Shipped, Prepared Feeds**
(thousand short tons)

	1947	1954	1958	1963*	1967
Poultry					
Complete feeds	10,887	13,438	13,896	14,463	15,320
Feed supplements and					
concentrates	832	1,557	2,449	2,772	1,925
Feeds, n.s.k.	207	400	325	474	1,757
Total poultry	11,926	15,395	16,720	17,709	19,002
Livestock					
Complete feeds	7,720	8,801	7,907	9,775	11,507
Feed supplements and					
concentrates	828	824	3,551	6,647	6,545
Feeds, n.s.k.	240	465	282	580	2,071
Total livestock	8,788	10,090	11,540	17,002	20,123
Dog and cat food	554	1,272	1,639	2,252	2,749
Feed materials					
Mineral mixtures	200	212	306	456	374
Alfalfa	1,000(e)	1,281	1,200	2,015	2,060
Processed grain	1,584	1,307	1,182	1,798	920
Total materials	2,796(e)	2,800	2,688	4,269	3,354
Total	24,064(e)	29,557	32,587	41,232	45,228

*Detailed data for 1962 are not available.

(e)—estimate; n.s.k.—not specified by kind.

Source: Bureau of the Census, *Census of Manufactures.*

Table 6-3. **Physical Output of Prepared Feeds**
(indexes, 1947 = 100)

	1947	1954	1958	1963	1967
Poultry feeds, supplements and concentrates	100	129.1	140.2	148.5	159.3
Livestock feeds, supplements and concentrates	100	114.8	131.3	193.5	229.0
Dog and cat food	100	229.6	295.8	406.5	496.2
Feeds materials*	100	100.1	96.1	152.7	119.9
Total	100	122.8	135.4	171.3	187.9

*Mineral mixtures, alfalfa and processed grains.

Source: Bureau of the Census, *Census of Manufactures.*

increase has been the rapid expansion of the livestock feeding industry. Firms specializing in the custom feeding of livestock have grown in size and number. Large-scale feedlots—lots with a capacity of 1,000 head or more—have grown almost 40% between 1962 and 1972. Part of the growth in output of the prepared feeds industry has been a response to the increase of the livestock feeding industry.

Efforts to increase the weight of animals have been successful, and have benefited both the meatpacking industry and the prepared feeds industry. Considerable research and experimentation to improve the quality and quantity of meat obtained from each slaughter performed has been done by the prepared feeds industry and still continues. Combination feeds are now made containing proteins, vitamins, drugs, minerals, etc., aimed at increasing and improving the meat supply. The results of these efforts are best exemplified by the meat yield of cattle. In 1947, the average dressed weight of cattle was 471 pounds; in 1971, the average dressed weight was 611 pounds. (Dressed weight refers to the meat yielded from a slaughter which is to be sold unprocessed or to be further processed and sold as prepared meat.)

The net increase of 30% in pounds yielded is partially due to improved breeding techniques; however, much of the advance can be accounted for by better quality feeds. Between 1947 and 1967, total pounds of livestock produced increased at an average rate of 2.5% per annum. If the average weight for each species held constant at the 1947 level, the increase in poundage produced would have been only 1.7% per annum.

The number of animals slaughtered increased at an average annual rate of 1.1% between 1947 and 1967, while the shipments of prepared feeds have advanced 4.2% per annum—indicating the shift to greater use of prepared feeds (complete feeds, supplements, or concentrates).

Due to more rapid growth of the red meats industry, prepared feeds for livestock have grown much faster than feeds for poultry. In conjunction with the growth of total output of livestock feeds, supplements and concentrates have gained in popularity. Thus, production of feeds in this form has expanded more than the production and shipments of complete feeds.

Chart 6-1 shows the value of shipments in constant 1967 dollars for the prepared feeds industry.

Energy Consumed

Between 1947 and 1967, total energy consumed (with electricity converted to BTUs on a useful energy basis) rose from 15.6 trillion to 48.7 trillion BTUs. This gain was fairly rapid—growing at an average annual rate of 5.9%. The amount of energy used by this industry has grown much faster than that in food manufacturing as a whole. Table 6-4 shows the energy used to manufacture prepared feeds as a per cent of total energy used by all of the foods industries.

Table 6-5 shows the amount of BTUs for each type of fuel and energy used. Electricity is converted on a gross energy as well as a useful energy

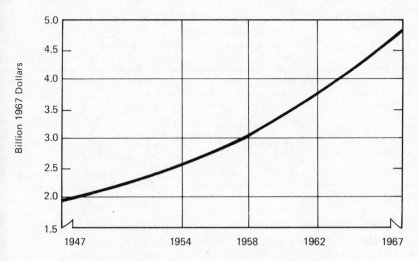

Chart 6-1. Value of Shipments Constant 1967 Dollars. Source: *Census of Manufactures.*

Table 6-4. Total Energy Consumed—All Foods and Prepared Feeds (trillion BTUs)*

	1947	*1954*	*1958*	*1962*	*1967*
All foods	619.4	777.4	829.9	856.2	926.4
Prepared feeds	15.6	23.1	22.3	33.0	48.7
Prepared feeds as a per cent of all foods	2.5%	3.0%	2.7%	3.9%	5.3%

*Electricity converted on a useful energy basis.

Table 6-5. Total Energy Consumed, by Source (trillion BTUs)

	1947	*1954*	*1958*	*1963*	*1967*
Coal	3.3	3.5	2.5	1.8	2.9
Coke and breeze	0.1	0.0	0.0	0.0	0.0
Total fuel oil	3.6	3.4	6.1	5.5	3.5
Gas	5.7	10.3	6.7	15.3	23.4
Other fuels	1.3	3.3	2.8	6.1	2.8
Fuels, n.s.k.*	0.0	0.0	0.7	0.0	10.7
Electric energy					
Useful	1.6	2.6	3.5	4.3	5.3
Gross	7.3	9.1	11.3	13.3	16.2
Total					
Useful	15.6	23.1	22.3	33.0	48.7
Gross	21.3	29.7	30.1	42.0	59.7

*n.s.k.—not specified by kind.

Source: Bureau of the Census, *Census of Manufactures.*

Table 6-6.   Energy Consumed (Useful), by Source
(per cent distribution)

	1947	1954	1958	1962	1967
Coal	21.2%	15.1%	11.2%	5.4%	6.0%
Coke and breeze	0.6	0.0	0.0	0.0	0.0
Total fuel oil	23.1	14.7	27.4	16.7	7.2
Gas	36.5	44.6	30.0	46.4	48.1
Other fuels	8.3	14.3	12.6	18.5	5.8
Fuels, n.s.k.	0.0	0.0	3.1	0.0	22.0
Electricity	10.3	11.3	15.7	13.0	10.9
Total	100.0%	100.0%	100.0%	100.0%	100.0%

Source: Bureau of the Census, *Census of Manufactures.*

basis. Gross consumption of energy has shown less rapid growth than energy measured on a useful basis due to increases in generating efficiency.

Types of Fuels Used

Energy from coal has been a declining proportion of the total amount of energy used by the prepared feeds industry. In 1967, it accounted for 6% of all energy consumed. Currently, its only major use is for space heating.

Fuel oil accounts for a modest proportion of total energy consumed. It is used for generating steam for processing operations, such as shaping the feeds—pelletizing, crimping, or flaking.

Use of gas by the industry is growing in importance. Gas is used primarily for drying of the grains. This process is being done more carefully and extensively to prevent spoilage.

Electric energy is utilized for grinding, processing, and pelletizing. The pelletizing process involves moving the feed in mash form, pulverizing the mash, and forcing it through appropriate-size holes to form the pellets.

Energy-Output Ratio

Energy consumed per constant 1967 dollar of shipments has been increasing at an average annual rate of 3.8% since 1958. Between 1947 and 1954, the energy-output ratio increased 1.8% annually; and then it declined by 4.8% a year between 1954 and 1958. Chart 6-2 illustrates the historical movements of the energy-output ratio.

The nation's livestock industry experienced a particularly rapid rate of growth between the late 1950s and mid-1960s, which created a high level of demand for prepared feeds. To further expand the supply of meat, attempts were made to increase the meat yield per animal. The prepared feeds industry directed considerable effort toward developing a more nutritious product in order to improve the quality and amount of meat produced. Currently, most medium- and larger-sized firms make use of the computer for selecting and determining the types and quantities of grain and additives necessary for each particular ration. Linear programming techniques had been introduced during the mid-1950s, but the use of computers within the industry did not become widespread until the 1960s.

During the 1960s, the variety of feeds offered by the industry proliferated. The increase in types of feeds available was not only a response to the high level of demand, but also a response to competition within the industry.

Sales of feed supplements and concentrates have increased more rapidly than sales of complete feeds. Because supplements and concentrates require mixing a greater variety of feedstuffs and additives, more energy is required to produce them than to make complete feeds. Also, the addition to the feed product of proteins, drugs, vitamins, minerals, etc., involves more steps in the manufacturing process. With competition keen, product improvement is an ongoing process necessitating many adjustments of input quantities as well as changeovers to accommodate different types of additives.

There is also a trend within the industry towards more crimping, flaking, and especially pelletizing the feeds. These processes, which gained popularity during the 1960s, require more energy inputs than simply bagging the mixed feedstuffs. But compacting the products in this fashion wastes less grain and feed both at the plant and when the product is consumed by the animal.

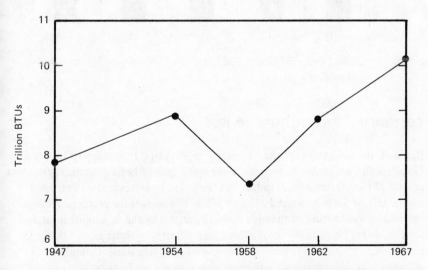

Chart 6-2. Energy Consumed (Useful) per Constant 1967 Dollar of Shipments. Sources: *Census of Manufactures;* Conference Board.

In sum, a larger variety of feeds available, more mixing of different types of additives, and rapid advances in product improvement have increased energy requirements in the manufacturing processes.

The energy-output ratio on a gross basis has not risen as fast as when measured on a useful basis. This is because the proportion of electricity used has held fairly steady at the same time that technological improvements over the years have reduced the energy needed to generate electrical power.

Chart 6-3 shows BTUs consumed per constant 1967 dollar of shipments with electricity converted on a useful basis vs. the same measure with electricity measured on a gross consumed basis.

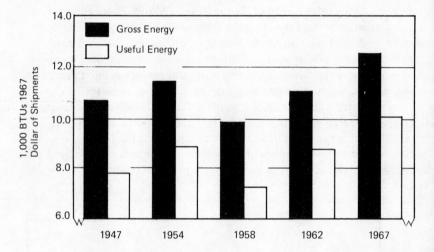

Chart 6-3. BTUs per 1967 Dollar of Shipments. Source: *Census of Manufactures.*

SECTION III.   PROJECTIONS TO 1980

Based on the projections of the University of Maryland Interindustry Forecasting Model (with Conference Board assumptions concerning key economic aggregates), output of the prepared feeds industry is projected to increase at an average annual rate of 3.3% between 1971 and 1980. The market for prepared feeds is currently good because of the high demand created by the expanding meat and fowl industry. Demand for meat is high, and industry analysts expect this condition to continue. Ownership of dogs and cats has gained tremendous popularity in the past decade and more than one pet per household is not uncommon. While household pet food is not a major portion of output, it has been the fastest growing segment of the industry. Because of the higher degree of processing involved, dog and cat food represented 15% of the value of shipments, although on a pound basis it is only 6% of total shipments.

Energy consumed per dollar of output is expected to continue to increase. The industry has not experienced any major technological changes in equipment or machinery, but increases in product variety have involved more energy utilization. More changes in the variety produced are likely, as research continues to improve the nutritional quality of feeds and the meat quality of animals. Land grant colleges are involved in projects to reduce the amount of feed necessary for an animal to add a pound of meat. But even should these efforts prove successful, an increase in the energy-output ratio may result based on the nature of the additives and number of inputs required. Equipment manufacturers are experimenting with more sophisticated machinery that will better handle the additives being used in feeds, supplements, and concentrates. This equipment, however, will be of a highly specialized nature and perhaps more energy consuming than equipment currently in use.

The trend towards more processing (i.e., pelletizing, flaking, and crimping) should also continue, as feed in this form is easier to handle as well as more economical for the buyer. Further processing of this nature should involve increases in the amount of energy consumed.

Table 6-7 shows projections to 1980 for output in constant dollars, total energy consumed, and for the energy-output ratios.

Table 6-7. Projections to 1980

	1971	*1975*	*1980*
Value of shipments			
1967 $ (millions)	$5,760	$6,383	$7,692
Total BTUs consumed (trillions)			
Useful energy.............................	61.6	71.5	92.3
Gross energy	73.7	84.3	104.6
1,000 BTUs/constant 1967 $ of shipments			
Useful energy.............................	10.7	11.2	12.0
Gross energy	12.8	13.2	13.6

Sources: Bureau of the Census, *Census of Manufactures*; The Conference Board.

SECTION IV.   APPENDIXES

A.   THE MANUFACTURE OF PREPARED FEEDS[b]

Receiving

A mechanical belt conveyor located beneath the receiving point discharges grains and ingredients into a pneumatic suction conveyor system, which takes them into the mill. A magnetic separator over the belt conveyor pulls out all tramp metal. The air and grains or ingredients are then separated in

[b]Krider, J. L. "Quality Feed Manufacturing," *International Animal Feed Symposium*, U.S. Dept. of Agriculture, Washington, D.C., 1959.

a cyclone. The grains or ingredients pass through a scalper, and the air goes through a stocking dust filter. From the scalper, the stream goes to a separate pressure fluidizing pneumatic system.

Storage

Multiple pneumatic conveyor lines move the fluidized stream to storage bins for mixing or to whole grain bins for grinding. The pneumatic lines elevate to a height in excess of 100 feet where turnheads direct the flow to spouts discharging into bulk storage bins.

Mixing

Mixing operations are carried out in three stages:

1. Mixing of high percentage ingredients and selected liquids.
2. Mixing of trace or low percentage ingredients.
3. Final blending of remaining liquid before bagging.

Formulation for desired feeds may be prepunched on cards. When cards are placed in a "reader," a master electronic control panel is actuated for an addition of high and low percentage ingredients.

After the proper amounts of ingredients are added, they are blended and the main mixer empties into a feed surge hopper. While the mixers are operating, the scale hoppers are "weighting" the next formulation.

Grinding

From bulk grain lines, whole grains are fed to a hammermill where they are ground and then conveyed to ground grain bulk storage bins. Where whole grains are called for in some feed, the grinding operation can be bypassed and the grains conveyed directly to ingredient storage bins.

Blending and Bagging

The feed is then conveyed to the top of the mill where it is scalped and discharged into feed surge bins. From these bins the feed flows through gravimetric feeders to the final blender. It is at this point that remaining liquids are metered into the mixture.

Addition of selected liquids may be accomplished by electronically proportioned metering into a tank. From this tank, the premixed liquids are handled as any other ingredient on the master programming console. Addition of final liquids may be electronically controlled. Preset proportion dials call for a definite amount of the final liquids.

The liquids involved in the dual blending and mixing operations are vitamin feeding oils, fats, condensed fish solubles, and molasses. Thermostatically controlled temperatures in the system vary from 80° during storage to as high as 180° F during delivery and mixing.

After final blending, the feed may be bagged off through automatic bagging scales, bypass the bagging scales and sent to bulk feed bins for truck or car loading, or conveyed to pellet supply bins.

Pelletizing

Feed to be pelleted is discharged from bins to a pellet mill, then through a pellet cooler. Following cooling they pass through a feeder to a crumbilizer, or may bypass it. Following pelleting or crumbilizing, the feed is graded to assure a dust-free pellet or a uniform size crumble.

Tests

Routine chemical analysis and other specified tests are made in laboratories to check incoming ingredients and finished feeds. These include tests for moisture, protein, fat, fiber, nitrogen-free extract, ash, certain minerals, vitamins, and undesirable substances.

Loading Out

Loading facilities may include both bagging and bulk forms for truck or rail shipment.

B.   LIST OF PRODUCTS

The following list of products is included in the Standard Industrial Classification of Industry 2042—Prepared Feeds for Animals and Fowls.

Alfalfa, prepared as feed for animals
Animal feeds, prepared
Bird food, prepared
Buttermilk emulsion for animal food
Chicken feeds, prepared
Citrus seed meal
Dog and cat food, canned
Dog food, dry
Dried citrus pulp
Feather meal, made from purchased
  materials
Feed concentrates
Feed prepared (including mineral):
  for animals and fowls

Feed supplements
Fish meal
Horse meat: canned, fresh or frozen
  from purchased carcasses
Kelp meal and pellets
Meal, alfalfa
Meal, bone: prepared as feed for
  animals and fowls
Oyster shells, ground: used as feed
  for animals and fowls
Shell crushing, for feed
Stock feed, dry

C. TYPES OF FEEDS

Livestock feeds and poultry feeds can basically be divided into two categories: complete feeds, and supplements and concentrates.

Complete Feeds
A product classified as a complete feed is a complete ration to be fed to an animal and no additional feed or other material is necessary as an additive or supplement.

Supplements and Concentrates
Products classified as supplements or concentrates are feeds that are not a complete ration, but are produced to be used with another feed or grain (for example, corn). Supplements and concentrates contain nutrients such as proteins, vitamins, and minerals, which are added during processing.

D. DATA LIMITATIONS

In the years covered by this report, the coverage ratio (proportion of total products covered by a particular SIC number within an industry) for SIC 2042 has been quite high. In 1954, the coverage ratio was 90%, in 1958—91%, in 1963—93%; and in 1967, the coverage ratio was 94%. If output of feeds for animals and fowls is examined for all industries, it is safe to assume that a fairly accurate portrayal of industry 2042 will be obtained.

The primary products of industry 2042 include poultry feeds, live stock feeds, dog and cat food, feed materials and feeds not specified by kind. The specialization ratio of this industry (primary products as a per cent of primary and secondary products) has also been high—95%, 97%, 96%, and 97% in 1954, 1958, 1963, and 1967, respectively.

SECTION V.   SELECTED BIBLIOGRAPHY

American Gas Association. *A Study of Process Energy Requirements in the Food Industries,* Columbus, Ohio.

Bickel, Blaine. "Meeting Consumer Demand for Beef—From Ranch to Roast," *Monthly Review.* Federal Reserve Bank of Kansas City, April 1973.

Department of Agriculture. *Agricultural Statistics,* 1971.

———. *Grain and Feed Statistics.* Agricultural Marketing Service, 1962, 1963, 1964, 1965.

Jennings, Ralph. *Consumption of Feed and Livestock,* Department of Agriculture, 1958.

Kastelic, J. "Higher Quality Meat Product." *International Feed Symposium,* Department of Agriculture, 1960.

Krider, J. L. "Quality-Feed Manufacturing." *International Feed Symposium,* Department of Agriculture, 1960.

Chapter Seven

Bread, Cake, and Related Products—SIC 2051

Saul Levmore

SECTION I.   INTRODUCTION AND SUMMARY

The Bread, Cake, and Related Products industry, SIC 2051, hereafter referred to as the Bread and Cake industry, includes all bakery products other than cookies and crackers.

The industry consists of firms that bake, package, and market perishable baked products in the United States. Production in this industry rose at a slow but steady rate until 1967, and since then has fallen off slightly. Bread has always been the industry's staple; and it has come to be produced almost exclusively by the very large baking companies.

The energy-output ratio has decreased at a very steady rate since 1954, and as a result total energy consumed has decreased as well. Gas has accounted for the lion's share of energy use.

It appears that although the shift to softer breads and to continuous baking processes has had something to do with these trends, the major factor has been innovations in the baking process itself. Gas usage is more efficient than the previously used coal and the use of convection through air agitation has revolutionized the industry. Not only is the quality of the product much improved as the baking is more even, but the energy required is far less than it had been previously.

Demand is expected to increase at about 2.5% annually through 1975 and then at a rate of 1.7% through 1980. These two projections are based on the Maryland Interindustry Forecasting Model (INFORUM).

The energy-output ratio is expected to drop at its already consistent pace. Taken together with the demand projections, it is expected that total BTU consumption will drop about 1% each year through 1980.

A serious limitation of this report is that reliable data for 1958 were unavailable. The Census information for that year contained too many incon-

153

sistencies to warrant its use. The only figures from 1958 appearing in this report are those we have found to be reliable from at least two separate sources. For the most part, trends were viewed as passing through that year.

SECTION II.   HISTORICAL DEVELOPMENT

The Bread and Cake Industry

Establishments producing bakery products primarily for direct sale on the premises to household consumers are not included in this industry. (In terms of Census data they are considered to be Retail Traders.) Otherwise, all bakers can be classified into one of four subgroups listed below.

Wholesale Bakeries: Bakeries selling primarily to other business concerns at the wholesale level, such as grocers, restaurants, and other establishments buying from them for resale.

Grocery Chain Bakeries: Bakeries operated by chain stores whose products are distributed through the chain's retail outlets.

Home Service Bakeries: Bakeries selling their goods through retail home service routes. The share of the industry attributed to this sector trends to be overstated, as shipments are generally valued at their retail cost.

Retail Multi-outlet Bakeries: Bakeries selling chiefly through non-baking outlets. An example of this would be a restaurant chain which operates its own bakeries.

The industry's specialization ratio is about 97%. Its coverage ratio is closer to 99%. About 90% of the industry's products are produced by plants specializing in just one product class. Very small establishments were excluded from many statistical sources, but the resulting error is probably no more than 1%.

Wholesale bakeries make up the overriding share of the industry. As Table 7-1 shows, the trend in energy use in the wholesale bakeries subgrouping is the crucial element for our purposes.

Table 7-1.   Relative Distribution of Value of Shipments, by Type of Bakery, 1958-1967

	1958	1963	1967
Wholesale bakeries	76.3	77.7	86.2
Grocery chain bakeries	9.3	9.4	9.2
Home service bakeries	9.9	8.4	2.0
Retail multi-outlet bakeries	4.3	4.5	2.6
Total	100.0	100.0	100.0

Note: Columns may not add to 100% due to rounding.
Source: Bureau of the Census.

The Demand for Bread and Cake

The demand for bread and cake over the last twenty-five years has risen at a slow but steady pace. From 1947 to 1967 the value of shipments for the industry rose from $4,002 million to $5,103 million. This is equivalent to an annual growth rate of 1.3%. From 1947 to 1954 the value of shipments rose only 0.3% a year. Then from 1954 to 1958 there was healthier rate of 2.7% a year, only to slow down for the 4-year period ending in 1962 to a rate of 0.7% annually. The more recent 1962 to 1967 period showed a growth rate of 1.8% a year. These figures are all computed on the basis of U.S. Census information. For the years following 1967 we have information gathered for the University of Maryland's input-output model that we make use of later on in this paper for demand projections. These figures show fluctuations beginning with positive growth rates for 1968 and 1969 and then negative rates for the next two years. The overall movement in value of shipments from 1967 through 1971 is slightly downward.

Within the industry itself there has been a substantial shift in composition. Bread has always been the primary product; but in 1954, for example, its value of shipments was 54.2% of the whole industry's, while in 1967 it was responsible for 65.0% of the total value of shipments.

Table 7-3 indicates that bread must have gained its share at the expense of secondary products. Within the primary products themselves, there has scarcely been a shift in composition.

Table 7-2. Value of Shipments*
(million 1967 $)

1947	1954	1958	1962	1967	1968	1969	1970	1971
$4,002	$4,082	$4,546	$4,672	$5,103	$5,133	$5,281	$5,075	$4,982

*Adjusted from sales volume for post-1967.
Source: Maryland Interindustry Forecasting Model; Bureau of the Census.

Table 7-3. Relative Distribution of Primary Products Shipments, by Product Class

	1958	1963	1967
Bread (includes rolls)	62.4%	65.3%	64.9%
Sweet yeast goods	8.3	8.6	9.1
Soft cakes	11.6	11.4	11.0
Pies	5.7	5.4	5.2
Pastries and handmade cookies	1.8	1.2	1.0
Doughnuts (cake type)	3.5	3.7	3.8
Other	7.3	4.4	4.9
Total	100.0%	100.0%	100.0%

Note: Columns may not add to 100% due to rounding.
Source: Bureau of the Census.

Energy Consumption

While the value of shipments for the Bread and Cake industry has risen over the years, the amount of energy used has not. There was a slight rise from 1947 to 1954, but by 1967 the total was about that of 1947.

Table 7-4 gives the total energy consumption of the Bread and Cake industry. It says nothing of whether the energy-output ratio is rising or falling. For this we need a measure of the amount of energy used by the industry for a set amount of product. Table 7-5 gives this in terms of BTUs per unit of output.

There has been an increasing reliance on gas in the industry. Most of this stems from the use of natural gas to bake the goods in the ovens. It seems that the use of gas has leveled off; however, accurate statistics are unavailable on this point. It is certain that electric energy is being used more than in the past. Fuel oil, on the other hand, is being used less.

Table 7-4.   Energy Utilization
(trillion BTUs)

	1947	1954	1962	1967
Useful energy[1]	51.3	53.9	50.8	49.0
Gross energy[1] consumed	58.6	62.3	59.6	59.1

Source: Bureau of the Census; appropriate conversion factors.

[1] See Chapter One, pages 14-15, for definitions of useful and gross energy.

Table 7-5.   Energy Consumption per Unit Shipped
(1,000 BTUs/1967 $)

	1947	1954	1962	1967
Useful energy	12.8	13.2	10.9	9.6
Gross energy consumed	14.7	15.3	12.8	11.6

Source: Bureau of the Census.

SECTION III.   PROJECTIONS TO 1980

Demand Projections

For the purpose of making demand projections we make use of the Maryland Interindustry Forecasting Model for SIC 2051. Despite the recent negative trend for the years 1967 to 1971, the forecast is for an overall positive rate of growth of output. Demand for bread and cake follows the general level of population for the most part, but at a faster rate. While competitive products (such as frozen baked goods) must also be considered, they generally are relatively expensive, and this price difference will almost certainly continue. The projection is for an annual rate of growth of 2.5% through 1975 and then a slow-down in the rate to a level of about 1.7% between 1975 and 1980.

Table 7-6. Projected Shipments to 1980
($ millions)

	1967	*1971*	*1975*	*1980*
Value of shipments (1967 dollars)	$5,103	$4,982	$5,602	$6,082

Source: Maryland Interindustry Forecasting Model; appropriate conversion factors.

Substantial increases in the price of bread will probably not alter the Maryland figures. It is true that many of the consumers now purchasing bread and cake will cease to do so at their previous level. However, many who are purchasing bread not included in SIC 2051, but rather in small bakeshops retailing on store premises, will switch to a cheaper product which is included in SIC 2051.

Energy Utilization Projections

For many years the classic method of commercial bread baking has been the sponge-dough process. Basically, this means that when the ingredients are mixed prior to fermentation, about 60% of the flour has been added and the mixing is of a sponge-like material. More recently, there have been enormous strides, especially among the larger bakers, towards a continuous process of baking. In this method, a ferment or broth is mixed with a portion of the flour. The result is that the flour is insufficient to form dough and remains in liquid form. It is thus pumped through the various processes. Definite statistics are unavailable, but the feeling in the industry is that the continuous bread-making process uses somewhat less energy than the classical method for the same amount of product.

The most marked changes in the industry involve the actual baking process itself. Previously, breads, for instance, were baked for about 30 minutes. With technological improvements this baking time has been cut down by at least one-third—to from seventeen to twenty minutes. First, natural gas has become the primary energy source for baking. It allows better control of the ovens and more efficient heating. It has been used together with air agitation to allow more evenness of temperature. Agitation implies the ability to move the air within the oven and thus heat the bread from many directions at the same time. The effect is the same as spreading the bread out and giving it more exposure to the heat source. Gas is important here, because it allows rapid control of the flame level and consequently can keep temperatures at a desired level. The agitation itself helps on this account because it requires lower temperatures (15 or 20 degrees Fahrenheit less), which makes the job of temperature control easier to begin with.

For the purposes of the industry, the benefit of all this is that the bread is baked evenly. There is little loss because of flash heat and resultant bread burning. From the point of view of energy utilization, there is an enormous saving of fuel by using gas and air agitation. The temperature requirements are lower and much of the heated air is reused as it is moved around in the oven. This explains the steadily decreasing energy-output ratio for the industry which we have observed (Table 7-5). This trend is expected to continue through 1980. The industry is not at all saturated with this process, nor is it a quick and simple matter for it to adapt to this type of baking. In general, as the old ovens wear out, they are replaced or updated with air agitation systems and gas heat.

From 1954 to 1962 the energy-output ratio dropped at a rate of about 2.5% annually in terms of useful energy. This rate was matched from 1962 to 1967. It appears that this simply corresponds to the rate of machine replacements by the industry (capital expenditures have maintained a fairly steady position). In terms of gross energy consumed, the energy-output ratio also maintained the same annual rate of decrease in the 1954-1962 period (2.5%), and then in the 1962-1967 span slowed to about 2.2%. If the projected shipments figures are correct, we can expect the industry's energy consumption for 1975 to be about the same as that of 1971, as shipments are expected to grow at a rate of 2.5% as well. By 1980, the industry's consumption of energy should be considerably decreased.

Table 7-7.   Projected Energy Consumption
(trillion BTUs)

	1967	1975	1980
Useful energy	49.0	44.4	42.8
Gross energy consumed	59.1	54.6	53.3

These projections were derived from the expected energy-output ratios shown in Table 7-8.

Table 7-8.   Projected Energy-Output Ratios
(1,000 BTUs/1967 $)

	1967	1975	1980
Useful energy	9.6	7.92	7.03
Gross energy consumed	11.6	9.74	8.77

Part Two

Paper Industries

(see also Chapter 32)

Chapter Eight

Corrugated and Solid Fiber Boxes—SIC 2653

Paul A. Parker

SECTION I. INTRODUCTION AND SUMMARY

The Corrugated and Solid Fiber Boxes industry, SIC 2653, hereafter referred to as Fibre Box industry, is defined in the 1972 Standard Industrial Classification codebook as:

> Establishments primarily engaged in manufacturing corrugated and solid fiber boxes and related products from purchased paperboard of fiber stock.

Products are listed as: Boxes corrugated and solid fiber; and Display Items, Shipping Hampers, Pads, Partitions, and sheets, all of corrugated and solid fiberboard.

This report is based on Department of Commerce, *Census of Manufactures* data for 1958, 1963, 1967; and Fibre Box industry data for 1958-71. Information on technology was supplied by the American Paper Institute, the Fibre Box Association, and corporate experts.

Mills in this industry are located close to markets, and rely on utility-supplied energy, primarily gas. Interruptions of gas and electric service are a current problem in the industry. Stand-by power plants, primarily run by fuel oil, are in service or under construction at some mills.

Production grew at an annual rate of 6.8% from 1958 to 1967, measured in Value of Shipments. (See Table 8-1, column A.)

Total energy used grew at an annual rate of 5.8% in 1958-67 to a level of 36.3 trillion BTUs consumed.[a] Gas and electricity used rose at annual

---

[a]Throughout this chapter, energy is measured on a gross basis. See Chapter One, pages 14-15, for definitions of gross and useful energy.

161

rates of 9.8% and 10.9%, respectively. Coal declined at −11.0% and Fuel Oil rose and fell. (See Table 8-2 for fuel use in BTUs, and Table 8-3 for fuel use in original units.)

The energy used per unit of output ratio, an estimate of energy efficiency in production, improved at an annual rate of 2.1% from 1962 to 1967. As no marked process or technological innovation occurred in this period, the improvement is an economy from improved production efficiency: faster handling of wider sheets, changing from one to two or three operating shifts, etc.

The outlook for the next eight to ten years is for continued growth of production and energy requirements at approximately their long-term historical rates. No energy saving innovations are foreseen. Interruptions of utility supplied energy will continue to be a problem.

Corrugated and Solid Fiber Boxes is a stable industry. No energy saving innovations have occurred in the past twenty years, nor are any expected in the near future. Production can be expected to grow at a projected rate of 5.5% annually, reaching $4,542 million by 1975, and $5,973 million by 1980, measured in value of shipments at 1967 prices. The energy-output ratio will probably not vary significantly from the 1967 ratio of 12.3 thousand BTUs per 1967 dollar shipped, and is projected to remain at about 12.2 thousand through 1980.

Energy requirements, therefore, will grow at approximately the 5.5% annual rate of increase in production that is expected. As a result, 55.4 trillion BTUs in 1975, and 72.4 trillion BTUs in 1980 would be required to meet this production demand. (See Table 8-1, columns D and E, for the above projections computed on a useful energy basis.)

SECTION II.   THE PRESENT INDUSTRY

In 1967, the industry had a coverage ratio (fibre box made in this industry to that made in all industries) of 98%. The primary product specialization ratio (primary to primary plus secondary product) was 98%.[1] Thus, the study of these establishments is limited to, and covers virtually all, fibre box production.

Production is divided into three sectors, Corrugated (SIC 2653-1 + −6), Solid (SIC 2653-5), and Corrugated and Solid Fiber Not Specified by Kind. In 1967 they amounted to 91.6%, 1.5%, 6.9%, respectively, of the value of shipments of the industry.[2] (On a square feet basis, corrugated fiber accounted for 99%, solid for 1%, of 1970 production.[3]) The industry thus consists almost exclusively of corrugated production.

Briefly, the corrugating process is as follows. Containerboard stock of varying width and weight is purchased in massive rolls. Three rolls are fed into a corrugating machine. First one roll is fluted. This "corrugating medium" is then bonded front and back to flat "facing sheets." Then the combined board is dried, cut, and scored for later folding. It is then further treated to meet end use requirements.[4]

The fibre box industry is not highly energy-intensive. Its 1967 energy-output ratio was 12.3 (measured in thousand BTUs per 1967 constant dollar shipped), in comparison with the entire paper industry ratio of 65.2, and the all manufacturing ratio of 27.8.

Because of the bulkiness of fibre box output, production facility locations are closely market oriented, usually within 100 miles. As a result, these mills are tied into the energy system of various regions, and specifically into the energy supplies of the local community. However, interruptions of gas and electric service have begun to appear as certain communities experience shortages. Some mills are constructing, or have in service, stand-by power plants as a consequence. These are primarily powered by fuel oil.

This is reflected in the 1967 distribution of types of fuel used: gas, 39.5%; electricity, 11.1% (of which purchased is 97.4%); fuel oil, 22.3%; misc. fuels, 22.6%; and coal, 4.7%.

SECTION III. HISTORICAL DEVELOPMENT, 1958-1967

The fibre box industry has been marked by the lack of radical change, either in growth rates or in technology.

Production (measured in value of shipments) grew at an annual rate of 2.4% in 1954-58, and at 6.9% in 1958-62 and 1962-67, or at an overall annual rate of 5.4% for 1954-67.

Total fuel used in 1958-67 (measured in BTUs) grew at an annual rate of 5.8% (versus 6.9% growth in production in the same period). (See Table 8-1, column B.) Electricity use grew at a 10.9% annual rate; misc. fuel at 10.2%; and gas at 9.8% in this period. Coal declined at a −11.0% annual rate, reflecting increased reliance on utility supplied power. Fuel oil use, after rising from 1958 to 1962, fell below its 1958 level at the end of the period (see Table 8-2).

The total energy-output ratio (measured in thousand BTUs per 1967 constant dollar shipped) remained virtually constant from 1958 to 1962. However, in 1962-67, the ratio declined at an annual rate of 2.1%. (See Table 8-1 column C.)

No marked change in technology or production processes has occurred in this period. Rather, gradual increases of machinery capacity have taken place. Operating speeds have risen from 350'/min. to 500'/min. over the period, with the changeover accelerating in recent years. Maximum width of processing sheets, 63" 20-25 years ago, is up to 87" today.

Thickness of facings has decreased over the last decade, leading to weight reductions in processing and lower energy requirements. But the weight

Table 8-1.   Energy and Output: Trends in the Fibre Box Industry, 1958-1980

Year	A Value of Shipments (million 1967 $)	B Total Energy Use (trillion BTUs)	C *Gross Energy Basis*[1] Energy-Output Ratio (thousand BTUs/$, B ÷ A)	D Total Energy Use (trillion BTUs)	E *Useful Energy Basis*[1] Energy-Output Ratio (thousand BTUs/$, D ÷ A)
			Actual		
1958	$1,632	21.9	13.4	19.0	11.6
1962	2,124	28.9	13.6	24.7	11.6
1967	2,960	36.3	12.3	29.6	10.0
			Projected		
1975	4,542	55.4	12.2	54.8	9.9
1980	5,937	72.4	12.2	71.7	9.9

[1] See Chapter One, pages 14-15, for definitions of gross and useful energy.
Note: Ratios off due to rounding.
Source: Bureau of the Census, *Census of Manufactures*, 1967, 1963.

Table 8-2.   Energy Use, by Source, 1958-1967

	Trillion BTUs (Useful Energy Basis)			
	1958	1962	1967	Annual Growth Rate 1958-67
Coal	2.8	1.9	1.4	−11.0%
Fuel oil, total	7.0	9.7	6.6	−0.6
Gas	5.1	7.3	11.7	9.8
Misc. fuels	2.8	3.9	6.7	10.2
Electricity, total	1.3	2.0	3.3	10.9
Total energy	19.0	24.7	29.6	5.1

	Relative Distribution of Useful Energy, by Source		
	1958	1962	1967
Coal	14.7%	7.7%	4.7%
Fuel oil, total	36.8	39.3	22.3
Gas	26.8	29.6	39.5
Misc. fuels	14.7	15.8	22.6
Electricity, total	6.8	8.1	11.1
Total energy	100%	100%	100%

Note: Columns may not sum to total due to rounding.
Source: Converted from Table 8-3.

of corrugating medium has remained fixed at 144 pounds per 1,000 sq. ft. And single wall corrugated paperboard is being partially replaced with double and triple wall, with concurrent weight gain.

The product mix of corrugated and solid fibre boxes has changed minimally, from a 1958 concentration of 97.2% of production in corrugated, to a 1970 concentration of 99.0%.[5]

Improvement in the energy-output ratio in the later years of the survey is attributable to increased concern for production efficiency. A change from one to two, and now three operating shifts has reduced energy overhead per production unit slightly. Also, faster handling of wider paper sheets has created energy efficiencies of scale. The combination explains the 2.1% average annual improvement in the energy-output ratio.

SECTION IV.   PROJECTIONS

No sharp changes are expected in the fibre box industry in the ensuing eight to ten years. Solid fibre box production, already minimal, is expected to virtually cease by 1980. No major technological or process innovations are expected.

The growth rate of production to 1980 is projected at 5.5% by the Fibre Box Association.[6] This is pegged to growth in customer industries' use of fibre box, particularly for food packaging (29.4% of total end use in 1967[7]). This growth rate is consistent with the 1954-67 growth rate of 5.4%. Therefore, production can be expected to reach $4,542 million, in value of shipments, at 1967 prices, by 1975, and $5,973 million by 1980.

Total fuel use grew at an annual rate of 5.8% in the 1958-1967 period. Though larger than the long-term growth rate of production, this figure obscures the slight decline in the energy-output ratio in 1962-67. It is not likely, however, that this decline will prevail in the future. Energy savings from improvements in production efficiency may have largely been realized. In addition, for the entire paper industry (no data are available for fibre boxes alone), paperboard production was at 100.9% of capacity in mid-1973.[8] Further energy savings from this source are unlikely.

In the light of this, the energy-output ratio will probably not change significantly from its 1967 level of 12.3 thousand BTUs per constant dollar shipped and is projected at 12.2 through 1980. Total energy requirements are expected to continue to grow at the rate of increased production, that is, 5.5%. The industry will therefore require approximately 55.4 trillion BTUs by 1975, and 72.4 trillion BTUs by 1980. Interruptions of power will remain a problem due to continued reliance on purchased electricity and gas. (See Table 8-1, columns D and E, for the above projections computed on a useful energy basis.)

Table 8-3.   Fuel Use in Physical Units, 1958-1967

Type of fuel	1958	1962	1967
Coal			
(thousand short tons)	110	73	56
Fuel oil, total			
(thousand barrels)	1,215	1,665	1,133
Distillate fuel oil			
(thousand barrels)	n.a.	228	442
Residual fuel oil			
(thousand barrels)	n.a.	1,438	691
Gas			
(million cu. ft.)	4,891	7,047	11,296
Miscellaneous fuels[1]			
(million current $)	1.0	1.4	2.4
Electricity, total			
(mkwh)	412	598	980
Purchased			
(mkwh)	375	586	955
Generated less sold			
(mkwh)	37	12	25

[1] Other fuels plus fuels not specified by kind.
n.a.—not available.
Source: Bureau of the Census, *Census of Manufactures*, 1967, 1963.

Notes

[1] Department of Commerce. *Census of Manufactures* 1967, Vol. II, Part II, p. 26c-13.
[2] *Ibid.* p. 26c-15.
[3] Fibre Box Association. *Fibre Box Industry Statistics*, p. 5.
[4] _____ . *Fibre Box Handbook*, pp. 6-7.
[5] See footnote 1.
[5,6] Fibre Box Association. *Fibre Box Industry Statistics*, p. 5.
_____ . *Fibre Box Industry—Annual Report* 1972, p. 8.
[7] Bureau of the Census. *Census of Manufactures* 1967, Vol. II, Part II, p. 26c-15.
[8] _____ . Industry Fact Sheet.

SECTION V.   SELECTED BIBLIOGRAPHY

American Paper Institute. *Industry Fact Sheet,* June 11, 1973. New York.

_____ . *Monthly Statistical Summary,* June 1973. New York.
_____ . *The Statistics of Paper.* New York, 1972.

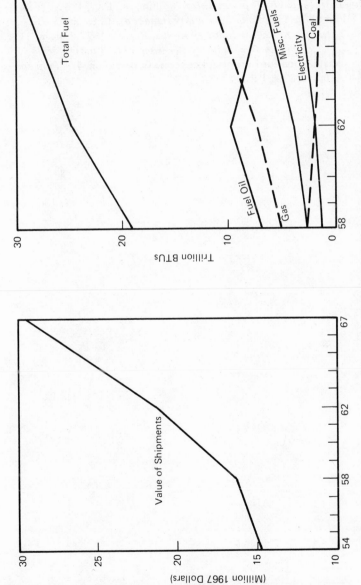

Chart 8-1. Production and Fuel Use, 1954–1967. Note: Electricity computed in BTUs produced by a kwh. Source: Table 2.

Britt, Kenneth (ed.), *Pulp and Paper Technology*. Reinhold Publishing Corp.: New York, 1964.

Bureau of the Census. *Census of Manufactures,* Vol. II, 1967 & 1963.

Bureau of Labor Statistics. *Impact of Technological Change and Automation in the Pulp and Paper Industry.* Washington, D.C., 1962.

Fibre Box Association. *Fibre Box Handbook.* Chicago, 1970.

————. *Fibre Box Industry Annual Report,* 1972. Chicago, 1973.

————. *Fibre Box Industry Statistics,* 1970. Chicago, 1971.

Organization for European Economic Cooperation. *The Pulp and Paper Industry in the USA.* Paris, 1951.

Chapter Nine

Building Paper and Board Mills—SIC 2661

Paul A. Parker

SECTION I. INTRODUCTION AND SUMMARY

The Building Paper and Board Mills industry, SIC 2661, (hereafter building paper and board) is defined, in the 1972 Standard Industrial Classification codebook, as:

> Establishments primarily engaged in manufacturing building paper and building board from wood pulp and other fibrous materials. Pulp mills combined with building paper and building board mills, and not separately reported, are also included. . . .

Primary products are: asbestos, asphalt, building and insulation paper and board; felts, dry, saturated, and unsaturated, Kraft sheathing paper; lath; roofing; tar paper; and wall tile and board. Before 1963, hardboard was also included.

Sources of data are the Department of Commerce, *Census of Manufactures*, 1963 and 1967, and the Maryland Interindustry Forecasting Model. The American Paper Institute, the Asphalt Roofing Manufacturers Association, and corporate experts provided technical information.

It should be noted that the definition of SIC 2661 changed in 1963; 1967 data are therefore not completely comparable with earlier years in the Census series.

This industry is composed of establishments manufacturing primarily paper and felt stock, usually saturated in asphalt or tar, and insulation board. In 1967, insulation board accounted for 55.8% of the total industry output, and construction paper for 42.6%.

Much of the construction paper, such as tar paper and shingles, has insulating properties. The products of this industry are extremely heat-intensive, requiring 271.6 thousand BTUs per dollar of value added in 1967.

In the same year, the entire paper industry required 140.1 thousand, and all manufacturing only 59.0 thousand BTUs per dollar of value added.

It should be noted that home insulation in place is very energy saving, and that most homes are currently under insulated. Therefore, greater production of insulation is net energy saving.

Building paper and board output is cyclical, pegged to the cycle of new housing units started, its primary demand. But alteration and repair, and nonresidential construction demand, create the continuing growth.

From 1954 to 1970, production rose at 2.1% annually. Total energy use grew at a 5.8% annual rate in the period 1954-1962, but declined in 1962-1967. (The gross energy basis is used throughout this report, except as noted.) [a] The decline may be due to the change in statistical coverage in 1963, and is therefore unreliable. The energy-output ratio rose from 1954 to 1962, at a 6.0% annual rate. (Again, the change in 1962-1967 is unreliable.) This was due to an upgrading of product composition which required more heat in production as a result. Other technological changes have been minimal.

Production of insulation materials creates large amounts of harmful effluents. The Environmental Protection Agency has imposed upon the industry the requirement to detoxify these effluents before release from the mill. As a result, large amounts of energy are being committed to pollution control techniques. The industry is committed to research in pollution control and energy conservation, but faces several years lag time before the effects of innovation will be felt.

Building paper and board are high energy-use products. This industry faces serious pollution control problems in the immediate future. Both these factors will act to limit growth. However, output is projected to continue to grow at a rate of 3.7% annually, paced by the nation's increasing need for insulation to assist in fuel conservation. At this rate of growth, value of shipments will reach $470 million, at 1967 prices, in 1975, and $560 million in 1980.

The energy-output ratio can be expected to increase at approximately 8% annually, reaching 204.0 thousand BTUs per 1967 constant dollar shipped by 1975. After that, fuel-saving innovations now envisioned will come into general application and the ratio should level off. Before 1980 the ratio should have begun to decline, standing at 190.0 thousand BTUs per 1967 constant dollar shipped in that year.

Total energy use, therefore, should rise very sharply to 1975 and continue rising thereafter, but at a much slower rate. By 1975 the industry's total energy demand should reach 96 trillion BTUs; by 1980, approximately 106 trillion BTUs.

[a]See Chapter One, pages 14-15, for definitions of gross and useful energy.

(See Table 9-3, columns D and E, for the above projections computed on a useful energy basis.)

SECTION II. THE PRESENT INDUSTRY

Establishments in this industry produce basically only building paper and board, and account for almost all building paper and board manufactured. The 1967 Primary Product Specialization Ratio (primary to primary plus secondary products) was 92%. In the same year, the Coverage Ratio (of building paper and board produced in this industry to that produced in all industries) was 96%. Both ratios have averaged over 90% in the period discussed.[1]

Although building paper and board products vary widely from company to company due to differences in brand name composition, the output can be described as primarily consisting of insulation materials.

Insulation board has made up over half of industry output since 1954 (Table 9-1). In addition, much construction paper has insulating properties, specifically tar paper and roofing shingles. (The 1962-67 drop in board output percentage is due to the removal of hardboard from SIC 2661 in 1963.)

This predominance of insulation output gives the industry its characteristic of high energy requirements.

Insulation production can be loosely summarized as follows:

(1) *Insulation Paper:* Waste materials—paper, rag and pulp—are processed into a rough grade of paper stock or felt, via blending, rolling, pressing and drying. This material is then usually soaked in asphalt, either in the mill or at the construction site. Large amounts of heat are required to melt the asphalt for soaking. If done in the mill, this energy increment is necessarily included in the industry total.

The asphalt must be heated to 450°F. At 100% efficiency, this requires 150 BTUs per pound of asphalt; under normal conditions, 230 BTUs per pound. One plant alone reportedly processes 15 tons of insulation paper

Table 9-1. Distribution of Value of Shipments, by Product Mix

Year	Insulating Board	Construction Paper	Other
1967	55.8%	42.6%	1.7%
1962	57.2	42.3	0.5
1958	57.5	41.0	1.5
1954	52.8	47.2	n.a.
1947	41.4	58.6	n.a.

Note: n.a. = Not available.

Source: Bureau of the Census, *Census of Manufactures*, Vol. II, 1967-Part II, p. 26A-22; 1963-Part I, pp. 26A-21, 26A-24, 26A-38.

per hour. At 33% asphalt content, and under normal conditions, this would require up to 2.3 million BTUs per hour. Also, the asphalt and tar used are products of crude petroleum. Thus, the raw materials (feedstocks) of this industry make further demands on hydrocarbon supplies. No data are available measuring total crude oil used as raw material.

As a final step, various finishing surfaces are often applied to the saturated paper and felt, requiring further energy use.

(2) *Insulation Board:*   Waste materials plus insulation fibers are blended, rolled, and pressed into board, and then dried. Drying of insulation board presents tremendous heating problems for, as the outer areas dry first, they insulate the still damp interior of the board from the applied heat.

These production techniques create large amounts of effluent, usually in the form of vapors. The Environmental Protection Agency has imposed upon the industry the requirement of cleaning this effluent before it is discharged out of the mill. The current cleansing technique involves burning of these vapors in furnaces. As they are not self-combusting, they require applications of heat of approximately 1,350-1,400°F. (At one plant alone, this consumes 10-15 million BTUs per hr.) At the present time, none of this heat is being recycled into production.

Thus, production in the industry is very heat-intensive. A measure of energy intensiveness, thousand BTUs per dollar of value added in 1967, is: Manufacturing, 59.0; Total Paper, 140.1; Building Paper and Board, 271.6. Further, with 1% of all paper production, building paper and board used 3.7% of total paper industry BTUs in 1967.

The 1967 distribution of fuel use in the building paper and board industry was: coal, 24.0%; oil, 11.6%; gas, 39.1%; misc. fuels, 13.6%; and electricity, 11.4%. This differed from the distribution of fuel in the entire paper industry (coal, 28.1%; oil, 20.5%; gas, 30.7%; misc. fuel 13.3%; electricity, 7.4%), primarily in building paper and board's reliance on gas, which is used in the heating of asphalt and tar.

Finally, it can be seen in Table 9-2 that building paper and board mills integrated with pulp mills predominate over nonintegrated mills. Yet little

Table 9-2.   Distribution of Value of Shipments, by Type of Mill

	Paper & Board Mill Integrated with Pulp	Paper & Board Mill Nonintegrated
1967	72.7%	27.3%
1962	84.4	15.6

Source: Bureau of the Census, *Census of Manufactures*, Vol. II, 1967: Part II, p. 26A-11; 1963: Part I, p. 26A-12.

use can be made of pulping by-products as fuel because of their use as raw materials for building grade paper and felt stock.

SECTION III.   HISTORICAL DEVELOPMENT

Building paper and board output is cyclical, pegged to the cycle of new housing units started, primarily privately owned, which provide the basic demand for the product. As can be seen in Chart 9-1 (at the end of this report), building paper, building board, and privately owned, newly started housing units have all troughed in the same year. Building paper and board have trailed peaks in new housing units started by one year. From 1959 to 1968 (peak year to peak year) privately owned, newly started housing units experienced virtually zero growth: 1,516.8 thousand units in 1959, and 1,507.7 thousand units in 1968.[2]

However, in approximately the same time period, 1954 to 1970, building paper and board production (measured in value of shipments) rose 2.1% annually (see Table 9-3, column A). The impetus for this growth lies in the supplemental product use for alterations and repairs to residential units, and nonresidential structures.

Total energy use, measured in BTUs, grew at an annual rate of 5.8% during the period 1954 to 1962: in 1954, it was 43.2 trillion BTUs; in 1962, 67.8 trillion. It is not known how much of the large drop in fuel use from 1962 to 1967 is due to the removal of hardboard from the coverage in 1963, or to the downswing in production in 1966 (see Table 9-3, column B).

The energy-output ratio (thousand BTUs per 1967 constant dollar shipped) increased greatly from 1954 to 1962 at an annual rate of 6.0%. Starting about 1958, the quality of tar papers and shingles was upgraded by employing more crude petroleum inputs and more heat to melt them. It is most probable that this change and others in building paper and board composition contributed to the rise in energy use per unit of product in this period. In 1962-67, an improvement occurred in the energy-output ratio at the rate of 10.1% annually. Again, how much of this can be attributed to the change in coverage is unclear at this time. The only major innovation in the technology of production occurred about 1958. This involved the heating of asphalt and tar, previously done in batches in large kettles, in a new and more efficient, continuous-flow, tube heater process. This innovation may not have come into general use in an amount great enough to affect the industry-wide statistics until after 1962 (see Table 9-3, column C).

Other technological changes have been minimal, consisting of gradual increases in production efficiency through the use of faster and larger machinery.

Table 9-3.   Energy and Ouput: Trends in the Building Paper and Building Board Industry, 1954-1970

	(A)	*(B)*	*(C)* Gross Energy Basis[1]	*(D)*	*(E)* Useful Energy Basis[1]
	Value of Shipments (million 1967 $)	*Total Fuel Use (trillion BTUs)*	*Energy-Output Ratio (BTUs/1967 $ of shipments)*	*Total Fuel Use (trillion BTUs)*	*Energy-Output Ratio (BTUs/1967 $ of shipments)*
			Actual		
1954	$283	43.2	152.6	36.8	130.0
1958	314	56.8	181.0	47.6	151.6
1962	280	67.8	242.3	57.7	206.1
1967	341	49.9	146.3	40.4	118.5
1970	392*	n.a.	n.a.	n.a.	n.a.
			Predicted		
1975	470	96.0	204.0	72.8	155.0
1980	560	106.0	190.0	78.4	140.0

[1] See Chapter One, pages 14-15, for definitions of gross and useful energy.

n.a. = Not available.

Sources: Bureau of the Census, *Census of Manufactures*, 1967 and 1963.
    *American Paper Institute, *Statistics of Paper* 1972.

Table 9-4.   Fuel Use in BTUs, 1954–1967

	1954	*1958*	*1962*	*1967*
		Trillion BTUs		
Coal	13.7	15.7	17.2	9.7
Fuel oil, total	4.3	4.5	6.0	4.7
Gas	15.9	20.7	26.0	15.8
Misc. fuel (1)	0.8	2.5	3.6	5.5
Electricity, total (2)	2.5	4.1	4.8	4.6
Total energy (3)	36.8	47.6	57.7	40.4
		Percentage Distribution		
Coal	36.1%	33.0%	29.8%	24.0%
Fuel oil, total	11.7	9.5	10.4	11.6
Gas	43.2	43.5	45.1	39.1
Misc. fuel (1)	2.2	5.3	6.2	13.6
Electricity, total (2)	6.8	8.6	8.3	11.4
Total energy (3)	100.0%	100.0%	100.0%	100.0%

(1) Other fuel and fuel not specified by kind
(2) Based on useful energy
(3) Sum off due to rounding.

Source: Table 9-5.

SECTION IV.   PROJECTIONS TO 1980

The building paper and board industry is currently facing many conflicting trends.

Environmental regulations are creating increasing fuel use and increasing operating costs. The effect is two-fold. First, there is a shift away from asphalt and crude petroleum saturated insulators. Second, operating techniques that were economically unfeasible when first invented years ago are now coming under reconsideration. For example, some companies are ending asphalt and tar product lines entirely. One is experimenting with radio-frequency drying of insulating board. Too expensive when first developed, it may now be cheaper than burning fuels for heat. Another company is starting to remodel its mills in order to recycle effluent burning heat into the production cycle.

Much research is being done in the fields of effluent control and fuel conservation as areas of prime concern in the industry. But the lag time from innovation to application will not prevent a further rise in the energy-output ratio in the near future.

The outlook for the residential construction for the period 1972-1980 (peak year to peak year), based on the Maryland Interindustry Forecasting Model, is for minimal growth at an annual rate of 0.9%, while additions and alterations are forecast to rise at an annual rate of 2.9%.

Plastic products are coming into increasing competition with building paper and board. In addition, the growth in mobile home construction, which does not use many of these products, may eliminate some of the demand created by residential construction. The Mobile Homes Manufacturers Association projects a 10% to 15% annual growth rate in units shipped after 1973. However, increased concern for fuel conservation throughout the economy will provide increasing demand for insulating materials per unit of construction or alteration and repair. This may prove the prime impetus for growth in the industry.

The Maryland Interindustry Forecasting Model projects growth in sales volume in the industry from 1972 to 1980 at an annual rate of 3.7%. The high pollution and energy requirements of asphalt and tar products will act as a factor limiting their growth. Insulation paper and board will probably experience the greatest growth among the industry's products. The Maryland estimate may be slightly high due to the adverse effects of energy and pollution requirements. However, the growth rate can be expected to exceed the 2.1% rate of 1954 to 1962.

The energy-output ratio will probably rise sharply in the near future due to pollution control demands. This rise should exceed the 1954 to 1962 increase of 6.0% annually, which was primarily due to a change in product composition. Projecting an 8.0% annual rise, the energy-output ratio should reach approximately 204.0 thousand BTUs per 1967 constant dollar shipped by 1975 (based on a tentative 1971 ratio of approximately 150).[3]

Thereafter, plant remodeling and production innovation should begin to come into general operation, and the energy-output ratio should consequently stabilize. General improvement in energy use per unit of output will take place only near the end of the period. The energy-output ratio in 1980 is therefore predicted to be approximately 190.0 thousand BTUs per 1967 constant dollar shipped.

Accepting the Maryland Interindustry Forecasting Model's growth rate in building paper and board of 3.7%, production will reach approximately $470 million in value of shipments, in 1967 prices, by 1975. With the above energy-output ratio projected for that year, this would require 96 trillion BTUs to produce. By 1980, production is estimated to reach $560 million; 106 trillion BTUs would be required to meet this production level. (See Table 9-3, columns D and E, for the above projections computed on a useful energy basis.)

Table 9-5.   Fuel Use in Physical Units

	1954	1958	1962	1967
Coal (thousand short tons)	514	610	667	375
Fuel oil, total				
(thousand bbls.)	743	778	1,038	811
Distillate (thousand bbls.)	n.a.	n.a.	121	105
Residual (thousand bbls.)	n.a.	n.a.	917	707
Gas (million cu. ft.)	15,341	19,983	25,136	15,270
Misc. fuel*				
(million current $)	.3	.9	1.3	2.0
Total electricity				
(million kwh)	934	1,805	2,041	1,432
Purchased (million kwh)	731	1,210	1,420	1,357
Generated less sold				
(million kwh)	203	595	621	75

*Other fuels and fuels not specified by kind.
n.a. = Not available.
Source: Bureau of the Census, *Census of Manufactures*, 1967, 1963.

Notes

[1] Bureau of the Census, *Census of Manufactures,* 1967, Vol. II, Part II, p. 26a-16.

[2] Department of Commerce, *Business Statistics,* 1971 ed., p. 51.

[3] Department of Commerce, unpublished data supplied to The Conference Board.

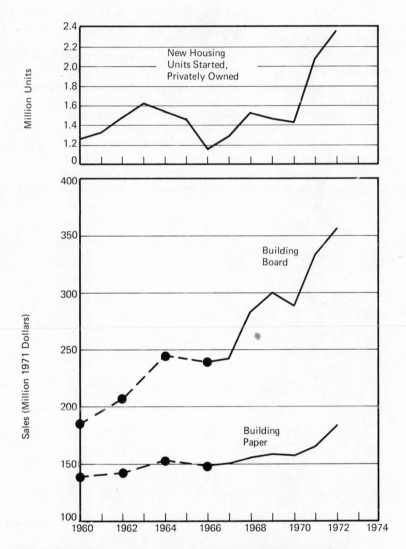

Chart 9-1. Cycles in New Housing Units Started, Building Paper and Board Sales. Sources: Dept. of Commerce, *Business Statistics 1971, Construction Review, May, 1973*; Maryland Interindustry Forecasting Model.

SECTION V.   SELECTED BIBLIOGRAPHY

American Paper Institute. *The Statistics of Paper.* New York, 1972.

Britt, Kenneth (ed.). *Pulp and Paper Technology.* New York: Reinhold Publishing Corp., 1964.

Bureau of Labor Statistics. *Impact of Technological Change and Automation in the Pulp and Paper Industry.* Washington, D.C., 1962.

Department of Commerce. *Business Statistics.* Washington, D.C., 1971 ed.

——————. *Census of Manufactures,* 1963 and 1967.

——————. *Construction Review,* May 1973.

Organization for European Economic Cooperation. *The Pulp and Paper Industry in the U.S.A.* Paris, 1951.

Strahan, J. L. *Manufacture, Selection and Application of Asphalt Roofing and Siding Products.* Asphalt Roofing Manufactures Association: New York, 1966.

Part Three

Chemicals Industries

Chapter Ten

Alkalies and Chlorine—SIC 2812

Mark Wehle [a]

SECTION I. INTRODUCTION AND SUMMARY

This chapter analyzes shipments and energy consumption in the alkalies and chlorine industry (SIC 2812) in 1954-1980 (Section II) and discusses chlorine-caustic soda and soda ash manufacture and their energy per ton of product (Sections III and IV).

Alkalies and chlorine ranked as follows among the nine heavy energy-using chemical industries in 1967:

- Eighth in value of shipments
- Fourth in energy use
- First in energy use per dollar of shipments.

It used 1% of the country's electric power.

The intensive use of energy is due to the nature of the chemical processes. Chlorine is produced by electrolysis of brine, and soda ash is produced by a complicated succession of operations including much baking at high heat.

Table 10-1 shows what the industry ships. Primary products assigned to it as their "home" industry by the Bureau of the Census accounted in 1967 for about two-thirds of shipments, consisting mostly of chlorine, caustic soda, and soda ash to roughly equal value.

The chlorine and caustic soda are nearly all produced jointly by electrolysis of brine by a technique that dates back to the 1890s. Chlorine is

[a] Especially helpful information and advice were received from Messrs. W. L. Amos of the U.S. Department of Commerce; H. Stuart Holden and Joseph Perret of Electrode Corporation; A. J. Lichota, D. J. Saunders, and Lawrence Walker of Allied Chemical Corporation; Robert L. Mitchell, Jr. of the Chlorine Institute; M. D. Rubin of Raytheon Co.; and A. E. Thompson of PPG Industries. They are not responsible for any errors.

181

Table 10-1.   Shipments of the Alkalies and Chlorine Industry in 1967

Product	Per Cent of Total Shipments
Chlorine, compressed or liquefied	20.0%
Caustic soda (sodium hydroxide, NaOH)	23.0
Soda ash (sodium carbonate, Na_2CO_3), including the quantity used to make sodium bicarbonate ($NaHCO_3$, "baking soda")	17.6
Other alkalies and alkalies and chlorine n.s.k. (not specified by kind)−two-thirds of this was caustic potash (potassium hydroxide, KOH)	4.0
Secondary products Four-fifths of these were primary to industrial inorganic chemicals n.e.c. (not elsewhere classified), industrial organic chemicals n.e.c., and plastics materials and resins	32.2
Miscellaneous receipts Mostly resales; some contract work	3.2
	100.0
Total value of shipments ($millions)...........................	$720

Source: Computed from Bureau of the Census, *Census of Manufactures*: 1967, Vol. II, *Industry Statistics*, Part 2, p. 28A-17.

made into vinyl chloride and thence into plastics, into household and industrial bleach (these were originally the chief uses), and into compounds for chlorinating swimming pools and drinking water.

Caustic soda (sodium hydroxide) is used in the home in oven cleaner and in industry in the manufacture of glass, rayon, and pulp and paper. In industrial use it increasingly supplants soda ash because of the rapid growth of chlorine output and the fixity of the electrolytic ratio (1.13 to 1) by which caustic soda has been produced alongside chlorine.

Soda ash (sodium carbonate, Na_2CO_3) is made from brine, limestone, and ammonia by the ammonia-soda ("Solvay") process, in use now for more than a century. Soda ash, like caustic soda, is used for making glass and in the pulp and paper industry. Recrystallized from water, it becomes washing soda ("sal soda," $Na_2CO_3.1OH_2O$). Treated with carbon dioxide in water solution, it becomes the bicarbonate used for medicine and in baking power (bicarbonate is included in Table 10-1 as soda ash equivalent). Manufactured soda ash has been in decline for many years because of competition from "natural" sodium carbonate made largely from sodium sesquicarbonate ($Na_2CO_3.NaHCO_3.2H_2O$) in Wyoming, as well as competition from caustic soda (as mentioned), and because of the difficulty in disposing of the waste product, calcium chloride, without polluting streams and lakes.

"Other alkalies" are mostly potassium hydroxide, which is produced alongside chlorine in electrolytic cells. It is used for making soap, detergents, and dyes.

Some of the secondary products are by-products made alongside the primary products, for instance, carbon dioxide made alongside soda ash or hydrogen alongside chlorine. More often, perhaps, the primary product is used as a raw material for further processing, as with organic chemicals made from chlorine.

The chief conclusions of this report are:

(1) Based on the 1954-1967 energy price trend, energy per ton shipped declines continuously. Energy per constant dollar of shipments rises to 1980 for chlorine and caustic soda as their shipments to production ratio falls due to competition from the Kel-Chlor process (which recovers chlorine from by-product hydrochloric acid), or because of possible shrinkage in vinyl chloride ($CH_2:CHCl$) production (due to cancer hazard).

(2) Kel-Chlor competition could cut the growth of chlorine and caustic soda shipments by half while increasing soda ash shipments. Otherwise, using the 1954-67 energy price trend, chlorine-caustic shipments might nearly double by 1980 (as they nearly did in 1954-67), while soda ash shipments stay level.

(3) For a 50% rise in the price of electric energy relative to plant and equipment cost, the use of electric energy in electrolysis to make chlorine may decline one-eighth, and this estimate would enable some correction to be made to forecasts based on 1954-67 energy prices.

SECTION II. SHIPMENTS AND ENERGY PER CONSTANT DOLLAR OF SHIPMENTS

Table 10-2 shows energy, shipments in current dollars, and energy per constant dollar of shipments in census years 1954-67 and projected to 1975 and 1980. (Data for 1947 are available but were not analyzed.) Chlorine, caustic soda, and caustic potash are lumped together as the "chlorine-caustic subindustry" and the rest of alkalies and chlorine is the "soda ash subindustry" (about 6% larger than soda ash itself).

The possibility of continued higher energy prices is not part of Table 10-2, but the reader may incorporate it by reducing energy to shipments ratios by, say, one-eighth per 50% expected rise in fuel and electricity prices relative to those for plant and equipment (an arbitrary figure—see below).

Uncorrected in this way, the chief trends in the alkalies and chlorine industry 1954-80 according to Table 10-2 are:

Table 10-2.   Energy and Shipments in the Alkalies and Chlorine Industry, 1954-1980

	Chlorine-Caustic[a]	Soda Ash[b]	(1) & (2) Primary Products	Secondary Products	Miscellaneous Receipts	(3), (4), & (5) Alkalies & Chlorine
	(1)	(2)	(3)	(4)	(5)	(6)
			Energy-to-Shipments Ratio (1,000 BTUs/1967 $)			
1980 H ...	541.2	409.7	518.0	134.0	0.0	357.7
L ...	597.6	409.7	550.0	134.0	0.0	375.0
1975	527.3	411.4	502.9	137.0	0.0	357.2
1967	526.2	413.1	493.1	164.5	0.0	371.6
1962	528.3	429.0	497.7	196.4	0.0	388.6
1958	530.7	437.5	499.0	230.7	0.0	415.4
1954	530.2	447.9	497.4	207.4	0.0	422.0
			Shipments (million 1967 $)			
1980 H ...	$589.5	$126.4	$715.9	$425.2	$35.8	$1,176.9
L ...	451.5	152.8	604.3	359.0	30.2	993.5
1975	471.1	125.2	596.3	335.0	29.2	960.5
1967	329.2	136.1	465.3	231.8	22.7	719.8
1962	275.2	122.9	398.1	184.2	20.5	602.8
1958	215.1	112.6	327.7	112.7	15.9	456.3
1954	184.2	122.0	306.2	79.5	14.4	400.1
			Energy (trillion BTUs)			
1980 H ...	319.0	51.8	370.8	50.2	0.0	421.6
L ...	269.8	62.6	332.4	40.2	0.0	372.6
1975	248.4	51.5	299.9	43.2	0.0	343.1
1967	173.3	56.2	229.5	38.1	0.0	267.6
1962	145.4	52.7	198.1	36.2	0.0	234.3
1958	114.2	49.2	163.4	26.0	0.0	189.4
1954	97.6	54.7	152.3	16.5	0.0	168.8

[a]Chlorine, caustic soda, and caustic potash.

[b]Soda ash, alkalies and chlorine not specified by kind, and other alkalies except caustic potash.

Notes: "H" and "L" refer to high and low chlorine-caustic production associated with low and high Kel-Chlor process production of 0.610 and 2.242 million tons of chlorine in 1980. Discontinuance of vinyl chloride production would have the same effect as going from the H to the L projection. See text. 1971 energy conversion factors are used as described for Tables 10.5, 10.6, and 10.7, including 10,500 BTUs per kwh for electricity for all years. "Constant" dollars are 1967 dollars.

Sources: Energy to Shipments Ratio. Alkalies and chlorine for 1954, 1958, 1962, and 1967: 1967 shipments in dollars were extrapolated back by a Census-derived output index to get constant-dollar shipments for 1954, 1958, and 1962. On a computer program, conversion factors were applied to industry consumption of fuel and electricity to get energy, which was divided by the constant-dollar shipments. (Actually, energy could have been divided by shipments in the present table directly, but the computer figure was available and is more accurate. See Chapter 1 and its Appendixes 2 and 3 regarding shipments and energy figures.) Alkalies and chlorine for 1975 and 1980, and all other columns for all years: energy was divided by shipments here.

Shipments. 1954, 1958, and 1962. Chlorine-caustic: the shipments in tons of chlorine, caustic soda, and caustic potash by all industries were each multiplied by the share of the alkalies and chlorine industry in their current-dollar value, and again by the 1967 price of the product—the ratio of the shipments of the product by all industries in dollars to the same in tons (Bureau of the Census, *Census of Manufactures*, 1954, 1958, 1963, and 1967—for after 1954, see Vol. II, part 1 or 2, tables 5A and 6A—and same author, *Annual Survey of Manufactures, 1962*, p. 395) and added to get "trial" shipments in constant dollars. Miscellaneous receipts and the shipments of secondary products were now subtracted from the alkalies and chlorine industry's total shipments, all in constant dollars (see below). Trial chlorine-caustic shipments and trial soda ash subindustry shipments (below) were added and their sum divided into this difference to get the "shipments correction factor," which was used to raise trial shipments by around 5% or 6% so all would add to the total. Soda ash: all industries' manufactured soda ash shipments in tons were multiplied by the alkalies and chlorine share and by the 1967 price of soda ash, as described for chlorine-caustic, and then raised in proportion to the ratio of the current-dollar shipments of "alkalies and chlorine, not specified by kind" plus "other alkalies" except caustic potash to those of soda ash, to get trial shipments in constant dollars for the soda ash subindustry. These were multiplied by the shipments correction factor as for chlorine-caustic. Secondary products: current-dollar shipments of secondary products by the alkalies and chlorine industry were obtained from each *Census of Manufactures*—in 1967 individually, though sometimes as a range, for practically every product and in 1954, 1958, and 1963 individually for some and in combination for the rest. Shipments in constant dollars had been obtained for a list consisting of all manufacturing and, within manufacturing, of six 2-digit groups and 37 4-digit industries (see "energy-shipments ratio," above). Each secondary product having current-dollar shipments individually available was arbitrarily assigned the price behavior of that one of the 44 groups on the list which it seemed most closely to resemble. Current-dollar shipments of that group from each Census were divided by its constant-dollar shipments and the resulting price index for the group was used to deflate the current-dollar shipments of the like secondary products. For products whose shipments were given only in combination with other secondary products, a composite price index was calculated on the assumption that the relative importance of the products in the combination was in proportion to that of the same or similar secondary products in 1967. 1962 shipments were interpolated on a straight line. Miscellaneous receipts: their ratios to alkalies and chlorine industry shipments in current dollars were applied to these shipments in 1967 dollars. Total: 1967 shipments were extrapolated back by a Census-derived output index (see "energy-to-shipments ratio," above).

1967. *Census of Manufactures* 1967, Vol. II, Part 1, p. 28A-17, table 5-A.

1975 and 1980. Chlorine-caustic: 1971 chlorine production from U.S. Bureau of the Census, *Current Industrial Reports: Inorganic Chemicals*, Series M28-A(72)-14 (December, 1973), p. 4, was extrapolated at 6½% (from range given in U.S. Dept. of Commerce, Bureau of Comparative Assessment and Business Policy, *U.S. Industrial Outlook, 1974*, p. 95). It was multiplied by the extrapolated share of the alkalies and chlorine industry in all industries' current-dollar chlorine shipments to get preliminary production and again by the extrapolated ratio of all industries' chlorine shipments to all industries' chlorine production in tons to get preliminary shipments (see "1954, 1958, and 1962" for sources). Kel-Chlor process chlorine of 160,000 tons in 1975 and 2,242,000 or 610,000 tons in 1980 (see text) was multiplied by the alkalies and chlorine industry's extrapolated share in chlorine shipments and the result subtracted from preliminary production and

(continued)

preliminary shipments. The reduced chlorine shipments were multiplied by the 1967 price of chlorine (see "1954, 1958, and 1962") and raised by the 1967 ratio of caustic soda and caustic potash to chlorine shipments. Soda ash: 1975 and low chlorine shipments projection for 1980—natural sodium carbonate production and manufactured plus natural for 1971 (*Current Industrial Reports*) were extrapolated at 8½% and 4½% (from ranges in *U.S. Industrial Outlook, 1974*, p. 95) and natural subtracted from manufactured plus natural to get manufactured. Manufactured was multiplied by the extrapolated share of the alkalies and chlorine industry in all industries' current-dollar soda ash shipments to get a preliminary soda ash production figure and again by all industries' extrapolated ratio of shipments to production in tons to get shipments in tons. These were multiplied by the 1967 price of soda ash (see "1954, 1958, and 1962") and raised by the ratio of the 1967 shipments of "alkalies and chlorine, n.s.k." and "other alkalies" except caustic potash to those of soda ash to get subindustry shipments in constant dollars. High chlorine shipments projection for 1980—same, except 1.325 times the difference in caustic soda production between the high and low Kel-Chlor assumption was added to all industries, 1980 manufactured plus natural soda ash production and prorated between natural and manufactured before multiplying by the alkalies and chlorine share. Secondary products and miscellaneous receipts: ratios for primary products in constant and current dollars, respectively, were extrapolated and applied to the sum of the projected constant-dollar chlorine-caustic and soda ash subindustry to the sum of the projected constant-dollar chlorine-caustic and soda ash subindustry shipments. Total: by addition.

Energy. 1954 and 1958. Chlorine-caustic: consists of lime-soda process caustic soda plus electrolytic process chlorine and caustic. No production figures are available for the alkalies and chlorine industry by itself. They must be estimated from all industries' production, from alkalies and chlorine's share in current-dollar shipments, and from energy data. A "trial production" figure for caustic soda made by the lime-soda process by the alkalies and chlorine industry was obtained by multiplying all industries' production of such caustic soda by the share of alkalies and chlorine in all industries' current-dollar shipments of all caustic soda, lime-soda plus electrolytic (see "shipments" references). Alkalies and chlorine's shipments of lime-soda process caustic soda were obtained in tons by multiplying that share by all industries' shipments of such caustic soda in tons. The shipments were subtracted from total production to get "trial production for further processing." Shipments and trial production for further processing were each multiplied by energy per ton (22.6 million BTUs, calculated from R. N. Shreve, *Chemical Process Industries*, 2nd edition, New York, McGraw-Hill, 1956, p. 297) to get "shipments energy" and "trial energy for further processing." Secondary products' energy and the shipments energies for three groups—lime-soda process caustic soda, electrolytic chlorine-caustic, and the soda ash subindustry (see below)—were now all subtracted from the total energy used by alkalies and chlorine and the difference was divided by the sum of the trial energies for further processing of the three groups to get the energy correction factor. This was multiplied into the trial production for further processing and the trial energy for further processing of each group and the results added to its shipments and shipments energy to get corrected production and corrected energy. (Trial production assumed that the alkalies and chlorine industry's share in the production of each of the three groups was the same as its share in the shipments. Apparently the share in production is less than the share in shipments. Furthermore, calculated energy adds up to more than the energy recorded by the Census, despite the fact that energy per ton is good practice rather than average practice. The energy correction factor cuts off the excess, prorating the cuts in production and energy among the groups in proportion to the BTUs by which, without the correction, each group's energy would exceed that needed to provide for its shipments.) For the electrolytic process, chlorine production by all industries was multiplied by the share of the alkalies and chlorine industry in all industries' current-dollar chlorine shipments to get trial chlorine production. Chlorine shipments by all industries in tons were also multiplied by that share to get those of the alkalies and chlorine industry. Shipments and trial production for further processing were each multiplied by energy per ton of chlorine from Table 10.6, and so forth as for the lime-soda process above. Soda ash: all manufactured soda ash production was multiplied by the share of the alkalies and chlorine industry in all industries' current-dollar soda ash shipments and raised by the ratio of the shipments of "alkalies and chlorine, n.s.k." and "other alkalies" except caustic potash to those of soda ash to get trial production for the subindustry. All industries' soda ash shipments in tons were also multiplied by the alkalies and chlorine industry's share and were raised as above to get subindustry shipments in tons. Shipments and final production for further processing were each multiplied by energy per ton of soda ash interpolated in Table 10.7, and so forth, as was done for chlorine-caustic. Secondary products: energy consumption per constant dollar of shipments had already been obtained for 44 groups. Shipments in constant dollars had been computed for many secondary products by deflating current-dollar shipments by the price index for an appropriate group. (See under "shipments.") The constant-dollar shipments of each of these secondary products was now multiplied by the energy per constant dollar of the same group that had been used for the price index. For the other secondary products, whose shipments were available only in combination, the 1967 relative composition of the combination was assumed (as for shipments). 1962 was interpolated on a straight line. Miscellaneous receipts: energy consumption was treated as zero because these are nearly all from resales. Total: conversion factors were applied to Census energy consumption (see under "energy-shipments ratio").

1962 and 1967. Same, except lime-soda process was omitted for lack of data.

1975 and 1980. Chlorine-caustic: preliminary production and preliminary shipments of chlorine in tons were reduced by the amount of the industry's sales loss due to the Kel-Chlor process (see "shipments"). The excess of the reduced production over the reduced shipments was multiplied by the 1967 energy correction factor and added to shipments energy. Soda ash: the preliminary production figure and the shipments figure for soda ash in tons were raised to the subindustry level (see "shipments"), and the excess of the raised production over the raised shipments was multiplied by the 1967 energy correction factor and added to shipments energy. Secondary products: energy per constant dollar was projected freehand. Miscellaneous receipts: energy assumed zero as above. Total: by addition.

---

1. Chlorine-caustic shipments in constant dollars nearly doubled from 1954 to 1967. From 1967 to 1980 they may experience anything from a one-half increase to another near doubling, depending on how much chlorine the organic chemicals manufacturers who buy chlorine from the industry are able to save by the Kel-Chlor process. Entire stoppage of vinyl chloride production due to the cancer scare in that industry would virtually convert the chlorine-caustic projection from the high to the low figure, but no such extreme effect seems likely.

Chlorine-caustic's energy-to-shipments ratio rises 1967-1980 because the loss of chlorine sales due to the Kel-Chlor process would reduce shipments and production by the same number of tons. Since shipments are smaller than production, they fall relatively to production and so to energy.

2. Manufactured soda ash shipments fluctuate within a narrow range

1954-1980 except under the high Kel-Chlor projection. Here the slump in chlorine sales reduces competition to soda ash from caustic soda, produced jointly with chlorine. Some dumping of wastes is assumed permissible to 1983. Energy falls for soda ash per constant dollar shipped and per ton produced.

3. Secondary products tripled their shipments 1954-67 and may again double them, against very much smaller increases in primary production. Their energy-to-shipments ratio fell one-fifth and may decline another fifth.

4. The whole alkalies and chlorine industry increased its constant-dollar shipments by three-fourths 1954-67 and could go up another one- or two-thirds, assuming vinyl plastics continue to enjoy their present growth rate Its energy-to-shipments ratio fell one-eighth to 1967 and thereafter will remain steady or rise, depending on the Kel-Chlor and vinyl chloride assumptions.

It should be pointed out that besides being influenced by these assumptions, the numerical conclusions of this chapter depend on the procedure used to estimate industry production and allocate discrepancies. Also, it is difficult to determine whether given observations are for best practice, good practice, or average practice of existing plants; therefore, the conclusion of what the trend in energy use per ton has been becomes very uncertain.

Energy Prices for Projections

From 1947 to 1972 the Bureau of Labor Statistics wholesale price index for fuels and related products and power rose practically parallel with that for all commodities—54% against 56%. The trend projections of energy per ton produced or shipped are necessarily based on a continuance of this parallel movement and do not take account of the Arab boycott or prospects of more energy "crunches."

To remedy this weakness, a one-eighth drop in the energy to shipments ratio was suggested above for a 50% rise in the ratio of the wholesale price index for fuel and related products and power to that for plant and equipment. The basis for this is that such an elasticity is used for electrolysis energy in chlorine production. Energy in chlorine-caustic is two-thirds purchased and generated electricity, one-third fuel if (as here) the electricity is measured by the BTUs needed to generate it. The electricity elasticity could be arbitrarily applied to the fuel portion if a search of the literature failed to turn up elasticities for evaporation and calcining, the major fuel-using operations. No corrections at all for higher energy prices have been applied here.

Procedure

Secondary products' shipments and energy are calculated 1954-67 by assigning to each product the energy use and price index of the industry group indicated by the first four digits of its product code. Miscellaneous receipts are assumed to use no energy and their shipments are assumed the same proportion of industry shipments in constant dollars as in current dollars. Energy and constant-dollar shipments for secondary and miscellaneous are subtracted from industry shipments and energy. Correction factors prorate the residues between chlorine-caustic and soda ash according to the shipments and energy of these subindustries as calculated independently from tonnages produced and shipped and from the good-practice energy per ton of Tables 10-6 and 10-7. Projections use the 1967 correction factors. (See Table 10-2's source note.)

Chlorine-Caustic Subindustry

The near-doubling of chlorine-caustic's constant-dollar shipments 1954-67 was due to sales of chlorine for making vinyl chloride ($CH_2:CHCl$), the starting material for vinyl plastics, and for chlorinating hydrocarbons for refrigerants and other uses. The energy-to-shipments ratio stayed nearly level to 1967. The lime-soda process for making caustic soda from soda ash and lime, which amounted to 9% of subindustry shipments in 1954, fell in 1958 to 6% and had disappeared from the Census statistics by 1962. Its energy to shipments ratio was only one-ninth below that for electrolytic chlorine-caustic so the closing-down of the process had little effect on the overall ratio. The 7% fall in energy per ton of production for the electrolytic process 1954–67 led to only a 1% fall in that ratio.

Going ahead now to the projections, the 6½% growth rate of chlorine production used here is based on a forecast in *U.S. Industrial Outlook, 1974.* Since that forecast was made, newspaper articles have appeared about liver cancer cases in plants that work with vinyl chloride.[1] About 17% of chlorine has been going into making vinyl chloride and its polymer[2] and a 12% to 15% annual growth rate had been forecast.[3] Elimination of the chemical would reduce chlorine's net growth rate 1971-1980 from 6.5% to 2.6% and alkalies and chlorine's 1980 chlorine shipments by about a quarter—about the same effect as going from the H to the L projection in Table 10-2.

The prospects for Kel-Chlor production are another uncertainty. The process enables organic chemicals manufacturers to decompose by-product hydrochloric acid (HCl) to recover the chlorine. In chlorinating a hydrocarbon, one atom of chlorine combines with a hydrogen atom to make hydrochloric acid. while another atom of chlorine takes the hydrogen atom's place in the hydrocarbon molecule. Thus, in most cases, a ton of chlorine goes into hydrochloric acid for every ton that goes into the product.[4] In the case of vinyl chloride production there was (ten years ago) no net waste of hydrochloric acid because 56% of vinyl chloride was made an alternate way by combining hydrochloric acid with acetylene (CH:CH),[5] but, in other chlorinations much acid is neutralized with lime and the calcium chloride dumped into streams.[6]

As to how much this is: organic chemicals in 1972 took 60% to 70%[7] of chlorine production of 9.87 million tons, or 5.9 to 6.9 million tons, and should have put 3.0 to 3.4 millions ton of chlorine into hydrochloric acid. The Census records 2.1 million tons of 100% HCl in by-product acid produced in that year,[8] or 2.0 million tons of chlorine. (Of this perhaps 0.8 million were in hydrochloric acid collected and recycled with acetylene by vinyl chloride plants.) The residue of 1.0 to 1.4 million tons of chlorine went into hydrochloric acid that was not recorded as having been produced, and it is this that may have been dumped or otherwise lost. Eliminating vinyl chloride plants, which apparently took 1.7 million tons of chlorine and dumped no acid, the range for the residue centers at 26% of chlorine consumption by organic chemicals manufacture except vinyl chloride (1.2 divided by (6.4 less 1.7)).

The Kel-Chlor process is now incorporated only in DuPont's plant under construction by M. W. Kellogg Co. at Corpus Christi, Texas. The hydrochloric acid will be treated with oxygen in the presence of nitrogen oxide and sulfuric acid as catalysts. Energy requirements to the user are listed as 40 kwh plus 40 pounds of steam per ton of recovered chlorine, or less than half a million BTUs compared with about 40 million for electrolytic chlorine with associated caustic soda. Cost is expected to be perhaps $16 to $20 per ton of chlorine compared with a current market price of $75. Practically all of the chlorine will be returned to the start of processing, replacing what would otherwise have to be bought from the outside (including the alkalies and chlorine industry).[9]

Turning now to the present forecasts: the 1975 forecast assumes that the DuPont plant will be the only one operating and that it will produce 160,000 tons of chlorine, about three-quarters of which will come out of the shipments and production of the alkalies and chlorine industry.

The high chlorine shipments ("H") forecast for 1980 uses a 6½% growth rate for chlorine and 8½% for its customers in organic chemicals manufacture, of whom a tenth will be using the Kel-Chlor process to recover an assumed half of their chlorine consumption that would otherwise go out of the plant as hydrochloric acid. (Vinyl chloride producers would presumably not be among this tenth because they would be consuming as much hydrochloric acid as they made.) 1980 Kel-Chlor production would be about four times 1975. This assumption seems to agree with *U.S. Industrial Outlook, 1974*, p. 95.

The low chlorine shipments ("L") forecast for 1980 assumes 2,242,000 tons of chlorine will be produced by the Kel-Chlor process. This can be interpreted as follows: using a 6½% growth rate for chlorine, 8½% for organic chemicals, and 13½% for vinyl chloride (see above and Table 10-2), 46% of 1980 chlorine production or 7.5 million tons of chlorine would be used in the manufacture of organic chemicals other than vinyl chloride. At the 26% wastage rate suggested for 1972, 1.7 million tons of chlorine might be discarded as waste hydrochloric acid. There would remain ½ times 7.5 less 1.7 or 1.9 million tons of hydrochloric acid being sold. If about a quarter of these sales were at give-away prices, there could well be a market for the Kel-Chlor process of 2.2 million tons of chlorine in 1980. This assumption agrees best with the other chapters in this volume.

Kel-Chlor units will presumably be parts of large petrochemical complexes and not be counted in the alkalies and chlorine industry or affect energy per ton of chlorine produced there. But they will raise energy per ton or per constant dollar shipped. For since alkalies and chlorine ships only part of the chlorine it produces, a loss of sales that reduces shipments and production by the same arithmetic amount must reduce shipments in greater proportion and so here it raises the energy-to-shipments ratio, even while energy per ton produced declines.

(It is taken for granted in the forecasts that Kel-Chlor production will be collected and measured and so be recorded as production by the Census Bureau.)

Soda Ash Subindustry

Shipments of the soda ash subindustry in constant dollars changed little 1954-62. To 1967 they rose about a tenth, somewhat more than production. The 1975 projection and the high chlorine shipments projection for 1980 would erase half of this gain. On the low chlorine shipments projection, 1980 caustic soda shipments would shrink enough to reserve to soda ash some of its present market. Energy per constant dollar of soda ash subindustry shipments fell 8% 1954-67 against perhaps 2% for energy per ton of production, reflecting a rise in the proportion of production retained for further processing. Energy per constant dollar of shipments and energy per ton are forecast to share the same rate of decline 1967-1980.

Secondary Products

Inorganic chemicals, n.e.c., organic chemicals, n.e.c., and plastics materials accounted in 1967 for a much larger fraction of the secondary products of the alkalies and chlorine industry in 1967 than they did of all chemicals: 83% against 34%. Agricultural chemicals accounted for another 5%, cyclic intermediates 3%, and industrial gases, mostly carbon dioxide, 2%.

Secondary products' past shipments and energy are known here with much less certainty than other groups' because of the assumption used in getting them: that each secondary product had the same energy-using and price experience as did the industry on the list it most resembles. This might hold for lime, which comes from a homogeneous industry on the list, but agricultural chemicals, SIC 2879, were not on the list and were likened to all chemicals, SIC 28. The projections are inexact because shipments of secondary products are forecast as a group in ratio to those of primary products.

Alkalies and Chlorine Industry

The alkalies and chlorine industry as a whole gains 3.9% a year in constant dollar shipments to 1980 on the high chlorine shipments projection and 2.5% on the low. This compares with 3.5% for the product group 2812– on the University of Maryland INFORUM model, which presumably does not take account of the Kel-Chlor process, and with the 4.4% current prices projection of *U.S. Industrial Outlook, 1974,* p. 95. Attention is drawn to the reservations about the Kel-Chlor process and the vinyl chloride cancer scare discussed under "chlorine-caustic."

SECTION III.   TECHNOLOGY AND ENERGY PER TON IN CHLORINE-CAUSTIC SODA MANUFACTURE

Here are explained the energy-per-ton-of-production figures in Sections I and II for chlorine-caustic soda manufacture and some of the underlying technology. The effect of higher energy prices is briefly discussed. (Tons are short tons of 2,000 pounds.)

This branch of the alkalies and chlorine industry has located near solid salt or brine deposits where electricity was cheap or could be made from cheap natural gas. Alternating current is converted to direct by solid-state rectifiers with 2½% to 4% loss (compared with 9% in the mercury-arc rectifiers used before 1968). The direct current passes to the electrolytic cells.

The cells are in series, the anode of one being connected to the cathode of the next. Saturated brine is treated with sodium carbonate to remove calcium, magnesium, and iron salts (see Fig. 10-1). It is piped to the cells at 140° F. and may be heated there to 190° F.

Two main kinds of cells are in use, diaphragm and mercury. In the diaphragm cell a porous partition surrounds the metal cathode to keep the sodium and hydroxyl ions that gather there from eddying back. The flow of brine is directed out of the cell past the cathode so as to carry these ions outside. The effluent, which may contain 11% caustic soda and 12% salt, is evaporated to 50% or 68-74% caustic soda and 1% salt, or to solid caustic soda with 2% salt. The salt removed is recycled.

Chlorine is discharged at the anode, which may be made of carbon, but those made of titanium coated with ruthenium oxide or similar combination are increasingly common. Hydrogen is discharged at the cathode and usually is either vented to the air or recycled for fuel.[10] The mercury cell needs no diaphragm, because no sodium hydroxide is formed in the brine, sodium being separated as an amalgam with mercury. A sheet of flowing mercury constitutes the cathode. Instead of hydrogen, sodium is discharged there and the mercury dissolves. The amalgam of sodium and mercury is usually pumped to a decomposer where the sodium in it reacts with pure water. Nearly salt-free sodium hydroxide solution results along with hydrogen. Alternatively, the sodium metal itself is recovered from the mercury for use in making organic chemicals.

Mercury cells need solid salt to replenish their spent brine. This still has 85% of its original salt content, so it is more economical to recycle it than dump it (especially with the concern about pollution). The salt may come from

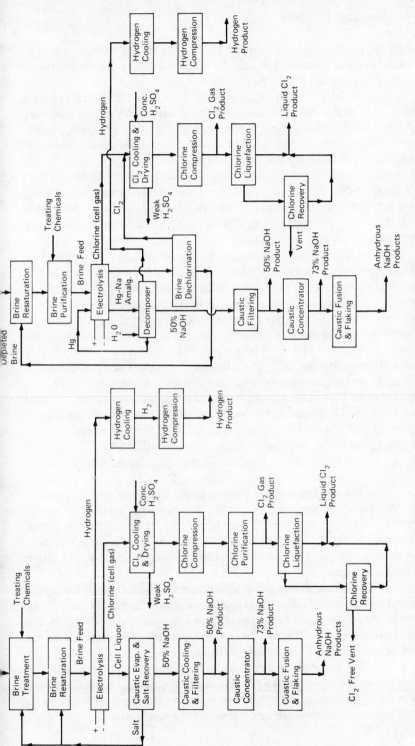

Figure 10-1. Flow Diagrams for Diaphragm Cell Plant (left) and Mercury Cell Plant (right), for Making Chlorine and Caustic Soda. Source: Kirk-Othmer Encyclopedia of Chemical Technology, 2nd ed., Vol. 1 (1963), pp. 699-700 (courtesy of Science and Technology Research Center, The New York Public Library, Astor, Lenox, and Tilden Foundations).

outside the plant, or mercury cells and diaphragm cells may be worked in combination, evaporation of the brine-caustic effluent from the diaphragm cell providing make-up salt for the mercury cells.

With the mercury cell, unlike the diaphragm cell, no evaporation is needed to bring the caustic soda solution to the usual 50% strength. And being salt-free, the solution is cheaper to evaporate further. Also, freedom from salt enables the mercury-cell product to be used in rayon manufacture without the purification needed for the diaphragm-cell product.

Despite these advantages, mercury cells are on the way out. They receded from early dominance to near extinction in this country around 1947. They returned to about a quarter of chlorine capacity in the late 1960s (Table 10-3). Because of the impossibility of altogether preventing the escape of some mercury, no more such cells are being built in the U.S.

Escaped mercury discharged into rivers and lakes is assimilated by marine vegetation, which in turn is eaten by food fish. It was the finding of mercury-contaminated fish in Lake St. Clair that put mercury cells on the defensive. The success of new technologies in eliminating mercury discharge seems to be only relative. Thus a plant of FMC Corp., producing 175 tons of chlorine a day at Squamish, B.C., got its mercury down to 28 parts per million of solid waste and to 3 parts per billion of liquid effluent, for a weekly discharge of only 1½ pounds of metal.[11] But is this small enough? General Technology, the contractor that has been working out regulations for adoption by the Environmental Protection Administration, has recommended a limit of 0.00014 pounds per ton of chlorine,[12] or about one-ninth of FMC's figure. Japan, more dependent than this country on fish for food, has ordered all mercury-cell operators to switch to diaphragm cells by September 1975.[13]

The lead pollution from diaphragm cells using graphite anodes is considered less serious than mercury pollution.

The chlorine gas from either type of cell may be used for other products, mainly organic chemicals, in the same or nearby plants, or it may be shipped. If the latter, it is dried by cooling and sulfuric acid treating, and then compressed or liquefied. Liquefying also removes the hydrogen that may be present in diaphragm-cell chlorine and which, in certain concentrations, creates an explosion hazard.

The main new technical development in the industry is the replacement of carbon by metal anodes, as mentioned above. Carbon anodes are eaten away by the solution with formation of carbon monoxide and other gases that must be separated from the chlorine, and the space between anode and cathode must be often readjusted or the cell overhauled.

The smoother surface of the metal anode and its resistance to crumbling enable narrowing the gap between the electrodes. A metal anode also forms fewer gas bubbles. Both these developments reduce cell resistance so that a 12% reduction in power can be obtained for the same current.

Table 10-3. U.S. Chlorine Capacity by Method of Production, 1946-1980

(per cent of U.S. chlorine capacity)

	Diaphragm Cells	Mercury Cells	All Other
1980	90.6%	6.0%	3.4%
1975	81.1	15.5	3.4
1972	72.4	24.2	3.4
1971	69.8	27.2	3.0
1967	69.8	26.7	3.5
1962	76.2	18.5	5.3
1956	81.6	12.4	6.0
1946	88.6	4.3	7.1

Source: Chlorine Institute, "North American Chlor-Alkali Industry Plants and Production Data Book" (Pamphlet No. 10; New York: The Institute, January 1973), p. 15. The Conference Board.

The 1973 Hooker catalog suggests that this power saving was not materializing on new installations before the Arab oil embargo. Instead, the current was increased (Table 10-4), presumably reducing the number of cells and so the maintenance and overhead, in line with the post-1947 trend, which has seen only moderate reductions in power along with rapid improvement in current-carrying capacity.

The last line of each half of Table 10-4 shows the ratio of energy use in each kind of cell to a theoretical minimum, which itself could be approached only at great expense. Ratios run from 1.5 to 2.3.

Besides the metal anode, other developments in chlorine cells are: bipolar diaphragm cells, developed by PPG Industries, which use only 2,575 kwh per ton chlorine including circuit losses; a new membrane material stronger than asbestos for diaphragm cells, introduced by DuPont; and PPG's electrolytic cell for removing iron, nickel, and lead from diaphragm cell effluent (in combination with the ammonia extraction process already being used to remove sodium chloride and sodium chlorate).[14]

Table 10-5 gives past and forecasted energy use per ton of chlorine by diaphragm and mercury cell plants separately (ignoring plants that mix the two types). The last line combines the results weighted by the relative importance of the two kinds of cells. The forecasts are simple trend extrapolations and do not incorporate the perhaps permanently higher relative prices of fuel and electricity accompanying the Arab oil embargo.

Higher prices of fuel and purchased electricity should shift the trade-off between operating cost and fixed capital in favor of fixed capital, with a saving of energy (even though it takes some energy to produce and maintain the fixed capital). With enough higher fuel prices a given quantity of caustic soda will be evaporated with one more evaporator effect in series, economizing on fuel. The effects and the piping leading in and out of them may be better

Table 10-4.　Changing Characteristics of Typical Electrolytic Cells, 1916-1973

	1916	1947	1962	1973
Diaphragm cell				
Name	Griesheim	Hooker S	Hooker S	Hooker H[a]
Voltage[b]	3.6 & 4.0	3.52	3.25-3.95	3.8
Current (1,000 amperes)	To 2.5	8	10-30	80-150
Estimated d.c. energy, 1,000 kwh per short ton of chlorine	3.1-3.9	2.64	2.34-2.82	2.69 & up
Same ÷ theoretical minimum[c]	1.99-2.51	1.71	1.52-1.83	1.74 & up
	1916	*1947*	*1962*	*1968*
Mercury cell				
Name	Castner-Kellner	I. G. 7-Meter	Krebs & DeNora	(Various)
Voltage[b]	4.4	4.25	4.15-4.30	4.23-4.70
Current (1,000 amperes)	4.0	13.4	40-150	100-300
Estimated d.c. energy, 1,000 kwh per short ton of chlorine	3.2	3.28	2.95-3.03	3.06-3.60
Same ÷ theoretical minimum[c]	2.07	2.12	1.91-1.96	1.98-2.33

[a]With "dimensionally stable" (metal) anode.

[b]Usual voltage applied under good practice, 1916 and 1947; rated voltage 1962 on.

[c]Theoretical minimum of 1,544 kwh per ton of wet chlorine is 1.322 kg. of dry chlorine per 1,000 ampere-hours (D. A. Kent, ed., *Riegel's Industrial Chemistry*, New York, Reinhold, 1965, p. 161) times 1.1025/1000 tons per kg., all divided into 2.25 decomposition voltage (Riegel, p. 160).

Sources: 1961: J. R. Partington, *The Alkali Industry* (2nd ed., London: Bailliere, 1925), p. 160, for cell names and C. Elliott, "Electrolytic Caustic Soda: A Comparative Study of Cell Design and Efficiency" (sixth of a series), *Chemical Trade Journal*, August 22, 1924, pp. 211-213, for cell data. 1947: R. B. MacMullin, "Diaphragm vs. Amalgam Cells for Chlorine-Caustic Production," *Chemical Industries*, July 1947, p. 45. 1962: same author, "Electrolysis of Brines in Mercury Cells," p. 185, and M. S. Kircher, "Electrolysis of Brines in Diaphragm Cells," p. 98, in J. S. Sconce, ed., *Chlorine: Its Manufacture, Properties, and Uses* (London: Chapman & Hall, 1962). 1968: H. A. Sommers, "Mercury Cell Anode and Anode Stem Design and Other Factors Relating to Lowered Power Consumption and Operating Cost," *Electrochemical Technology*, March-April 1968, pp. 126-127. 1973: Hooker Chemical Corp. brochure, "Hooker's New H-4 150KA Diaphragm Cell" (1973?).

insulated and steam leaks repaired more promptly. Similar economies will be sought in the generation of electricity from the fuel.

In using electricity, the trade-off between current and number of cells is shifted towards less current and a longer string of cells. Chlorine production per cell is less in proportion to the shrinkage in current. But since it takes less voltage per cell to drive through a smaller current, power, which is voltage times current, shrinks more than in proportion to current; and energy per ton of

Table 10-5.   Steam and Electricity Consumed in Chlorine-Caustic Soda Manufacture (Good Practice for Existing Plants), 1925-1980 (million BTUs per electrochemical unit[a])

	1925	1947	1971	1975	1980
Diaphragm cell plants					
Steam (1,000 lbs.)		10.64	9.79	9.68	9.60
Electricity (kwh)	3,628	3,329	3,043	3,016	2,990
Total at 1971 conversion[b]					
(million BTUs)		46.0	42.1	41.7	41.4
Mercury cell plants					
Steam (1,000 lbs.)		1.12	.49	.47	.45
Electricity (kwh)		3,959	3,718	3,694	3,670
Total at 1971 conversion[b]					
(million BTUs)		43.1	39.7	39.4	39.1
Both plants					
Total at 1971 conversion[b]					
(million BTUs)		45.8	41.4	41.4	41.2

[a]An electrochemical unit is 1 ton of dry chlorine and 1.13 tons of caustic soda in 50% solution.

[b]1971 conversion factors: 1,350 BTUs to make a pound of steam and, in a diaphragm cell plant, 9,500 BTUs to generate 1 kwh of electricity, from G. L. Decker and R. S. Spencer, "Energy Crisis Drives Up Chemical Costs," *Chemical Engineering Progress*, Feb. 1972 p. 16; and 10,500 BTUs to generate 1 kwh of electricity in a mercury cell plant, this being taken as the average electric utility plant heat rate in the U.S. (see Chapter One, Appendix 3). It takes less BTUs to generate electricity in a diaphragm cell plant because much of it is a by-product from making the process steam for evaporating the caustic soda to 50%. The ratios of diaphragm cell capacity and mercury cell capacity to their sum were used as weights to get "both plants."

Note: A 1916 total energy figure, not broken down by steam and electricity, can be calculated from J. R. Partington, *The Alkali Industry* (London: Bailliere, 1918), pp. 105 and 127, and J. A. Kent, ed., *Riegel's Industrial Chemistry* (New York: Reinhold, 1962), p. 47. Other figures, not used here because too extreme, were found in *Kirk-Othmer Encyclopedia of Chemical Technology*, Vol. 1 (1963), p. 698, and W. L. Faith and others, *Industrial Chemicals* (3rd ed.; New York: Wiley, 1965), p. 248.

Sources: 1925: Computed from J. R. Partington, *The Alkali Industry* (2nd ed.; London; Bailliere, 1925) p. 185, where 1 kilogram active chlorine for making bleach is said to require 4 kwh of electricity. May contain 12½% rounding error. The 1947 drying and liquefaction cost was added in.

1947: Computed from R. B. MacMullin, "Diaphragm vs. Amalgam Cells for Chlorine-Caustic Production," *Chemical Industries*, July 1947, p. 49.

1971: Diaphragm cell—Computed by A. E. Thompson of PPG Industries from G. L. Decker and R. S. Spencer, "Energy Crisis Drives Up Chemical Costs," *Chemical Engineering Progress*, February 1972, pp. 16-17. The chlorine is assumed here to be dry. Mercury cell—estimated from 1947 source and the information that the mercury cell with DSA anode may use 3,300 DC kwh per ton chlorine compared with 2,600 for the diaphragm cell similarly equipped.

1975 and 1980: Estimated by extrapolating trends.

chlorine shrinks. To get the same production, more cells have to be used. Energy per ton of chlorine might fall roughly one-eighth for a 50% rise in the ratio of fuel price to the cost of plant and equipment.[15]

The end products for Table 10-5 are chlorine and 50% caustic soda. Actually, the chlorine is a slightly changing product: only 50% of it was liquid in 1972 compared with 55% in 1954. This is because relatively more chlorine is retained in the plant for further processing and less is shipped out. The proportions of shipped chlorine that went out as liquid and as compressed gas were the same in 1972 as in 1954. No adjustment was made to chlorine production for the decline in the importance of liquid.

With caustic soda, there is such an adjustment: some of the 50% solution, which is the end product for Table 10-6, is evaporated to 68 to 74% or

Table 10-6.   Extra Energy Needed to Evaporate 50% Caustic Soda to 68-74% and to Dryness (Good Practice for Existing Plants), 1954, 1971, 1975, and 1980

	1954	1971
Unit energy needed to make steam for caustic soda evaporation (million BTUs per ton of 100% NaOH)		
1 From cell liquor to 50% solution *or* from 50% solution to dryness .	12.37	11.70
2 0.3 x (1): From 50% solution to 68-74% solution	3.71	3.51
U.S. caustic soda production (1,000 tons of 100% NaOH)		
3 In solutions other than 68-74%	2,051	8,319
4 In 68-74% solution	537	755
5 Solid caustic	343	544
Total extra energy used to make concentrated or solid caustic soda (million BTUs)		
6 (2) x (4): To concentrate 50% solution to 68-74%	1.99	2.65
7 (1) x (5): To evaporate 50% solution to dryness	4.25	6.36
8 (6) + (7): Total extra energy needed	6.24	9.01
9 All industries' chlorine production (000 tons)	2,904	9,352

	1954	1971	1975	1980
	(trillion BTUs per ton chlorine)			
10 Extra energy	2.15	0.96	0.76	0.66
11 Energy to produce chlorine with 50% caustic (Table 10-5 data) . .	44.35	41.44	41.35	41.23
12 (10) + (11): Energy to produce actual chlorine-caustic soda mix	46.50	42.40	42.12	41.89

*Solutions other than 68-74% are assumed all 50%.

Sources: Lines 1 and 2: 1,350 BTU/lb. of steam times steam interpolated in Table 10.5 times relative fuel consumption of about 1:1.3:2 from an industry source and from J. P. Kapur, "Evaporation of Liquid from Diaphragm Cells" and N. S. S. Rajan, "Caustic Fusion and Packaging," *Chemical Age of India*, November-December 1961, pp. 485-486 and 488-492. Lines 3, 4 and 9: 1954 and 1958–U.S. Bureau of the Census, *Census of Manufactures, 1958*, Volume II, part 1, table 6-A; 1962: *Annual Survey of Manufactures*, 1962, p. 395; 1967 and 1972: *Current Industrial Reports, Inorganic Chemicals*.

to dryness. This fraction in 1954-67 fell from a third to an eighth (Table 10-6). The dry form is used to save freight, or where water would be an inconvenience, as in glass manufacture. It was formerly baked in pots over an open flame, but now superheated steam or molten salt is used for drying. The extra energy required fell from 4½% to 2¼% of the total in 1954-71.

SECTION IV. TECHNOLOGY AND ENERGY PER TON IN SODA ASH MANUFACTURE

Manufactured soda ash is nearly all made by the ammonia-soda (Solvay) process. It is called "manufactured" to distinguish it from natural soda ash made from sodium sesquicarbonate (trona) and other deposits in Wyoming and California, which is classified by the Census in mining.

Like chlorine-caustic soda plants, Solvay plants are located near brine wells or salt deposits. Calcium, magnesium, and iron salts are separated in settling tanks and the brine is saturated first with ammonia and then with carbon dioxide obtained by calcining limestone with coke (Fig. 10-2). Crude sodium bicarbonate precipitates out. The crystals are filtered and baked to the carbonate, recovering the carbon dioxide for recycling along with that from the limestone. The filtrate, containing ammonium chloride, is heated with the lime that was obtained when the limestone was calcined. Ammonia gas is recovered, leaving calcium chloride. Some calcium chloride can be sold for melting snow, for "brine" for commercial refrigerators, etc. The rest of it, along with perhaps a third of the sodium chloride that came in the brine, has to be dumped into rivers—about 1½ tons of waste to a ton of soda ash.

A recent process improvement is that superheated steam is substituted for direct heat in baking the bicarbonate, saving 10% to 15% of the heat formerly used for this and 2% to 3% of overall energy.

The fuel for the limestone seems to have always been metallurgical coke, since the fuel must actually be mixed with the limestone. Coal was formerly used for the other operations, but now has been partly replaced by oil and gas. Practically all electricity is generated in the plant.

Table 10-7 shows the continuous decline since 1868 in the energy needed to make a ton of soda ash. Great latitude exists in classifying the data. For 1942, the figure used here of 13.0 million BTUs per ton, derived from Hou's figure for "good conditions," could plausibly be changed to 19.5 million, the bottom of the "average conditions" range. The data chosen for the table do have the virtue, though, of lying on a curve and flattening off about now. The forecasts must flatten off because it is hard to secure additional fuel economy without new plants, and none are expected.

The lack of new plants is for two reasons. First, natural soda ash has already displaced the ammonia-soda process product over two-fifths of the U.S. markets and the rate of displacement is slowing only slightly. Reserves of

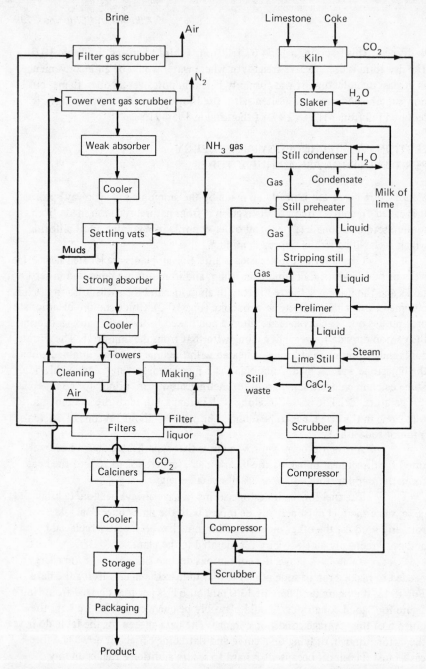

Figure 10–2. Flow Diagram for Ammonia-Soda (Solvay) Process for Making Soda Ash. Source: Kirk-Othmer Encyclopedia of Chemical Technology, 2nd ed., Vol. 1 (1963), p. 718 (courtesy of Science and Technology Research Center, The New York Public Library, Astor, Lenox, and Tilden Foundations). Updated by putting settling vats ahead of strong absorber.

Table 10-7.   Energy Used to Manufacture a Ton of Soda Ash by the Ammonia-Soda Process (Good Practice for Existing Plants), 1868-1980

| | Weight (short tons) | | Heat Content (million BTUs) | | |
	Coke	Coal	Coke	Coal	Sum
	(1)	(2)	(3)	(4)	(5)
1980					12.2
1975					12.2
1967	0.102	0.375	2.6	9.7	12.3
1942	.095	.41	2.5	10.5	13.0
1925	.065	.50	1.7	12.9	14.6
1911	.20	.75	5.2	19.3	24.5
1894	.14	.90	3.6	23.2	26.8
1868	.72	1.28	18.7	33.1	51.8

Notes: Electricity is generated in the plant. Table excludes estimate in *Kirk-Othmer Encyclopedia of Chemical Technology*, Vol. I (1963), article "Alkali and Chlorine Industries (Sodium Carbonate)," p. 729, of 145 lb. coke and 5.5 million BTUs of other fuels per ton of soda ash for an efficient, fully loaded plant, because they seem too low compared with the level of the other estimates, suggesting that they are for "best practice" in a new plant rather than "good practice" for existing plant. It is hard to tell in the sources whether any particular figure represents average, good, or best practice and is for existing or new plant; hence this table is only roughly valid.

Sources: *Cols. 1 and 2.*
    1868 and 1925: J. R. Partington, *The Alkali Industry* (2nd ed.; London, Bailliere, 1925), pp. 127-128.
    1894 and 1911: Georg Lunge, *Manufacture of Sulfuric Acid and Alkali*, 3rd ed., Vol. III (New York: Van Nostrand, 1911), pp. 182, 184.
    1942: Te-Pang Hou, *Manufacture of Soda* (2nd ed.; New York: Reinhold, 1942), p. 444 (took "good conditions" figure).
    1967: R. N. Shreve, *The Chemical Process Industries* (third ed.; New York: McGraw-Hill, 1967), p. 227, averaging the ranges given.
    Cols. 3 and 4.
    Fuel conversion factors assumed same as in 1967: 26.0 million BTUs per ton for coke, 25.8 for coal—see Chapter One, Appendix 3.

trona are estimated as 200 million tons of contained sodium, which is over 60 years' supply at the present rate of consumption.[16] Second is pollution. Mathieson closed its Saltville, Virginia plant in 1971 because meeting state standards would have been too expensive. General Technology, a contractor for the Environmental Protection Agency, has recommended that the Federal Government close all ammonia-soda plants.[17]

    Researchers at the University of California at Berkeley propose substituting magnesia (MgO) for lime in the ammonia-recovery process. One ends up with magnesium chloride, which can be evaporated to regenerate the magnesia. The hydrochloric acid driven off can be oxidized to chlorine and water by the Kel-Chlor process (see Section II), dispensing with any dumping of wastes.[18] Apparently this way out is considered too costly at present.

The forecasts assume continuation of past trends and so do not take account of the rise in energy prices that followed the Arab oil embargo.

Notes

[1] *New York Times,* February 15, 1974, p. 1; February 20, 1974, p. 23; and February 22, 1974, p. 35.

[2] "Big Boom in Vinyl Gets Chlorine on the Move Today," *Chemical Week,* June 28, 1972, p. 37.

[3] "Chlorine: A Battle To Meet Fast-growing Demand," *Chemical Week,* February 28, 1973, p. 27.

[4] H. B. Hass, article "Chlorine," *Kirk-Othmer Encyclopedia of Chemical Technology,* 2nd edition, Supplement (1971); p. 169.

[5] J. A. Kent, editor, *Riegel's Industrial Chemistry* (New York: Reinhold, 1962), p. 897.

[6] Hass, *loc. cit.*

[7] From an industry source. 1967 *Census,* Vol. II, Part 2, Table 7-A, gives about 60% in 1967.

[8] U.S. Census Bureau, *Current Industrial Reports: Inorganic Chemicals.*

[9] C. P. Van Dijk and W. C. Schreiner, "Hydrogen Chloride and Chlorine via the Kel-Chlor Process," *Chemical Engineering Progress,* April 1973, pp. 57-61.

[10] If all the 9.4 million tons of chlorine produced in 1971 were electrolytic, which is nearly true, one thirty-fifth of this, or 270,000 tons of hydrogen, could have been produced with it (this being the ratio of relative densities). But in all the U.S. in that year only 56.000 tons were produced (excluding amounts vented or burnt as fuel, but including amounts produced for consumption in the same plant otherwise than for fuel).

In 1960 less than 10% of industrial consumption of hydrogen came from the alkalies and chlorine industry. Z. G. Deutsch and others, "Alkali and Chlorine (Chlorine)," *Kirk-Othmer Encyclopedia of Chemical Technology,* second ed. revd., I (1963), p. 677. If this percentage held also in 1971, it would mean that less than 6,000 out of the 270,000 tons of hydrogen emerging as cell gas in 1971 were consumed otherwise than as fuel where produced. (The burned hydrogen is not counted in fuel here, however, because the energy to make it has already been counted in electricity.)

[11] "Chementator" column, *Chemical Engineering,* February 5, 1973, p. 27.

[12] "Plant Effluent Guidelines Get Rush Job," *Chemical Week,* August 15, 1973, pp. 33-34.

[13] "Japan's Fishermen Force Chlorine Makers To Switch," *Chemical Week,* August 1, 1973, pp. 31-32.

[14] "More Life for Diaphragm Cells," *Chemical Week,* May 14, 1973, p. 32 and R. E. Feathers and J. E. Wyche, III, "Caustic Purification," *Chemical Engineering,* May 14, 1973, pp. 122-123.

[15] Calculated from Fumio Hine, "Economic Studies on the Amalgam-Type Chlorine Cell," *Electrochemical Technology*, Jan.-Feb. 1968, pp. 69-73, combining equations (4) and (15) to get the relation i (current) moves inversely with the 1.74th root of c (price of electricity). The relations are assumed to be roughly applicable to diaphragm cells. The article gives diaphragm cell references from which a more applicable figure could be calculated.

[16] R. T. MacMillan, article "Sodium," in U.S. Bureau of Mines, *Mineral Facts and Problems, 1970* (Bulletin No. 650; Washington: U.S. Government Printing Office, 1970), p. 201.

[17] L. C. Fuhrmeister and A. T. Emery, "Report of the Electrochemical Industries for the Year 1971," *Journal of the Electrochemical Society*, January 1973, pp. 7ff. "Plant Effluent Guidelines Get Rush Job," *Chemical Week*, August 15, 1973, pp. 33-34.

[18] *Chemical Week*, October 18, 1972, p. 47 and December 6, 1972, p. 41.

Chapter Eleven

Industrial Gases—SIC 2813

Leonard Nakamura

SECTION I. INTRODUCTION AND SUMMARY OF FINDINGS

According to the U.S. Bureau of the Census Standard Industrial Classification, Industrial Gases (SIC 2813) is defined as follows:

> Establishments primarily engaged in manufacturing gases for sale in compressed, liquid and solid forms. Establishments primarily engaged in manufacturing fluorine, ammonia, and sulfur dioxide are classified in Industry 2819; and chlorine in Industry 2812.

In addition to the above-mentioned exclusions from this category, important quantities of acetylene (acetylene made from hydrocarbons), carbon dioxide (produced and consumed in plants making soda ash and urea), hydrogen (produced and consumed for synthetic ammonia, methanol, and in oil refining) and nitrogen (produced and consumed for synthetic ammonia) are excluded; they are conceptually included in the industries in which they are intermediate products.

The Industrial Gases

The major gases included in SIC 2813 are the compound gases, acetylene (C_2H_2) and carbon dioxide (CO_2), and the elemental gases, argon (A), helium (He), hydrogen (H), nitrogen (N_2), and oxygen (O_2). Of these, acetylene, carbon dioxide, nitrogen, and oxygen have over the period studied accounted for over 80% of shipped value of output. (Important quantities of acetylene, carbon dioxide, hydrogen, and nitrogen are omitted from this industry because they are produced as intermediate products in the manufacture of various other chemicals or in petroleum refining.)

205

Historical Demand and Energy Utilization

Over the last twenty years, the industrial gases industry has grown very rapidly. Between 1947 and 1967, the industry's shipments rose from $93 million to $589 million, a six-fold increase (computed on a 1967 constant dollar basis by linking the *Census of Manufactures* indexes of production to 1967 value of shipments).

For making intraindustry comparison between products, it was necessary to create a second index. This measure weights physical volume by their 1967 prices. This second measure omits some products included in the indexes of production, and so the totals disagree somewhat.

Within the industry, this rapid increase in value shipped has been accompanied by a marked shift in industry composition. In 1954, the compound gases, acetylene and carbon dioxide, accounted for some 55% of total value shipped at current prices. Oxygen and nitrogen accounted for 32%. In 1971, acetylene and carbon dioxide accounted for only 22% of total value shipped, and oxygen and nitrogen for 59%.

This shift becomes even greater if we price physical shipments at 1967 prices, since prices of both oxygen and nitrogen dropped sharply during the period. On this basis, acetylene and carbon dioxide accounted for 68% of the industry in 1954, with oxygen and nitrogen just 17%. In 1971, acetylene and carbon dioxide accounted for 20% of total value shipped, and nitrogen and oxygen for 62%.

Energy utilization for power and heat by the industrial gases industry rose rapidly from 1947 to 1967 although not as rapidly as shipped value. Energy use per unit of output declined from 1947 to 1958, rising there-

Table 11-1.   Shipments at 1967 Prices
($ millions)

Basis	1947	1954	1958	1962	1967	1971
Industrial production index	93	136	202	354	589	684*
Physical volume		130	180	304	568	672

*Estimated
Sources: Bureau of the Census, *Census of Manufactures* and *Current Industrial Reports* M28c.

Table 11-2.   Energy Utilization, 1947-1967
(trillion BTUs)

Basis	1947	1954	1958	1962	1967
Useful energy[1]	11.8	14.8	14.4	31.7	64.7
Gross energy consumed[1]	19.4	27.4	27.4	56.7	112.3

[1] See Chapter One, pages 14-15, for definitions of useful and gross energy.
Source: Bureau of the Census, *Census of Manufactures*.

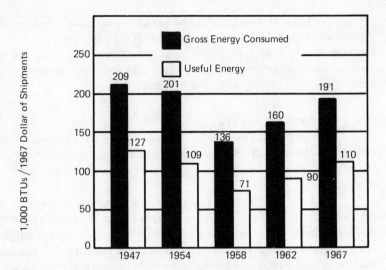

Chart 11-1. Energy Utilization per Unit Shipped: 1947–1967.

after to about the 1954 level. The rise in the latter part of the period, from 1958 to 1967, is 50% in nine years. This rise was caused by the change in product mix.

Projections

The Industrial Gases industry is expected to continue to grow quite rapidly through the 1970s at an accelerated rate of 13.2% from 1971 to 1975, and at a slower 6.9% rate from 1975 to 1980. The growth rate for the entire period is 9.7%. These figures are based on the Interindustry Forecasting Model of the University of Maryland, a highly flexible input-output model of the U.S. economy, using Conference Board estimates of Gross National Product.

A second projection was based on estimates for individual chemicals, using trends from 1966 to 1971. This does not incorporate the full effects of a return to full employment, particularly in the period 1971 to 1975. The total is shown because the product-by-product estimates were used to obtain a crude picture of product mix changes for the 1970s.

Table 11-3. Projected Shipments to 1980
(millions, 1967 constant $)

Basis	1971	1975	1980
INFORUM			
Shipments	$684	$1,125	$1,568
Index (1967 = 100)	116	191	266
Product by product			
Shipments	697	929	1,280
Index (1967 = 100)	118	158	217

Although energy utilization per unit of output has been increasing in the Industrial Gases industry since 1958, we do not expect this trend to continue. Although we expect energy utilization to continue to rise, we believe it will rise less rapidly than the industry as a whole, and that as a consequence energy utilization per unit of output will drop.

Summary Analysis

The period 1947 to 1967 was one of very rapid growth for the Industrial Gases industry. As would be expected, energy utilization also rose very rapidly, although not quite so rapidly overall as output measured in shipments.

From 1947 to 1958 energy consumption per unit of output declined, but rose between 1958 and 1967. Our analysis of this pattern of energy utilization is as follows: On a gas-by-gas basis, energy demand per unit of output has fallen throughout the period. However, since 1958, growth within the industry has favored high energy-using gases, particularly oxygen and nitrogen, and it is this shift in the product mix that has driven up energy demand per unit of output.

Although the low energy-using gases, acetylene and carbon dioxide, will continue to decline as a per cent of the industry's output, their share of the industry is now small enough so that shift in product mix will no longer play a major role in determining the level of energy utilization. Our projection, therefore, is that future energy utilization will reflect the underlying trend of increased efficiency of energy use, and that energy utilization per unit of output will decline.

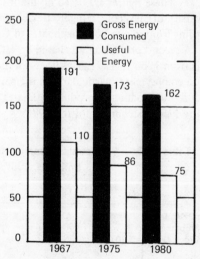

Chart 11-2. Energy Utilization per Unit Shipped, Projections to 1980.

Table 11-4. Energy Utilization to 1980

	1967	1975	1980
Useful energy			
Trillion BTUs	64.7	96.8	117.6
Index (1967 = 100)	100.0	149.6	181.8
Gross energy consumed			
Trillion BTUs	112.3	194.6	254.0
Index (1967 = 100)	100.0	173.3	226.18
INFORUM shipments projection			
Million 1967 $	$589	$1,125	$1,568
Index (1967 = 100)	100.0	191.0	266.2

SECTION II. TRENDS IN ENERGY UTILIZATION: 1954-1971

Change in Product Mix

Within any growing industry, there will be variations in the growth rates of various products, which will alter the industry's product composition. During the period 1954 to 1971 this was particularly true of the Industrial Gases industry, where the elemental gases (measured in terms of physical volume at 1967 prices) grew far more rapidly than the compound gases, as the entire industry rose at an average annual rate of over 10%.

The compound gases, acetylene and carbon dioxide, which had dominated the industry in 1954, grew at an annual rate of 2.6%, and fell to an industry share of just 20%.

The elemental gases as a group rose at a rate of 16.3% per year, and their share of the industry rose from 32% in 1954 to 80% in 1971. The largest part of this group were the joint products of the air separation process, oxygen, nitrogen, and argon.

Trends in Energy Utilization: Quantitative Analysis

The compound gases, acetylene and carbon dioxide, use much less energy in production than do the elemental gases. On a gross consumption of energy basis,[1] it is estimated that the production of the compound gases required as little as 3% of total industry energy use in 1954, and less than 1% in 1971.

Thus, the change in product mix in the Industrial Gases away from compound gases towards elemental gases was a shift from very low-energy-using products towards relatively high-energy-using products.

Since there has been a large increase in the proportion of high-energy-using gases, it is surprising that there has not been a large increase in overall energy utilization per unit of output. It is thus hypothesized that very large

Table 11-5.   Average Annual Growth Rates of Shipments,
1954-1971

(physical units)

Industrial gases (product shipment basis)	10.1%
Compound gases ....,.........................	2.6
Acetylene	2.4
Carbon dioxide	3.0
Elemental gases	16.3
Argon	18.3
Helium.......................................	20.4
Hydrogen.....................................	3.8
Nitrogen	28.8
Oxygen	16.1

Source: Appendix Tables 11A-1 and 11A-2.

increases in efficiency of energy utilization were realized in the Industrial Gases
industry on a product-by-product basis. In order to test the plausibility of this
hypothesis, estimates of energy use by product[2] were made, and these estimates
were multiplied by physical production by product to obtain total energy
requirement trends, assuming no increase in efficiency.

These estimates are based primarily on engineering data on a best-
practice-as-of-1958 basis, rather than on plant data. As such they involve considerable understatement and these results should be regarded as highly tentative.

Had there been no increase in efficiency of energy utilization, the
increase in energy utilization per unit of output would have been over 50%. The
actual slight decline in energy utilization per unit of output over the period
corresponds to a decrease in energy utilization due to increased efficiency of
3.5% per year.

Table 11-6.   Shipments at 1967 Prices—Compound and Elemental
Gases, Group Totals

(million 1967 $)

	1954	1958	1962	1967	1971
Total	$130	$180	$304	$568	$672
Compound gases	89	112	132	134	138
Share of total	68%	62%	43%	23%	20%
Elemental gases	41	68	172	434	534
Share of total	32%	38%	57%	77%	80%
Oxygen, nitrogen, argon	24	43	140	334	455
Share of total	18%	24%	46%	59%	· 68%

Source: Appendix Table 11A-2.

Chart 11-3 compares the trend of our theoretical model of energy utilization (assuming 3.5% as the annual decrease in energy use per product) with the actual energy utilization, both on a per unit of output basis.

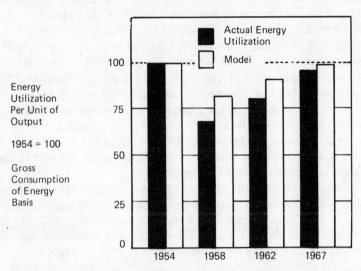

Chart 11-3. Comparative Model of Energy Utilization.

The estimates presented in Chart 11-3 show a decrease in the period 1954 to 1958, which is less sharp than the one which actually occurred. It seems reasonable to speculate on this basis that increases in efficiency were greater during that period (1954-1958). Since the estimates of energy utilization by product are based on engineering estimates rather than on actual production data, it would be wise to limit such speculation.

Trends in Demand for Industrial Gases

As we have seen, output of the industrial gases industry as a whole has risen very rapidly. Most broadly speaking, this rise in output has had two sources of demand driving it: the Federal Government's space program, and the steel industry's switch toward the basic oxygen steelmaking process.

The space program (and related missile development) created huge direct demands for hydrogen, oxygen, and helium. Liquid oxygen is the main oxidant for missile fuels; hydrogen is a major fuel, liquid hydrogen having the greatest energy per pound of non-nuclear fuels. Helium is required to maintain the pressure in fuel tanks during and after the rapid exodus of liquid hydrogen, helium being the only substance that will remain gaseous at that temperature (around $-400°$ F). Demand for these uses has decreased in recent years.

An extraordinary rise in helium shipments occurred between 1962 and 1967, resulting from the implementation of the Bureau of Mines helium conservation program.

The steel industry's demand for oxygen, however, has perhaps been the major factor. Between 1961 and 1969, steel production using the basic oxygen steelmaking process rose from 4 million to 60 million tons. At the end of that period, steel accounted for 60% of total demand for oxygen. As a direct result of this demand, gaseous oxygen shipped by pipeline (as opposed to liquid and gaseous oxygen shipped by truck or in pressurized containers) became the primary mode of delivery, resulting in dramatic price declines (from $3 per 1,000 cubic feet to less than $.60 per thousand cubic feet, average prices).

The rise in oxygen production and concomitant technological advances have helped lower the prices of nitrogen and argon. These price reductions have spurred development of their use in a variety of industries. In particular, liquid nitrogen has found wide use as a refrigerant and inert atmosphere for frozen and chilled fruits and vegetables.

The acetylene in SIC 2813 is used primarily for welding metals, and since 1967 demand has fallen as other welding processes began replacing it.

Carbon dioxide, which is used in carbonating soft drinks and as a refrigerant, has about kept pace with the soft drink industry. Compressed liquid CO_2 has replaced dry ice as the major form of shipment and use.

Trends in Industrial Gas Production Processes

A perusal of the literature on the industrial gases indicates a very broad range of advances in technology, including improvements in heat transfer, distillers, compressors, chemical and metallic absorbers, screens, piping materials, control apparatus, valves, and reaction catalysts.

One of the few major prospective changes in overall processes is the increasing popularity of the partial oxidation process of hydrogen production over the steam reforming of natural gas process. This process decreases fuel requirements because the oxidation of the feedstock creates heat. Fuel requirements decrease from 210 BTUs per cubic foot to 35 BTUs per cubic foot.[3]

An "early 1960's" Bureau of Mines study (Katell and Faber), cited in a 1967 article[4] on oxygen production, found power requirements for oxygen (separation of air) of 1.9 kwh per 100 cubic feet of high purity oxygen. Earlier that same year, a state of the art article on "Distillation of Air"[5] reported actual power requirements at about 1.2 kwh per 100 cubic feet of high purity oxygen for a new plant using latest screens and distillation techniques. If it is assumed that the Bureau of Mines study reflects best practice for 1958, this is a decrease in power requirements of 37% in nine years (this is a faster rate than the hypothesized 3.5% annual decrease).

Since nitrogen and argon are produced with the same process they have presumptively increased in efficiency to the same degree. Moreover, if the increase in their production (relative to oxygen production) has meant that a greater proportion of separation plants produce joint products (both nitrogen and oxygen, for instance, instead of just oxygen), these efficiencies would multiply. Unfortunately, statistics that would permit analysis of this question are not available.

Liquefaction of gases has benefited from the increase in understanding of physical properties at low temperatures that has come about as the result of governmental support of research in this area. The expander cycle of liquid hydrogen production requires 5 kwh per pound, as compared to simple and complex Joule-Thompson cycle requirements of 16 and 14 kwh per pound, respectively.

SECTION III. PROJECTIONS TO 1980

Demand for Industrial Gases

The projection of demand at any time is a very difficult task. This is particularly true of the industrial gases industry, because of two factors. One is the influence of Federal Government demand. Congressional decisions on specific programs can completely change the trend of output and have done so in this industry.

The other is that particularly nitrogen and oxygen have benefited from industrial changeovers of production technique; oxygen, in the steel industry switch from open-hearth to the basic oxygen process; nitrogen, in a switch from mechanical refrigeration to liquid nitrogen refrigeration in food industries.

During a change in technique, the new materials of choice grow much more rapidly than the industry using the materials as a whole, until the switch is completed. Once the switch is completed, demand grows only as rapidly as the industry itself does.

The projections of production (based on shipments at 1967 prices) shown in Table 11-7 are extrapolations of trends in physical shipments from 1966 to 1971, with the following exceptions:

Hydrogen production has been particularly affected by decreases in government demand. As it seems most of the damage has been done, it is assumed that hydrogen production will stabilize.

Table 11-7.   Projected Growth Rates to 1980, Individual Gases (shipments in physical units)

	Growth Rate per Year
Carbon dioxide	4%
Acetylene	−4
Oxygen	8
Nitrogen	14 through 1975; 8 thereafter
Argon	12
Helium	0
Hydrogen	0

Oxygen demand in 1971 was particularly affected by a slowdown in steel production. Because production has since rebounded, and new uses of oxygen appear imminent in pollution control and metallurgy, the trend from 1966 to 1970 was used.

Nitrogen cannot grow forever. Although new uses for nitrogen continue to develop (for instance, joint use with oxygen in stainless steel production), it was arbitrarily assumed that nitrogen after 1975 would slow to the oxygen rate of increase.[6]

Demand for Energy

The projections of demand for energy by the Industrial Gases is presented in Table 11-4, and the energy utilization rates per unit of output on Chart 11-2.

These were based on the assumption that additional production would utilize state of the art 1967 energy utilization rates, based on engineering data. Engineering data tend to understate actual production requirements. However, since no allowance has been made for new plant construction replacing outmoded units, the overall totals may not be biased.

No allowance was made for old plant replacement, because some of the industries, notably helium and acetylene, are suffering from over-capacity. Also, air separation plants are quite new and will not display a great deal of retirement over the coming decade.

One possible source of major error is a large switchover in the hydrogen industry to different techniques, particularly if a hydrocarbon shortage of major proportions occurs. There are many possible techniques for making hydrogen.

Some of the products of this industry are sources of energy for other industries. These include acetylene used in welding, liquid nitrogen and solid carbon dioxide used as refrigerants, and hydrogen used as a rocket fuel. A more consistent accounting system would allocate the energy consumption due to these uses to the purchasing industry rather than to the Industrial Gases. Unfortunately, there was insufficient data to permit such a breakdown in this report.

Table 11-8.   Projected Shipments to 1980
(million 1967 $)

	1971	1975	1980
Total	$672	$896	$1,235
Acetylene	82	70	57
Carbon dioxide	56	66	80
Argon	40	63	111
Helium	54	54	54
Hydrogen	25	25	25
Nitrogen	161	272	400
Oxygen	254	346	508

Notes

[1] These are based on energy coefficients discussed below. See Appendix Table 11A-4 for actual coefficients assumed.

[2] Large quantities of oxygen, nitrogen, and argon are produced in liquid form. Since liquefaction requires additional power input, these gases were further subdivided into gaseous and liquid shipments.

[3] A problem which has been omitted from this study is the use of feedstocks. The steam reforming of natural gas requires some 240 BTUs per cubic foot of hydrogen produced in natural gas feedstocks not counted as fuel. The partial oxidation of process requires some 350 BTUs per cubic foot of hydrogen produced, if fuel oil is used as the feedstock. *Hydrocarbon Processing and Petroleum Refiner,* "What Hydrogen Costs," September 1961, Vol. 40, No. 9, p. 165.

[4] *33, The Magazine of Metal Producing.* "Oxygen, Steelmaking's Nourishing Gas," Vol. 5, No. 10, October 1967, pp. 71-94.

[5] R. E. Latimer. "Distillation of Air," *Chemical Engineering Progress,* Vol. 63, No. 2, February 1967, pp. 35-58.

[6] Data received too late for incorporation indicate that nitrogen and hydrogen may in fact grow more rapidly than the rates assumed. This should not materially affect energy-output projections.

SECTION IV. APPENDIX

Table 11A-1. Physical Shipments and Growth by Product

	1971	1967	1962	1958	1954
Acetylene (M)*	7,684 (149.8)	8,176 (159.4)	8,528 (166.3)	7,157 (139.5)	5,129 (100.0)
Carbon dioxide (T)*	1,147 (166.5)	971 (140.9)	846 (122.8)	741 (107.5)	689 (100.0)
Argon (M)	2,986 (1,736.1)	1,910 (1,110.5)	821 (477.3)	379 (220.4)	172 (100.0)
Helium (M)	4,459** (2,346.9)	4,667** (2,456.3)	677** (356.3)	352 (185.3)	190 (100.0)
Hydrogen (M)	17,460 (188.7)	27,666 (298.9)	12,578 (135.9)	11,939 (129.0)	9,255 (100.0)
Nitrogen (M)	148,453 (7,389.4)	91,941 (4,576.5)	34,950 (1,739.7)	5,478 (272.7)	2,009 (100.0)
Oxygen (M)	268,845 (1,260.0)	220,802 (1,034.8)	96,411 (451.8)	33,495 (157.0)	21,337 (100.0)

*M = million cu. ft.; T = 1,000 short tons.

**Includes amounts added to conservation stockpile.

Figures in parentheses are index numbers; 1954 = 100.

Sources: Bureau of the Census, *Census of Manufactures, 1954, 1958, 1963, 1967;* Bureau of the Census, *Current Industrial Reports, M28c,* 1962, 1967, 1969, 1971, 1972.

Table 11A-2. Physical Shipments at 1967 Prices
(million $)

	1971	1967	1962	1958	1954
Total	$672 (100)	$568 (100)	$304 (100)	$180 (100)	$130 (100)
Acetylene	82 (12)	87 (15)	91 (30)	76 (42)	55 (42)
Carbon dioxide	56 (8)	47 (8)	41 (13)	36 (20)	34 (26)
Argon	40 (6)	25 (4)	11 (4)	5 (3)	2 (2)
Helium*	54 (8)	61 (11)	14 (5)	8 (4)	4 (3)
Hydrogen	25 (4)	39 (7)	18 (6)	17 (9)	13 (10)
Nitrogen	161 (24)	100 (18)	38 (13)	6 (3)	2 (2)
Oxygen	254 (38)	209 (37)	91 (30)	32 (18)	20 (15)

Figures in parentheses represent per cent of total.
*Includes amounts added to storage at $11 per 1,000 cu. ft.; conservation program began 1961.

Table 11A-3. Value Shipped
(million $)

	1971*	1967*	1962*	1958	1954
Total	$617 (100.0)	$572 (100.0)	$358 (100.0)	$263 (100.0)	$195 (100.0)
Acetylene	98 (15.9)	87 (15.2)	93 (26.0)	89 (33.8)	65 (33.3)
Carbon dioxide	38 (6.2)	47 (8.2)	49 (13.7)	43 (16.3)	43 (22.1)
Argon	29 (4.7)	25 (4.4)	19 (5.3)	13 (4.9)	6 (3.1)
Hydrogen	34 (5.5)	39 (6.8)	16 (4.5)	9 (3.4)	6 (3.1)
Nitrogen	135 (21.9)	100 (17.5)	38 (10.6)	17 (6.5)	7 (3.6)
Oxygen	231 (37.4)	209 (36.5)	125 (34.9)	80 (30.4)	56 (28.7)
Residual, incl. helium .	52 (8.4)	64 (11.2)	18 (5.0)	12 (4.6)	12 (6.2)

Figures in parentheses represent per cent of total.
*Data based on CIR M28c.
Source: Bureau of the Census, *Census of Manufactures*, 1967, 1953, 1958.

Table 11A-4   Parameters of Energy Use—Best Practice as of 1958

Oxygen[1] —separation of air—19 kwh per 1,000 cubic feet
Nitrogen[1] —separation of air—10 kwh per 1,000 cubic feet
Argon[1] —separation of air —19 kwh per 1,000 cubic feet
Liquid oxygen[2] —.39 kwh per lb.
Liquid nitrogen[2] —.50 kwh per lb.
Liquid argon[2] —.39 kwh per lb.
Helium—17.0 kwh and 3,830 thousand BTUs per 1,000 cubic feet
Oxygen and hydrogen—electrolysis of water—140 kwh per 1,000 cubic feet of hydrogen
    and 500   cubic feet of oxygen
Hydrogen—steam reforming of natural gas—210,000 BTUs per 1,000 cubic feet (not counting
    240,000 BTUs per 1,000 cubic feet in natural gas feedstock)
Acetylene—1 kwh per 1,000 cubic feet
Carbon dioxide—40 kwh per short ton

[1] As mentioned in the text, oxygen, nitrogen, and argon are joint products, and to assign individual costs in terms of energy use is very difficult, particularly since a given plant may produce any one or more of three products. As such, these are conservative figures (actual costs or lower).
[2] All these figures exceed current practice and, therefore, probably resemble more closely 1958 average practice. On this basis, the datum for liquid argon is probably too low. We would like to express our appreciation to Maxwell Hill and J. W. Hall of Union Carbide for their comments on this matter.

SECTION V.   SELECTED BIBLIOGRAPHY

American Society of Heating, Refrigerating and Air Conditioning Engineers. *ASHRAE 1971 Guide and Data Book.*

Bureau of Domestic Commerce, *U. S. Industrial Outlook 1972.*

Bureau of Mines, *Mineral Facts and Problems,* 1970 Ed.

Compressed Gas Association. *Handbook of Compressed Gases.* New York: Reinhold Publishing Corporation, 1966.

Hardie, D. W. F. *Acetylene: Manufacture and Uses.* Oxford, 1965.

Kent, James A., Ed. *Reigel's Industrial Chemistry.* New York: Reinhold Publishing Corporation, 1962.

Kirk-Othmer. *Encyclopedia of Chemical Technology,* 2nd Edition. New York: Wiley-Interscience, 1972.

Kline, C. H. & Co. *Marketing Guide to the Chemical Industry,* Kline, 1971.

Sittig, Marshall. *Nitrogen in Industry.* Van Nostrand, 1965.

Vance, R. W., Ed. *Cryogenic Technology.* Wiley, 1963.

Serials:
Cryogenic Technology
Cryogenics and Industrial Gases
Proceedings of the Annual Meeting, Compressed Gas Association
33, The Magazine of Metal Producing

Chapter Twelve

Cyclic Intermediates and Crudes—SIC 2815

Anthony D. Apostolides

SECTION I. SUMMARY OF FINDINGS

According to the Standard Industrial Classification code, industry SIC 2815 is defined as "Establishments primarily engaged in manufacturing cyclic organic intermediates, dyes, color lakes and toners, and coal tar crudes." By far the dominant class in this industry, however, is the cyclic intermediates. In 1968, for example, cyclic intermediates accounted for over 90% of total production of SIC 2815. The cyclic intermediates group encompasses many products. The most important ones, however, have been ethylbenzene, styrene, cyclohexane, and phenol; chlorobenzene, cumene, dodecylbenzene, and phthalic anhydride have also been important.

      The cyclic intermediates group includes many products which can be made by a variety of chemical processes that have been changing over time. These changes in production techniques have contributed to the lowering of the industry's energy-output ratio. Decreases in energy utilization per unit of output can be attributed to changes in technology in the industry rather than to changes in the product mix. The energy-output ratios of this industry in the past and those predicted for the future are presented in Table 12-1.

Table 12-1.   Energy-Output Ratio, 1954-1980
(1,000 BTUs per 1967 $ of shipments)

	1954	1958	1962	1967	1975	1980
Gross energy[1]	132	133	98	94	74	62
Useful energy[1]	122	124	88	82	65	54

[1] See Chapter One, pages 14-15, for definitions of gross and useful energy.
Sources: Table 12-2 and Table 12-4.

219

The industry has experienced relatively high growth of output. This growth was significantly influenced by the input of cyclic intermediates in the production of plastics and fibers, both of which have experienced high rates of output expansion.

Output of SIC 2815 is projected to grow at 9.75% per year over 1971-80; the growth rate is to decline from 11.58% for 1971-75 to 8.30% during 1975-80. We assume a continuation of the decline in the energy-output ratio: of 3.0% over 1967-71 and 3.5% during 1975-80. The ratio decreased at an annual rate of 2.6% over 1954-67. When the projected output figures are related to the energy-output ratio, they provide an indication of energy consumption that can accompany possible output expansion in SIC 2815 (see Table 12-1).

The future growth of output in cyclic intermediates should be significantly affected by the expected high levels of output expansion in the production of plastics and man-made fibers. With respect to the energy input, considerable attention is presently being paid in industry to increase the efficiency of energy utilization. This can be done by the adoption of energy-saving techniques in plants already in operation, or by the building of such techniques in new plants. This latter policy can be the more important factor in the long run.

SECTION II.   TRENDS IN PRODUCTION AND ENERGY UTILIZATION

Production Processes

In general, the manufacture of a chemical requires one or more chemical reactions and physical operations such as mixing and separation. A chemical reaction involves:[1]

1. Preparation of raw materials.
2. Production (i.e., the actual reaction).
3. Recovery: separation of the products of the reaction, such as filtering crystals out of a liquid.
4. Purification, to meet specification of different grades.

The main chemical processes in the production of cyclic intermediates are nitration, amination by reduction, amination by ammonolysis, halogenation, sulfonation, hydrolysis, oxidation, alkylation, and condensation and addition reactions.[2]

It should be pointed out that a cyclic intermediate—or any chemical, for that matter—can be made by a number of processes using different inputs, and that these processes change over time. Thus, to present a production process for a given chemical does not mean that 100% of the chemical is produced by this process at a given period of time, or that the process has been used to the same extent over a period of years.

Most of the intermediates are produced from petrochemicals; the remainder are derived from tar distillers and coke-oven operators. In order to show how cyclic intermediates are produced, Figure 12-1 presents a diagram of a refinery with facilities for the manufacture of aromatics and derivatives.[3] Aromatics such as benzene, toluene, and ethylbenzene are the basis in the production of cyclic intermediates. Most of the raw material for the production of intermediates comes from the reforming unit. For the entire industry, relatively small amounts of raw material are obtained from ethylene plant by-products and from catalytic cracking cycle oil.

The material from the reformer is channelled into an extraction unit in which aromatics are separated from the paraffins and residual naphthalenes by dissolving in a solvent, such as aqueous diethylene glycol or sulfolane. The aromatics are then stripped of the solvent and are separated by distillation into benzene, toluene, mixed xylenes, and alkylnaphthalenes.

Benzene is used for the manufacture of cyclohexane, styrene, and phenol. Cyclohexane can be obtained from benzene by a relatively simple hydrogenation process. On the other hand, the manufacture of styrene is more complex. The manufacture of phenol can be achieved by a number of processes, though the cumene process and the toluene-based process are the only two considered to be petrochemical processes.

The dominant use of toluene is in the manufacture of benzene by hydrodealkylation. In this process, hydrogen reacts with toluene to form benzene and methane. The mixed xylenes are used as raw material in the production of ethylbenzene. Ortho-xylene and ethylbenzene can be separated by distillation; while para-xylene is separated by crystallization.

Thus, a wide range of chemical processes is used in the production of cyclic intermediates, including hydrogenation, dehydrogenation, alkylation, dealkylation, oxidation, and isomerization, along with separation steps such as crystallization and distillation.

Over time a shift has been taking place in raw materials and petroleum has become the dominant source, rather than coal, in the production of aromatics and cyclic intermediates. Thus, although most of benzene was initially produced from coal, by 1959 more benzene was being produced from petroleum. This trend continued and, by 1963, 81% of benzene production was obtained from petroleum. Production of benzene from petroleum was significantly affected by the introduction of the hydrodealkylation process.

With respect to phenol, prior to World War 1, nearly all the phenol manufactured in the United States was natural phenol derived from coke-oven operations and coal tar distillation. In 1962, less than 5% of phenol production was natural phenol; the remainder was synthetic.[4] In the manufacturing of phenol, there has been a trend toward captive plants. In 1945, 15% of phenol capacity was captive; in 1963 the figure was over 50% and the trend was expected to continue.[5]

Phthalic anhydride is another synthetic organic chemical once based

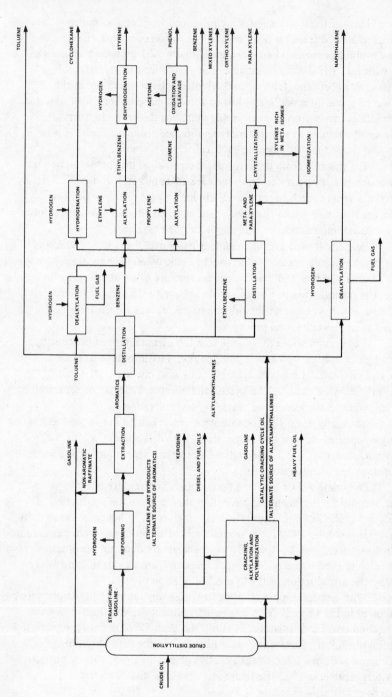

Figure 12-1. Manufacturing of Aromatics and Derivatives. Source: R.B. Stobaugh, Jr., *Petrochemical Manufacturing & Marketing Guide*, p. 204.

on the by-product coke industry, but presently largely dependent on petroleum.

Markets

Cyclic intermediates have a diverse set of market outlets (see Figure 12-2), and they are used widely in the production of plastics and fibers. Phenol is used in the production of the phenol-derived plastics of epoxies, caprolactam, and polycarbonates. Cyclohexane is an input for nylon. Phthalic anhydride is used largely for the manufacture of plasticizers, alkyd resins, and polyesters. The biggest market for styrene is the production of polystyrene, with the production of SBR (styrenebutadiene rubber) being a second important market.

Energy-Output Relationship

It can be seen in Table 12-2 that the energy-output ratio of the cyclic intermediates has been declining over the period of analysis. Energy is measured in terms of BTUs and includes inputs of coal, coke and breeze, fuel oil, gas, other fuels, fuel n.s.k., and electric energy. Output is measured by the value of shipments at 1967 constant dollars. The major energy-producing inputs for intermediates have been fuels, coal, gas, and electricity. The relative importance of coal has declined, while that of gas and electricity has been increasing. Over 1954-1967, real output of cyclic intermediates grew at an annual rate of 6.90% while the energy input grew at 4.17% a year.

The decline in the energy-output ratio over the 1954-67 period could have been affected by increased efficiency of energy utilization in products whose share in the industry increased during the period of analysis or, alternatively, by a general improvement of energy utilization in the industry with no particular importance to changes in the product mix. The latter situation appears to be applicable to cyclic intermediates. It can be seen in Table 12-3 that the relative shares of the three largest products, ethylbenzene, phenol, and styrene, did not change significantly over time. Thus, it would seem that it was general improvements in energy utilization in cyclic intermediates that affected the energy-output ratio rather than changes in the product mix.

The energy-output ratio experienced its most noticeable decline between the years 1958 and 1962. Notwithstanding shortcomings in the energy and output data, it may be pointed out that the growth rate of output over 1954-58 was 2.87%, while over 1958-62 it was 10.48%. Energy (useful) input, on the other hand, grew at an annual rate of 3.33% over 1954-58 and 1.23% over 1958-62. These figures would seem to suggest that some form of economies of scale was in operation during the 1958-62 period that could have resulted in better utilization of capacity in the industry.

Available information indicates that improvements in process technology led to reduction in energy consumption per unit of output over the period of analysis. Considering the production of cyclohexane, a major intermediate whose share in the industry total has been increasing, there are data for

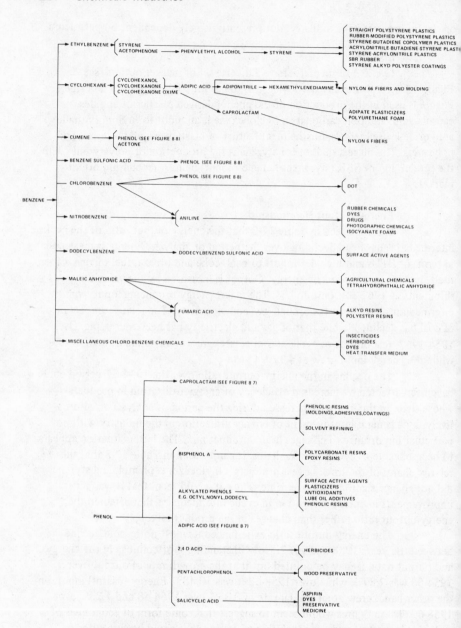

Figure 12-2. Major Markets for Benzene, Cyclohexane, Styrene, and Phenol. Source: Petrochemical Manufacturing & Marketing Guide, pp. 212, 213.

Table 12-2.   Energy Utilization and Energy-Output Ratio

	1954	*1958*	*1962*	*1967*
Gross energy (trillion BTUs)	88.3	100.4	110.1	149.8
Shipments (million 1967 $)	$670.0	$752.0	$1,119.0	$1,597.0
Energy/shipments (1,000 BTUs per 1967 $ of shipments)	131.7	133.5	98.4	93.8
Useful energy (trillion BTUs)	81.8	93.4	98.3	131.7
Energy/shipments (1,000 BTUs per 1967 $ of shipments)	122.1	124.2	87.8	82.5

Source: Appendix Table 12A-1.

Table 12-3.   Cyclic Intermediates—Percentage Distribution Total Industry Production Volume

	1947	*1954*	*1958*	*1962*	*1967*
Aniline	5%	2%	2%	1%	1%
Chlorobenzene	13	8	6	5	2
Cumene	–	1	3	3	5
Cyclohexane	–	5	5	8	8
Dodecylbenzene	–	8	7	5	–
Ethylbenzene	–	18	18	18	16
o-Xylene	–	–	–	2	2
p-Xylene	–	1	2	2	4
Phenol	10	9	8	7	6
Phthalic anhydride	5	6	4	4	3
Styrene	12	15	18	17	16
Subtotal	45	73	73	72	63
Rest of SIC 2815	55	27	27	28	37
Total	100%	100%	100%	100%	100%

Source: Output data were obtained from U.S. Tariff Commission, *Synthetic Organic Chemicals* (several years).

three points in time—1963, 1965, and 1971—for the same process from the same organization.[6] These data show that for a 100,000 metric tons/year cyclohexane unit, the electricity input in 1963 was 2,376 thousand kwh; in 1965 it was 1,500 thousand kwh; for 1971 the required electricity input was 963,000 kwh. The gas input figures for 1963 and 1965 were about the same, and there were no data given for 1971. Concerning figures for required steam input, the figure for 1963 was 56.8 million pounds; for 1965, 35.8 million pounds, for 1971, 40.3 million pounds.

In phenol production, one can also observe an increase in the efficiency of energy utilization. Figures for 1951 show that to produce one ton of phenol, there was an input of 252 kwh of electricity and 4,000 pounds of steam. By 1967, the electricity requirement was 80 kwh with the same input of steam.[7]

Finally, changes in styrene production have also contributed to the decreasing energy-output ratio of cyclic intermediates. Data for 1962 show that to make 100 pounds of styrene, the input demand was 295 pounds of steam, 7 kwh of electricity, and 875 cu. ft. of gas. In 1973, for 100 pounds of styrene, input demand was 299 pounds of steam, 9.6 kwh of electricity, and 72.5 cu. ft. of gas.[8] The savings in gas are significant. And it may be pointed out that styrene has had the second largest share in the cyclic intermediates group, and that this share has been increasing significantly over the period of analysis.

SECTION III.   PROJECTIONS TO 1980

In this section, projections are made of the energy-output ratio. These figures are subsequently related to projected output data in deriving an estimate of the drain in energy resources accompanying possible expansion of output in cyclic intermediates.

Projected output[9] data are obtained from calculations, carried out by computer, based on the INFORUM input-output model of the University of Maryland (see Table 12-4). These figures indicate growth of 9.75% per year over 1971-80; during 1971-75, growth is expected to take place at 11.58% per year, which is to decline to 8.30% over 1975-80.

In projecting the energy-output ratio, we assume an annual decrease of 3.0% over 1967-71 and 3.5% over 1975-80. Concerning its past trend, the ratio has declined over 1954-67 at an annual rate of 2.58% (2.97% when useful energy is used). The results of relating projected output to the energy-output ratio are shown in Table 12-4.

Cyclic intermediates should enjoy a good growth rate of output in the future since they are important inputs in the production of plastics and fibers. There may, on the other hand, be an adverse effect as a result of increasing prices of gas, oil, and coal, which may result in increased allocation of these energy-creating inputs to the utilities industry. This may cause price increases, in the energy input and feedstocks, that tend to reduce or, perhaps, even eliminate the production of certain plastics. However, this does not appear to be a likely possibility.

Demand for Energy

With respect to energy consumption, considerable attention is presently being paid in industry to increase efficiency in energy utilization through two basic ways: first, in adopting energy-saving techniques and devices in plants already in operation; second in building into the construction of new plants appropriate energy-conservation factors. Substantial amounts of energy

Table 12-4. Output, Energy, and Energy-Output Ratio to 1980

	1967	1975	1980
Output (million 1967 $)	$1,597	$3,380	$5,036
Gross energy (trillion BTUs)	149.8	248.4	309.8
Gross energy/output (1,000 BTUs/1967 $)	93.8	73.5	61.5
Useful energy (trillion BTUs)	131.7	218.4	272.4
Energy/output (1,000 BTUs/1967 $)	82.5	64.6	54.1

savings appear to be relatively easy to attain, and it has been stated that "Our experience, both inside and outside Du Pont, shows that a significant conservation effort on an operating industrial plant will normally yield a 7-15% reduction within a reasonably short time. Part of this reduction will require capital expenditure, but some will result simply from improved operation."[10] Furthermore, it appears important that ways of conserving energy be built into a new plant or a production process at the beginning, because changes may not be economically justifiable at later stages.

Notes

[1] M. J. Harkins, *et al.*, "The Chemical Industry", in *The Development of American Industries*, p. 316.

[2] For description of processes, see N. R. Shreve, *Chemical Process Industries*, chapter 39.

[3] The description which follows comes from Robert B. Stobaugh, Jr., *Petrochemical Manufacturing & Marketing Guide, Volume I*, chapter 8.

[4] W. L. Faith, D. B. Keyes, and R. L. Clark, *Industrial Chemicals*, p. 593.

[5] Ibid., p. 594.

[6] The data came from *Hydrocarbon Processing*, for November 1963, 1965, and 1971; the production process was that of the Institut Francais du Petrole.

[7] Data for 1951 came from *Chemical Engineering*, March (p. 314) and April (p. 315), 1951. Data for 1967 came from Shreve, *Chemical Process Industries*, p. 677.

[8] Data for 1962 were obtained from M. Sittig, *Organic Chemical Processes*, p. 97. Data for 1973 were obtained from Stanford Research Institute, *Styrene*, Process Economic Program report, 1973.

[9] These data pertain to total supply; that is, domestic production plus import, minus exports. However, this should not have significantly adverse effects on the calculations: data, for several years over 1958-68, from the

Commerce Department (*U.S. Commodity Exports and Imports as Related to Output*) show that the difference between imports and exports in relation to shipments is 5% or less.

[10] G. F. Moore, *Energy Management in The Industrial Community*, p. 2.

SECTION IV.　APPENDIX

Table 12A-1.　Shipments and Energy Consumption

	1954	1958	1962	1967
Shipments (million 1967 $)	$670.0	$752.0	$1,119.0	$1,597.0
Gross energy (trillion BTUs)	88.3	100.4	110.1	149.8
Useful energy (trillion BTUs)	81.8	93.4	98.3	131.7

Source: Bureau of the Census, *Census of Manufactures* (several years).

Table 12A-2.　Growth of Shipments and Energy Consumption (average annual percentage rates)

	Shipments (1967 $)	Gross Energy (BTUs)	Useful Energy (BTUs)
1954-67	6.90%	4.17%	3.73%
1958-67	8.71	4.53	3.89
1962-67	7.42	6.34	6.03
1954-58	2.87	3.33	3.33
1958-62	10.48	2.41	1.23

Table 12A-3.　Energy Consumption (trillion BTUs)

	1954	1958	1962	1967
Coal, coke, and breeze	45.5	49.8	28.7	28.5
Fuel oil	8.0	6.8	10.9	11.5
Gas	23.8	32.5	45.1	64.5
Other fuels	2.0	0.7	7.7	10.4
Fuels n.s.k.	0	0.7	0	8.1
Electric energy	9.0	10.1	17.4	26.9
Total	88.3	100.4	110.1	149.8

n.s.k.—not specifed by kind.
Source: Bureau of the Census, *Census of Manufactures* (several years).

SECTION V. SELECTED BIBLIOGRAPHY

Department of Commerce. Bureau of Domestic Commerce. *U.S. Industrial Outlook 1972 with Projections to 1980.* Washington, D.C., 1972.

Domestic and International Business Administration. *U.S. Industrial Outlook 1973 with Projections to 1980.* Washington, D.C. 1973.

Faith, W. L., Keyes, Donald, B.; and Clark, Ronald, L. *Industrial Chemicals.* New York: John Wiley & Sons, Inc., 1965.

Harkins, Malcolm, Jr. and Wallace, Charles E. Manufacturing Chemists Association, Inc. "The Chemical Industry" in *The Development of American Industries.* Glover, J. G. and Lagai, R. L., eds. New York: Simmons-Boardman Publishing Corporation, 1959.

Hydrocarbon Processing (serial)

Kent, James, A., ed. *Riegel's Industrial Chemistry.* New York: Reinhold Publishing Corporation, 1962.

Kirk-Othmer. *Encyclopedia of Chemical Technology,* 2nd Edition. New York: Wiley-Interscience, 1972.

Long, R. ed. *The Production of Polymer and Plastics Intermediates from Petroleum.* London: Butterworths, 1967.

Mercier, Claude. *Petrochemical Industry and the Possibility of its Establishment in the Developing Countries.* Paris: Institut Francais du Petrole, 1966.

Moore, G. Frank. *Energy Management in the Industrial Community.* A talk presented at National Energy Forum, Washington, D.C.

Encyclopedia of Polymer Science and Technology. Vol. 10, Polyamides and Polyelectrolytes, edited by Mark, H. F. et al. New York: Wiley-Interscience, 1969.

Shreve, Norris R. *Chemical Process Industries,* 3rd Edition. New York: McGraw-Hill, 1967.

Sittig, Marshall. *Organic Chemical Processes.* Pearl River, N.Y.: The Noyes Press, Inc., 1962.

Stobaugh, Robert B., Jr. *Petrochemical Manufacturing & Marketing Guide Volume I: Aromatics and Derivatives.* Houston, Texas: Gulf Publishing Company, 1966.

Tariff Commission. *Synthetic Organic Chemicals.* Washington, D.C., for several years.

U.N. *Report of the First United Nations Interregional Conference on the Development of Petrochemical Industries in Developing Countries.* New York, 1966.

_____ . *Petrochemical Industries in Developing Countries.* New York, 1970.

Serial:
Chemical Engineering Progress

Chapter Thirteen

Industrial Organic Chemicals n.e.c.—SIC 2818

Leonard Nakamura

SECTION I. INTRODUCTION AND SUMMARY OF FINDINGS

This chapter examines an industry which the Census Bureau entitles, "Industrial Organic Chemicals, not elsewhere classified" (SIC 2818). As the title suggests, it is a catch-all industry composed of several hundred chemical products. The great bulk of the industry consists of acyclic hydrocarbons (*acyclic* means that the molecules lack a ring structure characteristic of benzene, and *hydrocarbons* means that the chemicals contain hydrogen and carbon) made from derivatives of petroleum and natural gas. Because of this origin, organic chemicals are frequently called petrochemicals.

Although some of the chemicals in this industry are used as end products, most of them are further processed before final sale. Ultimate uses of petrochemicals include plastics, synthetic fibers and synthetic rubber, fertilizers, pesticides, detergents, solvents, and gasoline additives.

The appendix to this chapter contains the assumptions, methodology and results of a detailed study, prepared as the basis for this report, of 21 major petrochemicals.

Unlike most manufacturing industries but like other major chemical industries, Industrial Organic Chemicals n.e.c., SIC 2818, contains far too many chemicals and processes for individual analysis. The Census definition alone requires half a page of print, and an incomplete listing of the chemicals included requires another page and a half.

Most briefly, these chemicals consist of compounds of carbon, generally with one or more of: hydrogen, oxygen, nitrogen, sulfur, chlorine, fluorine, or lead.

231

Historical Demand and Energy Utilization

The base period for this study is 1954 to 1967. During this time the industry grew very rapidly, with shipments rising from $1,857 million to $6,378 million, a rate of 10.0% a year (computed on a 1967 constant dollar basis by linking the *Census of Manufactures Industrial Production Index* to 1967 value of shipments).

Since the basic calculations in this study on chemical production processes are conducted on a weight basis, we have included in Table 13-1 total production in millions of pounds.

As the ratio between the two shows, production measured in pounds and the shipments in constant dollars have moved more or less together, varying around $0.10 of shipments per pound of production. This fact is significant, because it enables us to use physical production in pounds as a proxy for constant dollar shipments, without too greatly straining credulity, later in this report.

The rapid rise in production for this industry has been due in large measure to long-term declining prices in an era of generally rising prices. In 1967 dollars, shipments in 1954 were valued at $1,857 million dollars, while the actual price of the shipments in 1954 was $2,199 million dollars, so that average prices have declined 15.6% between 1954 and 1967. These declining prices, achieved through rapid technological progress and economies of scale, have enabled the end products based on these chemicals to develop an excellent competitive position for a broad spectrum of consumer and industrial uses ranging from clothes, tires, and carpeting to piping, electronic equipment, and synthetic flavorings.

Energy use for heat and power has also increased rapidly, although not as rapidly as production. Energy use per unit of output has shown a consistent decline of not quite 1% per year.

Energy use for heat and power is not the only demand this industry places on total fuel resources. The basic feedstocks for this industry are petroleum and natural gas. Unfortunately, Census data on feedstock use of fuels and fuel derivatives (ethylene, propane, methane, etc.) are very incomplete.

Table 13-1.　Output, 1954 to 1967

	1954	1958	1962	1963	1967
Shipments (million 1967 $) ..	$1,857 (100.0)	$2,575 (138.7)	$4,099 (220.7)	$4,638 (249.8)	$6,378 (343.5)
Production (million lbs.)	18,293 (100.0)	28,250 (154.4)	39,392 (215.3)	43,059 (238.4)	62,385 (341.0)
Ratio (cents per lbs.)	10.2	9.1	10.4	10.8	10.2

Figures in parentheses are index numbers 1954 = 100.
Sources: Bureau of the Census, *Census of Manufactures*; U.S. Tariff Commission, *Synthetic Organic Chemicals*.

Table 13-2.   Total Energy Consumption and Energy per Unit of Output

	1954	1958	1962	1967
Gross Energy[1]				
Total energy consumption (trillion BTUs)	304.2	406.4	624.8	952.1
Energy/Unit shipped (1,000 BTUs/1967 $ of shipments)	163.8	157.8	152.4	149.3
Useful energy[1]				
Total energy consumption (trillion BTUs)	273.7	371.2	572.3	858.1
Energy/Unit shipped (1,000 BTUs/1967 $ of shipments)	147.4	144.2	139.6	134.5

[1] See Chapter One, pages 14-15, for definitions of gross and useful energy.
Source: Bureau of the Census, *Census of Manufactures.*

In the time available for this study, it was not possible to develop a complete survey of feedstock utilization by this industry. Indirect estimates were obtained by using engineering data on process yields for a sample of 21 major petrochemicals. This study indicates that net feedstock utilization (BTUs available in feedstock less BTUs available in products and by-products) does not have any systematic relationship to energy utilization for heat and power, and that in the past (for the period 1954 to 1967) net feedstock utilization per unit of output declined less rapidly than did energy utilization for heat and power.

Projections

Projecting total production and energy use by this industry is difficult, because the industry is so vitally affected by energy supplies. Our projections were made based on the assumptions that (1) 1980 will be a full employment year, (2) energy prices will rise more rapidly than construction costs, (3) present petroleum shortages will be relieved by additional refinery capacity or imports, and (4) adequate new capacity will be in place.

Production projections were prepared on two different bases. The first is based on the Interindustry Forecasting Model of the University of Maryland (INFORUM), a highly flexible input-output model of the U.S. economy as a whole. A special run was made for the Energy Policy Project, using Conference Board forecasts of total U.S. Gross National Product for 1975 and 1980.

The INFORUM figures imply a 9.5% growth rate from 1967 to 1975, slowing somewhat thereafter to a 7.3% growth rate to 1980. For the entire period the annual growth rate is 8.8%. This figure has been adjusted to 8.3% to allow for imports of methanol. This is a slightly higher figure than most industry sources give and reflects a real growth for the economy higher than past trends indicate due to the rapid growth in labor force expected in the 1970s.

A second estimate, based on the appendix study, is shown here primarily to provide a bridge between the appendix data and our overall real projections. It was obtained by projecting the 21 major petrochemicals as individual products, and by assuming that total industry real shipments retained a fixed ratio to physical production of the 21 petrochemicals as it has in past years. The individual estimates are for the most part based on recent trends (to 1971) and industry "guesstimates." As such these projections have a conservative bias, since they do not account for the more rapid rate of growth the economy should attain as the size of the labor force spurts forward.

Projections of energy utilization for heat and power for this industry have been based on the detailed study of 21 major petrochemicals in the appendix to this chapter. Trend rates of energy utilization were made using the "21 Petrochemicals" projection of total output, and this overall rate of energy utilization was then applied to the INFORUM model total output.

Within the scope of the study it was not possible to obtain estimates of feedstock uses of fuels. For further discussion of this problem and estimates of feedstock uses of fuels, see the appendix.

Table 13-4 shows energy utilization for heat and power projected to 1975 and 1980. Using the INFORUM projections for total shipments, adjusted for imports, energy use by this industry will grow at a rate of 5.5% for the period 1967 to 1980. This is a considerably less rapid rate of increase than the 8.3% growth rate of shipments.

Table 13-3.   Projected Shipments to 1975 and 1980
(million 1967 constant $)

Basis	1967	1975	1980
INFORUM	6,378	13,126	18,000*
Index	(100.0)	(205.8)	(282.3)
21 Petrochemicals	6,378	11,461	15,922*
Index	(100.0)	(179.7)	(249.6)

*Adjusted to allow for importation of methanol at the rate of 4 billion lbs. per year.

Table 13-4.   Energy Utilization for Heat and Power, 1967 to 1980
(trillion BTUs, gross energy consumed)

Basis	1967	1975	1980
INFORUM	952.1	1,619.4	2,000.0
Index	(100.0)	(170.1)	(210.0)

Table 13-5. Energy Utilization* for Heat and Power per Unit Shipped, 1967 to 1980

(1,000 BTUs/1967 $)

	1967	1975	1980
Price changes	149.3	123.4	108.7
Index	(100.0)	(82.7)	(72.8)
No relative price changes	149.3	140.3	134.3
Index	(100.0)	(94.0)	(90.0)

*Gross energy consumed.
Source: The Conference Board.

Table 13-5 shows energy use per unit shipped. The table also shows, for comparative purposes, the effect of the assumption of rising energy prices, by showing estimates for energy use rates if energy prices did not rise relative to construction prices. With price changes, the energy-output ratio is projected to decline at a rate of 2.2% per year. Without price changes, the ratio would decrease at less than 1% per year.

Summary

Chart 13-1 shows the levels of energy utilization per unit shipped for this industry historically to 1967 and projected to 1975 and 1980. From 1954 to 1967, the level dropped steadily but slowly. These declines occurred despite the fact that low energy prices offered little incentive to conserve energy.

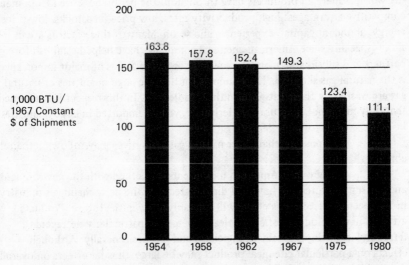

Chart 13-1. Energy Utilization for Heat and Power per Unit Shipped. Sources: Bureau of the Census, *Census of Manufactures;* The Conference Board.

Since 1967, energy prices have been rising, and the outlook is for them to continue to do so. As a result, it is becoming economically necessary to cut down on energy use wherever possible. Although the greatest savings will be effected in new plants, older plants will also be able to effect savings, particularly those that will still be in operation in 1980. For these and other reasons, substantial decreases in energy use per unit shipped are projected for 1975 and 1980.

SECTION II.   HISTORICAL DEVELOPMENTS, 1954 TO 1967

Trends in Demand

Industrial Organic Chemicals n.e.c. is an industry that is still maturing. During the period 1954 to 1967 demand, fueled by declining prices, grew at an annual rate of about 10%. Much of this growth was due to replacement of natural materials such as cotton, wood, metal, soap, manure, natural solvents, and rubber by synthetic materials such as synthetic fibers, plastics, detergents, urea, synthetic solvents, and synthetic rubber. Natural materials, just as Malthus and Ricardo suggest, could not keep up with the pace of demand. The petrochemicals could and, aided by stable fuel and feedstock prices, did lower prices as total output rose.

From its beginnings in 1920 through 1950, the petrochemical industry was virtually an American monopoly. During the 1950s, substantial petrochemical industries arose in Europe, and in the 1960s spread throughout the world. American producers have throughout the period benefited from many competitive advantages: high productivity rates, low price feedstocks, low price energy, abundant capital, experience, and so on. Many of these factors are in flux (especially since American chemical companies have helped establish foreign partners and subsidiaries), but the only factor which seems of major importance is the natural gas shortage. This is important because large quantities of natural gas are wasted by flaring at wells in the Middle East. In this respect it is assumed that only methanol, a natural gas derivative, will be imported in large quantities in 1980.

It is possible that other natural gas derivatives may follow methanol abroad.

The growing American movements concerned with the environment and consumer protection have had direct effects on the petrochemicals industry in the recent past, and this effect will probably grow in the future. Products affected have included pesticides, cleansing agents (particularly detergents), tetraethyl lead, vinyl chloride, fungicides, and plastics generally. Although effects on a particular chemical product may be large, thus far effects on overall demand have been negligible.

Trends in Production Processes

Broadly speaking, production processes have exhibited four major trends: (1) increasing realization of economies of scale; (2) more direct routes to products (fewer intermediate products); (3) eliminating by-products and co-products; and (4) replacement of acetylene by ethylene, propylene, and butadiene.

Economies of scale. There are a multitude of economies of scale from which this industry has benefited as it has grown. At the small end of the scale, the switch from batch processing to continuous processing generally allows less waste, less manpower, and lower process heating. Higher cost of processing control is offset by improvements in quality and speed of handling. Large rotary compressors are less expensive and more efficient than reciprocal compressors. Vertical integration reduces merchandising and transportation costs and frequently allows reductions in heating costs due to cooling and reheating.

The study of 21 major petrochemicals shows that much of the decline in energy use for heat and power per unit of output is due to the large petrochemicals. This reflects a greater research and engineering effort directed to large volume products.

Direct routes to products. Although direct routes to products (such as the direct reduction of ethylene to ethyl alcohol as compared to the indirect route via ethyl sulfate) in the short run generally offer lower yields and greater utilities costs, capital cost reductions and elimination of secondary materials have been powerful incentives to the more direct routes. Over time, yields improve, and more efficient capture of process heat release ensures long-run improvement in energy use.

Elimination of by-products and co-products. Unless a process allows considerable control over yields of co-products, a process which involves the production of large amounts of more than one product increases the complexity of operations and risks of production. If, as will often happen, demand for the major product becomes much larger than demand for the co-product, the co-product becomes an economic burden instead of an economic asset. More direct routes to products will sometimes involve an increase in co-product or by-product production, as the search for an economic method for the direct oxidation of propylene to propylene oxide has demonstrated. (Co-products of possible methods that have been studied include acetaldehyde, formaldehyde, acetic acid, styrene, ethylbenzene, and tertiary butyl alcohol.)

Shift from acetylene to ethylene and propylene. Acetylene (C_2H_2) has a triple bond between the carbon atoms, which gives it a greater chemical activity than ethylene (C_2H_4) or propylene (C_3H_6), each of which has a double bond. As a result, acetylene processes have generally had low utility and feedstock requirements. However, acetylene has been more expensive to produce, generally over 10¢ per lb., compared to ethylene and propylene costs of less than

4¢ a lb. In addition, acetylene is far more difficult to handle safely. As a result, ethylene and propylene have been highly favored as feedstocks, a factor that has impeded the decline of energy use by some chemicals.

Trends in Energy Utilization

The major trend in energy utilization has been in energy savings realized by the major petrochemicals. This is documented in the appendix. Three major factors have contributed to this effect: physical economies of scale (including plant integration), economies of research effort, and process experience.

Process experience is a very difficult concept to quantify even roughly Qualitatively, it involves the following elements: (1) a new process in a new plant may take ten years to achieve best yield on operating costs; (2) capital improvements, such as corrosion resistant steels and plastics; (3) more public or shared information; (4) standardization of product; and (5) standardization of process leading to more accurate engineering evaluation.

SECTION III.   PROJECTIONS TO 1980

Demand Projections

Demand projections based on the INFORUM model for this industry show a growth rate of almost 9% per year between 1967 and 1980. These projections reflect an assumption of full employment growth somewhat higher than standard industry projections.

Projections for 21 major petrochemicals are shown in Table 13A-1 of the appendix. These have not been adjusted to reflect the higher overall projections in the INFORUM model with Conference Board assumptions.

High growth rates reflect continued replacement of traditional materials by petrochemical-based materials. Ultimate uses of petrochemicals are covered more adequately in other reports, but particularly rapid future growth is expected in plastics, which will more than quadruple between 1967 and 1980, and in noncellulosic fibers, which will more than triple. These are reflected most directly in chemical products such as acrylonitrile, vinyl chloride monomer, vinyl acetate monomer, caprolactum, formaldehyde, urea, adipic acid, DMT, TPA, and hexamethylene diamine.

Increasing energy prices will clearly require petrochemical prices to rise. Even though direct cost effects will be offset to a considerable extent by decreases in utilization rates for energy, the decreases will be purchased via capital expenditures, so that the total offset may be relatively small.

These price changes will have two effects. In the short run, there appear to be capacity shortages developing, as product prices have lagged behind operating costs, discouraging construction. In the long run, price rises will eventually have a retarding effect on rate of growth of the industry as a whole.

It has been assumed that pollution controls on cars will result in the removal of lead from most gasoline, causing declines in tetraethyl lead production and ethyl chloride production. This assumption has recently come into question and should lead content stay at present levels, some changes should be made in the projection.

Projections of Energy Utilization

Energy utilization rates in this industry in 1980 will broadly be affected by two factors: (1) price changes and (2) process improvements. Process changes will broadly follow past trends, although it is possible that some outmoded processes that had high yields and low energy use rates may be revived. For the 21 major petrochemicals studied, it did not appear likely that any would "revert." There may be a greater movement in the direction of European and Japanese processes, since their energy prices have been considerably higher than American prices and, as a result, their processes are more energy conserving.

Price changes will affect energy utilization rates in two ways, in terms of feedstock yields and in terms of energy for heat and power. Feedstock yields in terms of BTUs will increase as price per BTU rises via additional recycling, additional capture of by-products, and increases in yield per run. As waste becomes more expensive, capital improvements to improve capture will become necessary.

Energy savings for heat and power will come out of a large variety of means of heat recovery. Although additional research will undoubtedly create refinements on techniques of heat recovery, the basic technology exists and is well known. Broadly speaking, only those chemical processes that have very large heat yields have had this technology applied to them as a matter of course.

For example, exothermic processes were typically cooled by water, which was then pumped out of the plant. This was economically efficient, because heat and water were cheap. A great deal of this heat can be recycled, either directly into process steam, or indirectly with waste tars or other sealed system heat transport processes. Distillation towers can be lengthened, additional steam traps installed, more insulation used, more electricity generated, and so on. More frequent maintenance, replacement, and repair of energy-related capital equipment can also contribute substantially to energy savings.

Three special cases should be mentioned:

(1) Ethylene is produced in substantial amounts in petroleum refineries. As the largest volume petrochemical, it greatly affects energy use. Traditionally, ethylene has been produced from ethane and propane, but substantial amounts are now being made with naphtha and by 1980 naphtha will be the dominant feedstock. Ethylene from naphtha is a low yield process with very large amounts of by-product, particularly residue gas and pyrolysis gasoline,

but also co-product propylene and butylene-butanes and fuel oil. As part of a chemical plant, ethylene from naphtha is a substantial net producer of utility energy. If one takes into account feedstock BTUs, however, ethylene is a substantial user of energy. In general, heavier feedstocks require more process energy; in the case of ethylene, this is obscured by the burnable by-products.

(2) Chlorine is generally produced by the electrolytic method. Recent improvements in the electrodes allow a substantial reduction in electric energy required, although for the most part the improvement has been utilized to reduce capital requirements. The Kel-Chlor process would permit further reductions in energy use, since it is a chemical reaction process. Thus far, difficulties in materials of construction have prevented any wide-scale use of this process. It appears that the high economic incentive in favor of the process (or one like it) will succeed, but timing is obscure, to say the least.

(3) Methanol (methyl alcohol) is traditionally made from methane via the synthesis gas route. It presently appears that due to the availability of large quantities of "free" natural gas (currently being flared) in the Middle East, almost all future growth will be via imports from that region, given current and presumably persisting shortages of natural gas in the United States.

SECTION IV.   APPENDIX: A DETAILED STUDY OF TWENTY-ONE MAJOR ORGANIC CHEMICALS

Industrial Organic Chemicals not elsewhere classified, (SIC 2818) is an industry producing several hundred chemical products, most of which it consumes itself, but which are also bought by virtually every other industry.

Because of the complexity of the industry, it is very difficult to study and analyze it as a whole. One possible course for studying energy utilization would be to consider the industry as a whole as a "black box," and to use total trend parameters to project energy use. Since there are so many products, the argument would go, the behavior of each as an individual is random; to study individual processes would be like studying the path of an individual electron as a means of measuring current flow.

The other extreme would be to study them all, to create an encyclopedia of energy use, studying every chemical and every process in every location over time. The collection of information on such a detailed basis is, however, unfeasible.

This report attempts to strike a middle ground between the two approaches. Detailed engineering data have been obtained for each of the major processes by which 21 of the largest industrial organic chemicals are produced. The total production of this group in 1967 was 35 billion pounds, more than half the estimated 63 billion pounds produced by the industry as a whole. The group includes all the chemicals for which individual production data were available and whose production was greater than 450 million pounds, with the exceptions of cellulose acetate, carbon tetrachloride, ethylene dichloride (other than used in vinyl chloride production), and tetraethyl lead. Inclusion of those chemicals would have increased the group total by about 3 billion for 1967, to 38 billion pounds. They were excluded primarily because data obtained for them was too sketchy for a time series analysis.

For the remainder of the industry, the "black box" assumption was employed. The supposition is that energy use patterns would change as they have in the past.

Two additional problems should be mentioned. These are the quantities of chlorine and ethylene that are produced and consumed in industry 2818; most chlorine is included in SIC 2813, Chlorine and Alkalies, and most ethylene in SIC 2911, Petroleum Refining. In 1967, SIC 2818 plants produced and consumed 4.7 billion pounds of ethylene and 6.2 billion pounds of chlorine.

Up to now, virtually all chlorine has been produced by a single process, electrolysis. Consequently the historical energy use pattern of chlorine is clear cut. By 1980, however, it is believed that a significant amount of chlorine will be produced by the Kel-chlor process. (The Kel-chlor process recovers chlorine from by-product hydrochloric acid.) The exact amount is difficult to assess at this point, but there should be substantial energy savings.

Ethylene production is much more complicated, because it is made from a variety of feedstocks and under a variety of operating conditions. Some very crude efforts have been made to estimate energy costs. These estimates are particularly important, because ethylene produced from any feedstock other than ethane results in a net production of utilities energy. Furthermore, large scale production of ethylene from naphtha feedstocks is becoming a more and more important factor, and ethylene production from naphtha results in a large amount of coproduct and by-product production. (In ethylene production, large amounts of by-product propylene result, a factor which has kept the price of propylene low and greatly enhanced propylene's usefulness as a petrochemical feedstock.)

Fuel and energy use in the organic chemicals industry takes two forms: fuels and energy used for heat and power, and fuels used as feedstocks. This distinction is in practice easy to make and clear cut, because they form distinct process flows; however, there is in fact a major conceptual problem. The conceptual difficulty in this classification can be shown most clearly in the following example:

Producing Acetylene from Methane by Partial Oxidation

This process invoves two reactions which take place simultaneously:

a) Methane + Oxygen → Carbon Dioxide + Water
$$CH_4 + 2O_2 \rightarrow CO_2 + 2H_2O$$

b) Methane $\rightarrow$ Acetylene + Hydrogen

$$2CH_4 \rightarrow C_2H_2 + 3H_2$$

The naive observer looking at this might say, "Why, this is silly. Why have the first reaction at all? It does not produce any acetylene, which the second reaction does very well." The reasons are: (1) the second reaction is highly endothermic (heat-absorbing) and requires large inputs of heat to sustain itself, and (2) the first reaction is the means of providing that heat. The first reaction, which amounts to simple burning, sneaks fuel used for heat into the feedstock (where, in the *Census of Manufactures*, it is counted as a raw material).

This is, of course, an extreme example, but because many chemical reactions produce heat (which can then be tapped for other uses), the problem is highly significant. In particular, it is believed that rising energy costs over the next decade will result in increased utilization of this type of waste heat, which in most processes is now unrecovered.

One way around this problem is to lump all manufacturing uses of fuel together, since they all make demands on the total supply of energy. Going back to the acetylene example, however, the acetylene might now be packed into high pressure cylinders and used for oxyacetylene welding, as a fuel source of heat. If you count that as fuel used as heat, you are now double-counting (since the BTUs have already been "used up" in manufacture). The double-counting problem is no trivial matter, since almost all the production of petroleum refineries would be double-counted this way.

Therefore, we are obliged to add up BTUs available in the end product, and subtract this from total BTU content of feedstock and fuel (total use of fuels).

Conceptually, then, we arrive at the following methodology:

1. Total net energy use is equal to energy inputs less energy outputs.
2. Energy inputs consist of:
   (a) Feedstock energy (measured in gross heat of combustion)
   (b) Fuel energy (direct fuel requirements, excluding steam requirements)
   (c) Electrical energy (purchased or generated, measured in fuel requirements for generation)
   (d) Steam energy (measured in fuel requirements, rather than heat content)
3. Energy outputs consist of:
   (a) Product energy (measured in gross heat of combustion)
   (b) By-product energy (measured in gross heat of combustion, excluding unrecovered by-products)
   (c) Produced steam (measured in fuel required for an equivalent amount of steam generation, excluding vented steam)

Census-defined fuel and electrical energy for heat and power will approximately equal inputs for fuel energy, electrical energy and steam energy less by-product energy (by-products used for heating) and produced steam.

Use of Engineering Data

Total net energy use was calculated from published engineering data, and as such is liable to many sources of inaccuracy as a proxy for actual total net energy use, or for comparison with *Census of Manufactures* data. Factors to be kept in mind in understanding and analyzing these data include the following:

(1) Regional differences in capital costs and fuel prices have a major effect on engineering practices. Thus, there is really no such thing as "fuel requirements" for a process, since these vary from one plant location to another. In particular, European and Japanese practice is more energy saving than American practice has been because energy costs have been far lower in America.

(2) Start-up costs, particularly for new processes, can cause large short-run increases in energy requirements.

(3) Declining product prices have meant a fine tuning of engineering practice as new processes have had to meet increasingly demanding economic justification. Thus, historical figures have probably had an upward bias in process costs, while most recent ones perhaps have a downward bias.

(4) Process energy requirements omit such energy uses as space heating, lighting, intraplant transportation, shipping, and automation. These uses have probably risen relative to process energy.

These problems seriously limit the usefulness of the data collected, particularly because we are attempting to use a residual category.

The Feedstock Problem

As far as is known, no detailed series on feedstock use in the petrochemical industry exists. This study attempts to begin to rectify this problem. Of particular interest is the fact that, within certain limits, efficiency of feedstock usage and efficiency of heat and power usage are substitutable. That is, one can lower the severity of process conditions, or decrease recycling of by-products, which will lower utility requirements but increase feedstock requirements.

Broadly speaking, data on yields were more plentiful and consistent than data on utility use, and it would seem possible to estimate feedstock use for a far larger sample than has been undertaken here. It is not the purpose of this study to perform such a thorough analysis of the feedstock problem, but to propose a methodology and examine that methodololgy for its interest and feasibility. The tentative conclusion is that the methodology is both feasible and useful.

The Double Counting Problem

A major problem in the petrochemical industry as a whole and in SIC 2818 in particular is the measurement of production. The measurement of any real variable in economics is of course subject to many problems both conceptual and statistical, but the problem takes a particularly acute form in chemical production because process variation can completely eliminate the production of intermediate chemicals.

For example, in 1954, most acetaldehyde was made from ethyl alcohol, itself in turn made from ethylene. By 1967, half of production was directly from ethylene, while half was from ethyl alcohol. Since the intermediate production of ethyl alcohol shows up as production of ethyl alcohol, we have the following production figures due to acetaldehyde:

1954		*1967*	
Ethylene	.53 million lbs.	Ethylene	1.00 million lbs.
Ethyl alcohol	.81 million lbs.	Ethyl alcohol	.81 million lbs.
Acetaldehyde	.70 million lbs.	Acetaldehyde	1.40 million lbs.
Total	2.04 million lbs.	Total	3.21 million lbs.

Thus total pounds produced of all petrochemicals increased only 58%, although the end result is that we have twice as much of the end product acetaldehyde. In general, because the trend in petrochemical processes is towards more direct routes with fewer intermediate steps, total physical production tends to understate the rate of growth of final production. A compensating trend, which has resulted in long-term stability of the ratio of value added to total shipments (in current prices), has been increases in efficiency of production that have generally been fully reflected in price decreases.

Tariff-Commission-defined "sales" and Census-defined "sales and interplant shipments" compound rather than clarify these problems, since they reflect not only changes in process but also changes in the degree of integration of plants.

Despite the described limitations, total pounds of production have been taken as the basic unit of measure of output. The only other reasonable measure (and admittedly a better one) would have been to use value added in production. Unfortunately, such a study was beyond the scope of this effort, particularly because of interregional differences in production cost structure and the difficulty of pricing a multitude of goods which may be alternatively purchased or produced within the same plant or company.

The Data

Table 13A-1 presents the 21 major chemicals studied and their production in the census years 1954, 1958, 1963, and 1967. Production of the sample was a remarkably stable proportion of total production. This is not surprising, since these chemicals represent the basis for production of many of the others, or are jointly required with other chemicals for various products such as plastics. Thus, cellulose acetate's fate is shared by the proportion of acetic anhydride used to produce cellulose acetate, and vinyl plasticizer growth is reflected in the vinyl chloride monomer it is added to in the production of polyvinyl chloride. For additional comparisons to be made later, the sample has

Table 13A-1. Production of the Sample of Twenty-one Major
Organic Chemicals, 1954 to 1980
(millions of pounds)

	1954	1958	1963	1967	1980
Acetaldehyde	700*	900*	800*	1,409	3,800
Acetic acid	442	546	1,028	1,560	3,400
Acetic anhydride........	691	965	1,272	1,559	1,700
Acetone	478	611	943	1,284	2,700
Adipic acid	200*	450*	670	971	2,500
Vinyl chloride monomer**..	653	1,211	2,666	5,424	23,600
Ethyl alcohol..........	1,152	1,525	·1,951	1,919	3,800
Ethylene glycol	638	1,145	1,600	1,989	5,100
Ethylene oxide	640*	1,169	1,889	2,308	5,600
Formaldehyde***	380	502	940	1,370	3,000
Isopropyl alcohol	859	1,029	1,466	2,069	2,100
Methyl alcohol	1,118	1,422	2,533	3,432	11,800
Urea	600*	1,061	2,183	4,182	10,300
Subtotal..............	8,551	12,536	19,741	29,476	79,400
Acrylonitrile	63	180	455	671	2,400
Carbon disulfide	476	462	652	694	900
Ethyl chloride............	547	537	592	618	100
Perchloroethylene	158	187	325	533	1,200
Trichloroethylene	297	295	368	490	300
Hexamethylene diamine	100*	170*	325*	498	1,700
Propylene oxide	75*	160	497	814	2,600
Vinyl acetate monomer	106	190	405	603	1,800
Subtotal..............	1,822	2,181	3,619	4,921	11,000
Total	10,373	14,717	23,360	34,397	90,400

*Estimate.
**Includes EDC production.
***100%.

been subdivided into those with a 1967 production greater than 950 million
pounds, and those with 1967 production between 450 and 950 million pounds.
    Table 13A-1 shows actual production for census years and projected
production for 1980. Projections for 1980 assume no change in the relative
price of fuel relative to construction costs. Projections for production of
individual chemicals have been based on past trends, expert opinion, journal
articles (chiefly *Chemical Engineering, Hydrocarbon Processing*, and *Oil and
Gas Journal*), and various expected developments (particularly that sufficient
capacity will be in place and that fire retardant plasticizers will permit smooth
growth of vinyl chloride demand).
    Table 13A-2 gives figures for "utilities" and "net feed" use in BTUs.
"Utilities" is an abbreviation for an approximate equivalent to Census-defined
fuels and energy for heat and power, converted to BTUs. "Net feed" is an
abbreviation for organic feedstock (gross heat of combustion) less organic
chemical products (including by-products except fuel oils and gases). Heats of

Table 13A-2.   Production, Fuels and Energy for Heat and Power ("Utilities") and Fuels for Feedstocks ("Net Feed"), 1954 to 1980

	1954			1967			1980		
	Production (billion lbs.)	Utilities (trillion BTUs)	Net Feed (trillion BTUs)	Production (billion lbs.)	Utilities (trillion BTUs)	Net Feed (trillion BTUs)	Production (billion lbs.)	Utilities (trillion BTUs)	Net Feed (trillion BTUs)
Acetaldehyde	.7	12.6	2.3	1.4	5.6	4.1	3.8	7.6	10.6
Acetic acid	.4	3.1	1.1	1.6	20.5	9.1	3.4	27.2	12.6
Acetic anhydride	.7	4.2	.6	1.6	11.2	.3	1.7	10.2	.2
Acetone	.5	3.8	2.4	1.3	4.4	1.6	3.0	6.0	.0
Adipic acid	.2	4.4	3.8	1.0	14.5	7.0	2.5	27.5	12.0
Vinyl chloride monomer*	.7	2.0	.4	5.4	11.7	4.5	23.6	33.3	21.3
Ethyl alcohol	1.2	8.5	2.5	2.0	10.7	2.0	3.8	19.0	3.4
Ethylene glycol	.6	6.0	.8	2.0	14.0	2.0	5.1	8.7	2.0
Ethylene oxide	.7	9.1	5.8	2.4	3.4	20.7	5.6	-6.2	28.7
Formaldehyde	.4	1.6	1.6	1.4	2.8	4.2	3.2	-3.2	8.3
Isopropyl alcohol	.9	7.2	1.8	2.0	12.0	2.2	2.1	9.4	2.7
Methyl alcohol	1.1	8.8	2.2	3.4	23.8	6.1	3.8	24.7	1.9
Urea	.6	3.0	.8	4.2	16.8	5.0	10.3	20.6	12.4
Subtotal**	8.5	74.3	26.1	29.5	151.4	68.8	71.9	184.8	116.1
Acrylonitrile..............	.1	1.0	.0	.7	3.0	6.1	2.4	.2	20.9
Carbon disulfide	.5	7.2	-1.7	.7	2.1	.1	.9	1.8	-2.1
Ethyl chloride	.5	1.6	1.1	.6	1.3	1.2	.1	.2	.2
Perchloroethylene	.2	1.0	.4	.5	1.4	.9	1.2	3.0	1.3
Trichloroethylene	.3	1.5	.5	.5	1.0	.7	.3	2.1	.5
Hexamethylene diamine ...	.1	.5	-.1	.5	17.0	2.4	1.7	30.0	-3.7
Propylene oxide	.1	1.1	.7	.8	3.6	3.6	2.6	39.0	3.9
Vinyl acetate monomer ...	.1	.4	.3	.6	2.6	1.8	1.8	12.6	5.0
Subtotal**	1.9	14.4	1.2	4.9	32.0	16.8	11.0	88.9	26.0
Total**	10.4	88.7	27.3	34.4	183.4	85.6	82.9	273.7	142.1

*Includes ethylene dichloride.

combustion of inorganic chemicals have been omitted, except in the case of urea, where ammonia heat of combustion was included

Negative or low net feeds generally represent endothermic processes (heat-absorbing), while negative or low utilities generally represent exothermic processes (heat-producing) where process heat is recovered.

The basic data from which these figures are derived are presented in Table 13A-3, where products are further subdivided by process. The process is usually indicated by the feedstock source, except where two different processes use the same feedstock, in which case the specific process is indicated in a parenthesis next to the feedstock. Thus, the chlorhydrin process for producing ethylene oxide is distinguished from the direct oxidation process by the initials (C1).

Discussion of Findings

Table 13A-4 presents the results of Table 13-2, imbedded in Census data for utilities, with corrections made for production of chlorine and ethylene. The 1980 ethylene projection is based on a total consumption by SIC 2818 of 19 billion pounds, of which 4 billion are produced by oil refineries. The 1980 chlorine projection assumes a total consumption of 25 billion pounds of chlorine by SIC 2818, of which 5 billion are produced by other industries.

Our sample of 21 major chemical products shows a sharp drop in utilities from 1958 to 1967. Two projections are shown for 1980. Projection A assumes a substantial rise in the price of oil and natural gas compared with capital construction costs; Projection B assumes no change in relative costs. Both projections show substantial decreases in BTUs per pound. With a price increase, increase in efficiency of energy use will be 45%, from some 5,300 BTUs per pound in 1967 down to some 2,950 BTUs per pound.

It should be pointed out that the decline in energy utilization between 1954 and 1967 was accompanied by a slight increase in feedstock utilization, which indicates that some of the energy decline was merely a trade-off between the two categories. Surprisingly, our figures do not indicate a decrease in the industry excluding our sample of 21 major chemicals (the Residue). This result in our opinion is somewhat artifactual, due to the data problems mentioned earlier which tend to overstate the increase in efficiency for the sample of 21 major chemicals and hence understate efficiency increase in the rest.

The much greater process requirements of the Residue agree with the findings of a quick study made of utility requirements of a sample of smaller chemicals whose production was less than 450 million pounds, the results of which are shown in Table 13A-5. Although these represent some of the larger chemical products outside of the sample of 21 major chemicals, utility requirements are comparatively quite high (over 13,000 BTUs per pound, compared

Table 13A-3.   "Utilities and "Net Feed" by Process, 1954 to 1980

Year	Chemical	Production (billion lbs.)	Process	Utilities (1,000 BTUs/lb.)	Total Utilities (trillion BTUs)	Feedstock Less Product (1,000 BTUs/lb.)	Total Net Feed (trillion BTUs)
1954	Acetaldehyde	.7	Ethyl alcohol	18	12.6	3.3	2.3
1967	Acetaldehyde	.7	Ethyl alcohol	4.5	3.15	2.9	2.0
	Acetaldehyde	.7	Ethylene	3.5	2.45	3.0	2.1
		1.4			5.60		4.1
1980	Acetaldehyde	3.8	Ethylene	2.0	7.6	2.8	10.6
1954	Acetic acid	.4	Acetaldehyde	7.0	3.1	2.6	1.1
1967	Acetic acid	.6	Acetaldehyde	5.0	3.0	2.5	1.5
	Acetic acid	1.0	Butane	17.5	17.5	7.6	7.6
		1.6			20.5		9.1
1980	Acetic acid	1.7	Butane	10.0	17.0	5.8	9.9
	Acetic acid	1.7	Carbon monoxide + methyl alcohol	6.0	10.2	1.6	2.7
		3.4			27.2		12.6
1954	Acetic anhydride	.7	Acetic acid	6.0	4.2	.9	.6
1967	Acetic anhydride	1.6	Acetic acid	7.0	11.2	.2	.3
1980	Acetic anhydride	1.7	Acetic acid	6.0	10.2	.1	.2
1954	Acetone	.5	Isopropyl alcohol	7.5	3.8	5.0	2.4
1967	Acetone	.8	Isopropyl alcohol	5.5	4.4	2.0	1.6
	Acetone	.5	Cumene*	—	—	—	—
		1.3					
1980	Acetone	1.2	Isopropyl alcohol	5.0	6.0	0	0
	Acetone	1.8	Cumene*	—	—	—	—
		3.0					

*Phenol is major product.

Year	Product		Raw material				
1954	Acrylonitrile	.06	Ethylene oxide	17.0	1.0	0	0
1967	Acrylonitrile	.07	Acetylene	20.0	1.4	1.7	.1
	Acrylonitrile	.6	Propylene	2.8	1.6	10.0	6.0
		<u>.7</u>			<u>3.0</u>		<u>6.1</u>
1980	Acrylonitrile	2.4	Propylene	.1	.2	8.7	20.9
1954	Adipic acid	.1	Cyclohexane (air)	24.0	2.4	21.0	2.1
	Adipic acid	.1	Cyclohexane (nitric)	20.0	2.0	17.0	1.7
	Adipic acid	<u>.2</u>			<u>4.4</u>		<u>3.8</u>
1967	Adipic acid	1.0	Cyclohexane	15.0	14.5	7.0	7.0
1980	Adipic acid	2.5	Cyclohexane	11.0	27.5	4.8	12.0
1954	Carbon disulfide	.5	Electro charcoal	15.0	7.2	-1.7*	—
1967	Carbon disulfide	.7	Methane	3.0	2.1	.1*	—
1980	Carbon disulfide	.9	Methane	2.0	1.8	-2.1*	—
1954	Ethyl chloride	.06	Ethyl alcohol	2.0	.1	1.5	.1
	Ethyl chloride	.49	Ethylene	3.0	1.5	2.0	1.0
		<u>.5</u>			<u>1.6</u>		<u>1.1</u>
1967	Ethyl chloride	.03	Ethyl alcohol	2.0	.1	1.0	0
	Ethyl chloride	.5	Ethylene	1.5	.8	2.0	1.0
	Ethyl chloride	.1	Ethane	4.5	.4	2.2	.2
		<u>.6</u>			<u>1.3</u>		<u>1.2</u>
1980	Ethyl chloride	.1	Ethylene	1.5	.2	2.0	.2

*Not counting sulfur.

Year	Product		Raw material				
1954	Perchloroethylene	.2	Acetylene	5.0	1.0	1.8	.4
1967	Perchloroethylene	.1	Acetylene	5.0	0.4	1.8	.2
	Perchloroethylene	.2	Propane/Propylene	2.0	.4	1.9	.4
	Perchloroethylene	.2	Ethylene dichloride	3.0	.6	1.3	.3
		<u>.5</u>			<u>1.4</u>		<u>.9</u>
1980	Perchloroethylene	1.2	Ethylene dichloride	2.5	3.0	1.1	1.3
1954	Trichloroethylene	.3	Acetylene	5.0	1.5	1.6	.5

(continued)

Table 13A-3.—Continued

Year	Chemical	Production (billion lbs.)	Process	Utilities (1,000 BTUs/lbs.)	Total Utilities (trillion BTUs)	Feedstock Less Product (1,000 BTUs/lb.)	Total Net Feed (trillion BTUs)
1967	Trichloroethylene ...	.3	Acetylene	2.0	.6	1.4	.4
	Trichloroethylene ...	.2	Ethylene dichloride	2.0	.4	1.6	.3
		.5			1.0		.7
1980	Trichloroethylene ...	.3	Ethylene	7.0	2.1	1.6	.5
1954	Vinyl chloride monomer	.4	Acetylene	5.0	2.0	.9	.4
1967	Vinyl chloride monomer	.6	Acetylene	1.5	.9	.5	.3
	Vinyl chloride monomer	1.8	Ethylene	6.0	10.8	2.2	4.2
		2.4			11.7		4.5
1980	Vinyl chloride monomer	4.5	Ethylene	5.0	22.5	1.5	8.3
	Vinyl chloride monomer	4.5	Ethane	2.4	10.8	2.9	13.0
		9.0			33.3		21.3
1954	Ethyl alcohol........	1.0	Ethylene (Sulf.)	5.6	5.3	1.8	1.8
	Ethyl alcohol........	.2	Ethylene (D.R.)*	16.0	3.2	3.6	.7
		1.2			8.5		2.5
1967	Ethyl alcohol........	1.5	Ethylene (Sulf.)	5.0	7.5	.8	1.2
	Ethyl alcohol........	.5	Ethylene (D.R.)*	7.0	3.2	1.5	.8
		2.0			10.7		2.0
1980	Ethyl alcohol........	3.8	Ethylene (D.R.)*	5.0	19.0	.9	3.4

*Direct Reduction (D.R.)

Year						
1954	Ethylene glycol	.6	Ethylene oxide	10.0	6.0	.8
1967	Ethylene glycol	2.0	Ethylene oxide	7.0	14.0	2.0
1980	Ethylene glycol	5.1	Ethylene oxide (carbonation)	1.7	8.7	2.0
1954	Ethylene oxide	.4	Ethylene (Cl)	17.0	6.3	2.3
		.3	Ethylene (Air)	10.0	2.8	3.5
		.7			9.1	5.8
1967	Ethylene oxide	.4	Ethylene (Cl)	10.0	4.0	1.6
		1.7	Ethylene (Air)	0	0	16.5
		.3	Ethylene (O_2)	-2.0	-.6	2.6
		2.4			3.4	20.7
1980	Ethylene oxide	5.0	Ethylene (Air)	-1.0	-5.0	26.0
		.6	Ethylene (O_2)	-2.0	-1.2	2.7
		5.6			6.2	28.7
1954	Formaldehyde (100%)	.4	Methyl alcohol	4.0	1.6	1.6
1967	Formaldehyde (100%)	1.4	Methyl alcohol	2.0	2.8	4.2
1980	Formaldehyde (100%)	3.2	Methyl alcohol	-1.0	-3.2	8.3
1954	Hexamethylene diamine	.1	Adipic acid	7.0	.5	-.1
1967	Hexamethylene diamine	.4	Butadiene	30.0	12.0	2.0
		.1	Acrylonitrile	50.0	4.5	.4
		.5			17.0	2.4
1980	Hexamethylene diamine	1.7	Butadiene	20.0	34.0	-3.7

(continued)

Table 13A-3.—Continued

Year	Chemical	Production (billion lbs.)	Process	Utilities (1,000 BTUs/lb.)	Total Utilities (trillion BTUs)	Feedstock Less Product (1,000 BTUs/lb.)	Total Net Feed (trillion BTUs)
1954	Isopropyl alcohol	.9	Propylene (Sulf.)	8.0	7.2	2.0	1.8
1967	Isopropyl alcohol	2.0	Propylene (Sulf.)	6.0	12.0	1.1	2.2
1980	Isopropyl alcohol	1.0	Propylene (Sulf.)	5.0	5.0	.7	.7
	Isopropyl alcohol	1.1	Propylene (D.R.)	4.0	4.4	1.8	2.0
		2.1			9.4		2.7
1954	Methyl alcohol	1.1	Natural gas–HP	8.0	8.8	2.0	2.2
1967	Methyl alcohol	3.4	Natural gas–HP	7.0	23.8	1.8	6.1
1980	Methyl alcohol	3.8	Natural gas–LP	6.5	24.7	.5	1.9
1954	Propylene oxide	.1	Propylene (Cl)	11.0	1.1	6.9*	.7
1967	Propylene oxide	.8	Propylene (Cl)	4.5	3.6	4.6*	3.6
1980	Propylene oxide	2.6	Propylene (oxirane)	15.0	39.0	1.5**	3.9
1954	Urea	.6	Ammonia	5.0	3.0	1.3	.8
1967	Urea	4.2	Ammonia	4.0	16.8	1.2	5.0
1980	Urea	10.3	Ammonia	2.0	20.6	1.2	12.4
1954	Vinyl acetate monomer	.1	Acetylene/acetic acid	4.0	.4	3.2	.3
1967	Vinyl acetate monomer	.5	Acetylene/acetic acid	3.5	1.8	3.0	1.5
	Vinyl acetate monomer	.1	Ethylene/acetic acid	8.0	.8	3.3	.3
		.6			2.6		1.8
1980	Vinyl acetate monomer	1.8	Ethylene/acetic acid	7.0	12.6	2.8	5.0

Table 13A-4. Reconciliation of Census and Sample Data for "Utilities," with Alternative Projections to 1980

	1954	1967	High Energy Price Projection A 1980	No Change in Energy Price Projection B 1980
Total, trillion BTUs	304.2	952.1	1,773.0	2,193.3
BTU/Unit output				
(1,000 BTUs/1967 $)	163.8	149.3	111.1	137.8
Chlorine, trillion BTUs	36.2	142.4	320.0	320.0
Production, billion lbs.	(1.3)	(6.2)	(20.0)	(20.0)
Ethylene, trillion BTUs	−2.0	−17.0	−126.5	−84.0
Production, billion lbs.	(1.7)	(4.7)	(15.0)	(15.0)
Net total,* trillion BTUs	270.0	826.7	1,579.5	1,957.3
Sample−21, trillion BTUs . . .	88.7	183.4	232.6	273.7
Production, billion lbs.	(10.4)	(34.4)	(82.9)	(82.9)
Residue, trillion BTUs	181.3	643.3	1,346.9	1,683.6
Production, billion lbs.	(8.0)	(28.0)	(73.2)	(73.2)
Shipments, million 1967 $ . . .	$1.857	$6,378	$15,922	$15,922

*Total excluding captive production of ethylene and chlorine.

with under 6,000 BTUs per pound for the sample). Chemicals whose production is smaller would, we anticipate, show even greater BTU requirements.

Even assuming a 20% error in our process data (which is larger than we believe exists), the Residue would decrease its utility requirements only to 21,700 BTUs per pound, which would represent less than a 10% increase in efficiency (the increase in efficiency under this assumption for the 21 major chemicals would be about 24%).

Thus our data clearly indicate that the overall increase in efficiency for the industry was due primarily to the improvements in production technique for the largest-volume chemicals in the industry.

The data for net feed shown in Table 13A-2 are particularly interesting. In the following discussion, Group 1 will refer to chemicals whose 1967 production was greater than 950 million pounds, and Group 2 will refer to those whose 1967 production was between 450 million and 950 million pounds.

Table 13A-6 shows utilities and net feed BTUs per unit of output in terms of thousand BTUs per pound.

Over the entire period from 1954 to 1980 the total sample shows a decline in net feed use of fuels, but the decline is much slower than for utilities. Over the period 1954 to 1967, there is a small rise per pound for the total group, with fivefold increase in net feed per pound in Group 2. As a result, total fuel and energy utilization (both utilities and net feed) decreased much more slowly

Table 13A-5. "Utilities" Requirements of a Sample of Small Chemicals, 1967

Chemical	1967 Production (billion lbs.)	Utilities (1,000 BTUs per lb.)	Total Utilities (trillion BTUs)
Ethanolamines	.2	10.0	2.3
Caprolactum	.3	26.0	8.0
Methyl ethyl ketone	.4	20.0	8.0
Methyl isobutyl ketone ...	.2	32.0	6.4
Methyl chloroform	.3	3.0	0.9
2 Ethyl hexanol	.4	11.0	4.4
Plasticizers*	.4	1.0	.4
Glycerine	.4	22.0	8.8
Ethylene glycol ethers ...	.3	5.0	1.5
Total	2.9	14.1	40.8

*di–(2 Ethyl Hexyl) Phthalate
di–(2 Ethyl Hexyl) Adipate
Epoxidized Soya Oils
Tricresyl Phosphate

Table 13A-6. "Utilities" and "Net Feed" Requirements of Large and Small Chemicals, 1954 to 1980

	1954	1967	1980
Group 1			
Utilities per lb.	8.48	5.13	2.88
Net feed per lb.	2.85	2.33	1.47
Group 2			
Utilities per lb.	8.00	6.53	7.78
Net feed per lb.	0.67	3.43	2.63
Total			
Utilities per lb.	8.40	5.33	3.45
Net feed per lb.	2.47	2.49	1.61

for this group of chemicals than the utility rate would indicate, and this holds true through 1980. It is also interesting to note that over the entire period, utility requirements for Group 2 per pound rise, due to the increased requirements of the oxirane process for propylene oxide and to the rapid growth of hexamethylene diamene.

Turning to projections for the Residue for 1980, projection A assumes a 20% increase in efficiency due to price changes, while projection B assumes that the past figure of 23,000 BTUs per pound continues.

The assumption of a 20% increase in efficiency is based not only on price effects, but also on the effects of increased volume of production, which will yield increasing economies of scale, both to engineering and basic research efforts. Increasing energy prices will also give a competitive edge to products having lower utility costs, causing them to grow more rapidly and thus assume a larger share of the industry.

SECTION V.   SELECTED BIBLIOGRAPHY

Brownstein, *The U.S. Petrochemical Industry*

Chemical Engineering. "Cost Estimating in the Chemical Process Industries."

Chemical Engineering. "107 Process Flowsheets."

Compression Gas Association. *Handbook of Chemistry and Physics.*

Faith,W. L.; Keyes, Donald B. and Clark, Ronald I. *Industrial Chemistry.* New York: John Wiley & Sons, Inc., 1965.

Goldstein and Waddams, *The Petroleum Chemicals Industry.*

Hahn, *The Petrochemical Industry.*

Industrial and Engineering Chemistry, *Modern Chemical Processes.*

Institut Francais du Petrole, *Recent Technological and Economic Developments in the Petrochemical Industry.*

Isard, *et al. Industrial Complex Analysis.*

Kent, James A., Ed. *Riegel's Industrial Chemistry.* New York; Reinhold Publishing Corporation, 1962.

Kirk-Othmer, *Encyclopedia of Chemical Technology.* 2nd Edition . New York: Wiley-Interscience.

Kline, C. H. & Co. *Marketing Guide to the Chemical Industry.*

Kobe and McKetta, *Advances in Petroleum Chemistry and Refining.*

Maxwell, *Data Book on Hydrocarbons.*

Mercier, *Petrochemical Industry.*

Sherwood, *Petrochemical Profits for Tomorrow.*

Shreve, Morris R. *Chemical Process Industries,* 3rd Ed. New York: McGraw-Hill, 1967.

Sittig, Marshall, *Organic Chemical Processes, Chemical Process Encyclopedia.*

Stanford Research Institute, *Chemical Conversions and Yields.*

Stobaugh, Robert E., Jr. *Petrochemical Manufacturing and Marketing Guide.* Houston, Texas: Gulf Publishing Company Inc.

Serials:
Hydrocarbon Processing
Chemical Engineering
Chemical Engineering Progress
Oil and Gas Journal
Petro/Chem Engineer
Industrial and Engineering Chemistry
European Chemical News (Supplements)
Chemical Economy and Engineering Review

Stanford Research Institute, *Process Economics Program Reports*
Stanford Research Institute, *Chemical Economics Handbooks*
U. S. Tariff Commission, *Synthetic Organic Chemicals*
Chemicals Statistics Handbook
U.S. Industrial Outlook

Chapter Fourteen

Industrial Inorganic Chemicals n.e.c.—SIC 2819

Barry Kolatch

SECTION I. INTRODUCTION AND SUMMARY OF FINDINGS

Introduction

The 1967 U.S. Bureau of the Census Standard Industrial Classification defines Industrial Inorganic Chemicals, not elsewhere classified—SIC 2819—as follows:

> Establishments primarily engaged in manufacturing industrial inorganic chemicals, n.e.c. Important products of this industry include inorganic salts of sodium (excluding refined sodium chloride), potassium, aluminum, calcium, chromium, magnesium, mercury, nickel, silver, tin; inorganic compounds such as alums, calcium carbide, hydrogen peroxide, phosphates, sodium silicate, ammonia compounds and anhydrous ammonia; rare earth metal salts and elemental bromine, fluorine, iodine, phosphorous, and alkali metals (sodium, potassium, lithium, etc.). Establishments primarily engaged in mining, milling, or otherwise preparing natural potassium, sodium or boron compounds (other than common salt) are classified in Industry 1974.

Industry Overview

Over the past 13 years, Industrial Inorganic Chemicals, n.e.c., has shown substantial growth. Between 1954 and 1967 industry shipments more than doubled, rising from $1,972 million to $4,280 million, in 1967 prices.

Comparisons between industry and product statistics indicate that the growth rate for all the chemicals in SIC 2819 has not been uniform. Value shipped rose at an annual average rate of 6.1% from 1954 to 1967. This rate was exceeded by the growth of many chemicals, among which were ammonia with an annual average growth rate of 12.2%; phosphoric acid, 12.1% per year; ammonium nitrate, 9.3% per year; and nitric acid, 8.0% per year. It was most

257

notably above the average growth rate of sulfuric acid which was 5.5% per year. Thus, during the period 1954 through 1967, SIC 2819 shifted slightly toward the production of agricultural chemicals.

Aside from a shift in the product mix, important changes in technology took place in the years 1954 through 1967. New processes included the wet process for the manufacture of hydrochloric acid. Modified processes included the replacement of reciprocal expanders with turbine expanders in the manufacture of nitric acid and lower conversion pressures in the manufacture of ammonia.

A difficulty for analysis arises from the inclusion of uranium diffusion plants in this industry. These plants use very substantial levels of electricity, and production has varied considerably over the years. Unfortunately, while the amount of electricity used is known, production remains a national defense secret. A very crude attempt has been made in this report to separate the diffusion plants from the rest of the industry.

When the uranium diffusion plants are removed, the growth rate for the remainder of the industry rises to 6.7% per year for the period 1954-1967. Moreover, the time pattern of growth changes remarkably.

As can be seen from Table 14-1, if the uranium plant production is included, the industry's growth appears to be slowing steadily. When uranium plants are removed, however, the industry growth rate appears to increase from 1954 to 1967.

Energy Utilization

Two types of energy measures are used in this study, gross energy consumed, and useful energy.[a] In terms of gross energy consumed, the amount of energy used by Industrial Inorganic Chemicals, n.e.c., rose by slightly more than 50% between the years 1954 and 1958, and then declined slightly in 1967. While output increased from 1954 to 1958, it did not keep pace with energy use, and thus energy per unit of output rose 11%. Between 1958 and 1967 energy use decreased, but output continued to increase, thus energy per unit of output decreased 42%.

Useful energy, however, yielded slightly different results. While gross energy consumed fell from 1958 to 1967, useful energy increased steadily from 1954, with the net increase coming to 47%. The useful energy-output ratio fell steadily throughout the period for a net drop of 31%.

As the only difference between these two measures concerns electric power, it follows that any significant difference between them stems from the use of extremely large amounts of electricity. As stated above, government-owned, privately operated plants—primarily the Federal Government's three gaseous diffusion plants used for the separation of U_{235} from U_{238}—are included in

---

[a] See Chapter One, pages 14-15, for definitions of gross and useful energy.

Table 14-1. Shipments of Inorganic Chemicals, n.e.c.

	Total Industry		Industry Less Uranium Diffusion	
	Shipments (million, 1967 $)	Average Annual Growth Rate (per cent)	Shipments (million, 1967 $)	Average Annual Growth Rate (per cent)
1967	$4,248	5.0%	$3,933	7.1%
1962	3,334	5.6	2,796	7.5
1958	2,679	6.3	2,095	5.5
1954	1,972		1,692	

the industry. At full capacity these plants use a total of 5.3436×10^{13} kwh of electricity a year. Although they have not operated near full capacity for some time, it is easy to see how a number even half this size could cause tremendous differences between useful energy and gross energy consumed.

Not only does the electricity used by the diffusion plants create large differences between useful energy and gross energy consumed, it also totally dominates energy use in the industry. The energy-output ratio for these plants is so high that, in general, any shift in energy per unit of output for the industry as a whole is governed by the amount of electricity used by the gaseous diffusion plants in that year and by the percentage of capacity at which they operate. During the years 1954 to 1958, two of the uranium enrichment plants were completed. Consequently, the energy-output ratio rose despite technological change in the manufacture of other chemicals that would have dictated otherwise. In the years 1958 to 1967, decreased production of enriched uranium combined with technological change to decrease the energy-output ratios.

After removing the uranium diffusion plants' energy and production data from the industry totals, a significant change occurs in the trend of the energy-output ratio. As can be seen in Table 14-3, the energy-output ratio now declines sharply from 1954 to 1962, and more slowly thereafter.

The primary reason for this slowdown is the rapid growth of

Table 14-2. Total Industry Energy Use, Inorganic Chemicals, n.e.c.

	Energy Use (trillion BTUs)		Per Unit Output (1,000 BUTs/1967 $ output)	
	Useful Energy	Gross Energy Consumed	Useful Energy	Gross Energy Consumed
1954	422.2	694.3	214.1	352.1
1958	528.2	1,047.8	197.2	391.1
1962	552.3	995.5	165.6	298.5
1967	620.8	971.?	146.1	228.6

Source: Bureau of the Census, *Census of Manufactures.*

Table 14-3.   Energy Use, Inorganic Chemicals Less Diffusion Plants

	Energy Use (trillion BTUs)		Per Unit Output (1,000 BTUs/1967 $ output)	
	Useful Energy	Gross Energy Consumed	Useful Energy	Gross Energy Consumed
1954	340.6	403.1	201.3	238.2
1958	358.1	495.3	170.9	236.4
1962	397.7	517.2	142.2	185.0
1967	536.0	712.1	136.2	181.1

Source: The Conference Board.

ammonia production between 1962 and 1967. Ammonia production is very energy-intensive. In 1967 it is calculated to have accounted for as much as 33% of all energy consumed by the industry excluding uranium, while accounting for only about 15% of the value shipped.

Projections to 1980

Unfortunately, the projections for SIC 2819 as they existed in the Maryland Interindustry Forecasting Model (INFORUM) were inappropriate, and thus could not be used in this report. The nature of the chemicals involved suggested that we should attempt instead to link expected growth in Industrial Inorganic Chemicals, n.e.c. to expected growth in GNP. According to Conference Board projections, GNP should rise 6.3% a year from 1971 to 1975, and 4.3% per year between 1975 and 1980. Modifying these projections to account for other factors that should affect the growth of Industrial Inorganic Chemicals, n.e.c. (aside from GNP), we arrive at a projected growth rate for SIC 2819 of 6.8% per year from 1971 to 1975, and an annual growth rate of 4.7% from 1975 to 1980. The resulting levels of output are shown in Table 14-4. Energy use per unit of output will decline from 1967 to 1975 at a 4.3% average annual rate.

Table 14-4.   Energy and Output, 1967-1980

	1967	1971	1975	1980
Volume of shipments (million 1967 $)	$4,248	$5,217	$6,783	$8,529
Total energy use (trillion BTUs)				
Gross energy	971.3	1,095.7	1,358.8	1,551.2
Useful energy	620.8	732.6	834.0	895.0
Energy use per value shipped (1,000 BTUs/1967 $)				
Gross energy	228.6	210.0	200.3	181.9
Useful energy	146.1	140.4	123.0	104.9

Energy use per unit of output in the manufacture of inorganic chemicals excluding uranium is expected to fall by 5% a year during this period, but this will be partly offset by a rising energy-output ratio in uranium diffusion.

From 1975 through 1980 the jump in electricity used in uranium enrichment should not be nearly as high as from 1971 to 1975. Furthermore, technological improvements scheduled for these plants during 1975-1980 should serve to sharply lower their astronomical energy-output ratio. However, the

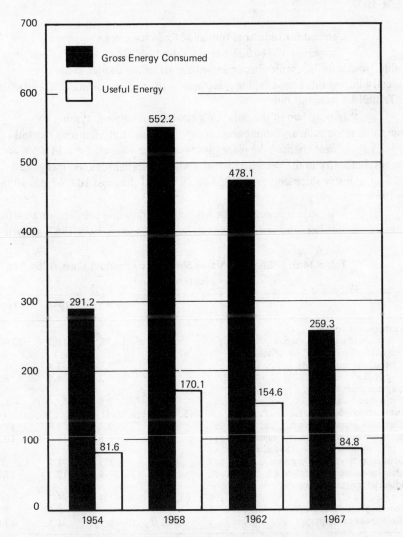

Chart 14-1. Electricity Used in the Enrichment of Uranium. Source: Unpublished Data from Atomic Energy Commission.[2]

relatively more rapid growth in uranium diffusion production will give its higher energy-output ratio greater weight in this later period. This will limit the decline in the entire industry's ratio to a 2.7% annual rate.

The resulting energy consumption levels and energy-output ratios are presented in Table 14-4.

SECTION II.   HISTORICAL ANALYSIS
1954-1967

Demand for Industrial Inorganic Chemicals, n.e.c.

The period 1954-1967 has generally been characterized as one of stable growth for inorganic chemicals, with most of the change in the chemical industry during this period taking place among the organic chemicals. The figures in Table 14-5 bear this out.

In only two of the industry's eleven subdivisions—synthetic ammonia, nitric acid, and ammonium compounds; and miscellaneous receipts— did any significant change take place. Synthetic ammonia, etc., gained 4.3% of the total industry in the years 1958-1967, while miscellaneous receipts gained 3.2% of industry shipments from 1954 to 1958, and then lost 10.8% from 1958 to 1967.

Synthetic ammonia, nitric acid, and ammonium compounds are used primarily as fertilizer and fertilizer inputs. During the years 1958-1967, growth

**Table 14-5.   Share of Value Shipped, by Product Class, 1954-1967
(current value)**

	1967	1962	1958	1954
Synthetic ammonia, nitric acid and compounds	14.3%	12.2%	10.0%	12.4%
Inorganic industrial and household bleaching compounds	3.6	4.1	3.4	3.7
Sulfuric acid	4.4	4.2	4.9	5.3
Inorganic acids except nitric and sulfuric	2.6	2.5	2.4	1.8
Aluminum oxide	(5.9-11.8)	(1)	(2)	(2)
Other aluminum compounds	2.6	2.7	9.9	11.1
Potassium and sodium compounds .... (except bleaches, alkali and alums)	8.8	8.8	10.0	10.3
Chemical catalytic preparations	2.3	(1)	1.7	(3)
Other Inorganic chemicals, n.e.c.	19.0	17.9	17.1	17.0
Industrial inorganic chemicals, n.e.c., n.s.k.	(0.5-1.2)	(4)	(4)	(4)
Secondary products	10.7	8.4	8.8	9.7
Miscellaneous receipts	21.0	28.1	31.8	28.6

(1) Not available. (2) Included in other aluminum compounds. (3) Not conceptually in SIC 2819 in 1954. (4) Included in other inorganic chemicals, n.e.c.

in the fertilizer industry accelerated sharply. Production of anhydrous ammonia, a highly energy-intensive chemical, rose from 3.9 to 12.2 million tons in this period. Two forces were behind this development. First, there was a continued contraction in the number of farms, with large farms becoming increasingly more dominant. In general, large farms with their larger capital bases are better able to make investments in fertilizers than smaller ones. Following this, an increase in the number of large farms should coincide with an increase in fertilizer use. Second, and perhaps more importantly, there was great substitution of fertilizers for land during this period. Federal farm support programs made it profitable for a farmer not to plant all of his land, yet it was profitable for the individual farmer to have as high an output as possible. As a result the farmer increased the amount of fertilizer he used in order to get a higher yield from a given plot of land, rather than increasing land use to increase output.

Miscellaneous receipts, the other category whose share of the product mix has changed significantly over time, seems to consist primarily of receipts from the government uranium enrichment plants. Prior to 1954, the AEC had gaseous diffusion facilities in Oak Ridge, Tennessee, and Paducah, Kentucky. In the early 1950s, the need for additional facilities led to further construction in Paducah, which was completed in 1954, and the construction of an additional plant in Portsmouth, Ohio, which was completed in 1956. The additional capacity allowed by these plants explains for the large part played by miscellaneous receipts between 1954 and 1958 shown in Table 14-5. Afterwards the proportion of SIC 2819 occupied by miscellaneous receipts is related to the arms race and the cold war. In 1963 the U.S. was still very busy arming itself, and thus miscellaneous receipts occupied over 28% of the industry. By 1967, however, the cold war was beginning to thaw, and the nuclear test ban treaty had already been in effect a number of years. Thus, by 1967, miscellaneous receipts fell off to 21% of SIC 2819 output.

Technological Change

Aside from any change in the product mix, changes in technology took place between 1954 and 1967. While the vast number of chemicals included in the industry (over 200) precludes the possibility of discussing every change in technology, a few will be included to give the reader an indication of this change.

At the beginning of this period, all phosphoric acid manufactured in the U.S. was made in electric furnaces. This process used around 30 million BTUs of gross electricity and around 9 million BTUs of coke per ton of acid. During this period, however, all newly built phosphoric acid plants employed "the wet process." A "wet process" phosphoric acid plant uses between 150,000 and 1 million BTUs of gross electricity, and around 500,000 BTUs of steam per ton.

In the manufacture of nitric acid, improvements were made in existing processes. High efficiency turbine expanders replaced the recriprocal expanders previously utilized. Thus, while typical power requirements for the manufacturers of nitric acid were formerly 2 million BTUs of gross electricity per ton, power requirements for nitric acid are now on the order of 100,000 BTUs of gross electricity per ton.

Change has also taken place in the production of ammonia. Previously, natural gas was used as reformer fuel, and electricity was used to power electric drives in ammonia production. The combined energy use of this process was 23 million BTUs of gross energy per ton. More modern processes, however, use air cooling and gas engine drives, and thus energy requirements are reduced to 20 million BTUs of gross energy per ton. Technological change in ammonia production did not stop there. In 1964, vertically split, barrel type centrifugal compressors for the handling of synthesis gas were introduced. The compressors allow the hydrogen-nitrogen synthesis to take place at pressures as low as 150 atmospheres. The energy saved by such a system can be as high as 15% of the energy used in a plant with conventional compressors.

These are just a few of the technological changes that have taken place in SIC 2819 between 1954 and 1967, but they do point out the general trend of increased energy efficiency in manufacturing.

Energy Consumption[1]

Three factors previously discussed have affected energy use in SIC 2819 over time: technological change, enriched uranium production, and ammonia production. Of these, uranium and ammonia production are by far the most important.

Uranium Diffusion. Because uranium diffusion production prior to the mid-1960s was primarily for defense purposes, it is not possible to obtain the precise data that would be needed to do a highly accurate analysis of the effect of the diffusion plants. No production data are available at all, and the only energy statistics readily available are the average electrical power levels at which the plants were operated.

However, since the plants have such a marked effect on the industry totals, it was necessary to approximate the data. This was done by (1) assuming that electricity consumption was the total energy consumption of the diffusion plants, and (2) by assuming that increases in energy efficiency were quite small. The first assumption appears fairly safe, if we assume that the plants' steam facilities are the only major use of nonelectric power. At rated capacities of one million pounds of steam per hour, energy use is only about 7% of the plants' rated electrical capacity measured in useful energy, and about 2% of electrical capacity measured in gross energy consumed. The second assumption is undoubtedly too conservative. However, our calculations suggest that uranium diffusion production is, at its greatest point, only 20% of the industry's total

---

[1] All energy calculations in this section were done on a gross energy consumed basis.

production. Thus even a 20% error in calculating the production creates only a 4% total error.

Value of shipments was calculated as follows: Separative Work Units produced (SWU) was derived from AEC charts on the uranium diffusion plants' current operating characteristics. (A Separative Work Unit is the unit by which the work done at the diffusion plants is measured. Crudely put, the buyer of the diffusion plants' contract service gives the plant uranium with a low U_{235} content. The plant concentrates the U_{235} content to the level required for use, and then hands it back. The difference in concentration levels is the separative work done.) The 1967 contract price of $26 is then applied to the estimated SWUs to arrive at a value of total contract work done in 1967 dollars. Contract work plus the raw material cost of the uranium would equal value of shipments. This method was rejected because, at 1967 prices, it would add about 100% to the contract cost, and extrapolating that back to 1954 would have meant that the diffusion plants were producing one-third of all the industry's products. But in that year adjusted shipments, as defined by the Census Bureau, for all government-owned plants represented only 28% of all shipments. It was decided, therefore, to assume that contract cost was equal to three-fourths of the value of shipments, since even then the 1954 uranium plants account for 22% of the total industry. (An alternate assumption might be simply to equate contract cost and value of shipments. A check indicated that this did not appreciably affect the shape of the energy-output trends, though it varied the levels, of course.) A further source of error is that some of the work was done for stockpiling, and this might have been excluded from the output index.

When the uranium plant data are removed from industry totals, the energy-output ratio, measured in gross energy consumed, is relatively flat from 1954 to 1958 and from 1962 to 1967, but declines sharply from 1958 to 1962. In useful energy, the ratio declines sharply from 1954 to 1962 and levels out from 1962 to 1967. It is our belief that the 1954 electricity datum is in error, either due to errors in Census processing or in the uranium diffusion plant data. The main reason for this belief is that of the 31.0 billion kwh purchased by the industry in that year, 23.9 billion kwh were used by the AEC. This leaves 7.1 billion kwh, of which 5-6 billion kwh were required by electric furnace phosphoric acid, and 2 billion kwh were required for ammonia production. Of course, some of this requirement was met by the 4 billion kwh generated within the industry, but we do not believe that the rest of the industry (outside these two processes) used so little electricity. In 1958, the SIC 2819 electricity purchased is 67.7 billion kwh, of which 48.8 is the diffusion plants, leaving 18.9 billion kwh for the rest of the industry. In 1962, the purchased electricity total is 62.0, with 45.3 billion kwh for the diffusion plants, leaving 16.7 billion kwh. The decline in electricity for the industry, excluding the diffusion plants, from 1958 to 1962 is plausible, because ammonia plants began switching to natural-gas-driven compressors. Also, wet process phosphoric acid began replacing electric furnace phosphoric acid.

If we assume that some fairly steady decline occurred from 1954 to 1962 in the energy-output ratio for the industry less uranium diffusion, we still must explain the flattening out of the ratio from 1962 to 1967.

Ammonia. The answer seems to be the awesome growth of production of synthetic anhydrous ammonia, primarily for fertilizer use. In 1958, with average price around $75 a ton, production was 3.9 million short tons. In 1962, production had increased to 5.8 million tons. Between 1962 and 1967, production leapt forward by 6.4 million tons to an annual level of 12.2 million tons. In this latter year, the average shipment price was down to $55 per ton, and the cost at the big new plants may have been as low as $30 per ton. With gas-driven compressors, natural gas consumption for heat and power was probably 18 or 19 thousand cubic feet per ton, or some 220 or 230 billion cubic feet all told.

Table 14-6 tells the story. Between 1958 and 1962, natural gas consumption rose from 184 to 210 trillion BTUs, and then leapt to 351 trillion BTUs in 1967. Of this 141 trillion BTU increase in natural gas use from 1962 to 1967, the bulk, possibly 120 trillion, must be attributed to increased ammonia production.

Table 14-6.   Energy Use, Industrial Inorganic Chemicals Less Diffusion Plants

Gross Energy Consumed, 1954-1967
(million BTUs)

	Coal	Coke & Breeze	Fuel Oil	Gas	Other Fuels	Fuels n.s.k.	Elec. Energy	Total
1967 ...	50.5	0.0	16.2	351.1	9.4	0.0	284.9	712.1
1962 ...	102.6	4.7	15.8	210.2	7.4	23.2	153.3	517.2
1958 ...	73.8	0.0	17.4	184.4	18.1	3.4	198.2	495.3
1954 ...	113.8	.3	14.3	183.1	4.7	0.0	86.9	403.1

Gross Energy Consumed per Unit of Output
(1,000 BTUs/1967 $)

	Coal	Coke & Breeze	Fuel Oil	Gas	Other Fuels	Fuels n.s.k.	Elec. Energy	Total
1967 ...	11.9	0.0	3.8	82.7	2.2	5.4	75.1	181.1
1962 ...	30.8	1.4	4.7	63.0	2.2	0.0	82.9	185.0
1958 ...	27.6	0.0	6.5	68.8	6.7	1.3	125.5	236.4
1954 ...	57.7	0.2	7.2	92.9	2.4	0.0	77.8	238.2

Source: Bureau of the Census, *Census of Manufactures.*

SECTION III. PROJECTIONS TO 1980

Output Projections

The nature of the chemicals in Industrial Inorganic Chemicals, n.e.c., dictates that the growth of the industry should move in the same direction as the economy as a whole. Between 1967 and 1971, GNP rose at an annual average rate of 2.5%, while Industrial Inorganic Chemicals, n.e.c., rose at a rate of 1.5% a year. According to Conference Board projections, GNP should rise at a 6.3% annual average rate from 1971 through 1975, and at a rate of 4.3% from 1975 to 1980. Taking into account expected movements in GNP as well as other parameters, among which is an expected large rise in enriched uranium output from 1971-1980, we project that Industrial Inorganic Chemicals, n.e.c., will grow at an annual average rate of 6.8% from 1971 to 1975, and at a rate of 4.7% per year from 1975 to 1980. The resulting levels of output are shown in Table 14-7.

While we have projected a growth rate of Industrial Inorganic Chemicals, n.e.c., the growth will not be uniform, and some change in the product mix will result. Sharply rising energy prices will limit the growth of the energy-intensive chemicals.

Perhaps the hardest hit of all inorganic chemicals will be ammonia. In the past, ammonia had led the growth in production among the chemicals in the industry. However, ammonia production uses natural gas both as a feedstock and as fuel. Therefore, growth in ammonia production is expected to be sharply curtailed. This, in turn, will draw down the average growth rate for all the chemicals in the industry. Any additional demands for ammonia which will emanate from increased demands for fertilizer due to a grain shortage will have to be met by imports. By the second half of the 1970s the industry should have adjusted, combining changes in technology with alternative feedstock, especially substitutes for natural gas, and domestic ammonia growth should start to increase. Of course, if the government decides to regard ammonia as a defense chemical (it is used in the manufacture of explosives), and to allot it the natural gas it needs, the picture will change.

In general, the same pattern will hold for all energy-intensive chemicals. Initially, their growth rate of production will fall off as imports or substitute chemicals take their place. By the middle to late 1970s, adjustments should be effected in the chemical industry to allow energy-intensive chemicals

Table 14-7.   Projected Value of Shipments
(million 1967 $)

1967	1971	1975	1980
$4,284	$5,217	$6,783	$8,529

that will recover to start making a comeback. Chemicals whose growth rate has not started to pick up by 1978 will probably never regain the share of the inorganic chemical market they once held.

Energy Use to 1980

Concern in the chemical industry over the energy shortage should lead to a sharp decline in the energy-output ratio in the manufacture of inorganic chemicals other than uranium in the next few years. From 1967 to 1975 energy use per unit of output should fall about 4.3% a year, and some estimates range as high as 7% per year. From 1975 to 1980 the decline in this ratio should taper off to 2.7% per year.

The initial drop will come as result of changes that the industry may execute immediately. One such change will be the switch in the product mix towards less energy-intensive chemicals already mentioned. This will be combined with the phasing out of energy-intensive processes where less energy-intensive processes exist for the same chemical, along with a careful watch over energy use to avoid wastage. The net result should thus be a saving of about 5% per year in energy use per unit of output for the nondiffusion sector of the industry until 1975.

By the end of 1975, however, most of the immediate changes will have been put into effect; energy conservation will have to await more substantial change. While it is difficult to say what the change may be, it will probably include changes in technology. Since any changes in technology will use the most available fuels, a change in the fuel mix may be expected during this period. Undoubtedly, natural gas will account for a smaller percentage of the fuel mix than it does at the present time. The fuel that will take its place will be the one most easily attained at the time. At the present time, this appears to be coal, or coal transformed to substitute natural gas.

However, the effects of technological change will be outweighed by changing product mix. To understand what will happen to energy use in SIC 2819, we must include projected electric energy use in the AEC's uranium enrichment plant until 1980. During this period, the government plans on putting into effect two programs. The first, known as the Cascades Improvement Program (CIP), is designed to implement technological advances and improvements developed through fiscal year 1970, as well as any advanced technology projected to be achieved by the mid-1970s. These improvements will both increase capacity and increase the efficiency with which additional power may be used. Aside from the additional capacity offered by the CIP, further increases in capacity will be possible by modifying the Cascades to utilize more power following the installation of the improvements. This second plan is known as the Cascades Uprating Program (CUP).

Both the CIP and the CUP will improve the energy-output ratio of enriched uranium production. However, the AEC projects uranium production to grow at a much faster rate than what is expected for the rest of the industry. Therefore, because it is so much more energy-intensive, energy used in gaseous diffusion plants will have a greater influence on energy use in SIC 2819 than it has had in previous years. The AEC's projections for electric energy use in the enrichment of uranium are shown in Table 14-8. This electricity will be used in the manufacture of enriched uranium to meet outstanding and anticipated commitments of the AEC to domestic central power stations, foreign central power stations, and government and other non-power applications.

Linking projected energy use in the manufacture of inorganic chemicals with projected electric energy use in the AEC's gaseous diffusion plants yields the energy use levels projected for SIC 2819, found in Table 14-9.

These figures were then combined with the output projections found in Table 14-7 to yield energy use per unit of output projections for Industrial Inorganic Chemicals, n.e.c. These projections are found in Table 14-10.

Table 14-8. Projected 3-Site Power Level
(megawatts per fiscal year)

1974	4,069
1975	4,588
1976	5,008
1977	5,567
1978	5,733
1979	6,199
1980	6,788
1981	7,110

Note: To convert to kwh multiply megawatts by $365 \times 24 \times 10^3$.
Source: *Report on Outstanding and Anticipated Commitments for Uranium Enrichment vs. Projected Enrichment Capability,* U.S. Atomic Energy Commission, March 1973.

Table 14-9. Projected Energy Use
(trillion BTUs)

	1967	1971	1975	1980
Gross energy consumed	971.3	1095.7	1358.8	1551.2
Useful energy	620.8	732.6	834.0	895.0

Table 14-10. Projected Energy Use Per Value Shipped
(1,000 BTUs/1967 $)

	1967	1971	1975	1980
Gross energy consumed	228.7	210.0	200.3	181.9
Useful energy	146.1	140.4	123.0	104.9

SECTION IV.   APPENDIX

Table 14A-1.   Useful Energy Statistics

| | | | | Energy Consumed (trillion BTUs) | | | | |
	Coal	Coke & Breeze	Fuel Oil	Gas	Other Fuels	Fuels n.s.k.	Purchased Electric Energy	Total
1967 ...	50.5	0.0	16.2	351.1	9.4	0.0	170.3	620.8
1962 ...	102.6	4.7	15.8	210.2	7.4	23.2	211.6	552.3
1958 ...	73.8	0.0	17.4	184.4	18.1	3.4	231.1	528.2
1954 ...	113.8	0.3	14.3	183.1	4.7	0.0	105.9	422.2

| | | | | Energy Use Per Unit of Output (thousand BTUs/constant 1967 $) | | | | |
	Coal	Coke & Breeze	Fuel Oil	Gas	Other Fuels	Fuels n.s.k.	Purchased Electric Energy	Total
1967 ...	11.9	0.0	3.8	82.7	2.2	5.5	401.0	146.1
1962 ...	30.8	1.4	4.7	63.0	2.2	0.0	634.8	165.6
1958 ...	27.6	0.0	6.5	68.8	6.8	1.3	862.5	197.2
1954 ...	57.9	0.2	7.3	92.9	2.4	0.0	537.0	214.1

Source: Bureau of the Census, *Census of Manufactures.*

Table 14A-2.   Shipments by Product Class
(million current $)

	1967	1963	1958	1954
Synthetic ammonia, nitric acid, & ammonium compounds	609.1	424.9	276.5	248.2
Inorganic industrial & household bleaching compounds	154.6	143.4	92.9	74.2
Sulfuric acid	188.4	145.2	136.3	106.9
Inorganic acids except nitric & sulfuric	111.7	85.8	66.0	36.1
Aluminum oxide	(250-500)	(1)	(2)	(2)
Other aluminum compounds	117.5	94.0	272.0	221.9
Potassium & sodium compounds (except bleaches, alkalies & alums)...................	374.7	308.2	274.7	206.8
Chemical catalytic preparations	99.2	(1)	46.8	(3)
Other inorganic chemicals, n.e.c.	807.5	627.1	470.0	338.9
Industrial inorganic chemicals, n.e.c., n.s.k.	(20-50)	(4)	(4)	(4)
Secondary products	453.9	294.9	243.5	194.8
Miscellaneous receipts	894.4	982.3	875.5	570.8
Total shipments	4,248.4	3,493.9	2,754.4	1,998.6

(1) Not available. (2) Included in other aluminum compounds. (3) Not conceptually in SIC 2819 in 1954. (4) Included in other inorganic chemicals, n.e.c.

Source: Bureau of the Census, *Census of Manufactures.*

Table 14A-3.   Diffusion Plant Power Levels
(megawatts)

1954	2,729	1964	4,598
1955	4,936	1965	3,823
1956	6,044	1966	3,332
1957	5,986	1967	2,838
1958	5,690	1968	2,332
1959	5,741	1969	1,999
1960	5,720	1970	1,861
1961	5,590	1971	2,196
1962	5,170	1972	2,862
1963	5,138	1973	3,210

To convert to kwh, multiply megawatts by $365 \times 24 \times 10^3$.

Source: Unpublished data courtesy of Atomic Energy Commission.

SECTION V.   SELECTED BIBLIOGRAPHY

Atomic Energy Commission. *Gaseous Diffusion.*

_____ . *Report on Outstanding and Anticipated Commitments for Uranium Enrichment vs. Projected Capability,* March 1973.

Department of Commerce. *U.S. Industrial Outlook.*

Faith, W. L.; Keyes, Donald B. and Clark, Ronald L. *Industrial Chemicals.* New York: John Wiley and Sons, 1965.

Hogertan, John. *The Atomic Energy Desk Book.* New York: Reinhold Publishing Corporation, 1963.

Shreve, Norris R. *Chemical Process Industries* (3rd. ed.). New York: McGraw-Hill, 1967.

Serials:
Chemical Engineering
Chemical Engineering News
Chemical Week

Chapter Fifteen

Plastics Materials and Resins—SIC 2821

Anthony D. Apostolides

SECTION I. SUMMARY OF FINDINGS

According to the Standard Industrial Classification code, SIC 2821 is entitled
"Plastics Materials, Synthetic Resins, and Nonvulcanizable Rubber" and it is
decribed as: "Establishments primarily engaged in manufacturing synthetic
resins, plastics materials, and nonvulcanizable elastomers." Important products
of this industry are: phenolic and other tar acid resins, urea and melamine resins,
polyethylene and polypropylene resins, styrene resins, and vinyl resins. Establishments engaged in manufacturing fabricated plastics products are classified under
industry SIC 3079.

  Plastics are synthetic organic chemicals; viz., they are built up from
a hydrocarbon base. Plastics and resin materials are typically produced from
intermediate organic chemicals such as styrene and phenol. Producers of resin
usually sell it to processing firms, a separate industry.

  Demand for plastics has increased rapidly over the period of analysis,
as is indicated by the average annual rate of growth in output of 12.8% between
1947 and 1967. Important markets for plastics are construction, packaging,
transportation, appliances, electronics, toys, and agriculture. Growth of plastics
output has been influenced by the high income elasticity of demand for plastics,
by the improvement in quality of existing plastics, and by the discovery of new
uses for plastics and of new plastics materials. Research and development activity
has resulted in the development of new types of plastics and new uses. Demand has
also been influenced by declining plastics prices. Output expansion of plastics
has, moreover, been affected by the substitution of plastics products for other
traditionally used ones. Besides the substitution between plastics and other
products, there is also competition among plastics themselves, as new resins or
new processes are developed.

  Plastics is an industry being affected by the present energy shortage

273

to a higher degree than most industries, since in plastics the materials used for energy creation, such as oil and gas, are also used as raw materials in production.

As growth of energy consumption took place at an annual rate of 8.9% from 1947 to 1967, the energy-output ratio declined by 3.6% per annum from 1954 to 1967, and 3.5% per annum from 1962 to 1967 (see Table 15-1). The decline in the ratio was influenced by changes in process technology which reduced the energy requirement.

Concerning the future, projections of output were derived from the INFORUM input-output model of the University of Maryland, on the basis of Conference Board assumption concerning key economic aggregates. These figures indicate growth of plastics of 11.0% per annum from 1971 to 1980 and 13.7% from 1971 to 1975. The energy-output ratio was projected by assuming an acceleration in its drop to an average annual decline of 4.0% per annum from 1967 to 1975 and to 4.5% from 1975 to 1980 (Table 15-1).

Table 15-1.   Energy-Output Ratio, 1954-1980
(1,000 BTUs/1967 Constant $ of Shipment)

	1947	1954	1958	1962	1967	1975	1980
Gross energy[1]	93	68	80	53	46	33	26
Useful energy[1]	81	60	70	45	37	27	21

[1] See Chapter One, pages 14-15, for definitions of gross and useful energy.
Sources: Tables 15-2 and 15-3.

It appears that plastics production should expand in the future at relatively high rates. Information at present indicates that consumption of plastics will expand significantly in the production of automobiles, construction, and furniture. Furthermore, new uses of plastics are expected to be found over time.

Energy consumption in the future can be expected to decline. Available information shows that there are new processes being adopted in production of plastics which have 25% to 60% lower energy requirements than other processes used today. Moreover, the emphasis currently placed on conservation of energy by both the industry and government should result in energy-saving advances of technology through research and development activity. It can be expected that the plastics industry will devote more resources to develop energy-saving measures, since increased costs for coal, gas, and petroleum affect this industry from both the side of energy and that of raw materials.

SECTION II. HISTORICAL DEVELOPMENTS

Production Processes

The chemical conversion for resin manufacture is polymerization, where single molecules react to form polymers. The two principal types of polymerization are condensation and addition.[1] In *addition* polymerization, when the monomer units polymerize, they do not completely break a chemical bond, but form a new bond between monomers. The result is a polymer which has an identical structural unit with the monomers from which it is formed. In *condensation* polymerization, the chemical bonds between atoms completely rupture; polymers formed by condensation reactions have structural units lacking certain atoms present in the monomers from which they are formed.

Polymerization can take place in a number of ways such as bulk, solution, emulsion, or suspension.[2] Products of condensation polymerization include phenolic resins, amino resins, and polyester resins. Products of addition polymerization encompass polyolefins (which include polyethylene and polypropylene), vinyl resins, vinyl alcohol resins, vinylidene chloride resins, styrene resins, and acrylic resins.

Market Demand

The plastics industry has experienced relatively high rates of output expansion, which are largely attributable to the high income elasticity of demand for plastics and to the substitution of plastics materials for other established ones. The major end-uses for plastics are in large markets, such as construction, packaging, and transportation. Other important markets are appliances, electronics, toys, and agriculture. In these and other markets, plastics continue to replace traditionally used materials such as tin, copper, zinc, wood, and paper. The substitution process has been influenced by improvements in the properties of plastics materials, by the development of new applications, and by the introduction of new products with specialized properties.

Moreover, prices in the plastics industry have declined in absolute terms and in relation to other products, thus further increasing demand and contributing to the process of substitution. Technical developments, brought about by research and development activity, have reduced production costs through new processes.

With respect to individual products, low-density polythylene, used widely in the packaging field, has made possible the manufacturing of unbreakable bottles, liquid-holding paper cartons, no-dent cans, and moisture-proof shipping bags—products not in existence at the time polyethylene was discovered. The single biggest use for low density polyethylene is flexible film and sheeting, most of which goes into packaging.

Changes in Output

The plastics industry has experienced a relatively rapid expansion of output, as is indicated by the 12% growth rate over the 1947-67 period (Appendix Table 15A-1). While the growth rate was the highest during the period from 1947 to 1954, it did not change significantly in subsequent periods.

Within the plastics group, there have been shifts in the product mix over the period of analysis. The relative shares of phenolic resins and urea and melamine resins have declined over time. On the other hand the shares of polyethylene (high and low density) and vinyl resins have increased. Low density polyethylene accounted for 18% of total plastics production in 1958 and for 20% in 1967. The share of high density polyethylene rose from 2% in 1958 to 8% in 1967. Vinyl resins (the most important of which is polyvinyl chloride) accounted for 14% of total plastics production; this figure rose to 19% by 1967. Styrene resins (the most important of which is polystyrene) have been a major product class of the plastics group, at about 17% of total plastics production, and have maintained their relative importance through the years. Thus, the three major product classes of plastics are polyethylene, polystyrene, and polyvinyl chloride.

Energy Input

The energy consumed in plastics production grew at an annual rate of over 8% from 1947 to 1967 (Table 15-2). Energy consumption had its fastest growth from 1954 to 1958.

The main energy sources during the period 1947 to 1967 were coal, fuel oil, gas, and electric energy (Appendix Table 15A-2). The consumption of all four inputs increased from 1947 to 1967; consumption of gas and electricity had the highest growth rates.

During the 1947 to 1967 period, output grew faster than energy and the energy-output ratio declined, as can be seen in Table 15-2.

Table 15-2.   Energy, Output, and Energy-Output Ratios

	1947	1954	1958	1962	1967
Gross energy[1] (trillion BTUs)	29.2	54.3	102.4	105.3	160.0
Shipments (million 1967 $)	$314.0	$798.0	$1,281.0	$1,988.0	$3,474.0
Energy/shipments (1,000 BTUs/1967 $ of shipments)	92.9	68.1	80.0	53.0	46.0
Useful energy (trillion BTUs)	25.5	48.0	90.0	88.9	130.0
Energy/shipments	81.2	60.2	70.3	44.7	37.4

Source: Data on energy and output were obtained from the Bureau of the Census, *Census of Manufactures* (several years).

SECTION III.   PROJECTIONS TO 1980

Growth of Output

In examining the possible future situation of energy and output in the plastics industry, projections of the energy-output ratio are related to projected output data in order to derive an indication of total future energy demand.

Projected output data are obtained from calculations based on the INFORUM input-output model of the University of Maryland (Table 15-3). These figures indicate an annual growth rate of 11.0% for the period 1971 to 1980. Growth is expected to be 13.7% a year during the 1971 to 1975 period; it is expected to be only 8.9% over the following period from 1975 to 1980.

Energy-Output Ratio

In projecting the energy-output ratio, we assume a decline of 4.0% per annum in the ratio from 1967 to 1975 and a decline of 4.5% from 1975 to 1980. It may be pointed out that the energy-output ratio declined at an annual rate of 3.6% between 1954 and 1967, and by 3.5% over the more recent 1962 to 1967 period. The resulting energy use figures for the future are presented in Table 15-3.

The big markets for plastics are construction, packaging, and transportation; and these markets have good growth potential in the future. Use of plastics in automobiles is expected to increase as added uses for plastics are found. Also, use of plastics in furniture is growing rapidly, and the furniture market is predicted to increase markedly along with the number of newly formed households.

It is also anticipated that future output expansion will be influenced by the development and introduction of new and more sophisticated plastics, which will have appeal to architects and designers. Though the use of plastics in these two areas increased during the 1960s, it is expected to rise to even higher levels in the 1970s. Concerning use of plastics in architecture and design, it has been stated that "Probably half of the resins [used] in design over the next decade do not exist commercially today."[3]

Table 15-3.   Projections of Output and Energy Utilization to 1980

	1967	*1975*	*1980*
Shipments (million 1967 $)	$3,474	$8,647	$13,235
Gross energy/shipments (1,000 BTUs/1967 $ of shipments)	46.0	33.2	26.4
Gross energy (trillion BTUs)	160	303	406
Useful energy/shipments (1,000 BTUs/1967 $ of shipments)	37.4	27.0	21.4
Useful energy (trillion BTUs)	130	233.4	283.8

The decline in consumption of energy per unit of output in plastics can be expected to accelerate for the following reasons: First, due to higher energy cost, there will be a drive for technological advances to reduce the amount of energy required. In this regard, one may reasonably expect that there will be a wider adoption of production techniques that require less energy. For example, the radiation-induced polymerization process for the production of low density polyethylene, which appears to be still in the initial stages of development, requires 25% less energy than the tubular reactor process.[4]

With respect to high-density polyethylene, recent versions of the Phillips process, which is used in 60% of U.S. capacity, have greatly reduced energy consumption. The required energy input in these recent versions is 13% to 25% lower than in the older ones.[5] Finally, in the production of polyvinyl chloride, a bulk process is gaining in importance over the suspension polymerization process. The requirement for energy per metric ton of polymer is 1,940 kwh for the suspension process and 750 kwh for the bulk process,[6] a decrease of about 61% in energy requirement.

Furthermore, there should be a wider adoption of, and improvement in, energy conservation measures, such as the capture and use of steam created as a by-product of an initial chemical reaction. Another possibility would be to use waste materials from plastics production as inputs in the creation of energy. Based on survey information, it has been estimated that almost $500 million worth of electricity can be generated annually in the U.S. from waste plastics, by incineration.[7]

Finally, it may be pointed out that the plastics industry uses coal, petroleum, and gas not only as sources of energy but also as raw materials, or feedstock. Thus, when prices of hydrocarbons rise, costs of the plastics industry are affected from both the standpoint of energy and that of feedstock. With respect to possible output expansion of plastics, it may be that the decline in availability of petroleum, caused largely by the rapid growth of energy consumption, will impede the future growth of the industry. The use of alternate sources of energy, such as fast breeder nuclear reactions, fusion power, solar power, and geothermal power, will have a beneficial impact on energy availability. As previously stated, "These sources offer the potential for much more energy than was ever available in coal, petroleum, and natural gas."[8] Furthermore, use of alternate energy sources would release raw materials for plastics production.

With respect to growth of plastics output and the feedstock problem, a process has been developed in Japan to convert waste polyethylene into fuel oil and gasoline.[9] In this process, polyethylene wastes in the form of film, sheet, pellets, and molded products are placed in a reactor with water. The heat and pressure built up by the steam from the boiling water cracks about 90% of the polyethylene into fuel oil, of which about 20% can be refined into gasoline. Reportedly, the process can be applied to other plastics. Technological advances, such as the above, can offset possible adverse effects on output growth, brought about by nonavailability of feedstock; they can also contribute to the energy input.

Notes

[1] These processes are explained in more detail in Kent, J. A., ed., *Riegel's Industrial Chemistry,* Chapter 10.

[2] For a description of these processes, see Shreve, *Chemical Process Industries,* pp. 660-662.

[3] "The Outlook: 1970-80," *Modern Plastics,* January 1970, p. 98.

[4] Stanford Research Institute, *The Plastics Industry in the Year 2000,* p. 56.

[5] *Ibid,* p. 57.

[6] *Ibid,* p. 59.

[7] *Ibid,* p. 42.

[8] *Ibid,* p. 29.

[9] *Modern Plastics,* January 1972, p. 116.

SECTION IV. APPENDIX

Table 15A-1. Growth of Shipments and Energy Consumption (compound annual percentage rates)

	Shipments (1967 $)	Gross Energy (BTUs)	Useful Energy (BTUs)
1947-67	12.77%	8.88%	8.44%
1947-54	14.24	9.27	9.44
1954-58	12.47	17.10	17.10
1958-62	11.58	0.74	−0.46
1962-67	11.84	8.73	7.86

Source: Bureau of the Census, *Census of Manufactures* (several years).

Table 15A-2. Energy Consumption, by Source (trillion BTUs)

	1947	1954	1958	1962	1967
Coal	19.9	27.1	38.2	40.0	37.0
Fuel oil	2.6	5.2	9.2	12.1	18.4
Gas	0.5	10.7	28.1	20.7	39.2
Other fuels	1.3	2.7	6.4	8.4	9.4
Fuels n.s.k.	0	0	2.7	0	10.4
Electric energy*	4.7	8.7	17.9	24.2	45.6
Total	29.2	54.3	102.4	105.3	160.0

*Refers to gross energy.

Source: Bureau of the Census, *Census of Manufactures* (several years).

SECTION V.   SELECTED BIBLIOGRAPHY

Faith, W. L.; Keyes, Donald B.; and Clark, Ronald L. *Industrial Chemicals.* New York: John Wiley & Sons, 1965.

Harkins, Malcolm J.; Wallace, Charles E. and Manufacturing Chemists Association, Inc. "The Chemical Industry" in *The Development of American Industries.* Glover, John G. and Lagi, Rudolph L. eds. New York: Simmons-Boardman Publishing Corporation, 1959.

Kent, James A., ed. *Riegel's Industrial Chemistry.* New York: Reinhold Publishing Corporation, 1962.

Kirk-Othmer. *Encyclopedia of Chemical Technology,* 2nd Edition. New York: Wiley-Interscience, 1972.

Mercier, Claude. *Petrochemical Industry and the Possibility of Its Establishment in the Developing Countries.* Paris: Institut Francais du Petrole, 1966.

"The Outlook: 1970-80". *Modern Plastics.* January 1970, p. 97.

Shreve, Norris R. *Chemical Process Industries,* 3rd Edition. New York: McGraw-Hill, 1967.

Sittig, Marshall. *Organic Chemical Processes.* Pearl River, N.Y.: The Noyes Press, 1962.

Stanford Research Institute. *The Plastics Industry in the Year 2000.* Menlo Park, California: April, 1973.

United Nations. *Studies in the Development of Plastics Industries.* New York, 1969.

————. *Studies in Plastics Fabrication and Application.* New York, 1969.

————. *Petrochemical Industries in Developing Countries.* New York, 1970.

U.S. Tariff Commission. *Synthetic Organic Chemicals,* for several years.

Vance, Stanley, "The Chemical Industry" in *American Industries.* New York: Prentice Hall, 1955.

Serials:
Chemical Engineering
Chemical Week
Hydrocarbon Processing
Modern Plastics

Chapter Sixteen

Synthetic Rubber—SIC 2822

Barry Kolatch

SECTION I. INTRODUCTION AND SUMMARY OF FINDINGS

Introduction

The Synthetic Rubber industry, as described under the 1972 Standard Industrial Classification, consists of establishments primarily engaged in the manufacture of synthetic rubber by polymerization or copolymerization. The elastomer (rubber-like) materials used are, among others, butadienes, acrylonitriles, styrenes, chloroprenes and isobutylene-isoprenes. Butadiene copolymers containing less than 50% butadiene are classified in Industry 2821. Natural chlorinated rubbers and cyclized rubbers are classified in Industry 3069.

The most popular kind of synthetic rubber is styrene-butadiene rubber (SBR). It is mostly used in the manufacture of passenger tires, and in 1967 accounted for 67.9% of total synthetic rubber consumption. In conjunction with SBR, stereo elastomer polybutadiene is used in passenger tire manufacture. In 1967, polybutadiene accounted for 10.4% of total synthetic rubber consumption. Other synthetic rubbers of note are polyisoprene, which is man's duplicate of natural rubber, butyl, nitrile rubber (N-type), chloroprene, and ethylene-propylene rubbers, among which the most popular is ethylene-propylene dimer rubber (EPDM).

Historical Overview, 1947-1967

The synthetic rubber industry grew at an annual average rate of 6.7% in the twenty-year period between 1947 and 1967. This growth had two driving forces behind it: (1) increased substitution of synthetic rubber for natural rubber; and (2) constant growth of the automobile industry, which consumes large quantities of synthetic rubber for tire use.

From 1947 through 1962, both the product mix and the technology of the synthetic rubber industry remained more or less constant. Thus it would be expected that the energy-output ratio for the synthetic rubber industry should be approximately constant for these years. This was indeed the case for 1947, 1958, and 1962. The 1954 figure, however, is considerably higher than the others, and this fact is largely unexplained.

In the early 1960s the product mix of the synthetic rubber industry changed somewhat, with the newly developed stereo elastomers, polybutadiene and polyisoprene cutting into SBR's share of the product mix. The stereo elastomers are polymerized in solution and thus require a higher steam load than does SBR. As a result, the energy-output ratio for the synthetic rubber industry rose 31.7% between 1962 and 1967.

Projections to 1980

Output projections used in this report were obtained from the Maryland Interindustry Forecasting Model (INFORUM). The growth levels that come out of the model for the synthetic rubber industry are 8.1% per year for the years 1971 through 1975, and 5.1% per year for 1975 through 1980. The projected levels of output are shown in Table 16-3.

During this time period, it is expected that the trend towards energy-intensive rubbers will continue. Polyisoprene growth should be aided by the increasing popularity of the radial tire. The SBR polybutadiene mix in passenger

Table 16-1.   New Rubber Consumption, 1947–1967
(1,000 long tons)

	1947	1954	1958	1962	1967
Synthetic rubber	560	634	872	1,256	1,628
Natural rubber	563	596	485	427	489
% New rubber = Synthetic rubber ...	49.9%	51.5%	64.3%	74.6%	76.9%

Source: *Rubber, Current Industrial Reports M30A.*

Table 16-2.   Energy Use, 1947–1967

	Total (trillion BTUs)		Per Unit of Output (1,000 BTUs/1967 $)	
	Useful[1] Energy	Gross Energy[1] Consumed	Useful Energy	Gross Energy Consumed
1947	11.4	14.9	44.7	58.1
1954	21.4	24.8	72.7	84.5
1958	22.7	27.4	46.0	55.4
1962	35.4	41.9	49.5	58.6
1967	60.5	71.6	65.3	77.2

[1] See Chapter One, pages 14-15, for definitions of useful and gross energy.

Table 16-3. Projected Value Shipped, 1967-1980
(million 1967 $)

1967	*1971*	*1975*	*1980*
$927.0	$1,086.4	$1,486.8	$1,910.5

Table 16-4. Projected Energy Use, 1967-1980

	Total (trillion BTUs)		*Per Unit of Output* (1,000 BTUs/1967 $)	
	Useful Energy	*Gross Energy Consumed*	*Useful Energy*	*Gross Energy Consumed*
1967	60.5	71.6	65.3	77.2
1971	76.4	90.7	70.3	83.5
1975	109.0	129.1	73.3	86.9
1980	147.4	174.4	77.1	91.3

tires may shift from 65-35 to 50-50, and new SBR plants may use the more energy-intensive solution polymerization rather than the emulsion polymerization presently employed. Further adding to energy use will be pollution-control devices, which have recently or will shortly become mandatory by law.

Faced with rising energy use and a prospective fuel shortage, the rubber companies are taking steps to combat a rise in their energy-output ratio. The use of heat exchangers to recover waste streams, as well as the recovery of waste heat, are steps the industry is taking; one company substituted waste tars for water in the making of steam and found it cut energy use by 20%.

It will be difficult, however, for energy conservation measures to offset a more energy-intensive product mix. Thus, the energy-output ratio for the industry is projected at a rise of 1% a year from 1971 through 1980. The projected energy levels and energy-output ratio are shown in Table 16-4.

SECTION II. HISTORICAL ANALYSIS
1947-1967

Demand for Synthetic Rubber

Over the twenty-year period from 1947 to 1967, the value shipped by the synthetic rubber industry jumped from $256 million to $927 million (computed in 1967 constant dollars), an increase of over 260%. This yielded an annual average growth rate of 6.7% per year. The growth rates of all synthetic rubbers, however, were not uniform, resulting in a few changes in the product mix. These changes may be seen in Table 16-3.

Three things of note come out of Table 16-3. The share of the product mix held by butyl fell consistently from 1947 through 1967. S-type rubbers' (this is mostly SBR) share of total consumption, which had been about 80% of the total from 1947 through 1958, dropped in 1962, and declined again in 1967.

A new breed of rubbers called stereo elastomers started to account for some synthetic rubber consumption in 1962.

Like most synthetic rubbers, butyl rubber is used in the manufacture of tires. Unlike SBR, however, butyl is not used in the manufacture of the outer tire, but is used in the manufacture of inner tubing. With the invention of the tubeless tire in the early 1950s, butyl's share of the synthetic rubber industry began to diminish.

The drop in the share of the synthetic rubber product mix experienced by SBR in recent years stems directly from the advent of stereo elastomers. The two most popular types of stereo elastomers are polyisoprene and polybutadiene. Polyisoprene is a duplicate of natural rubber, and it was expected to cut into natural rubber consumption significantly. While polyisoprene has grown and should continue to grow, it has not had as significant an effect on natural rubber as originally expected. Polybutadiene, however, has enjoyed greater success, and by 1967 it accounted for 10.4% of synthetic rubber consumption. Originally it was thought that polybutadiene, with its low heat buildup and abrasive resistance, would replace natural rubber in the manufacture of heavy duty tires. Pure polybutadiene, however, exhibited inferior wet traction, and inferior resistance to chipping, so its use in tire manufacture has been restricted to blends with SBR and natural rubber. Instead of replacing natural rubber, polybutadiene has gradually encroached on SBR's share of the passenger tire market. At first polybutadiene replaced 15% to 20% of the SBR used in passenger tire compounds. At the present time, polybutadiene accounts for 35% of the rubber used in passenger tire manufacture. The use of polybutadiene in tires contributes excellent resilience, good aging properties, and low temperature flexibilities, as well as abrasive resistance and low heat buildup. It is the substitution of polybutadiene for SBR that has accounted for the growing share of the product mix occupied by stereo elastomers, and the diminishing share of the product mix occupied by SBR since 1962.

Energy Use[1]

Table 16-6 shows that natural gas is the fuel used in greatest abundance by the synthetic rubber industry, while electricity is the industry's second largest source of power. Most of the natural gas as well as other fuels, excluding electricity, goes into the making of steam to be used during the manufacture of synthetic rubber, while the electricity is used to power machinery.

With the exception of the year 1954, the energy-output ratio for the

Table 16-5.   Rubber Consumption, by Type, 1947-1967
(1,000 long tons)

	1947	1954	1958	1962	1967
S-type	448.6	500.3	730.2	974.1	1,106.3
Share of total	80.2%	78.6%	83.0%	74.5%	67.9%
Butyl	68.8	61.5	53.4	71.3	81.0
Share of total	12.3%	9.7%	6.1%	5.5%	5.0%
Neoprene	37.7	57.2	69.7	(2)	(2)
Share of total	6.7%	8.9%	7.9%		
N-Type	0.45	17.7	26.6	39.6	55.4
Share of total	0.8%	2.8%	3.0%	3.0%	3.4%
Stereo polybutadiene elastomers	(1)	(1)	(1)	108.4	169.5
Share of total				8.3%	10.4%
Other stereo elastomers	(1)	(1)	(1)	(3)	78.8
Share of total					4.8%
Other elastomers	(1)	(1)	(1)	113.4	137.1
Share of total				8.7%	8.5%
All synthetic rubber	559.6	636.7	879.9	1,306.8	1,628.3
Share of total	100%	100%	100%	100%	100%

(1) Not yet developed
(2) Included in other elastomers
(3) Included in stereo polybutadiene elastomers.

Source: *Rubber, Current Industrial Reports M30A.*

Table 16-6.   Gross Energy Consumed, 1947-1967
(trillion BTUs)

	Coal	Fuel Oil	Gas	Other Fuels	Fuels n.s.k.	Purchased Electric Energy	Total
1967	7.3	0.3	37.5	8.1	2.0	16.4	71.6
1962	7.5	0.2	16.2	8.4	0.0	9.5	41.9
1958	2.8	0.2	9.9	6.7	1.0	6.7	27.4
1954	3.8	0.1	11.4	4.7	0.0	4.8	24.8
1947	2.7	0.0	7.8	0.0	0.0	4.4	14.9

Note: n.s.k.—not specified by kind.
Source: Bureau of the Census, *Census of Manufactures.*

synthetic rubber industry remained relatively unchanged from 1947 through 1962. Between 1947 and 1954, however, the energy-output ratio rose from 58.0 thousand BTUs per 1967 constant dollar to 84.5 thousand BTUs per 1967 constant dollar. This 45% increase is largely unexplained. No significant change in the product mix took place in 1954, and there was no major change in technology to cause a major shift in the energy-output ratio. The relative

Table 16-7.   Gross Energy Consumed per Unit of Output,
1947-1967

(1,000 BTUs/1967 $)

	Coal	Fuel Oil	Gas	Other Fuels	Fuels n.s.k.	Purchased Electric Energy	Total
1967	7.9	0.3	40.5	8.7	2.2	17.7	77.2
1962	10.5	0.3	22.7	11.8	0.0	13.3	58.6
1958	5.7	0.4	20.1	13.6	2.0	13.6	55.4
1954	12.9	0.3	38.8	16.0	0.0	16.4	84.5
1947	10.3	0.1	30.4	0.0	0.0	17.1	58.0

Note: n.s.k.—not specified by kind.
Source: Bureau of the Census, *Census of Manufactures.*

consistency of energy utilization per unit of output in 1947, 1958, and 1962
reflects the fact that there was little change in technology or in the product mix
from 1947 to 1962.

Between 1962 and 1967, the energy-output ratio increased from
58.5 thousand BTUs per 1967 constant dollar of output to 77.2, an increase of
over 31%. The switch in the product mix from SBR to stereo elastomers was
largely responsible for this shift. In 1967, one ton of SBR required 5,040 pounds
of steam and 493 kwh of electricity. Thus 6.9 million BTUs of fuel and 5.1
million BTUs of electricity were consumed in the manufacture of SBR.
Polybutadiene, however, the most popular of the stereo elastomers can use as
much as 35,840 pounds of steam and 896 kwh of electricity per ton, or a total
of over 49 million BTUs for the manufacture of steam, and electricity
consumption of about 9.3 million BTUs. Other stereo elastomers have similarly
high energy requirements, and thus the shift in the product mix from SBR to
stereo elastomers caused a high rise in the synthetic rubber industry's energy-
output ratio from 1962 to 1967.

SECTION III.   PROJECTIONS TO 1980

Output

Output projections made in this study are made on the basis of the
Maryland Interindustry Forecasting Model (INFORUM). The growth levels that
come out of the model for the synthetic rubber industry are 8.1% per annum for
the years 1971 to 1975, and 5.1% per annum for the years 1975 to 1980. The
resulting output levels are shown in Table 16-3.

Two or possibly three changes should occur in the synthetic rubber
industry by 1980. First, the emergence of radial tires is expected to shift some
rubber demand patterns. The possibility of uneven stretching between cord
material and carcass rubber is higher in the manufacture of a radial tire than a

bias ply tire. The radial tire maker thus attaches a premium on the green (uncured) strength of the rubber he uses. Of all rubbers, natural rubber has the highest green strength, and thus natural rubber's share of the new rubber market is expected to grow with the popularity of the radial tire. Of the synthetic rubbers, polyisoprene, which is regarded as man-made natural rubber, has the highest green strength, though not as high as that of natural rubber. Because polyisoprene's processibility and flow properties are better, and because its price is more stable, its growth should at least keep pace with that of natural rubber.

The second trend that may be expected is the gradual switch towards solution polymerization of SBR as opposed to emulsion polymerization. The advantage of solution SBR, however, is that its production costs are no greater than those of emulsion SBR, and the cost of building a new plant is less. Until the rise of an energy shortage, this made solution polymerization the most probable process for all new SBR plants. However, solution SBR uses more energy than the emulsion polymer as additional steam is necessary for solvent recovery; so if the price of fuel gets high enough, solution SBR plants may no longer be economical. Consequently, their growth will be seriously impeded.

The third change that may come about in the synthetic rubber product mix by 1980 is the rise of EPDM from a specialty rubber to a general purpose tire rubber. Since the 1960s EPDM has been hailed as the rubber of the future. It has been held in high esteem due to qualities such as high tolerance of cost-cutting carbon black and oil extenders, high heat and abrasion resistance, and its formation of a superior base for retreading. Yet poor building tack and low compatibility with other blend polymers during curing have caused EDPM's growth to be far below all expectations. If the need for polymer tack is reduced through new tire-building techniques or chemical additions, and if EPDM is modified to overcome incompatibility, it may rise to the heights originally predicted for it and be an important tire rubber by 1980. If this is not the case, EPDM will remain in its present position as a specialty rubber.

Energy Use

Almost all the stereo elastomers and ethylene-propylene rubbers are polymerized in solution and thus require more energy than older elastomers such as emulsion SBR. If the trends toward these rubbers continue, especially if solution SBR becomes more prevalent, the energy-output ratio of the synthetic rubber industry will rise.

Faced with a prospective fuel shortage, the rubber industry is taking steps to combat rises in the energy-output ratio and shortage of natural gas. As an immediate reaction to a lack of natural gas, rubber companies have already begun to convert their steam-making facilities so that they may use oil. If the natural gas shortage worsens, the trend will continue, and we will expect to see a marked change in the fuel mix from natural gas to oil. If oil becomes scarce, the next step would probably be towards coal. Most rubber companies, however, would try to avoid this because of the added costs of pollution control on the high-sulfur-content coal that would be available.

To keep their energy-output ratio down, the rubber companies are trying to use all the energy-saving devices they now have available. The use of heat exchangers to recover heat streams should become increasingly prominent over the next few years, as should the recovery of waste heat. To further reduce energy use, it is expected that economizers will be put on all boilers that do not already have them. A slightly less conventional method for saving fuel may be the heating of waste tar instead of water to provide steam. Dow Chemical Company tried this in their latex manufacturing plant in Midland, Michigan, last winter and found that it reduced energy consumption by 20%.

All in all, however, it appears that energy-saving techniques will be hard pushed to keep up with rising energy needs over the next few years. The push from solution elastomers raised the energy-output ratio between 1962 and 1967, and again between 1967 and 1971. While solution SBR growth may be significantly stunted by an energy shortage, other solution elastomers such as polyisoprene and polybutadiene have desirable properties not found in less energy-intensive substitutes. Thus, barring massive rises in price, their growth rates should not be impeded by an energy shortage. Furthermore, pollution-control devices that have already become or will soon become mandatory by law should add to energy usage during the next decade.

Assuming that technology remains constant, and that solution SBR does not become an important product within the next few years, we project that the energy-output ratio for the synthetic rubber industry will rise at an annual average rate of 1% between 1971 and 1980. The levels of energy use, and the energy-output ratios for the years 1967 through 1980, are shown in Table 16-4.

Notes

[1] All energy measurements in this section are computed on a gross energy consumed basis.

SECTION IV. APPENDIX

Table 16A-1. Useful Energy, 1947-1967
(trillion BTUs)

	Coal	Fuel Oil	Gas	Other Fuels	Fuels n.s.k.	Purchased Electric Energy	Total
1967	7.3	0.3	37.5	8.1	2.0	5.4	60.5
1962	7.5	0.2	16.2	8.4	0.0	3.1	35.4
1958	2.8	0.2	9.9	6.7	1.0	2.1	22.7
1954	3.8	0.1	11.4	4.7	0.0	1.3	21.4
1947	2.7	0.0	7.8	0.0	0.0	1.0	11.4

Useful Energy per Unit of Output 1947-1967
(1,000 BTUs/1967 $)

	Coal	Fuel Oil	Gas	Other Fuels	Fuels n.s.k.	Purchased Electric Energy	Total
1967	7.9	0.3	40.5	8.7	2.2	17.7	77.2
1962	10.5	0.3	22.7	11.7	0.0	13.3	58.6
1958	5.7	0.4	20.1	13.6	2.0	13.6	55.4
1954	13.0	0.3	38.8	16.0	0.0	16.4	84.5
1947	10.4	0.1	30.5	0.0	0.0	17.1	58.1

Note: n.s.k.—not specified by kind.
Source: Bureau of the Census, *Census of Manufactures.*

Table 16A-2.   Energy Use per Long Ton for Selected Synthetic Rubbers

Styrene-Butadiene

	Emulsion Process		Solution Process
	Without Expander Dryer	*With Expander Dryer*	
Steam	5,040 lbs.	2,665 lbs.	10,816 lbs.
Electricity	493 kwh	600 kwh	493 kwh

Polybutadiene

	Cobalt Complex	*Iodine Ziegler*
Steam	22,400 lbs.	35,840 lbs.
Electricity	672 kwh	896 kwh
	Nickel Complex	*n-Butyllithium*
Steam	31,360 lbs.	19,040 lbs.
Electricity........	784 kwh	784 kwh

Polyisoprene

	Ziegler	*n-Butyllithium*
Steam	25,760 lbs.	22,400 lbs.
Electricity........	716 kwh	588 kwh

Butyl

	Butyl
Steam	22,064 lbs.
Electricity	3,203 kwh
Natural gas........	67 scf.

Chloroprene

	From Acetylene	*From Butadiene Oxychlorination*
Steam	8,326 lbs.	2,979 lbs.
Electricity........	97 kwh	69 kwh

SECTION V.   SELECTED BIBLIOGRAPHY

Stanford Research Institute. *Chemical Economics Handbook.*
——— . *Process Economics Program Reports.*
U.S. Department of Commerce. *U.S. Industrial Outlook.*

Serials:
Chemical Engineering.
Rubber Age.
Rubber World.

Chapter Seventeen

Man-Made Fibers—SIC 2823 and 2824

Anthony D. Apostolides

SECTION I. SUMMARY OF FINDINGS

This chapter deals with two industries: that of cellulosic man-made fibers (SIC 2823) and that of synthetic organic fibers, except cellulosic (SIC 2824). The Standard Industrial Classification manual defines SIC 2823 as follows: "Establishments primarily engaged in manufacturing cellulosic fibers (including cellulose acetate and regenerated cellulose such as rayon by the viscose or cuprammonium process) in the form of monofilament, yarn, staple or tow suitable for further manufacturing on spindles, looms, knitting machines or other textile processing equipment." The same manual defines SIC 2824 as "Establishments primarily engaged in manufacturing synthetic organic fibers, except cellulosic, in the form of monofilament yarn, staple or tow."

Important markets for man-made fibers are home furnishings (absorbing about 30% of production), industrial uses (23%), women's and children's apparel (21%), and men's and boy's wear (13%).

The energy-output ratios of both industries steadily declined between 1958 and 1967 (see Table 17-1). The ratio of SIC 2823 declined by an annual rate of 2.97% (3.07% for useful energy[a]), while that of SIC 2824 declined at 2.44% per year (3.55% for useful energy). It is suggested that decreases in energy utilization per unit of output can be attributed to advances in process technology and the pressure of competition from abroad to reduce production costs. Furthermore, the rapid growth of SIC 2824, at 18.7% over 1958-67 (versus 3.9% for SIC 2824), may have brought about economies of scale in production, contributing to more efficient utilization of energy.

With respect to the components of energy input in SIC 2823, by far the most important has been coal; but the relative share of electricity, though small, has been steadily increasing over 1958-67. In SIC 2824, the two most

[a]See Chapter One, pages 14-15, for definitions of useful and gross energy.

Table 17-1.   Energy–Output Ratio, 1958-1980
(1,000 BTUs/1967 $ of shipments)

	1958	1962	1967	1975	1980
			Cellulosic (2823)		
Gross energy	146	128	112	84	69
Useful energy	143	125	108	81	67
			Noncellulosic (2824)		
Gross energy	66	58	53	42	36
Useful energy	61	52	44	32	25

Source: Tables 17-2 and 17-3.

important classes of energy have been coal and gas. However, the importance of electricity increased rapidly during 1958-67, and in 1967 its relative share, in energy consumption, was second—similar to that of gas.

Total energy use in 1975 and 1980 was estimated for each industry by projecting the energy-output ratio and relating it to projected output figures. These output figures were obtained from calculations, carried out by computer, based on the INFORUM input-output model of the University of Maryland. According to these data, output of SIC 2823 is expected to grow at 4.0% per annum over 1971-80, and 5.7% over 1971-75. Output of SIC 2824 is predicted to grow at 10.9% over 1971-80, and 15.0% over 1971-75. It is expected that the energy-output ratio will continue to decline. This appears justified in view of the steady decrease in the ratio, for each industry, in the past. The projected energy-output ratios are shown in Table 17-1, along with those of the past.

SECTION II.   TRENDS IN PRODUCTION AND ENERGY UTILIZATION

Production Processes

Cellulosic fibers are produced when natural polymeric materials such as cellulose are brought into a dissolved state and then spun into fine filaments. Cellulosic fibers are rayon and acetate. Noncellulosic synthetic fibers result from the formation of long chain molecules, by two methods: addition polymerization and condensation polymerization.[1] The polymer is taken from its solution and processed into fiber form. Important product classes are nylon, acrylics (such as Orlon), and polyesters (such as Dacron). Noncellulosic synthetic fibers begin with the preparation of a polymer which consists of very long, chainlike molecules. The polymer is spun in one of four ways: melt, dry, wet, or core. The polymer is then stretched and crystalline lattices are formed. A single polymer can be used to make a number of different fibers by controlling the degree of orientation when stretching the molecules, crystallinity, and average chain length.

For the production of rayon and acetate, the general outline of both the viscose and cuprammonium processes is as follows: solution of the cellulose through a chemical reaction, aging or ripening of the solution, filtration and removal of air, spinning of the fiber, combining the filaments into yarn, and finishing (which entails bleaching, washing, oiling, and drying).

The single largest user of man-made fibers is the home furnishings market, accounting for 30% of production. Industrial users absorb 23%, women's and children's apparel 21%, men's and boy's wear 13%, and other consumer uses 14%.[2]

Energy-Output Relationship

The energy-output ratio of SIC 2823 steadily declined between 1958 and 1967 (see Table 17-2). This decline can be observed in terms of either gross energy or useful energy data.

With respect to the components of the ratio and their change over time, output (shipments in 1967 dollars) of cellulosic fibers (SIC 2833) grew at an annual rate of 3.89% over 1958-67 while energy grew at 0.75% (0.65% for useful energy) over the same period (Appendix Table 17A-1). Output growth rose from about 2% during 1958-62 to well over 5% during 1962-67. Energy consumption also increased at an annual rate of 2.47% (2.29% for useful energy) over 1962-67; it had a negative growth rate during the previous 1958-62 period. Among the components of the energy input of cellulosic fibers, by far the most important class has been coal (see Appendix Table 17A-2). Also, the relative share of electric energy, though small, steadily increased over 1958-67.

Table 17-2.   Output, Energy Consumption, and Energy-Output Ratio

	Cellulosic (2823)			Noncellulosic (2824)		
	1958	*1962*	*1967*	*1958*	*1962*	*1967*
Shipments (million 1967 $)	641	695	903	435	968	2,033
Gross energy (trillion BTUs)	93.9	89.3	100.8	28.7	56.7	107.4
Energy/shipments (1,000 BTUs/1967 $ of shipments)	146.4	128.4	111.6	65.9	58.6	52.8
Useful energy (trillion BTUs)	91.7	86.9	97.5	26.5	50.5	89.6
Energy/shipments (1,000 BTUs/1967 $ of shipments)................	143.1	125.0	108.0	60.9	52.2	44.1

Source: Data for shipments and energy were obtained from the Bureau of the Census, *Census of Manufactures* (several years).

With respect to noncellulosic fibers (SIC 2824), the energy-output ratio in this industry also declined steadily over the 1958-67 period (Table 17-2). Output over this period grew at 18.7% a year, while energy consumption grew at 15.8% (14.5% for useful energy). Both output and energy consumption in this industry grew faster during 1958-62 than they did during the subsequent 1962-67 period (Appendix Table 17A-1). Of the components of the energy input, coal and gas have been the two most important classes (Appendix Table 17A.3). However, the importance of electricity increased rapidly during 1958-67 and in 1967 its relative share was second—similar to that of gas. Coal was the single most important energy input over 1958-67.

It may be pointed out that the rate of 18.7%, at which output of SIC 2824 grew over 1958-67, was a significantly higher rate than the 3.9% rate at which output of SIC 2823 grew over the same period. And although the difference of the two growth rates has decreased over time, it has remained quite substantial. Thus, demand for synthetic noncellulosic fibers seems to have grown considerably faster than for cellulosic ones.

The steady decrease over 1958-67 in the energy-output ratio of both industries would indicate advances in process technology that decreased the energy requirement per unit of output. Also, emphasis on increasing production efficiency was probably influenced by foreign competition. Since textiles (and thus fibers) are one of the first industries developed during a country's economic development, domestic textile products usually have to compete with those made abroad, often in developing countries. This provides an impetus to increase overall production efficiency, which can result in lower rates of energy utilization.

SECTION III.   PROJECTIONS TO 1980

In examining the possible future situation of energy and output in cellulosic (SIC 2823) and other man-made fibers (SIC 2824), projections of the energy-output ratio will be related to projected output data, and thereby elicit an indication of the energy requirement that may accompany future output expansion of the two industries.

Growth of Output

Projected output data are obtained from calculations, carried out by computer, based on the INFORUM input-output model of the University of Maryland, and they are shown in Table 17-3. These figures indicate an annual growth rate of 4.0% for cellulosic fibers from 1971 to 1980. Over 1971-1975, output is predicted to grow at 5.7%, and then at a rate of 2.7% over 1975-80. Output of noncellulosic fibers is expected to grow at 10.9% over 1971-80. Furthermore, the growth rate is predicted to drop from 15.0% during 1971-75 to 7.7% over the subsequent 1975-80 period.

Table 17-3. Projections of Output and Energy Utilization to 1980

	Cellulosic (2823)			Noncellulosic (2824)		
	1967	*1975*	*1980*	*1967*	*1975*	*1980*
Shipments (million 1967 $)	903	1,194	1,366	2,033	5,518	7,994
Gross energy/shipments (1,000 BTUs/1967 $ of shipments	111.6	83.9	69.2	52.8	42.3	36.3
Gross energy (trillion BTUs)	100.8	100.2	94.5	107.4	223.2	290.1
Useful energy/shipments (1,000 BTUs/1967 $ of shipments)	108.0	81.2	66.7	44.1	31.8	25.5
Useful energy (trillion BTUs)	97.5	96.9	91.4	89.6	175.4	203.5

Energy-Output Ratio

In projecting the energy-output ratio, we expect that there will be a continuation in the steady decline of the ratio in both industries, partly because the rising cost of energy is expected to motivate companies to adopt energy-saving measures in their plants. Thus, for cellulosic fibers (SIC 2823), we assume a decline in the energy-output ratio of 3.5% a year over 1967-75, and 3.8% over the subsequent 1975-80 period. For noncellulosic fibers (SIC 2824), we assume an annual decrease in the gross energy-output ratio of 2.75% for 1967-75 and 3.0% for 1975-80. With respect to the useful energy-output ratio in the same industry, the assumed rates of decline are 4.0% for 1967-75 and 4.35% for 1975-80. The two sets of assumed figures for SIC 2824 seemed warranted in view of the large disparity between past declines in the energy-output ratio. That is, over 1958-67 the gross energy-output ratio declined at an annual rate of 2.44%, while the useful energy-output ratio declined at 3.55% a year. The rates of decline for 1962-67 were 2.07% for gross energy and 3.32% for net energy. The results of relating the projected energy-output ratios to projected output figures are shown in Table 17-3.

With respect to expanding the output of man-made fibers, experts anticipate a steady growth, and no new synthetic organic fibers, in the near future. Instead, modifications of existing fibers are expected; advances already being made in synthetic fibers include flame resistance, better and more efficient dyeability, and new aesthetic effects.

At the present time, there is high demand for domestically produced man-made fibers. It has been boosted by the devaluation of the dollar and by current fashions, such as longer skirts and sweaters. On the supply side, trade agreements restricting imports of synthetic fiber products are benefiting production activity of domestic producers. Although the industry is at present not adding capacity at a fast pace, it is expected to do so after 1975.[3]

Finally, though not directly related to the energy situation in man-made fibers, recent testimony in the U.S. Senate holds that the production of cotton fiber requires less energy than the production of either cellulosic or synthetic fibers.[4] Assuming that the figures presented as evidence are correct, it could be suggested that energy savings can be realized by increasing the cotton fiber input in the manufacturing of textiles, whether these textiles are completely based on cotton or on a mixture of cotton and man-made fibers.

Notes

[1] For description of processes, see N. R. Shreve, *Chemical Process Industries*, Chapter 35.

[2] *Standard and Poor's Industry Surveys, Chemicals*, October 25, 1972, p. C35.

[3] "The Sprightly Outlook for Synthetic Fibers," *Business Week*, April 14, 1973, p. 30.

[4] "Senate Agricultural Committee Hearings," Hearing, First Session on S. 517, March 1973.

SECTION IV.   APPENDIX

Table 17A-1.   Growth of Output and Energy
(average annual percentage rates)

	Output	Energy (gross)	Energy (useful)
Cellulosic (2823)			
1958-67	3.89	0.75	0.65
1958-62	1.94	−1.25	−1.32
1962-67	5.39	2.47	2.29
Noncellulosic (2824)			
1958-67	18.68	15.79	14.49
1958-62	22.06	18.62	17.41
1962-67	16.00	13.58	12.10

Source: Bureau of the Census, *Census of Manufactures* (several years).

Table 17A-2. **Energy Consumption, Cellulosic Fibers (2823) (trillion BTUs)**

	1958	1962	1967
Coal	79.7	74.0	85.1
Coke + breeze	0	0	0
Fuel oil (total)	0.6	1.4	0.7
Gas	10.0	9.0	10.0
Other fuels	0.3	1.3	0
Fuel, n.s.k.	0	0	0
Electric energy	3.2	3.5	4.9
Total	93.9	89.3	100.8

Source: Bureau of the Census, *Census of Manufactures* (several years)

Table 17A-3. **Energy Consumption, Noncellulosic Fibers (2824) (trillion BTUs)**

	1958	1962	1967
Coal	11.9	28.8	46.1
Coke + Breeze	0	0	0
Fuel oil (total)	1.5	3.0	4.4
Gas	11.7	15.6	26.8
Other fuels	0.3	0	3.4
Fuels, n.s.k.	0	0	0.3
Electric energy	3.2	9.2	26.5
Total	28.7	56.7	107.4

Source: Bureau of the Census, *Census of Manufactures* (several years).

SECTION V. SELECTED BIBLIOGRAPHY

Chemical Engineering (serial)

Faith, W. L.; Keyes, Donald B: and Clark, Ronald L. *Industrial Chemicals.* New York: John Wiley & Sons, 1965.

Harkins, Malcolm J,; Wallace, Charles E. and Manufacturing Chemists Association, Inc. "The Chemical Industry" in *The Development of American Industries.* Glover, John G. and Lagai, Rudolph L., eds. New York: Simmons-Boardman Publishing Corporation, 1959.

J.M.N. "Textile Fibers: What Next?" *Chemical Engineering*, March 19, 1973, p. 74.

Kent, James A., ed. *Rigel's Industrial Chemistry.* New York: Reinhold Publishing Corporation, 1962.

"Senate Agricultural Committee." Hearings, First Session on S. 517, March 1973.

Shreve, Norris R. *Chemical Process Industries*, 3rd Edition. New York: McGraw-Hill, 1967.

Sittig, Marshall. *Organic Chemical Processes*. Pearl River, New York: The Noyes Press, 1962

"The Sprightly Outlook for Synthetic Fibers." *Business Week.* April 14, 1973, p. 30.

Standard and Poor's Industry Surveys, Chemicals. October 26, 1972.

Textile Organon (serial).

United Nations. *Textile Industry*. New York, 1969.

Part Four

Petroleum Refining

Chapter Eighteen

Petroleum Refining—SIC 2911

Leonard Nakamura

SECTION I. INTRODUCTION AND SUMMARY

Petroleum Refining, SIC 2911, is defined by the Bureau of the Census as follows:

> Establishments primarily engaged in producing gasoline, kerosene, distillate fuel oils, lubricants, and other products from crude petroleum and its fractionation products, through straight distillation of crude oil, redistillation of unfurnished petroleum derivatives, cracking, or other processes. Establishments primarily engaged in producing natural gasoline from natural gas are classified in mining industries. Those manufacturing lubricating oils and greases by blending and compounding purchased materials are included in Industry 2992.

The industry takes crude oil, either domestic or imported, and natural gas liquids from natural gas plants and transforms them mainly into a variety of fuels for use in various engines, motors, and heaters. To a much lesser extent, industry products find such non-fuel uses as chemical feedstocks, roofing, road surfaces, and lubricants.

The dominant product is gasoline, used primarily in cars and trucks. Distillate fuel oil, used primarily for home and commercial heating and as diesel fuel for railroads and trucks, and jet fuel are also produced in huge quantities.

Demand for Petroleum Refining Products and Energy Utilization in Refining

Petroleum refining is a mature, large industry, with relatively well-defined markets. It has grown at about the rate of growth of the economy as a whole.

301

Between 1947 and 1971, the industry's shipments rose from $8,544 million to $24,353 million in 1967 prices, a real growth rate of about 4.5% per year. Another measure of production is the output of refined products, measured in 42-gallon barrels. Refined output has risen from 1,919 million barrels to 4,562 million barrels, a growth rate of about 3.7% a year.

The discrepancy between the two measures occurs because the barrel measure does not take into consideration quality improvements, such as the rise in octane number in gasoline. Production of barrels of refined product is shown here and will be used at various places in this report, primarily because it is the standard unit of the industry.

Table 18-2 shows in detail the input and outputs of the industry. Throughout the period, gasoline (motor and aviation) has been the dominant product, moving slowly from 42.5% of physical production in 1947 to 48.3% in 1971. Distillate fuel oil also rises slowly in importance, from 16.3% to 20.0%. Jet fuel was not listed in 1947, but rose from 1.7% in 1954 to 6.7% in 1971. Residual fuel oil fell in importance, from 23.3% in 1954 to 6.0% in 1967. The decline of residual fuel oil, which is a major source of industrial process and space heating, is due to its low value in the market place. In 1967, residual fuel oil averaged $2.08 a barrel, while the crude oil from which it was made was $3.11 (averages from *Census of Manufactures*). Hence refiners were not loath to let imported oil take this market.

Crude oil is a mixture of chemical compounds, primarily hydro-carbons, but it also contains impurities such as water, sulfur compounds, nitrogen compounds, and particulate matter. The hydrocarbon compounds vary from methane, the lightest with just one carbon atom and four hydrogen atoms, to thick waxes and tars, composed of long chains of carbon and hydrogen.

The job of the refiner is to eliminate impurities, distill the remainder into workable fractions (grouping the hydrocarbons by weight), and rework these fractions by breaking them down and building them up as necessary to produce the groups of hydrocarbons it is desired to market.

For example, a simple refinery that merely removed impurities and distilled a medium crude oil (and used some viscosity breaking of the heaviest

Table 18-1.   Output, 1947 to 1971

	1947	1954	1958	1962	1967	1971
Value of shipments (million 1967 $)	8,544	12,047	14,041	16,570	20,294	24,353
Refined products (million barrels)	1,919	2,674	2,983	3,344	3,968	4,562

Sources: Bureau of the Census; Bureau of Mines.

fraction to produce residual fuel oil) might produce about 15% gasoline with an octane number of about 75 or 80, and 80% fuel oil, mainly residual. If the refiner is a gasoline maker, a 50% or higher yield of gasoline is needed, and this—to sell on the American market—must have an octane number of 90 to 100. The heavier oils must be cracked to get a larger percentage of light hydrocarbons, and these hydrocarbons must be reformed (having their configurations changed and often hydrogen removed), alkylated (a process which produces very high octane gasoline by joining light hydrocarbons), distilled, blended, and so on. The greater the difference between the crude oil the refiner begins with and the products the refiner markets, the greater the amount of processing and the more energy is used.

W. L. Nelson, whose writings in the *Oil and Gas Journal* on refinery cost engineering have virtually defined the field, has created a measure of degree of processing called complexity. Although refinery complexity most directly relates to construction costs, energy utilization rates (per barrel) also are positively correlated with complexity. Complexity has risen steadily throughout the period from a low of around six in 1947 to about ten as of 1973, as one would expect, given the implicit quality increase in Table 18-1.

Although petroleum refining is a mature and slowly changing industry, it has undergone a process of continuous technological advancement, in large part due to the increasing demands for higher quality gasolines. Innovation in the last twenty-five years has centered around catalytic reforming (platinum and bimetallic catalysts) and hydrogen processing (hydrocracking, hydrorefining, and hydrotreating).

These innovations have accelerated reactions and improved product quality, which in turn have resulted in increases in energy saving that have more than counterbalanced increases in complexity. As a result, energy utilization for heat and power has declined per unit of output.

Table 18-3 shows the basic series for the total energy requirements for heat and power of the petroleum refining industry, as published by the Bureau of Mines, alongside the comparable series from the *Census of Manufactures* for the years 1958, 1962, and 1967. Total energy for both series is expressed both in useful energy (BTU content of fuels and electricity) and gross energy consumed (BTUs required to generate purchased electricity).[a]

As the table shows, the energy utilization rate has shown a very consistent downward trend since 1954. Over the period 1954 to 1971, the annual rate of decline has been 1.3%, measured in useful energy, and 1.1% in gross energy consumed, the difference being primarily in the increase in purchased electricity's share of total energy use. However, there has been a major shift in trend in the last nine years. Between 1962 and 1971 the annual rates of decline were 2.0% in useful energy and 1.8% in gross energy consumed,

---

[a]See Chapter One, pages 14-15, for definitions of useful and gross energy.

Table 18-2.   Input and Output of the Petroleum Refining Industry, 1947 to 1971
(million barrels)

	1947	1954	1958	1962	1967	1969	1971
Input							
Crude petroleum input	1,852.2	2,539.6	2,776.1	3,069.6	3,582.6	3,879.6	4,087.8
Unfinished oils rerun	.2	8.0	32.5	27.7	34.2	34.3	43.6
Natural gas liquids	70.7	117.5	150.6	182.8	244.7	264.6	284.9
Other hydrocarbons & hydrogen			.4	.1	.1	4.2	6.1
	1,923.1	2,665.1	2,959.2	3,280.2	3,861.6	4,182.7	4,422.4
Output							
Motor gasoline	} 814.8	1,233.0	1,412.0	1,570.6	} 1,801.4	1,995.9	2,179.1
Aviation gasoline		46.6	73.7	102.3	37.1	26.5	18.5
Jet fuel					273.2	321.7	304.7
Ethane (incl. ethylene)					7.0	9.2	9.3
Liquefied refinery gas	18.7	34.2	57.6	76.8	104.5	114.4	121.0
Kerosene	110.4	122.3	110.0	156.4	99.1	101.7	86.3
Distillate fuel oil	312.2	542.3	631.4	719.6	804.4	846.9	910.7
Residual fuel oil	447.8	416.8	363.4	295.7	276.0	265.9	274.7
Petrochemical feedstocks:							
Still gas					9.5	10.0	16.2
Naphtha—400°				Included in other items	50.6	57.4	54.1
Other					27.4	31.0	40.7
Special naphthas				37.3	26.9	28.4	28.3
Lubricants	51.8	53.2	51.3	61.5	64.9	65.1	65.5
Wax	3.6	5.3	5.3	5.4	5.7	6.0	6.9
Coke	12.1	24.3	37.8	78.7	90.9	102.9	109.1
Asphalt	49.3	74.9	89.4	109.6	127.8	135.7	157.0
Road oil	7.1	7.2	5.9	7.1	7.0	9.1	8.8
Still gas for fuel	85.6	102.6	126.0	130.8	140.0	160.4	157.0
Miscellaneous	5.7	11.0	18.7	29.8	14.9	17.1	14.3
	1,919.1	2,673.7	2,982.5	3,344.3	3,968.3	4,305.3	4,562.2
Less: processing gain	−4.2	8.5	23.2	63.9	106.6	122.4	139.4
	1,923.3	2,665.2	2,959.3	3,280.4	3,861.7	4,182.9	4,422.8

Thous. BTUs per bbl. of refined

Table 18-3. Fuel and Energy Used for Heat and Power, 1947 to 1971

(trillion BTUs)

Source and Concept	1947	1954	1958	1962	1967	1971
Bureau of Mines						
Useful energy	1,199	1,718	1,976	2,266	2,481	2,790
Gross energy consumed .	1,246	1,777	2,055	2,361	2,603	2,955
Bureau of the Census						
Useful energy			1,937	2,304	2,508	
Gross energy			2,007	2,391	2,631	

Table 18-4. Energy for Heat and Power per Unit Shipped, 1947 to 1971

(1,000 BTUs/1967 $)

Concept	1947	1954	1958	1962	1967	1971
Useful energy	140.3	142.6	140.7	136.8	122.2	114.6
Gross energy	145.8	147.5	146.4	142.5	128.3	121.3

Sources: Bureau of Mines; Bureau of the Census.

while the rates of decline from 1954 to 1962 were just 0.5% and 0.4%, respectively.

The major factor in decline of energy use per unit of output has been the expectation of increases in energy costs, which some companies reportedly anticipated as early as 1961, and the actual sharp rises in energy costs between 1967 and 1971. Other contributing factors have been the switch to jet fuel from aviation gasoline, and a phasing out of older refineries, which occurred more rapidly between 1962 and 1967 than in the preceding eight years.

These energy inputs measure both purchased fuels and energy, and captive consumption of fuels and energy from process by-products. A more complete measure of the effect of the petroleum refining industry on the energy resources of the domestic economy would be to measure the BTU content of all feedstocks and purchased fuel and electric energy against the BTU content of produced fuels and feedstocks. This would give us a true measure of BTU losses due to processing, and would include BTU gains and losses due to chemical changes during refining, as well as direct refinery losses.

Such a study would entail detailed estimation of the types of crude oil processed as well as variations in products produced, particularly gasolines. No such study has been attempted here, but it should be noted that crude oil consumption per constant dollar of output has declined more rapidly than energy for heat and power per constant dollar of output over the period 1954 to 1971.

Projections to 1980

The uncertainties over future automobile engines and emission control devices have cast a deep smog-like haze over forecasts of gasoline demand. The clash between environmentalists and oil producers over the Alaskan pipeline, and over the location of deep-water ports and associated refineries on the East Coast, has helped blur information on the future supply of domestic crude oil. Finally, the level of future energy use in the United States in the long run as well as the medium term has been obscured by the awkward domestic and foreign politicization of energy. Political decisions are the most difficult to predict.

Projections herein for total petroleum refining output and for energy use rest on the basic assumptions that lightning (such as an Alaskan earthquake, or a major breakthrough on fusion power) won't strike, that needed capacity will be built, that crude oil will be available from somewhere, that new cars will somehow or other be built and will more or less meet expected pollution-control standards with a mileage penalty of less than 20%.[1]

The basic projections, which are based on the University of Maryland INFORUM input-output model, do not take into account in any explicit way the effect of future changes in the gasoline engine, except insofar as they are reflected in changes already underway. However, the model incorporates Conference Board assumptions of relatively rapid growth in the labor force and an unemployment rate of 4½%.

Factors which affect growth rates of demand for petroleum products are multitudinous and will not be gone into here. The INFORUM model projects a growth rate of 5.0% between 1971 and 1980, and 5.4% in the short run to 1975. Table 18-5 shows this growth rate, which we consider to be the most likely trend to 1980. However, we also project lower and upper brackets to the forecast, to reflect the limits of uncertainty. Factors taken into consideration are discussed further in Section III of this report.

As the price of energy rises with respect to other prices (particularly the price of construction), we can see a two-fold effect on petroleum refining operations. First, a general focussing of attention on energy use, with concomitant changes in the trend rate of decline of energy use per dollar of output. That is, the trend rate of decline from 1962 to 1971 was 1.8% on a gross energy consumed basis. Greater attention to maintenance, repair, and more systematic review of operating practices, as well as a higher rate of innovation, should contribute to boost the trend rate to about 2%. Second, there presently exists a large stock of capital improvements that have until now not been economic to install. These particularly include heat-recycling and heat-conserving devices for flue and other waste streams: heat exchangers, waste-heat recovery convection coils, pre-heaters, CO boilers, hydraulic turbines, etc. These represent one-time improvements that will reduce energy use per unit 7.0% over the period to 1980. Such improvements are already seeing use in some recently built plants, but the greatest improvement will be in the units which will come on stream between 1975 and 1980, since these will be designed from the ground up with energy conservation in mind.

Table 18-6 shows the forecast of total demand for energy for heat and power by the petroleum refining industry on a gross consumption of energy basis. The gross consumption of energy basis is a more realistic measure for energy use because the refiner has a viable alternative of self-generation of electricity, and the gross consumption basis places the alternatives of self-generated electricity and utility-generated electricity on an equal footing.

Summary

The petroleum refining industry is a very large energy user, a mature industry with well-defined markets and techniques of production. Since 1954, the industry has been able to rely on fuel prices lower than those of any other industrialized nation, and there has, therefore, been little incentive to install fuel-saving capital equipment. Nevertheless, a slow but steady decline in the energy-output ratio occurred. Since 1962 there appears to have been a substantial increase in the trend rate of decline, due to rising energy prices and other factors.

Since 1971 projections of future energy costs and management attention to energy consumption have taken a quantum jump, as a result of which further energy savings, at least in the medium term, are expected. Projections for changes in the energy-output ratio are shown in Chart 18-1, which gives the ratio in both gross energy consumed and useful energy.

Table 18-5. Production Forecasts, 1971 to 1980
(million 1967 $)

Basis	1971	1975	1980
INFORUM	24,353	30,027	37,518
Lower limit	24,353	27,024	33,766
Upper limit	24,353	31,529	41,270

Table 18-6. Gross Consumption of Energy for Heat and Power, 1971 to 1980
(trillion BTUs)

Basis	1971	1975	1980
INFORUM	2,955	3,252	3,479
Lower limit	2,955	2,927	3,131
Upper limit	2,955	3,414	3,827

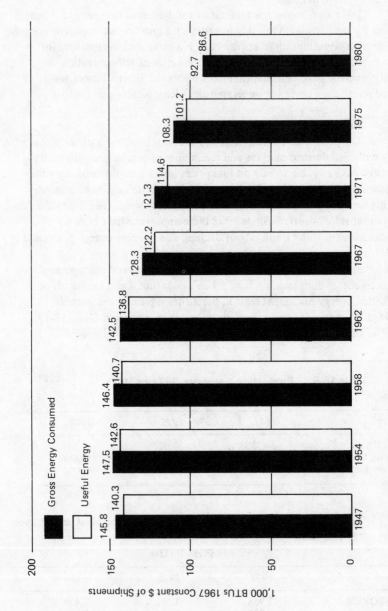

Chart 18–1. Fuel and Electric Energy for Heat and Power per Unit Shipped.

1,000 BTUs 1967 Constant $ of Shipments

- Gross Energy Consumed
- Useful Energy

Year	Gross Energy Consumed	Useful Energy
1947	145.8	140.3
1954	147.5	142.6
1958	146.4	140.7
1962	142.5	136.8
1967	128.3	122.2
1971	121.3	114.6
1975	108.3	101.2
1980	92.7	86.6

SECTION II. HISTORICAL DEVELOPMENTS

Trends in Demand for Petroleum Products

Table 18-7 shows the products of Table 18.2 as percentages of total physical production in barrels. We can group physical production into major products and minor products by separating gasoline, jet fuel, and residual and distillate fuel oils from all others. These four major products have accounted for over 80% of all production in the postwar period.

Gasoline. Gasoline is primarily consumed by cars, trucks, and aircraft. Truck consumption has been relatively declining, due to replacement by diesel fuel; aviation consumption has been declining due to replacement by jet fuel. The increases in this category have been due to the automobile engine, with increases in number of miles driven and decreases in gasoline mileage per gallon (due to larger cars with larger engines).

Quality of automotive gasoline has been consistently upgraded, as larger engines with higher compression ratios have demanded higher octane gasoline (octane number measures the amount the air-fuel mixture can be

Table 18-7. Relative Distribution of Refinery Products, 1947 to 1971

	1947	1954	1958	1962	1967	1971
Gasoline (motor and aviation)	42.5	46.1	47.3	47.0	46.3	47.9
Jet fuel.....................	n.a.	1.7	2.5	3.1	6.9	6.7
Liquefied refinery gas	1.0	1.3	1.9	2.3	2.6	2.7
Kerosene	5.8	4.6	3.7	4.7	2.5	1.9
Distillate fuel oil	16.3	20.3	21.2	21.5	20.3	20.0
Residual fuel oil	23.3	15.6	12.2	8.8	7.0	6.0
Petrochemical feed-stocks (including ethane and ethylene)	Included in other items				2.4	2.7
Lubricants	2.7	2.0	1.7	1.8	1.6	1.4
Coke	0.6	0.9	1.3	2.4	2.3	2.4
Asphalt	2.6	2.8	3.0	3.3	3.2	3.4
Still gas	4.5	3.8	4.2	3.9	3.5	3.4
Other (including special naphtha, wax, and road oil) ..	0.9	0.9	1.0	1.3	1.4	1.3
Total	100.0	100.0	100.0	100.0	100.0	100.0
Gasoline, jet fuel, and fuel oils	82.1	83.7	83.2	80.4	80.5	80.6
All other	17.9	16.3	16.8	19.6	19.5	19.4

n.a. = Not available.
Source: Table 18-2.

compressed without pre-ignition). Recent trends in gasoline consumption have become more ambiguous as new cars have had their compression ratios drastically dropped due to environmental regulation, and there is a growing trend towards smaller cars.

Jet fuel. Jet fuel has been replacing aviation gasoline as jets have replaced piston airplanes. Aviation gasoline required very high octanes and was relatively energy-intensive; jet fuel, which is primarily kerosene type, requires less processing.

Distillate fuel oils. The major uses of distillate are for home and commercial heating and diesel fuel for trucks. Truck diesel consumption has been rising rapidly, replacing gasoline. Other uses of diesel fuel by tractors, busses, railroads and ships have been declining. Oil for home and commercial heating has been losing out to natural gas and electric heating, but its relative decline has been slow; from 1958 to 1971, the absolute rise was about 30%, while the industry has risen about 70%.

Residual fuel oil. Total consumption of residual fuel oil has risen about as rapidly as production of the entire industry, but domestic production of residual has declined. The major reason has been that natural gas prices have kept the price of residual very low, which made it relatively unprofitable to produce. Imports, benefiting from the industry's lack of interest, were allowed to enter the country duty-free to fill the gap. Recently, increases in natural gas prices have changed this situation entirely, and residual production is expected to increase.

Demand for Energy

Automotive gasoline dominates this industry. Until very recently, the industry trend was to more octane, which was provided by tetraethyl lead and by extensive processing.

Tetraethyl lead added to gasoline increases the octane rating. The extent of increase varies depending on the composition of the gasoline; aromatics, for instance, have a relatively high susceptibility.

In general, the higher the octane desired, the more processing is required. This means a greater degree of cracking, reforming, aromatization and alkylation, which in turn required more energy use. Consequently, given constant technology, energy use per barrel of refined products should rise, since more processing goes into each barrel. Table 18-8 shows energy use per barrel of refined oil, which has not risen.

The technical innovations that have made this possible include the following:

Table 18-8. Energy-Output Ratios, 1947 to 1971

	1947	1954	1958	1962	1967	1969	1971
Total energy input (trillion BTUs)	1,198.6	1,718.2	1,976.0	2,266.2	2,480.7	2,732.0	2,789.7
Crude runs to stills (million bbls.)	1,852.2	2,539.6	2,776.1	3,069.6	3,582.6	3,879.6	4,087.8
BTUs/bbl. of crude (thous.)	647	677	712	738	692	704	682
Refined products, (output, million bbls.)	1,919.1	2,673.7	2,982.5	3,344.3	3,968.3	4,305.3	4,562.2
BTUs/bbl. of refined prod. (thous.)	625	643	663	678	625	635	612

Note: Useful energy basis.
Source: Bureau of Mines.

Catalytic cracking. Catalytic cracking is essentially a thermal process, but the cracking takes place in the presence of a catalyst which (1) creates additional catalytic decompositions, and (2) absorbs coke, preventing undesirable reverse reactions (polymerizations). As a result, less energy is needed and yields are higher. A drawback is the loss of hydrocarbons to coke and the need to regenerate the catalyst, which is quickly covered with coke.

Catalytic reforming. Catalytic reforming uses platinum or bimetallic catalysts to rearrange hydrocarbon molecules, producing mainly highly desirable aromatic compounds and isomers of straight chain hydrocarbons. Useful hydrogen is produced as a by-product. The reactions are more desirable ones than in thermal reforming, producing higher yield, and temperatures and pressures are lower. Catalyst life is much longer than in catalytic cracking.

Hydrogen processing. The addition of hydrogen to processing steps can occur at many points in petroleum processing. The cracking stage is the point at which the hydrogen is most valuable, since the hydrogen saturates the cracked hydrocarbons and thus prevents the tendency towards recombination. (When a straight chain hydrocarbon is cracked, a chemical bond is broken. The hydrogen atom uses up the "extra" bond.)

An additional factor in the decline of energy utilization per unit of output in the period 1962 to 1967 was a more rapid than usual phasing out of outmoded capital stock. It is difficult to measure this factor, because the different units of a refinery complex may be built at widely differing times, and so a refinery has no specific "age". During the 5-year period from 1962 to 1967, the number of operating refineries declined from 287 to 260, while in the earlier 8-year period from 1954 to 1962 the number declined from 308 to 287. Thus, the rate of decline in number was about twice as fast during 1962-67 than during 1954-62.

Overall energy costs in the United States have been very low. As a result, there has been little incentive to save on energy costs. Nevertheless, technological innovations and changes in capital stocks have acted to restrain a rise in total energy use per physical unit, and have in fact caused a decline in the energy-output ratio when quality improvements (as measured in constant-dollar output per barrel of refining products) are taken into account.

SECTION III. PROJECTIONS TO 1980

Trends in Demand for Petroleum Products

The major question concerning demand for petroleum products is: Whither the automobile engine?

The prime problem the automobile producers must solve is pollution, specifically the requirements set down by the Environmental

Protection Agency under the Clean Air Act of 1970. The problem is not clear-cut, because EPA might be persuaded to change its requirements and because the automobile manufacturers' apparent ability to meet the requirements is a major factor in what EPA can demand.

The first question is whether a major change in the engine will take place. Although production of new types of engines can only be very limited by 1975, a lot can happen between now and 1980. The best alternatives are steam and electric engines, but unless major design breakthroughs occur, these cannot be anticipated until some time after 1980. Likely alternatives are the turbine engine, the new Honda CVCC, and the Wankel rotary engine.

The turbine engine would burn kerosene-type fuels, and a major shift towards it would have staggering effects on the gasoline market. A great deal of research has gone into the Chrysler turbine engine, and it is considered a major hope by EPA.

The Honda CVCC is the closest of the three to a conventional engine, and while the others are basically simpler engines, the CVCC is more complicated. The CVCC, also called the stratified charge engine, has two combustion chambers for each cylinder with ignition occurring in the smaller upper chamber which ignites the lower main chamber and induces very complete burning. Very sketchy reports indicate that gasoline consumption is increased very little. Widespread adoption of the CVCC would mean, if its claims are borne out, less consumption of gasoline than most estimates based on conventional engines with catalytic converters.

The Wankel rotary engine, the only one of these engines to have made an appearance on the American market, is clearly going to have a substantial share of the market. The Wankel-powered Mazda is selling very well, and, even more significantly, General Motors is developing the Wankel for its own cars and will apparently be introducing it not only in its subcompact Vega but also in its full-sized Impala. The current Mazda has a high compression ratio, so the performance characteristics of a low compression, pollution-control engine equipped for the 1975 and 1976 EPA standards are unclear. The major known factor is that the Wankel is significantly lighter and smaller than conventional engines, and that the car it is installed in would presumably have less weight to drag around.

The second question is what form pollution-control devices will take. The catalytic converter, which is the base point, poses a problem because the gasoline must be very pure in order to avoid poisoning the catalyst. In particular, the gasoline must be as lead-free as possible.

Ninety-one octane lead-free gasoline is the reference point for the catalytic converter. In general, the converter is expected to have a substantial mileage penalty. Worse, if 91 octane creates poor performance in the engine attached to the converter, oil companies may be forced to produce clear octanes of 94 or 95. So the catalytic converter may create mileage and octane penalties.

(Most recent reports indicate that penalties due to emission control devices may have peaked out as of the 1973 model year. A stabilization of the penalty will continue to have a downward effect on miles per gallon as older cars without emission controls are slowly replaced.)

Alternatives to the catalytic converter have been proposed, including some that would filter lead out of the exhaust, permitting use of low lead rather than unleaded gasolines.

The third question is how are consumers going to react to the combination of higher gasoline prices with lower mileage cars. Presumably there will be a trend towards smaller cars, alternative forms of transportation, less moving around, and more car pooling; that is, less demand. How much less is a very open question.

The recent spectacular increases in the price of gasoline combined with greatly increased national concern for energy conservation have combined to set a new goal for the automotive industry of reversing the current downward trend of gasoline mileage. The increase in gasoline consumption in 1973 over 1972 will probably be in the 4% to 5% range, far lower than predicted and resulting in a sharp reversal of the trend to more gasoline per barrel of crude.

The final question about demand for petroleum products is how fast demand for fuel oils will increase. The lack of natural gas has already drastically affected residual fuel oil and will affect distillate, although not as greatly.

Trends in Energy Utilization

Energy utilization is a function of how much of what is made, and of the price of energy.

If production should equal demand, the above discussion of demand would be all of the answer; at least all of the answer this report was going to supply. To the above considerations these must be added:

(1) For the last few years, petroleum refining capacity has been growing less rapidly than consumption. As a result, product importation has been rising, and will continue to increase in the short run, probably through 1976.

(2) Now that residual prices have gone up, tariff barriers are on their way in, and a swing towards residual production will occur. This will lower the quality mix of petroleum products, since residual is the bottom of the barrel. It will also reduce energy requirements, since residual requires less processing.

Now we encounter the question of the price of energy.

In detail, the price of energy involves a further barrage of questions, including the rate of production of Alaskan crude, the actions of Arab political leaders, the strength of the dollar on international markets, antitrust action against oil companies, new natural gas discoveries, off-shore drilling, the price of tea in China.

The price of energy will rise.

In recently built refineries, more energy-saving capital equipment will be installed. But this can occur only after sufficient additional capacity is created to allow refineries to be idled temporarily. Refineries constructed between now and 1980 will have large amounts of energy-saving design and construction.

Oil companies recently have reported exceeding annual energy reduction targets of as high as 3% a year and reductions in energy costs in newly constructed refineries and plants of 10% and higher. Since the largest companies and refineries are the greatest users of energy, and since they are most heavily dependent on natural gas energy, necessity and capital availability should conspire to create rapid short-term changes in the level of the energy-output ratio.

Afterword

This chapter was completed prior to the international crude oil price increases of late 1973. These sweeping changes in the price structure of energy increase the degree of uncertainty previously discussed. However, at this date, it is not clear, *a priori*, that these price increases must invalidate the *projections*, although they certainly change the analysis.

It is our opinion that while the increased price of petroleum will lower demand, the primary effect will be a decline in projected imports. This is because domestic crude supply will increase. Already, the Alaskan pipeline and leasing of off-shore lands have been expedited, and the new prices will induce both domestic exploration and increased rates of recovery from known oil-in-place. As domestic crude supply increases, some of the refinery capacity that otherwise would go abroad will be located in the U.S.

Note

[1] The Arab oil boycott, and concomitant uncertainties over input supply price and availability, are discussed in a brief note at the end of this chapter.

SECTION IV. APPENDIX

1. Sources of Data

Essentially two sources of data were used to estimate past consumption of fuels and electric energy in the petroleum refining industry (SIC 2911).

(a) *Bureau of Census* data on fuels and electric energy purchased by Industry 2911 are available as part of the *Census of Manufactures* for the years 1954, 1958, and 1967. Data for 1962 were collected in connection with the *Annual Survey of Manufactures* of that year. (Census Bureau data for the census year 1947 are available only for purchased fuels and electric energy and not for fuels produced and used within the same establishment.)

The data on fuels and electric energy are given in physical units by major types of fuel, and also at cost in (current) dollars if purchased from outside (and not produced within the establishment).

(b) *Bureau of Mines* data on fuels consumed at refineries in the United States are published in the Bureau's *Mineral Industry Surveys*, "Petroleum Statement, Annual." The data are given in physical units (by major types of fuel, and for purchased electricity and purchased steam), and converted to BTUs.

These statistics cover the total consumption of energy whether purchased from outside, or produced and consumed within the same petroleum refinery. Data are available for the years 1947 to 1971.

2. Description of the Industry
Description of Processes[b]

A flow sheet of the basic petroleum refining processes is attached. The source is: Frank E. Walker, *Estimating Production and Repair Effort in Blast-damaged Petroleum Refineries*, July 1969.

Refineries may be classified as simple, complex, or fully integrated depending on the processes they perform. In nearly all of the processing units shown in the flow sheet, energy is required in the form of direct heat to raise the temperature of the oil being processed. Additional energy is required for mechanical drives to force the oil through the process.

Essentially all crude oil is subjected first to a distillation at near-atmospheric pressure known as topping or crude distillation. The straight-run products of topping with the lowest boiling point, known as light naphthas, usually go directly into gasoline. The other straight-run products (kerosene, diesel fuel or light distillate) are usually desulfurized or treated with hydrogen, and the heavy (gasoline) naphtha must be catalytically reformed to improve its octane number. The highest boiling straight-run product, gas oil, constitutes the feedstock to catalytic cracking, or hydrocracking. Through the cracking process (decomposition of hydrocarbon materials at high temperatures) the yield of gasoline from heavier materials is further increased.

The residue or topped crude oil is further reduced or processed in five main ways: (1) viscosity breaking, coking, or vacuum distillation, which is followed by (2) catalytic cracking, (3) hydrocracking, (4) lubricating oil manufacture, and (5) asphalt manufactures. Amounts of residue may also be directly hydrocracked for the production of low-sulfur residual fuel oil. Olefinic gases are assembled from all decomposition processes for polymerization, or more often alkylation, into the boiling range of gasoline. In the case of

[b]The description of processes is based partly on Kirk-Othmer, *Encyclopedia of Chemical Technology*, Volume 15, Second Edition, New York, 1968.

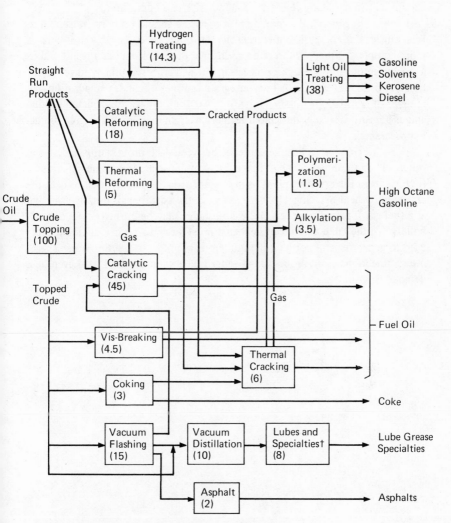

Notes: *Process capacity indices (with crude topping = 100)
applicable to all complete processing refineries.
†Including naphthenic lubes and specialties processes.

Figure 18-1. Petroleum Refining Processes. Source: *Estimating Production and Repair Effort in Blast-damaged Petroleum Refineries* by Frank E. Walker, July 1969.

alkylation, the isobutane is also assembled from catalytic hydrocracking and catalytic refining. Many refineries conduct all these operations.

In general, the refining processes in a simple refinery consume the least amount of energy in converting the raw crude oil to saleable products. A more complex refinery will require additional processes, and as a result will use a greater amount of energy in processing but will correspondingly have a greater range of products for sale. A fully integrated refinery includes an additional number of complex processing units to make a full range of petroleum products, and as a result, the fully integrated refinery uses an even greater degree of energy in processing.

There is an interdependence between each process unit and all the others. The interdependence in fuel use can be illustrated by some examples: (a) heat from the cracking plant or lube-plant streams may be used to heat the crude oil by heat exchange; (b) dry gas from the adsorbers is usually employed as a fuel gas for the furnaces; (c) the acid sludge may be burned under the boilers; (d) the large amount of heat that must be removed in cracking plants is used to generate steam or heat the numerous reboilers of fractionators. These interconnections of all process units cannot be completely indicated even on a detailed flow sheet.

Table 18A-1.   Census Data: Useful Energy by Major Source, 1958 to 1967

Energy Sources	1958	1962	1967
	In Physical Units		
Purchased			
Coal, million short tons	1.069	.789	.777
Petroleum, million bbls.	1.933	7.334	7.263
Gas, billion c.ft.	783.694	942.488	1,100.756
Other fuels, million $*	7.300	11.200	20.600
Electric energy, billion kwh	9.115	12.147	17.474
Captive Consumption			
Residual oil, million bbls.	43.147	34.582	41.638
Other fuels, incl.			
petroleum coke million bbls.	17.415	40.827	42.055
Refinery (still) gas, billion c.ft.	676.970	776.351	714.568
	In Trillions of BTUs		
Total Energy	*2,093*	*2,283*	*2,508*
Purchased	904	1,115	1,336
Coal	28	20	20
Petroleum	11	43	42
Gas	811	975	1,139
Other fuels*	23	35	76
Electric energy	31	41	60
Captive Consumption	1,033	1,189	1,172
Residual oil	271	217	262
Other fuels, incl.			
petroleum coke	82	192	198
Refinery (still) gas	680	780	711

*Includes gasoline, LPG, wood and purchased steam, and fuels not specified by kind.

Source: Bureau of the Census, *Census of Manufactures,* Fuels and Electric Energy Consumed, 1967.

Table 18A-2.   Bureau of Mines Data: Total Energy Use, by Major Source, 1947 to 1971

Energy Source	1947	1954	1958	1962	1967	1971
Fuel oil, mil. bbls.	38.717	47.410	43.661	41.718	39.626	38.072
LPG, mil. bbls.	n.a.	n.a.	3.695	5.502	3.043	6.850
Acid sludge, mil. bbls.	5.824	2.474	1.101	.360	.237	—
Natural gas, bil. cft.	363.892	563.315	681.384	789.877	936.085	1,062.938
Refinery gas, bil. cft.	324.737	501.574	715.152	769.069	838.529	1,013.117
Petroleum coke, mil. s. tons	.721	1.895	4.498	10.263	10.462	10.444
Coal, mil. s. tons	2.273	.876	1.027	.736	.859	.405
Purchased electricity, bil. kwh	2.958	5.364	8.632	11.420	15.106	20.720
Purchased steam, bil. lbs.	n.a.	n.a.	18.837	18.749	23.318	23.890
BTU equivalent, total*, in trillion BTUs	*1,999*	*1,718*	*1,976*	*2,266*	*2,481*	*2,790*
Fuel oil	n.a.	n.a.	274	262	249	239
LPG	"	"	5	2	1	—
Acid sludge	"	"	16	24	13	27
Natural gas	"	"	715	817	966	1,096
Refinery gas	"	"	751	771	834	1,003
Petroleum coke	"	"	135	309	315	315
Coal	"	"	27	19	22	10
Purchased electricity	"	"	29	39	52	71
Purchased steam	"	"	23	22	28	29

Source: U.S. Department of the Interior, Bureau of Mines, *Mineral Industry Surveys, Petroleum Statement, Annual*, Various issues.

*Calculated by Bureau of Mines.

n.a.—not available.

Part Five

Stone, Clay, and Glass Industries

Chapter Nineteen

Basic Glass—SIC 3211, 3221, and 3229

Bernard A. Gelb

SECTION I.   INTRODUCTION AND SUMMARY

The Industry

Basic Glass industries is the name we have given to the combination of the Flat Glass industry, SIC 3211, the Glass Container industry, SIC 3221, and the Pressed and Blown Glass, n.e.c., industry, SIC 3229. We have combined these because all three begin by making glass, which is then made into the products of the separate industries. In the manufacture of glass products, it is the melting of the raw material to a molten glass state that consumes a major portion—70% to 80%—of total energy used. The annealing process—also common to almost all production of glass products—accounts for a substantial part of remaining energy consumption.

Establishments primarily engaged in manufacturing flat glass are classified in SIC Industry No. 3211. The two main types of flat glass are sheet glass and plate glass (float glass is a type of plate glass). This industry also produces laminated glass, but establishments primarily engaged in making laminated glass from purchased flat glass are not included. SIC Industry No. 3221 comprises establishments primarily engaged in manufacturing glass containers for commercial packing and bottling and for home canning. As regards physical characteristics, the industry uses "narrow neck" and "wide mouth" for its main classifications. The major products that commercially packed glass containers hold are, of course, food, beverages (including beer, wine, and liquor), and medicines and toiletries. Establishments not elsewhere classified and primarily engaged in manufacturing glass and glassware that is pressed, blown, or shaped from glass produced in the same establishment are classified in SIC Industry No. 3229. Also included in this industry are establishments primarily engaged in manufacturing textile glass fibers, but not those primarily engaged in producing glass wool insulation products.

323

Table 19-1.   Relative Sizes of the Basic Glass Industries
(as per cent of total shipments)

Year	Flat Glass (SIC 3211)	Glass Containers (SIC 3221)	Pressed and Blown Glass n.e.c. (SIC 3229)	Total Basic Glass Industries
1947	22.4%	50.8%	26.8%	100.0%
1958	22.0	48.5	29.5	100.0
1971	21.7	48.0	30.2	100.0

Note: Figures may not add exactly to 100 due to rounding.
Source: Table 19-5.

As shown in Table 19-1, the glass container industry is now about 60% larger, in terms of output, than the pressed and blown glass (n.e.c.) industry, and more than twice as large as the flat glass industry.

In addition to having a common basic process, Industries Nos. 3211, 3221, and 3229 all have high degrees of coverage of their primary products. For 1967, these relationships were as follows:

Industry	Specialization Ratio	Coverage Ratio
SIC 3211	85*	(D)*
SIC 3221	99	99
SIC 3229	97	98

*The specialization ratio for SIC 3211 is a "minimum percentage"; additional information is withheld by the Census Bureau to avoid disclosure of data from individual companies. For the same reason, no figure at all is published for the coverage ratio.
Source: Bureau of the Census, *Census of Manufactures*, 1967.

In case it is not clear, it should be specifically stated that these three industries do not include establishments primarily engaged in manufacturing glass products from purchased glass. Such establishments constitute a fourth glass glass industry not discussed in this report.

Summary of Developments

The basic glass industries have grown less rapidly than the economy as a whole during the postwar period. Total output of SIC 3211, 3221, and 3229 in 1967 dollars increased 116% between 1947 and 1971, compared with a 141% rise in real gross national product. This performance is partly the result of slower growth in the major markets of the basic glass industries, especially their two largest markets—construction and food. But it also reflects some losses of domestic markets to two types of competitors: producers abroad and domestic producers of substitute materials. Incursions have been most severe in window glass, containers, and fine glassware.

Aggregate energy use by the basic glass industries has increased slower than output in the past two and a half decades. In contrast with the 116% gain in production between 1947 and 1971, aggregate useful[a] energy consumed by SIC 3211, 3221, and 3229 increased 71%. Implicitly, useful energy required per unit of output has dropped; the decline, from 107,400 BTUs per 1967 dollar of output to 85,100 BTUs per 1967 dollar of output, was at a moderate average annual rate of 1.0% a year. Aggregate gross energy demanded by the industry increased 78% between 1947 and 1971, and gross energy demanded per 1967 dollar of output declined from 118,500 BTUs to 98,000.

A number of technological and marketing developments can be credited for these movements in aggregate and per unit useful energy consumption by the basic glass industries. Gains in energy efficiency have come about mainly through (1) economies from the use of increasingly larger furnaces; (2) growing reuse of waste heat; (3) the introduction of an auxiliary heating unit inside the body of molten glass in the furnace; (4) advances in glass forming; (5) advances in process control; (6) a shift to lighter weight bottles by the glass container industry. Increases in energy consumption by pollution control equipment and increased mechanization have partly offset the savings won.

As in most industries, the movement in gross energy demanded per unit of output reflects all the above developments plus (1) a shift to more use of purchased electricity (tending to increase BTUs per unit) and (2) a steep decrease in the heat loss rate at electric utilities between 1949 and 1969, and the small increase since then (tending to decrease and then to increase BTUs per unit).

Changes in the mix of energy sources used by the basic glass industries have been notable. The contribution by coal to total BTUs used by glass producers dropped from 18% to 1% between 1947 and 1971. Gas increased its share from 65% to 84%; and oil's proportion fell from 13% to 4%. Basic glass producers' relative use of electricity (purchased) rose from 3% to 7%.

Projections

Some of the developments that affected energy use per unit of output over the past two decades will, we expect, persist through 1980, although with less force. The use of electric boosters will spread a little more; the flat glass industry will complete its conversion from the plate process to the float process; furnaces will get a little bigger and a little better. However, more stringent enviromental regulations will tend to offset some of the savings from the above. Further increases in real energy prices will, we also believe, provide a

[a]See Chapter One, pages 14-15, for definitions of useful and gross energy.

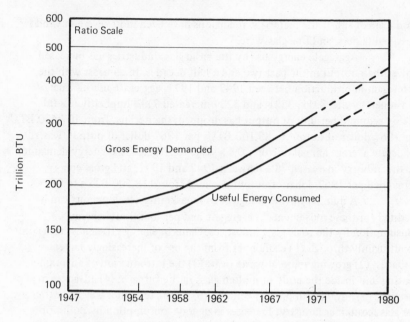

Chart 19-1. Aggregate Energy Use. Source: Table 19-5; Table 19-6.

Table 19-2.   Output, Energy Use, and Energy Use per Dollar of Output—Total, Basic Glass Industries

	1947	1971	1980
Output, million 1967 $	$1,495	$3,225	$4,750
Energy use, trillion BTUs			
Useful	161	274	381
Gross	177	316	461
Energy use per $ of shipments, thousand BTUs			
Useful	107	85	80
Gross	119	98	97

Sources: Table 19-5; Table 19-6.

strong cost incentive to encourage innovations and investments that will have similar effects.

Overall, we project further declines in energy use per unit of output. When the details of these expectations regarding per unit energy use are applied to production and aggregate energy use by the basic glass industries, the results are as follows: aggregate useful energy consumption is projected to increase from 274 trillion BTUs in 1971 to 381 trillion BTUs in 1980, a rise of 39%;

aggregate gross energy demanded is projected to grow from 316 trillion BTUs to 461 trillion BTUs, an increase of 46%. Useful energy consumed per 1967 dollar of output is projected to fall from 85,100 BTUs in 1971 to 80,300 BTUs in 1980, or an average drop of 0.6% a year—a slower rate than that experienced in the 1950s and 1960s. Aggregate gross energy demanded per dollar of output is anticipated to decline from 98,000 BTUs to 97,000 BTUs, or 1% altogether.

The postwar shift of energy use by source is expected to reverse slightly. Coal's share, which had shrunk to 1% of total useful BTUs consumed by the basic glass industries, is projected to grow marginally. The proportion accounted for by gas should drop moderately. It is anticipated that the relative contribution of oil will grow appreciably, and that the proportion accounted for by electricity will increase further, albeit moderately.

SECTION II.   HISTORICAL DEVELOPMENTS

Demand

Since the end of World War II, growth of the basic glass industries has been less rapid than that of the economy as a whole. Output (shipments in 1967 dollars) by the three basic glass industries combined increased 116% between 1947 and 1971, an average of 3.3% a year. During the same period, real gross national product expanded by 141%, or at an average annual rate of 3.7%.

The broad major markets for these industries are automobiles, construction, food, and housewares. By a rough measurement, these major markets have grown slower than the economy as a whole. A weighted total of real gross auto product, construction of buildings, food purchases at stores, and housewares purchased at stores rose 116% between 1947 and 1971, as against the 141% increase in GNP. But these numbers are not an accurate gauge of the glass industries' markets. Probably, shipments would have increased more than the 116% were it not for two major retarding factors: incursions by competing materials—particularly in the case of containers; and incursions by imports—which have been notable in sheet, or window glass.

Since the early 1960s, production by the basic glass industries has grown faster than the broad markets mentioned above. Total output in 1967 dollars by SIC 3211, SIC 3221, and SIC 3229 rose an estimated 45% between 1962 and 1971, versus 38% for the markets.

Trends in the demand for the basic glass industries' collective products and in the collective production of the basic glass industries are, of course, a summation of the respective trends in the individual industries themselves.

Output by the flat glass industry (SIC 3211) rose from $336 million (1967 dollars) in 1947 to an estimated $700 million in 1971—an average of 3.1% a year. In contrast, construction of buildings and production of automotive

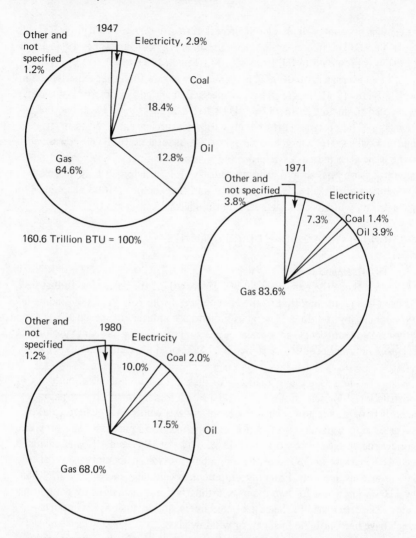

Chart 19-2. Distribution of Energy Consumed (Useful) by Source.
Sources: U.S. Bureau of the Census, *Census of Manufactures, 1947
Annual Survey of Manufactures, 1971*; Table 19-7; Table 19A-1.

vehicles—which probably use 80% of the output of SIC 3211—together increased
4.2% a year on average between 1947 and 1971. A rapid expansion of imports is
largely responsible for slower growth in output by SIC 3211 than in the flat
glass markets. Imports of flat glass soared from an amount equal to less than 1%
of domestic shipments in 1947 to an estimated 15% in 1971.[1]

Between 1947 and 1971, the glass container industry (SIC 3221)

Table 19-3.   Trends in Major Markets of the Basic Glass Industries

Product Group	Output			1963 Relative Importance (per cent)
	1947	*1962*	*1971*	
	(Index numbers: 1962 = 100)			
Motor vehicles & equipment	47	100	163	24%
Buildings	64	100	121	12
Food for off-premise consumption	69	100	123	51
China, glassware, tableware, etc.	77	100	170	13
Average (weighted by relative importance) ...	64	100	138	x

Note: Product group data are: gross auto product in 1958 dollars; value put in place of new construction of private and governmental buildings (residential and nonresidential) in 1957-1959 dollars; personal consumption expenditures for food purchased for off-premise consumption (including beverages) in 1958 dollars; and personal consumption expenditures for china, glassware, tableware, utensils, and other durable household furnishings in 1958 dollars. Relative importance figures are from the 1963 input-output tables of the Department of Commerce.

Sources: U.S. Department of Commerce, *Survey of Current Business; Construction Reports.*

boosted its production from $759 million (1967 dollars) to an estimated $1,550 million in 1971, or 3.0% annually on average. During the same period, consumer purchases of food (including soft drinks and beer) for other than restaurant eating—the major broad market for glass containers—increased an average of 2.4% a year. Consumer purchases of toiletries, drug preparations, and cleaning and polishing preparations—the second broad market for glass containers—grew an average of 5.2% a year. To be sure, consideration of food purchases as a whole does not focus on the fastest growing markets for glass bottles—soft drinks and beer—but neither does it focus on common uses of glass bottles, such as for dairy products and canned fruits and vegetables, that have shown relatively little growth due to slow increases (or decreases) in per capita consumption. In both food and the other category, however, glass has lost out in relative terms to other materials—metals, paper, and plastics. Except perhaps, for some specialties, imports are not a factor in this industry.

The third basic glass industry, pressed and blown glass, n.e.c., has enjoyed growth comparable to that of the total economy; SIC 3229 output increased 144% between 1947 and 1971. While imports have gained large portions of the domestic market for fine food, beverage, and art glassware, U.S. producers account for nearly all domestic supplies of lighting and electronic glassware and of textile glass fibers. The electronics industry has, of course, grown especially rapidly; and production of fiberglass has burgeoned along with the number of uses found for fiberglass. Largely due to the growth in these two areas, production by SIC 3229 (in 1967 dollars) increased by almost one half between 1962 and 1971.

Table 19-4.   Product Mix of Individual Basic Glass Industries

	Per Cent of Total
Flat glass (SIC 3211) 1967	
Sheet (window) glass	22%
Plate & float glass	30
Laminated glass	13
Other & n.s.k.	20
Secondary products	15
Glass containers (SIC 3221) 1971	
Food	35
Medicinal, toiletries, cosmetics	15
Household & industrial	2
Beverages (including beer)	33
Liquor & wine	13
Secondary products	2
Pressed and blown glass, n.e.c. (SIC 3229) 1967	
Table, kitchen, art, & novelty	30
Lighting and electronic	37
Textile fiber	14
Other & n.s.k.	15
Secondary products	4
	Total (millions of dollars)
Flat glass, 1967	$ 611.3
Glass containers, 1971	1,352.4
Pressed and blown glass, n.e.c., 1967	886.2

n.s.k.—not specified by kind.

n.e.c.—not elsewhere classified.

Sources: Bureau of the Census, *Census of Manufactures, 1967; Current Industrial Reports*, "Glass Containers," Summary for 1971.

Energy Use

Aggregate useful energy consumed by the basic glass industries increased 71% between 1947 and 1971, from 160.6 trillion BTUs to 274.4 trillion BTUs. Since, during the same period, real output by the industries (measured in 1967 dollars) grew 116%, this means that energy consumption (useful) per dollar of output dropped 21%, from 107,400 BTUs to 85,100 BTUs.

The relative as well as absolute use of electrical energy by the basic glass industries is, as in most industries, growing. In 1971, the useful energy content of electricity used by the three industries in 1971 accounted for 7% of total useful energy consumed by them compared with 3% in 1947. Consequently, the growth from 177.2 trillion BTUs to 316.1 trillion BTUs of gross energy demanded by SIC 3211, 3221, and 3229 was slightly faster than that of useful energy—78% versus 71%—between 1947 and 1971.

Other shifts during the postwar period in the mix of energy sources

Table 19-5. Output, Aggregate Energy Use, and Energy Use per Dollar of Output

Industry & Year	Output (millions of 1967 $)	Aggregate Energy Use		Energy Use per 1967 Dollar of Output	
		Useful (trillion BTU)	Gross	Useful (thousand BTUs)	Gross
Flat glass (3211)					
1947	336	44.4	48.4	132.1	144.1
1954	414	42.3	46.5	102.1	112.3
1958	393	42.3	47.0	107.6	119.5
1962	541	47.2	53.1	87.2	98.1
1967	611	53.6	60.5	87.7	99.1
1971	700	59.4	66.0	84.9	94.3
Glass containers (3221)					
1947	759	77.1	86.2	101.6	113.5
1954	759	81.0	89.7	106.7	118.1
1958	867	89.2	99.2	102.9	114.5
1962	1,037	100.8	112.7	97.2	108.7
1967	1,352	119.1	135.5	88.1	100.2
1971	1,550	143.6	167.1	92.6	107.8
Pressed & blown glass, n.e.c. (3229)					
1947	400	39.1	42.6	97.7	106.4
1954	528	39.6	44.1	74.9	83.4
1958	526	39.6	43.9	75.3	83.5
1962	663	50.6	56.7	76.3	85.6
1967	886	65.7	74.1	74.2	83.6
1971	975	71.4	83.0	73.2	85.1
Three combined (3211 + 3221 + 3229)					
1947	1,495	160.6	177.2	107.4	118.5
1954	1,701	162.9	180.3	95.8	106.0
1958	1,786	171.1	190.1	95.8	106.4
1962	2,241	198.6	222.5	88.6	99.3
1967	2,850	238.4	270.1	83.6	94.8
1971	3,225	274.4	316.1	85.1	98.0

Sources: Bureau of the Census, *Census of Manufactures* (several editions); *Annual Survey of Manufactures, 1962 & 1971*; Table 19-6.

used by basic glass producers as a group have been about as moderate as the shift to electricity. In 1971, gas accounted for 84% of total useful energy consumed, as against 65% in 1947. The proportions attributable to coal and oil have dropped from 18% to 1% and from 13% to 4%, respectively.

Of the three basic glass industries, aggregate energy consumption has increased slowest in flat glass manufacture. Aggregate useful BTUs used by SIC 3211 rose 33.8% between 1947 and 1971. Aggregate gross energy demanded increased only slightly faster (36.4%), because the flat glass industry uses relatively little electricity. These slow rises are largely attributable to the rapid decline in energy use per unit of output in the industry. Useful energy consumption per dollar of output fell from 132,100 BTUs in 1947 to 84,900 BTUs in 1971—35.7%. Most of the relative and absolute decline occurred earlier in the postwar period; there has been little improvement since the early 1960s. However, operating rates were relatively low in 1971, tending to raise per-unit energy inputs; energy use per dollar of output, therefore, might well have been less were demand levels closer to optimum operating rates, especially in view of the growing use of the float glass process (discussed in the next section).

Glass container manufacturing has experienced the fastest increase in aggregate energy use among the basic glass industries during the postwar period. Between 1947 and 1971, aggregate useful energy consumed by SIC 3221 rose 86.3%; and it now accounts for more than half of aggregate useful energy consumed by all three basic glass industries combined. Aggregate gross energy demanded by the glass container industry increased 93.8% during the 24-year period. As shown in Chart 19-3, energy use per dollar of output declined much slower in SIC 3221 than in the other two industries—only 8.9% between 1947 and 1971. Probably because furnaces in the glass container industry cannot be as large as most in flat glass and many in pressed and blown glass, less can be done to reduce per unit use of furnace heat (which accounts for three-fourths of total energy used) through economies of scale. Glass container making attained a very high level of automation many years ago; recent improvements in the process have been largely in labeling, coloring, and strengthening (through surface treatments), most of which tend to add little to per-unit energy inputs.

Aggregate energy use by SIC 3229 (pressed and blown glass, n.e.c.) has increased almost as rapidly as in the glass container industry during the postwar period. Pressed and blown glass producers consumed 71.4 trillion BTUs in 1971, 82.6% more than in 1947. Partly because use of electricity by SIC 3229 has grown faster than in the other two industries, aggregate gross energy demanded by pressed and blown glass makers has grown faster.

The rapid rise in aggregate energy consumed is largely attributable to the rapid increase in output by the industry. Improvements in per-unit energy use were substantial, although not as rapid as in flat glass. Useful energy consumed per dollar of output by SIC 3229 dropped from 97,700 BTUs in 1947 to 73,200 BTUs in 1971, or 25.1%. While most of the products of the pressed and blown glass industry are machine made, many are partly hand made. In both cases, smaller furnaces than in flat glass manufacture are appropriate; and in the latter instance, potential savings in energy costs are very small in relation to the value of the final product. Rapid expansion of the electronics market and of glass fiber production, with attendant savings from economies of scale as production increased, probably tended to lower energy use per dollar of shipments. Of the three basic glass industries, the absolute level of energy use per dollar of output is lowest in SIC 3229. Probably, this is ascribable to the high value per unit of many of the table and art glassware items produced by the industry, value that is added through design, coloring, and other attributes not related to energy inputs.

Technological and Marketing Developments

A few technological and marketing trends can be offered as explanation for these movements in aggregate and per-unit energy use by the basic glass industries. Most are common to all three industries.

Increases in the size of the typical glass melting furnace have been a significant factor in the decline in energy use per dollar of shipments. As furnace size increases, the ratio between the interior area and the length of the walls increases, decreasing the relative opportunity for loss of heat by radiation

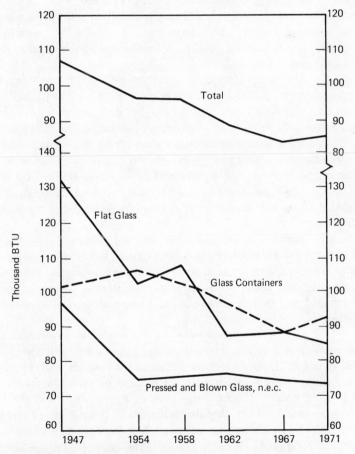

Chart 19-3. Energy Consumption (Useful), per 1967 Dollar of Output. Source: Table 19-5.

through the walls. Moreover, larger furnaces make feasible the recuperative regeneration procedure—which recirculates much of the hot waste gases and uses air pre-heated by these gases to facilitate fuel combustion.

Less important has been the development of refractories—the material that lines the inside of the furnace—that can better withstand high temperatures and corrosion. Better refractories reduce average yearly down-time by lengthening furnace lives and campaigns,[2] and, therefore, they lower energy use per unit of output by reducing the total amount of start-up energy required per year.

A third factor is the introduction and use of electric "boosters" in fuel-fired furnaces. By introducing more heat near the bottom of the furnace (through passing current between electrodes placed there), a stirring action is created. This is said to increase furnace output by much more than the relative amount of additional energy; in addition, it helps to mix the molten glass and, consequently, to improve its homogeneity. Undoubtedly, the spread in the use of electric boosters has accounted for some of the relative increase in electricity use by the basic glass industries.

Completely electric furnaces have won some scattered use, but their output relative to total glass melt is very small. While their thermal efficiency is higher than that of fuel-fired furnaces and they are excellent for some specialized applications, high energy costs of electricity (per useful BTU) and present limitations on the size of electric furnaces (ruling out use in large plants) discourage further adoption for glass making. Areas where electric power is extremely cheap and pollution control requirements are very strict are the most suitable locations for glass plants with electric furnaces. Increased use of electric furnaces would, of course, substantially raise gross energy demanded by the basic glass industries.

Advances in mechanization (including automation) have tended to lower energy use per unit of output. Such changes have included improvements in glass forming systems (e.g., in bottle making); automation of many non-container systems; use of control instruments (including computers) for blending raw materials and furnace operation; and improvements in methods of heat recovery.

The trend to lighter weight bottles (especially nonreturnables) in the glass container industry has also contributed to the lowering of energy use per dollar of output. Lighter weight bottles mean less basic material required, and it is the melting of the basic materials that accounts for three-fourths of total energy consumption. Because energy costs are a small proportion of total costs, and other elements of cost stay almost the same, a possibly large relative drop in energy costs barely affects total costs and, therefore, the value of production.

It should be noted, however, that greater use of lighter weight bottles does not necessarily mean that *total* energy consumed is, or will be, less, even though energy use per unit of output is lowered. In the absence of large scale recycling, relatively greater use of nonreturnables means that more bottles have to be produced, requiring more total energy. On the other hand, the public brings back only a small proportion of returnables; so it is not clear how much the marketing of beverages in nonreturnables actually affects aggregate energy use in glass container manufacturing.

Development and adoption of the "float" process of making plate glass has been considerably important in the flat glass industry. Previously, the production of flat, fire-finished, distortion-free glass involved extensive grinding and polishing, which consumed 10% to 20% of the glass. In the float process, the molten glass leaves the furnace in a continuous strip and floats directly upon the surface of an enclosed pool of molten tin. By surrounding the glass with a controlled atmosphere (to prevent oxidation of the metal) and with sufficient heat, irregularities on both surfaces of the glass flow out, permitting both surfaces to be flat, smooth, and parallel. Elimination of the grinding and polishing steps saves the direct energy needs for power, and indirectly the energy required for melting the glass that was ground into waste. The float process (developed in England) was not perfected until the late 1950s, and there was little commercial use of it in the United States until the late 1960s.

SECTION III. PROJECTIONS TO 1980

Projections of production and of aggregate energy use by the basic glass industries as a whole are made by (1) forecasting output and energy consumption (useful) per dollar of output for each of the three industries; (2) deriving therefrom aggregate energy consumption (useful) for each industry; (3) combining the three sets of results; (4) projecting the distribution of aggregate overall useful energy consumption; and (5) applying the proper multiple to the BTUs attributable to electricity in order to derive aggregate gross demand for energy.

The projections for the individual industries are obtained first because we believe that their respective specific markets, although parts of common broader markets, are sufficiently different to mandate this approach.

Demand and Output

The three basic glass industries, as a whole, are projected to increase their production 47% between 1971 and 1980, from a total of $3,225 million (1967 dollars) to $4,750 million in 1980. When calculated from 1967, a year less affected by recession than 1971, the increase amounts to 67%.

Output of the flat glass industry is projected to increase 50% between 1971 and 1980, or 74% between 1967 and 1971. Thus, output of SIC 3211 is estimated to total $1,050 million dollars (1967) in 1980. Demand for flat glass is projected by using the forecast of the computerized INFORUM input-output model of the University of Maryland based on Conference Board projections of

Table 19-6.   Output, Energy Use, and Energy Use per Dollar of Output

	SIC 3211 Flat Glass	SIC 3221 Glass Containers	SIC 3229 Pressed and Blown Glass, n.e.c.	Total
Output (million 1967 $)				
1967	$ 611	$1,352	$ 886	$2,850
1971	700	1,550	975	3,225
1980	1,050	2,200	1,500	4,750
Energy use (trillion BTUs)				
Useful				
1967	53.6	119.1	65.7	238.4
1971	59.4	143.6	71.4	274.4
1980	78.7	183.7	103.5	381.4
Gross				
1967	60.5	135.5	74.1	270.1
1971	66.0	167.1	83.0	316.1
1980	x	x	x	460.7
Energy use per dollar of output (thousand BTUs)				
Useful				
1967	87.7	88.1	74.2	83.7
1971	84.9	92.6	73.2	85.1
1980	75.0	83.5	69.0	80.3
Gross				
1967	99.1	100.1	83.6	94.8
1971	94.3	107.8	85.1	98.0
1980	x	x	x	x

x Not projected.

Sources: Table 19-5; Chart 19-4; Table 19-7; University of Maryland, INFORUM Input-output projection model, July & August, 1973; The Conference Board.

gross national product. The Maryland model actually forecasts domestic supplies (imports plus shipments by domestic producers). But we have used its percentage change because we do not anticipate any appreciable change in the share of the market accounted for by imports.

Glass container industry production is projected to grow from the $1,050 million (1967 dollars) total of 1971 to $2,200 million in 1980, or 42%. The 42% full-period increase is the result of assuming a 4% average annual rise in output—slightly higher than its average rate of growth between 1967 and 1971. This is not a real acceleration, inasmuch as industry output in 1971 was below trend, and it matches a curve fitted to plottings of historical per capita production (in 1967 dollars) by the glass container industry (see Chart 19-4). The Maryland model could not be used for SIC 3221 because of faulty data in the memory bank.

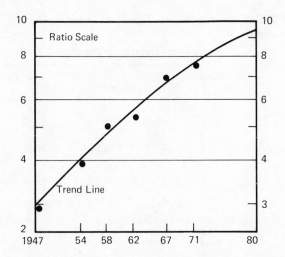

Chart 19-4. Per Capita Output by the Glass Container Industry.
Source: Table 19A-3.

Demand for products of the pressed and blown glass, n.e.c., industry are projected by the Maryland model to increase 70% between 1971 and 1980. Imports have, however, been increasing their share of the market for these products, although these incursions are limited to certain types of products. It is roughly estimated that production by domestic producers will increase an average of 5% a year, or 54% altogether, rather than the 6% implicit in the 70% rise in domestic supplies. Recent as well as historical increases in output by SIC 3229 have been in the order of 5% a year.

Energy Use

Aggregate energy use in 1980 by the basic glass industries is arrived at by first projecting energy use per dollar of output for each industry separately. This procedure is necessary because the industries exhibit different patterns of change in energy use per unit of output. This ratio has been in a clear downtrend in all three industries, but accelerations and decelerations have differed. Also, individual industry developments indicate varied rates of technological change and varied opportunities for adoption of such changes.

As a whole, there does not appear to be any ongoing technological shift or new development on the horizon that will drastically affect energy use per unit of output between now and 1980. Average furnace size may increase further, but less rapidly than previously, since there are limitations to the ability of present systems and forming machinery to receive and process the molten glass. The use of electric boosters probably will become more widespread. Prospects for energy savings seem to be best in the flat glass industry. There,

Table 19-7.   Projections of Aggregate Energy Use by Source, Useful and Gross

Basic Glass Industries Combined

	Coal	Oil	Gas	Electricity	Total*
			Trillion BTU		
Useful energy consumed					
1967	10.7	10.9	184.8	15.4	238.4
1971	3.8	10.8	229.3	20.1	274.4
1980	7.6	66.7	259.5	38.0	381.4
Gross energy demanded					
1967	10.7	10.9	184.8	47.1	270.1
1971	3.8	10.8	229.3	61.9	316.1
1980	7.6	66.7	259.5	117.0	460.7
Per cent distribution of energy consumption (useful) by source					
1967	4.5%	4.6%	77.7%	6.5%	100.0%
1971	1.4	3.9	83.6	7.3	100.0
1980	2.0	17.5	68.0	10.0	100.0

*Totals include small percentages of energy from "other" sources and from sources not specified by kind.
Sources: Table 19-5; Table 19-6; Appendix Table 19A-1; The Conference Board.

further conversion to the float process of making plate glass should reap benefits. Glass container manufacturing and other pressed and blown glass making do not have a development with comparable impact.

All three industries should benefit somewhat from a likely rise in the recycling of used glass, but glass container makers would gain more than the others. Because glass melts faster than its individual ingredients, crushed glass has long been used in the batch of materials to speed melting. Therefore, any increase in the proportion of used glass in the batch will lower energy require-ments per ton of molten glass produced by the furnaces.

Should the use of electric furnaces spread significantly, there would be a considerable increase in gross energy demanded by the basic glass industries. This, however, does not seem likely to occur during the next seven years.

Based on these considerations and on the historical perspective, it appears reasonable to project further declines in energy use per dollar of output in the three industries, but at different rates. Flat glass manufacturing seems to have the greatest promise of improvements in energy input per unit of output; the glass container industry is placed second. Thus, the lines used to fit the respective series and to project energy use per dollar of output have different slopes and degrees of curvature (see Chart 19-5).

The resulting projections indicate a decrease in per unit consumption of useful energy in flat glass production from 84,900 BTUs per 1967 dollar of output in 1971 to 75,000 BTUs in 1980. Useful energy consumption by glass container manufacturers is projected to decline from 92,600 BTUs per dollar of

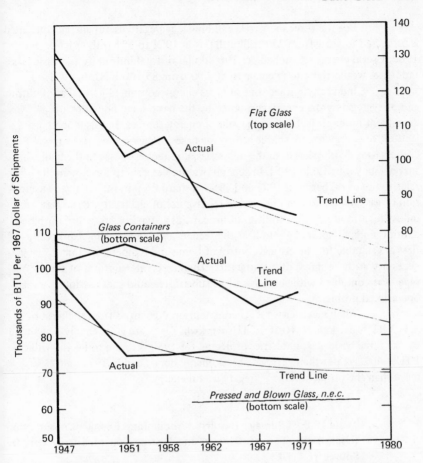

Chart 19-5. Projections of Energy Use per Dollar of Output.
Source: Table 19-5.

output to 83,500 BTUs. Per dollar use by SIC 3229 is projected to drop from 73,200 to 69,000. As in most industries that are heavy energy users, a continuation of the recent increases in real prices of energy and the threat of supply difficulties will provide cost incentives to lower energy use per unit of output.

When these per unit useful energy projections are applied to the forecasts of production for each of the industries, projections of aggregate useful energy consumed by each of the industries, are, of course, derived. For SIC 3211, aggregate useful energy consumed is projected to increase from 59.4 trillion BTUs in 1971 to 78.7 trillion BTUs in 1980; useful energy consumed by SIC 3221 is projected to reach 183.7 trillion BTUs in 1980, versus 143.6 trillion BTUs in 1971; and establishments in SIC 3229 are projected to increase their energy use from 71.4 trillion BTUs to 103.5 trillion BTUs.

For the three industries combined, aggregate useful energy consumed is projected to grow from 274 trillion BTUs in 1971 to 381 trillion BTUs in 1980. Useful energy consumed per 1967 dollar of total output by the basic glass industries would therefore decline to 80,300 from 85,100 BTUs in 1971.

Indirectly, projections of gross energy consumed per dollar of output and of aggregate gross energy consumed by the basic glass industries are dependent upon projections of the mix of energy sources. In this report, projections of energy use by source are on the bases of past trends in the mix, conversations with persons in the industries, and the responses to the mail survey (shown in Table 19-8). In general, we project a sharp increase in the relative use of oil between 1971 and 1980, a sharp drop in the relative consumption of gas, and a moderate rise in the relative use of electricity. Basic glass industries also use small quantities of propane as a standby substitute for piped natural or manufactured gas to heat the feeders and the annealing lehrs. Only gas fires are suitable for the critical control of flame and temperature that is necessary at these stages of manufacture. Therefore, interruptions of supply of piped gas combined with shortages of its substitute could cause serious operational problems.

When electricity's BTU contribution is changed from the basis of 3,412 BTUs per kwh to 10,500 BTUs per kwh, aggregate gross energy demanded by the three basic glass industries projected for 1980 is found to be 461 trillion BTUs—46% greater than aggregate gross energy demanded in 1971 and 21% more than the projection for aggregate useful energy.

Table 19-8.   Survey Results: Production, Energy Consumption (Useful) per Ton of Output, and Distribution of Energy Use, by Source

	1971	1975	1980
		Index Numbers, 1971 = 100	
Production	100	135	169
Energy use per unit of output	100	96	92
Distribution of energy use, by source		*Per Cent*	
Light fuel oil	4.0%	11.5%	22.3%
Heavy fuel oil	2.1	4.0	7.4
Natural gas	72.4	57.1	40.2
Electricity	20.4	24.9	27.0
Total	98.9	97.5	96.9

Note: Distribution percentages add to less than 100 because respondents were asked to report figures for their three main fuels only. Data for production cover six companies; data for energy use per unit of output and for distribution by source cover seven companies.

Source: The Conference Board, "Survey of Future Energy Demand, U.S. Manufacturing."

The projections are summarized in Table 19-7. To be comparable with data for earlier years, a small allowance for "other" fuels and fuels not specified by kind has been included.

Notes

[1] Bureau of the Census, *U.S. Commodity Exports and Imports As Related to Output, 1958, 1967/1968; U.S. Foreign Trade: Imports—SIC-Based Products, Annual 1971* (FT-210-71); U.S. Bureau of the Census, *Annual Survey of Manufactures,* 1971; The Conference Board.

[2] A furnace campaign is the length of time between the installation of a new furnace and its first overhaul, or between overhauls.

SECTION IV.   APPENDIXES

A.   DETAILED INDUSTRY AND PRODUCT CLASSIFICATION, 1972

Industry
3221 Flat Glass

Establishments primarily engaged in manufacturing flat glass. This industry also produces laminated glass, but establishments primarily engaged in manufacturing laminated glass from purchased flat glass are classified in Industry 3231.

Building glass, flat
Cathedral glass
Float glass
Glass, colored: cathedral and antique glass, flat
Insulating glass, sealed units: mitse*
Laminated glass, mitse*
Multiple-glazed insulating units, mitse*
Opalescent flat glass
Ophthalmic glass, flat
Optical glass, flat

Picture glass
Plate glass blanks for optical or ophthalmic uses
Plate glass, polished and rough
Sheet glass
Sheet glass blanks for optical or ophthalmic uses
Skylight glass
Spectacle glass
Structural glass, flat
Tempered glass, mitse*
Window glass, clear and colored

3221 Glass Containers

Establishments primarily engaged in manufacturing glass containers for commercial packing and bottling, and for home canning.

*mitse—made from glass produced in the same establishment

Ampoules, glass
Bottles for packing, bottling and
   canning: glass
Carboys, glass
Containers for packing, bottling and
   canning: glass
Cosmetic jars, glass
Fruit jars, glass

Jars (packers' wares), glass
Jugs (packers' wares), glass
Medicine bottles, glass
Milk bottles, glass
Packers' ware (containers), glass
Vials, glass: made in glass-making
   establishments
Water bottles, glass

3229 Pressed and Blown Glass and Glassware, Not Elsewhere Classified

Establishments primarily engaged in manufacturing glass and glassware, not elsewhere classified, pressed, blown, or shaped from glass produced in the same establishment. Establishments primarily engaged in manufacturing textile glass fibers are also included in this industry, but establishments primarily engaged in manufacturing glass wool insulation products are classified in Industry 3296. Establishments primarily engaged in the production of pressed lenses for vehicular lighting, beacons, and lanterns are also included in this industry, but establishments primarily engaged in the production of optical lenses are classified in Industry 3832. Establishments primarily engaged in manufacturing glass containers are classified in Industry 3221, and establishments engaged in producing complete electric light bulbs in Industry 3641.

Art glassware, made in glassmaking
   plants
Ash trays, glass
Barware, glass
Battery jars, glass
Blocks, glass
Bowls, glass
Bulbs for electric lights, without
   filaments or sockets, mitse*
Candlesticks, glass
Centerpieces, glass
Chimneys, lamp: glass-pressed or
   blown
Christmas Tree ornaments from glass;
   mitse*
Clip cups, glass
Cooking utensils, glass and glass
   ceramic
Drinking straws, glass
Fibers, glass

Flameware, glass and glass ceramic
Frying pans, glass and glass ceramic
Glass blanks for electric light bulbs
Glass brick
Glassware: art, decorative, and novelty
Glassware, except glass containers
   for packing, bottling, and home
   canning
Goblets, glass
Illuminating glass: light shades,
   reflectors, lamp chimneys, and
   globes
Industries glassware and glass
   products, pressed or blown
Inkwells, glass
Insulators, electrical: glass
Lamp parts, glass
Lamp shades, glass
Lantern globes, glass: pressed or
   blown

Lens blanks, optical and ophthalmic
Lenses, glass: for lanterns, flashlights,
  headlights and searchlights
Level vials for instruments, glass
Light shades, glass: pressed, blown
Lighting glassware, pressed or blown
Novelty glassware
Ophthalmic glass, except flat
Optical glass blanks
Reflectors for lighting equipment,
  glass: pressed or blown
Refrigerator dishes and jars, glass
Scientific glassware, pressed or blown:
  made in glassmaking plants

Stemware, glass
Tableware, glass and glass ceramic
Teakettles, glass and glass ceramic
Technical glassware and glass products,
  pressed or blown
Textile glass fibers
Tobacco jars, glass
Trays, glass
Tubing, glass
Tumblers, glass
TV tube blanks, glass
Vases, glass
Yarn, fiberglass: made in glass plants

*mitse—made from glass produced in the same establishment

Source: U.S. Bureau of the Budget, *Standard Industrial Classification Manual, 1972.*

B. GLASS AND ITS MANUFACTURE

What is referred to as glass in everyday language is one of any number of substances that are at once a liquid (in a technical sense) and viscous to the point of rigidity.

Chemically, common glass is a mixture of inorganic oxides. The basic ingredients are silica (from sand), calcium monoxide (from limestone), and sodium monoxide (from soda ash). Not all of these are in all types of glasses, however; and some types of glass that we use include other ingredients, such as oxides of aluminum lead, and boron. In the actual manufacture of glass, crushed waste glass (cullet) of the same type as that being made is added to the batch of materials. Because glass of all types melts at a lower temperature than any of its separate ingredients, the addition of cullet speeds the melting process.

The production of glass involves: (1) mixing the ingredients; (2) heating the mixture in a furnace until the ingredients combine and melt; (3) forming the product to be made by one or more of such means as drawing, blowing, molding, pressing, floating, and casting; (4) annealing, or reheating and slowly cooling the products to relieve stresses caused by the unavoidable cooling that takes place during the forming process; and (5) inspection. (See the flow diagram, Figure 19-1, Appendix C.)

In all basic glass industries, melting practices are essentially the same, regardless of the type of end product. Most glass is produced with a continuous furnace converting the raw materials into the molten state. Products such as flat glass, bottles and jars, and drinking glasses are made in large volumes in a continuous process from melting to packing. Glass melting for smaller volume products is often done in "pots," "day tanks," etc., which generally are much smaller than the continuous furnaces.

The melting of the raw materials consumes a major portion of the energy used to produce glass products. According to a study made by the American Gas Association,* the melting operation accounts for 70%-80% of process energy requirements. If non-process uses are considered also, the proportion accounted for by melting amounts to 65%-75%. Forming (which consumes largely electrical energy) and annealing account for most of the remainder of energy used by the basic glass industries. (When tempering is performed, it also consumes a considerable amount of energy.)

Efficiencies of furnaces vary widely, depending on such factors as their basic design and age, the type of glass being melted, and the end use of the product. For example, flat glass cannot have any noticeable amounts of bubbles, unreacted raw materials, or other substances; the addition of color affects the absorptivity of the mixture and, thus, the rate at which it melts. Furnaces are subject to considerable stress. Because molten glass is highly corrosive, the insides of furnaces and tanks must be lined with materials that retard erosion. These linings, called refractories, are made of composite clays, which may contain one or more of several different minerals—such as alumina, silica, or zircon. Gradual erosion does occur, however; and small fragments of tank lining occasionally break off into the molten glass. Eventually, the furnace lining becomes deeply scored, and has to be renewed; when this is required, operation of the furnace must, of course, be halted. The length of time between installation of a new furnace and its first renewal, or between renewals, is called a furnace "campaign."

Since the wide variety of glass products entails a wide variation in the production and formation processes required, the energy used to produce finished glass products ranges from about 14 million BTUs per ton of mechanically and continuously formed window glass to five or six times that per ton for handmade glassware.

*American Gas Association, *A Study of Process Energy Requirements in the Glass Industry*, p. 9.

C. FLOW DIAGRAM

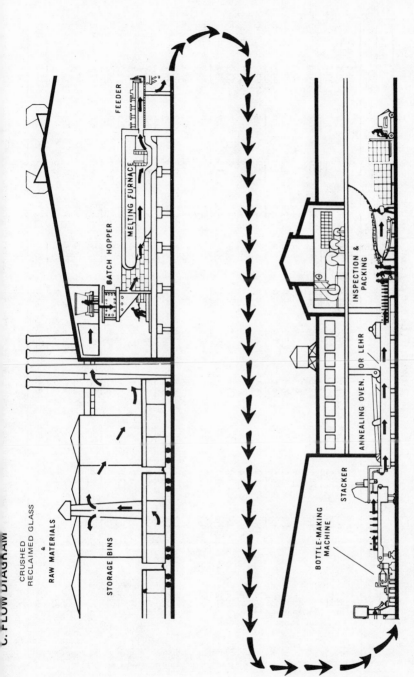

Figure 19-1.   Flow Diagram of the Manufacture of Glass Containers. Source: Glass Container Manufacturers Institute.

D. TABLES

Table 19A-1.   Aggregate Energy Consumption (Useful) by Source—Individual Basic Glass Industries (trillion BTUs and per cent of total)

Year	Industry	Coal BTU	Coal %	Oil BTU	Oil %	Gas BTU	Gas %	Electricity BTU	Electricity %	Other & NSK BTU	Other & NSK %	Total BTU	Total %
1947	3211	14.1	31.8%	0.4	0.1%	28.8	64.9%	1.1	2.5%	–	–	44.4	
	3221	10.3	13.4	13.8	17.9	49.0	63.6	2.5	3.2	1.5	1.9%	77.1	
	3229	5.2	13.3	6.4	16.4	26.0	66.5	1.0	2.6	0.5	1.3	39.1	
	Total	29.6	18.4	20.6	12.8	103.8	64.6	4.6	2.9	2.0	1.2	160.6	100
1954	3211	10.1	23.9	0.1	0.2	30.5	72.1	1.6	3.8	–	–	42.3	
	3221	4.8	5.9	7.1	8.8	63.9	79.0	3.4	4.2	1.7	2.1	80.9	
	3229	3.4	8.6	1.6	4.1	31.6	80.0	1.7	4.3	1.2	3.0	39.5	
	Total	18.3	16.2	8.8	5.4	126.0	77.4	6.7	4.1	2.9	1.8	162.7	100
1958	3211	9.9	23.4	–	–	30.1	71.2	2.1	5.0	0.2	0.5	42.3	
	3221	2.7	3.0	9.0	10.1	72.1	80.8	4.4	4.9	1.0	1.1	89.2	
	3229	1.8	4.6	2.0	5.1	29.9	75.7	1.9	4.8	3.9	9.9	39.5	
	Total	14.4	8.4	11.0	6.4	132.1	77.3	8.4	4.9	5.1	3.0	171.0	100
1962	3211	8.7	18.5	0.5	1.1	33.9	72.0	2.8	5.9	1.2	2.5	47.1	
	3221	1.8	1.8	8.9	8.8	83.6	83.0	5.7	5.7	0.7	0.7	100.7	
	3229	1.1	2.2	1.9	3.8	40.9	81.0	2.9	5.7	3.7	7.3	50.5	
	Total	11.6	5.8	11.3	5.7	158.4	79.8	11.4	5.7	5.6	2.8	198.3	100
1967	3211	8.0	14.9	1.1	2.1	37.9	70.7	3.4	6.3	3.2	6.0	53.6	
	3221	2.4	2.0	8.3	7.0	97.6	82.2	7.9	6.7	2.5	2.1	118.7	
	3229	0.3	0.5	1.5	2.3	49.3	75.2	4.1	6.3	10.4	15.9	65.6	
	Total	10.7	4.5	10.9	4.6	184.8	77.7	15.4	6.5	16.1	6.8	237.9	100
1971	3211	3.7	6.2	0.3	0.5	52.2	87.9	3.2	5.4	z	–	59.4	
	3221	–	–	8.6	6.0	120.3	83.8	11.3	7.9	3.4	2.4	143.6	
	3229	0.1	0.1	1.9	2.7	56.8	79.7	5.6	7.9	6.9	9.7	71.3	
	Total	3.8	1.4	10.8	3.9	229.3	83.6	20.1	7.3	10.3	3.8	274.3	100

z – Less than 50 billion BTU.

Sources: Bureau of the Census, Census of Manufactures, 1947, 1954, 1958, 1967; Annual Survey of Manufactures, 1962, 1971.

D. TABLES (continued)

Table 19A-2.   Glass Containers: Distribution of Shipments and Shipped Value per Gross

	Per Cent of Shipments		Shipped Value per Gross
	1950	1971	1971 (dollars)
Narrow neck......................	62.1%	75.2%	$ 7.70
Food	10.5	9.5	9.12
Medicinal & health	14.0	6.0	6.85
Household & industrial	7.0	1.2	7.41
Toiletries & cosmetics	5.7	2.9	6.73
Beverage, returnable	6.0	3.8	12.52
Beverage, nonreturnable	0.2	22.7	7.32
Beer, returnable	3.0	0.7	7.67
Beer, nonreturnable	3.1	20.1	5.02
Liquor	9.2	5.2	11.61
Wine	3.6	3.1	13.70
Wide mouth	37.9	24.8	6.79
Food	28.3	22.4	6.61
Medicinal & health supplies	3.3	1.3	6.55
Household & industrial	1.3	0.4	9.20
Toiletries & cosmetics	1.5	0.6	9.65
Dairy products	3.5	0.1	20.87
Total shipments in thousands of gross	105,254	255,261	

Note: Data include shipments for direct exports, which account for less than 1% of total shipments.

Sources: Bureau of the Census, *Current Industrial Reports*, "Glass Containers, Summary for 1972," M32G(72)-13; Glass Container Manufacturers Institute, *Glass Containers*, 1972.

Table 19A-3.   Per Capita Output by the Glass Container Industry

	Output SIC 3221 (million 1967 $)	Total U.S. Population (millions)	Output Per Capita (dollars)
1947	$ 422.6	144.13	2.93
1954	646.1	163.03	3.96
1958	862.1	174.88	4.93
1962	987.6	186.54	5.29
1967	1,352.4	198.71	6.81
1971	1,550.0	207.05	7.50

Sources: Table 19-5; Bureau of the Census, *Current Population Reports*.

SECTION V.   SELECTED BIBLIOGRAPHY

American Gas Association, *A Study in Process Energy Requirements in the Glass Industry.* New York: American Gas Association, *circa* 1967.

Berlye, Milton K. *The Encyclopedia of Working with Glass.* Dobbs Ferry, N.Y.: Oceana Publications, 1968.

Bureau of the Budget. *Standard Industrial Classification Manual, 1967.* Washington: 1967.

Corning Glass Works. *This is Glass.* Corning, N.Y.: Corning Glass Works, 1956.

Giegerich, W., and Trier, W., Editors. *Glass Machines: Construction and Operation of Machines for the Forming of Hot Glass.* New York: Springer-Verlag New York, Inc., 1969.

Glass Container Manufacturers Institute. *Glass Containers, 1970 and 1972 Editions.* New York: Glass Containers Manufacturers Institute, 1972.

Jones, G. O. *Glass,* 2nd Edition. New York: Chapman & Hall, 1969.

Maloney, F. J. Terence. *Glass in the Modern World.* Garden City, N.Y.: Doubleday & Company, 1968.

Shand, Errol B. *Glass Engineering Handbook,* 2nd Edition. New York: McGraw-Hill, 1958.

Stanford Research Institute. *Patterns of Energy Consumption in the United States.* Washington: Office of Science and Technology, 1972.

Chapter Twenty

Hydraulic Cement—SIC 3241

Bernard A. Gelb

SECTION I.   INTRODUCTION AND SUMMARY

The Industry

The Hydraulic Cement industry, SIC 3241, is defined as that group of establishments primarily engaged in manufacturing hydraulic cement—which includes portland, natural, masonry, and pozzolan cements. It is one of the most "specialized" manufacturing industries, and one with the greatest coverage of its primary product. Almost all (99%) of the output of this group of establishments is hydraulic cement; and these establishments account for almost all (99%) hydraulic cement produced in the United States. Moreover, 96% of the industry's production of hydraulic cement (by weight) is in the form of portland cement.

Because the proportion of hydraulic cement production accounted for by portland cement is so large, the overall energy-to-output relationship of the industry is to all intents and purposes determined by the relationship in portland cement production. Output of masonry cement, with slightly less energy requirements than portland, has increased much faster in the postwar period than portland output, yet it still accounts for less than 4% of the total hydraulic cement production. A brief description of the technology of cement manufacture, especially regarding energy use, is provided in Section IV; a flow diagram is included.

Summary of Developments

In the postwar period, the hydraulic cement industry has grown less rapidly than the economy as a whole. Output by SIC 3241 in 1967 dollars increased 103% between 1947 and 1971, compared with a 139% rise in gross national product. This is partly the result of slower growth in construction activity—to which cement sales are closely tied—than in other economic activity. But it is also a case of capacity not keeping pace with domestic demand. As a result, the country has switched from being a net exporter of cement to a net importer. The deceleration in additions to domestic cement capacity and production has occurred mainly in the past ten years.

Aggregate energy use by hydraulic cement producers has increased more slowly than output in the past two and a half decades. In contrast with the 103% gain in the value of production (in constant dollars) between 1947 and 1971, aggregate useful[a] energy consumed by SIC 3241 increased just 53%. Implicitly, useful energy required per dollar of output has dropped rapidly; the decline, from 458,000 BTUs per 1967 dollar of output to 345,000 BTUs per 1967 dollar of output, was at an average annual rate of 1.2% a year. Aggregate gross energy demanded by the industry increased 57% between 1947 and 1971, and gross energy demanded per 1967 dollar of output declined from 500,000 BTUs to 385,000 BTUs.

Several technological and marketing trends, some of them offsetting, are responsible for these movements in aggregate and per unit useful energy consumption by SIC 3241. Gains in energy efficiency have come about mainly through (1) growing reuse of waste heat, (2) economies of scale won through the use of increasingly larger plants, (3) advances in mechanization, (4) advances in process control, and (5) a shift from on-site power generation to the purchase of electricity. These developments have been partly countered by the greater per unit energy requirements of increased mechanization, of finer grinding, and of pollution control equipment.

The movement in gross energy demanded per unit of output reflects all the above developments plus (1) the shift to much more use of purchased electricity (tending to increase BTUs per unit) and (2) the steep decrease in the heat loss rate at electric utilities between 1949 and 1969, and the small increase since then (tending to decrease and then to increase BTUs per unit).

Changes in the mix of energy sources used by the hydraulic cement industry have been substantial. Between 1947 and 1967, coal's contribution to total BTUs used by SIC 3241 dropped from two-thirds to less than one-half; gas's share increased from one-fourth to two-fifths; and oil's proportion started at 8% and fell to 3%. Cement producers' relative use of electricity (purchased) rose from 2½% to 5½%.

Projections

We expect that most of the developments affecting energy use per barrel of cement produced will continue to be operative through 1980. In addition, we believe that the cost incentive of higher real energy prices has begun, and will continue, to encourage a shift from wet process manufacture to the less energy-intensive dry process. Such an incentive should further lower—through innovation—the theoretical limits of energy use per barrel produced. We therefore project further declines in useful energy consumed per unit of output.

[a] See Chapter One, pages 14-15, for definitions of useful and gross energy.

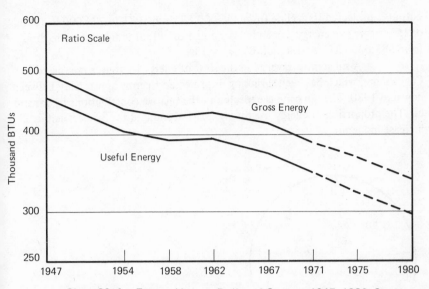

Chart 20-1. Energy Use per Dollar of Output, 1947-1980. Source: Table 20-1.

Table 20-1. Output, Energy Use, and Energy Use per Dollar of Output

	1947	1954	1958	1962	1967	1971	1975	1980
Output (million 1967 $)	$684	$930	$1,053	$1,092	$1,246	$1,391	$1,547	$1,767
Energy use (trillion (BTUs)								
Useful	313	375	410	428	463	480	496	519
Gross	342	407	449	471	515	536	564	594
Energy use per dollar of output (1,000 BTUs)								
Useful	458	403	390	392	371	345	321	294
Gross	500	438	426	431	413	385	365	336

Sources: Bureau of the Census, *Census of Manufactures* and *Annual Survey of Manufactures*. Bureau of Mines, *Minerals Yearbook*, 1971, Table 20-2.

When the specifics of these expectations regarding per unit energy use are applied to output and aggregate energy use by SIC 3241, the results are as follows: Aggregate useful energy consumption is projected to increase from 480 trillion BTUs in 1971 to 519 trillion BTUs in 1980, a rise of 8%; aggregate gross energy demanded is projected to grow from 536 trillion BTUs to 594 trillion BTUs, an increase of 11%. Useful energy consumed per 1967 dollar of output is projected to decline from 345,000 BTUs in 1971 to 294,000 in 1980, or 15%; aggregate energy demanded per dollar of output is anticipated to drop from 385,000 BTUs to 336,000 BTUs, or 13%.

A substantial reversal in the shift of energy by source is expected. Coal's share, which has been shrinking, is projected to grow appreciably between now and 1980. The opposite is expected of the relative contributions by gas and oil. The proportion of energy use by SIC 3241 accounted for by electricity will increase moderately.

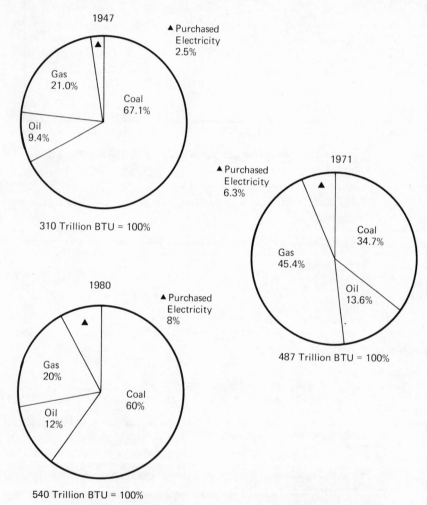

Chart 20-2. Distribution of Energy Consumption (Useful) by Source, 1947, 1971, 1980, All Portland Cement Manufacture. Source: Table 20-3; Appendix Table 20A-4; Pages 361, 364.

SECTION II.   HISTORICAL DEVELOPMENTS

Demand, Production, and Capacity

Virtually all cement is used for construction. Therefore, demand for it is closely tied to fluctuations in the building of roads, bridges, other public works, most commercial structures, and large residential structures. *Pit and Quarry* (a cement industry trade magazine) stated that, in 1969, 47% of the end use of cement was for public buildings and other public works, 20% for industrial and commercial construction, 24% for residential construction, and 9% for farm and other construction.[1] Reflecting sharp gains in these types of construction, domestic consumption of cement spurted in the early 1950s, late 1950s, middle to late 1960s and early 1970s.

In the postwar period as a whole, apparent consumption of cement has increased about 10% faster than construction activity, but U.S. cement *production* has increased at about the same rate as construction activity, as we have changed from a net exporter to a net importer of cement. In the past decade or so, construction has grown less rapidly than it did earlier; and average yearly growth in domestic production of hydraulic cement has mirrored this. Slower growth in construction does not, however, appear to be the sole or main cause of slower increases in domestic cement output.

Growth in capacity has decelerated also. In contrast with most of the history of the industry, undercapacity seems to be a serious problem now. Production of portland cement equaled 88% or more of capacity in 1970, 1971, and 1972—the first time the utilization rate has been this high for three consecutive years since 1954-1956. Below-par profitability has discouraged capital investment. Additionally, environmental regulations have also had an effect. Plant closings have been more numerous than normal largely as a result of pollution control regulations, which would have made many marginal establishments unprofitable had the required changes in facilities been undertaken.

A major consequence of the slowdown in growth of capacity has been a rapid increase in imports of cement. In the four years after 1967, imports of cement rose 23%, 33%, 43%, and 19%, respectively. This boosted them to a rate of 16.4 million barrels in 1971—three and a half times their average for 1955 through 1967. They jumped another 59% in 1972, to a level equal to 6% of domestic consumption. Because of the local nature of the cement industry, imports have grown rapidly even though average capacity utilization has not approached 100%.

Energy and Output—Summary Measures

Total useful energy consumed by the "hydraulic cement" industry increased 47.6% between 1947 and 1967 from 313.3 trillion BTUs to 462.5 trillion BTUs. During the same period, real output by the industry measured in constant 1967 dollars grew 82.2%. Implicitly, energy consumption (useful) per dollar of output dropped 19% from 458,063 BTUs to 371,222 BTUs.

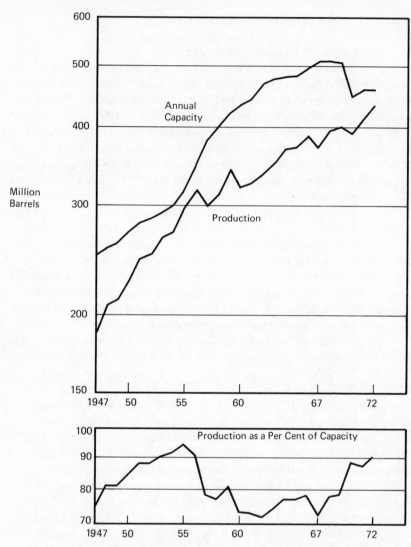

Chart 20-3. Portland Cement, Capacity and Production, 1947–1972. Source: U.S. Bureau of Mines, *1971 Minerals Yearbook.*

The relative as well as absolute use of electrical energy by SIC 3241 is, as in most other industries, growing rapidly; but the useful energy content of electricity accounted for only 5½% of total useful energy consumed by the industry in 1967. Consequently, the growth of *gross* energy demanded, from 342.1 trillion BTUs to 515.2 trillion BTUs, by SIC 3241 has been only slightly faster than that of *useful* energy—50.6% versus 47.6% between 1947 and 1967.

There has been a much more extensive shift in the mix of fuels used by hydraulic cement producers than the shift to electricity. In both 1947 and 1967, coal and gas together accounted for 89% of total useful energy consumed by SIC 3241; but in the twenty-year period gas increased its proportion from 23% to 41%, while coal's proportion dropped from 66% to 48%. Total useful energy accounted for by oil declined from 8% to 5%, offsetting the rise of electricity from 2½% to 5½%.

On the basis of data from the Bureau of Mines, some of these trends continued from 1967 through 1971, but some were altered—and even reversed. As previously, aggregate energy use increased less rapidly than output. Energy use per unit of output declined at an average annual rate of about 1%. Aggregate useful energy consumed grew 2.5%; production of cement (in barrels) rose 10.9%. Useful energy consumed per barrel of cement produced dropped from 1.32 million to 1.22 million BTUs; the 1947 level was 1.66 million. Aggregate gross energy consumed by establishments making portland cement increased 4.1% between 1967 and 1971.

Electricity use continued to grow steadily in relative terms between 1967 and 1971, increasing from 5.6% to 6.3% of total useful energy consumed by all portland cement producers (based on Bureau of Mines data). However, the relative drop in coal use accelerated, and a larger part of the drop was made up by oil (which had reversed its long-term relative decline during the mid-1960s) than by gas. Bureau of Mines figures show that coal-derived energy (useful) consumed by portland cement producers plummeted from 46.6% of the total in 1967 to 34.7% in 1971; gas energy rose from 41.5% to 45.4%, and oil from 6.4% to 13.6%.

Because both the specialization and the coverage ratios of SIC 3241 are extremely high (99% for both in 1967), Bureau of Mines data can be used as a proxy for Census data with a high degree of confidence and accuracy in the case of this industry. For example, the total value of cement shipped by SIC 3241 in 1967 is recorded in the *Census of Manufactures* as $1,217 million; and 99% of the total value of cement shipments recorded by the Bureau of Mines equals $1,226 million, only 0.7% greater than the Census figure.

Technological and Marketing Developments

These movements in aggregate and per-unit energy use by SIC 3241 are the consequence of several technological and marketing trends, some of them offsetting others.

A major development tending to reduce energy use per unit of output has been the increase in the size of the typical plant. In 1971, nearly half of establishments producing portland cement had an annual capacity of 3 million or more barrels, compared with less than one-fifth in 1948. There are technical cost incentives to make plants as large as possible. The sources of savings are primarily labor and overhead, the costs of which grow less than proportionately as plant size increases. For example, construction costs per barrel of capacity do not rise in proportion to the size of plant. Less building space is required, per unit of capacity, and less steel is needed. Savings in fuel are among the advantages of reducing the number of kilns per barrel of output, along with better quality control. Greater grinding efficiency is one of the dividends of larger grinding mills with greater horsepower; better adaptability to computer process control is another.

In approximating the cost per barrel of producing cement at plants of various levels of annual capacity, Joseph Wynen of Bendy Engineering Company recently found that establishments with a 3-million barrel capacity (annual) experienced 10% lower total cost than establishments with a 1-million barrel capacity, and 12½% lower fuel costs.[2] The advantages of size cannot, however, be fully exploited in cost terms unless output is near capacity. Lower operating rates may well result in higher costs per unit than those associated with smaller plants.

Advances in mechanization (including automation) and other gains in technology over the years have also tended to lower energy use per unit of output. Such changes have included the following: improvements in materials handling equipment; use of control instruments (including computers) for blending raw materials, for kiln operation, and for finish grinding; improvements in the methods of flue dust recovery; improvements in the systems that move the "meal" through the kiln; and the introduction of the oxy-fuel burner, which increases fuel-burning efficiency. One plant was able to reduce fuel requirements by 300,000 BTUs per barrel of clinker by installing an adequate chain system.

It should be noted that, despite rapid mechanization in the industry, which has increased use of electrical machinery, consumption of electricity per barrel of portland cement produced rose only slightly between 1947 and 1971—from 22.5 kwh to 24.5 kwh. The main reason for this rise is the trend toward increased grinding of the clinker to produce smaller particles and hence a finer powder.

A major development has been the introduction and spreading use of preheaters, which reduce (a) energy requirements per unit of output and (b) the size of the kiln, by using heat from waste gas to heat the mix before it enters the kiln. One industry analyst has reported energy use by a kiln with a suspension preheater at 537,000 BTUs per barrel, compared with 726,000 BTUs per barrel used by a conventional kiln without a preheater. The Bureau of Mines cites another comparison in which new modern dry process kilns with suspension preheaters used 550,000 BTUs per barrel of clinker, compared with 900,000 used by new large wet process kilns.[3]

These improvements affected energy use in dry process more than in wet. Postwar technological improvements have been more applicable to dry than to wet process production. Perhaps, also, wet process may have more closely approached its theoretical maximum energy efficiency by the late 1940s than

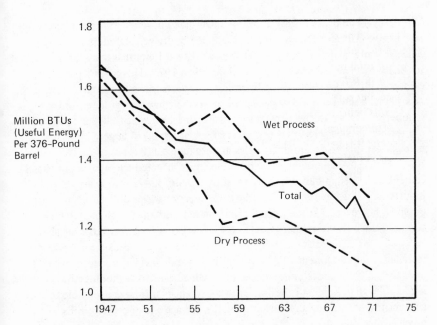

Chart 20-4. Energy Use per Unit of Output in the Production of Portland Cement. Note: Wet and dry process plotted only for 1947, 1950, 1954, 1958, 1962, 1967, and 1971. Source: Appendix Table 20A-4; Appendix Table 20A-8.

dry process. Between 1947 and 1971 average useful energy consumed per barrel of portland cement produced by dry process dropped 33.8%, from 1.64 million BTUs to 1.09 million BTUs, according to Bureau of Mines data; average per barrel use of energy consumed by wet process manufacturers declined 22.7%, from 1.68 million BTUs to 1.30 million BTUs. Thus, toward the end of the period, dry process required 15%-20% fewer BTUs per barrel of cement produced than wet.

The overall drop in energy use per unit of output by cement producers probably would have been greater were it not for a moderate shift from dry to wet process during most of the postwar period. Wet process portland cement mills accounted for 61.6% of total portland cement producing capacity in 1967, compared with 53.4% in 1947. If it were assumed that there was no change between 1947 and 1967 in wet and dry process shares of production, but that energy efficiency improvement by process did occur as described above, aggregate and per unit energy (useful) consumption by portland cement producers would have been 2% less than it actually was. The shift from dry to wet occurred largely because of continuing problems of dry process in handling high alkali materials.

The process shift appears, however, to have reversed itself since the late 1960s. Portland cement clinker produced in dry process mills accounted for 38.8% of total portland clinker in 1968—a postwar low; then the proportion rose to 39.1% in 1969, 39.9% in 1970, and 40.2% in 1971. This is scanty statistical evidence, but it is corroborated by industry reports. As many as five of eight new plants being built are designed for dry rather than wet process; and a number of companies are considering converting from wet to dry process with preheaters. It is believed that this reversal is being spurred largely by sharp increases in fuel costs and difficulties in obtaining some types of fuels.

Environmental regulations also have affected energy use per barrel of cement produced, albeit relatively recently. In SIC 3241, as in nearly all industries, pollution control facilities raise energy use per unit of output. It is possible, however, that the overall effect on per-unit energy use may be less severe in the cement industry due to the closing of a relatively large number of very old marginal plants—with high energy-output ratios—because necessary installation of equipment such as precipitators and glass bag collectors would have forced costs above competitive levels. Since cement technology has changed less rapidly than in most other industries, cement plants have been able to stay competitive as long as 70 years, causing the average age of cement mills to be much higher than that of other kinds of manufacturing plants.

A major change in the form in which cement is marketed, as a result of changes in the distribution system, has probably tended to lower energy use—though the effect may be exceedingly small. At the outset of the postwar period, most cement was shipped from mills in containers (mainly paper bags) directly to users (who prepared their concrete themselves) or to building supply dealers (who then sold it to eventual users). Partly due to the rapid growth of the ready-mixed concrete industry, mills now distribute preponderantly in bulk. In 1971, 91.4% of portland cement shipments were in bulk form, as against 36.8% in 1947. Nearly two-thirds of cement shipments went direct to "ready-mixed" concrete companies in 1971, and less than one-tenth to building supply dealers.[4] Elimination, or avoidance, of bagging operations probably reduces overall energy use to some degree.

SECTION III.   PROJECTIONS TO 1980

Some Considerations

Because of actual and potential limitations on output, factors bearing on the capacity situation must be discussed in relation to future aggregate use of energy by SIC 3241. Annual portland cement production capacity actually dropped in 1970, and for the last three years has been below that of any year from 1962 through 1969. (Part of the decline in 1970 was, however, not "real," but due to a change in definition by the Bureau of Mines in its compilation of data.) Although portland cement mills operated at over 90%

of capacity in 1972, domestic production had to be supplemented by 26.4 million barrels of imported cement.

Probably, more new capacity would have been built were it not for the long slump in profitability of cement manufacturing. Very low return on investment discourages additions to capacity by dampening profit expectations, and it often prevents capital outlays through actual shortages of funds. That profitability has indeed been poor seems to be borne out by data from the Federal Trade Commission[5] and the First National City Bank of New York,[6] which show the rate of return on stockholder equity, or net worth, to have been one of the lowest of all manufacturing industries since the mid-1960s. These data also show that the relative profitability of cement manufacturers has increased over the past few years, but it is still well below the average for all manufacturing.

A second consideration, prices, comes into play at this point. Overcapacity in the cement industry had been a major factor in holding down prices and hence capacity. When price controls were instituted, the "base period" selected was particularly unfortunate for the industry, since it covered part of the era of depressed prices. The improvement in profitability noted above has occurred despite the existence of price controls since August 1971. Lifting of price controls on the cement industry (in late 1973) should be

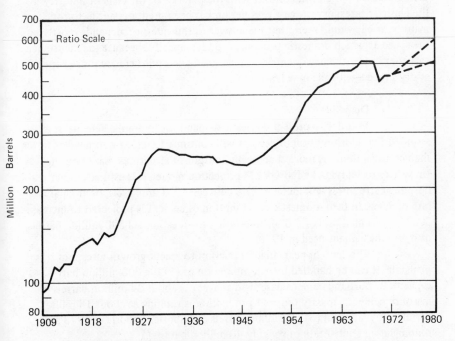

Chart 20-5. Manufacturing Capacity—Portland Cement. Source: U.S. Bureau of Mines, *Minerals Yearbook, 1971.*

beneficial to profit margins. This is not to say that return on investment will necessarily approach its level of the 1950s.

Overall, it appears to us that the combination of further improvements in profitability, continued operation near full capacity, and likely apprehension about further loss of markets to foreign producers will encourage expansion of capacity not now contemplated, partly through modernization and small additions. Capital investment by portland cement producers should be sufficient to at least attain by 1980 the 510-million barrel capacity level of the late 1960s once more. This capacity would yield 434 million barrels of output at an 85% operation rate. However, we do not believe it is optimistic to expect portland cement capacity to return to the level of its long-term growth curve.[7] Such an expansion would put annual capacity at about 600 million barrels in 1980, with potential output of 510 million barrels at 85% of capacity.

A third question concerning future aggregate use of energy by the cement industry is the extent to which producers will adopt already developed technological improvements capable of sharply curtailing energy use per unit of output. Such improvements, generally described in Section II, focus on dry process operations and are moving in the direction of more use of preheaters and shorter kilns. They are said to have their origins in Europe and Japan and to be used extensively there. In contrast with the practice of the cement industry in the United States, dry-process production has been predominant in Europe for many years. It would seem that the answer to this question depends mostly on the speed at which domestic producers add to capacity, because—as mentioned earlier—most of the new plants being designed and built here are indeed specified as dry process with the new features.

Demand

In order to project domestic demand for hydraulic cement, it is assumed that consumption of cement will continue to increase somewhat faster than construction, or, more specifically, output of structures. Based on the University of Maryland's INFORUM projection model, it is estimated that real output of structures will increase 27% between 1971 and 1980, or at an annual rate of 2.7%. In turn, domestic consumption of cement is projected to increase 30.5% (an annual rate of 3.0%), amounting to an estimated 590 million barrels of hydraulic cement used in 1980.

This level appears high in relation to recent growth rates, but it is plausible. It can be handled by a combination of (1) the 600-million barrel capacity of portland cement described above; (2) about 24 million barrels of masonry cement capacity (current production is running at about 18 million barrels per year); and (3) 50 million barrels of imports (imports in 1973 are running at an annual rate of roughly 40 million barrels).

The 30.5% increase in consumption projected between 1971 and 1980 is very closely paralleled by the average production increase expectations of three large cement companies (31.8%) that supplied tonnage figures in responding to the survey of future energy use.[8] Total output (in 1967 dollars) by the industry is projected to increase 27% between 1971 and 1980, allowing for a relative increase in imports—most of which has already occurred in 1972 and 1973.

Energy Use

Aggregate energy use by SIC 3241 in 1980 is arrived at by first projecting energy use per unit of output under wet process and under dry process portland cement production separately. This procedure is necessary because (1) improvements in energy use per unit of output have been at different rates in each of the processes, and (2) we believe that the proportion of total output made by dry process is going to continue to increase.

Because energy use per unit of output in both production processes has been in a clear downtrend with no appreciable acceleration or deceleration, and because industry reports indicate continued adoption of new technological developments, it was decided to project energy use per unit of output by extrapolating straight lines that were fitted to the series by the least squares method. This is shown in Chart 20-6. The resulting projections indicate a decrease in consumption of useful energy in wet process portland cement production from 1.30 million BTUs per barrel in 1971 to 1.19 million BTUs in 1980. Dry process useful energy consumption is projected to decline from 1.09 million BTUs per barrel to 0.85 million BTUs per barrel. We believe that these projected declines are guaranteed by a continuation of the recent increases in real prices of energy through 1980, which will provide a cost incentive to further lower, through innovation, the theoretical limits of energy use per unit of output.

Since *Census of Manufactures* shipments figures are not broken down by process of manufacture, it is necessary to obtain an average energy-output ratio for both processes combined in order to estimate the projected change in aggregate energy use. To do this, the two relationships are multiplied by anticipated physical production by mills using the respective processes, and the results are added.

Anticipated physical production by process is arrived at by projecting total portland cement production to 1980 (by applying the 27% growth figure), and then applying the estimated proportion of total 1980 output accounted for by each of the processes. These proportions are estimated by assuming that dry process will increase its proportion of total portland cement output by 0.5 percentage points a year between 1971 and 1980, resulting in a percentage of 44.7 in 1980, compared with 40.2 in 1971. The projection of total portland cement output comes out to 520 million barrels in 1980, compared with 409.6 million in 1971. Overall energy use per barrel of output in 1980 is determined to be 1.038 million BTUs, versus 1.218 million in 1971. Aggregate energy use by portland cement producers is projected to increase from 499 trillion BTUs to 540 trillion BTUs. These steps and results are summarized in Table 20-3.

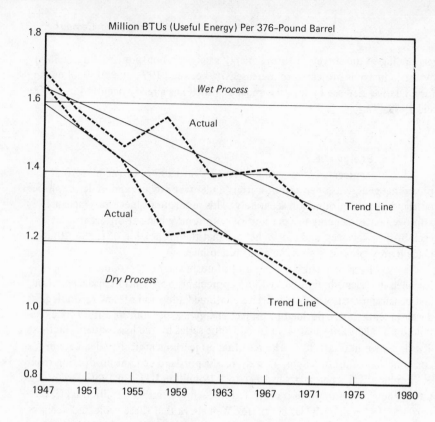

Million BTUs (Useful Energy) Per 376–Pound Barrel

Note: Wet process trend—Y = 1.650 – .0134t
Dry process trend—Y = 1.611 – .0224t

Chart 20-6. Projections of Energy Use per Unit of Output in the Production of Portland Cement to 1980. Sources: Appendix Table 20–8; The Conference Board.

Table 20-2. Projections of Output, Energy Use, and Energy Use per Dollar of Output

	1967	1971	1975	1980
Output, (million 1967 $)	1,246	1,391	1,547	1,767
Energy use (trillion BTUs)				
Useful	463	480	496	519
Gross	515	536	564	594
Energy use per dollar of output, (1,000 BTUs)				
Useful	371	345	321	294
Gross	413	385	365	336

Sources: 1967, 1971—Table 20-1; 1975, 1980—The Conference Board.

Table 20-3. Projected Portland Cement Production and Energy Use, by Process

	Wet Process			Dry Process			Total	
	Production (thousand barrels)	Energy Use per Barrel of Output (million BTUs)	Aggregate Energy Use (Useful) (trillion BTUs)	Production (thousand barrels)	Energy Use per Barrel of Output (million BTUs)	Aggregate Energy Use (Useful) (trillion BTUs)	Production (thousand barrels)	Aggregate Energy Use (Useful) (trillion BTUs)
1971	245,151	1.297	318	164,465	1.088	179	409,617	499
% of Total	59.8	x	x	40.2	x	x	100.0	x
% Change 1971-1975	x	x	x	x	x	x	11.0	3.4
1975	263,000	1.261	332	192,000	0.961	184	455,000	516
% of Total	57.8	x	x	42.2	x	x	100.0	x
% Change 1971-1980	x	x	x	x	x	x	27.0	8.2
1980	287,600	1.194	343	232,400	0.849	197	520,000	540
% of Total	55.3	x	x	44.7	x	x	100.0	x

Million BTUs per barrel of output for both processes combined are: 1971, 1.218; 1975, 1.134; 1980, 1.038.

Sources: Bureau of Mines, *Minerals Yearbook,* 1971; University of Maryland, INFORUM projection, February 1973 forecast; Conference Board estimates of production by process; Chart 20-6.

Projections of *gross* energy consumed per barrel of portland cement produced and of aggregate gross energy consumed by SIC 3241 in 1980 are dependent upon projections of the mix of energy sources for that year. These were made first for portland cement, by applying approximately half the relative changes in shares expected by the six large cement companies responding to the survey of future energy demand that supplied distributions of fuel or energy used by type. (The weighted average of the responses are shown in Table 20-4.) Thus, coal's contribution to total useful BTU consumption is projected to grow substantially—from 34.7% in 1971 to 60% in 1980; oil's share is projected to drop from 13.6% to 12%; gas's proportion is reduced from 45.4% to 20%; and electricity's contribution is projected to increase from 6.3% to 8.0%. When electricity's BTU contribution is inflated to gross energy consumption through the required arithmetical steps, total gross energy consumption by portland cement manufacture projected for 1980 is found to be 17% higher than useful energy consumption, or 630 trillion BTUs.

Since the specialization and coverage ratios of the industry are very high, it is reasonably safe to apply the projected increase in total hydraulic cement production to constant-dollar output of SIC 3241. By applying the per cent growth in total shipments of cement in physical terms between 1967 and 1971 (using Bureau of Mines data) to the *Census of Manufactures* output figures for 1967, we estimated 1971 output in constant dollars. Projected 1971-1980 growth in total cement production was then used to estimate 1980 production (in 1967 dollars). And the projected 8.2% increase in aggregate useful energy consumed in portland cement manufacture was applied to aggregate energy consumed by SIC 3241. With these calculations done, the results show aggregate useful energy consumed by SIC 3241 at an estimated 519 trillion BTUs

Table 20-4.   Survey Results: Energy Use per Unit of Output and Distribution of Energy Use, by Source, 1971, 1975, 1980

Source of Energy	Energy Use by Source			Energy Use per Barrel of Output		
	1971	*1975*	*1980*	*1971*	*1975*	*1980*
	(Per Cent)			(million BTUs)		
Coal	16.5%	29.3%	48.0%	x	x	x
Heavy fuel oil	13.9	20.1	20.7	x	x	x
Natural gas	51.1	30.6	10.8	x	x	x
Electricity (purchased)	11.2	16.9	18.3	x	x	x
Total	92.7	96.9	97.8	1.136	1.108	1.085

Note: Distribution percentages do not add up to 100 because respondents were asked to report figures for their three main fuels only. Data for distribution by source cover six large companies; data for energy per unit of output cover four large companies.

Source: The Conference Board, "Survey of Future Energy Demand, U.S. Manufacturing."

in 1980. Aggregate gross energy consumed is projected at 594 trillion BTUs for 1980, or 11% greater than in 1971. Aggregate energy (useful and gross) by source, actual and projected, consumed by SIC 3241, is shown in Table 20-5.

Table 20-5. Energy Use, by Source, SIC 3241, 1947-1980 (trillion BTUs)

	1947	*1967*	*1975*	*1980*
Coal	207	227*	293	343
Oil	25	15	15	15
Gas	73	193*	156	125
Electricity				
Useful	8	27*	33	37
Gross	37	82*	101	111
Total				
Useful	313	463	496	519
Gross	342	515	564	594

*Adjusted, to include prorated portion of fuels not specified by kind.
Sources: 1947 and 1967 from Appendix Table 20A-2; 1975 and 1980 projected on the basis of text pages 361 and 364, and Table 20-3.

Notes

[1] *Pit and Quarry*, July 1971, p. 100.

[2] Wynen, Joseph P., "Economics of Cement Plant Design," *Rock Products*, February 1971.

[3] *Minerals Yearbook, 1971*, p. 271.

[4] Most cement is ultimately used as an ingredient of concrete. Ready-mixed concrete producers have largely taken over from the ultimate users the function of mixing the cement with the other concrete ingredients.

[5] U.S. Federal Trade Commission, *Rates of Return in Selected Manufacturing Industries—1959-1968*, Table 8; *Rates of Return—1961-1970*, Table 8. New York, *FNCB Corporate Profits Tabulations: Historical Summary, 1925-1971*.

[6] First National City Bank of New York, *FNCB Corporate Profits Tabulations—Historical Summary, 1925-1971; Monthly Economic Letter*, April 1973, p. 6.

[7] Due to unusually long accelerations and decelerations in capacity expansion, the growth "curve" is difficult to ascertain. High and low extrapolations to 1980 were made by extending the imaginary lines connecting the low and the high points on the actual curve, and a point halfway between the high and low intersections with 1980 was arbitrarily chosen.

[8] A fourth large company indicated absolutely no change in output between 1971 and 1980; this response was not included above because the company also indicated absolutely no change in aggregate energy use, leading us to believe that no effort was made to estimate future output or energy use.

SECTION IV.   APPENDIX

The Manufacture of Cement

Essentially, the production of hydraulic cement involves (1) proportioning a lime-containing substance and a material containing silica, alumina, and iron; (2) grinding these to a slurry or powder; (3) "burning" the mixture in a rotary kiln, until fused; and (4) grinding the "clinker" that comes out of the kiln with gypsum into a fine powder. Most of the energy required is used in the kiln for heat. Substantial amounts are also used for mechanical processes: crushing and grinding the rock and ores that are the sources of the lime and other materials; blending them; moving the mixture through the kiln; and grinding the "clinker" that comes out of the kiln. Energy is also used in the extraction, or mining, of the materials from the earth. Most of the energy so required is included in the energy consumption data for SIC 3241, since about 75% of cement manufacturing establishments include mining operations.

Either a "wet" or a "dry" process may be used in the manufacture of portland cement, the difference being in the state of the mixture during and after the blending procedure. Wet process has the advantage of easier movement of the materials during and after blending, but the kiln must eliminate the moisture before proper burning can take place. Therefore, much more heat is required. Conversely, dry process boasts lower energy needs, but it poses problems in grinding, mixing, and moving. Because energy in the United States has, historically, been relatively cheap, domestic cement producers have had less incentive than foreign producers to innovate or adopt improvements in the direction of greater efficiency in energy use. Thus, wet process production has been more popular here than dry process.

STONE IS FIRST REDUCED TO 5-IN. SIZE, THEN 3/4-IN., AND STORED

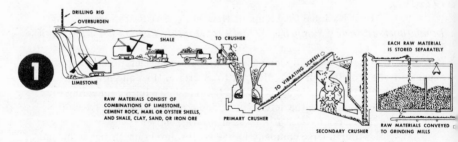

Figure 20–1. Steps in the Manufacture of Portland Cement.
© Portland Cement Association 1965.

RAW MATERIALS ARE GROUND TO POWDER AND BLENDED

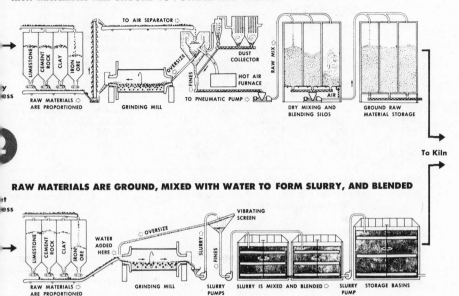

RAW MATERIALS ARE GROUND, MIXED WITH WATER TO FORM SLURRY, AND BLENDED

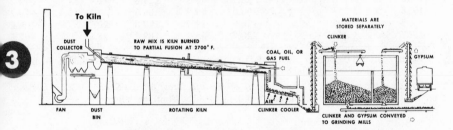

BURNING CHANGES RAW MIX CHEMICALLY INTO CEMENT CLINKER

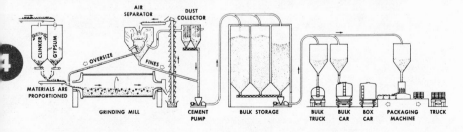

CLINKER WITH GYPSUM ADDED IS GROUND INTO PORTLAND CEMENT AND SHIPPED

Figure 20-1. (continued)

Table 20A-1.   Output, and Fuels and Energy Purchased in Original Units

| | Output (million 1967 $) | Fuels and Energy Purchased | | | |
		Coal (thousand short tons)	Oil (thousand barrels)	Gas (million cubic feet)	Electricity (million kwh)
1947	684	8,002	4,341	70,688	2,364
1954	930	7,701	5,774	125,202	3,643
1958	1,053	7,983	3,420	160,945	5,017
1962	1,092	7,631	3,053	185,494	5,913
1967	1,246	8,554	2,611	182,987	7,495

Note: Other fuels and fuels not specified by kind not shown.

Sources: Bureau of the Census, *Census of Manufactures*, 1947, 1954, 1958, 1967; *Annual Survey of Manufactures*, 1962.

Table 20A-2.   Output, and Fuels and Energy Purchased by Source

| | Output (million 1967 $) | Fuels and Energy (trillion BTUs) | | | | |
		Coal	Oil	Gas	Electricity	Total
1947	684	206.5	25.2	73.2	8.1	313.3
1954	930	198.7	33.5	129.6	12.4	375.2
1958	1,053	206.0	19.8	166.6	17.1	410.2
1962	1,092	196.9	17.7	192.0	20.2	428.2
1967	1,246	220.7	15.1	189.4	25.6	462.5

Note: Total BTU figures include BTUs attributable to "other" fuels and to fuels not specified by kind, which are not shown separately.

Sources: Bureau of the Census, *Census of Manufactures, Annual Survey of Manufactures*; Bureau of Mines; conversion to BTUs by The Conference Board.

Table 20A-3. Production, Capacity, Fuels and Energy Used (Original Units) Portland Cement Mills, 1947-1972

	Production	Capacity	Fuels and Energy Used		
			Coal	Oil (thousand	Gas (million	Electricity (million
	(thousand barrels)		(short tons)	barrels)	cubic feet)	kwh)
1947 ..	186,519	249,107	7,938	4,624	63,180	2,300
1948 ..	205,488	254,272	8,554	4,658	73,313	2,578
1949 ..	209,727	258,948	7,988	4,587	84,689	2,688
1950 ..	226,026	268,273	7,943	5,261	97,165	2,877
1951 ..	246,022	281,532	8,525	6,352	102,740	3,214
1952 ..	249,256	284,014	8,073	6,506	111,712	3,383
1953 ..	264,181	291,798	8,362	6,782	117,142	3,652
1954 ..	272,353	298,026	8,124	6,584	126,053	3,648
1955 ..	297,453	315,299	8,728	8,506	131,402	4,022
1956 ..	316,438	349,442	9,270	7,926	144,192	4,527
1957 ..	298,424	380,386	8,853	5,415	146,166	4,524
1958 ..	311,471	402,786	8,427	4,475	164,994	4,897
1959 ..	339,091	420,395	8,668	4,512	190,519	5,420
1960 ..	319,009	432,941	8,368	4,032	171,602	5,589
1961 ..	324,114	443,022	7,768	3,910	180,354	5,902
1962 ..	336,488	468,974	7,907	4,018	187,747	6,194
1963 ..	352,543	477,585	8,322	4,026	198,388	6,684
1964 ..	368,633	479,618	8,824	4,302	201,672	7,255
1965 ..	371,422	482,439	9,136	4,463	198,507	7,485
1966 ..	384,632	495,171	9,336	3,911	203,805	7,988
1967 ..	369,399	508,952	9,096	4,956	195,717	7,940
1968 ..	394,999	509,286	9,508	5,762	202,921	8,359
1969 ..	399,602	507,286	9,183	6,074	201,295	8,688
1970 ..	389,190	445,079	7,966	10,028	211,813	8,717
1971 ..	409,617	456,336	7,182	10,754	219,973	9,179
1972 ..	429,489	456,371	7,339	12,231	223,351	9,702

Sources: Bureau of Mines, *Minerals Yearbook*, 1971, and by telephone.

Table 20A-4.   Useful Energy Consumption, by Source, Portland
Cement Mills, 1947-1971

| | Fuels and Energy Used (trillion BTUs) | | | | | Energy Used per Barrel Output (million BTUs) |
	Coal	Oil	Gas	Electricity	Total	
1947	208	29	65	8	310	1.662
1948	224	29	76	9	338	1.645
1949	209	29	89	9	336	1.602
1950	208	33	101	10	352	1.557
1951	223	40	106	11	380	1.545
1952	212	41	116	12	381	1.529
1953	219	43	121	12	395	1.495
1954	213	41	130	12	396	1.454
1955	229	53	136	14	432	1.452
1956	243	50	149	15	457	1.444
1957	232	34	151	15	432	1.448
1958	221	28	171	17	437	1.403
1959	227	28	197	18	470	1.386
1960	219	25	178	19	441	1.382
1961	204	25	187	20	436	1.345
1962	207	25	194	21	447	1.328
1963	218	25	205	23	471	1.336
1964	231	27	209	25	492	1.335
1965	235	28	205	26	494	1.330
1966	237	25	211	27	500	1.300
1967	227	31	202	27	487	1.318
1968	236	36	209	29	510	1.291
1969	226	38	208	30	502	1.256
1970	193	63	218	30	504	1.295
1971	173	68	227	31	499	1.218

Sources: Bureau of Mines, *Minerals Yearbook* (most editions between 1948 and 1971);
conversion to BTUs by The Conference Board.

Table 20A-5.   Size Distribution of Portland Cement Plants

| Year-end | (annual capacity in millions of barrels) | | | | | | |
	Less than 1	1-2	2-3	3-4	4-5	5 & Over	All sizes
	Per Cent of Total Capacity						
1948*	8%	56%	17%	19%			100%
1954*	4	43	37	17			100
1958	2	22	34	19	9	13	100
1962	1	19	33	20	10	18	100
1967	1	17	25	27	10	20	100
1971**	1	16	35	21	11	16	100

*Estimated on the basis of size distribution of number of plants.
**Data are for daily clinker capacity.
Sources: Bureau of Mines, *Minerals Yearbook* (several years); The Conference Board.

Table 20A-6. Distribution of Portland Cement Shipments, by Form

| | Per Cent of Total | | |
	In Bulk	*In Containers*	*All Shipments*
1947	36.8%	63.2%	100%
1958	79.2	20.8	100
1971	91.4	8.6	100

Source: Bureau of Mines, *Minerals Yearbook*, 1948, 1958, 1971.

Table 20A-7. Capacity of Portland Cement Plants, by Type of Process

| | Per Cent of Total | | |
Year-end	*Wet Process*	*Dry Process*	*Total Capacity*
1948	53.7%	46.3%	100%
1954	56.8	43.2	100
1958	58.1	41.9	100
1962	58.8	41.2	100
1967	61.6	38.4	100

Source: Bureau of Mines, *Minerals Yearbook*, 1948, 1954, 1958, 1962, 1967.

Table 20A-8. Energy Consumption (Useful) per Unit of Output, by Process in Portland Cement Manufacture

Year	*Type of Process*	*Energy Use (trillion BTUs)*	*Cement Production (thousand barrels)*	*Energy Use per Barrel (million BTUs)*
1947	Wet	169	100,697	1.678
	Dry	141	85,822	1.643
1950	Wet	200	127,316	1.571
	Dry	151	98,710	1.530
1954	Wet	230	156,070	1.474
	Dry	167	116,283	1.436
1958	Wet	261	167,044	1.562
	Dry	176	144,427	1.219
1962	Wet	272	195,745	1.390
	Dry	175	140,743	1.243
1967	Wet	318	224,752	1.415
	Dry	169	144,647	1.168
1971	Wet	318	245,151	1.297
	Dry	179	164,465	1.088

Sources: Bureau of Mines, *Minerals Yearbook*, 1948, 1950, 1954, 1958, 1962, 1967, 1971; conversion to BTUs by The Conference Board.

SECTION V.   SELECTED BIBLIOGRAPHY

Bureau of Mines. *Minerals Yearbook* (a number of editions). Washington, D.C.

Bureau of the Census. *Census of Manufactures* (several editions). Washington, D.C.

Federal Trade Commission. *Economic Report on Mergers and Vertical Integration in the Cement Industry.* Washington, D.C., 1966.

Loescher, Samuel M. *Imperfect Collusion in the Cement Industry.* Cambridge: Harvard University Press, 1959.

Stanford Research Institute. *Patterns of Energy Consumption in the United States.* Washington: Office of Science and Technology, 1972.

Serials:
Pit and Quarry
Rock Products

Chapter Twenty-One

Brick and Structural Clay Tile–SIC 3251

Hirohiko Chiba

SECTION I. SUMMARY OF FINDINGS

The Industry

The Brick and Structural Clay Tile industry, SIC 3251, consists of brick and tile making. The major product groups are brick (SIC 32511), glazed brick and structural hollow tile (SIC 32512), and brick and structural clay tile not specified by kind (SIC 32510).

Demand and Energy Use

During the period 1947-1971, the brick and structural clay tile industry grew at an average annual rate of 1.7%. Between 1947 and 1971 the industry's shipments rose from $260 million to $392 million, only a 50% increase (computed on a 1967 constant dollar basis by linking the *Census of Manufactures* indexes of production to 1967 value of shipments).

The slow rate of increase in value of shipments has been accompanied by a relatively rapid growth in competitive industries.

Within the brick and structural clay tile industry, the share of brick (SIC 32511) in primary product shipments rose from 81% in 1954 to 94% in 1971. This shift is almost the same even when one measures physical shipments at 1967 prices.

Table 21-1. Shipments
(million 1967 $)

	1947	1954	1958	1962	1967	1971
Total	260	343	327	323	362	392
Primary products	n.a.	326	302	301	340	368

n.a.–not available
Sources: *Census of Manufactures* and *Annual Survey of Manufactures*; Table 21-13.

Energy utilization for power and heat by the brick and structural clay tile industry grew from 1947 to 1967 at an average annual growth rate of 0.8%, while value of shipments rose at an average annual growth rate of 1.7% during the same period. Consequently, energy use per unit of output declined from 331,000 BTUs per 1967 constant dollar of shipments in 1947 to 281,000 in 1967 (on the basis of gross energy consumed). But the energy ratio did not decline consistently; during the period 1958-1962 it showed a considerable rise.

Projections

The brick and structural clay tile industry is expected to grow more rapidly during the 1970s than in the 1960s as a result of total new construction growth. But the relative share of brick and structural clay tile within building materials will decline compared to hydraulic cement, concrete block and brick, and ready-mixed concrete.

We assume that the future elasticity of shipments of brick and structural clay tile with respect to total new construction is 0.7. Total new construction will grow at an average annual growth rate of 8.4% from 1971 to 1975 and 7.6% from 1975 to 1980, based on the projections in *U.S. Industrial Outlook 1973*. This results in an average annual growth rate in the brick and structural clay tile industry of 5.9% from 1971 to 1975 and 5.3% from 1975 to 1980.

The projections presented in Table 21-3 are in constant 1967 dollars; they are derived from the above projections by deflating by the projected wholesale price index, based on the latest trend.

Energy utilization per unit of output has been fluctuating since 1958, when it was at its lowest point throughout the period. Although efforts to save on energy costs will continue, we assume that energy utilization per unit of output will decline only to the 1958 level.

Summary Analysis

During the 1947-1967 period, energy utilization increased at an average annual rate of 0.8%, which was slower than the 1.7% growth of output (as measured by shipments). During the first part of the 1947-1958 period, energy consumption per unit of output declined, but rose between 1958 and 1962; during the third period, 1962-1967, it declined again. The decline in the first period was mainly due to reduced energy use per unit in the drying process, and that of the third period mainly to the introduction of tunnel kilns, which use less energy than periodic kilns. On the other hand, the rise in energy utilization of the second period was due to the shift in product mix towards high-energy-using bricks and to the introduction of automated production processes in order to save on labor costs.

Our projection assumes that future energy utilization will keep the

Table 21-2.   Energy Utilization 1947-1967
(trillion BTUs)

	1947	1954	1958	1962	1967
Useful energy[1]	83.1	101.8	84.9	95.0	96.7
Gross energy consumed	86.1	105.1	88.5	99.0	101.6

[1] See Chapter One, pages 14-15, for definitions of useful and gross energy.
Sources: Bureau of the Census, *Census of Manufactures* and *Annual Survey of Manufactures.*

Table 21-3.   Projected Shipments to 1980
(million 1967 $)

	1971	1975	1980
Totals	392	429	468
Primary products	368	403	440

Sources: Tables 21-1, 21-9, and 21-13, assuming 1967 ratio of primary products to total.

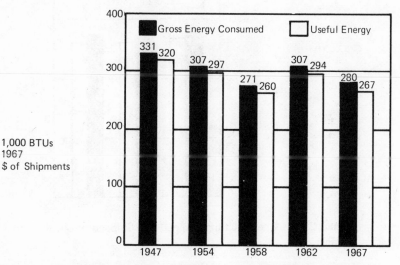

Chart 21-1.   Energy Utilization per Unit Shipped: 1947-1967.
Source: Table 21-7.

most efficient use of the last period and this implies the same level as in 1958.
The reasons are as follows: the introduction of tunnel kilns will continue to
some extent, but it will be limited because of the inflexible nature of tunnel
kilns. In addition, the continuing introduction of automation in production will
counterbalance energy saving by the introduction of tunnel kilns.

Table 21-4.   Energy Utilization to 1980

	1967	1975	1980
Useful energy			
(trillion BTUs)	96.7	112	122
Index (1967 = 100)	(100)	(116)	(126)
Gross energy consumed			
(trillion BTUs)	101.6	116	127
Index (1967 = 100)	(100)	(114)	(125)
Shipments–based on			
production index (million 1967 $)	$ 362.0	$ 429	$ 468
Index (1967 = 100)	(100)	(119)	(129)

Sources: *Census of Manufactures*; Tables 21-7, 21-13; Section III, "Energy."

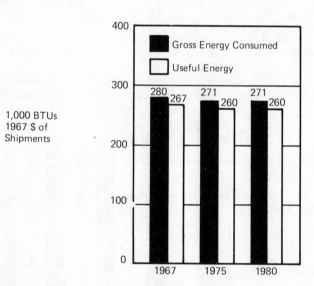

1,000 BTUs
1967 $ of
Shipments

Chart 21-2. Energy Utilization per Unit Shipped: Projections to 1980.

SECTION II.   HISTORICAL DEVELOPMENTS

Change in Product Mix

During the period 1965-1971, brick,   which was dominant in 1954, grew far more rapidly than the other components within the brick and structural clay tile industry, so that the share of brick (measured in terms of primary product shipments) rose from 81% in 1954 to 94% in 1971. A similar trend can be observed in terms of physical shipments at 1967 prices, shown in Table 21-6.

Table 21-5.   Primary Product Shipments in Current Dollars
($ millions)

	1954	*1958*	*1962*	*1967*	*1971*
Primary products	$ 238	$ 265	$ 299	$ 340	$ 427
Brick, except ceramic					
glazed and refractory	192	210	245	296	403
(share of total)	(81)	(80)	(85)	(87)	(94)
Glazed brick and					
structural hollow tile	42	42	38	28	17
(share of total)	(17)	(16)	(13)	(8)	(4)
Brick and structural clay					
tile, n.s.k.	4	12	7	16	7
(share of total)	(2)	(4)	(2)	(5)	(2)

Sources: *Census of Manufactures, Annual Survey of Manufactures*; and (for 1962) Table
21-6 and Appendix Table 21A-1.

Energy Utilization

As the product mix in the brick and structural clay tile industry has
been changing, the brick subgroup, a relatively high energy-using product, has
become more dominant. In spite of an increase in the proportion of high energy-
using brick, there was a decline in overall energy utilization per unit of output
from 1947 to 1958. This is mainly because of very large increases in the efficiency of energy utilization in the drying process and the firing process.

During the period 1958-1962, there was a rise in overall energy
utilization per unit of output to about the 1954 level. It is hypothesized that the

Table 21-6.   Primary Product Shipments
(million 1967 $)

	1954	*1958*	*1962*	*1967*	*1971*
Primary products, total	332	318	334	340	375
(share of total)	(100)	(100)	(100)	(100)	
Brick, except ceramic					
glaze and refractory	264	251	280	296	354
(share of total)	(79)	(79)	(84)	(87)	(94)
Glazed brick and structural					
hollow tile	62	53	46	28	15
(share of total)	(19)	(17)	(14)	(8)	(4)
Brick and structural clay					
tile, n.s.k.	6	14	8	16	6
(share of total)	(2)	(4)	(2)	(5)	(2)

Note: Shipments for the three product groups were obtained by independent deflation and
so do not add to the totals from Table 21-1.

Sources: Tables 21-1 and 21-5, Appendix Table 21A-1; *Census of Manufactures* and *Annual
Survey of Manufactures.*

Per Cent of Primary Products

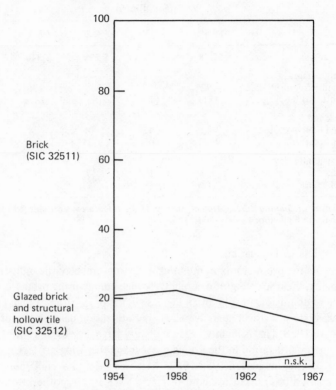

Chart 21-3. Change in the Product Composition of the Industry.
Source: Table 21.6.

shift in product mix towards more energy-using brick and the introduction of automation processes that use energy in place of manpower caused the rise.

As for the trend during the 1962-1967 period, the decline in the overall energy utilization per unit of output may be due to more efficient utilization of energy in the firing process brought about by the introduction of tunnel kilns in place of periodic kilns.

Generally speaking, most efforts have been concentrated on saving labor costs in all manufacturing processes. Of course, saving energy costs has also been a very important problem for this industry. This problem has been met not only by improvement of production utilization per unit of output but also by using cheaper fuel sources. A steep and continuing rise in oil prices, the discovery of North Sea natural gas, large supplies of liquefied petroleum gas, and increasingly stringent clean air requirements have resulted in the shift in fuel source from coal and oil to natural gas.

**Table 21-7.   Energy Use per Unit of Shipments
(1,000 BTUs/1967 $)**

	1947	1954	1958	1962	1967
Coal, coke and breeze	183.2	85.3 (−10.3)	48.6 (−13.1)	43.9 (−2.5)	31.3 (−6.6)
Fuel oil (total)	33.7	39.8 (2.4)	20.4 (−16.8)	13.6 (−10.2)	10.4 (−5.3)
Gas	92.8	160.5 (7.8)	161.2 (0.1)	205.8 (6.1)	186.4 (−2.0)
Other fuels and .... fuels n.s.k.	6.7	7.3 (1.1)	24.4 (35.3)	24.7 (0.3)	32.4 (5.6)
Electric energy (gross)	14.8	13.6 (−1.1)	15.9 (3.9)	18.6 (3.8)	20.2 (1.7)
Electric energy (useful)	3.2	3.8 (2.4)	4.9 (6.2)	6.0 (5.0)	6.6 (2.0)
Total (gross energy)	331.2	306.5 (−1.1)	270.5 (−3.1)	306.6 (3.1)	280.7 (−1.8)
Total (useful energy)	319.6	296.7 (−1.1)	259.5 (−3.4)	294.0 (3.1)	267.1 (−1.9)

Note: Figures in parentheses are average annual growth rates computed from unrounded data.
Sources: Tables 21-1 and 21-8.

Demand

Looking back over the years it can be observed that the brick and tile industry experienced a vigorous growth from 1849 to 1906 and that this growth was checked by the rise in competitive materials. Growth was slowed primarily by changes that took place in other industries, namely, the rapid development of portland cement manufacturing and cement products such as concrete blocks. Much of the expansion of the cement industry was at the expense of the brick industry, especially in construction of roads, pavements, and industrial buildings for which cement was regarded as superior to the older materials. Thus, the growth of the brick and tile industry was checked by the vigorous growth of the cement industry and by the introduction of cheap steel, which made revolutionary changes in construction methods.

As one can see in Table 21-9, shipments of bricks and structural clay tile have increased recently because of the rapid increase of total new construction. But the average annual growth rate (or elasticity) of brick and structural clay tile was lower than that of other competitive materials, such as concrete block and brick, concrete products (except block and brick), and ready-mixed concrete. This implies that the relative share of brick and structural clay tile within the building materials industries has been declining.

Table 21-8.   Energy Utilization
(trillion BTUs)

	1947	1954	1958	1962	1967
Coal, coke & breeze	47.7 (55.4)	29.2 (27.8)	15.9 (18.0)	14.2 (14.3)	11.3 (11.1)
Fuel oil (total)	8.8 (10.2)	13.6 (12.9)	6.7 (7.6)	4.4 (4.4)	3.8 (3.7)
Gas	24.1 (28.0)	55.1 (52.4)	52.7 (59.5)	66.5 (67.1)	67.5 (66.5)
Other fuels and fuels n.s.k.	1.7 (2.0)	2.5 (2.4)	7.9 (9.0)	8.0 (8.1)	11.7 (11.5)
Electric energy (gross energy consumed basis)	3.8 (4.4)	4.7 (4.5)	5.2 (5.9)	6.0 (6.1)	7.3 (7.2)
Electric energy (useful energy)	0.8	1.3	1.6	1.9	2.4
Total (gross energy consumed basis)	86.1 (100)	105.1 (100)	88.5 (100)	99.0 (100)	101.6 (100)
Total (useful energy)......	83.1	101.8	84.9	95.0	96.7

Note: Figures in parentheses represent per cent distribution of total gross energy. Coke and breeze were less than 2% of coal. Because of rounding, data will not necessarily add to the totals.

Sources: Appendix Table 21A-3 and Chapter One, Appendix 3.

Production Processes

(1) Process of Manufacture: The manufacture of brick and tile involves the mining of the raw material, the forming of the brick or tile, and the burning to give the products rigidity and strength. The actual forming of brick and tile may be accomplished by one of three methods: the stiff-mud process, the soft-mud process, and the dry-press method (Figure 21-1).

Bricks made by the stiff-mud and the soft-mud processes contain much moisture and are therefore so fragile that they must be dried before being placed in the kiln for firing, Formerly, the green bricks were dried by open-air methods, which required from five to twelve days; but in the late 1950s drier kilns, heated by steam heat or by waste heat from the burning kilns, reduced the drying time to two days[1] and supplanted the earlier method.

In the overall process, the firing (burning) of ceramic wares is the most important and energy-intensive process. It is during the firing that the final

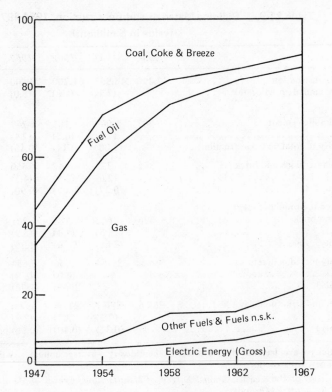

Chart 21–4. Energy Utilization. Source: Table 8.

properties and the final usefulness of the ceramic product are developed. A variety of kilns and furnaces are utilized to carry out the firing of ceramic wares. The furnace in which firing takes place, commonly called a kiln, can be classified as either a periodic (intermittent or batch) kiln or a tunnel (continuous) kiln, depending upon its construction and mode of operation.

The periodic kiln is the more flexible type since its time-temperature cycle can be tailored to a wide variety of different ceramic products. The tunnel kiln is more economical of fuel and labor, but is relatively inflexible, being limited to firing long runs of one kind of product. Many plants employ both kinds of kilns. The periodic ones are used for special products, and the tunnel kilns are for standard product lines. Initial investment for a tunnel kiln is high and more sophisticated control systems are usually required than for a periodic kiln.

(2) Advances in Technology: Major developments have occurred in the use of tunnel kilns and in the automation of preparation, cutting, and setting of the machines.

Table 21-9.   Building Materials and Construction, 1954-1971
(value in $ millions)

	1954	1958	1962	1967	1971
Total new construction	37,200	48,903	61,200	77,500	109,400
(average annual growth rate)		(7.1)	(5.8)	(5.0)	(8.9)
Shipments of:					
3241 Hydraulic cement	807	1,063	1,103	1,247	1,575
(a.a.g.r.)		(7.1)	(0.8)	(2.4)	(6.0)
(elasticity to total new construction) ..		(1.00)	(0.14)	(0.48)	(0.67)
3271 Concrete block and brick	342	379	442	550	745
(a.a.g.r.)		(2.6)	(3.9)	(4.5)	(7.9)
(elasticity)		(0.37)	(0.67)	(0.90)	(0.89)
3272 Concrete products except					
block and brick	336	662	785	1,201	1,640
(a.a.g.r.)		(18.5)	(4.4)	(8.9)	(8.1)
(elasticity)		(2.61)	(0.76)	(1.78)	(0.91)
3273 Ready-mixed concrete	n.a.	1,464	1,756	2,684	3,400
(a.a.g.r.)		–	(4.0)	(8.9)	(6.1)
(elasticity)		–	(0.69)	(1.78)	(0.69)
3251 Brick and structural clay tile	262.6	286.7	313.4	362.0	459.8
(a.a.g.r.)		(2.2)	(2.3)	(2.9)	(6.2)
(elasticity)		(0.31)	(0.40)	(0.60)	(0.70)

Note: elasticity = average annual growth rate of the industry ÷ average annual growth rate of total new construction.

Sources: Bureau of the Census, *Annual Survey of Manufactures; Census of Manufactures, U.S. Industrial Outlook.*

a) In brick making, a variety of improvisations and improvements have occurred between the extruder mouthpiece and the cutter.

b) Driers and the mechanical handling systems that are used for bricks have been progressively refined over the years. The handling equipment involves such items as gathering and storage frames, multitired finger cars, walking beams, automatic pallet storage elevators and pallet magazines. Ways have been found to reduce drying times inside the driers. Fully or semi-automatic control systems are used and there is maximum exploitation of excess kiln heat.

c) The drier handling system for bricks in many cases now leads straight on to an automatic setting machine.

d) Tunnel kilns are now by far the most popular choice for new or modernized walks, and they continue to undergo refinement. The conditions most sought after are fuel economy, even heat distribution, ease of control, and low maintenance requirement.

e) One of the most significant recent changes has been the trend toward gas firing in tunnel kilns and even in traditional intermittent ones.

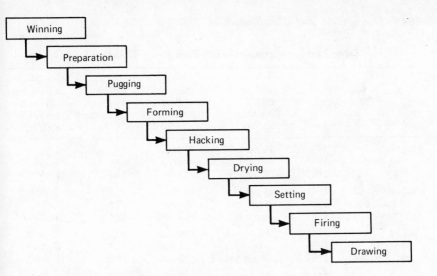

Figure 21-1. Work Flow in a Typical Plant Making Brick and Tile by the Stiff Mud Process. Source: Bureau of Labor Statistics Report No. 43.

Table 21-10. Comparison of Kiln Firing Costs in Periodic Kilns

Fuel	Year	(1) Million BTU per Unit of Fuel	(2) Units of Fuel per M Brick *	(3) Million BTU per M Brick *	(4) Kiln & Fuel Labor Cost per Million BTU
Bituminous coal, hand-fired	1954 ..	26 per ton	1.6 tons	42	$ .12
	1959 ..	26 per ton	1.6 tons	42	$ .19
	1967 ..	26 per ton	1.6 tons	42	$ .19
Bituminous coal, stoker-fired	1954 ..	26 per ton	1.3 tons	34	$ .128
	1959 ..	26 per ton	1.3 tons	34	$ .12
	1967 ..	26 per ton	1.3 tons	34	$ .12
Fuel oil distillate No. 2 or No. 3	1954 ..	.14 per gal.	228 gals.	32	$ .033
	1959 ..	.14 per gal.	228 gals.	32	$ .06
	1967 ..	.14 per gal.	228 gals.	32	$ .06
Fuel oil residual No. 5 or No. 6	1954 ..	.15 per gal.	213 gals.	32	$ .036
	1959 ..	.15 per gal.	213 gals.	32	$ .06
	1967 ...	.15 per gal.	213 gals.	32	$ .06
Natural gas	1954 ..	1 per M cu. ft.	33 M cu. ft.	33	$ .031
	1959 ..	1 per M cu. ft.	33 M cu. ft.	33	$ .05
	1967 ..	1 per M cu. ft.	33 M cu. ft.	33	$ .05

*Must be adjusted to suit the particular plant, kiln, and fuel under consideration.

M = thousand; 1 ton = 2,000 lbs.

Source: *Ceramic Data Book* Suppliers' Catalog–Buyers' Directory 1954-55, 1959-60, 1963-64, 1967-68 (a Cahners publication).

Table 21-11.   Comparison of Kiln Firing Costs in Tunnel Kilns

Fuel	Year	(1) Million BTU per Unit of Fuel	(2) Units of Fuel per M Brick *	(3) Million BTU per M Brick *	(4) Kiln & Fuel Labor Cost per Million BTU (a)
Bituminous	1954 ..	26 per ton	75 tons	19.5	$ .067
coal, hand-	1959 ..	26 per ton	75 tons	19.5	$ .19
fired	1967 ..	26 per ton	75 tons	19.5	$ .19
Anthracite	1954 ..	24 per ton	86 tons	20.6	$ .056
or coke in gas	1959 ..	24 per ton	86 tons	20.6	$ .17
producers	1967 ..	24 per ton	86 tons	20.6	$ .17
Fuel oil	1954 ..	.14 per gal.	111 gals.	15.5	$ .053
distillate	1959 ..	.14 per gal.	111 gals.	15.5	$ .14
No. 2 or No. 3	1967 ..	.14 per gal.	111 gals	15.5	$ .14
Fuel oil	1954 ..	.15 per gal.	103 gals.	15.5	$ .056
residual	1959 ..	.15 per gal.	103 gals.	15.5	$ .16
No. 5 or No. 6	1967 ..	.15 per gal.	103 gals.	15.5	$ .16
Natural gas	1954 ..	1 per M cu. ft.	16 M cu. ft.	16	$ .05
	1959 ..	1 per M cu. ft.	16 M cu. ft.	16	$ .14
	1967 ..	1 per M cu. ft.	16 M cu. ft.	16	$ .14

M = thousand; 1 ton = 2,000 lbs.
Source: See Table 21-10.

SECTION III.   PROJECTIONS TO 1980

Demand

The future growth of this industry will be determined not only by the trend in construction activity but also by the ability of the industry to compete with other building materials—notably cement, lumber, and concrete block. This competition involves both price and style factors. The price factor involves the cost of labor not only at the plant but also on the construction site. The greater amount of labor required for building a brick house compared with that required for a building frame house places brick under a disadvantage. Taking these elements into consideration along with the past trend of the elasticity of brick and structural clay tile, we assume the future elasticity of this industry with respect to total new construction to be 0.7, which is the same elasticity as that from 1967 to 1971.

The projections of total new construction and other building materials industries are based on the projections by *U.S. Industrial Outlook, 1973,*[2] and they are shown in Table 21-12. The projection of the wholesale price index shown in Table 21-13 enables us to derive future total shipments of the brick and structural clay tile industry at 1967 prices shown in Table 21-3.

Table 21-12. **Building Materials and Construction, 1971, 1975, 1980**

(value in $ millions)

	1971	*1975*	*1980*
		Projection	
Total new construction...................	$109,400	$150,500	$220,000
(average annual growth rate)		(8.4)	(7.6)
Shipments of:			
3241 Hydraulic cement	1,575	2,150	3,100
(a.a.g.r.)		(8.2)	(7.8)
(elasticity to total new construction)......		(0.98)	(1.03)
3271 Concrete block and brick	745	989	1,350
(a.a.g.r.)		(7.3)	(6.3)
(elasticity)		(0.87)	(0.83)
3272 Concrete products (except			
block and brick)	1,640	2,445	3,500
(a.a.g.r.)		(10.5)	(7.9)
(elasticity)		(1.25)	(1.04)
3273 Ready-mixed concrete	3,400	4,375	6,000
(a.a.g.r.)		(6.5)	(6.6)
(elasticity)		(0.77)	(0.87)
3251 Brick and structural clay tile..........	459.8	578	749
(a.a.g.r.)		(5.9)	(5.3)
(elasticity)		(0.70)	(0.70)

Sources: Table 21-9. Projections (except brick and structural clay tile) based on projections in *U.S. Industrial Outlook 1973*.

Energy

Much more energy is required to manufacture a ton of building bricks than to manufacture other products of the industry. With the continual increase in construction activity, bricks (and especially building bricks) will become relatively more important in the industry and energy use per unit of output will rise. But as the figures show (Table 21-5), the share of bricks within the brick and structural clay tile (SIC 3251) was over 90% in 1971. The continuing shift in product mix will no longer play an important role in determinig the level of energy utilization. On the other hand, the improvement of production processes has been pursued for a long time, and it will still continue to affect energy utilization. The introduction of tunnel kilns, which use less energy than periodic kilns, has been prevalent. The decrease of BTU per unit of shipment from 1962 to 1967 can to some degree be attributed to this factor. We may safely assume that continuing attention will be paid to efficient use of labor and energy.

Utilization of tunnel kilns will be more prevalent but there still exist strong demands for intermittent (periodic) kilns. Continuous non-tunnel

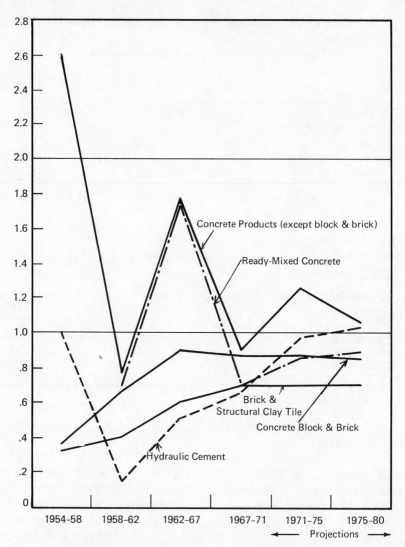

Chart 21-5. Elasticity of Building Materials to Total New Construction. Sources: Table 21-9 and Table 21-12.

kilns in the form of modified Hoffmans are also still in operation. These have a rationalized working space internally, which lends itself to efficient fork-lift loading and unloading, and they also have relatively sophisticated control systems. It is pointed out by their advocates that cost is considerably lower than that of a tunnel kiln. Considering these elements, we assume that future overall energy utilization per unit of output will be the same (271,000 BTUs per unit of

Table 21-13.   Price Index, 1954 to 1980
(1967 = 100)

	1954	1958	1962	1967	1971	Projection 1975	1980
Brick and structural clay tile	76.6	87.7	97.0	100	117.4	134.7	159.9
Average annual growth rate (%)		(3.4)	(2.6)	(0.6)	(4.1)	(3.5)	(3.5)

Note: (1) As the price index, we use the wholesale price index of Masonry brick (common and face).
  (2) The projection is based on the assumed average annual rate of increase of 3.5% which is the same rate as that from 1971 to 1972.
Sources: Bureau of Labor Statistics and Bureau of Domestic Commerce.

shipment on a gross energy basis) as that in 1958, when the most efficient level of energy utilization during the entire 1947-1967 period was recorded.

Notes

[1] Alderfer & Michl. *Economics of American Industry*. McGraw-Hill, 1957, p. 200.
[2] Department of Commerce. *U.S. Industrial Outlook 1973—with projections to 1980.* Chapter 3, "Building Materials," p. 13.

SECTION IV.   APPENDIX

Table 21A-1.   Price Indexes for Brick and Structural Clay Tile Products (1967 = 100)

Product		1954	1958	1962	1963	1967	1971
32511	Brick, except ceramic glazed and refractory brick						
32511-11	Building or common, and face	72.9	93.9	90.8	91.9	100.0	114.0
32511-19	Other brick (paving, floor and sewer)	68.5	60.1	(58.4)	58.0	100.0	(114.0)
	Total weighted by 1967 value	72.8	83.8	(90.6)	91.7	100.0	(114.0)
32512	Glazed brick and structural hollow tile						
32512-11	Structural clay tile, except facing	54.4	63.7	60.2	63.1	100.0	134.1
32512-31	Ceramic glazed facing tile and ceramic glazed brick	70.3	84.6	89.8	86.8	100.0	105.5
32512-51	Unglazed and salt glazed facing tile	88.9	91.1	81.9	103.6	100.0	94.4
	Total weighted by 1967 value	67.3	80.2	83.2	82.1	100.0	111.4
32510	Brick and structural clay tile, n.s.k.						
	Weighted average of 32511 and 32512	72.4	83.5	(90.0)	90.9	100.0	113.8

Note: Seven-digit product indexes are value of product shipped by all manufacturing establishments divided by the physical quantity. The indexes are put on the base 1967 = 100 and are combined into groups by weighting by 1967 values. For "other brick," 1962 was interpolated and 1971 was assumed the same as "building brick."

Sources: *Census of Manufactures, Annual Survey of Manufactures,* and U.S. Bureau of the Census, *Current Industrial Reports: Clay Construction Products.*

Table 21A-2.   Energy Purchases
($ millions)

	1947	1954	1958	1962	1967
Purchased fuel and electricity	24.8	35.7	38.2	43.7	44.7
Purchased fuels	21.1	29.9	31.1	35.1	35.2
Coal, coke, and breeze*..........	11.6	8.4	4.9	4.1	2.9
Fuel oil (total)	4.6	7.9	4.4	2.7	2.5
Distillate	n.a.	n.a.	n.a.	1.4	1.8
Residual	n.a.	n.a.	n.a.	1.3	.7
Gas	4.3	12.5	18.6	25.1	25.1
Other fuels and fuels n.s.k.	.7	1.0	3.2	3.2	4.7
Electricity purchased	3.7	5.8	7.1	8.6	9.5

*Coke and breeze were less than 5% of cost.

n.a.–not available.

Source: *Census of Manufactures.*

Table 21A-3. **Energy Utilization in Physical Quantities**

	Unit of Measure	1947	1954	1958	1962	1967
Coal, coke and breeze* .	1,000 tons	1,846	1,134	616	549	439
Fuel oil (total)	1,000 bbls	1,511	2,353	1,148	755	649
Distillate	1,000 bbls	n.a.	n.a.	n.a.	313	448
Residual	1,000 bbls	n.a.	n.a.	n.a.	443	202
Gas	million cu.f.	23,307	53,200	50,930	64,245	65,186
Purchased electric energy	million kwh	246	384	470	568	702
Electricity, generated less sold ...	million kwh	4	5	4	3	2

*Coke and breeze were less than 2% of cost.

n.a.—not available.

Source: *Census of Manufactures.*

SECTION V.   SELECTED BIBLIOGRAPHY

Alderfer & Michl. *Economics of American Industry*. New York: McGraw-Hill, 1957.

Bureau of Labor Statistics. *Case Study Data on Productivity and Factory Performance: Brick and Tile*. Washington D.C., 1953.

Department of Commerce. *U. S. Industrial Outlook*. Washington, D.C. 1973.

Ford, R. W. *The Drying of Bricks*. Brick Development Association, 1967.

International Ceramic Industries Manual 1971. Turret Press Limited.

Jones, J. T. and Berard, M. F. *Ceramic Industrial Processing and Testing*. The Iowa State University Press, 1972.

Rowden, E. *The Firing of Bricks*. Brick Development Association, 1964.

Chapter Twenty-Two

Ready-Mixed Concrete—SIC 3273

Bernard A. Gelb

SECTION I. SUMMARY

The Ready-Mixed Concrete industry, SIC 3273, is defined as that group of
establishments primarily engaged in manufacturing portland cement concrete
and delivering it to the purchaser in a plastic and unhardened state. The industry
includes production and sale of central-mixed, shrink-mixed and truck-mixed
concrete.

Only after World War II did the industry emerge as a significant
manufacturing industry. It grew very rapidly and is still growing appreciably
faster than general economic activity. Between 1958 and 1967, output of the
industry (measured by shipments in 1967 dollars) increased from $1.75 billion
to $2.68 billion, or an average of 4.9% a year. Rapid growth by SIC 3273 is
attributable to the industry's success in being able to supply builders with
concrete already prepared at a lower total cost (to the builders) than if they
prepared the concrete themselves.

This success is partly the result of a considerable increase in the
mechanization of the industry and in the relative extent of truck mixing (as
opposed to central mixing). These trends have boosted energy use by the industry
even faster than production. Per unit of output, useful energy consumption
doubled between 1958 and 1971; in the aggregate, useful energy consumption
tripled.

We expect the industry to continue to increase its share of the concrete preparing market, and we project that constant-dollar output will grow at
about the same rate between 1971 and 1980 as it did in the past decade. Energy
use, we anticipate, will increase less rapidly in relation to output than it has. We
project useful[a] energy consumption per dollar of output to rise about 4% a year
between 1971 and 1975, and 3% a year between 1975 and 1980. This compares

[a]See Chapter One, pages 14-15, for definitions of useful and gross energy.

391

with a 5% annual average recently, and 6% annually in the late 1950s and early 1960s.

SECTION II.   DEMAND, OUTPUT, AND ENERGY USE

The Industry

The degree of specialization of the ready-mixed concrete industry is not as high as that of the hydraulic cement industry (93% vs. 99% in 1967), but its coverage of its primary product is almost the same as that industry. Their coverage ratios were 98% and 99%, respectively, in 1967.

Ready-mixed concrete manufacturing is also characterized by the small size of the typical establishment. In 1967, establishments in SIC 3273 had an average of 15.7 employees, compared with 60.5 for all manufacturing (excluding administrative and auxiliary units). The average number of employees per establishment in SIC 3273 has changed relatively little since 1958. The ready-mixed concrete industry was not defined as a manufacturing industry or included in the *Census of Manufactures* until 1958.

Demand

Although all concrete is used for construction, and demand for it is related to the level of and fluctuations in such activity, the ready-mixed concrete industry has grown considerably faster than construction activity during the postwar period. Total production of ready-mixed concrete in 1971, at 199 million cubic yards, was more than four times its estimated 1950 level. Output (in 1967 dollars) by SIC 3273 more than doubled between 1954 (earliest reliable estimate available) and 1971. In contrast, construction activity, measured by real gross

Table 22-1.   Output, Energy Use, and Energy Use Per Dollar of Output

	1958	1962	1967	1971	1975	1980
Output						
(million 1967 $)	1,745	2,232	2,684	2,675	3,250	4,150
Energy Use						
(trillion BTUs)						
Useful.	14.8	24.2	37.4	44.8	63.4	93.8
Gross	17.3	28.7	41.3	49.4	70.2	104.2
Energy use per dollar of Output						
(1,000 BTUs)						
Useful.	8.5	10.8	13.9	16.7	19.5	22.6
Gross	9.9	12.9	15.4	18.5	21.6	25.1

Sources: Bureau of the Census, *Census of Manufactures*; Table 22-3; The Conference Board.

product in the form of structures, increased by about one-half between 1950 and 1971.

The rapid growth by SIC 3273 is attributable to the industry's success in replacing concrete prepared by building contractors at construction sites with the ready-mixed variety. Such substitution shifts labor and capital requirements from on-site construction to the ready-mix plants or trucks and increases opportunities for economies of scale in the production of ready-to-pour concrete. Improvements in material mixing at the batching plant, partly through instrument control, have helped to raise product quality. Automation of concrete mixing operations has reduced labor requirements appreciably. In addition, ready-mix companies have been able to reduce delivery costs and widen their market areas; this has been accomplished through the use of larger capacity and higher speed trucks and through the growing use of dispersed "portable" plants that are assembled and dismantled as market needs dictate. The number of cubic yards produced per truck has increased 50% since 1958, according to the National Ready-Mixed Concrete Association, while the average number of cubic yards produced per plant per month has not changed.

Benefits to users from the productivity gains behind such improvements are in the form of lower ready-to-use cost per yard of concrete. Part of the increases in product quality, reductions in delivery time, and widening of availability, however, do incur additional costs; and these additional costs are reflected in the amount of value added by the industry, and in value of shipments. Hence, as is plain from the growth comparisons above, output by SIC 3273 in constant dollars has risen much faster than output of concrete in cubic yards. Between 1954 and 1971, constant dollar output rose at an average rate of 5.1% compared with 4.0% for physical output (cubic yards).

Success of the ready-mixed concrete industry in substituting its services for on-site preparation of concrete is also indicated by the increases in the proportion of total cement shipments that go to ready-mixed concrete companies. Bureau of Mines figures show that 63.1% of total shipments of portland cement went to ready-mixed companies in 1971, as against 53.5% in 1959.

Despite increasing competition from precast concrete recently, ready-mixed concrete companies have continued to enlarge their share of total concrete preparing at about the same rate as before. We believe that this indicates continuing expansion of markets and achievement of economies that are passed on to customers. We project that the ready-mixed concrete industry will further enlarge its share of total concrete preparing to at least 69% in 1980, compared with 63.1% in 1971 and 64.4% in 1972.

Since, unlike the cement industry, capacity is not a problem for SIC 3273, the industry should have little difficulty reaching the output levels implicit in this expansion of its share. Combining an assumed 30.5% increase in cement consumption between 1971 and 1980 (see Section III of Chapter Twenty,

Hydraulic Cement) with the 9.35% increase in share by the ready-mixed concrete industry, we get a projected rise of 42.7% in cubic yardage output between 1971 and 1980, or 4.0% annually, on average (1.305 x 1.0935 = 1.427). Allowing for product quality improvements of approximately 1% a year, constant dollar output by SIC 3273 is therefore expected to increase 5% a year, or 55.1% altogether.

Energy Use

Based on rough estimates by The Conference Board (in consultation with industry representatives), useful energy consumed by the ready-mixed concrete industry totaled about 37 trillion BTUs in 1967 and 45 trillion in 1971. Useful energy consumption per 1967 dollar of output was about 16,700 in 1971. The largest part of energy consumption in SIC 3273 is accounted for by the trucks, which both mix (about three-fourths of the industry) and deliver the concrete. Other substantial energy uses are the electricity needed to power the mixing machinery in those cases where the concrete is "centrally" mixed, and gas and oil to heat the concrete during cold weather.

As a consequence of difficulties in using and interpreting fuel and electricity purchase figures collected by the Census Bureau, this industry analysis can only provide the roughest estimates and projections of energy use. The difficulties are briefly described in Section III. The estimation procedure used to try to overcome these difficulties is shown in Table 22-3.

While the special estimating procedure results in much lower energy totals than if the regular method were used, the increases in energy use by SIC 3273 are still extremely rapid. But in view of the technological and marketing developments in the industry over the past fifteen years, it is not surprising that rapid increases per unit of output did occur. The major changes have been growth in the size of road equipment and a shift to relatively more truck mixing, both of which raise fuel use per unit of output. Larger trucks (with larger engines) burn more fuel per mile; and because internal combustion engines are less efficient than electric motors, truck mixing uses more energy per cubic yard produced than central mixing. In addition, further modest substitution of mechanical for human power has occurred; and the industry has improved and enlarged its capacity to provide concrete during sub-freezing weather, both of which tend to increase per unit energy use. Better control of material mixing increases product quality and therefore value per unit, with virtually no boost in energy use; this, of course, tends to lower energy use per dollar of output.

Because some of the above developments are continuing, future energy use by the ready-mixed concrete industry is likely to continue to increase in relation to output. However, in the absence of anything approaching firm data, we are assuming a further slowdown in this increase on a natural law basis. Useful energy consumption per constant dollar of output increased about 6% a year on average between 1958 and 1962, a little more than 5% between 1962 and 1967,

Table 22-2. Estimated Production

	Shipments of Portland Cement (million barrels)	Shipments of Cement to Ready-mixed Concrete Companies (per cent of total shipments)	Shipments of Cement to Ready-mixed Concrete Companies (million barrels)	Output of Ready-mixed Concrete Total (million cubic yards)	Output of Ready-mixed Concrete SIC 3273 (million cubic yards)
	(1)	(2)	(3)	(4)	(5)
1958	307.1	53.3*	163.7	123.1	119.4
1959	335.5	53.5	179.5	135.0	130.9
1960	312.3	56.2	175.5	132.0	128.7
1961	320.8	56.9	182.5	137.2	133.8
1962	331.8	57.9	192.1	144.4	141.5
1963	349.3	57.9	202.2	152.0	149.0
1964	366.3	59.0	216.1	162.5	159.3
1965	374.1	59.1	221.1	166.2	162.9
1966	380.7	59.5	226.5	170.3	166.9
1967	374.0	60.2	225.1	169.2	165.2
1968	397.4	61.4	244.0	183.5	179.8
1969	409.8	60.3	247.1	185.8	182.1
1970	390.5	61.9	241.7	181.7	178.1
1971	420.2	63.1	265.1	199.3	195.3

*Estimate based on trend line.

Sources and methods of estimation:

Column (1) U.S. Bureau of Mines, *Minerals Yearbook*, 1971.

Column (2) U.S. Bureau of Mines, *Minerals Yearbook*, 1958-1969, 1971; per cent for 1970 estimated by National Ready-Mixed Concrete Association.

Column (3)—Column (2) + Column (1).

Column (4)—Column (3) ÷ 1.33. (There are an estimated 1.33 barrels of cement in each cubic yard of concrete.)

Column (5)—1958-1959:—Column (4) x .97;1960-1961:—Column (4) x .975;—1962-1971:—Column (4) x .98. The factors .97, .975, and .98 are the actual or estimated coverage ratios for the respective years.

and a little less than 5% between 1967 and 1971. We project that the increase will average 4% a year between 1971 and 1975, and 3% a year between 1975 and 1980.

SECTION III.   CENSUS OF MANUFACTURES
ENERGY DATA

The nature of *Census of Manufactures* data on fuel and energy purchases by SIC 3273 has necessitated the changing of our procedure for estimating BTU equivalents of these figures, and the making of very rough estimates of energy use by the industry.

Problems arise because of the following: (1) Census reporting forms instruct that gasoline (a very expensive—per BTU—form of energy) be reported in the "Other" category in dollar terms, along with other, less expensive, fuels; (2) inasmuch as diesel fuel is a road fuel also, some companies probably report this, too, under "Other"; (3) the Census Bureau does not collect fuel and electricity purchase data from very small companies, but makes estimates and includes such estimates in the "Other" or "Not specified by kind" (nsk) column; (4) the Census Bureau is not consistent in its categorization of expenditures for fuels that are not specified by kind or that have been estimated. It appears that expenditures for fuels nsk are sometimes added in with other fuels.

These problems are serious in energy analyses of SIC 3273, because "Other" fuels and fuels "nsk" account for such a large proportion of total energy purchases by this industry. In nearly all the other energy-intensive manufacturing industries, energy use for transportation is a much smaller proportion of total energy use, so that categorization of gasoline as an "Other" fuel is relatively unimportant.

Table 22-3 shows the procedure developed by The Conference Board to try to adjust for these data problems. We do not present the results as anything more than rough estimates. We are satisfied, however, that they are in the range of reality, because the gasoline and diesel fuel estimates approximately jibe with figures that are obtained by using an industry rule of thumb for road fuel consumption per cubic yard produced.

SECTION IV.   CONCRETE AND ITS MANUFACTURE

Concrete is essentially a mixture of cement, sand, gravel (or a variant), and water. Additional materials are usually added in small amounts for various purposes—such as to accelerate setting (or hardening), retard setting, ease mixing, increase strength, or add color.

Producers of ready-mixed concrete assemble and proportion the ingredients at a "central" plant. Some establishments mix the materials with the

Table 22-3. Estimated Aggregate Energy Consumed

	1958	1962	1967	1971
1. Purchases of specified fuels (BTU equivalent–trillions)	8.5	12.7	23.8	28.4
2. Purchases of electricity (BTU equivalent–trillions)	1.1	2.1	1.9	2.2*
3. Purchases of "other" fuels and fuels "nsk" ($ millions)	$11.0	$19.9	$25.6	$34.0*
4. Purchases of gasoline and diesel fuel[1] (assumed equal to line 3) ($ millions) . .	$11.0	$19.9	$25.6	$34.0
5. Approximate average retail price of gasoline and diesel fuel per barrel, including taxes ($)	$11.70	$11.70	$12.15	$13.25
6. Barrels of gasoline and diesel fuel purchased (line 4 ÷ line 5) (millions) . .	.94	1.70	2.11	2.57
7. BTU content of gasoline and diesel fuel purchased (line 6 x 4.62 x 10^6) . . (trillions)	5.2	9.4	11.7	14.2
8. Aggregate useful energy consumed (line 1 + 2 + 7) (trillions)	14.2	24.2	37.4	44.8
9. Gross energy equivalent of electricity purchases (kwh purchases for respective years x heat rate for those years) (trillions) . . .	3.6	6.6	5.8	6.8*
10. Aggregate gross energy demanded (line 1 + 7 + 9) (trillions)	18.4	30.5	43.8	53.1

*Estimate based on trend line.
[1] In equal volumes
Sources: Bureau of the Census; Bureau of Labor Statistics; Bureau of Mines; The Conference Board.

appropriate equipment at the central station only; this is called "central-mixing." Some load the materials into mixing trucks, which have rotating drums that mix the batch en route to the delivery site or mix the batch at the site; this is called "transit-mixing"; some establishments perform both central- and transit-mixing. Whichever type of mixing is done, the concrete is delivered by truck to the construction site and poured.

Whether mixing is done centrally or in transit, energy is required at the central plant for unloading, storing, and proportioning the materials. The equipment used is almost exclusively electrically driven. Central-mixing requires additional electrical energy to turn the mixing drum. Truck-mixing is done off the truck's propelling engine. In either case, additional energy is required to turn the mixing drum.

In those cases where ready-mixed concrete establishments undertake to supply concrete in extremely cold or warm weather, energy is required to fuel the burners or power the refrigeration unit in order to keep the concrete at the appropriate temperature.

Note

The author wishes to acknowledge a special indebtedness to Richard D. Gaynor, Director of Engineering of the National Ready-Mixed Concrete Association, for his extensive assistance in the way of advising on operational, technical, and quantitative aspects of the ready-mixed concrete industry.

SECTION V.   SELECTED BIBLIOGRAPHY

Bureau of the Census. *Census of Manufactures*, 1958, 1963, 1967. *Annual Survey of Manufactures*, 1962, 1971.

Bureau of Labor Statistics. *Technological Trends in Major American Industries*, BLS Bulletin No. 1474. Washington, D.C.: Government Printing Office, 1966.

Bureau of Mines. *Minerals Yearbook*, 1971. Washington, D.C.: Government Printing Office, 1973.

Department of Commerce. *U.S. Industrial Outlook*, 1973, Washington D.C.: Government Printing Office, 1973.

National Ready-Mixed Concrete Association. *Production and Value of Ready-Mixed Concrete in 1970*, Silver Spring, Md.: 1972.

Pit and Quarry Publications. *Concrete Industries Yearbook*, 1972/73. Chicago: Pit and Quarry Publications, 1973.

Serials:
Pit and Quarry
Journal of the American Concrete Institute.

Chapter Twenty-Three

Lime—SIC 3274

Hirohiko Chiba

SECTION I.   SUMMARY OF FINDINGS

The Industry

The products included in SIC 3274 are quicklime (CaO), hydrated lime (Ca(OH)$_2$) and "dead-burned" dolomite (CaMgO), which are made from limestone, dolomite, or other substances.

The analysis in this study is based on a physical unit production basis, with output data from the U.S. Bureau of Mines *Minerals Yearbook*. This has been done because the proportion of lime used within the industry has been increasing.

The total value of shipments increased at an average annual rate of 2.09% from 1947 to 1971, and quantity of product increased at 4.52% (Appendix Table 23A-3). Within the products, the share of quicklime has been rising.

Energy Utilization

Between 1947 and 1967, energy utilization for power and heat by the lime industry (on a gross basis)[a] grew at an average annual rate of 2.0%. Consequently, energy utilization per 1967 dollar of shipments declined from 478,000 BTUs in 1947 to 465,400 BTUs in 1967 (on the basis of gross energy consumed). The energy-output ratio fell during this period at an average annual rate of 0.1%.

When related to tons of product, however, the energy-output ratio declined rapidly during this period—at an average annual rate of 3.4% (see Chart 23-1). This difference was due to a change in proportion of lime used within the industry. Internal use of lime has grown rapidly due to increased need for it for pollution control.

[a]See Chapter One, pages 14-15, for definitions of gross and useful energy.

Table 23-1.   Energy and Output, 1947-1980

		Gross Energy Consumed		Useful Energy Consumed	
	Value of Shipments (million 1967 $)	Total Energy Use (trillion BTUs)	Energy per 1967 Dollar of Shipments (1,000 BTUs)	Total Energy Use (trillion BTUs)	Energy per 1967 Dollar of Shipments (1,000 BTUs)
Actual					
1947	119.0	56.9	478.0	54.5	458.0
1954	137.0	55.9	408.0	53.5	390.5
1958	149.0	52.5	352.4	50.2	336.9
1962	157.0	61.4	391.0	58.9	375.2
1967	176.0	81.9	465.4	78.3	444.9
*Projected					
1975	233.3	86.2	369.5	82.0	351.5
1980	279.7	98.2	351.1	93.2	333.2

*These figures are based on Projection Case 1 (See Table 23-7).
Source: Bureau of the Census, *Census of Manufactures*, 1963 and 1967.

Projections

The growth of the lime industry depends on chemical uses and construction uses, especially on the demand by the steel industry and for road construction.

We projected the quantity of product on two bases. Case 1 is based on an average annual growth rate of 4.01% and Case 2 is based on 2.16% (Table 23-7). If the share of lime sold within total product remains constant (63% in 1971), volume of shipments will also grow at the same rate.

Energy utilization per unit of product has been declining consistently since 1947. In order to meet cost increases, especially fuel cost increments, efforts to save energy will continue. Energy utilization per ton of product declined at an average annual rate of 1.31% (gross energy consumed) and of 1.37% (useful energy) from 1962 to 1967. We assume these trends will continue in the future. If the share of lime sold within total product remains constant, energy utilization per unit of shipments will also decline at the same rate.

Summary Analysis

During the 1947-1967 period, energy utilization rose at an average annual rate of 1.53%, which was slower than the 5.0% growth of quantity of product. From 1947 to 1967, energy consumption per unit of product declined at an average annual growth rate of 3.4% (gross energy consumed basis). The decline was mainly due to great technological change in the calcining process, especially to efficient energy use in rotary kilns.

Our projection assumes that future energy utilization per unit of product will also decline at 1.4% in gross energy consumed and at 1.4% in useful energy, which are the latest trend values (1962 to 1967). The reason for the decline is that increasing costs of fuel and air pollution control will require efficient energy utilization for this energy-intensive industry.

SECTION II.   HISTORICAL DEVELOPMENT

Trends in Production and Use

The total value of lime sold or used by producers set a new record of $308.1 million in 1971 (Table 23-2). The quantity of lime produced, however, decreased and was 3% below the 1969 record. During the period 1947-1971, the total value increased at an average annual growth rate of 6.78% and the quantity increased at 4.52%. This means that the average value per ton rose from $9.42 in 1947 to $15.73 in 1971, or an average annual increase of 2.26%.

Among the products, the share of quicklime rose from 59.4% in 1954 to 77.3% in 1971, and the share of hydrated lime and dolomite lime declined. The share of lime, used by producers rose from 16.8% in 1954 to 37.0% in 1971.

Table 23-2.   Lime Sold or Used by Producers

	Unit of Measure	1947	1954	1958	1962	1967	1971
Total.........	1,000 short tons	6,779	8,629	9,211	13,753	17,985	19,591
		(100)	(100)	(100)	(100)	(100)	(100)
Quicklime.....	1,000 short tons	5,021	5,128	5,538	9,509	13,449	15,138
		(74.1)	(59.4)	(60.1)	(69.1)	(74.8)	(77.3)
Hydrated lime..	1,000 short tons	1,758	1,980	2,014	2,386	2,656	3,446
		(25.9)	(23.0)	(21.9)	(17.4)	(14.8)	(17.6)
Dolomite.....	1,000 short tons		1,521	1,659	1,858	1,880	1,007
			(17.6)	(18.0)	(13.5)	(10.4)	(5.1)
Lime sold.....	1,000 short tons		7,180	7,388	8,145	11,461	12,337
			(83.2)	(80.2)	(59.2)	(63.7)	(63.0)
Lime used.....	1,000 short tons		1,449	1,823	5,608	6,524	7,254
			(16.8)	(19.8)	(40.8)	(36.3)	(37.0)
Value........	millions of dollars	63.8	101.8	121.2	186.8	240.2	308.1
Average value per ton.....	dollars/ton	9.42	11.79	13.16	13.58	13.36	15.73

Note: Figures in parentheses represent percentage distribution of total.
Source: Bureau of Mines, *Minerals Yearbook.*

**Table 23-3.   Lime Sold or Used by Producers, by Use
(thousand short tons)**

Use	1967			1971		
	Sold	Used	Total	Sold	Used	Total
Agriculture............	174		174	80	–	80
	(1.5)		(1.0)	(0.7)		
Construction...........:	1,433	w̄	1,433	1,499	w̄	w̄
	(12.5)		(8.0)	(15.2)		
Chemical and industrial..	8,290	6,198	14,488	9,836	w̄	w̄
	(72.3)		(80.6)	(79.5)		
Refractory dolomite.....	1,565	315	1,880	965	42	1,007
	(13.7)		(10.4)	(4.6)		
Total*...............	11,461	6,513*	17,974	12,380	7,254*	19,635*
	(100)		(100)	(100)		

w̄ Withheld to avoid disclosing individual company's confidential data.
*Includes uses indicated by symbol w̄.
Note: Figures in parentheses represent percentage distribution of total.
Source: Bureau of Mines, *Minerals Yearbook.*

The four principal uses of lime sold by producers in 1971 were chemical, 79%; construction, 15%; refractory, 5%; and agricultural, 1% (Table 23-3). Looking back over the years, agricultural use of lime has been declining and recently refractory use has also been declining (Chart 23-1).

The leading individual uses were basic oxygen steel furnaces, alkalies,

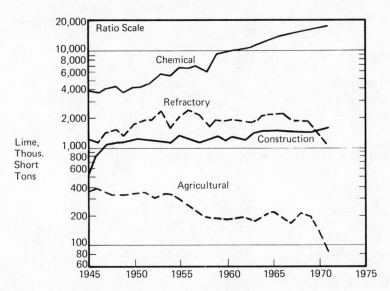

Chart 23-1. Trends in Major Uses of Lime.

water purification, refractory dolomite, and other chemical uses. Each of these required more than one million tons of lime.[1]

Trends in Energy Utilization

Energy utilization (gross energy) increased at an average annual rate of 1.53% between 1947 and 1967. The latest available figures showing the type of fuel used in the lime industry (Table 23-4) indicate that the largest share of the industry, 51%, is furnished by coal, 38% comes from natural gas, and 11% from fuel oil or some other fuel.

During the period of 1947-1967, quantity of lime production increased at an average annual rate of 5.0%. This means there was a decline in overall energy utilization per unit of product at an average annual rate of 3.4% during the same period (Table 23-5). This is mainly because of very large increases in the efficiency of energy utilization in lime kilns. The change in product mix did not affect the decline because all products are almost the same energy per unit of product.

Trends in Production Processes

Lime is basically calcined limestone. Either plain or dolomitic limestone may be used. The former yields high calcium quicklime and the latter yields dolomitic quicklime. The two types are interchangeable in many uses, but dolomitic quicklime is preferred for refractory use. Production techniques for the two types are identical.

Table 23-4. Distribution of Energy Utilization, by Source (trillion BTUs, and percentages)

	1947	1954	1958	1962	1967
Coal, coke, & breeze	44.6 (78.4)	35.2 (63.0)	29.4 (56.0)	39.6 (64.5)	42.0 (51.3)
Fuel oil (total)	1.9 (3.3)	2.4 (4.3)	1.7 (3.2)	1.8 (2.9)	2.3 (2.9)
Gas	6.0 (10.5)	14.5 (25.9)	15.9 (30.3)	15.7 (25.6)	31.1 (38.0)
Other fuels & fuels n.s.k.	1.2 (2.1)	0.5 (0.9)	2.2 (4.2)	0.5 (0.8)	1.2 (1.0)
Electric energy (gross energy consumed basis)	3.0 (5.7)	3.3 (5.9)	3.3 (6.3)	3.7 (6.2)	5.3 (6.9)
Electric energy (useful energy)	0.7	0.9	1.0	1.2	1.7
Total (gross energy consumed basis)	56.9 (100)	55.9 (100)	52.5 (100)	61.4 (100)	81.9 (100)
Total (useful energy)	54.5	53.5	50.2	58.9	78.3

Note: Figures in parentheses represent percentage distribution of total which is based on gross energy consumption.

Source: Tables 23A-2 and 23A-3.

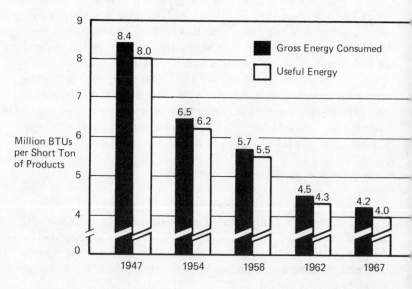

Chart 23-2. Energy Utilization per Unit of Product, 1947–1967.

**Table 23-5.   Energy Utilization per Unit of Product
(million BTUs per short ton)**

	1947	1954	1958	1962	1967
Coal, coke, & breeze	6.579	4.079	3.192	2.879	2.144
Fuel oil (total)	0.280	0.278	0.185	0.131	0.117
Gas....................	0.885	1.680	1.726	1.142	1.588
Other fuels, fuels n.s.k.	0.177	0.058	0.239	0.036	0.062
Electric energy (gross energy consumed basis)	0.457	0.382	0.358	0.269	0.271
Electric energy (useful energy)	0.103	0.104	0.109	0.087	0.087
Total (gross energy consumed basis)	8.394	6.478 (−3.64)	5.700 (−3.15)	4.465 (−5.92)	4.181 (−1.31)
Total (useful energy)	8.040	6.200 (−3.64)	5.450 (−3.17)	4.283 (−5.30)	3.997 (−1.37)

Note: Figures in parentheses represent average annual growth rates.
Sources: Tables 23-2 and 23-4.

Limestone is mined or quarried and is transported to the mills, where it is crushed and screened. The sized limestone is then calcined in either rotary, vertical, or rotary-hearth kilns.[2]

The product that comes from the kiln is called *quicklime*. It has a high affinity for airborne moisture and carbon dioxide, and so cannot be stored for more than a few weeks. Water may be added to quicklime, under controlled conditions, to produce *hydrated lime*. This product can be stored safely for longer periods, and in many cases is interchangeable with quicklime in terms of ultimate use. Hydrated lime is also known as *slaked lime*.

Quicklime is generally a pebble or lump-sized granular material, though certain types of limestone produce quicklime in powder form. Hydrated lime generally breaks down when the water is added into a fine light powder.

The chemical reactions are as follows:

Calcination

High calcium lime:

$$CaCO_3 + heat \longrightarrow CaO \text{ (quicklime)} + CO_2$$

Dolomitic lime:

$$CaCO_3 \cdot MgCO_3 + heat \longrightarrow CAMgO_2 \text{ (dolomitic lime)} + 2CO_2$$

Hydration

$$CaO + H_2O \longrightarrow Ca(CH)_2 \text{ (hydrated lime)}$$

Although the fuel consumption per ton of product is somewhat higher in the rotary kiln (Table 23-6) and although there is generally a higher capital investment required for a rotary, by far the greatest percentage of product is handled in this type of kiln. The advantages claimed for the rotary kiln are: the utilization of all sizes of limestone; better control of feed and temperature; and greater production per man-hour due to much higher production rate per unit.

Considering the energy use in the calcining process and another heat requirement,[3] overall energy utilization per unit of product seems to be underestimated. Nevertheless, one can admit that the decline of the overall energy utilization was due to the reduction of energy utilization in kilns, especially in rotary kilns.

SECTION III.   PROJECTIONS TO 1980

Demand

The future growth of this industry will be determined mainly by the leading individual uses. In particular, the demand by the steel industry for larger quantities and higher quality lime, and the increasing use of lime for road construction, are the main factors among many which point to a healthy outlook for the lime producers.

Quantity of product and average value per unit of product are projected first, and value of production is derived by multiplying them

Table 23-6.   Change in Rate of Energy Utilization in Kilns (million BTUs per short ton of limestone)

	1950's	*1960's*
Rotary kilns	10 ~ 14 million BTUs per ton of quicklime ↓ 6 ~ 8 million BTUs	5 ~ 5.5 million BTUs per ton of quicklime ↓ 4.5 ~ 5 million BTUs
Vertical kilns	4 ~ 6 million BTUs	4 ~ 5.5 million BTUs ↓ 4 million BTUs
Fluid-bed kiln		4 ~ 4.5 million BTUs

Sources: Robert S. Boynton. "Rotary Kiln," *Chemistry and Technology of Lime and Limestone*, 1966; W. L. Faith, Donald B. Keynes and Ronald L. Clark, "Lime," *Industrial Chemicals*, 1965, page 482-487; Bureau of Mines, *Minerals Yearbook*, 1954, 1958, 1962.

(Table 23-7). The quantity of product is projected on two bases. Case 1 is based on an average annual growth rate of 4.01%, which is the same increase as that from 1962 to 1971. Case 2 is based on 2.16%, which is the same annual increase as that from 1967 to 1971. The average value per unit of product is based on an average annual rate of increase of 1.71%, which is the same increase as that from 1962 to 1971.

Energy Use

One of the most important trends in the lime industry is the increasing demand for quicklime of higher purity. This single factor has initiated considerable research and development into new types of kilns, new methods of

Table 23-7. Projected Production to 1980

	Unit	1971	1975 Case 1	Case 2	1980 Case 1	Case 2
Quantity ...	Thousand short tons	19,591	22,919	21,373	27,884	24,354
Value	Millions of dollars	308.1	403.8	376.6	543.5	474.7
Average value ...	Dollars per short ton	15.73	17.62 (1.71)	376.6	19.49 (1.71)	474.7

Note: Regenerated lime excluded; production for own use included. Figures in parentheses represent the assumed average annual growth rate (%).

Sources: Bureau of Mines, *Minerals Yearbook*; The Conference Board.

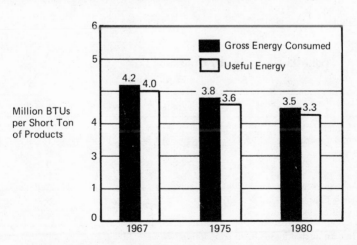

Chart 23-3. Energy Utilization per Unit of Product: Projections to 1980.

firing, and other refinements to existing vertical shaft kilns and rotary kilns. Since natural gas is the most suitable fuel for producing lime of higher purity, it is likely that relatively more gas will be used by SIC 3313 in 1980 than at present.

Higher grade lime commands a higher price, and with an industry as competitive as this one, it seems likely that the technology of lime production may change rapidly in the future. Furthermore, many lime plants have installed dust control equipment in order to meet air pollution regulations. Some plants have closed rather than try to meet the standards. Rising fuel costs are directly reflected in increased costs of manufacturing lime. Fuel shortages have been reported at several plants.

Combating these pressures of cost increase, this industry will still continue to concentrate on reducing energy utilization. We assume that future overall energy utilization per unit of production will continue to decline at an average annual rate of 1.31% in gross energy consumed base and of 1.37% on a useful energy basis, which are the same annual rates as those from 1962 to 1967.

Notes

[1] Bureau of Mines, *Minerals Yearbook, 1971,* "Lime."

[2] *A Study of Process Energy Requirements in the Cement and Lime Industry,* American Gas Association, Inc.

[3] This is the retention of the dissociation temperature until all of the CO_2 has been expelled, 2.77 million BTU/ton for high calcium and 2.60 million BTU/ton for dolomitic quicklimes. See *Chemistry and Technology of Lime and Limestone,* p. 136.

SECTION IV.   APPENDIX

Table 23A-1.   Energy Utilization (1)
($ millions)

	1947	1954	1958	1962	1967
Purchased (fuel & elec.)	16.0	18.8	22.1	21.3	31.4
Coal, coke, & breeze	11.4	10.5	11.8	11.1	13.8
Fuel oil (total)	0.8	1.3	1.3	0.9	1.3
Distillate	0	0	0	0.2	0.3
Residual	0	0	0	0.7	1.0
Gas	1.0	3.4	4.5	5.1	10.3
Other fuels & fuels n.s.k.	0.5	0.2	0.9	0.2	0.5
Electricity purchased	2.2	3.3	3.6	4.0	5.5

Source: Bureau of the Census, *Census of Manufactures.*

Table 23A-2.   Energy Utilization (2)

	Unit of Measure	1947	1954	1958	1962	1967
Purchased (Fuel & elec.) ...	Mill kwh	n.a.	n.a.	n.a.	n.a.	23,062
Coal	1,000 tons	1,677	1,330	1,140	1,535	1,626
Coke & breeze	1,000 tons	50	36	0	0	0
Fuel oil (total)	1,000 bbls	336	413	293	318	401
Distillate	1,000 bbls	0	0	0	57	72
Residual	1,000 bbls	0	0	0	261	329
Gas	Million cft	5,827	13,993	15,338	15,154	30,001
Other fuels	$ Million (cur)	n.a.	n.a.	n.a.	n.a.	n.a.
Fuels nsk	$ Million (cur)	n.a.	n.a.	n.a.	n.a.	n.a.
Electric energy	Million kwh	198	270	295	355	512

n.a.–not available.

Source: Bureau of the Census, *Census of Manufactures.*

Table 23A-3.   Total Lime Production*

	Unit	1947	1954	1958	1962	1967	1971
Quantity	1,000 short tons	6,779	8,629	9,211	13,753	17,985	19,591
Value	Millions of dollars	63.8	101.8	121.2	186.8	240.2	308.1
Average value ..	Dollars per short ton	9.42	11.79	13.16	13.58	13.36	15.73

Source: Bureau of Mines, *Minerals Yearbook.*

*Sold and used, excludes secondary product.

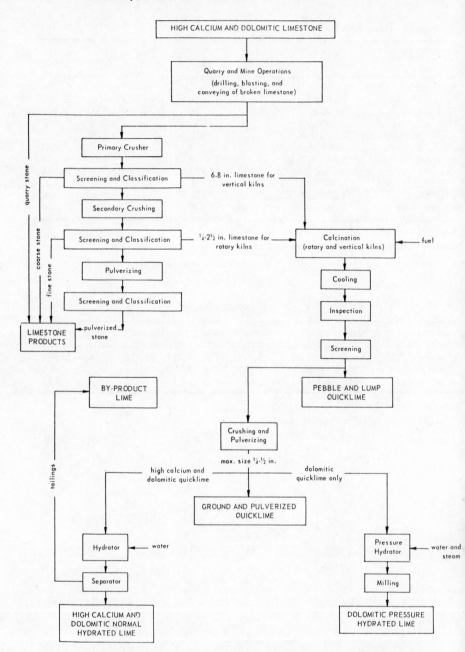

Figure 23-1. Flow Sheet for Lime Production. Source: *Chemistry and Technology of Lime and Limestone*, Robert S. Boynton, 1966, Wiley.

SECTION V.   SELECTED BIBLIOGRAPHY

Azbe, Victor J. *The Rotary Kiln*. Azbe Corporation, August 1954.

————. *Theory and Practice of Lime Manufacture*. Azbe Corporation, 1946.

Boynton, Robert S. *Chemistry and Technology of Lime and Limestone*. Wiley, 1966.

Clark, Ronald; Keynes, D. B.; and Faith, W. L. *Industrial Chemicals*. Wiley, 1965.

Gee, B. J. and Knibbs, N. V. S. *Lime and Limestone*. Toronto, Ont.: H. L. Hall Corporation Ltd., 1955.

Serials:
Rock Products
Pit and Quarry

Chapter Twenty-Four

Blast Furnaces and
Steel Mills — SIC 3312

Elisabeth K. Rabitsch

SECTION I. INTRODUCTION AND SUMMARY

The Bureau of the Census Standard Industrial Classification defines
the Iron and Steel industry, SIC 3312, as follows:

> Establishments primarily engaged in manufacturing hot metal, pig
> iron, silvery pig iron, and ferroalloys from iron ore and iron and steel
> scrap; converting pig iron, scrap iron and scrap steel into steel; and in
> hot rolling iron and steel into basic shapes such as plates, sheets,
> strips, rods, bars, and tubing. Merchant blast furnaces and by-
> product or beehive coke ovens are also included in this industry.
> Establishments primarily engaged in manufacturing ferro and
> nonferrous additive alloys by electrometallurgical processes are
> classified in Industry 3313.

In addition to the above mentioned exclusions from SIC 3312, there
are also those establishments primarily engaged in producing finished products
from *purchased* iron and steel (non-integrated producers of steel products)
classified in Industries 3315 (Steel Wire-Drawing and Steel Nails and Spikes),
3316 (Cold Rolled Steel Sheet, Strip, and Bars), and 3317 (Steel Pipe and
Tubes).

A flowline on steelmaking, Figure 24-1, shows in simplified form the
basic processes of iron and steel making from iron ore, coal, and limestone to
finished steel products. The source of this flowchart is the American Iron and
Steel Institute.[1]

The scope of the study was confined to measuring utilization of
energy within an iron and steel works complex. Requirements of energy by iron
ore mines, off-site ore beneficiation plants, producers of industrial gases
(oxygen) and other raw materials (calcined fluxes, refractories, etc.) are not

415

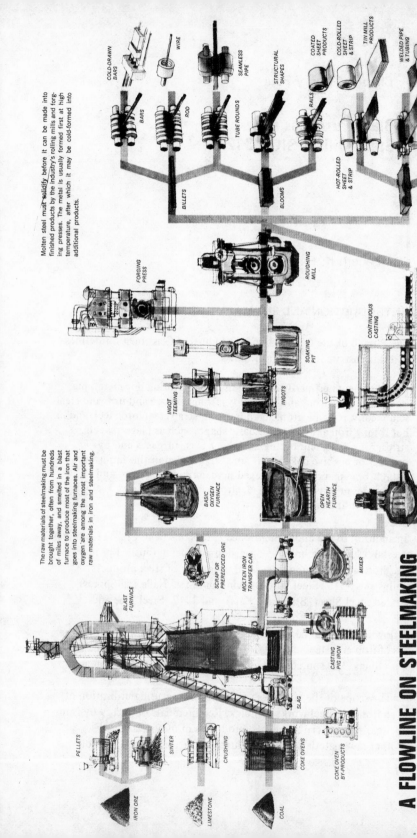

A FLOWLINE ON STEELMAKING

This is a simplified road map through the complex world of steelmaking. Each stop along the routes from raw materials to mill products contained in this chart can itself be charted. From this overall view, one major point emerges: Many operations—involving much equipment and large numbers of men—are required to produce civilization's principal and least expensive metal.

The raw materials of steelmaking must be brought together, often from hundreds of miles away, and smelted in a blast furnace to produce most of the iron that goes into steelmaking furnaces. Air and oxygen are among the most important raw materials in iron and steelmaking.

Molten steel must solidify before it can be made into finished products by the industry's rolling mills and forging presses. The metal is usually formed first at high temperature, after which it may be cold-formed into additional products.

Reproduced with permission of the American Iron and Steel Institute

PELLETS

IRON ORE

SINTER

LIMESTONE

CRUSHING

COAL

COKE OVENS

COKE OVEN BY-PRODUCTS

BLAST FURNACE

SLAG

CASTING PIG IRON

SCRAP OR PREREDUCED ORE

MOLTEN IRON TRANSFER CAR

MIXER

BASIC OXYGEN FURNACE

OPEN HEARTH FURNACE

ELECTRIC FURNACE

INGOT TEEMING

INGOTS

SOAKING PIT

CONTINUOUS CASTING

FORGING PRESS

ROUGHING MILL

BILLETS

BLOOMS

SLABS

COLD-DRAWN BARS

BARS

WIRE

ROD

TUBE ROUNDS

SEAMLESS PIPE

STRUCTURAL SHAPES

RAILS

COATED SHEET PRODUCTS

COLD-ROLLED SHEET & STRIP

TIN MILL PRODUCTS

HOT-ROLLED SHEET & STRIP

WELDED PIPE & TUBING

SKELP

LARGE-DIAMETER PIPE

included in this study. Energy used in transportation of raw materials to steel mills was also not considered. However, energy consumed by ore beneficiation plants or sinter plants located within an integrated iron and steel complex is included in total energy utilization, as is energy consumed in steel processing to final mill products.

The Iron and Steel Industry

This chapter examines the energy utilization of four major manufacturing operations included in SIC 3312. These are the coke oven and blast furnace operations, the basic steelmaking processes, and the rolling mill sector of the iron and steel industry. The large, vertically integrated iron and steel mills in the United States combine all of these operations. Smaller steel mills may be specializing in one or more of the basic steelmaking processes. Descriptions of the major operations of the iron and steel industry are given in Section II of this chapter.

Historical Demand and Energy Utilization

The iron and steel industry is, as is well known, a highly cyclical industry with fairly wide variations in volume of output from year to year. The all-time high of the industry's volume of output was reached in 1969, with raw steel production at 141 million short tons.[2] The production of raw steel increased in the 20-year period 1947 to 1967 from 85 million tons to 127 million tons, or by 49%, and in the 25-year period 1947 to 1972 from 85 million tons to 133 million tons, or by 56%. The average growth rate over both time spans was about 2% a year.

Between 1954 and 1967, the industry's shipments rose from $14.5 billion to $19.6 billion, a 35% increase (computed on a 1967 constant dollar basis by linking the *Census of Manufactures* indexes of production to 1967 value of shipments). Shipments in 1969 and in 1972 amounted to $22.2 billion and $21 billion, respectively, when measured on a 1967 constant dollar basis (Table 24-1).

Energy utilization for heat and power by the iron and steel industry increased from 1947 to 1967, although not as rapidly as either raw steel production or constant dollar shipments. According to Bureau of the Census data, energy use per unit of output declined from 1958 to 1967 at an average annual rate of 1.0%. Energy-output ratios, based on American Iron and Steel Institute data, reflect the cyclical nature of the industry. The lowest energy-output ratio seems to have occurred in 1969, at the time of a cyclical peak in output, and at an accordingly high rate of capacity utilization in the industry.

Between 1947 and 1972, gross energy[a] utilization per short ton of produced raw steel declined at an average rate of about 1.2% per year. The

[a]See Chapter One, pages 14-15, for definitions of gross and useful energy.

Table 24-1.   Volume of Production and Shipments, 1947-1972

Basis	1947	1954	1958	1962	1967	1969	1971	1972
Raw steel production[1] (million short tons) ..	84.9	88.3	85.3	98.3	127.2	141.3	120.4	133.2
Shipments (at 1967 prices, $ billions)	n.c.	14.5	13.5	15.7	19.6	22.2	18.8	21.0
Volume index[2] 1967 = 100	n.c.	73.9	68.9	86.2	100.0	110.9	95.9	106.9

n.c.—not comparable.
Sources: [1] American Iron and Steel Institute.
    [2] Bureau of the Census, *Census of Manufactures, 1967;* Federal Reserve Board, *Index of Industrial Production.*

energy-output ratio between two peak production years, 1954 and 1969, declined at an average annual rate of about 1.1%.

Bureau of the Census data are available (on a comparable basis) for the years 1958, 1962, 1967, and 1971 (Table 24-2), but account in 1971 only for purchased energy by the establishments of the iron and steel industry. Data for the years 1958, 1962, and 1967 show captive consumption of energy as well.

The American Iron and Steel Institute provides data on fuels consumed and electric energy purchased by the iron and steel industry during the years 1947 to 1972. These are shown in Table 24-3 and Chart 24-2.

The difference between useful energy and gross energy is comparatively small, and in 1972 accounted for about 8% of gross energy consumed. In the iron and steel industry, purchases of electric energy are small in comparison with the utilization of other energy sources.

Estimates of energy utilization based on Bureau of the Census data Table 24-2) are somewhat higher (8% in 1967) than those based on American Iron and Steel Institute information (Table 24-3). Part of this discrepancy arises from different factors used to convert the various unit measures of energy into BTUs.[3]

Data on total energy utilization, of course, do not reveal important changes in energy consumption patterns that have occurred over the past decades. Consumption of electric energy and of natural gas have grown rapidly relative to the use of other fuels. Between 1947 and 1972, consumption of electric power has tripled, while consumption of natural gas has grown almost four-fold. During the same period, the use of coal in production of steam and for purposes other than coking has declined markedly. Both natural gas and fuel oil have been used increasingly as injectants in blast furnaces, contributing importantly to the lowering of the coke rate. The relatively low cost of these fuels, particularly of natural gas, made their use attractive. Fuel oil #6 has also

Table 24-2. **Energy Utilization, 1958-1971**

Basis	1958	1962	1967	1971
Total energy utilization (trillion BTUs)				
Useful energy				
Total (incl. captive)	2,423	2,768	3,223	n.a.
Purchased	1,143	1,471	1,566	1,472
Gross energy consumed*				
Total (incl. captive)	2,548	2,930	3,467	n.a.
Purchased	1,268	1,633	1,810	1,802
*Per Unit Shipped** (thousand BTUs/1967 $)*				
Useful energy, total	179	176	164	n.a.
Purchased	85	94	80	78
Gross energy, total	189	187	177	n.a.
Purchased	94	104	92	96

n.a.—not available.

*Average heat rate for fossil-fueled steam-electric plants estimated for 1958 at 11,085 BTU/kwh; 1962 at 10,558 BTU/kwh; 1967 at 10,432 BTU/kwh; and 1971 at 10,500 BTU/kwh.

**A graphic presentation is given in Chart 24-1.

Source: Bureau of the Census, *Census of Manufactures.*

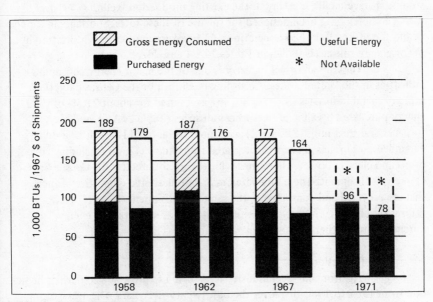

Chart 24-1. Energy Utilization per Unit Shipped: 1958–1971.
Note: This chart is based on Bureau of the Census data.

Table 24-3. Energy-Output Ratios, 1947-1972

Basis	1947	1954	1958	1962	1967	1969	1971	1972
Useful energy total (trillion BTUs) ..	2,741	2,465	2,409	2,535	3,007	3,218	2,878	3,050
Per unit shipped (1,000 BTUs/1967 $) .	n.c.	170.0	178.4	161.5	153.4	145.0	153.1	145.2
Per short ton of raw steel (million BTUs)	32.3	27.9	28.2	25.8	23.6	22.8	23.9	22.9
Gross energy consumed total (trillion BTUs) ..	2,845	2,608	2,532	2,687	3,222	3,478	3,144	3,330
Per unit shipped (1,000 BTUs/1967 $) .	n.c.	179.9	187.6	171.1	164.4	156.7	167.2	158.6
Per short ton of raw steel (million BTUs)	33.5	29.5	29.7	27.3	25.3	24.6	26.1	25.0

n.c.—not comparable.
Source: American Iron and Steel Institute.

been used as a back-up fuel for natural gas and by-product gases because of large volume storage facilities. Many of the existing production facilities in a steel works complex have been designed for the use of these fuels. Shortages in supply would therefore affect plant operations. (A breakdown of energy utilization by major energy sources is shown in Tables 24A-4 and 24A-5.)

The iron and steel industry is one of the major energy consuming industries in the United States. According to Bureau of the Census data, the primary metal industries (SIC 33) in 1967 accounted for about 21.3% of total energy purchased by all manufacturing industries (Table 24A-6), and blast furnaces and steel mills (SIC 3312) accounted for about 11.4% of total dollars expended on purchased energy. Integrated iron and steel mills (including coke ovens and electric power generating facilities) are counted by the Census Bureau as *one* establishment. These integrated mills produce large quantities of fuels that are recycled and consumed in the same establishment. In fact, captive utilization of energy in integrated mills is at least as important as energy purchased from other establishments.[4]

Projections

The iron and steel industry is expected to grow at a somewhat higher rate from 1967 to 1980 than over the past twenty-five years. The average annual growth rate from 1967 to 1980 is estimated at 2.5%. Projections of shipments in real terms, at 1967 prices, result in 1975 shipments of $24 billion, and 1980 shipments of $27 billion. These projections are shown below in Table 24-4.

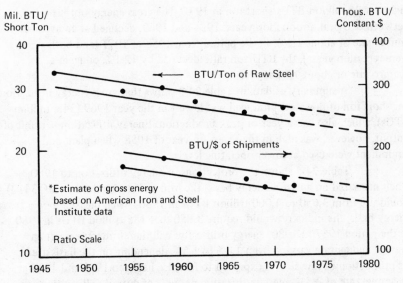

Chart 24-2. Gross Energy Utilization per 1967 Dollar of Shipments and per Short Ton of Raw Steel Produced.

Table 24-4.   Volume of Production and Shipments to 1980

	1967	*1971*	*1972*	*1975*	*1980*
Raw steel production, (million short tons)	127.2	120.4	133.2	155	175
Shipments (at 1967 prices) ($ billions)	$ 19.6	$ 18.8	$ 21.0	$ 24.0	$ 27.0
Index, 1967 = 100	100.0	95.9	106.9	122	138

Sources: Table 24-1; The Conference Board.

Production of raw steel is projected to grow to about 155 million short tons in 1975, and to about 175 million short tons in 1980.

Projections of demand for iron and steel products (SIC 331, 332, 3391 and 3399) made by the INFORUM input-output model of the University of Maryland show a growth rate of 2.4% per year from 1967 to 1980. Shipments and demand projections are, therefore, in fairly close correspondence.

Summary Analysis

In the period 1947 to 1972, energy utilization per unit of production (total BTUs used per short ton of raw steel produced) declined at a rate of about 1.2% per year. In 1947, gross energy utilized in the iron and steel industry amounted to 33.5 million BTUs per short ton of raw steel produced; this ratio dropped to 24.6 million BTUs/short ton in 1969, and was slightly higher at 25 million BTUs/short ton in 1972. The gross energy-output ratio between two peak production years, 1954 and 1969, declined at an average annual rate of about 1.2%. In the period from 1958 to 1971 (and both years were recession years), the BTU/ton ratio declined by 12.1%, or again at an average rate of about 1% per year.

A summary of data in Table 24-3 shows that gross energy utilization per short ton of raw steel produced was lowest in the year 1969 (24.6 million BTUs), which also was a year of peak production. Energy utilization per unit of output, however, was high in the recession year of 1958 when plant and equipment were used at lower operating levels.

Table 24-5 shows the projections of energy utilization to 1980. When measured on a useful energy basis, the iron and steel industry (SIC 3312) would use from 3,650 to 4,000 trillion BTUs in 1980. When measured on a gross energy basis, the industry would require 3,850 to 4,185 trillion BTUs in 1980. In the period 1967 to 1980, energy utilization will therefore increase at an average annual rate varying from 1.4% to 1.5%, depending on the basis used. As production of raw steel is expected to increase between 1967 and 1980 at an annual rate of 2.5%, energy utilization per unit of output will continue to decline.

Energy utilization per unit shipped, using Census of Manufactures data, will decline from 164,000 BTUs in 1967 to 148,000 BTUs in 1980, a 0.8% rate when measured on a useful energy basis, and from 177,000 BTUs to

Table 24-5. Energy Utilization to 1980

	1967	*1975*	*1980*
AISI Data			
Useful energy (trillion BTUs)	3,007	3,360	3,650
Index (1967 = 100)	100	112	121
Gross energy consumed (trillion BTUs)	3,222	3,600	3,850
Index (1967 = 100)	100	112	119
Raw steel production (million short tons)	127.2	155	175
Index (1967 = 100)	100	122	138
Census Data			
Useful energy (trillion BTUs)	3,223	3,650	4,000
Index (1967 = 100)	100	113	124
Gross energy consumed (trillion BTUs)	3,467	3,960	4,185
Index (1967 = 100)	100	114	121
Shipments (billion 1967$)	$19.6	$24.0	$27.0
Index (1967 = 100)	100	122	138

Sources: American Iron and Steel Institute (AISI); *Census of Manufactures*; The Conference Board.

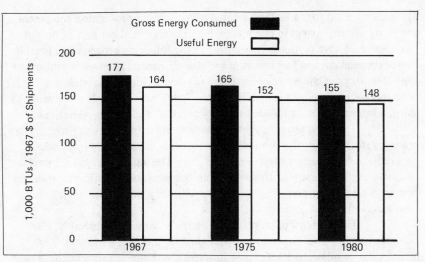

Chart 24-3. Energy Utilization per Unit Shipped—Projections to 1980.

Table 24-6. **Gross Energy Utilization per Ton of Steel Produced—Projections to 1980**

(Million BTUs per short ton of raw steel)

Source of Energy Data	1967	1975	1980
Census Bureau	27.6	26	24
American Iron & Steel Institute	25.3	23	22

Source: Table 24-5; Projections: The Conference Board.

155,000 BTUs, a 1.0% rate when measured on a gross energy consumed basis (Chart 24-3).

Energy utilization per short ton of raw steel produced in 1980, using AISI data, is expected to be 21 million BTUs for useful energy, and 22 million BTUs for gross energy consumed (Chart 24-2 and Table 24-6).

SECTION II. TRENDS IN ENERGY UTILIZATION: 1947-1972

General Remarks About Technological Change and Energy Utilization

During the past fifteen to twenty years, major technological changes have taken place in the steel industry that can be considered revolutionary.

These changes led to markedly increased efficiencies of production equipment and to significant savings in raw materials and energy used per unit of output. Improvements have particularly occurred in the following processes: (1) better charge preparation and fuel injection for blast furnaces; (2) development of the top-blown oxygen converter process; and (3) development of continuous processes for casting, rolling and finishing of steel. New methods of control and automation have been introduced in many areas of steelmaking operations.

The rapid progress in steel production technology was necessary in order for steel to meet the competition from other substantially improved materials, such as plastics, aluminum, and glass. The quality of finished steel products, and the variety of these products, has increased significantly over the past decade as higher performance, greater reliability, and closer tolerances have been achieved.

The capacity of blast furnaces has also grown considerably. For example, in 1960 blast furnaces were designed for a capacity of about 2,000 tons per day, while capacities of new furnaces now being constructed have been increased to as much as 7,000 tons per day. Steel melting furnaces have also become much larger and, with recently installed facilities, output has often increased to four or five times the volume of the early 1960s. Productivity in the rolling mill sector and of pipe-making facilities (for both welded and seamless pipes) has increased sharply.

The major shift in product mix to the production of high-strength, lightweight steels, which took place in recent years, reduced output on a tonnage basis. If steel output is quantified by means of tonnage statistics, which are not adjusted to reflect the changes in product mix, the savings in raw material and energy utilization might be understated. Value of shipments, measured in constant dollars, would also inadequately reflect the change in product mix and might therefore also result in underestimating the decline in energy use per unit of output. The projections of energy savings to 1980, discussed in Section I and Section III of this study, are probably conservative in view of these considerations.

Coke Ovens

(a) **Description of process.**[5] There are basically two types of coke produced: oven coke (made in by-product coke ovens) and "beehive" coke. (The beehive oven took the name from its resemblance to a beehive.) Today, more than 99% of all coke produced is made in by-product coke ovens. These by-product coke plants bake solid bituminous coal until it is porous. This fuel, called coke, is used in blast furnaces to make pig iron. Coke, unlike coal, burns inside as well as outside; it does not fuse into a solid mass and retains its strength under the weight of iron ore and limestone charged with it into blast furnaces.

By-product coke ovens are rather complicated pieces of equipment.

In iron and steel works they are usually located at the blast furnace plant and are part of the blast furnace area. Over the years, there have been some revolutionary changes in various aspects of coke technology. Coking capacity has been increased by making the ovens higher, and by decreasing coking time in the new ovens substantially. At present, coke ovens in the United States iron and steel industry average about 40 feet in length and up to 20 feet in height. Each oven is very narrow, with the width varying from twelve to 22 inches. In a battery of such ovens, the temperature of the coal is raised to about 2,000 degrees Fahrenheit. The heat separates the gas and other by-products. The coke oven gases are captured and passed through a pipe into a recovery plant where tar and other by-products are recovered. Part of the gas is then returned to the coke ovens as fuel for coking new charges of coal. Surplus gas is used as fuel in other operations of the steel plant. Use of the by-products contributed to the development of the fully integrated steel mill.

Coal is loaded into the ovens from the top. Coking time in the new ovens has been decreased substantially. The best time is about twelve hours, against sixteen or eighteen hours for older ovens. Because of larger size and shorter coking time, the new ovens are capable of a 75% to 80% higher coal throughput than the ovens used in the late 1940s. This substantial increase in volume was made possible also through the use of improved refractories that permit higher oven temperatures. In addition, the new ovens have better heating designs that allow for more uniform heating of the charge from bottom to top, and are also automatically controlled. The finished coke is discharged from the side of the oven.

(b) Production of coke, and coal used as raw material. The carbonization of bituminous coal for coke production is at the present time the second largest end-use of this fuel (after electric utilities, which rank first as a consumer of bituminous coal). In 1971,[6] coke producers (including iron and steel industry) charged 83.2 million short tons of bituminous coal into coke ovens. (This was about 1/6 of the total bituminous coal produced in the United States.) An additional 421,000 short tons of anthracite was blended with bituminous coal at oven coke plants and carbonized, chiefly to produce foundry coke (Table 24A-7).

There are three classifications of bituminous coal which are used to manufacture coke: high volatile, medium volatile, and low volatile, depending on the amount of volatile or gaseous material contained in the coal. High volatile coal, which is used most extensively in the production of coke since it constitutes from 65% to 85% of the coke oven burden, has between 29% and 39% volatile matter.

An overall average of 1.45 tons of coal was used for each ton of coke produced in 1971; that is, approximately 2,900 pounds of coal are required to produce one ton (or 2,000 lbs.) of coke. This ratio has changed very little in the past 25 years and the average yield of coke from coal carbonized has varied only between 69% and 70%. However, the quality and uniformity of metallurgical coke have become increasingly important with the improvement in blast furnace burdens and operating practices. Under these conditions, and with the continuing decrease in the amount of coke required to produce a ton of pig iron (see section on Blast Furnaces), small changes in the character of the coke can have a relatively large influence on blast furnace performance. (Breeze is coke that passes through a ½ inch screen and, because of its small size and high ash content, is not suitable for most metallurgical applications, but is used as a fuel to raise steam in many of the integrated iron and steel mills.)

(c) **Use of fuels in coke production.** Coke oven gas is one of the primary co-products in the carbonization of coal in slot ovens. After tar, ammonia, and light oil have been removed from the gaseous streams, coke oven gas remains as the final product. On the average, about 10,500 c.ft. of gas is produced for each ton of coal carbonized at high temperatures in slot ovens, or about 15% of the weight of coal.

Because of its high heat value (500 to 550 BTU/c.ft.) producers recycle a large part of it as fuel for heating coke ovens. In 1971, about 38% of the gas produced was recycled to heat coke ovens. "Surplus" gas is used as source of fuel for the many other fuel consumers in the integrated steel plant. Waste is flared gas (Table 24A-8).

Approximately 3.6 million BTUs are required in the production of one short ton of coke. This represents a slight increase in the energy output ratio from the early 1950s, because of higher oven temperatures required in modern, high-volume coke ovens (Table 24A-9).

The American Iron and Steel Institute publishes data on gases used by iron and steel mills for coke oven underfirings (Table 24A-10). The Institute assumes a heat value of 500 BTU/c.ft. in contrast to the 550 BTU/c.ft. coke oven gas conversion factor used by the Bureau of Mines. The energy required to convert coal into one ton of coke is therefore lower when the estimate is based on Iron and Steel Institute figures. Another reason for the lower energy input per unit of output might be that iron and steel mills are using more modern, and therefore more heat-efficient, coke ovens than those in operation outside the industry. In any case, both the Bureau of Mines and the AISI data based estimates show a slightly increasing energy-output ratio for the period 1967 to 1971, and 1972 respectively.

Blast Furnaces

(a) **Description of process.**[7] The blast furnace performs the first major operation in the steel industry as it transforms iron ore into molten metal. Essentially a tapered, giant cylindrical shell lined with refractory brick, it reduces the iron ore to molten iron and slag. (The resulting metal, free of most of the original impurities, is called *pig iron*.) This is accomplished by introducing three basic materials, iron ore, coke and limestone, at the top of the vertical shaft or stack. These materials, sometimes supplemented with a small amount of scrap, are met as they descend by a rising volume of preheated gas. This gas is formed by the combustion of coke with hot air blown in under pressure through openings at the base of the stack, called tuyeres.

Most of the integrated iron and steel complexes operate ore-processing plants. Crude iron ore, varying in size from dust to boulders and mixed with earth or sand, must be processed before it can be charged into blast furnaces for ironmaking. Ore processing plants are performing different tasks: some ore is simply washed, screened and sorted; some is crushed into fine powder and made into pellets by pellet furnaces; some powdered ore recovered from the blast furnace is mixed in sinter plants with other materials (powdered coal) and agglomerated into porous lumps to be recharged into furnaces. Low grade ore is processed in beneficiating plants to increase its iron content. With the growing use of lower grade ores in the United States, ore beneficiation has become more and more important. Increasing energy requirements in beneficiation may, therefore, partially offset the energy savings achieved in blast furnace operations.

The ore, which is fed into the furnace, contains in addition to iron, small quantities of phosphorus, silica, alumina, manganese and a considerable amount of moisture. In order to remove some of these elements from the ore, limestone is introduced into the blast furnace. At a temperature of over 2,000 degrees Fahrenheit, the limestone combines with the silica, alumina, and part of the manganese in the ore, as well as the ash and the sulphur in the coke, to form a molten mass lighter than iron called slag. The slag is drained off at time intervals through the cinder notches, which are openings in the furnace located a short distance above the tapping hole.

Coke has two purposes in the blast furnace process: (1) to provide carbon for the reduction of the iron oxide, and (2) to provide heat which is necessary to carry out the process.

Air is blown into the furnace at the tuyeres and reacts with the carbon in the coke to form a gas which rises through the descending column of coke, iron ore, and limestone. After a series of chemical reactions, the gas passes off at the furnace top and is then cleaned and used to provide heat required in various sections of the blast furnace and steel plant. (See Figure 24-2, a flow sheet of blast furnace ironmaking.)

Although the blast furnace process has remained basically unchanged, revolutionary technological developments have taken place in the past fifteeen years. Major factors contributing to the increase in blast furnace output were:

(1) Improvement of blast furnace burdens, including the increasing use of beneficiated and washed iron ores with higher iron content and lower rate of impurities.

(2) Operation of large size furnaces with pig iron production up to

BLAST FURNACE IRONMAKING

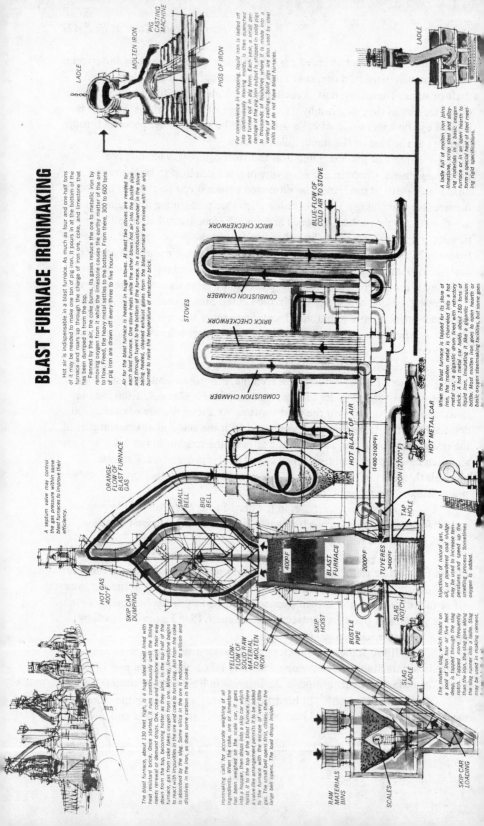

Hot air is indispensable in a blast furnace. As much as four and one-half tons of it may be needed to make one ton of pig iron. It pours in at the bottom of the furnace and roars up through the charge of iron ore, coke, and limestone that has been dumped in from the top.

Fanned by the air that blows through it, its gases reduce the ore to metallic iron by removing oxygen from it while the limestone causes the earthy matter of the ore to flow. Freed, the heavy metal settles to the bottom. From there, 300 to 600 tons of pig iron are drawn off every three to five hours.

Air for the blast furnace is heated in huge stoves. At least two stoves are needed for each blast furnace. One stove heats while the other blows hot air into the bustle pipe and through tuyeres to the bottom of the furnace. In a combustion chamber in the stove being heated, cleaned exhaust gases from the blast furnace are mixed with air and burned to raise the temperature of refractory brick.

For convenience in shipping, liquid iron is tapped off into continuously moving molds, is then quenched and turned out in pig form. Each year, a small percentage of the pig iron output is shipped in solid pigs to thousands of foundries where it is made into a variety of castings. Solid pigs are also used by steel mills that do not have blast furnaces.

A ladle full of molten iron joins limestone, scrap steel and alloying materials. A load of metal is poured into a hot metal car, a gigantic drum lined with refractory brick. A hot metal car holds about 160 tons of liquid iron, insulating it like a gigantic vacuum bottle. Most molten iron goes to open hearth or basic oxygen steelmaking facilities, but some goes

When the blast furnace is tapped for its stove of iron, the molten metal is channeled into a hot metal car, a gigantic drum lined with refractory brick.

A septum valve may control the gas pressure within some blast furnaces to improve their efficiency.

The blast furnace, about 130 feet high, is a huge steel shell lined with heat resistant brick. Once started, it runs continuously until the lining needs renewal or demand drops. Ore, coke and limestone work their way down from the top, becoming hotter as they sink. In the top half of the furnace, gas from burning coke takes oxygen from the iron ore and gets rid of it. The molten iron and slag run down to the bottom of the furnace where the ore is reduced to silicon and dissolves in the iron, as does some carbon in the coke.

Ironmaking calls for accurate weighing of all ingredients. When the coke, ore or limestone has been weighed on the scale car, it goes into a hopper, then drops into a skip car which hoists it to the top of the blast furnace. Here a valve-like arrangement permits it to be added to the furnace with the loss of very little gas. The small bell opens first, closes, then the large bell drops inside. The load drops inside.

The molten slag, which floats on a pool of iron four or five feet deep, is tapped through the slag notch. Tapped more frequently than the iron, the slag goes along the slag runner into a ladle. Slag may be used in making cement,

Injections of natural gas, oil, or powdered coal sludge may be used to increase temperatures and speed up the smelting process. Sometimes oxygen is added.

LADLE
MOLTEN IRON
PIG CASTING MACHINE
PIGS OF IRON
LADLE

BLUE-FLOW OF COLD AIR TO STOVE
BRICK CHECKERWORK
COMBUSTION CHAMBER
BRICK CHECKERWORK
COMBUSTION CHAMBER
STOVES

HOT GAS 400°F
ORANGE-FLOW OF BLAST FURNACE GAS
SKIP CAR DUMPING
SMALL BELL
BIG BELL

HOT BLAST OF AIR
HOT METAL CAR
IRON (2700°F)
(1400-2100°F)
TAP HOLE
BLAST FURNACE
400°F
2000°F
TUYERES 3400°F
BUSTLE PIPE
SLAG NOTCH
SKIP HOIST
SLAG LADLE

YELLOW-FLOW OF SOLID RAW MATERIAL TO MOLTEN IRON

RAW MATERIALS BINS
SCALES
SKIP CAR LOADING

7,000 tons per day, compared with average capacities of 2,000 tons per day in the early 1960s. Since 1971, two giant furnaces with capacities of up to 10,000 tons per day have been constructed in the United States.

(3) Injection of hydrocarbons (natural gas and oil), together with oxygen enrichment of the furnace blast and the use of higher operating pressures, have also increased the output and tended to lower furnace costs by partially replacing coke, a more expensive input.

(4) Improvements in refractories have made higher blast temperatures possible, to 2,000 degrees Fahrenheit, and extended periods between relining of furnace walls.

(5) Widespread use of instrumentation, and more precise methods of furnace control as well as improvements in auxiliary equipment.

(b) Production of pig iron and energy utilized. The coke rate, or the amount of coke required to produce one ton of pig iron, has been drastically reduced over the years. The reduction in the coke rate was possible through (a) improved ore charges, (b) higher blast temperatures, (c) fuel injection (natural gas, oil and tar), and (d) oxygen enrichment of the blast. (Coke rates for selected years and corresponding coal requirements are shown in the following tabulation.)

Lbs. Used per Short Ton of Pig Iron

Year	Coking Coal	Coke
1913	3,247	2,173
1947	2,755	1,926
1967	1,850	1,290
1969	1,816	1,260
1971	1,827	1,260
1972	1,780	1,230
1980 Projected	1,450	1,000

Chart 24.4 shows how coke utilization per short ton of pig iron has decreased, particularly since the mid-1950s.

The American Iron and Steel Institute summarizes the utilization of fuel at blast furnaces (Table 24A-11). Converting the fuel used at blast furnaces into BTU equivalent, and relating it to blast furnace production, the energy-output ratio in 1972 was 18.4 million BTU/short ton. The energy-output ratio has not changed significantly in the period 1967 to 1972. A reduction in the coke rate was partly offset by higher inputs of fuel oil and of tar. Comparable data for the period prior to 1967 are not available.

The reduction in coke rates, effected by burden beneficiation and higher hot blast temperatures, has reduced the BTU content of blast furnace gas from about 95 BTU/c.ft. to 85 BTU/c.ft., requiring at times the addition of

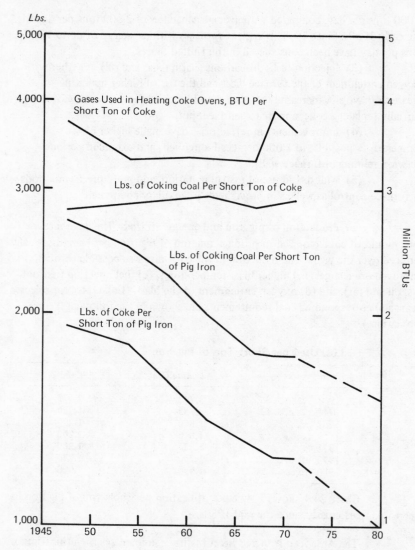

Chart 24-4. Utilization of Coke in Production of Pig Iron, 1947–1971. Source (historic data): Bureau of Mines, *Minerals Yearbook.*

natural gas to the blast furnace gas when it is used to heat the blast furnace stoves. Coke oven gas is also used to heat blast furnace stoves.

An estimate of fuels required in blast furnace operation was published in a study, "Reference Energy Systems and Resource Data for Use in the Assessment of Energy Technologies," submitted to the Office of Science and

Technology, Executive Office of the President, by Associated Universities Inc., Upton, New York, in April 1972. This estimate of total fuel demand by blast furnaces can be compared with data available from the American Iron and Steel Institute. Both estimates arrive at a 1969 total fuel demand in blast furnace operations of about 2,400 trillion BTUs (based on 95.5 million tons output).

Blast Furnaces (trillion BTUs)	1969 Estimates by:	
	AISI	Associated Universities
Coke	1,565	
Coal equivalent	2,177	2,291
Fuel oil	16	20
Tar & pitch	6	n.a.
Gas	215	51
Electricity	n.a.*	40
Total	2,414	2,402
Million BTU/short ton of pig iron**	25	25

*AISA reports consumption of electric power in total for all iron and steel mills and not broken down by use in blast furnace or other operations.
**Based on pig iron production of 95.5 million short tons.

(c) **Future developments.** The alternative to blast furnace expansion would be the installation of direct reduction plants. Various methods of direct reduction of iron ore are now being developed, and the future of the blast furnace will depend on the success achieved by these processes. Several of the direct reduction processes are now under active consideration and, in a few special situations, may be preferable to the conventional blast furnace process. Probably the most likely challenge to the blast furnace, which may well grow in importance during the next decade, is the use of prereduced pellets directly in steelmaking furnaces, thus bypassing the blast furnace completely.

The economics involved in the future of the blast furnace-basic oxygen furnace method of steelmaking were compared with the direct reduction-electric furnace production in a recently published engineering study.[8] According to this study, the blast furnace seems to have the highest economic advantage when producing about 3 million tons per year or more of hot metal. Under coke and electricity costs prevailing at the present time, and assuming that coke continues to be available, the blast furnace is expected to remain as the principal hot-metal-producing process in all major steel-producing countries for the next two or three decades. In the United States, the rapidly increasing price and decreasing availability of natural gas might defer, or possibly even prevent, the change from blast furnace operations to direct reduction processes.

Steel Melting Furnaces
a. Description of Major Processes

Innovation of new processes has affected steel melting more than any other operation of the iron and steel industry. The most significant development over the past fifteen years has been the gradual replacement of conventional open-hearth steelmaking by the basic oxygen process (BOF).

There are three major processes by which raw steel is produced: Open-Hearth, Basic Oxygen (BOF) and Electric. At the present time, more than 56% of raw steel produced in the United States is made in basic oxygen furnaces although it was only in the mid-1950s that the BOF process was introduced on a commercial scale (Table 24A-12).

The *open-hearth* and the Bessemer processes are the oldest used in steelmaking. The open-hearth furnace is so named because the steelmaking process takes place in a large rectangular structure lined with brick containing a shallow basin or "hearth" into which limestone, scrap steel, and molten iron are charged. The charge is exposed to a sweep of fuel flames. The fuel is introduced through an opening at the end of the furnace. The open-hearth makes use of the regenerative process whereby the heated gases are passed through bricks arranged with openings in the form of a checkerboard which are called "checkers." During the passage, the gases on their way to the stack transfer most of the heat to the brick work. After a short time, the gas fuel is shut off on one end of the furnace and introduced at the other end, having first been forced through the heated checkers. The name "open-hearth" was most probably derived from the fact that the steel, though melted in a shallow hearth enclosed by a roof and walls, was accessible through the furnace doors for test and inspection. A fairly typical furnace that produces 250 tons of steel in five to eight hours may be about 90 feet long and 30 feet wide. When tests of samples show that the steel is of the specified chemistry, the tap hole is opened by an explosive charge and the steel is poured into a ladle. With the advent of the basic oxygen furnace, the importance of open-hearth steelmaking began to decline although open-hearth technology has also been significantly improved. Introduction of oxygen, faster charging, high firing rates, and the use of supplementary fuel with oxy-fuel lances have increased output rates at low additional cost. The last open-hearth furnace was built in 1960, and before 1980 open-hearth steel will drop to third place (flow chart, Figure 24-3).

The *electric* furnace has been used in the past mostly for the production of alloy steels, but in the last decade electric furnaces also became economical in the production of standard steels. Output increased from 9 million short tons in 1962 to almost 24 million in 1972. The largest operating electric furnace in the United States has a capacity of 400 tons per heat. The electric furnace can use a 100% cold scrap charge and/or reduced materials to bypass the use of hot metal. Electric furnaces are therefore very flexible and are

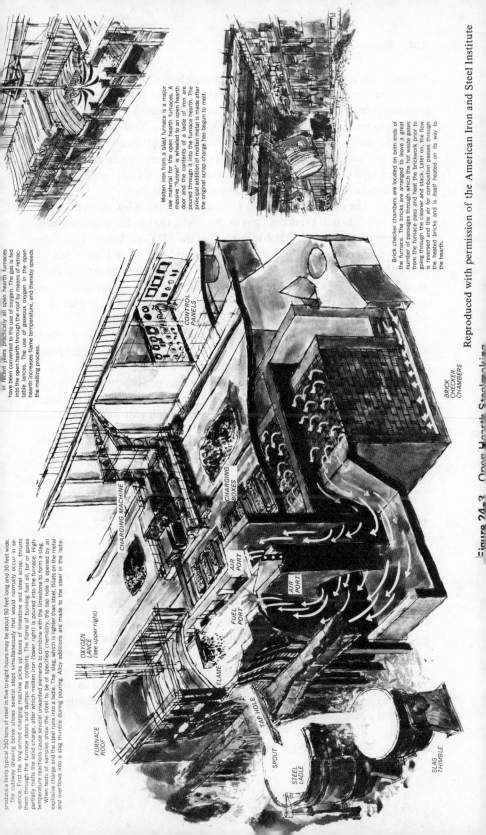

produce a fairly typical 350 tons of steel in five to eight hours.

The cutaway drawing below shows several steps simultaneously that would normally occur in sequence. First the long-armed charging machine picks up boxes of limestone and steel scrap, thrusts them through the furnace doors and dumps the contents. The flame of burning fuel oil, tar or gases partially melts the solid charge, after which molten iron (lower right) is poured into the furnace. High-temperature reactions cause several unwanted elements to combine with the limestone to form a slag.

When tests of samples show the steel to be of specified chemistry, the tap hole is opened by an explosive charge and the steel runs into a ladle. The slag, which is lighter than steel, floats on the metal and overflows into a slag thimble during pouring. Alloy additions are made to the steel in the ladle.

In recent years practically all open hearth furnaces have been converted to the use of oxygen. The gas is fed into the open hearth through the roof by means of retractable lances. The use of gaseous oxygen in the open hearth increases flame temperature, and thereby speeds the melting process.

Molten iron from a blast furnace is a major raw material for the open hearth furnaces. A massive "turnel" is wheeled to an open hearth door and the contents of a ladle of iron are poured through a door into the furnace hearth. The principal addition of molten metal is made after the original scrap charge has begun to melt.

Brick checker chambers are located on both ends of the furnace. The bricks are arranged to leave a great number of passages through which the hot waste gases from the furnace pass and heat the brickwork prior to going through the cleaner and stack. Later on, the flow is reversed and the air for combustion passes through the heated bricks and is itself heated on its way to the hearth.

FURNACE ROOF

OXYGEN LANCE (see upper right)

CHARGING MACHINE

CONTROL PANELS

CHARGING BOXES

AIR PORT

AIR PORT

FUEL PORT

FLAME

BRICK CHECKER CHAMBERS

TAP HOLE

SPOUT

STEEL LADLE

SLAG THIMBLE

Figure 24-3. Open Hearth Steelmaking

Reproduced with permission of the American Iron and Steel Institute

at present the most efficient and lowest cost melter of scrap iron and steel. The electric furnace provides a source of heat that does not contain impurities, and therefore impurities are not imparted to steel in the melting process. This fact, in addition to mechanical and electrical improvements in furnace design and operation, results in the production of consistently high-quality electric steel. Electric furnaces are also ideal for small-scale producers who do not have hot-metal facilities, and for larger steelmaking plants that can use this process to take advantage of the scrap market (flow chart, Figure 24-4).

The development of the *basic oxygen* furnace was one of the greatest technological breakthroughs in the steel industry. Early development work done in Austria in the 1940s resulted in the LD (Linz-Donawitz) process, which became commercial by 1953 and was introduced in the United States steel industry in the middle 1950s. After 1958, it became apparent that the oxygen steelmaking process would be acceptable for many grades of steel, and that—because of its potential advantages in low installation costs as well as operating costs—it would be the steelmaking process of the future.

The basic oxygen furnace is a pear-shaped converter that is tilted to receive the scrap and hot metal charge. It is then placed into an upright position, an oxygen lance is lowered into the converter from the top and placed at a distance of about 6 ft. above the metal, from which position it pours out 1,700 to 1,800 c. ft. of oxygen for each ton of steel produced. The injection of high purity oxygen into the converter results in a significant reduction in process time per heat:

Tap to tap time BOF . . . . 45 minutes
Tap to tap time open-hearth (using oxygen) . . . . 6½-7 hours
Tap to tap time open-hearth (without oxygen) . . . . 10-12 hours

The average length of time during which oxygen is blown is 22-24 minutes.

The converter size has increased substantially over the years. In 1954, capacity was about 35 tons per heat, in 1960, 300 tons, and in 1967, 325 tons. The average heat size in 1970 in the United States was 200 tons. A converter with a heat size of 200 tons can produce 6,400 tons per day as compared with a maximum of 1,800 tons per day from the 40-ton basic Bessemer converter normally used some years ago. An open-hearth shop (10-14 furnaces) equals approximately the output of a 2 or 3 BOF shop.

Basic oxygen furnaces use 25% to 35% scrap with 75% to 65% of hot metal, depending on the particular charge. Preheating or premelting of scrap permits a higher scrap charge than the standard 30% and may lead to cost savings depending on the relationship of scrap cost to hot metal cost. Computer-controlled operations make it possible to meet exact specifications of the end product.

The basic oxygen process is also more efficient in energy

STEELMAKING

A long-deserved reputation for producing alloy, stainless, tool, and other specialty steels belongs to America's electric furnaces. Operators have also learned to make larger heats of carbon steels in these furnaces; this development helps account for the record tonnage outputs of recent years.

The heat within the electric furnace is intense and rigidly controlled. Modern electric furnaces have top sections that can be moved away so that special containers can charge scrap into them from above. Sometimes pig iron is also charged and prereduced iron ore, in various forms, is rich enough in iron to be used as an electric furnace steelmaking charge.

Pure oxygen may be injected to speed up carbon removal from the molten metal.

CHARGING BOX

Limestone and flux are charged on top of the molten bath. Through a chemical interaction, impurities in the steel rise into the molten slag, which floats on top of the metal. The furnace is tilted slightly and the slag is raked off. Electric furnace steel can be made either with single-slag or a double-slag practice. In the double-slag method, an oxidizing slag is first formed, raked off, and a reducing slag formed.

SLAG

Alloying elements, which come from many parts of the world, are usually added to the molten steel in the form of ferroalloys. Typical elements include chromium from Brazil, tungsten from the Philippines, nickel from Canada, and cobalt from Africa.

LADLE

When the chemical composition of the steel meets specifications, the furnace tilts forward so that molten metal may pour out through the spout. The slag comes after the steel and serves as an insulating blanket during tapping.

ELECTROMAGNET

Steel scrap may vary widely in quality. It is carefully sorted and weighed before it goes to the electric furnace.

STEEL SCRAP

With its carbon electrodes attached to electrical cables, this electric furnace is shown mounted on 'rockers' so that it can be tilted toward the tapping spout, through which molten steel emerges.

The electrodes are lowered through the roof of the furnace and the electric power is turned on. The current in an electric furnace arcs from one electrode to the metallic charge and from the charge to the next electrode.

ELECTRODES

The entire top of an electric furnace may swing to the side, electrodes and all, so that a charging basket of steel scrap may be lowered into the furnace. The bottom of the basket is opened, thus charging the furnace.

CHARGING BASKET

DOOR

TAPPING SPOUT

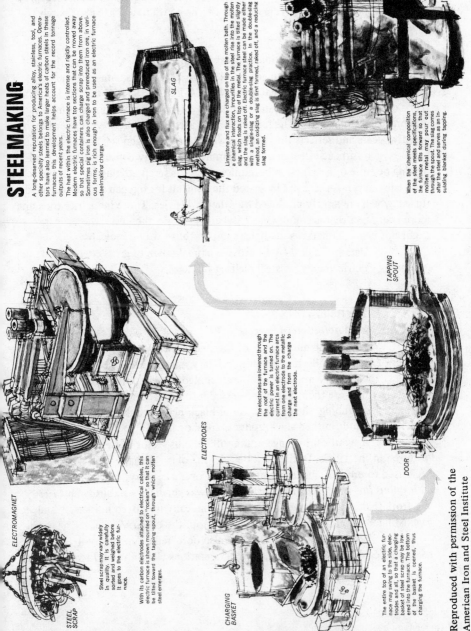

Reproduced with permission of the American Iron and Steel Institute

Figure 24-4. Electric Furnace Steelmaking.

consumption than the open-hearth process as the oxidation reactions in the process provide the source of heat for melting the scrap charge. (Flow chart, Figure 24-5.)

Over the next decade, the basic oxygen furnace is expected to replace essentially the older and less efficient open-hearth installations throughout the world. The advent of the very efficient BOF for steelmaking has partly reduced the incentive for the development of new steelmaking processes. Nevertheless, development work is under way and some of these methods (spray steelmaking, IRSID method) are intended to be continuous instead of batch processes.

b. Energy Utilization in Steel Melting

The American Iron and Steel Institute provides data on fuel utilization in steel melting furnaces (Table 24A-13). In 1972, about 0.85 million BTUs of melting fuel were required per short ton of raw steel, down from 1.7 million BTU/ton in 1967. The rate of decline averaged 13% per year over the past five years and reflects the rapid growth in basic oxygen steelmaking. The basic oxygen furnace effected a reduction in total energy consumption in steelmaking because of a reduction in requirements for scrap melting fuels. However, the basic oxygen furnace has increased the demand for oxygen and for calcined fluxes, which are largely produced by other industries. Those industries consume more energy on that account. On a total energy basis, therefore, the savings might not be as dramatic as the figures shown above would indicate.

Data in Table 24A-14 provide a breakdown of gross energy used (including electric energy) in steel melting furnaces.

The Rolling Mills Sector
a. Description of Process[9]

The rolling mills sector of the steel industry is composed of a number of types of mills ranging from primary mills to the various finishing facilities. The primary mills reduce the steel ingots to blooms, slabs, billets, and sheet bars which are then further processed into finished steel products such as rails, pipes and tubing, sheets, wire, tin or black plate, etc. Net shipments of semi-finished and finished steel products are shown in Table 24A-16.

A significant change in the rolling mills sector of the steel industry occurred in the 1920s. During that decade, the old style hand mill, which had been used to produce sheet and tin plate for over a century, was replaced by the *continuous hot strip mill*. The hot strip mill was generally established by 1930, and from that time on, larger, faster and technically improved units were added to existing installations in steel mills throughout the country.

However, in the 1930s there also occurred a fundamental technological breakthrough in sheet mill operations when the *cold reduction*

This schematic drawing of a BOF facility shows the emphasis the steel industry places on air quality control. A hood over the furnace catches the dirty waste gases from the steelmaking process. The gases are conducted to air treatment facilities which occupy most of the space to the left of the crane-held ladle in the diagram.

enormously from small beginnings during the middle 1950's. The high tonnage of steel now made in basic oxygen furnaces—commonly called BOF's—requires the consumption of large amounts of oxygen to provide operational heat and to promote the necessary chemical changes. No other gases or fuels are used.

The basic oxygen process produces steel very quickly compared with the other major methods now in use. For example, a BOF may produce up to 300-ton batches in 45 minutes as against 5 to 8 hours for the older open hearth process. Most grades of steel can be produced in the refractory-lined, pear-shaped furnaces.

During the oxygen blow, lime is added as an essential ingredient. Most of the impurities leave the furnace as a floating layer of slag. Lime is consumed at a rate of about 150 pounds per ton of raw steel produced.

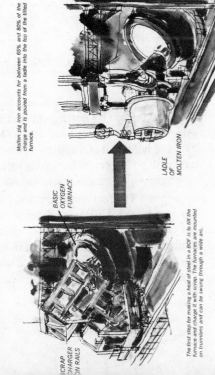

ALLOY
ADDITION

LADLE OF MOLTEN STEEL

TAP
HOLE

After steel has been refined, the furnace is tilted and molten steel pours into a ladle. Alloy additions are made into the ladle.

Oxygen combines with carbon and other unwanted elements, eliminating these impurities from the molten charge and converting it to steel.

OXYGEN
LANCE

REFRACTORY
LINING

STEEL
SHELL

The furnace is returned to upright position. A water cooled oxygen lance is lowered into the furnace and high purity oxygen is blown onto the top of the metal at supersonic speed.

Molten pig iron accounts for between 65% and 80% of the charge and is poured from a ladle into the top of the tilted furnace.

LADLE
OF
MOLTEN IRON

The principal material used in manufacturing steel by the basic oxygen process is molten iron. Therefore, most BOF facilities are built near blast furnaces. Some scrap steel is used in the process. Oxygen producing facilities are usually built in the same plant.

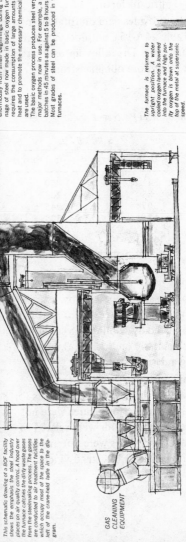

GAS
CLEANING
EQUIPMENT

BASIC OXYGEN FURNACE

SCRAP
CHARGER
ON RAILS

The first step for making a heat of steel in a BOF is to tilt the furnace and charge it with scrap. The furnaces are mounted on trunnions and can be swung through a wide arc.

Reproduced with permission of the American Iron and Steel Institute

process was introduced. In this process a long cold strip form is fed through a series of rolls at room temperature, and by means of great pressure and tension between the stands the strip is reduced by as much as 50% to 75% in thickness.

Major efficiencies in rolling and finishing have been achieved during the 1960s. Improvements in productivity were mainly brought about through increases in rolling speed, automation, and other rationalization measures. New rolling mills for the hot rolling of wide strip are designed for an output of as much as 4.5 million tons per year. Cold rolling mills are now reaching an output of one million tons per year. The latest units for the production of drawn wire will produce more than 400 thousand tons per year.

b. Energy Utilization in Rolling and Finishing

The rolling and finishing sectors of the integrated steel mill are highly energy-intensive, with electricity being a significant factor.

The American Iron and Steel Institute provides data on total use of electric energy by the iron and steel industry (Table 24A-15), but does not give a breakdown of electricity used by major operating areas. The following estimates of electric energy utilization in rolling mills were therefore obtained from industry sources:

Use of Electric Energy per Short Ton of Steel Processed

Process	kwh	1,000 BTUs Useful Energy	Gross Energy
Hot strip mill	100	341	1,050
Slab mill	25	85	263
Plate mill (large)	90	307	945
(small)	50	171	525
Cold reduction mill	100	341	1,050
Rod mill (high speed, 5,000 ft/minute)	275	938	2,889

The American Iron and Steel Institute, however, publishes data on fuel consumption by heating and annealing furnaces, and by heating ovens for wire rods (Tables 24A-17 and 24A-18). Annealing furnaces are used for heating steel and holding it at a suitable temperature, followed by cooling at a suitable rate, with the object of improving softness, machinability and coldworking properties, or of removing stresses and obtaining a desired structure.

The fuel consumption by heating and annealing furnaces (as reported by the AISI) was related to net shipments of finished steel products for the years 1967 and 1969 to 1972 as corresponding production figures were not available. Likewise, the fuels used in heating ovens for wire rods were related to the net shipments of wire rods plus wire as production figures were not available. The energy utilization to net shipments ratios show a slight but steady increase for heating and annealing furnaces over the years to 1972. The ratios for wire rod ovens have not shown a consistent change over the past years.

Continuous Casting

A major technological change affecting primary mills is taking place at the present time. The *continuous casting process* bypasses several steps in steel-making as it eliminates the pouring of steel into ingot molds, stripping the molds from the ingots, placing the ingots into soaking pits to develop an even temperature, and finally, the primary rolling stage by which the ingot is rolled down into semi-finished forms, such as slabs, or blooms and billets. In the continuous casting process the steel is tapped from the furnace into a ladle and then poured directly from the ladle into the continuous caster. It solidifies as it passes through and emerges as a semi-finished form. Although the process eliminates several intermediate steps, the initial capital outlays for continuous casting units are substantial. However, there would be a major saving in operating costs. By the early 1970s, practically all of the large steel companies in the United States had some type of continuous casting unit in operation. Approximately 18 million tons of steel were processed by continuous casting in 1972. Although the advantages of the continuous casting techniques are questioned from time to time, the process seems to be gaining ever wider acceptance.

a. Energy Utilization in Continuous Casting

During the 1970s, continuous casting might become the single most important energy-saving innovation in the steel industry. The potential savings of energy are estimated at 1.3 million BTUs per ton, or at 5.2% of total energy used (25 million BTUs) to produce one ton of raw steel in 1972. As the initial capital requirements for the installation of continuous casting units are substantial, major projects might be deferred, however, because of shortage of capital. There is a time lag of approximately eighteen months between planning and operation of a continuous casting unit.

SECTION III.   PROJECTIONS TO 1980

Demand for Steel

The projections to 1980 of demand for steel in the United States were partly based on the results obtained from an econometric forecasting model of the United States economy, and partly on information received from the industry.

(1) The INFORUM input-output model of the University of Maryland provides projections of demand for iron and steel products (SIC 331, 332, 3391, and 3399). According to these projections, in the period 1967 to

1980, the demand for steel products in the United States will grow at 2.4% per year.

(2) Industry forecasts indicate that the demand for raw steel in the United States will increase to 155 million short tons in 1975, and to 175 million short tons in 1980, up from 127 million tons in 1967. The average annual growth rate from 1967 to 1980 would be 2.5%. (These long-term trend projections are, of course, disregarding any cyclical swings in the economy which might affect demand in any one specific year.)

The comparatively high growth rate in steel demand projected for the 13-year period, 1967 to 1980, by both the INFORUM model and the industry, seems to be reasonable. Major steel consuming sectors of the economy are foreseen to expand rapidly during the second half of the 1970s. The construction industry, in particular, will require a large volume of steel for building and improving mass-transit facilities in big cities, for elevated (double-deck) highways, for pipelines for the oil and gas industry, for port facilities, and for major industrial projects connected with increasing the supply of energy. Competition from alternate materials, such as aluminum, plastics, glass, etc., particularly in industries such as automobiles and packaging, will remain keen but will also provide the incentive for a series of new developments throughout the iron and steel industry. New products with improved characteristics have been designed to better meet the users' needs at prices competitive with other materials. The application and usefulness of steel, and the markets for the product, seem to be expanding fairly rapidly, and seem to justify the expected growth in demand to 175 million short tons by 1980.

Demand for Energy

The projections of demand for energy by the iron and steel industry (SIC 3312) are presented in Table 24-5 (in Section I) of this report, and the energy-output ratios per short ton of raw steel produced in Table 24-6.

These projections were based on the assumption that energy utilization per short ton of raw steel produced will continue to decline at a long-term rate of 0.9% to 1.1% per year. Further significant improvements before 1980 in energy-output ratios are expected to occur in:

(1) Blast furnace operations (through prereduction of iron ores, the use of high-quality pellets and self-fluxing sinter, as well as the use of hydrocarbon injection into the furnace which by 1980 might reduce the coke rate to 1,000 pounds per short ton of pig iron from 1,230 pounds average at the present time);

(2) Steel melting operations (as the basic oxygen process will account for a continuously increasing proportion of total U.S. steel production, and the use of oxygen in the open-hearth furnace will reduce its process time); and

(3) Continuous casting operations (which bypass several intermediate steps in steelmaking).

In 1972, according to data available from the industry, a vertically integrated iron and steel mill in the United States utilized an average of 25 million BTUs (gross basis) per short ton of raw steel produced. Table 24-7 provides a rough approximation of the gross energy utilized by each of the major operating areas.

Industry sources estimate that, between 1972 and 1980, energy requirements could be reduced by 2 million BTUs per ton of raw steel. Over the 8-year period, potential energy savings per ton would therefore amount to 8%, or about 1% per year. (See Table 24-7.)

In the *blast furnace* area (including agglomeration and coke plants) the overall savings would amount to about 5%-6%. There will be some improvement in blast temperatures, but increasing energy requirements for agglomerating a higher percentage of lower grade ores. Environmental control will increase energy requirements.

In *steel melting* the overall savings are estimated at 5%-10%. The increased output of BOF steel will reduce energy requirements, but additional electric furnace steel will partially offset this reduction when energy is measured on a gross basis.

In *steel processing* the overall savings are estimated at 10%. Some energy savings will be achieved through continuous casting, and some through additional waste heat recovery, as higher relative energy cost will justify increased capital expenditures. Energy savings, however, will be partially offset by increasing environmental control requirements and increasing process requirements.

These estimates might appear conservative in view of the steel-

Table 24-7. Gross Energy Utilization in an Integrated Iron and Steel Plant, 1972

(million BTUs per short ton of raw steel)

	Approximate Utilization 1972 Average	*Potential Savings by 1980*
Blast furnaces, coke plant and agglomerating, minus surplus coke oven gas and blast furnace gas to other operations Net	12.4	−.74
Steel melting furnaces (OH, BOF, electric)	2.2	−.22
Steel processing to final mill products	10.4	−1.04
Gross energy utilization, 1972	25.0	−2.00
Approximate utilization, 1980	23.00	

making experience in some foreign countries and of technological changes now in progress in the United States. However, seven to eight years do not provide enough lead time to effect major additions to existing facilities. It is therefore unlikely that by 1980 substantially larger savings could be achieved than the 8% or 9% shown in the above estimate.

Notes

[1] American Iron and Steel Institute, *Steel Making Flow Charts*, Washington, D. C., 1972.

[2] The volume in 1973 was approximately 150 million tons.

[3] It is believed that the Census estimates are higher for three reasons: (a) The Census statistics report purchases of gas, which include natural gas and manufactured gas, in total as measured in cubic feet. The heat content of natural gas, however, is almost twice that of gas manufactured from coal: 1,035 BTU/c. ft. against 550 BTU/c. ft. The Census data might therefore lead to overestimating the BTU content of gas purchased by iron and steel mills. (b) The Census statistics include purchases of gasoline, diesel oil, etc., which are apparently used for transportation. It seems that fuels consumed in transportation are not included in the AISI data. (c) Merchant coke ovens are included in Census statistics but not in AISI data. The Census and AISI estimates might also differ for a fourth reason which might increase or narrow the gap between the two sets of data. The Census statistics report the dollar cost of "undistributed fuels," that is, of "other" fuels and fuels "not specified by kind." The conversion factors used might not adequately measure either the heat content or the mix of these fuels included in the "undistributed" category.

[4] The purchase of coal from coal mines to produce coke in the integrated mills is, according to Census Bureau definition, considered the purchase of a raw material.

[5] The description of process is based on Wm. T. Hogan, *Economic History of the Iron & Steel Industry*, 1971 (five volumes).

[6] Source: Bureau of Mines, *Minerals Yearbook*, 1970, and *Mineral Industry Survey*, Coke and Coal Chemicals in 1971.

[7] The description of process is based on Hogan, *op. cit.*

[8] Cartwright, W. F., *The Economic Survival of the Blast Furnace*, Journal of the Iron & Steel Institute, February 1971, pp. 89-95.

[9] Based on Hogan, *op. cit.*

SECTION IV. APPENDIX

Table 24A-1. Production and Shipments of the Iron and Steel Industry

Year	Production of Pig Iron (million short tons)	Production of Raw Steel (million short tons)	Shipments at 1967 Prices (billion dollars)	Volume Index (1967 = 100)
1947 ...	58.3*	59.3**	84.9	n.c.	n.c.
1954 ...	58.0	58.7	88.3	14.5	73.9
1958 ...	57.2	57.8	85.3	13.5	68.9
1962 ...	65.6	66.3	98.3	15.7	86.2
1967 ...	87.0	87.6	127.2	19.6	100.0
1969 ...	95.0	95.5	141.3	22.2	110.9
1970 ...	91.4	91.8	131.5	20.9	106.8
1971 ...	81.3	81.7	120.4	18.8	95.9
1972 ...	88.9	89.4	133.2	21.0	106.9

*Excluding ferro alloys.
**Including ferro alloys.
n.c.—not comparable.
Sources: American Iron and Steel Institute, *Annual Statistical Reports*; Bureau of the Census, *Census of Manufactures*.

Table 24A-2. Census Data: Energy Utilization 1958-1971, by Major Energy Source, Physical Units

Energy Source	1958	1962	1967	1971
Purchased				
Coal, million short tons	6.741	6.899	5.719	5.085
Coke, million short tons	11.282	14.011	11.017	10.240
Petroleum, million bbls.	36.332	34.394	30.894	27.780
Gas, billion cu.ft.	361.270	595.441	722.566	632.800
Other fuels, million dollars	13.5	15.7	19.4	41.2
Fuels n.s.k., million dollars	2.1	n.a.	18.9	3.7
Electric energy, billion kwh	16.350	22.595	34.795	46.5*
Captive				
Coke & breeze, million short tons ..	36.221	38.194	47.542	n.a.
Blast furnace gas, billion cu. ft.	4,224.600	3,703.200	4,850.800	n.a.
Coke oven gas, billion cu. ft.	614.000	553.400	765.700	n.a.

*Estimated on basis of total energy purchased.
n.a.—not available.
n.s.k.—not specified by kind.
Sources: Bureau of the Census, *Census of Manufactures, Fuels and Electric Energy Consumed*, 1958, 1967. (1962 data are from *Annual Survey of Manufactures* and 1971 data are preliminary.)

Table 24A-3.   Census Data: Energy Utilization 1958-1971, by Major Energy Source, BTUs

(trillion BTUs)

Energy Source	1958	1962	1967	1971
Useful energy	2,423	2,768	3,223	n.a.
Purchased	1,143	1,471	1,566	1,472
Coal	174	178	148	131
Coke	293	364	286	266
Petroleum	211	200	179	161
Gas	374	616	748	655
Other fuels*	30	36	44	93
Fuels, n.s.k.**	5	n.a.	43	8
Electric energy	56	77	119	158
Captive consumption	1,280	1,297	1,657	n.a.
Coke & breeze	942	993	1,236	n.a.
Blast furnace & coke .... oven gas***	338	304	421	n.a.
Gross energy	2,548	2,930	3,467	n.a.
Purchased	1,268	1,633	1,810	1,802
Captive consumption	1,280	1,297	1,657	n.a.

Estimates based on Bureau of the Census data.

*Includes gasoline, LPG, wood and purchased steam.

**Fuels not specified by kind.

***Blast furnace gas is a coke by-product and included in the coke energy.

n.a.—not available.

Table 24A-4. AISI Data: Energy Utilization 1947-1972, by Major Energy Source, Physical Units

Energy Source	1947	1954	1958	1962	1967	1969	1971	1972
Coal, million short tons*	12.088	6.441	7.158	6.994	6.878	5.893	4.627	4.363
Coke, million short tons	57.758	52.518	47.818	46.724	56.435	60.424	51.745	54.832
Electric, billion kwh**	11.811	16.373	15.934	21.229	30.557	36.691	37.481	39.358
Fuel oil, billion gal.	2.168	1.798	1.607	1.418	1.254	1.238	1.112	1.313
Tar and pitch, billion gal.	.266	.309	.309	.284	.303	.264	.171	.232
LPG, billion gal.	n.a.	.008	.008	.008	.015	.015	.016	.015
Natural gas, billion cu. ft.	148.936	213.703	278.700	434.491	534.461	634.520	603.473	636.104
Coke oven gas, billion cu. ft.	720.612***	660.654	675.158	690.467	886.228	915.641	872.783	916.643
Blast furnace gas, billion cu. ft.	2,775.942	2,757.857	2,720.164	3,123.893	4,131.003	4,757.049	4,075.469	4,240.908

*Coal used in production of steam and for other purposes, but *not* used in production of coke.

**Purchased electric energy.

***Blast furnace gas is a coke by-product and included in the coke energy. Data for the years 1947, 1954, 1958, and 1962 are estimated on basis of pig iron production.

Source: American Iron and Steel Institute, *Annual Statistical Reports*, various volumes.

**Table 24A-5.   AISI Data: Energy Utilization 1947-1972, BTUs
Useful Energy and Gross Energy Consumed
(trillion BTUs)**

*Energy Source**	*1947*	*1954*	*1958*	*1962*	*1967*	*1969*	*1971*	*1972*
Useful energy	2,741	2,465	2,409	2,535	3,007	3,218	2,878	3,050
Coal**	312	166	185	180	178	152	119	113
Coke***	1,502	1,366	1,243	1,215	1,467	1,571	1,345	1,426
Electric****	40	56	54	72	104	125	128	134
Fuel oil	299	248	222	196	173	171	154	181
Tar and pitch	38	44	44	41	43	38	25	33
LPG	n.a.	1	1	1	1	1	2	2
Natural gas	154	221	289	450	553	657	625	657
Coke oven gas	396	363	371	380	488	503	480	504
Gross energy consumed ..	2,845	2,608	2,532	2,687	3,222	3,478	3,144	3,330
Electric	184	199	177	224	319	385	394	413

Estimates based on American Iron and Steel Institute data.

*In addition to energy shown here, the steel industry purchased in 1972 about 89% of its oxygen supply. Energy required to produce oxygen is discussed in Chapter Eleven, "Industrial Gases".

**Coal used in production of steam and for other purposes but *not* used in production of coke. In the latter case, coal is considered a raw material while coke is considered a fuel.

***Blast furnace gas is a coke by-product and included in the coke energy.

****Purchased electric energy. (Useful energy at 3,412 BTU/kwh.)

**Table 24A-6.   U.S. Manufacturing Industry—Total Cost of Purchased
Fuels and Electric Energy
(million current $)**

Industry	*1958*		*1962*		*1967*		*1971**	
	Mil.$	*%*	*Mil. $*	*%*	*Mil. $*	*%*	*Mil. $*	*%*
All manufacturing .	5,067.0	100.0	6,184.1	100.0	7,691.7	100.0	5,360.6	100.0
SIC 33	1,113.3	22.0	1,379.8	22.3	1,635.7	21.3	1,151.4	21.5
SIC 3312	676.2	13.3	809.4	13.1	877.3	11.4	741.7	13.8

*Excluding electric energy.

Sources: Bureau of the Census, *Census of Manufactures, Fuels and Electric Energy Consumed, 1958, 1967.* (1962 data are from *Annual Survey of Manufactures*, and 1971 data are preliminary.)

Table 24A-7. Coal Utilized in Production of Coke

(million short tons)

Raw material and yield	1947	1954	1958	1962	1967	1969	1970	1971
Coal carbonized	105.1	85.6	76.8	74.7	91.4	93.4	96.5	83.2
Bituminous	104.8	85.4	76.6	74.3	90.9	92.9	96.0	82.8
Anthracite	.3	.2	.2	.4	.5	.5	.5	.4
Coke produced	73.4	59.7	53.6	51.9	64.6	64.8	66.5	57.4
Oven coke	66.8	59.1	53.6	51.1	63.8	64.1	65.6	56.6
Beehive coke	6.7	.6	.6	.8	.8	.7	.9	.8
Average yield of coke in % of coal	69.91	69.68	69.77	69.51	69.59	69.30	68.95	68.99
Ton of coal used/ton of coke produced	1.43	1.43	1.43	1.44	1.42	1.44	1.45	1.45

Note: Data cover all oven-coke plants in the United States (not only those operated by the iron and steel industry).

Sources: Bureau of Mines, *Minerals Yearbook 1971*, Coke and Coal Chemicals, and *Mineral Industry Surveys*, Coke and Coal Chemicals in 1971.

Table 24A-8. Coke Oven Gas Produced and Used

(billion cubic feet)

Coke Oven Gas	1947	1954	1958	1962	1967	1969	1971
Produced	971.3	869.9	789.8	766.1	959.4	962.0	861.7
Used in heating coke ovens	366.3	298.5	274.7	271.3	341.7	347.9	336.0
"Surplus"	592.9	558.3	502.0	483.9	606.0	594.7	506.6
To steel & allied plants ...	348.3	408.6	374.5	363.1	399.7	391.6	339.3
For boiler heating	38.0	46.0	61.4	73.4	100.1	104.9	100.8
For other ind. use	38.8	27.0	25.2	24.7	86.3	84.3	55.6
To city mains	167.9	76.7	40.9	22.7	20.0	13.8	10.8
Waste	12.0	13.0	13.1	10.9	11.6	19.4	19.1

Source: Bureau of Mines, *Minerals Yearbook 1971*, Coke and Coal Chemicals. Data cover total United States production and consumption of coke oven gas by oven-coke plants.

Table 24A-9.   Gases Used in Heating Coke Ovens (billion cubic feet*)

Gases used	1947	1954	1958	1962	1967	1969	1971
Coke oven gas	366.3	298.5	274.7	271.3	341.7	347.9	336.0
Blast furnace gas	41.5	56.4	53.0	47.8	61.7	100.6	31.9
Natural gas	–	–	6.7	2.7	2.3	2.0	3.0
Other	36.1	19.5	6.4	2.3	–	–	–
Total (coke oven gas equivalent)	443.9	374.3	340.8	324.1	405.7	450.5	370.9
Trillion BTUs	244.1	205.9	187.4	178.3	223.1	247.8	204.0
BTU/ton of coke, millions	3.6	3.5	3.5	3.5	3.5	3.9	3.6

*Adjusted to an equivalent of 550 BTU/c.ft. of gas.

Source: Bureau of Mines, *Minerals Yearbook 1971*, Coke and Coal Chemicals. Data cover all oven-coke plants in the United States (not only those operated by the iron and steel industry).

Table 24A-10.   Gases Used for Coke Oven Underfiring by the Iron and Steel Industry

Gases Used for Underfiring	1967	1969	1970	1971	1972
Coke oven gas, million cu. ft.* ..	237,541	254,991	274,603	254,773	281,313
Blast furnace gas, million cu. ft.**	334,068	345,270	286,402	254,353	225,033
Natural gas, million cu. ft.*** ..	5,766	7,247	10,262	12,770	16,186
Coke oven gas equivalent, mil. cu. ft.	312,546	335,886	349,543	328,640	356,467
BTU equivalent, trillion	156.273	167.943	174.772	164.320	173.234
Coke produced, million short tons	57.465	58.205	59.777	51.476	53.184
BTU/ton of coke, million	2.72	2.89	2.92	3.19	3.25
BTU/ton of raw steel produced, million	1.23	1.19	1.33	1.36	1.30

*500 BTU/cu. ft.

**95 BTU/cu. ft.

***1,000 BTU/cu. ft.

Note: A small quantity of fuel oil is also used for coke oven underfiring. (Natural gas used in coke oven underfiring not reported separately.)

Source: American Iron and Steel Institute, *Annual Statistical Report*, 1972, p. 59.

Table 24A-11.   Energy Utilization in Blast Furnaces, 1967-1972

	1967	1969	1970	1971	1972
Physical Units					
Coke, million short tons	56.205	60.176	58.151	51.497	54.607
Fuel oil, million gal.	67.225	116.770	146.031	194.568	288.515
Tar & pitch, million gal.	20.936	43.351	42.500	17.182	64.185
Natural gas, million cu. ft.	44.255	44.355	44.474	37.447	36.855
Coke oven gas, million cu. ft.	13.433	11.021	9.177	10.072	12.887
Blast furnace gas, million cu. ft.	1,400.147	1,733.763	1,592.038	1,512.008	1,424.570
BTU Equivalent (trillion BTUs)					
Coke	1,461.330	1,564.576	1,511.926	1,338.922	1,419.782
Fuel oil	9.283	16.125	20.166	26.869	39.844
Tar & pitch	2.991	6.193	6.071	2.455	9.172
Natural gas	44.255	44.355	44.474	37.447	36.885
Coke oven gas	6.716	5.510	4.588	5.036	6.443
Blast furnace gas	133.014	164.707	151.244	143.641	135.334
Total BTU, trillion	1,657.589	1,801.466	1,738.469	1,554.370	1,647.430
Blast furnace production (pig iron plus ferro-alloys) (million short tons)	87.6	95.5	91.8	81.7	89.4
BTU/short ton of blast furnace production (millions)	18.9	18.9	18.9	19.0	18.4
BTU/short ton of raw steel production (millions)	13.0	12.7	13.2	12.9	12.4

Note: Natural gas at 1,000 BTU/cu.ft., coke oven gas at 500 BTU/cu.ft. and blast furnace gas at 95 BTU/cu.ft.

Source: American Iron and Steel Institute, *Annual Statistical Report*, 1972, pages 54 and 59.

Table 24A-12.   Production of Raw Steel, Total and by Type of Furnace

(million short tons)

Raw Steel Production	1947	1954	1958	1962	1967	1969	1971	1972
Total	84.9	88.3	85.3	98.3	127.2	141.3	120.4	133.2
Carbon	77.5	81.1	78.6	89.2	113.2	124.8	107.0	117.7
Stainless	.5	.8	.9	1.1	1.4	1.6	1.3	1.6
Other alloy	6.9	6.3	5.8	8.1	12.6	14.9	12.2	14.0
By type of furnace								
Open-hearth	76.9	80.3	75.9	83.0 }	70.7	60.9	35.6	34.9
Bessemer	4.2	2.5	1.4	.8 }				
Basic oxygen (BOF) ..	n.a.	n.a.	1.3	5.5	41.4	60.2	63.9	74.6
Electric	3.8	5.4	6.7	9.0	15.1	20.1	20.9	23.7

Sources: Bureau of Mines, *Minerals Yearbook*; American Iron and Steel Institute, *Annual Statistical Report*, 1972 and earlier volumes.

Table 24A-13.   Melting Fuel* Used in Steel Melting Furnaces, 1967-1972

Energy Source	1967	1969	1970	1971	1972
Physical Units					
Fuel oil, million gal.........	567.663	504.673	416.822	298.536	305.667
Tar & pitch, million gal.......	248.222	205.548	176.902	110.998	116.933
Natural gas, million cu. ft.	85,932	92,446	57,797	46,517	48,215
Coke oven gas, million cu. ft...	32,762	29,946	22,056	13,093	11,310
BTU Equivalent (trillion BTUs)*					
Fuel oil	78.391	69.693	57.569	41.226	42.213
Tar & pitch	35.460	29.364	25.272	15.857	16.710
Natural gas	85.932	92.446	57.797	46.517	48.215
Coke oven gas	16.381	14.973	11.028	6.546	5.655
Total....................	216.164	206.476	151.666	110.146	112.793
Raw steel production (million short tons)	127.2	141.3	131.5	120.4	133.2
BTU/short ton of raw steel produced, millions** ...	1.70	1.46	1.15	.91	.85

*Heating values used by American Iron and Steel Institute: natural gas at 1,000 BTU/cu. ft., coke oven gas at 500 BTU/cu. ft., blast furnace gas at 95 BTU/cu. ft.

**Average melting fuel, all types of steel. Not included is energy (electric or steam) required for waste gas handling and cleaning, cooling water, materials handling and other minor usages. Also does not include electric energy used for melting in electric furnaces.

Source: American Iron and Steel Institute, *Annual Statistical Report*, 1972, page 59.

Table 24A-14. Gross Energy Utilization in Steel Melting Furnaces, 1972, by Type of Furnace

1. Approximate Fuel Utilization*

Process	Raw Steel Produced (Million Tons)	BTUs per Ton of Raw Steel (Million)	Approximate Total Fuel (Trillion BTUs)
Open-hearth	34.9	2.7	93.2
Basic oxygen (BOF) ...	74.6	0.2	14.9
Electric	23.7	0.2	4.7
Total	133.2	0.85	112.8

2. Approximate Electric Energy Utilization*

Process	Raw Steel Produced (Million Tons)	Kwh per Ton of Raw Steel	Approximate Total Electric Energy (Million kwh)	(Trillion BTUs)
Open-hearth	34.9	13	454	4.8
Basic oxygen (BOF) ...	74.6	28	2,089	21.9
Electric				
Alloy	5.7	710	4,047	42.5
Other	18.0	500	9,000	94.5
Total	133.2	117	15,590	163.7

3. Fuel and Electric Energy, Total .... Trillion BTUs 276.5

Plus some minor volume of energy consumed in producing oxygen and calcined fluxes at integrated steel mills .... Trillion BTUs 18.5**

Sum .... Trillion BTUs 295.0

Gross energy consumed per ton of raw steel: Million BTUs 2.2***

*Based on average performance of large furnaces operated in integrated mills.

**The steel industry produced in 1972 approximately 11% of its supply of oxygen.

***See text Table 24-7 for comparison with estimates for other operating areas.

Source: Estimates derived from information provided by the industry.

Table 24A-15.   Utilization of Electric Energy by the Iron and Steel Industry, 1967-1972

	1967	*1969*	*1970*	*1971*	*1972*
Electric energy, billion kwh					
Total	42.5	48.4	49.6	48.6	51.6
Purchased	30.6	36.7	37.8	37.5	39.4
Generated	11.9	11.7	11.7	11.2	12.2
Kwh per short ton of raw steel	334.1	342.5	377.2	403.6	387.4
Electric energy, billion BTUs					
Useful (purchased and generated)	145.0	165.1	169.2	166.0	176.1
Gross* (purchased and generated)	443.4	508.2	520.8	510.3	541.8

Source: American Iron and Steel Institute, *Annual Statistical Report*, 1972.

Electric Energy Utilized by Process, 1972
    (kwh per short ton of product):

1) Coke ovens, modern 27 kwh/ton of coke
                older 20 kwh/ton of coke
2) Blast furnaces, modern 15 kwh/ton of pig iron
                older 10 kwh/ton of pig iron
                average 10 kwh/ton of pig iron
3) Open-hearth, modern 13 kwh/ton of raw steel
                older 8-9 kwh/ton of raw steel
                average 13 kwh/ton of raw steel
4) BOF 27-28 kwh/ton of raw steel
5) Electric furnace, carbon 500 kwh/ton of raw steel
                alloy 700-720 kwh/ton of raw steel
6) Finishing facilities
    Hot strip mill   100 kwh/ton of steel
    Slab mill   25 kwh/ton of steel
    Plate mill   50-90 kwh/ton of steel
    Cold reduction   100 kwh/ton of steel
    Rod mill (high speed of 5,000 ft./minute) 275 kwh/ton of steel.

Source: Estimates derived from information provided by the industry.

Table 24A-16.   Net Shipments of Steel Products, 1967-1972
(1,000 short tons)

	1967	1969	1970*	1971	1972
Net shipments of:					
Ingots and steel castings	.289	.500	.918	.412	.413
Blooms, slabs, billets, sheet bars	2,505	4,243	4,787	2,942	2,579
Wire rods	1,266	1,623	1,681	1,587	1,919
Total semifinished	4,062	6,373	7,386	4,962	4,917
Total all steel products	83,897	93,877	90,798	87,038	91,805
Finished (less semifinished)	79,835	87,504	83,412	82,076	86,888
Less production of companies not included in 1967 and 1969 figures (million short tons)	79.8	87.5	81.6	81.0	85.4

*Beginning with the year 1970, shipments statistics compiled by American Iron and Steel Institute include estimates for a relatively small number of companies which report raw steel production but not shipments to the Institute. The companies shipped an estimated 1.8 million net tons of steel products in 1970, 1.1 million net tons in 1971, and 1.4 million net tons in 1972.

Source: American Iron and Steel Institute, *Annual Statistical Report, 1972,* Table 14.

Table 24A-17.   Fuel   Utilization   in   Heating   and   Annealing
Furnaces,   1967-1972

Energy Source	1967	1969	1970	1971	1972
Fuel oil, million gal.	403.426	314.064	377.593	344.158	396.524
LPG, million gal.	11.112	7.404	6.555	8.048	7.147
Natural gas, million cu. ft.	277,322	337,307	306,097	329,176	354,821
Coke oven gas, million cu. ft.	352,236	378,028	363,899	323,941	352,007
Blast furnace gas, million cu. ft. . .	162,898	185,223	164,693	162,523	123,073

Natural gas at 1,000 BTU/cu. ft., coke oven gas at 500 BTU/cu. ft. and blast furnace gas at 95 BTU/cu. ft.

BTU Equivalent (trillion BTUs)					
Fuel oil	55.711	43.371	52.144	47.526	54.760
LPG	1.058	.705	.624	.766	.681
Natural gas	277.322	337.307	306.097	329.176	354.821
Coke oven gas	176.118	189.014	181.950	161.970	176.003
Blast furnace gas	15.475	17.596	15.646	15.440	11.692
Total	525.684	587.993	556.461	554.878	597.957
Net shipments* of finished steel products (million short tons)	79.8	87.5	81.6	81.0	85.4
Million BTU/short ton of finished steel shipments	6.58	6.72	6.80	6.84	7.00

*Data on production of finished steel products were not available.

Source: American Iron and Steel Institute, *Annual Statistical Report, 1972,* page 59. (Revised data for 1972.)

Table 24A-18.   Fuel Utilization in Heating Ovens for Wire Rods, 1967-1972

Energy Source	1967	1969	1970	1971	1972
Fuel oil, million gal.	n.a.	.857	1.648	2.561	3.309
Natural gas, million cu. ft.	5,682	4,805	4,403	4,760	7,456
Coke oven gas, million cu. ft. ...	9,681	12,606	9,217**	6,729	8,372

Natural gas at 1,000 BTU/cu. ft., coke oven gas at 500 BTU/cu. ft.

BTU Equivalent (trillion BTUs)					
Fuel oil	n.a.	.118	.228	.354	.457
Natural gas	5.682	4.805	4.403	4.760	7.456
Coke oven gas	4.841	6.303	4.610	3.365	4.186
Total	n.a.	11.226	9.241	8.479	12.099
Net shipments of wire rods plus wire (million short tons)*	4.4	4.9	4.7	4.4	4.9
Million BTU/short ton of wire shipped	n.a.	2.30	1.97	1.94	2.48

*Data on production of wire rods were not available.
**Adjusted estimate.

Source: American Iron and Steel Institute, *Annual Statistical Report, 1972*, page 59.

SECTION V.   SELECTED BIBLIOGRAPHY

American Iron and Steel Institute (AISI). *Directory of the Iron and Steel Works of the United States and Canada.* Washington, D.C., 1973.

————. *The Making of Steel.* (Raw Materials; Iron Manufacture; Steel Making Processes; Specialty Steels; Steel Mill Products; Testing and Inspection). Washington, D.C., 1971/72.

————. *The Picture Story of Steel.* New York, 1969.

————. *Steel Making Flow Charts.* Washington, D.C., 1972.

————. *Steel Processing Flow Charts.* Washington, D.C., 1972.

Economic Commission for Europe. *Development of Production Technology and New Properties of Steel Products.* New York: United Nations, 1970.

Hogan, William T. *Economic History of the Iron and Steel Industry* (five volumes). 1971.

————. "Productivity in the Steel Industry." Published in *Center Lines*, Steel Service Center Institute, Vol. VII, January 1972.

Osborne, A. K. *An Encyclopedia of the Iron and Steel Industry.* 2nd edition. London: The Technical Press Ltd., 1967.

United States Steel Corporation. *The Making, Shaping and Treating of Steel*, 7th edition. Pittsburgh, Pa., April 1957.

Serials:

Annual Statistical Report, 1972 (and earlier editions), American Iron and Steel Institute (AISI), Washington, 1973.

Minerals Yearbook, 1971 (and earlier editions), Bureau of Mines, U.S. Department of the Interior, Washington, 1973.

Mineral Industry Surveys, Coke and Coal Chemicals in 1971, Bureau of Mines, U.S. Department of the Interior, Washington, 1972.

Chapter Twenty-Five

Electrometallurgical Products— SIC 3313

Nancy Garvey and Bernard A. Gelb

SECTION I.   INTRODUCTION AND SUMMARY

The Industry

As defined by the 1967 *U.S. Standard Industrial Classification Manual,* the Electrometallurgical industry, SIC 3313, consists of "establishments primarily engaged in the manufacturing of ferrous and nonferrous additive alloys by electrometallurgical or metallothermic processes, including high percentage ferroalloys and high percentage nonferrous additive alloys." Excluded from this industry are ferroalloys, such as ferromanganese and silvery iron, produced in blast furnaces and classified in industry 3312, and all aluminum, magnesium, and copper electrometallurgical products classified elsewhere.

The industry is highly specialized and has been so for the entire postwar period: in 1967, as in 1947 and all other Census years in between, about 90% of output was accounted for by the several primary products. In contrast, the proportion of total U.S. output of electrometallurgical products accounted for by this industry (SIC 3313) has gradually risen since 1947, from about 70% to about 80%.

Industry Overview

The electrometallurgical industry has experienced very slow growth since 1947. Industry production grew at an annual rate of 1.6% between 1947 and 1967, rising from $339.0 million (in constant 1967 dollars) to $467.9 million. Because a large majority of electrometallurgical products (85%) are consumed by the iron and steel industry, output of SIC 3313 follows movements in the steel industry very closely, and therefore has fluctuated widely.

On a product basis, there are considerable differences in growth rates. Of the three major ferroalloys produced, production of ferrosilicon almost

Table 25-1.   Summary: Output, Energy Use, Energy-Output Ratios

	1947	1967	1980
Shipments (million 1967 $)	$339.0	$467.9	$398.2
Useful energy consumed (trillion BTUs)	40.3	76.0	74.0
Energy-output ratio (useful) (1,000 BTUs/1967 $ of output)	118.8	162.2	185.0
Gross energy consumed (trillion BTUs)	84.5	131.0	127.4
Energy-output ratio (gross) (1,000 BTUs/1967 $ of output)	249.3	280.0	319.9

Sources: Bureau of the Census, *Census of Manufactures*; The Conference Board.

tripled between 1947 and 1967. Ferromanganese and ferrochromium output increased 27% and 39%, respectively.

Total fuels and electricity consumed by the industry grew faster than output between 1947 and 1967. Shifts to production of more energy-intensive grades of alloys increased per-unit process energy requirements; more coal and coke was used for non-energy purposes than previously; and relatively more generation of power within the industry boosted BTU consumption per unit aside from any change in process requirements. Total useful energy[a] consumption rose 89% in the twenty years, from 40.3 trillion BTUs to 76.0 trillion BTUs. Gross energy consumed increased from 84.5 trillion BTUs to 131.0 trillion BTUs, or 55%.

Projections

Production of electrometallurgical products in constant dollars is expected to decline at a 2.3% average annual rate between 1967 and 1975. It is believed this trend will reverse after 1975, and output will increase 2.5% overall between 1975 and 1980. The upshot of this down-up movement is that the level of output in 1980 will be 14.9% lower than in 1967. Any growth in the demand for ferroalloys originating in the iron and steel industry is expected to be met by imports. Tonnage output is projected to decline at a 2.0% annual average rate to 1975, and to show no change from 1975 to 1980.

We expect energy use per ton of product to increase 14% between 1967 and 1975, and then remain unchanged between 1975 and 1980. Any savings in energy from the use of large furnaces and the automation of mixing and charging operations are expected to be more than offset by the continuing product shift to silicon alloys and the complete installation of pollution-control equipment industry-wide by 1975.

[a] See Chapter One, pages 14-15, for definitions of useful and gross energy.

SECTION II.   HISTORICAL DEVELOPMENT

Demand for Electrometallurgical Products

Ferroalloys have two major end uses: (1) they are introduced into steel by steel makers in order to give the steel certain physical properties such as hot hardness, wear-resistance, and strength, and (2) they are used by steel makers and foundrymen as cleansing, deoxidizing, or inoculating agents.

Alloys used for imparting special properties to steel or for the formation of alloy steels are ferromanganese, ferrosilicon, ferrochromium, ferrotungsten, ferromolybdenum, and ferrovanadium. Those alloys used as deoxidizing or inoculating agents are ferromanganese, ferrosilicon, silicomanganese, calcium-silicon, magnesium-ferrosilicon, and to a smaller extent ferrotitanium and silicon-zirconium.

Output of the electrometallurgical industry is considerably affected by the heavy dependence of SIC 3313 on sales to the iron and steel industry. Almost any changes in steel production will affect purchases from producers of electrometallurgical products. Such changes may be due to labor disputes, changes in steelmaking practices, fluctuations in the demand for steel, and other developments far removed from the electrometallurgical industry. Output of electrometallurgical products paralleled the general decline in steel production and gray iron and steel castings between 1947 and 1958. After 1958, production in the steel industry increased and, as a result, output of electrometallurgical products rose.

The second major factor indirectly affecting output is importation. Until the mid-1950s, most imports in the electrometallurgical industry were the ores used in the smelting operations. Although it has frequently been more economical to produce ferroalloys at the source of the ore, it was not until the mid-1950s that extensive facilities were built abroad. Part of the present cost difference in production is explained by the fact that most foreign producers are not required to install pollution-control equipment (which is necessary in the United States), thereby avoiding the capital costs and higher per-unit energy consumption. As a consequence, U.S. producers of alloys find it difficult to compete with foreign manufacturers.

Between 1947 and 1971 the dollar value of imports of ores and ferroalloys grew at an average annual rate of about 8.5%. Since 1969, however, as increasing amounts of ferroalloys (of higher value than ores) have been imported, the growth rate has been 14.4%. Until 1970, growth in total demand for ferroalloys by the U.S. iron and steel industry was sufficient to more than offset the increase in imports, and domestic production of electrometallurgical products continued to expand. This is not expected to hold true between now and 1980.

A third factor which has affected the level of demand for domestic and foreign electrometallurgical products is the cessation or curtailing of the U.S.

Table 25-2.   Imports of Ferroalloys and Alloy Metals

Total Imports	1947	1954	1958	1962	1967	1971
Value ($ millions)	$ 13.1	$17.7	$ 37.9	$ 35.7	$ 56.7	$ 92.5
Quantity (1,000 short tons)	105.9	92.4	103.0	182.7	347.3	417.5

Source: U.S. Bureau of Mines, *Minerals Yearbook*.

government stockpiling programs. In the past, the government has maintained two types of stockpiles of ferroalloys and alloy ores: (1) the national strategic stockpiles, and (2) the U.S. Department of Agriculture Commodity Credit Corporation stockpiles. Both of these stockpiles were supplied from foreign sources, and were responsible for the expansion in foreign production during the 1950s. As the government has terminated the national strategic stockpile program and reduced its activity in the U.S. Department of Agriculture's barter programs, it has further depressed activity in the ferroalloy markets, more so in the foreign than in the domestic markets. Because the termination dates of the programs coincided with the Census years, the level of imports shown in Table 25-2 are lower than in contiguous years.

Characteristics of Energy Use

Of total energy consumed by an electrometallurgical establishment with installed pollution-control equipment, the smelting operations account for between 80% and 85%; approximately 10% is consumed by air-pollution control equipment; and the remaining 5% to 10% is used in the other procedures. For those firms that do not have pollution-control equipment, smelting accounts for 90%-95% of energy use, and other procedures and needs account for the remainder.

As far as the actual production processes are concerned, electricity—used in the smelting operations—is the major form of energy used by the electrometallurgical industry. In addition to the BTUs attributable to purchased electricity, which account for about one-third of total useful energy consumed, most of the coal BTUs consumed by the industry are used for steam generation by those plants that produce their own electric power, and thus indirectly represent use of electricity. This is roughly confirmed by the fact that, in 1967, establishments in SIC 3313 generated 3.4 billion kwh of electricity for their own use, or 30% of their total electric energy consumption. Much smaller proportions of coal are used for such purposes as reduction and the manufacture of electrodes.

Compared with electricity and coal, very small quantities of fuel oil, natural gas, and coke are consumed. Natural gas is used for space heating, for curing the ladles that hold the molten products, and, in some plants, for igniting burners on steam stations. Fuel oil is primarily used in the rotary kilns and

Table 25-3. **Energy Use by Source**
(trillion BTUs)

Energy Source	1947	1954	1958	1962	1967
Total useful energy	40.3	40.1	51.5	83.8	76.0
Coal	16.5	24.8	31.7	46.4	33.9
Coke & breeze	10.7	2.2	1.2	13.4	6.9
Fuel oil	.2	.4	1.0	1.0	.4
Gas	.3	.2	1.0	2.0	4.4
Other fuels	.2	.2	.2	2.5	3.4
Fuels n.s.k.	.0	.0	.0	.0	.2
Electricity (purchased)	12.4	12.3	16.4	18.5	26.8
Total gross energy	84.5	71.7	88.5	122.7	131.0
Electricity (purchased) (gross energy basis)	56.5	43.9	53.4	57.4	81.9

Source: Bureau of the Census, *Census of Manufactures.*

sintering machines, although a few plants collect and clean the waste gases (e.g., carbon monoxide) released from the furnaces and use these gases in their rotary kilns and other auxiliary operations. Fuel oil and natural gas make up less than 6% of total useful energy consumed by the industry. Coke, which accounts for 9% of total useful energy consumed, is utilized as a reducing agent in the charge to the furnace.

Energy-Output Ratios

At a given level of technology, energy consumption per unit depends on the size of the furnace employed, the particular product manufactured, and the degree of refinement in the final product. Changes in the last two variables during the 1950s and 1960s were largely responsible for an increase in energy use per unit of output in the electrometallurgical industry.

Throughout the 1947-1967 period, little technological change occurred in SIC 3313 and furnaces were operated at about the same near-peak thermal efficiency. However, apparent energy consumption on a useful basis per constant 1967 dollar of output rose steeply between 1954 and 1962, and then declined between 1962 and 1967, but not so far as to reach the levels of the early 1950s.

In part, these movements reflect changes in industry operations; in part, they reflect industry idiosyncrasies in fuel and energy use; and, in part, they reflect faults in Census data. When allowance is made for the last factor, the picture becomes clearer. It is the opinion of the Bureau of the Census and industry representatives that the 1958 and 1962 fuel purchase figures for coal, coke, and (possibly) fuel oil are too large, and as a result, the 1958 and 1962 energy-output ratios are too high. While the extent of overstatement is unknown, it can be seen (in Chart 25-1) that a reasonable adjustment would result in a more gradual rise in the energy-output ratio between 1947 and 1967.

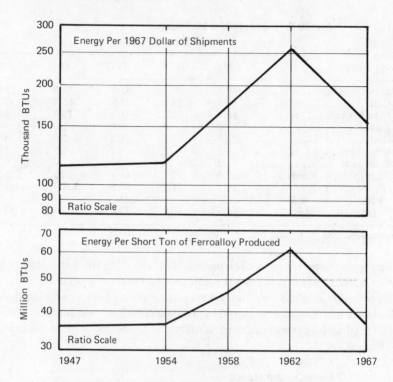

Chart 25-1. Two Ratios of Useful Energy per Unit of Output.
Sources: U.S. Bureau of the Census, *Census of Manufactures*, U.S.
Bureau of Mines, *Minerals Yearbook*.

Four distinct changes in industry operations constitute the more
basic analytical problem, and appear to have been responsible for the increase in
energy use per unit of output.

Part of the apparent long-term increase, particularly in the 1950s, in
energy use per 1967 dollar of output in SIC 3313 can be attributed to a change
in the product mix among the three major types of alloys toward those with
lower unit prices (the silicon alloys). Other things being equal, lower value per
unit will, of course, increase energy use per dollar of output. However, when
energy use is related to tonnage, the rise in the energy-output ratio, although less
steep,[1] is still there. This is because the silicon alloys, aside from their lower cost,
are more energy intensive than the chromium and manganese alloys.

In addition to the shift to lower cost alloys, there was also a trend to
relatively more production of higher grades of each type of alloy, which tend to
use more energy. For example, whereas 50% ferrosilicon (half silicon and half
iron, by weight) requires about 4,700 kilowatt hours of electricity per ton to
produce, 75% ferrosilicon requires about 10,000 kwh, and silicon metal as much

Table 25-4.   Changing Product Mix
(short tons)

	1947	1954	1958	1962	1967	1971
Total production	1,129,080	1,100,246	1,128,879	1,386,135	2,040,075	1,827,282
Total of three major alloys	850,000e	783,614	796,748	934,229	1,392,944	1,331,584
Ferrochromium	150,000e	181,673	304,406	261,559	446,137	355,658
Ferromanganese	215,120	315,591	205,946	252,929	273,272	288,760
Ferrosilicon	484,456	286,350	286,396	419,741	673,535	687,166
Three major alloys as % of total production	75%	71%	71%	67%	68%	73%

e–estimated.

Note: Production at blast furnaces has been subtracted from total U.S. ferroalloy output to arrive at output of the electrometallurgical industry.

Source: Bureau of Mines, *Minerals Yearbook*.

as 14,000 kwh per ton. Ferrochromium and ferromanganese require, on average, 5,000 kwh per ton and 3,500 kwh per ton, respectively.

Since smelting accounts for up to 95% of energy consumption in the production of ferroalloys, any increase in kilowatt-hour requirements for a given amount of tonnage of a ferroalloy is almost entirely translated into greater per unit energy use. In general, alloy shifts and their effects on total energy use are difficult to quantify due to inadequate statistical data. Judging by industry statements and some data from the Bureau of Mines, however, the impact of these shifts on energy use per unit of output was substantial.

A second operational change in the industry has been a shift to relatively more generation of electric power by establishments in the industry. In 1967, 31% of electric power used by SIC 3313 was self-generated, compared with 25% in 1947. Such a shift results in relatively more BTUs "consumed" in heat loss being attributed to the industry instead of the electric utility sector, and it increases the industry's (useful) energy-output ratio. We have estimated that useful energy consumed by SIC 3313 in 1967 was three trillion BTUs, or 4% greater than it would have been without the shift to self-generation of electric power (see Table 25-5). While the shift is irrelevant insofar as process use of energy per unit of output is concerned and, of course, has virtually no effect on gross energy consumption per unit of output, it still must be accounted for. Since, according to industry experts, not all establishments in SIC 3313 have a realistic option to generate their own power, both gross and useful energy measures must be examined, and compared.

Table 25-5. Useful Energy Consumption Adjusted for Shift to On-site Power Generation

		1967	
	1947	Actual	Hypothetical[1]
Total electricity used (billion kwh)	4.903	11.206	11.206
Purchased (billion kwh)	3.621	7.852	8.276
Generated (billion kwh)	1.282	3.354	2.930
Approximate energy used for on-site generation[2] (trillion BTUs)	20.00	34.99	30.57
Useful energy content of purchased electricity (trillion BTUs) ...	12.35	26.79	28.24
Total useful energy consumed by SIC 3313 (trillion BTUs)	40.3	75.9	72.9[3]

[1] Assuming no change in proportion of electricity accounted for by on-site generation.
[2] Average heat rates for utility steam-electric generating plants for the respective years were used to approximate generating energy requirements.
[3] Actual total, less difference between hypothetical and actual generation BTUs, plus difference between actual and hypothetical useful energy content of purchased electricity.
Sources: Bureau of the Census, *Census of Manufactures*; The Conference Board.

A third development in the industry that has tended to raise apparent energy consumption per unit of output is the increase in the use of carbonaceous materials (largely coal and coke) for non-energy purposes. This increase is partly attributable to the shift to higher grade silicon alloys—which require more coal and coke in the furnace charges—and partly to the rapid spread of the practice by industry establishments of making their own electrodes (from coal) rather than buying them. A change in the technique of baking electrodes in the 1960s made such a practice much more economical than it had been before. These increases in uses for coal and coke had, however, a comparatively minor effect on total or per unit energy consumption by the electrometallurgical industry.

The one exogenous factor which has directly affected energy requirements in the electrometallurgical industry has also tended to increase per-unit energy consumption. This is the legislation by the Federal, state, and local governments of air pollution standards beginning in 1963. This legislation is particularly pertinent in the electrometallurgical industry, where large emissions of dust particles are caused by the electric furnaces. Pollution-control equipment may have accounted for part of the rise in per-unit energy use between 1962 and 1967. But, since only 40% of the industry had installed such equipment as late as 1971, very little of that rise can be attributed to pollution control. The full impact of pollution control will not be felt until 1975, when 100% of the industry must comply with government standards. It is estimated that, at that time, pollution-control equipment will account for 10% of total energy consumption by SIC 3313.

Other Factors Affecting Energy Use

Little occurred in the industry between 1947 and 1967 to offset the trends that have tended to increase energy use per unit of output. It was not

Table 25-6. Output, Energy Use, and Energy Use per Unit of Output

	1947	1954	1958	1962	1967
Output (million 1967 $)	$339.0	$335.5	$295.3	$332.0	$467.9
Useful energy consumed (trillion BTUs)	40.3	40.1	51.5	83.8	76.0
Energy-output ratio (useful) (1,000 BTUs/1967 $ of output) . . .	118.8	119.8	174.7	253.2	162.2
Gross energy consumed (trillion BTUs)	84.5	71.7	88.5	122.7	131.0
Energy-output ratio (gross) (1,000 BTUs/1967 $ of output) . . .	249.3	214.2	300.0	269.6	280.0

Source: Bureau of the Census, *Census of Manufactures.*

until the middle or late 1960s that new larger furnaces that had been introduced in the late 1950s were in common use in the industry. These were supposed to be more economical with respect to per-unit energy use, but reports to us indicate that such energy savings are still to appear.

Within the past three or four years, electrometallurgical plants have begun to use computers to automate mixing operations and control power inputs to different machinery. This automation reduces per-unit energy use by automatically adjusting fuel supplies.

Both of these factors should contribute somewhat to savings in per-unit energy use, but their implementation has been too recent for the effect to be reflected in the Census data.

SECTION III.   PROJECTIONS TO 1980

Demand

Output by the electrometallurgical industry is not expected to grow during the 1970s, primarily because imports of ferroalloys are anticipated to increase further. Between 1962 and 1971, imports (in value terms) grew at an 11.2% average annual rate. There may be future periods of peak world demand for steel, such as in 1973, when foreign electrometallurgical products will not be easily available. But developing countries in particular are continuing to expand their ferroalloy capacity; and it is the opinion of industry analysts that imports will continue to increase throughout the 1970s and meet most of the rise in demand for ferroalloys, especially ferrochromium and ferromanganese.

When based on Conference Board assumptions regarding trends in economic aggregates during the 1970s, the Maryland Interindustry Forecasting Model (INFORUM) predicts a 1.9% annual average rate of decline in constant-dollar shipments between 1967 and 1975 and a 1.3% rate of growth from 1975 to 1980. The major assumptions are: (1) sufficient capacity will exist in 1975 and 1980, (2) full employment will exist in 1975 and 1980, and (3) present trends in imports and exports will remain the same. Since the growth rate of imports is expected to accelerate in the 1970s, the projections of INFORUM are considered high. Based on conversations with industry analysts, a 2.3% average annual decline in constant-dollar output is projected from 1967 to 1975, and a 0.5% average annual increase from 1975 to 1980.

Energy Use

Per-unit energy use is expected to be affected in the next few years by two, already ongoing, developments: (1) the continuing shift in product mix to the high-energy silicon alloys and away from low-energy ferrochromium and ferromanganese, due to increases in demand for ferrosilicon and increases in imports of the chromium and manganese alloys; (2) industry-wide installation of pollution-control devices by 1975, as dictated by law. It is estimated that the

Table 25-7.   Projections of Output and Energy Use

	1967	1975	1980
Physical output (million short tons)	2.04	1.74	1.74
Useful energy consumed (trillion BTUs)	76.0	74.0	74.0
Energy-output ratio (useful) (trillion BTUs/short ton)	37.3	42.5	42.5
Gross energy consumed (trillion BTUs)	131.0	127.4	127.4
Energy-output ratio (gross) (million BTUs/short ton)	64.2	73.2	73.2
Output value (million 1967 $)	$467.9	$388.4	$398.2
Energy-output ratio (useful) (1,000 BTUs/1967 $ of output)	162.2	190.5	185.8
Energy-output ratio (gross) (1,000 BTUs/1967 $ of output)	280.0	328.0	319.9

Sources: Bureau of Mines, *Minerals Yearbook*; Bureau of the Census, *Census of Manufactures*; Maryland Interindustry Forecasting Model; The Conference Board.

combined effect of these two factors will have boosted energy use per ton of product 14% between 1967 and 1975.

Because both factors will have made almost all of their impact by 1975, no change in the energy-output ratio, on a tonnage basis, has been projected for the 1975-1980 period.

In order to estimate total BTUs consumed on a useful and gross energy basis, it was also necessary to estimate tonnage in 1975 and 1980. Tons produced are expected to decline between 1967 and 1975 (2.0% annual average rate), but it is believed this decline will be slower than the decline in shipments (2.3% annual average rate). Tonnage is projected to decline, partly because the mandated installation of pollution-control equipment apparently has made or will make some furnaces uneconomical to operate, and has forced or will force some establishments to shut down. No change in tonnage is projected between 1975 and 1980. On the basis of these estimates, total BTUs consumed will fall at a 1.2% rate from 1967 to 1980, on either a gross or useful energy basis.

Note

[1] Data on physical output of metallurgical products were obtained from the Bureau of Mines *Minerals Yearbook*. Since the data there are organized by product rather than by industry, it is necessary to subtract blast furnace production of ferroalloys (classified as SIC 3312) from total ferroalloy production in order to obtain ferroalloy output by SIC 3313. In 1958, 1962, and 1967, blast furnace production was stated separately from electric furnace production of ferroalloys. For these years, the blast furnace figures were simply subtracted from the totals. SIC 3313 product output for 1947 and 1954 was estimated by

applying the average ratio of blast furnace production for 1958, 1962, and 1967 to the totals for 1947 and 1954.

SECTION IV.   APPENDIX

The Manufacture of Ferroalloys

The production of ferroalloys is a smelting operation. Various ores of the alloying materials—e.g., silica, manganese, vanadium—are weighed and mixed in the right proportion. They are mechanically transported to an electric furnace where they are continually fed in at the top. If too wet, the ores of the furnace charge are dried in rotary kilns before becoming part of the charge. The charge typically consists of ores (oxides of the metals), carbonaceous reducing agents in the form of coal or coke, and sometimes slag-forming materials and steel scrap.

In the three-phase submerged arc furnace, where ferrosilicon, ferro-manganese, high carbon ferrochrome, and other ferroalloys reduced by carbon are smelted, the molten products are intermittently tapped from a hole that is at hearth level. These units may operate for a period of years without lining or hearth repairs. The other major type of electric furnace employed in the electro-metallurgical industry is the open arc furnace, in which low carbon grades of ferrochrome and ferromanganese, ferrocolumbium, ferrovanadium, and ferro-molybdenum are produced. Production with this type of furnace is run either in batches (as in the steel industry), where the furnace is tapped and lining repaired after each heat, or in a semicontinuous operation of feeding and tapping.

After the molten product is tapped it is poured by ladle into flat molds. Once the product solidifies, it is crushed and sized, and then is ready to be shipped.

SECTION V.   SELECTED BIBLIOGRAPHY

Bureau of Mines. *Minerals Yearbook.* Government Printing Office, Washington, D.C.

Environmental Quality. U.S. Government Printing Office, 1972, 1971, 1970.

Mantell, Charles. *Electrochemical Engineering.* McGraw-Hill Book Company, Inc., 1960, 1950, 1940.

McGannon, Harold E., ed. *The Making, Shaping and Creating of Steel.* Herbich & Held, Pittsburgh, Pennsylvania: 1971.

Serial.

American Metals Market

Chapter Twenty-Six

Gray Iron and Steel Foundries—
SIC 3321 and 3323

Nancy Garvey

SECTION 1.   INTRODUCTION AND SUMMARY

Description of the Industry

Gray iron foundries, SIC 3321, are defined as "establishments primarily engaged in manufacturing gray iron castings, including cast iron pressure and soil pipes and fittings." Steel foundries, SIC 3323, are defined as "establishments primarily engaged in manufacturing steel castings." Although not specified in the general description, castings of ductile iron (another ferrous metal of which castings are made) are a primary product of the gray iron foundry industry.

There are a substantial number of ferrous and nonferrous castings not included in the gray iron and steel foundry industries. Malleable iron castings are classified in SIC 3322 and all nonferrous castings are classified elsewhere. Of those gray iron and steel castings excluded from SIC 3321 and SIC 3323, most are produced in establishments classified in other industries that operate their own foundry departments (captive foundries), and incorporate these castings into their final product. Captive foundry production constitutes about 41% of the total output of all gray iron foundries and 18% of the total production of steel castings. The remainder of steel castings excluded from the steel foundry industry is produced in establishments that primarily manufacture and roll steel. These establishments are classified in SIC 3312.

Gray iron and steel foundries are covered in the same report because the processes involved in the production of the two types of castings are very similar.

Process Description

Disregarding minor differences, the production of gray iron and steel castings involves the same general principles. The metal is heated to fluidity, poured into a mold of the desired shape, and allowed to solidify. If necessary, the resulting casting may be heat-treated to relieve internal stresses, to alter the mechanical properties of the casting, or both.

Metal for gray iron castings is melted in cupola, electric, or reverberatory furnaces; metal for steel castings is melted in open-hearth or electric furnaces.

Industry Overview

Gray iron and steel foundries showed little secular growth until the early 1960s, when demand for castings rose strongly. Output by gray iron foundries (in constant dollars) grew at an average annual rate of 5.5% between 1962 and 1967, and production by steel foundries increased 5.9% a year. This rise in demand is also responsible for a long awaited technological renaissance that occurred in these industries beginning in the early 1960s. During years of high demand prior to 1963, some foundries were able to mechanize many of their operations and implement new developments such as basic-lined cupolas, electric furnaces, shell molding machines, and high-pressure molding machines. Wide-scale mechanization and adoption of new equipment, however, did not begin until 1963, when higher sales levels helped raise the funds required for the capital investment.

Normally, greater mechanization would cause a rise in energy consumption and energy utilization per unit of output. This was the case in the gray iron foundry industry. The energy-output ratio rose 18% on a useful energy[a] basis between 1947 and 1967, but due to reporting errors, this estimate is a little high. However, in the steel foundry industry, energy utilization per unit of output fell 1% on a useful energy basis.

Another factor that has accounted for some of the increase in fuel and electrical energy consumption is pollution abatement equipment. This equipment will account for an increasing proportion of energy consumption as more firms strive to comply with federal, state, and local air pollution regulations.

Total useful energy and total gross energy consumed are shown in Chart 26-1 for the gray iron foundry industry and Chart 26-2 for the steel foundry industry. In the gray iron foundry industry, gross energy consumed increased faster than useful energy consumed despite the increase in efficiency of generating electricity. In 1967, 10,396 BTUs were required to generate a kwh of electricity, compared with 15,600 BTUs in 1947. The faster increase in gross energy consumed is due to the rise in the proportion of useful electricity consumed in relation to total useful energy consumed. Consumption of electricity, on a useful basis, tripled between 1947 and 1967. In 1947, 3.2 trillion BTUs of electricity were consumed, which made up 4.4% of total useful

[a]See Chapter One, pages 14-15, for definitions of useful and gross energy.

energy consumption. In 1967, 9.6 trillion BTUs of electricity were consumed. This consumption of electricity made up 9.6% of total useful energy consumed.

In the steel foundry industry, although consumption of electricity, on a useful basis, increased 120%, from 3.5 trillion BTUs in 1947 to 7.6 trillion BTUs in 1967, this rise was too small to offset the decline in BTUs required to produce a kwh of electricity. Consequently, gross energy consumed increased at a slower rate than useful energy consumed.

Projections to 1980

Growth in output of each of these industries is expected to continue through 1980. Production by the gray iron foundry industry is estimated to increase at an average annual rate of 5.2% between 1967 and 1975. Two estimates have been made for 1975 to 1980: one of a 3.1% rate of growth, and one of a 3.5% rate of growth. Production by the steel foundry industry is expected to grow at a 3.5% rate to 1975 and 4.4% thereafter.

Projection of two different growth rates for gray iron foundries was necessitated by the uncertainties surrounding the introduction of the rotary automotive engine. Because approximately 20% of the sales of SIC 3321 are for automobile engine parts, widespread use of a much lighter weight engine of a nonferrous metal will certainly affect shipments of gray iron castings. But it has not yet been determined whether the rotor housings will be of aluminum or cast iron.

The foundry industries are expected to continue to install pollution-control equipment until they have met government standards and to continue to

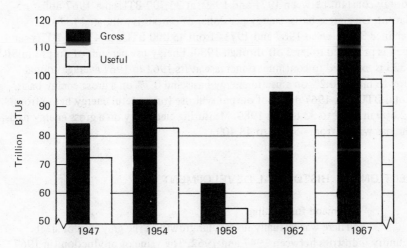

Chart 26-1. Gray Iron Foundries Industry, Useful and Gross Energy Consumed. Source: U.S. Department of Commerce, *Census of Manufactures.*

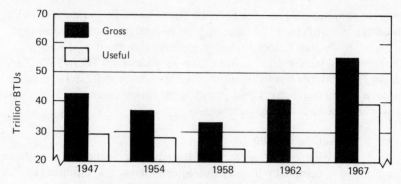

Chart 26-2.   Steel Foundry Industry, Useful and Gross Energy Consumed. Source: U.S. Department of Commerce, *Census of Manufactures.*

automate their production processes, but the latter should have only a small upward impact on the energy-output ratios. Much of the automation will be in the form of modernization of processes that have already been mechanized; in addition, it is anticipated that economies in energy use will be gained by the industries as a whole, as many smaller foundries close down and tonnage melted in the larger, more energy-efficient foundries increases.

The decline in energy consumption (useful) per dollar of output that the gray iron foundry industry (SIC 3321) experienced between 1962 and 1967 is estimated to have slowed between 1967 and 1971, and energy use is projected to stay constant between 1971 and 1980, at 35,700 BTUs per 1967 dollar of output. On a gross basis, energy per dollar of output is estimated to have declined 3% between 1967 and 1971—from 45,000 BTUs to 43,700 BTUs—and then is projected to level off through 1980. Energy use per unit of output in SIC 3323 is expected to continue to increase at its 1962 to 1967 average annual growth rate of 0.2% on a useful energy basis and 0.7% on a gross energy basis. Total BTUs per 1967 dollar of output will rise (on a useful energy basis) from 32,800 in 1967 to 33,600 in 1980. Measuring electricity on a gross energy basis, the rise will be from 45,800 to 48,400.

SECTION II.   HISTORICAL DEVELOPMENT

Demand for Castings

There was virtually no secular growth in the gray iron or steel foundry industries between 1947 and 1962. The value of production (in 1967 dollars) by gray iron foundries was $2,282 million in 1947 and $2,021 million in 1962. Output by steel foundries was $892 million in 1947 and $911 million in 1962. Demand for foundry products increased after 1962, and growth in these casting industries was sustained at least through 1970. Between 1962 and 1967, output by gray iron foundries increased 30% and production by steel foundries increased 33%. These percentage increases represent 5.5% and 5.9% average annual growth rates, respectively. (See Chart 26-3.)

The trends in output of gray iron and steel foundries are explained by changes in the sales levels of the industries they serve. The major markets of gray iron foundries are motor vehicles, farm machinery and equipment, and off-highway construction equipment. Steel foundries serve the same major markets, except that railroad equipment replaces farm machinery and equipment among the top three markets served. Sales by the major markets served by gray iron and steel foundries were relatively constant between 1947 and 1962. Consequently, foundry activity followed a similar trend.

The automotive market is the largest consumer of castings. Thirty-five per cent of the tonnage of gray iron castings and somewhat less of the tonnage of steel castings go into automotive parts. Chart 26-4 shows domestic factory sales of passenger cars from 1947 to 1971. From this chart, fluctuations in the activity of SIC 3321 and SIC 3323 can be deduced.

Of the remaining factors affecting output by gray iron and steel foundries, material substitution is perhaps most responsible for the retardation of growth between 1947 and 1962. Molded plastics, steel weldments, die castings, metal stampings, ceramics, and aluminum were all substituted for gray iron and steel castings. In some cases, gray iron or steel castings were substituted for forgings or malleable iron castings, offsetting some of this loss.

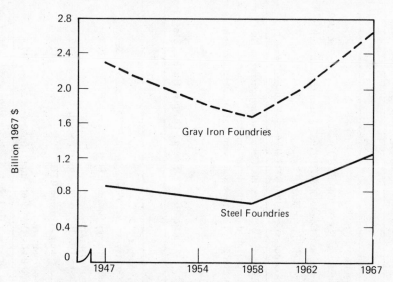

Chart 26-3. Value of Output of Gray Iron and Steel Foundries.
Source: U.S. Department of Commerce, *Census of Manufactures.*

Table 26-1.   Energy-Output Ratios, Gray Iron Foundry Industry

	1947	1954	1958	1962	1967	1975	1980[1]	1980[2]
Value of output (million constant 1967 $)	2,282	1,848	1,650	2,021	2,637	3,957	4,867	4,975
Total useful energy (trillion BTUs)	72.6	83.0	55.0	83.5	99.1	141.3	173.7	164.4
Energy-output ratio (1,000 BTUs/1967 $ of output) (useful)	31.7	44.8	33.4	41.3	37.6	35.7	35.7	35.7
Total gross energy (trillion BTUs)	83.9	92.3	63.5	94.7	118.8	172.9	212.7	217.4
Energy-output ratio (1,000 BTUs/1967 $ of output) (gross)	36.8	50.0	38.5	46.8	45.0	43.7	43.7	43.7

Sources: Bureau of the Census, *Census of Manufactures*; The Conference Board.
[1] Output projected on the assumption that rotary engine housing will be of aluminum.
[2] Output projected on the assumption that rotary engine housing will be of cast iron.

Table 26-2.   Energy-Output Ratios, Steel Foundry Industry

	1947	1954	1958	1962	1967	1975	1980
Value of output (million constant 1967 $)	892	731	663	911	1,213	1,597	1,980
Total useful energy (trillion BTUs)	29.7	27.3	24.0	29.3	39.8	53.2	66.5
Energy-output ratio (1,000 BTUs/1967 $ of output) (useful)	33.2	37.3	36.0	32.3	32.8	33.3	33.6
Total gross energy (trillion BTUs)	42.3	37.5	33.4	40.7	55.5	75.7	95.8
Energy-output ratio (1,000 BTUs/1967 $ of output) (gross)	47.4	51.3	50.4	44.7	45.8	47.4	48.4

Sources: Bureau of the Census, *Census of Manufactures*; The Conference Board.

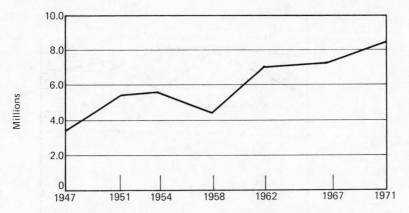

Chart 26-4. Factory Sales of Domestic Passenger Cars. Source: U.S. Department of Commerce, *Business Statistics*. 1971 edition.

Trends in Energy Utilization

The energy-output ratios measured in BTUs per 1967 dollar of output are fairly accurate indicators of trends in energy use in these industries. This is because specialization in the primary products is very high. The primary product specialization ratio has remained within two percentage points of 93% in SIC 3321, and 88% in SIC 3323 throughout the period. Since this ratio is so high, the energy-output ratio of secondary products is not likely to have a significant effect on the overall energy-output ratio.

Energy-Output Ratios

There are no continuous upward or downward trends in the energy-output ratios in either gray iron or steel foundries. In SIC 3321, energy utilization per unit of output fluctuates between census years—from 31,800 per dollar of production in 1947 to 44,800 in 1954, to 33,400 in 1958, etc. In SIC 3323, the energy-output ratio first rises, then falls from 1954 to 1962, rising again in the final period.

Because all castings require the same preparations, movements in the energy-output ratios cannot be explained by changes in the mix of castings produced.

A possible explanation for the fluctuations in the energy output ratios between 1947 and 1958 in both gray iron and steel foundries is the technological changes that took place outside of and within the industries. Those that occurred in industries served by gray iron and steel foundries have to do with the development of heavier and faster operating equipment (such as machine tools and farm equipment). Not only was the productivity of the new units of equipment greater, but each new unit replaced several units of older equipment. This new equipment required heavier gray iron or steel castings, but

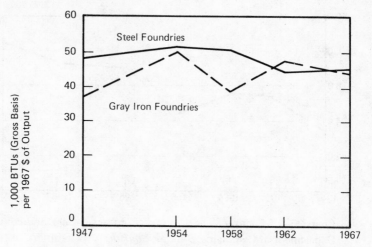

Chart 26-5. Energy-Output Ratios in Gray Iron and Steel Found-ries. Source: U.S. Department of Commerce, *Census of Manufactures.*

one casting might replace two or three castings previously demanded for the older equipment. Since the quantity of metal melted to produce fewer but heavier castings remains approximately the same, there is no increase in fuel requirements. Because the price of one heavier casting is not higher than the combined price of the two to three lighter-weight castings it replaces, per unit energy use will rise.

The technological change within the industry that affected the energy-output ratios was the development and production of lighter-weight castings of less dimensional variability—and hence of higher quality—through the increasing use of higher strength-to-weight steels. Because less metal is melted to produce the same number of lighter-weight castings, less fuel is required. Since the price of these higher quality castings would be either comparable to or higher than the older castings, the energy-output ratio would decline.

If the relevant technological development in the industries that SIC 3321 and SIC 3323 supply had greater effect between 1947 and 1954, and if the trend toward lighter-weight castings had greater effect in the latter period, this would explain the rise in the energy-output ratio between 1947 and 1954 and the decline between 1954 and 1958.

It should be noted that the gas and coke consumption figures from 1947 to 1962 may be too high. Because coke is consumed solely for melting, and gas is primarily utilized in heat treatments, molding, and coremaking, it is most improbable that consumption of these fuels was increasing in years when shipments, and hence production, were down. The consensus of industry and Bureau of the Census representatives is that these figures are overstated. The

Table 26-3.   Energy, Value of Output, and Energy-Output Ratios

	1947	1954	1958	1962	1967
SIC 3321					
Useful energy consumed (trillion BTUs)	72.6	83.0	55.0	83.5	99.1
Value of output (million constant 1967 $)	$2,282.0	$1,848.0	$1,650.0	$2,021.0	$2,638.0
Energy-output ratio (1,000 BTUs/1967 $ of output)	31.8	44.8	33.4	41.3	37.6
SIC 3323					
Useful energy consumed (trillion BTUs)	29.7	27.3	24.0	29.3	39.8
Value of output (million constant 1967 $)................	$892.0	$731.0	$663.0	$911.0	$1,213.2
Energy-output ratio (1,000 BTUs/1967 $ of output)	33.2	37.3	36.0	32.3	32.9

Source: Bureau of the Census, *Census of Manufactures.*

alternating up and down movements in the energy-output ratios prior to 1962 were probably less extreme than indicated by the Census data.

Part of the rise in electricity consumed is explained by the trend toward electric melting. Despite the development of energy-saving devices utilized in conjunction with the cupola furnace, the trend toward electric melting has increased. Table 26-4 presents data on the fuel and electrical energy requirements (in physical units and BTUs) to melt a ton of iron by type of furnace.

Table 26-4.   Energy Requirements to Melt a Ton of Iron, by Type of Furnace in SIC 3321

	Cupola	Electric Arc	Electric Induction	Reverberatory
Coke				
lbs.	250	–	–	–
BTUs (thousands)	3,250			
Gas				
cu. ft.	483	–	–	11,694
BTUs (thousands)	500			12,103
Electricity				
kwh................	40	550	600-650	–
BTUs (useful) (thousands)	136	1,877	2,047-2,218	2,218

More recent methods of operating the cupola are all means of increasing the efficiency of combustion and saving coke. These methods include the use of gas-fired air preheaters, forced draft blowers powered by electricity, and stack gas cleaning systems that utilize waste gas from the cupola and convert it into usable heat. The implementation of these techniques has reduced total coke requirements from 334 pounds per ton of iron melted to 250 pounds per ton of iron melted, and has reduced total BTUs required to melt one ton of iron by 456,000 BTUs between 1940 and 1965, even though electricity and gas are now required.

In spite of this saving in coke consumption and the higher energy costs involved in using electric furnaces, the trend toward electric melting has grown. It is likely that it will continue to grow because of better quality control (with lower-cost charge materials), less air pollution, shortages of high-quality coke, and the more pleasant working environment offered by electricity. In 1964, 94% of all melting in gray iron foundries was done in the cupola and 5% in electric furnaces. Today electric furnace melting accounts for 10% of the tonnage melted in gray iron foundries.

When looking at overall levels of energy utilization per unit of output in SIC 3323, we see a very small decline between 1947 and 1967. On a useful energy basis, the fall in the energy-output ratio is an almost insignificant 1%. On a gross energy basis, the decline is slightly larger, measuring 3%.

While the overall energy output ratio has changed very little, the gray iron and steel foundry industries have substituted increasing quantities of electricity and gas for other fuels.

Approximately 75% of total energy consumed is utilized in melting operations. Of the total tonnage of steel melted for castings, 50% was melted in the open-hearth furnace in 1957 and 50% in electric furnaces. In 1964, these figures were 45% and 55%, respectively. The trend toward electric melting has continued so that today the tonnage melted in electric furnaces is even higher. This trend partially accounts for the increases in consumption of electricity. Trends in energy use in the open-hearth furnaces account for the majority of the increase in gas consumption. Open-hearth furnaces are fired with either gas or oil. When producer gas made from coal is used as fuel, consumption is in terms of coal. Since 1947, consumption of oil and coal has been declining. This is explained by the increasing use of gas instead of oil in heating the open-hearth furnace and the conversion of coal-fired open-hearth furnaces to gas.

In Table 26-5, fuel and electric energy requirements are given for melting a ton of steel by type of furnace. The figures given for gas, oil, and coal are not to be totaled but represent operation of the open-hearth with different fuel sources.

Aside from changes in the melting operations there were many other technological advances in the foundry industry—high pressure molding machines, synthetic resin core binders, and basic lined cupolas—that caused consumption

Table 26-5. Energy Requirements to Melt a Ton of Steel, by Type of Furnace in SIC 3323

Furnace Type	Energy Requirements
Open-hearth	
Gas	
cu. ft.	48
BTUs (thousands)	50
Oil	
Gallons	28-35
BTUs (thousands)	4,453
Coal	
lbs.	550-600
BTUs (thousands)	7,418
Electric arc	
kwh	550
BTUs (useful) (thousands)	1,877
Electric induction	
kwh	600-650
BTUs (useful) (thousands)	2,132

Sources: Heine, Loper, Rosenthal, *Principles of Metal Casting*, McGraw-Hill Book Company, 1967; Telephone conversations with industry representatives.

of gas and electricity to rise after 1962. Since over 80% of all ferrous and nonferrous foundries finance expenditures on new equipment internally, they were not able to mechanize their operations until 1962, when funds became available. The trend toward mechanization in the gray iron and steel foundry industries may explain some of the change in the energy-output ratios, even though the consumption of fuels and electricity in automated operations exclusive of melting and heat treatment accounts for only 3% to 5% of total energy requirements (on a useful basis).

Another development that has affected per unit energy consumption in the gray iron and steel foundry industries in the increase in typical plant size. The number of establishments in SIC 3321 declined continuously between 1947 and 1967, from 1,655 in 1947 to 1,061 in 1967. But the majority of plants that closed were small family-operated firms whose costs and investment per ton of castings were generally three to six times higher than the costs for larger producers. The closing of these plants has probably decreased the per unit energy requirements of gray iron foundries and lowered the energy-output ratio.

In the steel foundry industry the number of establishments has increased from 203 in 1947 to 296 in 1967. As new plants were constructed they were able to take advantage of new technology and the economies of scale resulting from larger firm size. Substantial increases in the energy-output ratio due to automation and pollution control equipment were probably offset by the less wasteful use of energy in these new plants.

A final factor that has affected trends in energy use during the past ten years is installation of pollution-control facilities to meet state and federal air pollution standards. Such equipment as baghouse filters, scrubbers, and high energy dry cyclones use a substantial amount of energy, mainly in the form of electricity. Although no data are available, it is expected that the energy requirements of this equipment have caused increases in the energy-output ratios and will continue to do so.

SECTION III.   PROJECTIONS TO 1980

Demand for Castings

It is assumed that growth in the output of gray iron and steel castings will continue to 1980. After 1975, growth in gray iron castings is expected to decelerate because of trends in the auto market. Sometime between 1976 and 1978, the rotary engine is expected to be rapidly adopted. Coinciding with this development will be an overall trend in the automotive market toward smaller auto engines. Both of these developments will reduce the casting weight per car.

Although the rotary engine is not on the assembly lines of any United States auto producers at this time, estimates of weight differences between the traditional reciprocating engine and the rotary engine are available. General Motors claims that its rotary engine is 30% lighter than a comparable piston engine; and the Mazda Motors Company, which is presently producing the Wankel, claims that its engine is half the weight of a conventional piston engine producing comparable horsepower.

Part of this weight reduction is due to the smaller number of parts in the rotary (70 basic parts in the rotary as opposed to 230 in the piston engine), and part is due to the use of aluminum in the rotor housing. General Motors has cited the failure of gray iron in the rotary—due to the high heat concentration on the combustion side of the engine—as the reason for using aluminum. However, General Motors foundrymen believe that the housing can eventually be made of cast iron, a less expensive material than aluminum.

The trend toward smaller auto engines that began in 1969 is expected to continue through 1980. Part of the impetus for this change has come from increasing traffic congestion and the rise in fuel prices, both of which are expected to persist. Therefore, through 1980, relatively fewer engines larger than 250 cubic inches, and relatively more 250 cubic inch and under engines, are foreseen.

To project the rate of growth in output of gray iron foundries, projections of castings for the automotive market and for the remaining output of the industry are made separately. Two separate projections of growth rates are made in the automotive market. One on the assumption that the rotor housing will be of aluminum, and one on the assumption that the difficulties can be resolved and cast iron used in the rotor housing. The separate projections for the automotive market are made only for the period between 1975 and

1980, because the rotary engine will not make up a significant portion of the market before 1975.

At present, each passenger car in use has about 600 to 700 pounds of gray iron castings in its structure, but not all of these castings are in the engine. Approximately 65% of the weight of a 200 horsepower engine consists of gray iron castings. The total weight of an engine is about 500 pounds; therefore, 325 pounds of it is gray iron castings. Using the General Motors estimate of a 30% reduction in engine weight for its version, the rotary engine would weigh about 350 pounds. If the rotor housing is made of aluminum, about 50% of these 350 pounds, or 175 pounds, will be iron castings. This amounts to a loss of 150 pounds of cast iron per passenger car. On the basis of interviews with industry analysts, it is estimated that 35% of the market will be rotary-powered cars in 1980. On the assumption that approximately 11 million domestically-produced cars will be sold in 1980 (forecast from *U.S. Industrial Outlook*), this amounts to production of 3,850,000 rotary engines and a loss of 577.5 million tons of iron castings.

Should the rotary engine not be introduced by 1980,[1] it is estimated that sales of castings for automotive engines would grow at an average annual rate of 3.3% a year between 1967 and 1980, paralleling the growth in the auto market. Due to the weight loss resulting from rotary engine production with the use of aluminum for housings, the tonnage of castings supplied to the auto engine market will grow at a 0.9% annual rate between 1975 and 1980.

If we assume that the rotor housing will be made of cast iron, the differential in weight between a comparable piston and rotary engine would be an estimated 128 pounds. In this case, the average annual growth rate of gray iron castings between 1975 and 1980 for engine parts would be 2.6%.

To project overall growth in output of the gray iron foundry industry, it was first assumed that the rotary engine will not affect the casting industry until after 1975, and projections of output in constant dollars were made to 1975 based on the Interindustry Forecasting Model of the University of Maryland (INFORUM). Second, projections of growth in SIC 3321 from 1975 to 1980 were made excluding sales of castings for auto engines. Third, projections of the tonnage of castings for auto engines were made, and it was assumed

Table 26-6.   Projected Value of Output of Gray Iron and Steel Foundries

	1967	1975	1980[1]	1980[2]
Gray iron foundries ($ millions)	$2,637	$3,957	$4,867	$4,975
Steel foundries ($ millions)	1,213	1,597	1,980	1,980

[1] Output projected on the assumption that aluminum rotor housings will be produced.
[2] Output projected on the assumption that cast iron rotor housings will be produced.
Source: The Conference Board.

that this growth rate will correspond fairly closely to growth in the value of shipments. And fourth, the growth rates estimated in steps two and three were averaged (weighted) to arrive at a final projection of ouput in the gray iron foundry industry to 1980. Steps two, three, and four were done twice, once on the assumption that the rotor housings will be of aluminum and once on the assumption that they will be of cast iron.

It is estimated that production of the gray iron foundry industry will grow at an average annual rate of 5.2% from 1967 to 1975, a figure very close to the rate between 1962 and 1967. (This estimate was derived from the INFORUM Maryland Model.) After 1975, growth in the gray iron foundry industry is projected to slow down somewhat, due to an anticipated deceleration in the growth of the industries supplied by SIC 3321, the expected introduction of the rotary engine, and to the continuing trend toward production of smaller auto engines. It is estimated that growth from 1975 to 1980 will be at an average annual rate of 4.3% if the rotor housings are made of aluminum, and of 4.7% if they are made of cast iron. Applying these figures, output in 1967 dollars by gray iron foundries is projected to total $3,957 million in 1975 and $4,867 million in 1980 if aluminum housings are produced, and $4,975 million in 1980 if cast iron housings are produced.

The steel foundry industry also supplies the automotive market with many castings, but the majority of these castings are not utilized in the engine. Therefore, the introduction of the rotary is not expected to have a significant impact on the steel foundry industry. When based on Conference Board assumptions regarding trends in economic aggregates during the 1970s, the Interindustry Forecasting Model of the University of Maryland predicts a 3.5% average annual rate of growth in production between 1967 and 1975 and a 4.4% average annual rate of growth from 1975 to 1980. The corresponding output figures are $1,597 million and $1,980 million, respectively.

Demand for Energy

While technological changes are occurring, no major changes are likely to be introduced by 1980 in either the gray iron foundry industry or the steel foundry industry that are expected to affect energy reqirements. A gas injection system developed for the cupola furnace used by the gray iron foundry industry was ready for use in 1969. This system is a practical way to reduce melting costs and increase melting rates by replacing up to half the normal coke consumption with less expensive natural gas. But because of difficulties in obtaining gas, it is uncertain to what extent this system will be used. The introduction and use of air-setting type sands for molds and cores is expected to increase. These, which will replace green sand molding in making large molds and cores, do not require ovens for heating. Therefore, it is unlikely that the use of these new sands will increase energy consumption.

A trend toward further automation of foundry activities—e.g., conveyorization, push-button control panels for more operations, automatic molding machines—is expected to extend through the 1970s. This is expected to boost the energy-output ratio in these industries only slightly, however. Some of the automation will be accounted for by modernization of previously mechanized activities. Also, the impact on energy use per unit of output due to any additional mechanization should be largely offset by a rise in tonnage per foundry, due to the attrition of smaller unmechanized establishments that are now marginal operations and that will be unable to modernize. Per unit of output, larger melts are more economical than smaller melts with respect to energy consumption.

Table 26-7.   Projected Energy-Output Ratio to 1980 (1,000 BTUs/1967 $ of output)

	1967	*1975*	*1980*
SIC 3321			
Gross energy	45.0	41.7	39.5
Useful energy	37.6	36.0	35.0
SIC 3323			
Gross energy	45.8	47.4	48.4
Useful energy	32.8	33.3	33.6

Sources: Bureau of the Census, *Census of Manufactures*; The Conference Board.

Table 26-8.   Projected Energy Consumption to 1980 (trillion BTUs)

	1967	*1975*	*1980*[1]	*1980*[2]
SIC 3321				
Gross energy	118.8	172.9	212.7	217.4
Useful energy	99.1	141.3	173.7	177.6
SIC 3323				
Gross energy	55.5	75.7	95.8	95.8
Useful energy	39.8	53.2	66.5	66.5

[1] Projections based on assumption of aluminum rotor housing.
[2] Projections based on assumption of cast iron rotor housing.
Sources: Bureau of the Census, *Census of Manufactures*; The Conference Board.

One more source of increase in energy consumption should be the continuing installation of air pollution devices. The increase in electrical energy consumed for pollution abatement coupled with the increase due to automation are being translated into higher energy-output ratios in the steel foundry industry, and have slowed and then halted the decline in the energy-output ratio in the gray iron foundry industry.

It is estimated that the level of energy utilization (useful) per unit of output by the gray iron foundry industry declined at an average annual rate of

1% between 1967 and 1971, and that it will level off between 1971 and 1980. Energy consumption (useful) per unit of output in the steel foundry industry is expected to increase at an average annual rate of 0.4% between 1967 to 1980. On a gross energy basis, the decline in SIC 3321 is expected to be 0.6% a year, and the growth rate in SIC 3323 is expected to be 0.2% a year.

On the basis of projections of value of output and energy utilization per unit of output, calculations were made to obtain estimates of total fuels and electricity consumed (in BTUs) through 1980.

Note

[1] Chevrolet is planning to install a rotor engine in the Vega, beginning with the 1975 model year. This, however, is expected to have little impact on energy use by gray iron foundries (SIC 3321); the present Vega engine (4-cylinder reciprocating) is made of aluminum.

SECTION IV.   SELECTED BIBLIOGRAPHY

American Gas Association, *A Study of Process Energy Requirements in the Iron and Steel Industry.*

Amner, Dean S. *Mechanization and Manpower in Gray–Iron Foundries.* Boston, Massachusetts: Northeastern University, 1965.

Borch, Einar A. "Foundries Look to the Future." *Foundry Magazine,* Penton Publishing Co., Cleveland, Ohio, January 1973.

Brown, J. W. "Electric Arc Furnaces–a $35 Million Annual Load." *Electrical World,* February 5, 1968.

Census of Manufactures, U.S. Department of Commerce, Bureau of the Census, Ekey and Winter, *Introduction to Foundry Technology,* McGraw-Hill Book Company, Inc., New York, 1958.

Gude, William G. "Foundries Face the Energy Crisis." *Foundry Magazine,* Penton Publishing Co., Cleveland, Ohio, February 1971.

Haecker, C. F. "Iron Melting and Pollution Control." *Foundry Magazine,* Penton Publishing Co., Cleveland, Ohio, February 1971.

Heine, Loper, and Rosenthal. *Principles of Metal Casting,* McGraw-Hill Book Company, New York, New York, 1967.

"How Emission Control Affects Melting Costs." *Foundry Magazine,* Penton Publishing Co., Cleveland, Ohio, May 1971.

Huskonen. "The Wankel Rotary Engine–What it Means to You." *Foundry Magazine,* Penton Publishing Co., Cleveland, Ohio, May 1973.

"Inventory of Foundry Equipment." *Foundry Magazine,* Penton Publishing Co., Cleveland, Ohio, May 1954.

McGannon, Harold E., ed. *The Making, Shaping, and Treating of Steel,* 9th ed. Pittsburgh, Pennsylvania: Herbick and Held, 1970.

Venendaal, Robert and Davis, J. A. "Equipping for Natural Gas

Cupola Injection." *Foundry Magazine*, Penton Publishing Co., Cleveland, Ohio, July 1969.

Weber, Herbert J. "Impact of Air Pollution Laws in the Small Foundry." *Air Pollution Control Association Journal*, February 1970.

"What Automation Can Do for Foundries." *Metal Progress,* February 1970.

Chapter Twenty-Seven

Copper Rolling and Drawing – SIC 3351

Paul A. Parker

SECTION I. INTRODUCTION AND SUMMARY[a]

The Rolling, Drawing and Extruding of Copper industry, SIC 3351, is composed of establishments converting copper, brass, bronze, and other copper base alloys into basic shapes such as plate, sheet, strip, bar and tubing. The production process is a cycle of pressure forming of metal rods, cooling, annealing, and pickling that is repeated several times. It should be noted that the definition of SIC 3351 has varied slightly throughout the period studied.

The 1967 distribution of fuel use was: coal, 7.5%; misc. fuel, 16.3%; electricity, 17.9%; fuel oil, 22.9%; gas, 35.4%. Annealing ovens are the greatest energy consumer and are usually gas or electrically fired.

Output, measured in value of shipments, grew at a 1.0% annual rate from a 1947 level of $1.960 billion to $2.391 billion in 1967 (1967 constant dollars). This rate is somewhat low due to a strike in the copper smelting industry in 1966-1967 (which greatly reduced copper supplies in the last year) and to changes in statistical coverage.

Energy use grew at a 0.7% annual rate in this same period, from 37.9 trillion BTUs in 1947, to 43.7 trillion BTUs in 1967.

The energy-output ratio fluctuated throughout the period, arriving in 1967 at 18,300 BTUs per dollar shipped.

Output is projected to grow at a 3.5% annual rate to 1980. Value of shipments, in 1967 prices, is expected to reach $3.184 billion by 1975, and $3.727 billion by 1980.

Because of past instablilities, the energy-output ratio can only be predicted to fluctuate through 1980 around an average level of about 18,000

[a] Valuable technical information for this study was provided by the Wire Association and corporate experts.

BTUs per 1967 constant dollar shipped on a gross basis[b] (or 13,000 on a useful energy basis).

At this ratio 57.3 trillion BTUs would be required by 1975, and 67.1 trillion BTUs by 1980, to produce the expected level of output. (On a useful energy basis, this would be 41.4 and 48.5 trillion BTUs respectively.)

SECTION II.   THE PRESENT INDUSTRY

The industry's 1967 primary product specialization ratio (primary to primary plus secondary products) was 90%. In the same year, the coverage ratio (the specified copper products produced in the industry to those produced in all industry) was 93%. Thus, these establishments deal almost exclusively in the specified copper products and account for nearly all production of those products.

Although many shapes and products are manufactured from copper, bronze, and brass in the industry, the production process is basically the same for each. This similarity is primarily due to the metallic properties of copper.

The production process runs as follows:

The basic metal arrives at the mill in the form of rods, billets, or ingots. It is then often recast into the form to be worked. In 1967, 66.2% of the establishments in the industry had casting departments, 33.8% did not.

The metal is then repeatedly run through machinery that gradually changes its form, one step at a time, through applications of pressure. This is done by passing between large rollers (rolling), pulling through dies (drawing), or forcing through dies or tubes (extruding). As a result of the great pressure applied, the metal becomes heated and must be cooled in water tanks between runs. (The water itself is then cooled in towers and recycled for further use.) After several runs under pressure, copper and copper based metals become brittle. The metal must be annealed, or heated to high temperatures, and then cooled to restore ductility and flexibility. Also, periodically, the metal must be pickled, in a heated chemical solution, to remove surface oxides. After many cycles of pressure and cooling, annealing, and pickling, the end product is formed.

SECTION III.   HISTORICAL DEVELOPMENT

Statistical coverage of the industry has varied throughout much of the period studied. Only the long-range trends can be safely discussed, and these show extremely low rates of change.

Output (value of shipments in 1967 dollars) grew from $1.960 billion in 1947, to $2.391 billion in 1967. This is equal to an annual growth rate of 1.0% (see Table 27-1, column A). It must be noted, however, that the copper

[b] See Chapter One, pages 14-15, for definitions of gross and useful energy.

Table 27-1. Output and Energy Use, 1947 to 1980

	(A)	(B)	(C)	(D)	(E)
		Gross Energy Consumed Basis		*Useful Energy Basis*	
	Value of Shipments (Million 1967 $)	Total Energy Use (Trillion BTUs)	(1,000 BTUs/1967 $): (B) ÷ (A)	Total Energy Use (Trillion BTUs)	Energy/Output Ratio (1,000 BTUs/1967 $): (D) ÷ (A)
Actual					
1947	$1,960	37.9	19.3	27.9	14.2
1954	1,783	29.7	16.7	21.8	12.2
1958	1,636	35.7	21.2	28.2	16.7
1962	2,133	36.8	17.2	27.7	13.0
1967	2,391	43.7	18.3	31.9	13.3
Projected					
1975	3,184	57.3	18.0	41.4	13.0
1980	3,727	67.1	18.0	48.5	13.0

Source: Bureau of the Census, *Census of Manufactures*, Vol. II, 1967 & 1963.

Table 27-2.   Energy Use, by Source, 1947 to 1967

Year	Total	Purchased[1] Electricity	Coal	Fuel Oil	Natural Gas	Other or Not Specified
			Trillion BTUs			
1947	27.9	2.8	12.2	6.5	5.8	0.7
1954	21.8	3.1	6.5	5.9	4.8	1.6
1958	28.2	3.3	8.8	7.5	7.9	0.7
1962	27.7	4.4	6.7	6.7	9.2	0.7
1967	31.9	5.7	2.4	7.3	11.3	5.2
			Per Cent			
1947	100	10.0	43.7	23.3	20.8	2.5
1954	100	14.2	29.8	27.0	22.0	7.3
1958	100	11.7	31.2	26.6	28.0	2.5
1962	100	15.9	24.2	24.2	33.2	2.5
1967	100	17.9	7.5	22.9	35.4	16.3

[1] Useful energy basis.

Source: Bureau of the Census, *Census of Manufactures*, Vol. II, 1967 & 1963.

mining and smelting industry underwent a major strike in 1966-1967. Copper supplies for manufacturing were therefore limited in 1967, and total output of SIC 3351 was affected. The growth rate of output is thus somewhat lower than it would have been if post-1967 data were available.

Total fuel use grew at a 0.7% annual rate in this same period, from 37.9 trillion BTUs in 1947, to 43.7 trillion BTUs in 1967 (see Table 27-1, column B).

The energy-output ratio fluctuated in a narrow range between 1947 and 1967 (see Table 27-1, column C). Much of this fluctuation is believed to be due to changes in data coverage. The best that can be said is that the ratio remained roughly constant over the twenty years.

The major technological change that occurred during this period was in the rolling sector of the industry. In 1958-1962 a new generation of machinery was introduced. Previously, copper rods were cast or purchased. They were then rolled down to a gauge suitable to be handled by the wiremaking or other end product machinery. The new process involved semi-continuous or continuous production. In this, the copper was cast directly into a narrow gauge suitable for processing. This eliminated several of the previous reducing runs, with resultant energy savings.

It is believed that this innovation accounts for much of the drop in the energy-output ratio between 1958 and 1962. The magnitude of the innovation's impact is unclear, however, due to the changes in statistical coverage in the same period (see Figure 27-1).

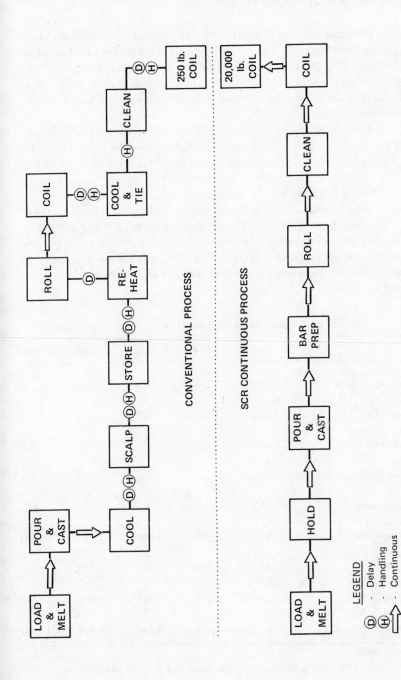

Figure 27-1. "Continuous Process" Innovation in Rolled Wire Production. Source: Southwire Co., Carrollton, Ga.

SECTION IV.   PROJECTIONS TO 1980

The major problem facing the industry is the maintenance of an adequate supply of copper for processing. Much of the world's copper ore reserves are located in countries with either political instability or popular movements toward expropriation of foreign holdings. Frequent strikes have marked the U.S. basic copper industry as well. However, large amounts of scrap copper are available and may serve to reduce any slack in supply.

The Maryland Interindustry Forecasting Model projects sales in constant prices to rise at an annual rate of 3.5%, from 1972 to 1980. This may prove slightly high due to the above-mentioned problems in raw material supply. Using this 3.5% growth rate, value of shipments, in 1967 prices, would reach $3.184 billion by 1975 and $3.727 billion by 1980.

An innovation in the extrusion die wiremaking process has recently been patented by Western Electric. The technique involves feeding a coated rod into a moving pressure chamber. The coating provides a better grip. The process requires only a single extrusion run (versus several runs in the previous system).[1] This promises significant energy savings but will take several years to become implemented throughout this segment of the industry.

Table 27-3.   Fuel Use in Physical Units

	1947	*1954*	*1958*	*1962*	*1967*
Coal (thous. short tons)	468	252	343	260	92
Fuel oil, total (thous. bbls.)	1,125	1,010	1,293	1,156	1,261
Distillate (thous. bbls.)	n.a.	n.a.	n.a.	190	525
Residual (thous. bbls.)	n.a.	n.a.	n.a.	966	736
Misc. fuel (million current $)	$.3	$.7	$.3	$.3	$2.3
Electricity, total (million kwh)	987	1,028	1,220	1,493	1,781
Purchased electricity (million kwh)	817	898	975	1,277	1,681
Generated less sold (million kwh)	170	130	245	216	100
Gas (million cu. ft.)	5,617	4,678	7,644	8,887	10,901

n.a. = not available.

Source: Bureau of the Census, *Census of Manufactures*, Vol. II, 1967 and 1963.

Because of its past instability, the energy-output ratio can only be predicted to fluctuate around its past average. This average may be slightly lower than the 1967 ratio, due to overall improvements in production efficiency, and effects of the above-mentioned innovation after a lag of several years.

Thus the energy-output ratio is projected about 18,000 BTUs per 1967 constant dollar shipped through 1980. Therefore, to produce the 1975 and 1980 output levels estimated above, approximately 57.3 and 67.1 trillion BTUs, respectively, would be required.

(See Table 27-1, columns D and E, for the above projections computed on a useful energy basis.)

Note

[1] *N.Y. Times,* June 30, 1973, "Improved Wire Making Machine Is Devised," p. 43.

SECTION V.   SELECTED BIBLIOGRAPHY

Battelle Institute. *A Study to Identify Opportunities for Increased Solid Waste Utilization,* Vol. II Aluminum, Vol. III Copper. Battelle Memorial Institute, Columbus, 1972.

Brown, Martin S. and Butler, John. *The Production, Marketing, and Consumption of Copper and Aluminum.* Frederick A. Praeger, Pubs.; New York, 1968.

Bureau of Mines, *Materials Survey—Copper.* Washington, D.C., 1965.

Bureau of the Census, *Census of Manufactures,* Vol. II, 1967 & 1963. Washington, D.C.

Houthakker, Hendrik S. "Copper: The Anatomy of a Malfunctioning Market." Remarks delivered at Duke Univ., Durham, North Carolina, March 11, 1970 for Executive Office of the President's Council of Economic Advisers.

"Improved Wire Making Machine Is Devised." *N.Y. Times.* June 30, 1972.

Wykes, R. and Duncan, W. F. "The Evolution of the Modern Copper Rod Mill." *Wire Journal.* September 1972, pp. 102-116.

Chapter Twenty-Eight

Nonferrous Wiredrawing, Insulating—SIC 3357

Paul A. Parker

SECTION I. INTRODUCTION AND SUMMARY

The Drawing and Insulating of Nonferrous Wire industry, SIC 3357, (hereafter drawn nonferrous wire) is defined in the 1972 Standard Industrial Classification Manual as:

"Establishments primarily engaged in drawing, drawing and insulating, and insulating wire and cable of nonferrous metals from purchased wire bars, rods, or wire." Primary products are listed as: wire and cable in general; plus aircraft, coaxial, communication, magnet, shipboard signal, and weatherproof wire and cable specifically.

The wire is made by a process of repeatedly drawing the rods through dies to reduce their diameter, and cooling after each run; then periodically annealing to restore ductility and flexibility, and pickling to remove surface oxides. The finished wire is coated by extruding it through tubes of melted plastic coating.

The 1967 distribution of energy use was: electricity, 25.9%; coal, 6.1%; fuel oil, 19.4%; gas, 29.1%; misc. fuel, 19.0%. The principal sources, electricity and gas, are used for the many heatings involved in annealing and pickling.

Output, measured in value of shipments, grew from $1.628 billion in 1954 to $3.591 billion in 1967; or at an annual rate of 6.3%. Fuel use grew from 25.6 trillion BTUs in 1958, to 37.9 trillion BTUs in 1967, an annual rate of increase of 4.5%.

The energy-output ratio declined from 13.5 thousand BTUs per 1967 dollar of output in 1958 to 10.6 thousand BTUs per dollar of output in 1967. This decline, at a 2.6% annual rate, was primarily due to a new generation of machinery introduced in the period 1958-1962. The new machinery significantly reduced the number of runs required to reduce the metal rods to a given wire gauge, thereby saving energy. The innovation has continued to spread throughout the industry, at a lower rate, ever since.

Output is projected to grow at a 5.9% annual rate, reaching about $5.019 billion (value of shipments in 1967 prices) by 1980. The energy-output ratio is expected to continue to improve, though at a slightly lower rate, reaching about 10.0 thousand BTUs per 1967 $ shipped by 1975 and 9.5 by 1980. At these ratios, the projected output would require 50.2 trillion BTUs in 1975 and 58.4 in 1980.

The drawing and insulating of nonferrous wire industry has been experiencing major technical innovations and still is. These innovations have worked to greatly simplify the production process. As a result, large energy savings have occurred in the past and probably will again in the future.

SECTION II.   THE PRESENT INDUSTRY

The industry's 1967 primary product specialization ratio (primary to primary secondary products) was 90%. In the same year, the coverage ratio (drawn nonferrous wire produced in this industry, to that produced in all industries) was 93%. Thus, these establishments produce principally drawn nonferrous wire, and account for almost all the production.

Drawn, nonferrous wire production has three stages: rod casting-rolling, wire drawing, and wire insulating. Mills are classified into four types: mills with casting, drawing and insulating; mills with wire drawing only; mills with drawing and insulating; mills with insulating only.

It is important to note the distribution. Major technological advances in the period studied have occurred in the rod casting-rolling and wire insulating sectors. Yet, because of the differences in mill types, their impact has not been felt throughout the industry. (These advances are discussed under Historical Development.)

Nonferrous wire is copper or aluminum wire. The production techniques are basically the same for both, and can be summarized as follows. The basic metal arrives at the mill in the form of rolled rods or, less commonly, billets. The rods are pointed at one end and fed into a conical orifice, usually of

Table 28-1.   Distribution of Value of Shipments, by Mill Type

	Nonferrous Wiredrawing, Insulating				
	With Rod & Insulating Mill	Without Rod or Insulating Mill	Without Rod, but with Insulating Mill	Insulating Mill Only	Total
1967	17.0%	6.0%	56.4%	20.7%	100%

Source: Bureau of the Census, *Census of Manufactures*, Vol. II, p. 5. 33D-19 & 20

tungsten carbide, in the drawing die. A clamp, called a "dog," is attached and the rod is pulled through. The drawing reduces the diameter of the rod, which is then cooled. This process is repeated several times, gradually reducing the size of the wire. After several runs, the metal becomes hardened and brittle. It must then be annealed, which involves heating the metal to restore ductility. The metal must then be pickled in heated chemical fluids to remove the surface oxides. The entire process is then repeated until a wire of the required gauge or hardness is produced.

The wire is then usually insulated in an extruding process. Plastic, paper pulp, or enamel is used as a coating base. Coloring, filler and other ingredients are added and the mix melted. The wire is drawn through a tube bearing the pressurized hot mix and emerges coated. The coated wire is then cooled in water troughs.

Major pollution problems are created in the production process. The copper-oxide-sludge and rinse water by-products of the pickling stage are the greatest problem, due to the presence of harmful salts. Once purified, these copper-oxides are marketable, which can serve to ameliorate this cost of pollution control.

In the enamel coating of magnetic wire, the final baking process drives off harmful solvents. Plating of wire with tin, silver, zinc, or gold often employs acids or cyanides for the electrolytic solution. These liquids pose severe toxicity problems in their disposal.

SECTION III.   HISTORICAL DEVELOPMENT

The drawn nonferrous wire industry has been marked by constant growth in the period studied.

Output, measured in value of shipments, has increased at a 6.3% annual rate, from $1.628 billion in 1954 to $3.591 billion in 1967 (see Table 28-2, column A).

Fuel use, measured in BTUs, grew at 4.5% annually, rising from 25.6 rillion in 1958 to 37.9 trillion in 1967 (see Table 28-2, column B).

The energy use per unit of output ratio (thousand BTUs per 1967 $ shipped) has declined as a 2.6% annaul rate, from 13.5 in 1958 to 10.6 in 1967 (see Table 28-2, column C).

In the period 1958-1962, a new generation of copper rod-producing machinery was developed. These new machines involved continuous or semi-continuous production. Originally, the large metal rods that arrived at a mill had to be reduced in diameter to a gauge that could be worked by the wire machinery. In the new process, metal arrives and is cast and rolled directly into rods of a narrow gauge suitable for the wire machinery. (The Southwire Continuous, the Properszi, and the Hazlett continuous casting machines are three of the new lines.)

Table 28-2.   Output and Energy Use, 1958-1980

	(A)	(B) Gross Energy Consumed Basis[1]	(C)	(D) Useful Energy Basis[1]	(E)
	Value of Shipments (million 1967 $)	Total Energy Use (trillion BTUs)	Energy/Output Ratio (1,000 BTUs/1967 $: B ÷ A)	Total Energy Use (trillion BTUs)	Energy/Output Ratio (1,000 BTUs/1967 $: D ÷ A)
Actual					
1958	$1,893	25.6	13.5	18.9	10.00
1962	2,435	26.5	10.9	17.8	7.31
1967	3,591	37.9	10.6	24.7	6.98
Projected					
1975	5,019	50.2	10.0	30.6	6.4
1980	6,149	58.4	9.5	35.6	6.1

[1] See Chapter One, pages 14-15, for definitions of gross and useful energy.

Source: Bureau of the Census, *Census of Manufactures*, 1967 & 1963.

Table 28-3. Energy Use by Source, 1958-1967

Year	Total	Purchased[1] Electricity	Coal	Fuel Oil	Natural Gas	Other or Not Specified
			Trillion BTUs			
1958	18.9	3.0	5.7	2.8	3.9	3.4
1962	17.8	4.2	3.1	5.6	3.8	1.1
1967	24.7	6.4	1.5	4.8	7.2	4.7
			Per Cent			
1958	100	15.9	30.2	14.8	20.6	18.0
1962	100	23.6	17.4	31.5	21.3	6.2
1967	100	25.9	6.1	19.4	29.1	19.0

[1] Useful energy basis.
Source: Bureau of the Census, *Census of Manufactures*, Vol. II, 1967 & 1963.

While statistical coverage of the industry does not include billet casting, it does include their reduction from billet to workable rod size. The new machinery thus eliminated several reducing runs on the production process. Significant energy savings per unit of output were realized.

The continuous casting machinery received its basic implementation in the years 1958-1962, and has since continued to spread throughout the industry, though at a somewhat slower rate. Thus, the greatest improvement in the energy-output ratio occurred in 1958-1962, and slower improvement has continued steadily thereafter.

At the present time, interest in this equipment is again rising, perhaps due to its energy conserving properties.

SECTION IV. PROJECTIONS TO 1980

Continued growth approximately equal to the historical rates can be expected to occur in the industry to 1980.

The Maryland Interindustry Forecasting Model projects a 5.9% annual growth rate in sales to 1980. When converted to value of shipments, this would mean a 4.2% annual rise to $5.019 billion by 1975 and to $6.149 billion in 1980 (both in 1967 prices). The only major inhibitor to growth will be the availability of a steady supply of copper (which is subject to many international political stresses). But the slack may be taken up with scrap copper or aluminum.

The new continuous process machinery will continue to spread to the remaining unconverted mills in the industry. Further refinements in the machinery can also be expected. In addition, a new, extrusion die wiremaking process requiring a single production pass[1] has been recently patented by Western Electric Co. While this is an extrusion process, it has applications for

Table 28-4.   Fuel Use in Physical Units, 1958-1967

	1958	*1962*	*1967*
Coal (thousand short tons)	222	122	59
Fuel oil, total (thousand bbls.)	490	964	825
Distillate (thousand bbls.)	n.a.	110	248
Residual (thousand bbls.)	n.a.	854	577
Misc. fuel (million current $)	$1.5	$.5	$2.1
Electricity, total (million kwh)	958	1,265	1,886
Purchased (million kwh)	874	1,221	1,885
Generated less sold (million kwh)	78	44	1
Gas (million cu. ft.)	3,794	3,640	6,954

n.a. = not available

Source: Bureau of the Census, *Census of Manufactures*, 1967, 1963.

drawn wire. An ongoing trend in the industry to switch from alkaline to acid electrolytic solutions in wireplating may produce some energy savings; as the acids are generally more efficient in their use of electric current, and both solutions require about the same amounts of detoxification before discharge.

Acting against these factors of improvement are the energy demands resulting from the onset of environmental regulation. The oxide sludge by-products of the pickling stage of production was previously used as landfill. In the future, the fluid component will have to be distilled before discharge to remove harmful salts, and the oxides dried for resale. The solvents from enamel baking and used electrolytic solutions must also be neutralized before discharge.

On balance, the energy-output ratio can be expected to continue declining but at a slower rate. The ratio should reach approximately 10.0 thousand BTUs per 1967 $ shipped by 1975, and 9.5 thousand BTUs per 1967 $ shipped by 1980. Combined with projected output, these ratios would result in a total fuel use of 50.2 trillion BTUs in 1975, and 58.4 trillion BTUs in 1980 (see Table 28-1, columns D and E, for the above projections computed on a useful energy basis).

Note

[1] *N.Y. Times,* June 30, 1973, "Improved Wire Making Machine Is Devised," p. 43.

SECTION V.   SELECTED BIBLIOGRAPHY

Battelle Memorial Institute. *A Study to Identify Opportunities for Increased Solid Waste Utilization*, Vol. II Aluminum, Vol. III Copper. Battelle Institute: Columbus, 1972.

Brown, Martin S. and Butler, John. *The Production, Marketing, and*

Consumption of Copper and Aluminum. New York: Frederick A. Praeger, 1968.

Bureau of Mines. *Materials Survey—Copper.* Washington, D.C., 1965.

Bureau of the Census. *Census of Manufactures.* Vol. II, 1967 and 1963. Washington, D.C.

Houthakker, Hendrik S. "Copper: The Anatomy of a Malfunctioning Market." Remarks delivered at Duke Univ., Durham, North Carolina, March 11, 1970 for Excutive Office of the President's Council of Economic Advisers.

N. Y. Times. "Improved Wire Making Machine Is Devised." June 30, 1972.

Wykes, R. and Duncan, W. F. "The Evolution of the Modern Copper Rod Mill." *Wire Journal,* September 1972, p. 102-116.

Chapter Twenty-Nine

Iron and Steel Forgings—SIC 3391

Nancy Garvey

SECTION I. INTRODUCTION AND SUMMARY OF FINDINGS

Description of the Industry

SIC 3391 is defined by the U.S. Standard Industrial Classification Code as consisting of those "establishments primarily engaged in manufacturing iron and steel forgings, with or without the use of dies. These establishments generally operate on a job order basis, manufacturing forgings for sale to others or for interplant transfer."

About one-fourth of all iron and steel forgings produced are made in industries other than SIC 3391. Most of these iron and steel forgings are produced by captive forge shops that make iron and steel forgings for use by other plants of the same company. If the captive forge shop is classified as a separate establishment, it is included in SIC 3391; otherwise it is classified in the industry of the specified product. Establishments classified in SIC 3312, Blast Furnaces and Steel Mills, also produce many forged parts.

Forgings are commonly found in machines and conveyances at points subject to severe shock or stress. By the process of forging, the structure of iron and steel is refined and controlled to provide improved mechanical properties such as high strength and impact and fatigue resistance. Forged parts, such as crank-shafts, wheel rim clamps for trucks, tractor-scraper hubs, cylinder caps, steering knuckles, and gear and ring drive assemblies, are commonly found in autos, airplanes, trucks, farm implements, earth-moving machines, and industrial engines and machines.

Process Description

Essentially, the production of forged parts is a process of shaping metal by hammering and pressing operations generally performed while the metal

503

is hot. This forming of metal is accomplished by a variety of forging techniques such as compression between dies, rolling, extrusion, and impression die forging. Figure 29-1 gives a more detailed breakdown of the typical operations involved in the production of forgings.

The forging process (shaping metal by applying impact or squeeze

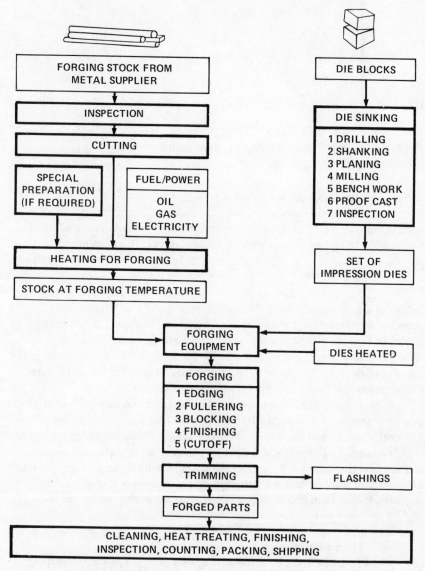

Figure 29-1. Flow Chart of Typical Operations Involved in the Production of Forgings. Source: *Forging Industry Handbook.*

pressure) differs from other techniques of shaping metal such as casting (where molten metal is poured into molds and allowed to solidify) or machining parts from bar stock or plate. In contrast to the latter two techniques, the forging process achieves the uniformity in grain flow required to develop the maximum strength potential of a particular material. Forgings are not subject to changes in chemical state or in volume, as are castings during solidification, and are less wasteful of material than the machining of parts.

Industry Overview

Output of the iron and steel forgings industry grew very rapidly toward the end of the historical period under study. Production in 1967 dollars rose 48% between 1962 and 1967, from $847 million to $1,262 million. Prior to 1962, output increased very gradually, only 12% over a 15-year period.

The fast increase in production since 1962 has been attributed to the expanding markets served by the iron and steel forgings industry. As jet engines were introduced and the Apollo space program was undertaken, many new forged parts of high structural integrity were required. Also, as the Vietnam war accelerated and defense requirements grew, the military sector required large quantities of forgings.

Energy Utilization

Energy utilization for power and heat by the iron and steel forgings industry was almost constant from 1947 through 1958 and rose slowly thereafter. Energy use per unit of output remained the same from 1947 to 1962, then it fell 26% between 1962 and 1967.

Since very small quantities of electricity are consumed in SIC 3391, trends in the energy-output ratio on a useful and gross energy basis[a] are the same. The energy-putput ratio, on a useful energy basis, declined from 56,100 BTUs per constant 1967 dollar of production in 1947 to 42,300 in 1967. Measuring electricity on a gross basis, BTUs per 1967 dollar shipped declined from 60,700 in 1947 to 46,500 in 1967.

Projections to 1980

The iron and steel forging industry is expected to continue to grow throughout the 1970s, but not quite as rapidly as it did between 1962 and 1967. The projections used here were generated by the University of Maryland's Interindustry Forecasting Model, on the basis of Conference Board assumptions regarding trends in key economic aggregates. Output by the industry, measured in constant 1967 dollars, is projected to rise from $1,262 million in 1967 to $2,077 million in 1980, or 65%.

It is expected that the energy-output ratio will decline between 1967 and 1980. Total useful BTUs consumed per constant 1967 dollar of output are

[a]See Chapter One, pages 14-15, for definitions of useful and gross energy.

Table 29-1. Value of Production and Energy Utilization per Unit of Output, Historical Data and Projections

	1947	1954	1958	1962	1967	1975	1980
Value of production (million 1967 $)	$750	$788	$705	$847	$1,262	$1,674	$2,077
Useful energy consumed (trillion BTUs)	42.1	43.3	41.6	48.5	53.4	66.8	79.8
Gross energy consumed (trillion BTUs)	45.5	47.5	45.1	52.4	58.7	72.0	85.2
Energy-output ratio (useful) (1,000 BTUs/1967 $ of output)	56.1	54.9	58.9	57.2	42.3	39.9	38.4
Energy-output ratio (gross) (1,000 BTUs/1967 $ of output)	60.7	60.3	63.9	61.9	46.5	43.0	41.0

Source: Bureau of the Census, *Census of Manufactures.*

expected to fall from 42,300 in 1967 to 38,400 in 1980. Measuring electricity on a gross energy basis, the energy-output ratio falls 11.8%, from 46,500 in 1967 to 41,000 in 1980.

Two factors account for the projected decline in per unit useful energy consumption. (1) Plants will be operating at closer to capacity levels throughout the 1970s. As a consequence, energy inputs will be more economically utilized in the slot furnaces, which must be maintained at a constant temperature regardless of the quantity of raw materials to be heated. (2) The increasing use of electrically powered induction and resistance furnaces is expected to continue. Energy is conserved by these furnaces, since they can be turned off when there is no raw material to be heated. However, to the extent that electric furnaces replace slot furnaces, the impact of higher operating rates on per unit energy use is diminished.

SECTION II.   ANALYSIS OF HISTORICAL TRENDS

Output

Growth in the iron and steel forgings industry was quite rapid. Between 1962 and 1967, the value of production grew at an average annual rate of 8.2%, rising from $847 million (1967 dollars) in 1962 to $1,262 million in 1967. Prior to that time (from 1947 to 1962), output of SIC 3391 increased at an average annual rate of only 0.7% (see Chart 29-1).

The aerospace, automotive (including trucking), and off-highway equipment industries are the largest markets for iron and steel forgings. The substantial growth in these industries in the post-1962 period largely accounts for the rise in demand for forged products. Coupled with the growth in demand are many technological developments outside of SIC 3391 which opened up new markets for forged parts. For example, forged products were heavily relied upon when the Boeing 707 and other jet airplanes were introduced. They were used for important structural and power plant components for all the Apollo trips and are currently being used in the Space Shuttle program.

Aside from commercial markets, the iron and steel forgings industry is a very large supplier of metal components to a variety of military markets. In addition to their widespread use in aircraft and missiles, forgings are found in virtually every implement of defense (e.g., rifle triggers and brackets, bomb casings, wheel drive flanges and other parts for armored personnel vehicles, and massive nuclear submarine drive shafts). Therefore, it is clear that the missile buildup in the late 1950s and 1960s and the Vietnam war contributed to the rise in shipments of SIC 3391 after 1962.

Lastly, part of the rise in shipments of SIC 3391 can be attributed to the increasing capabilities of forged products to meet a variety of design and performance requirements. As this technological progress within the iron and

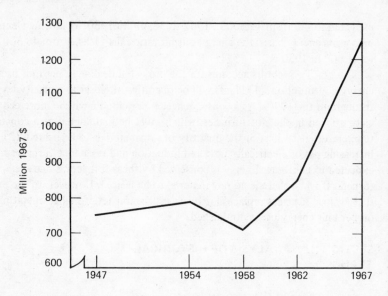

Chart 29-1. Value of Shipments of Iron and Steel Forgings.

steel forgings industry was made, new uses were discovered for forgings. One example is the use of forged valve bodies in nuclear power plants (beginning in 1962).

Energy-Output Ratio

There is little difference in the quantity of total useful energy consumed and that of total gross energy consumed by the iron and steel forgings industry; electricity makes up less than 4% of total useful energy requirements (see Chart 29-2). Due to this fact, the energy-output ratios on a gross or useful basis are virtually equal.

Energy utilization per unit of output remained nearly constant between 1947 and 1962. On a useful energy basis the ratio fluctuated around 56,000 BTUs per 1967 dollar of output. On a gross energy basis, the energy-output ratio fluctuated around 61,000 BTUs per constant 1967 dollar of production.

After 1962, the energy-output ratio declined 26% (on a useful energy basis) from 57,200 in 1962 to 42,300 in 1967. On a gross energy basis the decline was 25%, from 61,900 in 1962 to 46,500 in 1967.

The major factor that has affected per unit energy use in the iron and steel forgings industry is the level of operation. Between 1962 and 1967, production of SIC 3391 increased and the rate of capacity utilization for the industry was higher than in the previous Census years. With operations closer to

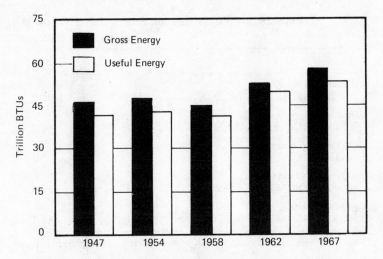

Chart 29-2. Energy Utilization: 1947–1967. Source: U.S. Department of Commerce; *Census of Manufactures.*

optimum levels, the energy-output ratio declined, as energy inputs were more economically utilized. The heating of metals in SIC 3391 is done largely in slot furnaces, fired with either oil or gas. These furnaces must be operated on a continuous basis (maintained at a certain temperature) regardless of the amount of stock (raw material) being heated. This implies that unless plants are operating near capacity, there will be periods of time when heated furnaces are less than full and occasionally even empty. Prior to 1962, this is probably a fairly accurate description of what was happening in most plants. By 1967, however, the situation had changed. A considerably larger tonnage of metal was heated with almost the same amount of energy as was used in earlier Census years. Clearly, the amount of stock heated in these furnaces increased and consequently the energy-output ratio declined.

Electrically powered furnaces (induction and resistance) were first used in the mid-1960s. Since then, their use has become more widespread. These furnaces are considerably less wasteful of energy than the slot furnace, because they can be turned off when there is no stock to be heated. The increased use of these furnaces has certainly been a factor in the decline of the energy-output ratio.

SECTION III.   PROJECTIONS TO 1980

Demand for Iron and Steel Forgings

It is expected that the output of the iron and steel forgings industry will continue to grow through 1980 in order to meet defense requirements and

Table 29.2.　Production and Energy Utilization per Unit of Output Projections to 1980

	1967	1975	1980
Value of production (million 1967 $)	$1,262	$1,674	$2,077
Useful energy consumed (trillion BTUs)	53.4	66.8	79.8
Gross energy consumed (trillion BTUs)	58.7	72.0	85.2
Energy-output ratio (useful) (1,000 BTUs/1967 $ of output)	$42.3	$39.9	$38.4
Energy-output ratio (gross) (1,000 BTUs/1967 $ of output)	46.5	43.0	41.0

Sources: Bureau of the Census, *Census of Manufactures*; The Conference Board.

industry needs. The projections of the University of Maryland Interindustry Forecasting Model (based on Conference Board assumptions concerning key economic aggregates) are for a 3.6% average annual rate of growth between 1967 and 1975, and a 4.4% average annual rate of growth from 1975 to 1980. The major assumptions are that: (1) sufficient capacity will exist to meet rises in demand, (2) the trend in imports and exports will remain the same, and (3) full employment will exist in 1975 and 1980.

On the basis of these projected growth rates, shipments of iron and steel forgings (in constant 1967 dollars), are expected to amount to $1,674 million in 1975 and $2,077 million in 1980.

One possible objection to these projections arises from the fact that there is a shortage of skilled manpower in the industry. Although this problem has existed for about eight to ten years, it did not become evident until the recent periods of peak production, when the industry has had to turn down some job orders. If the industry does not solve its manpower problem—or, in other words, does not have sufficient capacity to keep pace with the growth in demand—the projection of the Maryland model will be a little high.

Demand for Energy

The economies in energy use resulting from higher operating levels are expected to continue in the future. Many plants intend to install new electric furnaces for heating because they are more economical with respect to the consumption of energy and because they are "cleaner," and thus will meet increasingly stringent environmental controls. As a result, the energy-output ratio is expected to decline further. Since these factors have already had their major impact, their future effects will not cause as much of a decline in per unit energy use as that witnessed in the 1962-1967 period.

On a useful energy basis, the energy-output ratio is expected to decline at an average annual rate of 0.8%, reaching 39,900 BTUs per 1967 dollar of production in 1975 and 38,400 BTUs in 1980. The energy-output ratio will decline slightly faster on a gross energy basis, falling from 46,500 BTUs per 1967 dollar of production in 1967 to 41,000 BTUs in 1980 (see Table 29-2).

Total BTUs consumed by this industry are calculated on the basis of the above estimates. They are derived by multiplying the energy-output ratio by the value of production figures.

SECTION IV.   SELECTED BIBLIOGRAPHY

Department of Commerce, Bureau of the Census, *Census of Manufactures*.

Jenson, Jon E., ed. *Forging Industry Handbook*. Ann Arbor, Michigan: Ann Arbor Press, Inc., 1966.

McGannon, Harold E., ed. *The Making, Shaping and Treating of Steel*. 9th Edition. Pittsburgh, Pennsylvania: United States Steel Corporation, 1964.

Part Seven

Intensive Studies of Energy Use in Manufacturing Industries

Chapter Thirty

Methodology

M. F. Elliott-Jones

A. PURPOSE

There are two primary purposes in the development of a methodology to measure energy use: (1) To obtain an accurate, detailed, and comprehensive picture of energy use which is, (2) amenable to economic analysis. This means development of a system wherein numeric information can be collected about the past; into which numeric and literate[a] knowledge about the future can be incorporated; and which can be integrated into the overall body of economic knowledge and methods of analysis.

B. CONCEPTUAL PERSPECTIVES

B.1. Energy

Initially when we speak of *energy* in this paper we are speaking of three basic things (1) electric energy, (2) heat energy, and (3) kinetic energy.

When we speak of *sources of energy* we are speaking mainly of fuels and hydro power. *Fuels* are defined as fossil and nuclear.[b]

Uses of energy is employed as usage of energy *qua* energy to produce some desired result.

Usage of fuel (a) may produce energy (heat, electricity, or motion), or it may produce a product which (b) may itself be a fuel (e.g., petroleum refinery products), or, (c) may be a non-fuel (e.g., chemicals produced from fossil fuel feedstocks).

[a] The term "literate knowledge" refers to non-quantified information about some phenomenon. This knowledge, or knowledge of the symptoms of a phenomenon, may be quantifiable in a probabilistic framework or used to modify some quantity.

[b] We recognize, but omit for simplicity's sake, such energy sources as geothermal, solar, etc.; such potential fuels as may be used in fusion processes, and such insignificant (in most cases) fuels as wood.

B.2.   Energy in an Economic Product Context

Energy may be classified in four categories which are not necessarily mutually exclusive:

(1) Some energy may be viewed as a *primary product*. Common examples are raw hydro and geothermal power. These are of relatively minor importance for the purpose at hand.

(2) Some energy may be viewed as an *intermediate output*. In these cases, fuels are the preceding product stage and energy is derived from their use. "Intermediate" refers to the fact that energy is obtained during (and used in) the process of manufacturing other products or services.

(3) Viewing (2) from the opposite perspective, energy is an *intermediate input* in the process of production.

(4) Some energy must be classified as a *final product* sold to consumers, particularly electricity.

Energy-use analysis also suffers from the frequent appearance of joint products—particularly electricity and heat. This drawback is a little less difficult to handle in energy, because one can usually measure a BTU loss through a turbo-generator and assign that loss to electrical generation. If, indeed, accounting systems followed engineering principles, this measurement would not be overly difficult. Our experience with the pulp and paper industry, however, indicates that most explicit requests are necessary. Unfortunately, our questions were not specific enough, and the proliferation of reporting bases, plus frequent omissions by respondents, prevented any definitive separation of electricity from steam.[c]

B.3.   Energy in an Economic Resource Context

A concept of energy resources differs from that of energy products, because products are most frequently defined in a flow context, whereas resources exist in a stock context. Broadly defined, energy resources refer to the stock of materials and sources from which energy can be drawn, given present knowledge. Difficulties of measurement and forecasting arise because this stock is subject to change as a result of changes in knowledge; i.e., discovery of (1) added materials (petroleum, gas, coal, nuclear fuel ores) and (2) better technology to use previously untapped sources.

Uses of energy resources may or may not involve the production of energy; viz., the feedstock example.

The *energy resource base* is defined as fossil fuels, hydro potential, etc. In the study of the pulp and paper industry (Chapter Thirty-Two) the use of

---

[c] The actual handling of this problem is reported in Chapters Thirty-One and Thirty-two, Aluminum, and Pulp & Paper. The experience leads us to suggest that analysts would benefit from conversations with several engineers *within* firms of the industry in question before energy questionnaires are designed, and moreover, that respondent firms be explicitly asked to submit questionnaires to engineering as well as other staff.

wood waste products becomes significant, and these wastes are viewed as an energy source *not* drawn from the energy resource base.

B.4.   Energy Transactions

At the aggregate economic level, the only energy transactions that could not be accounted for via fuel transactions are (1) energy from primary sources—hydroelectric, etc. and (2) imports of electricity (such as those from Canada) because all other domestic energy use is provided by (originates in) fuels.

At the firm level, transactions involving energy *per se* are generally confined to electricity and steam heat. Other uses of energy most often, but not always, involve a transaction in fuels.[d]

This leads to a question of whether the study should, (1) concentrate only upon energy and fuels that are used to produce energy, or (2) the total use of fuel products regardless of whether they are converted to energy or converted to some other product. In this study, we have chosen the latter, but continually attempt to specify whether the result of fuel use is energy or a non-energy product—see, especially, the examples of anthracite, petroleum coke, and petroleum pitch that are used to manufacture carbon cathodes and carbon anodes that are consumed in the electrolytic Hall process of smelting aluminum. This also leads to the problem of double-counting, its measurement, and its elimination. Consequently, in what follows, we view firms as purchasing fuel and/or energy, the latter being confined to electricity and steam purchased from utilities or subsidiaries classified in other industries.

B.5.   Homogeneous Criteria and Convention of Measurement

Among the several available measures for energy (e.g., kwh, barrel of fuel oil equivalents, etc.), we have selected BTUs, the basic heat energy measurement. Consequently, we must convert electrical energy to heat equivalent (motive to heat conversions can be omitted for our purposes).

A distinct difference of opinion exists among analysts as to whether one should convert electricity to heat on the basis of the heat a kwh will deliver, or the heat required to produce a kwh. The former can be viewed as *useful energy*; the latter as *gross energy*. The resolution of this question depends on the analyst's purpose.

In this paper, we generally opt for gross energy. Although our primary focus is industrial sectors, we are concerned with the *demands upon the entire energy producing system* made by each industry, given its present and possible future energy demand patterns. If these patterns include use of electricity, then for each kwh used, a kwh must be produced.

[d] The primary exception is "captive" or internal-to-the-firm hydroelectric generation; see the discussion of wastes in pulp and paper.

And, since domestic U.S. production of electricity is based primarily on fossil fuel generating plants, we employ the average BTUs required to produce a kwh as a standard conversion.

When this convention of energy consumed is applied to PURCHASED electricity, it incorporates demand actually exercised by the producing utility, but derived from the industry under study. If this methodology is to fit into a system having an explicit utilities sector, the 10,500 BTUs consumed per kwh convention is not appropriate for purchased electricity. Consequently, we offer data on both bases defined as:

Gross Energy Consumed (GEC) basis: i.e., 10,500 BTU/kwh (1971)
Useful Energy (UE) basis: i.e., 3,412 BTU/kwh (atemporal)

With respect to electricity *generated* within industries (self-, or captive-generation), the analyst may (a) if given data for kwh generated, use the average utility heat rate of 10,500 BTUs, (b) if given units of fuels used for generation, convert those fuels to BTUs, using Bureau of Mines conversion factors, (c) if given both kwh generated and fuels input, convert fuels and derive apparent heat rate, or BTU/kwh, (d) whenever electricity can be identified as originating in a captive hydroelectric generator, one may employ the Bureau of Mines heat equivalent, and (e) where electricity is identified as originating in a specific type of generating engine and we can obtain the BTU rate, we use those data. As a rule, where joint energy products are absent, we request kwh generated and fuels used, base our data on GEC from fuel inputs, and use the ratio BTU/kwh as a check.

One other reason for using the "gross energy consumed" convention exists in the appearance of bias if useful energy (UE basis) is used. This can best be illustrated by an example. Say that an industry uses 1 kwh of electricity and 20,000 BTU of heat per unit of product. Conversion to homogeneous energy units on each basis results in:

Original Condition	Useful Energy Basis	Gross Energy Basis
	BTUs	
Electricity (1 kwh)	3,412	10,500
Heat from fuels	20,000	20,000
Total energy used	23,412	30,500

Say that, over time, the industry shifts toward electricity from heat by changing its processes increasing from one to two kwh, and by reducing heat from 20,000 to 10,000 BTUs per unit of output. Measuring changes we derive:

New Condition	Useful Energy Basis	Gross Energy Basis
	BTUs	
Electricity (2 kwh)	6,824	21,000
Heat from fuels	10,000	10,000
Total energy used	16,824	31,000
Absolute change	−6,588	+500
Percentage change	−28.1%	+1.6%

One may then suggest, assuming 100% efficiency in converting electricity and fuels to heat, that the industry uses 6,588 BTUs less in the new condition. But its shift in use pattern from heat to electricity increases the demand on the energy resource base by 500 BTUs. Thus, the industry has become less *energy using*, but more *energy demanding*.

This type of bias also exists in the converse case where a shift away from electricity occurs.

C. ECONOMIC CONTEXT

C.1. Fuel-Energy as an Input to Production

Perhaps the simplest manner of showing the relative position of fuel-energy in a microeconomic context is to use an input-output schema explicitly listing a firm's current inputs of non-labor services

$$q_j = x_{1j} + x_{2j} + \cdots + x_{nj} + v_j \tag{1}$$
$$= \sum_{i=1}^{n} x_{ij} + v_j$$

where q_j is the output of the jth firm in a given year; x_{ij} are purchases of the ith input by the jth industry; v_j is the value added term representing the value of labor, management, and entrepreneurial inputs. Extension to include capital inputs is omitted temporarily.

Input coefficients are derived by dividing through (1) by q_j such that $a_{ij} = x_{ij}/q_j$ and $w = v_j/q_j$

$$1 = \sum_{i=1}^{n} a_{ij} + w_j \qquad 0 \leqslant a_{ij} \leqslant 1 \tag{2}$$

The a_{ij} suggests that, given the structure of operations in the firm during the period in question, a_{ij} was required of the ith input to produce one unit of the jth output. One or more of these a_{ij} may represent fuels and energy.

In these terms, some of the crucial questions of this study can be clearly illustrated. To simplify, divide $i = 1, \ldots, n$ inputs into non-fuel-energy and fuel energy inputs, such that subscript i refers to all inputs, and subscript k

refers only to fuel-energy inputs: $(k \supset i)$ Say that a_{kj} has an observable value for one or more historical periods.

The questions are:

(1) What are the factors determining the observed value of a_{kj}?

(2) Will, and how will, a_{kj} change in response to changes in these factors?

(3) How will a_{ij}, $i \neq k$, change when a_{kj} changes?

Rephrasing the first, why does the firm have the energy purchase and use pattern it is observed to have rather than some other pattern? Three general classes of reasons may be suggested: (a) The technical requirements (chemical, physical, etc.) of the processes used by the firm demand one energy type—e.g., heat is the main energy input to steel making, but in making aluminum the only proven large scale method is electrolytic. (b) The practices of the industry in question. Fuel use patterns may have originated in some firm in the past, and since equipment changes would be required if switches are to be made, no change occurs. (c) The relative prices of various fuels. Natural gas is the best historical example—low cost per BTU relative to other energy sources will cause a firm to prefer gas even if it is completely indifferent on other criteria. Relative prices, of course, are frequently related to the location of the firm.

To broach the question of whether changes in these factors will indeed change a_{kj}, the original system shown in equations (1) and (2) should be extended to include capital inputs. Define:

$$q_j = \sum_{i=1}^{n} x_{ij} + [y_1\delta_1 + y_2\delta_2 + \cdots + y_m\delta_m] + z_j$$

$$= \sum_{i=1}^{n} x_{ij} + \sum_{\ell=1}^{m} y_\ell\delta_\ell + v_j \tag{3}$$

where y_ℓ is the stock of the ℓth capital input to production of the jth product, and δ_ℓ is the reciprocal of the average life of that capital input, adjusted for utilization in the period in question. In turn, v_j are payments or returns to other primary inputs. In this context, the input per unit output relationships can be derived by dividing through by q_j obtaining $b_{\ell j}$ coefficients analogous to a_{ij} defined as the apparent input of the ℓth capital good required to produce a unit of the jth output. (The $b_{\ell j}$ are essentially disaggregated average capital output ratios.)

$$1 = \sum_{i=1}^{n} a_{ij} + \sum_{\ell=1}^{m} b_{\ell j} + w_j \tag{4}$$

The reason that a capital term is needed is simply that use of fuel and energy virtually always requires some specific equipment—furnaces, boilers, wiring, switching, piping, etc. Moreover, much of this equipment is specific to some kind of fuel. Consequently, it is usually necessary that at least some change occur in the composition of the b vector if a change in fuel use is undertaken.

One may, therefore, posit that a_{kj} may change, but at first approximation, that change will depend on the cost of changing the composition of $b_{\varrho j}$, and the higher the cost of changing the composition, the less likely a change in a_{kj}.

We may generally suggest that there are two causes of possible change in a_{kj} arising out of the factors (a) – (c) listed above.

First, a change in technology or practices in the jth industry which the firm expects to reduce costs of production. It follows that such changes in a_{kj} will be undertaken if the expected return exceeds the cost of changing the composition of capital (the $b_{\varrho j}$), other things being equal.

Second, a change in relative prices. This factor has two aspects: a change in fuel-energy price relative to prices of other inputs, and a change in relative prices among fuels and energy. For the time being, these two can be treated as one, and we may again suggest that if the increased cost of using fuels within the present pattern (a_{kj}) exceeds the cost of changing the composition of capital $(b_{\varrho j})$, the change in a_{kj} will be undertaken.

Up to this point, the price of output sold by the jth firm has been ignored, but to bring the above closer to a realistic perspective, it is necessary to view the costs of changeover and expected returns in relation to the price of output. Moreover, since these would have to be translated into total revenue and total cost concepts, it would also be necessary to deal with the price elasticity of demand for output of the jth industry.

This leads to the generalization that a change in energy use patterns by a firm will depend on (1) prospects for change in the technology used by—and practices of—the firm; (2) changes in the price of fuels relative to (a) each other, (b) the prices of other inputs, (c) the price of capital used by the firm, (d) the price of the output of the firm. Translated, (2) means *all other prices*.

This, in turn, leads to the virtually inescapable conclusion that the only comprehensive manner of studying industrial fuel and energy use (or, for that matter, use of any intermediate input), is within a disaggregated general equilibrium system—Walrasian, Leontief, von Neuman, etc.

Such systems do not exist at present, and are approached only in I-O models that suffer from doubtful data inputs with respect to fuels (as is demonstrated below), lack of continuous series, and lack of explicit price systems. Thus, this study is reduced to an attempt to measure energy use, obtain information about its likely direction, and fit both into a coherent system of behavior with respect to fuel and energy demand.

C.2.   General Description of Methods Used

The methodology used follows from the prior discussion in that it provides a framework for the collection and processing of data based on an input-output scheme. It does not purport to be a behavioral model. The basic framework is a matrix that in concept is applicable to any industry. It may be termed a "sources and uses of energy" table, or a "product input-process" matrix. Each table or matrix carries flow data for one time period; in the studies below, one year. Each row is identified as an energy source. Each column is identified as an energy-using process.[e] The sum over any one row is defined as total usage of energy within an economic unit—a firm, industry, or sector— during the period. The sum over any one column is defined as total usage of energy in the process identified in the column. The sum of row (or column) sums is defined as total energy used within the economic unit from all sources, for all uses in the period.

The other basic piece of information required is output, measured where possible in physical terms, and otherwise in constant dollar value. In this study we have ignored changes in inventories of fuels, and of outputs.

Specific definitions of these measures, the conversions, and resulting concepts are given in the list of definitions given in Appendix 1 of Chapter Thirty-One. In this list and the following, lower case Latin symbols with two subscripts are elements of matrices; with one subscript are elements of vectors. Lower case Latin symbols with no subscripts represent vectors; capital Latin symbols represent matrices. Lower case Greek symbols represent scalars (single numbers). Each symbol should be viewed as representing some flow-type magnitude—i.e., defined as some amount per period of time.

[e] The process labels in this study are heterogeneous and are directly related to the industry under study. A more generalized set of process labels can be conceived into which virtually all energy uses would fit; e.g., Electrolysis, Electric drive, Process Heat (Steam, Radiant, Other), Direct drive (Turbine, Reciprocating Engine), etc.

Chapter Thirty-One

Aluminum—SIC 3324 and 3352

M. F. Elliott-Jones

SUMMARY OF MAJOR FINDINGS

Since its introduction as a commercially produced metal at the beginning of this century, aluminum has continued to show very rapid growth. During the years 1947 to 1972 total U.S. output of aluminum metal increased at an annual average rate of 8.2% — a seven-fold increase. This rate of growth is almost triple the rate of real GNP growth experienced during these years. During the years to 1980, we project demand for aluminum to increase at a rate of between 5% and 6% per annum.

      Aluminum is also a major energy user. Estimates made here suggest that total usage of energy in the production of aluminum in the U.S. during 1971 approximated between 5.5% and 6.0% of total energy use by manufacturing. Of the total energy estimated to have been used in the Primary Metals industries (SIC 33), aluminum accounted for approximately 28%.

      While we do not have sufficient data to determine the exact extent of the decrease in energy use per unit of aluminum produced over the past years since 1947, we do have data for the main component—electricity. Data obtained from the industry and from the Bureau of the Census indicate that in 1947 the aluminum industry used approximately 9.1 kwh of electricity per pound of aluminum metal produced. By 1971, this coefficient had been reduced to approximately 8.2 kwh/lb., a decline of 10%. This decrease in the energy coefficient has taken place without any major technological shift. The basic Hall-Heroult process remains unchanged in principle from its introduction in the late 1880s. Although there is now the possibility of a technological shift— introduction of the Alcoa Smelting Process—the basic process remains electro- lytic. Our study does not reveal that any major changes in the average energy use per unit of production are likely to appear prior to 1980, even though some minor declines are projected. The reason is simply that although introduction of

523

the Alcoa Process would result in smelters producing aluminum at approximately 5.0 kwh/lb., by 1980 the bulk of aluminum metal will still be produced in the older type Hall smelters. Moreover, by 1980, it is unlikely that there will be more than one commercial size smelter using the Alcoa process in operation.

Our projected changes in average per-unit energy usage originate in (1) incremental (vis-à-vis radical) technological change, and (2) conservation measures to reduce waste of energy—particularly heat.

Initially, our findings concerning the present condition of energy use within the aluminum industry indicate that production of one pound of aluminum ingot requires an average of 78,300 BTU (1971). Addition of the energy use in fabrication raises the total to approximately 98,000 BTU. (These data, and those presented below should be viewed as being the midpoint of a range having a span of 5% on either side. This span results from a number of assumptions that were made during the course of this study that might be made otherwise. The most important of these is the assignment of all imported alumina to non-metal purposes. It could well be argued that one should assign all imported alumina to the aluminum metal industry, thereby lowering the energy requirements for the manufacture of alumina in the United States. This is tantamount to "exporting" the energy requirement to the country in which the alumina is refined from bauxite.)

Projections to 1980 suggest that the above measures are likely to decline to 72,000 and 94,500, or by 8.0% and 3.8% respectively.

All of the above data refer to the production of aluminum from the average mixture of virgin materials and secondary scrap. One notable finding of this study was that production of a pound of aluminum ingot from used scrap aluminum requires some 6,000 BTU. Addition of the fabrication energy raises the total to about 31,000 BTU. Compared with the above data, these findings suggest that the energy required to produce a pound of aluminum from scrap aluminum is roughly 6% of that required to produce a pound of aluminum from bauxite. Similarly to produce a pound of semi-fabricated aluminum product from scrap materials requires approximately 25% of the energy required to produce the same product from virgin materials.

Total energy use by the aluminum industry in 1971 was 975.5 (10^{12}) BTU. If one were to assign all imported alumina to the aluminum metal industry, this amount would be reduced to 945.1 (10^{12}) BTU—or by 3.1%.

Our projections of demand for aluminum, depending upon the assumptions used, show an increase in shipments of between 5.3% per year and 5.9% per year, 1969-1980. Combined with our various findings concerning likely reductions in the energy-output coefficient, capacity considerations, and scrap recovery we project total energy use by the aluminum industry in 1980 at 1,531.4 (10^{12}) BTU. This projection makes the assumption that increased production of alumina takes place entirely within the United States. Conversely, one might argue that the increase in alumina production would take place entirely within the bauxite-producing nations, in which case the total usage would be decreased from 1,531.4 (10^{12}) BTU to 1458.4 (10^{12}) BTU—a 4.8% decline.

In 1971 demand for fuels was highly concentrated in natural gas, which accounted for some 30% of total energy inputs to the industry. Based on the results of our survey, which was made during the first half of 1973, we obtained information leading to the conclusion that by 1980 natural gas would account for somewhat less that 17% of total energy inputs. The subsequent events of late 1973 and early 1974 (that led one to the conclusion that the equilibrium price of natural gas is over \$1.50/Mcf) probably render this estimate on the high side. The conclusions of our survey also show that the greatest change in demand for fuel would be in oil. Demand for oil was projected to increase by a factor of almost 40. Again, events of late 1973 and early 1974 may well change this conclusion.

Our demand and capacity projections indicate that a shortage of aluminum metal productive capacity will appear about the middle of the 1970s. Considering the rather small additions to domestic capacity that are on the drawing boards, it is possible that imports of aluminum ingot may increase at a rate as high as 10% between 1969 and 1980. These factors cause the energy use for the prefabrication stages to decline more than the energy for the complete process of manufacturing aluminum.

Total demand for energy by the aluminum industry in the very short term, to 1975, will not be greatly affected by energy price changes. Over any longer period, the industry should show considerable responsiveness to changes in energy price, responding by one of two means. First, by maximizing production per unit of energy; by rebuilding existing plants and installing new pot lines, electricity requirements for the Hall process can be reduced from the existing 8.0 kwh per pound average down to 6.5 kwh per pound, a reduction of almost 20%. Second, pilot plants embodying a new technology, the chloride process, are now under construction; these promise to reduce energy requirements by a further 30%. High energy prices will provide sharp new impetus to commercialization of these new processes.

The projection of use of individual fuels has been greatly complicated by non-market constraints imposed (or threatened) by the federal government, and by rapid changes in the supply prices of individual fuels as a consequence of both market forces and foreign government actions.

One consequence of this uncertainty has been the installation of equipment that can use two or more fuels alternatively, a trend that is undoubtedly accelerating. This, of course, sharply increases the short-term cross elasticities between fuels. Such technological flexibility is difficult to measure in the current economic situation, where price controls create market discontinuities—available supplies at low prices suddenly becoming either very high priced or unavailable at any price.

A.　DATA COLLECTION

A.1　Sources and Samples

We requested and received the cooperation of five companies in this study: Alcoa, Reynolds, Kaiser, Martin Marietta, and Eastalco.[1] These firms are, or are part of, vertically integrated organizations having operations in many nations. Production includes bauxite mining, alumina refining, aluminum smelting and fabrication. In sampling terms, these account for 76.6% of U.S. primary aluminum smelting capacity, or 3.02 out of 3.94 million metric tons as of mid-1971.[2] While we have been unable to determine the proportion of U.S. alumina refining capacity accounted for by these firms, it appears to be over 95%. With respect to fabrication, while much of the heavy fabrication—manufacture of plate, sheet, bar, and heavy extrusions—takes place in the firms surveyed, there are a large number of smaller, non-integrated fabricators who purchase ingot and semi-fabrications from these companies. Patterns of energy use may be quite different in these from the pattern we found in the fabrication operations of the integrated companies.

In terms of representativeness, our alumina refining data appear valid; our data for aluminum smelting may be slightly skewed by inclusion of virtually all of the smelters built before 1960, but not all of those built since. Since several of those built in the last twelve years are likely to have lower electricity use per pound of metal, our survey data may be slightly higher than the actual average. On the other hand, in our expansion from the sample to the industry, we have allowed for this difference on the basis of general knowledge of the likely usage levels in newer plants supplied by several industry sources. With respect to fabrication energy use, our data are likely to be biased above the overall average for aluminum fabricators. At this stage, the degree of bias is unknown, since time did not permit a survey of the smaller fabricators.

A.2　Form of the Data Supplied

Three companies, Alcoa, Reynolds and Kaiser, stated that corporate policy did not permit release of data for individual plants. Data supplied were composite figures for operations of all smelters in each firm, and for all, or groups of fabricating plants. In terms of the data requested (see questionnaires in Appendix 3) the firms were able to provide virtually all figures for the year 1971. Most data were also produced for 1967. For intervening and prior years, data were frequently limited to electricity usage in smelting, and gross fuel purchases.

All data in this report are composites of the figures provided by these firms, or expansion of these data to total industry data, and are identified accordingly. Data for the companies are not presented, since the firms supplied statistics under the condition that they remain confidential. In some instances, single measures are quoted and cited as having their source in interviews. These are generally measures that have appeared in conversations with several persons in the industry and are taken by us to be accurate and representative.

A.3. Scope

In this study, we take a somewhat broader view of the aluminum industry than requested. Our proposal originally suggested a study of energy use in Primary Aluminum SIC 3334 and Fabricated Products SIC 3352 (1967 SIC basis, which in a 1972 basis includes SIC 3353, 3354, 3355 and part of 3359). This was expanded backward in the production process to include alumina and bauxite. Briefly, these stages start with mining bauxite ore which then undergoes crushing, washing and drying. Bauxite is then refined by a heat process to alumina (Al_2O_3). Alumina is then smelted by an electrolytic process to aluminum metal.[3] Subsequently, it was determined that in 1971, 85% of the bauxite, and 15% of the alumina used in the U.S. was imported. Consequently, the bauxite stage was omitted on the grounds that a very large proportion was imported; thus, the energy demand for its production is not a part of U.S. energy demands. On the other hand, since some 85% of alumina needs are produced in the U.S., energy demand derived from alumina production is relevant to the study. Thus, we also present data for energy demand derived from production of SIC 28195, alumina.

A.4. Preliminary Problems in Concepts

A preliminary step involved deciding what to do with the inevitable question of self-generated electricity. To illustrate, the matrix F is shown in Figure 31-1. with the double-counting explicitly included.

Since our measures exclude use of electricity in the generator, the cells in rows 1 and 2 of column 1 will be zero. The sum of row or column sums of this matrix will count both electricity generated and the fuels used for generation. To determine the net usage either of two procedures may be followed:

1. remove generated electricity, or
2. remove fuels used to generate electricity.[4]

In actual practice we are unable to specify the elements in rows 1 and 2, because the use of generated electricity cannot be separated from the use of purchased electricity—we can only determine their sum. On the other hand, data from Questionnaire Table 2 allows us to specify the total of each of these rows. Thus, the f vector of row sums provides us with the pattern of demand exercised by the firm or industry, and the f' vector of column sums provides us with the energy use pattern of the firm or industry. Within the matrix, we can distinguish usage by fuel, by process from the data requested in Questionnaire Tables 3 and 4 except for the distinction in process usage between

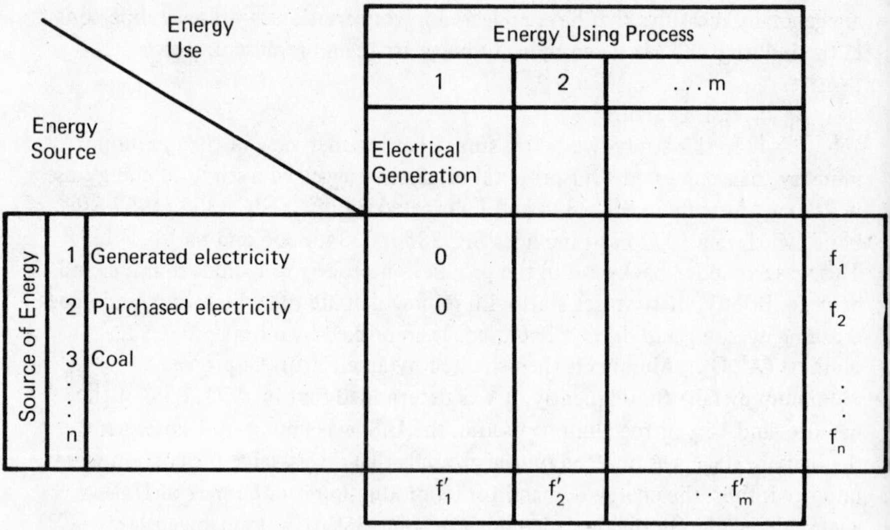

Energy Use	Energy Using Process		
Energy Source	1	2	...m
	Electrical Generation		

Source of Energy			1	2	...m	
	1	Generated electricity	0			f_1
	2	Purchased electricity	0			f_2
	3	Coal				
	.					.
	.					.
	n					f_n
			f'_1	f'_2	$...f'_m$	

Figure 31-1. Energy Utilization Matrix, Including Double Counting.

purchased and generated electricity. For most purposes, the double-counting problem is of minor importance, *except* when we make projections. It is then necessary to take a total demand for electricity, to split it into purchased and generated, and then to determine the pattern of fuel demands for that generation.

With these provisos in mind, the principles of manipulating the data are described. Given the F matrix for a firm or an industry, for any one year, we introduce the conversion factors—the c vector.[5] Using these factors we transform the heterogeneous fuel and energy data in F to homogeneous BTU data. The resulting matrix is termed H.

$$H = [h_{ij}] = [f_{ij} * c_i] = \hat{c}F \qquad i = 1, \ldots, n; \quad j = 1, \ldots, m$$

Where $\hat{c}$ denotes a diagonalized vector. Having homogeneous elements in H, column sums as well as row sums may be derived to obtain h_i, h_j and ϕ where

$$h_i = \sum_{j=1}^{m} h_{ij} \qquad h_j = \sum_{i=1}^{n} h_{ij} \qquad \text{and} \qquad \phi = \sum_{i=1}^{n} \sum_{j=1}^{m} h_{ij}$$

represent gross energy demand or use including double counting for generated electricity.

To eliminate the double counting, the procedure outlined in footnote 4 is necessary, and the result can be termed ϕ'. Depending upon whether we require information on energy demand or energy use, we eliminate either the generated electricity, or the fuels going to generated electricity. While both procedures produce ϕ', they will produce differences in h_i, h_j, and h_{ij}.

Given the H measures, the basic comparator—output—can be introduced. This measure, termed λ, is used to derive the coefficients or "energy input per unit of output" data resulting in the data ϵ, e_i, e_j and E. In some instances it is possible to divide the H matrix into column vectors or sets of column vectors consistent with portion of λ. In this industry, alumina refining, anode baking, and smelting are frequently separable in the company data in terms of energy use and output. Consequently, more detailed submatrices of coefficient data can be derived. These coefficients provide such measures as BTUs per pound of alumina, per pound of prebaked anodes, etc.—the fundamental material for projection of energy demand into the future.

B. HISTORICAL DATA

The basic energy use data for the five firms in the sample are presented in Table 31-1. This table shows the homogeneous, or H matrix of measures. Data are in (10^{12}) or trillion BTUs.

While this table represents firms producing 74% of U.S. aluminum metal output, this 74% does not apply across all columns of the table. Sections B.1 through B.5, below, discuss these variations.

Some explanation of the row and column headings may be in order. Broadly speaking, rows indicate sources of, and columns indicate uses of, energy.

Rows
1. Generated Electricity: includes thermal (turbine and engine) and hydro generation of electricity by the sample firms.
2. Purchased Electricity: includes electricity obtained by transaction.
4. Coal: includes bituminous and lignite.
5-9. Oil, Gas, LPG and Gasoline: as defined by U.S. Bureau of the Census in its Census of Manufactures MC forms, and its Survey of Manufactures MA. 100 (1971) forms.

Columns
1. Generation of Electricity: includes fuels used for generation of electricity; but not (as far as we can determine) fuel use for generation of electricity as a joint product with steam in alumina refining. This electricity is implicitly included in column 2.
2. Alumina Refining: includes fuels inputs into the alumina refinery, regardless of whether alumina is used for metal or sold for other purposes.
3. Anode Prebake: fuels for baking anodes regardless of whether anodes are used in smelting by the sample firm, or sold to other firms.
4. Smelting: electricity into the smelting plant; excludes electric furnaces.

Table 31-1.   Aluminum Industry Sample, Matrix of Sources and Uses of Energy, 1971 (all data (10¹²) BTU except as marked)

	Generation of Electricity	Alumina Refining	Anode Prebake	Smelting	Heat for Holding & Remelt Furnaces Casting, etc.	Elec. for Rolling, Drawing & Extension	Other Fabrication	Vehicles	All Other	Gross Total Input	% of Net[a]	Net Total Input	% of Net
Generated electricity	[b]									190.2[c]	n.a.	190.2	25.9%
Purchased elec.										379.3	51.8%	379.3	51.8
Total elec.		18.3		497.9[1]	15.9	36.5	.9			569.5	51.8	569.5	77.7
Coal					3.9					3.9	0.5	3.9	0.5
Distillate oil	0.1		*		1.8		*	*	0.1	2.2	0.3	2.1	0.3
Residual oil		0.8			0.6		0.3			1.7	0.2	1.7	0.2
Gas	89.3	88.6	5.3		49.7		0.4	*	1.9	235.2	32.1	145.9	19.9
LPG					3.4			2.0		5.4	0.7	5.4	0.7
Gasoline								3.5		3.5	0.5	3.5	0.5
n.s.k.	85.9									88.9	12.1	0.0	n.a.
Gross total usage	175.3[d]	107.7	5.4	497.9	75.3	36.5	1.6	5.6	2.0	907.3		732.0	100.0%
Net total usage		107.7	5.4	497.9	75.3	36.5	1.6	5.6	2.0		98.2	732.0	
Percentage of net		14.7%	0.7%	68.0%	10.3%	5.0%	0.2%	0.8%	0.2%	100.0%			

*Denotes less than 0.05 (10¹²) BTU.

n.s.k.—Not specified by kind.

[a]Detail will not add to 100% due to use of Net as a basis for calculation. Net electricity includes hydro power in self generation, but this column contains only the fuels going to self generation, and excludes row 1 containing the inputation of BTUs for hydro. Where available, data for purchased hydro electricity has been converted to BTU at the Bureau of Mines equivalent heat rate. Where available, heat equivalent of generated electricity has been assigned on the basis of the actual BTU content of the fuel used. For heat rates and conversion factor see Appendix 2.

[b]Some electricity is generated in alumina refining plants as a joint product with steam used in the process. Fuel input is included in the Gas row; the amount of electricity generated is not known.

[c]Derived by subtraction: (569.5 − 379.3).

[d]Derived from actual fuel use data.

5. Heat for Furnaces: essentially a catch-all for all fuels used to produce heat (vis-à-vis electricity or motive power) in both (a) smelters wherein holding furnaces are the prime use, and (b) fabricating plants, including casting. Electric furnaces are included here.

6. Electricity for Rolling, Drawing, Extruding: includes all electricity for motive power used as inputs in fabricating plants. Presumably, some of this amount is related to electric finishing processes. There is a minor amount of magnesium and titanium fabricated in some of the sample plants; no attempt has been made to remove this usage due to lack of data. (Data do not exist due to multi-use machinery and lack of single machine metering.)

7. Other Fabrications: essentially a catch-all for items not allocable to columns 5 or 6.

8. Vehicles: includes plant vehicles; cranes are apparently included in ancillary electricity to smelters (4) and to fabrication (6).

9. All other: an item included on the questionnaires to allow the sample firms to enter residuals.

B.1   Alumina

Data gathered from some of the firms in the sample, and other sources indicate that the process of refining bauxite ores to calcined alumina requires a total of 5,800-6,100 BTU per pound of alumina produced. This range includes all fuel inputs plus electricity. Electricity generated in the refining operation is implicit in the fuels input, and purchased electricity is added to the fuels input on a GEC basis.[6]

Historical series for this measure are not available, but a rough approximation of the total energy usage for 1971 in alumina refining can be made by reconstruction of bauxite and alumina production (Table 31-2).

The resulting measure—94.2 (10^{12}) BTU—compares with a figure of 107.7 (10^{12}) BTU shown in the sample data (Table 31-1) with the difference caused by alumina sold to chemicals, abrasives, ceramics, and other industries. If one uses the domestic absorption figure of 19.3 (10^9) pounds from Table 31-2, and assumes that energy requirements of 6,000 BTU per pound relevant to preparation of alumina for metal apply, the resulting input is 115.8 (10^{12}) BTU, or 8.1 (10^{12}) BTU more than the figure appearing in the H matrix (Table 31-1). Most of this difference can be accounted for by the heat inputs to calcining alumina for metal production. Alumina sold to chemicals, etc., is primarily non-calcined and would require less energy input.

This procedure amounts to an arbitrary assignment of much of the energy used to refine alumina to the aluminum metal. It is indeed an arbitrary assumption that has its roots in the practical impossibility of determining whether a particular carload of alumina going into an aluminum smelter originated in a domestic or a foreign alumina refinery. One could alternatively assign all imported alumina to domestic aluminum metal. This would be tantamount to

Table 31-2.   Reconstruction of Sources of Aluminum Ores and Energy Use in Alumina Refining, 1971

		Volume	Distribution
Bauxite	U.S. Production[a]	4.453(10^9) lbs.	14%
	Imports[b]	28.264(10^9)	86
		32.717(10^9)	100
Assuming average extraction rate of 0.5 lb. Al_2O_3 from each lb. of bauxite implies an Al_2O_3 equivalent of		16.358(10^9) lbs.	85
Imports of alumina[b]		+ 4.822(10^9)	25
Imports of alumina from USVI[b]		+ .240(10^9)	1
Exports of alumina[b]		− 2.116(10^9)	−13
Domestic absorption of alumina		19.304(10^9)	100
Assuming average extraction rate of 0.5 lbs. Al metal per lb. of Al_2O_3 implies metal content of		9.652(10^9) lbs.	100
Published primary metal production		7.850(10^9) lbs.	81
Implied volume of alumina assigned to metal		15.700(10^9) lbs.	
Total energy inputs to production of alumina for 15.7(10^9) lbs. aluminum metal @ 6,000 BTU/lb. Al_2O_3		94.20(10^{12})BTU[c]	

[a]Source: Bureau of Mines.

[b]Source: U.S. Department of Commerce.

[c]If one were to assume that all imported alumina were destined for aluminum metal, the figure for total energy inputs to production of alumina of 94.2(10^{12}) BTU would decrease to 63.8(10^{12}) BTU; a decrease of 328. Both this and the assumption used in the table are arbitrary. If we use the latter assumption here, then it would be necessary to make sure that the energy used in refining alumina that is destined for the chemicals, ceramics, and abrasives industry is indeed included in the energy use of those industries.

saying that the alumina destined for chemical, abrasives, ceramics, etc., was all of domestic origin.

B.2   Anodes

As discussed in earlier sections, two basic anode systems are commonly used: Soderberg and prebaked. In each case, a paste of petroleum pitch and anthracite is made. In the former system, the paste is continuously fed into the pot and the heat of the smelting pot bakes out the volatiles. In the prebake system, a separate operation is carried on wherein natural gas is used to bake anodes which are then used in the smelter. Consequently, anode baking energy use in Soderberg systems is included in the electricity to smelting measurement. Our survey indicates that a Soderberg system uses between 0.5

and 0.7 kwh per pound of metal more than a comparable prebake system, with the difference attributable mainly to heat to bake the paste. Converting 0.5 to 0.7 kwh on a GEC basis for 1971 gives a range of 5,250-7,350 BTU/lb metal produced.[7]

Anode baking energy consumption in prebake is substantially lower than in Soderberg systems. Physical usage of anodes per pound of metal produced is lower, but this is partially accounted for by the volatiles being included in the weight in the Soderberg paste measure, and excluded from the prebake data. When converted to energy use for anodes per pound of aluminum metal, however, the results are still substantially lower; our data showing a range of 1,200-1,600 BTU/lb. metal, with a mean of approximately 1,300 BTU/lb. metal.

The little data we have on historical change in this energy use suggest that the 1,300 BTU figure is some 14% above the level existing in 1967. The causes of this increase and the likely future direction of this ratio were not determined in this study. Table 31-3 presents a summary.[8]

Notably, these data cannot be directly derived from the data shown in the H matrix reproduced in Table 31-1, because we found that some larger producers of aluminum that bake their own anodes also manufacture and sell anodes. Thus, the data in Table 31-3 are based on *production* of prebaked anodes—not *usage* by the firms in the sample. In other words, while the sample firms produced 76% of 1971 primary metal production, they produced more than 76% of the total output of anodes for smelting. To obtain an estimate, we require estimates of outputs of metal by both processes, shown in Table 31-4.

As of mid-1971, published capacity of U.S. smelters totalled 3.94 million metric tons (4.34 million short tons). Of this 3.94 million, approximately 1.3 million was produced in horizontal or vertical type Soderberg systems. With the exception of one smelter of 159,000 tons, all this capacity is included in The Conference Board's sample. Consequently, the sample data include 1.95 million tons of prebaked capacity (Table 31-4).

On the assumption that each pound of primary aluminum produced in a prebake smelter requires 0.5 pound of anode, we obtain total anode usage of 0.9 million metric tons in 1971. If we ignore inventories, we find that production of anodes in the sample firms is within 7% of 0.9 million metric tons (exact data not given due to disclosure agreements with firms). Even if we consider that there was probably some net depletion of inventories in 1971, we come to the

Table 31-3.   Energy Use in Anode Baking
(BTU per pound of aluminum metal produced)

System	1967	1971
Soderberg	5,700	5,700
Prebake	1,140	1,300

Note: Data are estimated mean U.S.

conclusion that over 90% of all prebaked anode production is included in The Conference Board's sample.

Viewing the energy use figure from Table 31-1 of 5.4 (10^{12}) BTU in anode baking for the sample firms as representing 90% of energy use in anode baking, we derive a value of 6.0 (10^{12}) BTU for anode baking in the U.S. aluminum industry.

With respect to the future, we shall later make the assumption that Soderberg systems will not be built in new facilities and may indeed be replaced with prebake systems in existing facilities. The basis for this assumption is that E.P.A. and similar regulations by states will cause prebake systems to be preferred in that the release of volatiles from anode paste can be better controlled in a prebake than in a Soderberg system. That the prebake is less energy-using does *not* appear to be a factor in the firms' judgement that Soderberg will not be used.

Further discussion of Soderberg systems is undertaken in section B.3.

B.3.   Smelting

While smelting is indeed the major energy-use item in aluminum, we have the impression that its dominance has become singular. We prefer to treat it as the major, but by no means only, energy transaction.

Our data are defined as electricity (D.C.) into the smelting pot, excluding losses from rectification, line losses, and minor uses such as lighting, and cranes and vehicles. Where purchased electricity data were received on a "plant gate A.C." basis, we have assumed a 2% loss based on silicon rectifiers. Where power is on an "at the generator" basis, we have assumed a total loss of 5%.

Table 31-4.   Aluminum Smelting Capacity and Estimates of Production, by Type of System, 1971
(millions of metric tons)

	Total	*Sample*	*Percentage*
Capacity			
U.S. All systems	3.94	3.02	76.6%
Soderberg	2.11	1.95	92.4
Prebake	1.83	1.07	58.5
Production			
U.S. All systems	3.57	2.64	73.9
Soderberg	1.77 e	1.64 e	92.4
Prebake	1.80 e	1.00 e	58.5

e—estimated on the basis of the ratios shown in capacity data, and details obtained in various interviews.

The reader should note the following warnings and qualifications concerning the data on smelting.

a. Aluminum smelting pots have an operating range within which two points are of interest, (i) maximum efficiency in terms of energy; defined as a minimum kwh/lb. produced in a time period t, and (ii) maximum output, defined literally. Graphically, this can be depicted as in Figure 31-2, wherein point B represents condition (i) and point C represents condition (ii). Left of point A, output is zero. Right of point C, arcing prevents operation and output is essentially zero.

The firm may make the decision that operation at B, or operation at C is desirable. A change in the rate of operation, however, requires rebuilding the smelting pot.

In the Pacific Northwest, where in 1971 power costs averaged 2.0-2.5 mills/kwh, point C appears to have been preferred. In other regions where costs appears to have averaged 6 mills, and in some instances exceeded 7 mills/kwh, point B may have been preferred, especially in slack years for aluminum demand. Moreover, some firms appear to have a general corporate policy of requiring plant managers to minimize kwh/lb. metal, and others have a policy of maximizing output.

b. The decision of most of the firms in the sample not to provide data for individual smelters prevents our offering any distribution data. Consequently, the averages given may well be those of skewed distributions. Where ranges are given, the information stems from interviews, and we attempt to specify our degree of confidence in the data in each instance.

c. Data for kwh/lb. metal produced are almost pure input-output coefficients in the Leontief sense. As such they should be viewed as composites. Productive capacity enters and leaves the calculation over time as old potlines are replaced and new smelters are brought on stream. Year-to-year comparisons are influenced by a host of exogenous factors—breakdowns, strikes, power

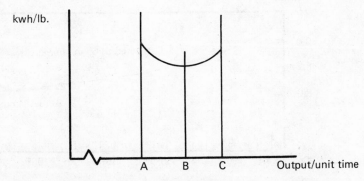

Figure 31-2. Aluminum Smelting—Operating Efficiency Curve.

shortages, start-up difficulties in new installations—and at this level of detail, even by such factors as changing personnel. Consequently, these data should be viewed in relatively long-term perspective, if one's interest concerns change in the coefficient.

Our calculations indicate that in 1971, among the sample firms, 7.97 kwh were required to smelt 1 pound of aluminum from the alumina to the metal stage. This figure is slightly below the trend value for the period 1963- 1971 of 8.05 kwh/lb. metal.

Using a linear trend from 1963-1971 shows a decline from 8.22 to 8.05. While a linear function may be a reasonable approximation for this period, data for the early post-World War II years indicate that over the longer period, the path of the kwh/lb. metal coefficient has been asymptotic. Figure 31-3 shows the approximate shape of the path based on fragmentary data (the trend path between 1947 and 1963 is interpolated and should be viewed as having low reliability).

One should also note that due to the entry of new firms, the coverage of the sample, from which data shown as "actual" in Figure 31-3 were drawn, declines from 85% in 1963 to 77% in 1971 in terms of the industry's capacity. Unfortunately, we were unable to gather sufficient data to expand this series from the sample to total U.S. aluminum smelting. Enough data have been collected, however, to expand the 1971 figures.

Total production of the sample firms in 1971 totalled 5,802 million lbs. (or 2.64 million metric tons), compared with total industry output of 7,850 million lbs. (or 3.57 million metric tons). The sample output was produced at a rate of 7.97 kwh/lb. Information gathered in interviews and from other sources leads us to make the relatively confident assumption that the balance of 2,048 million lbs. were produced at an average rate of 7.2 kwh/lb. Consequently, U.S. smelting usage may be derived (Table 31-5).

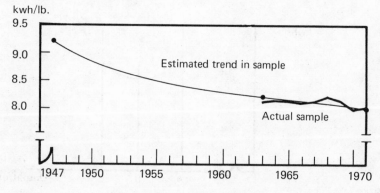

Figure 31-3. Trend in Aluminum Smelting Electricity Utilization.

Table 31-5A.   Electric Energy Usage in Aluminum Smelting, 1971[a]

	Production (million lbs.)	Energy Usage		
		kwh/lb.	(10^9) kwh	Equiv. (10^{12}) BTU
Sample firms	5,802	7.97	46.261	460.6[b]
Other firms	2,048	7.20	14.746	154.8[c]
Total U.S.	7,850	7.77	60.987	615.4

[a]Electricity into pot lines only.

[b]This figure differs from the datum of $497.9(10^{12})$ BTU shown in the Smelting column of the H matrix (Table 31-1). The $497.9(10^{12})$ figure includes ancillary uses of electricity in the smelting plants of $37.3(10^{12})$ BTU; the difference of $460.6(10^{12})$ BTU implies an average heat rate of 9,957 BTU/kwh $[460.6(10^{12})/46.261(10^9)]$.
See notes to Table 31.6, for derivation of the $497.9(10^{12})$ figure.

[c]Equivalent of electric energy calculated on a GEC basis using 1971 national average utility heat rate of 10,500 BTU/kwh.

Table 31-5B.   Ancillary   Electric   Energy   Usage   in   Aluminum Smelting, 1971

	Production (million lbs.)	Equiv. (10^{12}) BTU	BTU/lb.
Sample firms	5,802	37.3	6,429[a]
Other firms	2,048	13.2	6,429[b]
Total U.S.	7,850	50.5	6,429

[a]Observation.

[b]Assumption.

There are two main causes of the balance of production being estimated at a lower kwh/lb. rate than the sample: (1) the virtually complete absence of Soderberg systems outside of the sample, and (2) the preponderance of new smelters in the unsampled portion, some of which are known to approach a rate of 6.5 kwh/lb. in their smelting operations.

To expand our sample data inclusive of ancillary uses of electricity in smelting, we assume that use in the unsampled portion is the same as that in the sample on a per unit of metal basis. We use this basis since ancillary usage is primarily for motive power related to tonnage output.

At this point, a summary of the national (total U.S.) data derived, and its relation to the sample is presented. (The reason for placing the summary before the discussion of fabrication is that the reliability of our national estimates declines in fabrication.)

Basic data for the summary are shown in Table 31-6. Note that they refer only to primary metal, not total metal output.

From Table 31-6 one can draw an interim conclusion: production of

Table 31-6.   Summary of Energy Usage in Primary Aluminum from Alumina through Smelting Stages, 1971 (data are (10^{12}) BTU except as marked)

	Alumina Refining	Anode Prebake	Smelting Potlines	Smelting Ancillary	Total
1. Sample data[a]	107.7	5.4	460.6	37.3	611.0
2. Sample as a percentage of total U.S. industry[b]	~100%	~90%	74%		
U.S. aluminum industry[c]					
3. Usage on metal produced basis	94.2	6.0	615.4	50.5	766.1
4. Usage on all products produced basis	107.7				799.6
U.S. aluminum industry					
5. BTU usage per lb. of ingot (Row 3 in (10^{12}) BTU/7.85(10^{9}) lbs.)	12,000	764	78,395	6,433	97,592

[a]Source, Tables 31-1 and 31-5.
[b]Production basis; see text, sections B.1, 2, 3.
[c]See text, sections B.1, 2, 3.

primary aluminum from raw materials involves the use of 97,600 BTU/lb., or 214.7 million BTU per metric ton (195.2 million BTU per short ton).[9]

B.4. Scrap Recovery

To expand the data in Table 31-6 to total U.S. production of aluminum, the subject of scrap must be broached. There are two basic kinds of scrap: (1) clean scrap, which consists of (a) "run around" scrap or pieces discarded by an integrated firm in its fabricating processes that are clean, and graded according to alloys, etc., and (b) scrap purchased under agreement from independent fabricators where, again, the metal is graded and clean. Energy usage for utilization of clean scrap is excluded from the primary ingot production data, but appears in the fabrication data under heat used for furnaces. The volume of this scrap is not determinable. (2) "Secondary" scrap; this consists of metal which has passed through its final, or end-use stage, and has been recycled. This metal usually carries finish materials—lacquer, paint, etc.—and is not graded. Data on the volume of this material are published by the Aluminum Association.

While we are not able to separate the energy use attributable to processing of scrap metal in the sample data, we have been able to determine that there are three main points of energy use: (1) shredding and other physical preparation, (2) cleaning via burning off coatings, and (3) melting. Our interviews indicated that on the average 6,000 BTU/lb. are used to bring scrap from the plant gate to the stage of molten metal fit for use.[10]

In a study prompted by questions of energy resource conservation the significance of this figure is immediately obvious when compared with the energy use datum for primary ingot from raw material. At this stage of processing, metal from secondary scrap recovery requires approximately 6% (6,000/97,592) of the energy calculated as necessary when raw materials are used.[11]

If the Aluminum Association's data for secondary scrap metal recovery are used, we may approach a more global energy use datum for 1971.[12] Table 31-7 presents the necessary calculations.

These data indicate that in 1971, when secondary recovery accounted for 21.1% of U.S. primary plus U.S. secondary recovery production, the radically lower energy use in secondary recovery reduced the average energy required per pound of metal from 97,592 BTU to 78,261 BTU, or by 19.8%.[13] Consequently, the issue of scrap becomes important in the projections undertaken in section C, below.

Total U.S. energy usages derived in Tables 31-5 and 31-7 serve as estimates of energy required in 1971 by two SIC products: SIC 28195 (Alumina) 107.7 (10^{12}) BTU, and SIC 3334 (Primary Aluminum) 684.5 (10^{12}) BTU.[14]

Table 31-7.   Energy Use in U.S. Aluminum Production, 1971 Metal from Primary and Secondary Scrap Sources (data are (10^{12}) BTU except were noted)

	Alumina	Anode	Smelting	Scrap Reduction	Total
			(10^{12}) BTU		
Primary metal	94.2	6.0	665.9	–	766.1
Secondary scrap recovery[a] . . .	–	–	–	12.6	12.6
Total U.S.	94.2	6.0	665.9	12.6	778.7
BTUs per lb. of metal produced[b]	–	–	–	–	78,261

[a]$2.1(10^9)$ lbs. @ 6,000 BTU/lb.

[b]$778.7(10^{12})/[(7.85 + 2.1)10^9]$

[c]Use of the assumption shown in footnote c to Table 31-2 would result in the total in row 1 declining from 766.1 to 735.7, and the total in row 3 declining from 778.7 to 748.3—a fall of 3.9%. The concomitant change in BTU/lb., would be from 78,261 to 75,200.

B.5.   Fabrication

Several difficulties arise in this section. Sample data in Table 31-1 are energy uses for products that may or may not undergo further processing within SIC 3353, 54, 55, or 59. When these SIC categories are defined as a product group or "industry," there is much intra-industry movement that we are unable to specify. Figure 31-4 illustrates the basic problem.

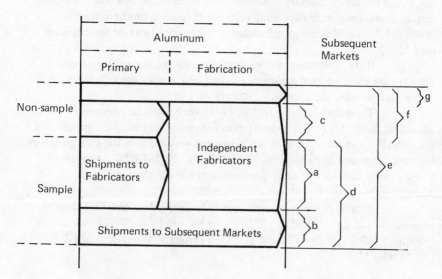

Figure 31-4.   Product Flows in Aluminum Production.

Magnitudes d and e only are known: 4.28 (10^9) and 7.84 (10^9) pounds, respectively; f cannot be derived, since a and c are not necessarily additive.

A second problem arises because processing may vary substantially in terms of product, and the energy use involved will also vary. For example, a pound of foil will require more energy to fabricate than, say, a pound of plate.

Data obtained from the sample firms indicate a range of from 15,000-30,000 BTU per pound of fabricated product. In the event that energy use in the processing performed by the independent fabricators were included with the energy use of the primary producers, the total energy use would be increased. Thus, we have arbitrarily selected a 25,000 BTU/lb. figure with the full understanding that it has little firm basis, and is indeed artificial, subject to influence by change in mix, etc.

Shipments of domestic mill products in 1971 totalled 7.84 (10^9) pounds.[15] Since inventories of all products of the industry increased by over half a million pounds in that year, production is likely to have exceeded shipments. Estimating conservatively we place output at 8.0 (10^9) pounds. Using the estimate of energy usage at 25,000 BTU/lb. we obtain a total U.S. usage of 200 (10^{12}) BTU.

Adding this figure to the total of 776.1 (10^{12}) BTU derived for ingot stage metal in Table 31-7, and scaling the vehicle column on the basis of production in the sample firms, we obtain a net total energy use figure of 975.5 (10^{12}) BTU for 1971. Net total energy use data shown in Table 31-1 constitute 75.0% of this 975.5 (10^{12}) estimate, close to the proportion of ingot output accounted for by the sample firms.

In 1971, 10.41 (10^9) pounds of all aluminum ingot, and domestic mill products were shipped. Inventories of all aluminum products increased 0.63 (10^9) pounds. Imports of ingot totalled 1.11 (10^9) pounds. These data imply production of 9.93 (10^9) pounds wherein intra-industry transactions have been removed. This figure of 9.93 (10^9) pounds, aluminum and products output from domestic sources, appears to be the best for comparison with dollar value of the shipments of SIC 3334, 3353, 3354, 3355, 3359. Since most imports are indistinguishable from domestic output when shipped, total 1971 availability of aluminum products in the U.S. industry would equal 11.04 (10^9) pounds. This differs from total industry supply of 11.35 (10^9) pounds by exclusion of imported scrap and mill products.

Tables 31-8 and 31-9 present estimates of the H and E matrices for total U.S. aluminum production. The H matrix—homogeneous measures of energy use— includes fabrication as a single column due to our lack of detail of the various aspects of fabrication. The E matrix in Table 31-9 shows the energy usage per unit of metal and metal products produced, i.e. Table 31-8 divided through by 9.93 (10^9) pounds.

Note that the measure ϵ = 98,237 BTU is only slightly higher than the datum of 97,592 BTU derived in Table 31-6, even after inclusion of fabri-

Table 31-8. Aluminum, Estimated U.S. Industry Matrix (H) of Sources and Uses of Energy, 1971 (data are (10^{12}) BTU except as marked)

	Alumina Refining	Anode Baking	Smelting	Fabrication	Vehicles	Other	Total Energy by Type	Percentage
Electricity	18.3	*	665.9	94.0	—	—	778.2	79.8%
Coal	—	—	—	6.9	—	—	6.9	0.7
Distillate oil	—	*	—	3.2	0.1	0.1	3.4	0.3
Residual oil	0.8	—	—	1.6	—	—	2.4	0.2
Gas	75.1	5.8	—	88.3	*	1.9	171.2	17.5
LPG	*	*	—	6.0	2.6	—	8.7	0.9
Gasoline	—	—	—	—	4.6	—	4.6	0.5
Total energy by use	94.2	6.0	665.9	200.0	7.4	2.0	975.5	—
Percentage	9.7%	0.6%	68.3%	20.5%	0.8%	0.2%	—	100%

Note: Distribution of data along the columns is based on proportions derived from Table 31-1. Data exclude fuel usage in production of alumina not sold to aluminum with the difference being taken from gas row. This single deduction is made on the assumption that the difference lies primarily in calcining alumina.

*Denotes less than $0.05(10^{12})$ BTU.

Table 31-9. Aluminum, Estimated U.S. Industry 1971 Matrix (E) of BTU/lb. Product Coefficients[a]
(data are BTUs)

	Alumina Refining	Anode Baking	Smelting	Fabrication	Vehicles	Other	Total Energy by Type
Electricity	1,843	*	67,059	9,466	–	–	78,368
Coal	–	–	–	695	–	–	695
Distillate oil	–	*	–	322	10	10	342
Residual oil	80	–	–	162	–	–	242
Gas	7,563	584	–	8,892	10	191	17,241
LPG	–	*	–	604	261	–	876
Gasoline	–	–	–	–	463	–	463
Total energy use	9,486	606	67,059	20,141	744	201	98,237

*Negligible.

[a]This is the E matrix (see List of Definitions, Appendix).

Note: Data are derived from the H. matrix shown in Table 31-8 by $E = H\lambda^{-1}$ where λ^{-1} is the inverse of $9.93(10^9)$ lbs.

cation, vehicles and other. The small difference results primarily from the inclusion of secondary scrap recovery offsetting addition of fabricating.

With respect to the future, if we could be assured that: (a) none of the elements of E are likely to change, and (b) the proportion of secondary recovery will remain constant, then future energy use could be easily calculated using a value of λ for a future year. In fact, we do expect several changes and these are discussed in C, below.

We also have the question of energy sources—from which fuels is energy likely to be derived? To lay a foundation for an answer we now turn to energy source patterns.

B.6. Energy Source Patterns

Electricity is the major source of power, which our sample shows to be 67% purchased and 33% generated, of which a small proportion is generated by captive hydro.

To expand this distribution to national U.S. aluminum industry data, we can be reasonably confident in stating that all captive hydro generation is in the sample, and the incidence of captive thermal generation in the unsampled portion is virtually nil. Consequently, we assume that the 208.7 (10^{12}) BTU difference between the 778.2 (10^{12}) BTU equivalent appearing in Table 31-8 and the 569.5 (10^{12}) BTU in Table 31-1 is purchased electricity.

Generation of electricity from thermal sources is dependent primarily upon natural gas. Of the 178.3 (10^{12}) BTU assigned to generation in Table 31-1, 50% is gas. Much of that listed as "not specified by kind" is known to be gas, and the residual is distributed between coal and oil.[16]

With respect to the future, we make the assumption with substantial confidence that within the period to 1985, the aluminum companies will not build additional captive generating capacity due to relatively large capital costs and long pay-back periods. Consequently additional electricity will be purchased.

Coal is presently a minor input to the fuel use pattern of aluminum accounting for under 3% of all BTU inputs. In the projection period it is likely to remain so, notwithstanding the large coal reserves held by the aluminum firms. We base this assumption on two foundations: (a) present fuel-using capacity of the aluminum industry is "specific" to other fuels and cannot be converted easily due to (i) need for clean fuels, and (ii) furnace design. (b) coal is likely to suffer from emission regulations during the forecast period to 1985; we assume that technological changes to render coal competitive with other fuels under emission criteria will not be widely available and/or not adopted by aluminum firms prior to 1985. On the other hand, we expect substantial use of coal reserves by aluminum firms after 1985 in gasification and other future uses not now commercially available.

Distillate and residual oils are also minor items in the 1971 fuel use patterns. We find, however, that increases are likely in providing heat for furnaces, albeit with a not insignificant capital input being required for modification and emission standard compliance.

Gas is without doubt the most widely used fuel. Our estimates suggest that 30% of all energy used in the U.S. aluminum industry in 1971 stemmed from natural gas.[17] In some uses, the processes are gas-specific. In alumina refining, for example, capital equipment essentially embodies a gas technology; a switch to oil will require some capital replacement. Specificity is less pronounced in fabrication, but substitution would require significant changes in capital equipment in some instances.

It has been suggested that the projection period would be a useful time to test the price elasticity of demand for natural gas by aluminum producers. When put to the firms, the essentials of this question elicited an answer suspected by some; in translation, the elasticity appears to be approximately zero, but it is probably discontinuous at some price at which the relative price of aluminum versus other materials rises high enough to affect demand adversely, and at which the relative costs of investment in alternate fuel capability are no longer critical.[18]

Zero elasticity is implied by the firms showing virtually no concern about gas prices within what they (the firms), consider an uncomfortable, but feasible range—up to $0.75/Mcf[a] (i.e., $0.75/1.035 (10^6) BTU), compared with $0.20/Mcf in 1971 (well-head basis). Gas price increases were viewed generally as something passed along to the customer. (Notably, when interviewed the firms were in the first period of near-capacity production seen in some years, and the demand outlook was, and remains optimistic.)

What was of concern was the possibility of unstable supplies—the F.P.C., in effect, rendering the aluminum companies' long-term gas contracts null and void. Interruptible gas may cause substantial costs if generators and, subsequently, pot lines are shut down. The possibility of building fuel flexibility into existing captive generating capacity is virtually nil. The possibility of building fuel flexibility into other capacity may exist in alumina refining and fabrication.

Liquid petroleum gas is used mainly as a substitute for natural gas, but necessities of building storage facilities, plus the higher price, render LPG an unattractive alternative for most firms to face.

Table 31-10 presents a summary of the industry's 1971 energy source pattern.

Further discussion of future possible changes in this pattern appears in section C., below.

[a]Thousand cubic feet.

Table 31-10.   Aluminum, U.S. Industry, Energy Source Patterns, 1971

	Percentage
Purchased electricity	60.6%
Coal	7.2
Distillate oil	0.5
Residual oil	
Natural gas	30.1
L.P. gas	1.0
Gasoline	0.5
Total	100.00

Note: Based on data from Table 31-1 with modifications according to data shown in Tables 31-6, 31-7, and 31-8, and information obtained in interviews.

B.7.   Comparison with U.S.
Bureau of Census Data

Table 31-11 presents energy data from prior *Census of Manufactures* for years 1947 to 1967. Data for 1971 in this table are constructed from The Conference Board sample data and estimates of the non-sampled portion of establishments classified in SIC 3334 with plants classified in SIC 3353, 54, 55, and 59 deleted as far as sample information permits.

First, a note on the 1967 Census data is warranted by our sample data for 1967 (sample data for 1967 are not presented due to disclosure problems). We have been informed by more than one firm in our sample that instances have arisen where they find data submitted to Census have been wrong. Most of these comments apply to 1971 data in the MA 100-forms submitted in the *Annual Survey of Manufactures*. As noted in Table 31-11, this problem must have also existed in 1967 since our survey data imply that the unsampled portion of the industry was producing at an absurd kwh/lb. rate. The existence of similar problems in earlier years is also possible. Given the implied unreliability of the Census figures, we forgo further comment and simply present the data.

C.   PROJECTIONS

Initially, the results appearing in this section are the outcome of "what if . . ." procedures. Results should not be viewed as an attempt to foretell what *will* occur, they are representations of what might occur, given the assumptions used.

The basic procedure is to:

(a) make projections of the E matrix, containing the BTU/lb. product measures.

	1971[2] Estimates	1967	1962	1958	1954	1947[3]
Production						
1 Primary metal production (10^9) lbs.	7.850	6.539	4.236	3.131	2.921	1.144
2 From scrap (domestic) (10^9) lbs.	2.100	1.756	1.164	.708	.626	.690
3 (imports) (10^9) lbs.	.113	.055	.012	.018	.015	.028
4 Total scrap (10^9) lbs.	2.213	1.811	1.176	.726	.641	.718
5 Total domestic production	10.063	8.350	5.412	3.857	3.562	1.862
GEC based data						
6 Heat rate for electricity GEC	10,500	10,432	10,558	11,085	12,180	15,600
7 Electricity purchased kwh(10^9)	45.3	41.957[1]	26.883	16.170	17.239	9.331
8 Row 6 × row 7 = BTU(10^{12})	475.7	437.69	283.83	179.24	209.97	145.56
9 Other fuels purchased BTU(10^{12})	160.0	151.90	141.00	124.20	111.50	11.00*
10 Total energy to SIC 3334 BTU(10^{12})	635.7	589.59	424.83	303.44	321.47	156.56*
UE based data						
11 Electricity generated kwh(10^9)	18.1	11.648[1]	9.387	8.968	9.044	1.070*
12 Total electricity row 7 + 11	63.4	53.605	36.270	25.138	26.283	10.401
13 Row 9 × (3412 BTU/kwh) UE (10^{12})	154.6	143.16	91.725	55.172	58.82	31.84
14 Total row 13 + 9 UE = BTU (10^{12})	314.6	295.06	232.725	179.372	170.32	42.84*
15 Row 14/row 1	40.076	45,123	54,940	57,289	58,309	37,447*
Ratios						
16 Row 10/row 1 BTU/lb	80.98	90,165	100,290	96,914	110,055	136,853
17 Row 10/row 5 BTU/lb	63.172	70,609	78,498	78,672	90,250	84,081
18 Row 12/row 1 kwh/lb	8.08	8.198[1]	8.562	8.029	9.00	9.092
Capacity						
19 Published U.S. capacity-thous. sh. tons	4,666	3,321	2,489	2,194	1,413	630
20 Ratio (Row 1/2000)/line 19	.84	.98	.85	.71	1.03	.91

[1] Data for 1967 are considered to be understated. We have obtained data covering roughly 80% of 1967 production, and we have estimates of the minimum datum for an added 6% of production. These imply that the balance of the industry was producing at under 6kwh/lb. metal in smelting, or under 6.5 kwh/lb. total usage in the relevant establishments. Such a low figure we view as highly improbable.

[2] Adjusted to match as closely as possible the establishments included in the Census of Manufactures.

[3] Data for 1947 are suspect and ought to be viewed as unreliable. Asterisks mark the anomalous data.

Sources: Rows 1-5, 19, 20, The Aluminum Association; Aluminum Statistical Review 1971; row 6, U.S. Bureau of Mines; Column 1, rows 7-18, The Conference Board; Columns 2-6, rows 7-18, U.S. Bureau of the Census, Census of Manufactures, 1947, 1954, 1958, 1967; Annual Survey of Manufactures, 1962.

(b) make projections of demand for aluminum, i.e., to obtain λ for the horizon year.

(c) derive the energy requirements.

(d) translate energy requirements into fuel demands.

In (a) and (c) we shall split the E matrix and project on the basis of metal at the ingot stage, and then go on to fabrication and the mill products stage in a separate step. The first step must also be split between primary and secondary scrap recovery sources. In (b) we shall present the two major alternative output projections that we feel have roughly equal probability of occurring. Projection I energy implications are presented in section C.2, and those for Projection II in C.3.

While a full discussion of output projections is given in section C.4, the results of these demand projections are used in the following pages. Consequently, we present here a brief summary of the projections of demand for aluminum.

There are two demand projections; Projection I differs from Projection II only in one instance. Projection I assumes a relatively uninterrupted growth of the can stock market. Projection II, on the other hand, assumes that legislation against disposable containers will be raised between now and 1980, and will become relatively widespread. The overall effect is to change the growth rate in the market for can stock from 12.0% annual average growth per year 1969-1980 in Projection I to an annual average rate of 3.4% in Projection II. The overall effect upon demand is to change the growth rate, 1969-1980, of total domestic shipments from 5.9% in Projection I to 5.3% in Projection II. These differences also result in a difference in the amount of scrap recovered. (Differing scrap recovery is the primary reason that it was necessary to develop projections of demand and shipments simultaneously with the projections of energy use.) The overall effect of reduction of the can stock market growth rate is to reduce the rate of growth of secondary scrap recovery from 5.6% per year to 4.4% per year, 1969-1980.

The overall impact of these differences between Projections I and II on primary U.S. metal production is negligible due to the expectation that capacity limitations will be reached prior to 1980, and that demand for metal above the U.S. capacity limits will be fed by imports. The data underlying these growth rates as shown in Table 31-28, with supporting data appearing in Tables 31-26 and 31-27.

In (a) we project on four bases: (i) projection of the 1971 magnitude (element of the H matrix, h_{ij}) with changes ($h_{ij}^{1980} = h_{ij}^{1971} + \Delta h_{ij}$), both of which result in a change in the corresponding e_{ij}, (iii) projection of a BTU/lb. coefficient (e_{ij}), unchanged at the 1971 level, and (iv) projection of a coefficient with changes ($e_{ij}^{1980} = e_{ij}^{1971} + \Delta e_{ij}$).

In the text, steps (b) and (c) are carried out roughly simultaneously, and the actual discussion of the demand projections follows derivation of the energy requirements.

In these projections, we continue to use the 1971 average utility heat rate for conversion of electricity to BTU equivalent (10,500 BTU/kwh, based on the assumption that this heat will indeed cease its long-term historical asymptotic decline due to the necessity of utilities diverting power into ancillary equipment to meet EPA standards).

C.1. Projections of Energy-Output Coefficients

In this section we consider each non-zero element of the E matrix shown in Table 31-9 individually. To do so, first, each column total is examined and the possible changes in the aggregate, obtained from interviews and other sources, are entered. Next, each element of the column is considered on the basis of information received from the firms on the likelihood of their switching fuels in the future.

(i) **Alumina refining.** Information obtained in interviews suggested strongly that increasing pressure to conserve energy was being brought to bear on operational personnel by the firms. In alumina refining, under existing technology, the main focus appears to be the steam systems. A (probably conservative) estimate puts possible saving at about 5% by 1980, reducing the total heat in our data from 4,839 to 4,560 BTU/lb. of alumina production. Interviews also suggested that usage of gas is likely to decline substantially, with gas to be replaced by oil. In alumina refining, a large proportion of heat is used to generate steam (and electricity) and furnaces can be converted to burn oil. In the calcining stage of refining, gas will probably be retained for manufacture of some chemical grade aluminas, but can probably be replaced by oil for metal grade alumina. By 1980, our estimates suggest, at least 45% and perhaps up to 70% of heat for refining will be derived from oil.

The breadth of this range results from the firms being unable to specify what proportion will have been reached by 1980. The basic reason for this inability to specify arises from lack of knowledge on four fundamental points: (a) the relative prices of gas and oil, and more important, the availability of gas, (b) whether or not oil will be a suitable substitute for gas in calcining, (c) the industry-wide availability of technology to move away from rotary kilns to other systems, and (d) the capital position of each firm over the decade as it relates to firms' willingness to undertake investment in equipment and machinery, which in turn is partially dependent on prices received for outputs relative to input costs.

Similarly, whether or not distillate or residual oil will be used is uncertain due to unstable supplies of low sulphur oil, EPA regulations, and relative prices of each.

Tables 31-12A and 31-12B present projections based on the assumption of 45% of heat from oil in Projection I columns, and 70% of heat from oil in Projection II. Note that the total declines 3% between the two

Table 31-12A.   Alumina Refining Energy Coefficients, Alumina Basis, 1971 and 1980 (BTU per pound of alumina produced)

	1971		1980 Proj. I		1980 Proj. II	
	Energy	Percentage	Energy	Percentage	Energy	Percentage
Electricity	1,161	19.4%	1,140	20%	1,040	20%
Coal	—	—	—			
Distillate oil	—	.8 }				
Residual oil	48	79.8 }	2,052	36	3,132	56
Gas	4,791		2,508	44	1,357	24
LP gas	*	*	*	*	*	*
Gasoline						
All heat	4,839	80.7	4,560	79.8	4,489	79.4
All sources	6,000	100.0	5,700	100.0	5,654	100.0

Note: Proj. I implies moderate shift to oil. Proj. II implies substantial shift to oil and includes consequent saving in energy due to shift from rotary calcining kiln; see text for details.

*Negligible.

Table 31-12B. Alumina Refining Energy Coefficients, Total Metal Basis[a], 1971 and 1980 (BTUs per pound of metal products)

| | 1971 | | 1980 | | | |
| | | | Proj. I | | Proj. II | |
	Energy	Percentage	Energy	Percentage	Energy	Percentage
Electricity	1,843	19.4%	1,840	20%	1,840	20%
Coal	—	—	—	—	—	—
Distillate oil	—	—				
Residual oil	80	.8	3,270	36	4,970	56
Gas	7,563	79.9	3,990	44	2,130	24
LP gas	*	*	*	*	*	*
Gasoline	—	—	—	—	—	—
All heat	7,643	80.7	7,260	79.8	7,100	79.4
All sources	9,486	100.0	9,100	100.0	8,940	100.0

Note: Proj. I implies moderate shift to oil. Proj. II implies substantial shift to oil and includes consequent saving in energy due to shift from rotary calcining kiln; see text for details.

*Negligible.

[a]Data consistent with Table 31-9.

projections due to the assumption of a widespread shift away from rotary calcining kilns to new techniques using less heat. Impressions obtained in interviews make us opt for Projection I implying a shift in some firms but not in others.

Electricity usage has been left constant. Although the actual refining process may use slightly less electricity by 1980, increasing use of ancillary equipment is likely to offset savings in the main process.

(ii) Anode baking. While oil can only be used in baking anodes subject to certain restrictions (e.g., oil containing vanadium, a serious contaminant of aluminum, cannot be used), it can be satisfactorily substituted for natural gas within limits. Overall energy usage may decline as much as 5% as a result of conservation measures.

Information gathered in interviews suggests that given the firms' present view of gas availability over the years to 1980, there will probably be serious attempts to convert anode baking furnaces to oil. In this case, the oil will probably be distillate, again with questions of sulphur content, EPA standards, availability, and price determining the actual mix that will be used.

Tables 31-13A and 31-13B present two projections, both under the 5% overall reduction assumption, the first showing a shift to 70% oil; the second showing a complete shift to oil, with the first having a somewhat higher probability in our view.

(iii) Electricity to smelting. To determine a likely possible future value for this coefficient, it is first necessary to broach the subject of capacity since additions and removals of capacity affect the total.

In Figure 31-5, projections of capacity are presented. These projections are based on known plans for expansion and rebuilding, and on other information. They result in a 1980 total capacity of 12.0 (10^9) lbs. Applying known and estimated kwh/lb. ratings to the components of this capacity, a 1980 electricity usage in smelting of 7.29 kwh/lb. is obtained.

The assumptions involved are:

(a) Rebuilt capacity will enter at 6.9 kwh/lb. prior to 1977 and at 6.8 kwh/lb. during 1978-1980.

(b) New capacity will enter at 6.8 kwh/lb. prior to 1977 and at 6.5 kwh/lb. thereafter, with one exception, i.e.,

(c) Chloride process capacity will enter at 4.6 kwh/lb.

(d) Removal of capacity to be rebuilt will reduce still existing capacity from 7.77 to 7.70 kwh/lb.

These capacity data ought to be qualified in that production can conceivably exceed capacity by as much as 8%. We assume that as production exceeds listed capacity, however, the relationship shown in Figure 31-2 applies and the average kwh/lb. would rise as production approached the maximum.

Table 31-13A. Anode Baking Energy, Anode-Primary Metal Basis, 1971 and 1980
(BTUs per pound of prebaked anode)

	1971		1980 Proj. I		1980 Proj. II	
	Energy	Percentage	Energy	Percentage	Energy	Percentage
Electricity	*	1%	*	2%	*	2%
Coal	—	—	—	—	—	—
Distillate oil	*	*	1,729	70	2,419	98
Residual oil	—	—	—	—	—	—
Gas	2,496	96	690	28	—	—
LP gas	*	*	*	*	—	—
Gasoline	—	—	—	—	—	—
All heat	2,550	99	2,419	98	2,419	98
All sources	2,600	100	2,470	100	2,470	100

*Negligible.

Sources: Table 31-3, Interviews.

Table 31-13B.   Anode Baking Energy Coefficients, Total Metal Basis, 1971 and 1980
(BTU per pound of metal products)

| | 1971 | | 1980 | | | |
| | | | Proj. I | | Proj. II | |
	Energy	Percentage	Energy	Percentage	Energy	Percentage
Electricity	*	1%	*	2%	*	2%
Coal	—	—	—	—	—	—
Distillate oil	*	*	400	70	570	98
Residual oil	—	—	—	—	—	—
Gas.	584	96	170	28	—	—
LP gas	*	*	*	*	—	—
Gasoline	—	—	—	—	—	—
All heat	600	99	570	98	570	98
All sources	606	100	580	100	580	100.

See notes to Table 31-12.

Data are consistent with Table 31-9.

*Negligible.

Estimates of the magnitude of this increase are based on the variance between trend and actual for years in the sample data during which production exceeded capacity ratings.

Consequently, 1980 capacity of 12.0 (10^9) pounds having an electricity to smelting (potline) energy usage of 7.29 kwh/lb. will be viewed as capable of producing 12.96 (10^9) pounds at an energy usage of 7.40 kwh/lb.

As noted in section B.3, time series for the electricity to smelting coefficient are available only for the sample firms. Consequently, we are unable to determine if the 7.29 kwh/lb. figure for 1980 falls on the curve depicted in Figure 31-3. By some elimination (based on company information), in the capacity data shown in Figure 31-5, however, we are able to obtain a figure for

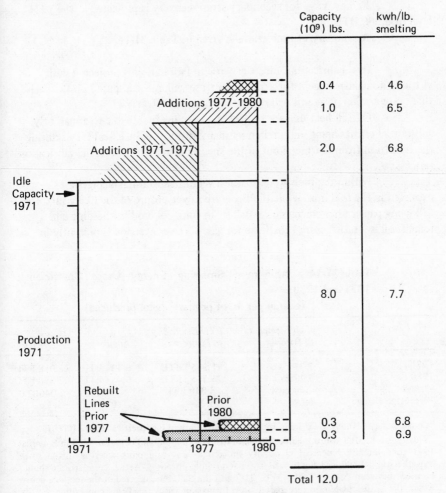

Figure 31-5. Aluminum Production Capacity, 1971-1980.

1980 roughly comparable in composition with data in Figure 31-3.[19] We find that when the chloride process is included, the kwh/lb. figure lies slightly below where the curve is estimated to lie in 1980. When the chloride process capacity is removed, the figure lies slightly above the curve. The latter overestimate may result from projection of kwh/lb. in capacity existing in 1971 and 1980 at a constant rate when, in fact, minor refinements of the process may reduce the 7.7 kwh/lb. figure by 1980.

Since introduction of the chloride process appears to have the potential to lower average industry usage of electricity sufficiently to shift the rate of descent of the kwh/lb. curve, it should be viewed as a significant technological change in terms of the path of the kwh/lb. input coefficient.

Energy usage for secondary scrap recovery is projected at the 1971 level of 6,000 BTU/lb.

A summary of projections is given in Table 31-14.

(iv) Fabrication. Electricity use in fabrication is projected with virtually no change except for a minor decrease which is computed on the basis that conservation programs will have some negative effect.

Overall heat usage is projected to decline by 6% due to apparently substantial efforts being undertaken by many firms to reduce heat losses during the transition from hot metal out of the smelter into and through the fabrication process.

Within the fuels to fabrication vector, substantial changes are expected in the fuel mix. While the firms are as yet unsure of the likely mix, the following pattern has emerged as possible. In furnaces used for holding and remelt, oil is a satisfactory substitute for gas. Some conversion is presently in

Table 31-14. Aluminum Smelting Energy Usage Coefficients, 1971 and 1980

(energy per lb. of primary metal produced)

	Kwh Electricity to Potlines	BTU Electricity to Potlines	Ancillary	All Electricity[a]
1971	7.77 kwh	81,585[b] BTU	6,433 BTU	88,018 BTU[b]
1980	7.29 kwh	76,545 BTU	6,433 BTU	82,978 BTU
Change	−.48 kwh	−5,040 BTU	0 BTU	−5,040 BTU
Percentage change . . .	−6.2%	−6.2%	0%	−5.7%

[a]Conversions at 10,500 BTU/kwh. Includes ancillary use of electricity at 6,433 BTU/lb.

[b]This figure 88,018 will not agree with data from Table 31-6 and others in section B, actual 1971 data include generated electricity on actual heat rate basis whereas this is on a hypothetical 10,500 BTU/kwh basis for comparison purposes. Actual comparisons should be made between data in Tables 31-6, 31-7 and the BTU data derived in the sections below where the actual heat rates are based on information from the firms concerning captive electrical generation by engines and includes hydro sources.

tentative plan form, and other conversions are feasible. Annealing furnaces and some other heat treatments of products will continue to require gas. In a few instances, coal is likely to be used for furnaces, but the extent of use will depend on sulfur content, EPA standards, availability of gas, and the price of oil. We assume that the incidence of coal use will increase only moderately by 1980 (but may increase substantially during the 1980s).

Based on rather vague possibilities offered by the firms, we project dependence on gas to decline considerably, from 83.3% of all heat (44.1% of all energy) to 37.2% of all heat (19.2% of all energy). This projection should be viewed as having relatively low reliability, and the author suggests that it probably represents a maximum switch out of gas; i.e., the usage of gas may well be higher in 1980, relative to other sources of heat; Table 31-15 presents the data.

Table 31-15 Aluminum Fabrication Energy Use Coefficients, 1971 and 1980

(BTU except as noted)

	1971 Energy	1971 Percentage		1980 Percentage		1980 Energy	1971–80 % Change
Electricity ...	9,466		47.0%		48.4%	9,400	−0.7%
Coal	695	6.5%	3.5	10.0%	5.2	1,004	44.5
Distillate oil ..	322	3.0	1.6 ⎫	45.8	23.6	4,596	950.0
Residual oil ..	162	1.5	.8 ⎭				
Gas	8,892	83.3	44.1	37.2	19.2	3,733	−58.0
LP gas	604	5.7	3.0	7.0	3.7	702	16.2
Gasoline	−	−	−	−	−	−	−
Total heat	10,676	100.0	52.9	100.0	51.6	10,035	−6.0
All sources	20,141	−	100.0	−	100.0	19,435	−3.5

N.B. Data based on and equivalent to 1971 coefficients shown in Table 31-9.

Table 31-16. Alumina Refining, Demand for Energy and Fuel, 1980

	$(h_{i1}^{1980})(10^{12})$ BTU	(f_{i2}^{1980}) Fuel Equivalent	Units
Electricity	27.4	2.61	(10^9) kwh
Coal	−	−	−
Distillate oil	49.2	8.20	(10^6) bbl.
Residual oil			
Gas	60.2	58.2	(10^9) cu. ft.
LP gas	*	*	−
Gasoline	−	−	−
Total	136.8	−	−

Sources: Table 31-12A and text; section C.2(i).

For conversion factors see Appendix.

*Denotes less than $0.05(10^{12})$ BTU.

(v) **Vehicles and other.** Coefficients in the last two columns of Table 31-9 are projected unchanged.

C.2.   The 1980 Energy Matrix under Output Projection I

Rather than constructing the E^{1980} matrix on a homogeneous product basis (as in Table 31-9) where all elements are divided through by a single metal output number, it is necessary to partition the matrix to account for the fact that not all alumina ends up in metal (viz chemical usage) and not all metal originates in alumina (viz scrap). Partitioning is on the basis of: (1) alumina, (2) anodes and smelting, and (3) fabrication. Consequently, to derive the energy used to make alumina, we employ the column vector of coefficients e_1 and the output of alumina λ_1, both expressed in pounds of alumina. To obtain the energy used in anode baking and smelting we use column vectors e_2 and e_3, and the output of primary metal λ_2, all expressed in pounds of primary metal. For fabricated products we use e_4 and λ_4, defined in terms of pounds of fabricated products. Energy used in vehicles and miscellaneous is derived from the vectors e_5 and e_6, and an output variable which in this case is defined as total metal output (marketed ingot plus mill products).

To do this, we need to know 1980 production of alumina, primary metal, and mill products. With respect to the first two, there is little difficulty involved since both demand projections (section C.4) imply substantial excess demand over U.S. capacity. Consequently, we can assume capacity output levels for 1980.

At this stage, a choice arose between using rated capacity of 12.0 (10^9) pounds or estimated maximum capacity of 12.96 (10^9) pounds. The former was chosen arbitrarily.

(i) **Alumina.** Production of 12.0 (10^9) pounds of primary metal in the U.S. during 1980 implies a requirement of 24.0 (10^9) pounds of alumina if a rate of 2.0 pounds Al_2O_3 per pound of aluminum is used. As in the historical discussion, we assume this amount to be produced in the U.S. Using the coefficients from Table 31-12A (Projection I), energy demands to produce 24.0 (10^9) pounds of alumina are calculated in Table 31-16.[20]

This procedure assumes that increased alumina production takes place within the United States. This is an arbitrary assumption. It may conversely be argued that most of the increase in alumina production by the international firms will be undertaken abroad. Indeed there is considerable pressure from both economic and political factors for the construction of alumina refineries near bauxite mines. On the other hand, in light of the experience of Alcan in Guyana, and increasing possibilities of nationalization of foreign companies' holdings in the Caribbean and Africa, it is also reasonable to expect the aluminum producing firms to be extremely cautious about making direct investments in the bauxite-producing countries. On the other hand, if the producing firms can work out arrangements whereby the capitalization of the alumina refineries is funded by the host nation, then an additional argument for placing the refineries near the bauxite sources arises.

(ii) **Anode baking.** Under the assumption that no further Soderberg capacity will be built in the U.S., all added U.S. primary production will require prebaked anodes. The exercise shown in Table 31-4 suggests that if 1980 primary production totals 12.0 (10^9) pounds, 7.7 (10^9) pounds will require prebaked anodes and 4.3 (10^9) pounds will be produced in Soderberg installations. On the basis that production of one pound of aluminum requires slightly more than half a pound of carbon (0.52 pound), production of anodes can be placed at 4.0 (10^9) pounds. Using the data in Table 31-13A, Projection I, 1980 demand is derived and shown in Table 31-17.

(iii) **Smelting.** Gross energy demand for smelting primary aluminum in 1980 is derived using U.S. primary output of 12.0 (10^9) pounds and coefficients from Table 31-18.

Table 31-17.   Anode Baking, Demand for Energy and Fuel, 1980

	(h_{i2}^{1980}) (10^{12}) BTU	(f_{i2}^{1980}) Fuel Equivalent
Electricity	0.2	0.02 (10^9) kwh
Coal	–	–
Distillate oil	6.9	1.15 (10^6) bbl.
Residual oil	–	–
Gas	2.7	2.61 (10^9) cu. ft.
LP gas	*	*
Gasoline	–	–
Total	9.9	–

*Denotes less than 0.05 (10^{12}) BTU.
Sources: Table 31-13A and text.
For conversion factors, see Appendix.

Table 31-18.   Aluminum   Smelting,   Gross   Electricity   Demand, 1980

	Rate	Kwh Total (10^9)	Rate	BTU^a Total (10^{12})
Potlines	7.29	87.5	76,545	917.4
Ancillary	.61	7.3	6,433	77.2
Total	7.90	94.8	82,978	994.6

[a]See note [b] to Table 31-14.
Sources: Table 31-14 and text.

(iv) **Fabrication.** Energy demand for fabrication in 1980 is based on a projection of mill product shipments of 13.3 (10^9) pounds. (See section C.4., below.) Data are shown in Table 31-19.

Recovery of metal from secondary scrap is projected to reach 4.2 (10^9) pounds by 1980, or 26% of total metal from domestic sources compared with 21% in 1971. At a constant projected energy use rate of 6,000 BTU/lb., energy demand for this component totals 25.2 (10^{12}) BTU.

Given the data derived thus far, a first approximation of the 1980 data comparable to those in Table 31-7 can be derived and is shown in Table 31-20.

A second approximation is made below after adjustments necessary for captive electricity generation heat rates.

At this point, the analog of Table 31-8, the H^{1980} matrix, can be built. A preliminary step is required concerning captive electrical generation. We assume on the basis of information obtained in interviews that additional captive generating capacity will not be in operation by 1980. We further assume that captive generation will supply 17.0 (10^9) kwh from all sources in 1980, and that inputs of fuel will be 205.2 (10^{12}) BTU.[21] According to data in Table 31-18,

Table 31-19.   Fabrication, Demand for Energy and Fuel, 1980

	(e_{i4}^{1980}) BTU/lb.[a]	(h_{i4}^{1980}) BTU (10^{12})[b]	(f_{i4}^{1980}) Fuel Equivalent
Electricity	11,676	168.1	16.01 (10^9) kwh
Coal	1,245	17.9	.69 (10^6) short ton
Distillate oil . . .			
Residual oil	5,694	82.0	13.67 (10^6) bbl.
Gas	4,632	66.7	64.44 (10^9) cu. ft.
LP gas	892	12.8	139.13 (10^6) gal.
Gasoline	–	–	–
Total	24,125	347.4	–

[a]Data derived from application of distribution and change 1971-1980 shown in Table 31-15 to the 25,000 BTU/lb. fabricated product discussed in B.5.

[b]Based on projected shipments of domestic mill products of 14.4 (10^9) lbs. in 1980. For conversion factors, see Appendix.

Table 31-20.   Energy Use in U.S. Aluminum Production, 1980
Metal from Primary and Secondary Scrap Sources

	((10^{12}) BTU)				
	Alumina	Anode	Smelting	Scrap Reduction	Total
Primary metal	136.8	9.9	994.6	–	1,141.3
Secondary scrap recovery	–	–	–	25.2	25.2
Total U.S.	136.8	9.9	994.6	25.2	1,166.5
BTUs per lb. metal produced[a]					72,006

[a][1166.5/(12.0 + 4.2)].

this leaves 77.8 (10^9) kwh to be purchased in 1980 for smelting. Conversion to BTU at 10,500 BTU/kwh yields 816.9 (10^{12}) BTU for purchased electricity, and addition of 205.2 (10^{12}) BTU yields 1,022.1 (10^{12}) BTU, which revises the total shown in Table 31-18.

Using this and data from Tables 31-16—19, the H^{1980} matrix is constructed and shown in Table 31-21; Table 31-22 shows the E^{1980} matrix comparable with Table 31-9.

C.3. The 1980 Energy Matrix under Output Projection II

Use of Projection II of output has no effect on the energy projections shown in columns 1, 2, and 3 of Table 31-21. Since demand still exceeds U.S. capacity, primary metal output remains at 12.0 (10^9) pounds, alumina refining, anode baking, and smelting still require the same energy inputs. Fabrication output, however, declines from 14.4 to 13.1 (10^9) pounds and secondary scrap recovery declines from 4.2 to 3.7 (10^9) pounds. The change in mix between Projections I and II is assumed to have negligible effects on the BTU/unit usage in fabrication. The calculations are presented in Table 31-23. The change in scrap recovery causes the total of 1,166.5 (10^{12}) BTU shown in Table 31-20 to decline by 4.2 (10^{12}) to 1,162.3 (10^{12}) BTU.

Table 31-24 shows the results of Projection II assumptions in a form comparable with Projection I data in Table 31-21, and 1971 data in Table 31-9. Basically it shows that while demand in Projection II is 6.6% lower than in Projection I, total energy demand by the U.S. industry is 2.1% lower, with the bulk of the difference being "exported," i.e., with imports substantially lower, demand for power in foreign smelters would also be lower.

Table 31-25 shows the changes in fuel dependence of the aluminum industry between 1971 and our projections of 1980.

Electricity is still preponderant due to the basic electrolytic process of smelting. In fuels, the overwhelming importance of gas disappears and a somewhat more balanced structure appears. Demand for gas declines absolutely by some 12% in these projections. The major increase appears in oil with demand projected to rise from 600,000 to 22 million or 23 million barrels.

C.4. Projections of Demand for and Output of Aluminum

Projections of demand for aluminum were derived from the INFORUM model and adjusted to categories defined in the trade association data. Three major markets required special attention:

(1) Construction, due to innovation of aluminum framing for residential structures and its penetration into a market previously held by lumber and wood products. Our projections of the rate of penetration of aluminum contribute to shipments of the metal to construction markets growing

Table 31-21.   Aluminum, Estimated U.S. Industry, Matrix (H) of Sources and Uses of Energy, 1980 (data are (10^{12}) BTU except as noted)

	Alumina[a] Refining	Anode Baking	Smelting	Fabrication	Vehicles	Other	Total[a]	Percentage
Electricity	27.4	0.2	1,022.1	168.1	–	–	1,217.8	79.5%
Coal	–	–	–	17.9	–	–	17.9	1.2
All oil	49.2	6.9	–	82.0	0.2	0.2	138.5	9.0
Gas	60.2	2.7	–	66.7	*	3.1	132.7	8.7
LP gas	*	*	–	12.8	4.2	–	17.0	1.1
Gasoline	–	–	–	–	7.5	–	7.5	0.5
Total	136.8	9.9	1,022.1	347.4	11.9	3.5	1,531.4	–
Percentage	8.9	0.6	66.7	22.7	0.7	0.1	–	100.0

*Denotes less than 0.05 (10^{12}) BTU.

Sources: Tables 31-16–19; Table 31-9 coefficients for columns 5 and 6 multiplied by 1980 total U.S. metal output of 16.2 (10^9) lbs. Element $h_{1,3}$ adjusted from Table 31-18 according to text, above.

[a]The data shown in the column under Alumina Refining are based upon the assumption that increases in the production of alumina take place within the United States. If one wishes to use the alternative assumption that the refining of additional supplies of alumina takes place within the bauxite-producing countries, the total in column 1 of 136.8 is reduced to 73.0. Similarly, the total of the matrix is reduced from 1,531.4 to 1,427.0, a 4.8% decline.

Table 31-22. Aluminum, Estimated U.S. Industry, Matrix (E) of BTU/lb. Product Coefficients[a]

	Alumina Refining	Anode Baking	Smelting	Fabrication	Vehicles	Other	Total
Electricity ..	1,691	*	63,092	10,376	–	–	75,172
Coal.......	–	–	–	1,105	–	–	1,105
All oil......	3,037	426	–	5,061	*	*	8,549
Gas	3,716	167	–	4,117	–	191	8,191
LP gas	*	*	–	790	259	–	1,049
Gasoline ...	–	–	–	–	463	–	463
Total ...	8,444	611	63,092	21,444	7,346	216	94,531

*Negligible.

[a]This is the E^{1980} matrix (see list of definitions).

Note: Data are derived from the H^{1980} matrix shown in Table 31-21 by $E^{1980} = H^{1980} \ \lambda - 1^{1980}$ where $\lambda - 1$ is the average of 16.2 (10^9) lbs. This table should be compared with Table 31-9.

Table 31-23. Fabrication, Demand for Energy and Fuel, 1980 Projection II

	e_{i4}^{1980} BTU/lb[a]	h_{i4}^{1980} BTU (10^{12})[b]	f_{i4}^{1980} Fuel Equivalent
Electricity	11,676	152.9	14.56 (10^9) kwh
Coal	1,245	16.3	.63 (10^6) short ton
Distillate oil .....⎱ Residual oil......⎰	5,694	74.6	12.43 (10^6) bbl.
Gas	4,632	60.7	58.65 (10^9) cu. ft.
LP gas	892	11.7	127.17 (10^6) gal.
Gasoline	–	–	–
Total	24,125	316.0	–

[a]Data derived from application of distribution and change 1971-1980 shown in Table 31-15 to the 25,000 BTU/lb./fabricated product discussed in section B.5.

[b]Based on projected shipments of domestic mill products of 13.1 (10^9) lbs. in 1980. For conversion factors, see Appendix 2.

at about twice the rate of output of the construction industry (based on constant dollars).

(2) Auto and trucks, due to probable shifts (caused by EPA regulations) to smaller vehicles made of lighter materials, and probable increases in the price of gasoline. Table 31-26 shows the assumptions concerning aluminum use in vehicles and the concomitant demand for the metal.

(3) Container usage, due to the likelihood of legislation being passed against disposable containers, and innovations appearing in the glass industry that may erode the rate of penetration of aluminum into container markets held by other materials. Table 31-27 presents two projections. Projection I shows continued penetration at near historical rates. This projection is apparently

Table 31-24. Aluminum, Estimated U.S. Industry, Matrix (H) of Sources and Uses of Energy, 1980, Projection II (data are (10^{12}) BTU except as noted)

	Alumina Refining[a]	Anode Baking	Smelting	Fabrication	Vehicles	Other	Total	Percentage
Electricity	27.4	0.2	1,022.1	152.9	–	–	1,202.6	80.2%
Coal	–	–	–	16.3	–	–	16.3	1.1
All oil	49.2	6.9	–	74.6	0.2	0.2	131.1	8.7
Gas	60.2	2.7	–	60.7	*	3.1	126.7	8.4
LP gas	*	*	–	11.7	4.2	–	15.9	1.1
Gasoline	–	–	–	–	7.5	–	7.5	0.5
Total	136.8	9.9	1,022.1	316.0	11.9	3.5	1,500.0	–
Percentage	9.2	0.7	68.1	21.1	0.8	0.2	–	100

*Denotes less than 0.05 (10^{12}) BTU.

[a]The data shown in the column under Alumina Refining are based upon the assumption that increases in the production of Alumina take place within the United States. If one wishes to use the alternative assumption that the refining of additional supplies of alumina takes place within the bauxite producing countries, the total in column 1 of 136.8 is reduced to 73.0. Similarly the total of the matrix is reduced from 1,500.0 to 1,427.0, a 4.9% decline.

Sources: Tables 31-16 to 31-19; Table 31-9 coefficients for Columns 5 and 6 multiplied by 1980 total U.S. Metal output of 15.7 (10^9) lbs. Element $h_{1,3}$ adjusted from Table 31-18 according to text above.

Table 31-25. Aluminum, Demand for Fuels and Purchased Energy, 1971, 1980

	1971	1980		1971	1980		
	est.	*Proj. I*	*Proj. II*	*est.*	*Proj. I*	*Proj. II*	*Units*
Purchased electricity ..	60.6%	67.1%	67.5%	56.0	96.4	95.0	(10^9) kwh
Coal	7.2	5.3	5.3	2.8	3.1	3.0	(10^6) sh. tons
Oil	0.4	9.2	8.9	0.6	23.1	21.9	(10^6) bbl.
Gas	30.1	16.8	16.7	278.3	244.2	238.4	(10^9) cu. ft.
LP gas	1.0	1.1	1.1	10.4	18.4	17.3	(10^6) gal.
Gasoline	.5	.5	.5	0.9	1.3	1.3	(10^6) bbl.
	100.0	100.0	100.0				

Includes demand for fuels for electrical generation; excludes imputations for captive hydrogeneration.

Table 31-26. Aluminum, Demand Projections, Vehicles Usage, 1969, 1975, 1980, 1982

	lbs. Aluminum per thous. 1958 constant $ of Auto Production	Production of Autos (billion 1958 constant $[c])	Aluminum for Auto and Truck Usage (10⁹ lbs)
1969 ..	34.4[a]	$31.4	1.066[a]
1975 ..	37.0[b]	37.7	1.394
1980 ..	50.0[b]	44.4	2.220
1982 ..	57.0[b]	46.2	2.633

[a]Mean of the 1967-1971 usage.

[b]Based on information obtained from interviews and other sources on a per auto basis and adjusted to constant 1958 $ basis.

[c]Based on INFORUM, adjusted to 1958 base.

Sources: The Aluminum Association, *Aluminum Statistical Review 1971*, New York, p. 25; *Survey of Current Business,* National Income Accounts, Table 1.16; Maryland Interindustry Forecasting Model (INFORUM), data adjusted to 1958 constant dollar basis.

similar to those current within the aluminum industry. Projection II shows a significant reversal in the growth of the lbs. aluminum/constant dollar of metal can output, and a slower growth of total can output. Projection II shows the legislation having an initial impact at about 1975, and affecting aluminum shipments significantly by 1980.

The complete set of demand projections and their conversion to output (net inventory change is assumed to be zero in 1980) are shown for the 1971 base year and the projection terminal year, 1980, in Table 31-28.

Table 31-27.   Aluminum, Demand Projections, Container Usage, 1960-1971, 1975, 1980

	Shipments of Metal Cans (million 1969 constant $)		Aluminum Shipments to Containers & Packaging (10⁹ lbs.)		Col. 2/Col. 1 (lbs./1969 constant $)		Shipments of Can Stock & Foil (10⁹ lbs.)		Col. 4/Col. 1 (lbs./1969 constant $)	
1960	2,276		.321		.141		n.a.		—	
1961	2,398		.351		.146		n.a.		—	
1962	2,407		.379		.157		n.a.		—	
1963	2,323		.496		.213		n.a.		—	
1964	2,491		.574		.230		n.a.		—	
1965	2,584		.656		.254		n.a.		—	
1966	2,778		.740		.266		n.a.		—	
1967	2,802		.868		.310		.409		.146	
1968	3,095		1.026		.331		.515		.166	
1969	3,241		1.194		.368		.637		.195	
1970	3,385		1.467		.433		.878		.259	
1971	3,361		1.514		.450		.905		.269	
	Proj. I	Proj. II	Proj. I	Proj. II	Proj. I	Proj. II	Proj. I	Proj. II	Proj. I	Proj. II
1975	3,929	3,700	2,307	2.109	.587	.570	1.281	1.083	.326	.292
1980	4,646	3,970	3.971	2.700	.855	.680	2.216	.945	.477	.238
1982	4,908	4,050	4.785	2.892	.975	.714	2.622	.729	.534	.180

Sources: Col. 1, INFORUM. Col. 2, The Aluminum Association, *Aluminum Statistical Review 1971*, New York. Projection II, col. 1, and Projections I & II, cols. 3, 5; The Conference Board. See text for discussion of projections.

Table 31-28.   Aluminum, Demand Projections, 1969, 1975, 1980, 1982
(10⁹ lbs.)

	Actual	Projection I				Projection II			
	1969	1975	1980	1982	Growth Rate 1969-1980	1975	1980	1982	Growth Rate 1969-1980
Building and construction	2.375	3.331	4.948	5.483	6.9%	3.331	4.948	5.483	6.9%
Transportation	1.986	2.462	3.496	3.984	5.3	2.462	3.496	3.984	5.3
Autos and trucks	1.066	1.395	2.220	2.633	6.9	1.395	2.220	2.633	6.9
Other	.920	1.067	1.274	1.351	3.0	1.067	1.274	1.351	3.0
Consumer durables	1.062	1.298	1.670	1.791	4.2	1.298	1.670	1.791	4.2
Electrical	1.425	1.734	2.463	2.687	5.1	1.734	2.463	2.687	5.1
Machinery & equipment	.701	.845	1.091	1.182	4.1	.845	1.091	1.182	4.1
Containers & packaging	1.194	2.307	3.971	4.785		2.109	2.700	2.892	
Can stock	.637	1.281	2.216	2.622	12.0	1.083	.945	.729	3.4
Other	.557	1.026	1.755	2.163	11.0	1.026	1.755	2.163	11.0
All other	1.075	.800	.850	.850		.800	.850	.850	
Total domestic shipments	9.818	12.777	18.488	20.762	5.9	12.579	17.217	18.869	5.3
Exports	1.007	.500	.800	.800		.500	.800	.800	
Total shipments	10.825	13.277	19.288	21.562		13.079	18.017	19.669	
Domestic mill product shipments	7.666	n.c.	14.400	n.c.	5.9	n.c.	13.100	n.c.	4.9
Ingot shipments	3.051	n.c.	4.500	n.c.	3.6	n.c.	4.500	n.c.	3.6
Imported mill products	.132	n.c.	.400	n.c.	10.6	n.c.	.250	n.c.	6.0
Imported ingot	0.937	n.c.	2.700	n.c.	10.1	n.c.	1.050	n.c.	1.1
Secondary scrap recovery	2.300	n.c.	4.200	n.c.	5.6	n.c.	3.700	n.c.	4.4
Primary U.S. metal production	7.586	n.c.	12.000	n.c.	4.3	n.c.	12.000	n.c.	4.3
Total U.S. metal production	9.886	n.c.	16.200	n.c.	4.6	n.c.	15.700	n.c.	4.3

n.c.—not calculated.

D.   ENERGY PRICES

In the process of interviewing the aluminum firms, a series of questions relating to prices of energy were advanced. The purpose was to discover if there is any apparent price elasticity in demand for total energy. Answers to our questions consistently indicated that both short- and long-term elasticities approach zero. Primary among reasons for the lack of any elasticity was the fact that the relationship between outputs of aluminum and inputs of energy was apparently viewed by the respondents as being technically determined and virtually rigid. Overall expectations concerning price of energy appear to lie in the region of a 75% increase by 1980, implying energy price increasing at an annual average rate of 6.4% to 8.5%. Compared with general price increase expectations of 3.5% to 4.5%, these imply relative price increase rates of 2.9% to 4.0%, or relative price increase magnitudes of 29% to 42%. Considering that overall average use per unit of production is projected to decline by 3.8%, the relative price elasticities of −0.09 to −0.103 can be obtained.

Whether these expectations will be fulfilled is not without question. In general, we believe our survey responses on future expectations of energy use with respect to price have been very conservative. As energy prices increase relative to construction prices, the power requirements of the Hall process can be reduced from the current 8.0 kwh per pound down to as low as 6.5 kwh per pound. Moreover, accelerated development of new processes, such as the chloride process, may reduce new plant energy requirements to 4 or 5 kwh per pound.

With respect to cross elasticities among fuels, responses indicated that short-term price elasticity of demand for individual fuels relative to prices of other fuels and energy sources were virtually zero in all but a few instances where facilities were capable of switching among fuels. Even in these cases, however, reaction to change in relative prices of energy forms was slow due to apparent habit, and due to practices of contracting for fuel supplies. A long-term price elasticity of demand for individual fuels relative to prices of other fuels and energy does appear to exist. In 1947, natural gas was a minor fuel input, but by 1971 it had attained a dominant position. As far as can be determined, this rise to dominance was caused by the lower price per BTU of natural gas (caused primarily by the F.P.C.'s regulatory procedures), as well as by increasing availability and superior qualities of gas as a fuel vis-à-vis coal, oil, etc.

On the other hand, the significant changes projected in aluminum industry fuel use to 1980 (Table 31-25) do not result solely, or even primarily, from expectation of price increase. Expectation of shortages of interruptible supplies of gas appears to be the main reason that gas declines in proportion by half, and oil becomes a major energy source.

One consequence of these expectations of supply dislocation, both of gas and other fuels, has been the installation of equipment that can use two or more fuels alternatively. This trend is undoubtedly accelerating. As a

Table 31-29. **Aluminum, Expected Rates of Energy Price Change, 1971-1980**

	Annual Average Rate		
	Maximum	*Minimum*	*Average*
Purchased electricity	8.9%	4.7%[a]	7.9%
Coal	b	b	b
Oil	10.8	6.0	8.6
Gas	15.0	6.0	13.0
LP gas	c	c	c

[a]Regional variation affects electricity prices and expectations. Firms depending solely on Bonneville power expect a much lower increase than firms depending on utilities in other areas and T.V.A.

[b]Several firms have large coal holdings, thus no market price expectations are given.

[c]Only a few persons chose to reply to the queries on LPG, but those suggested that LPG prices would follow natural gas.

Sources: Interviews. Maximum and minimum are general averages of high and low responses with apocalyptic visions removed. Data are the result of subjective questions and an informal averaging procedure.

consequence, cross elasticities between fuels is sharply increased, since capital costs have been sunk.

Table 31-29 presents results of our exploration of aluminum companies expectations of energy prices.

Notes

[1] Time necessitated omitting the other firms, Anaconda, Conalco, Gulfcoast, Intalco, Noranda, National Southwire, Ormet, and Revere, which account for 26% of U.S. smelting capacity.

[2] Based on data supplied by firms in the industry. Excludes smelters brought into operation during 1971.

[3] For a brief description of the process, see Sterling Brubaker, *Trends in the World Aluminum Industry*, (Baltimore: The Johns Hopkins Press, 1967), Chaps. 4, 7, 8.

[4] Gross and net usage (α and β), may be defined on the basis of (1) as:

$$\alpha = \sum_{i=1}^{n} \sum_{j=1}^{m} f_{ij}$$

$$\beta = \sum_{i=2}^{n} \sum_{j=1}^{m} f_{ij} = \sum_{i=1}^{n} f_i - f_1$$

and on the basis of (2) as:

$$\beta = \sum_{i=1}^{n} \sum_{j=2}^{m} f_{ij} = \sum_{j=1}^{m} f'_j - f'_1$$

In terms of the F matrix, α and β are only conceptual measures since the rows are heterogeneous in definition. However, β is analogous to ϕ.

[5] The vector c may carry a conversion factor for electricity based on either the GEC or UE basis; see Chapter Thirty.

[6] Inclusion of purchased electricity on a UE basis would reduce the range to 2,470-2,583 BTU/lb. alumina produced.

[7] Based on a range of 0.56 to 0.68 lbs. of anode paste consumed per pound of metal produced.

[8] To be comprehensive, one may wish to include energy inherent in the materials used for anodes and cathodes in the smelting process. Ignoring the cathodes, consumption of which in the process is minor, and using Bureau of Mines conversion rates for petroleum pitch and coke, and anthracite, we estimate this magnitude at approximately 6,700 BTU per pound of aluminum metal produced.

[9] N.B., comparative use of these data with weight-based energy use figures for other materials in The Conference Board's study may not be valid, and should be avoided unless specific physical properties are accounted for and end uses are explicitly defined.

[10] Energy use in collection and transportation of scrap is not included. Note that the criterion being used here is energy only; not comparative cost as calculated by a corporation.

[11] Note that this percentage will rise as processing continues through until the final product is reached.

[12] The Aluminum Association, *Aluminum Statistical Review 1971*, New York, 1972, p. 29.

[13] One may wish to suggest that had this 2.1 (10^9) pounds come from primary production in 1971, the additional energy required would have totalled 192.3 (10^{12}) BTU, i.e., $[(2.1 \ (10^9) * 97,592) - 12.6 \ (10^{12})]$; the equivalent of 32.05 million bbl of fuel oil, or 18.3 (10^9) kwh.

[14] 778.7 (10^{12}) − 94.2 (10^{12}) = 684.5 (10^{12}) BTU; see Tables 31-6 and 31-7.

[15] Mill products shipments data from the Aluminum Association are described as having had intra-industry shipments removed, and are thus preferable to data collected in The Conference Board's sample.

[16] Data not given due to disclosure agreements.

[17] Based on the addition of gas usage in electrical generation to other uses, and information obtained in interviews.

[18] See section D.

[19] Data not given due to disclosure agreements.

[20] Data in Table 31-16 constitute the h and f measures: for Col. 1 $h_{il} = e_{il} \lambda_l$ and for Col. 2 $f_{il} = h_{il} c_i$.

[21] Derivation omitted due to disclosure agreements. Note; includes an inputation for hydro at Bureau of Mines 1971 equivalent heat rate of 10,583 BTU/kwh.

APPENDIXES

1. List of Definitions

d_{ijk} — use of the ith fuel in the jth process of production within the kth establishment during a given year, t.

$$D = [d_{ijk}]$$

$f_{ij} = \sum_{k=1}^{\ell} d_{ijk}$ — use of the ith fuel in the jth process of production within the firm having $k = 1, \ell$ establishments during t.

$$F = [f_{ij}].$$

c_i — conversion factor to convert the ith fuel to homogeneous units; kwh or BTU equivalent.

$H = [h_{ij}] = [f_{ij}*c_i]$ where h_{ij} is a homogeneous measure of fuel inputs such that the following may be derived:

$h_i = \sum_{j=1}^{m} h_{ij}$ — the row sum, or total use of the ith fuel in $j = 1,m$ processes during t.

$h_j = \sum_{i=1}^{n} h_{ij}$ — the column sum, or total use of $i = 1,n$ fuels in the jth process during t.

$\phi = \sum_{i=1}^{n} \sum_{j=1}^{m} h_{ij}$ — total use of all fuels in all processes during t.

λ — a scalar value of output of the firm, measured in physical units (eg. gross tonnages) or constant \$, during t.

$\epsilon = \phi/\lambda$ — gross energy/output ratios for all establishments in the firm during t.

$e_i = (h_i/\lambda)$ — energy-output ratios, by energy source, for all establishments during t.

$e_j = (h_j/\lambda)$ — energy-output ratios, by using process, for all establishments in the firm during t.

$E = [e_{ij}] = [h_{ij}/\lambda]$ — energy-output ratios by energy source, by using process, for all establishments in the firm during t.

2. Conversion Factors

Fuel-Energy	BTUs	Unit
Distillate fuel oil	5.825 mil.	42 gal. barrel
Residual fuel oil	6.287 mil.	42 gal. barrel
Petroleum coke	6.024 mil.	42 gal. barrel
Natural gas	1,035	cu. ft.
Propane	92,000	U.S. gallon
Anthracite	25.4 mil.	Short ton
Coal	25.8 mil.	Short ton
Electricity (gross energy)		
Utilities fossil fuel standard U.S. mean 1971	10,500	kwh
Hydro & nuclear heat equivalent	10,583	kwh
Electricity, (useful energy)	3,412	kwh

Table 31A-1. Purchased Fuels

All Alumina and Aluminum Operations

This table requests the basic fuel data. Please fill in as many years as possible.

		1971	1970	1969	1968	1967	1966	1965	1964	1963	1962
TOTAL COAL	thou. short tons										
	$ thous.										
DISTILLATE FUEL OIL	thou. 42 gal. bbls.										
	$ thous.										
RESIDUAL FUEL OIL	thou. 42 gal. bbls.										
	$ thous.										
GAS	million cu. feet										
	$ thous.										
OTHER a. Gasoline	thou. gals.										
	$ thous.										
b. L. P. Gas (specify—	$ thous.										
c. ———(specify—	$ thous.										
d. All other	$ thous.										
TOTAL EXPENDITURES ON ALL FUELS (exclude purchased electricity)	$ thous.										

Table 31A-1a.   Purchased Fuels

Alumina Refining only

		1971	1970	1969	1968	1967	1966	1965	1964	1963	1962
TOTAL COAL	thou. short tons										
	$ thous.										
DISTILLATE FUEL OIL	thou. 42 gal. bbls.										
	$ thous.										
RESIDUAL FUEL OIL	thou. 42 gal. bbls.										
	$ thous.										
GAS	million cu. feet										
	$ thous.										
OTHER a. Gasoline	thou. gals.										
	$ thous.										
b. L. P. Gas (specify—	$ thous.										
c. _____ (specify—	$ thous.										
d. All other	$ thous.										
TOTAL EXPENDITURES ON ALL FUELS (exclude purchased electricity)	$ thous.										

574

Table 31A-1b. Purchased Fuels

Aluminum Smelting only

		1971	1970	1969	1968	1967	1966	1965	1964	1963	1962
TOTAL COAL	thou. short tons										
	$ thous.										
DISTILLATE FUEL OIL	thou. 42 gal. bbls.										
	$ thous.										
RESIDUAL FUEL OIL	thou. 42 gal. bbls.										
	$ thous.										
GAS	million cu. feet										
	$ thous.										
OTHER a. Gasoline	thou. gals.										
	$ thous.										
b. L. P. Gas (specify—	$ thous.										
c. _____ (specify—	$ thous.										
d. All other	$ thous.										
TOTAL EXPENDITURES ON ALL FUELS (exclude purchased electricity)	$ thous.										

575

Table 31A-1c. Purchased Fuels

Aluminum Fabrication only

		1971	1970	1969	1968	1967	1966	1965	1964	1963	1962
TOTAL COAL	thou. short tons										
	$ thous.										
DISTILLATE FUEL OIL	thou. 42 gal. bbls.										
	$ thous.										
RESIDUAL FUEL OIL	thou. 42 gal. bbls.										
	$ thous.										
GAS	million cu. feet										
	$ thous.										
OTHER a. Gasoline	thou. gals.										
	$ thous.										
b. L. P. Gas (specify—	$ thous.										
c. _____ (specify—	$ thous.										
d. All other	$ thous.										
TOTAL EXPENDITURES ON ALL FUELS (exclude purchased electricity)	$ thous.										

576

Table 31A-2. Electricity—Purchased and Generated

This table requests the basic electricity input data.

The purposes are to: a. measure purchased electricity, b. determine the volume and source of generated electricity and c. to measure net usage of electricity. Please include electricity generated in alumina plants.

		1971	1970	1969	1968	1967	1966	1965	1964	1963	1962
PURCHASED ELECTRICITY	million KWh										
	$ thousands										
TOTAL GENERATED* ELECTRICITY	million KWh										
from HYDRO	million KWh										
from PURCHASED FUELS	million KWh										
from OTHER specify (_____)	million KWh										
TOTAL GENERATED PLUS PURCHASED	million KWh										
TOTAL SOLD	million KWh										
NET USAGE (Purchased + generated − sold)	million KWh										

*Excluding electricity generated in alumina plants.

Table 31A-3.   Electricity—Usage

This table requests data to be used in determining the proportions of electric energy used as inputs to the major industrial processes. We request that you make every possible effort to separate power inputs to smelting operations from power inputs to fabrication. While we realize that power inputs to rolling and drawing in integrated plants are unlikely to be representative of all producers of rolled and drawn products, we hope to be able to provide some indication of relative energy use from the data requested here.

		1971	1970	1969	1968	1967	1966	1965	1964	1963	1962
USAGE IN SMELTING (SIC. 3334)	Million KWh										
USAGE IN ANODE PRE-BAKING OPERATION	Million KWh										
USAGE IN FABRICATION (Rolling, Drawing, Extrusion, Etc.)	Million KWh										
ALL OTHER USAGE (Residual)	Million KWh										
TOTAL USAGE*	Million KWh										

*Data in this line should match those in last line of Table 2.

578

Table 31A-4a. Percentage Distribution of Fuels by Using Process   Year 1971

This table has been divided into a separate sheet for each year to make it more readable. Its purpose is to obtain data which will enable us to determine specific uses of various fuels, and will be one of our most important sources of information.

Data are requested in percentages, defined as: the percentage of total use of the fuel named in the row that is used as an input to the process named in the column. Rows should add across to 100%. If you prefer to enter physical unit data, please do so, but it is vital that the units of measure be entered—use the last column for tons, bbls, etc.

We would appreciate having figures for years 1971 and 1967 minimum, however, a full time series would enable us to avoid interpolating between these points, and would provide superior results.

PERCENTAGE USE OF THE FUEL NAMED IN THE ROW IN THE PROCESS NAMED IN THE COLUMN:

	GENERATING ELECTRICITY	ALUMINA REFINING	ANODE PREBAKING	HOLDING FURNACE	FABRICATION	VEHICLES	ALL OTHER	TOTAL USAGE
COAL								100%
GAS								100%
DISTILLATE OIL								100%
RESIDUAL OIL								100%
GASOLINE								100%
L. P. GAS*								100%
OTHER								100%

*Please note here the proportion of LP GAS which is a standby fuel in case of interruption of GAS _____ %.

Addendum: KWh generated as a by-product in alumina operations only _____ million.

580   Intensive Studies of Energy Use in Manufacturing Industries

Table 31A-4b.   Percentage Distribution of Fuels by Using Process   Year 1967

PERCENTAGE USE OF THE FUEL NAMED IN THE ROW IN THE PROCESS IN THE COLUMN:

	GENERATING ELECTRICITY	ALUMINA REFINING	ANODE PREBAKING	HOLDING FURNACE	FABRICATION	VEHICLES	ALL OTHER	TOTAL USAGE
COAL								100%
GAS								100%
DISTILLATE OIL								100%
RESIDUAL OIL								100%
GASOLINE								100%
L.P. GAS*								100%
OTHER								100%

*Please note here the proportion of LP GAS which is a standby fuel in case of interruption of GAS_____%.
Addendum: KWh generated as a by-product in alumina operations only_____ million.

Table 31A-5.   Outputs and Shipments

In this table, we request the basic output data. These data are vital to our study since virtually all analytical measures we derive must be based on a per unit of output convention.

		ALUMINUM PRODUCTION & SHIPMENTS									
	1971	1970	1969	1968	1967	1966	1965	1964	1963	1962	
PRIMARY ALUMINUM PRODUCTION IN U.S.											
OTHER INGOT RECEIPTS											
OTHER METAL RECEIPTS											
TOTAL METAL PRODUCED AND AVAILABLE											

FABRICATED PRODUCT
SHIPMENTS—TOTAL

    SIC 3353
    SIC 3354

    All other

FABRICATED PRODUCT EXPORTS

INGOT SHIPMENTS (U.S.)

INGOT EXPORTS

TOTAL SHIPMENTS

TOTAL NET SALES $ $ $ $ $ $ $ $
(millions of dollars)

ALUMINA*
PRODUCTION (thous. tons)

PREBAKED ANODES

PASTE FOR SODERBERG
ANODES

ANODE PRODUCTION**

*Please include all alumina whether destined for aluminum metal or other purposes.
**Please include all anode production regardless of whether prebakes are used, or sold.

Chapter Thirty-Two

Pulp, Paper, and Paperboard Mills—SIC 2611, 2621, 2631

Paul A. Parker

SECTION I.   INTRODUCTION AND SUMMARY

Introduction

This report is the second of two pilot studies of energy consumption in manufacturing industries. As in the other pilot study, Aluminum, it is based largely upon data collected directly from firms, combined with other sources of information. Its purpose is two-fold: to gain methodological insights for future studies, and to gain knowledge about the specific industry studied—the Pulp, Paper, and Paperboard industry.

The Paper and Allied Products industry group, SIC 26, is composed of four sectors, Pulp, Paper, Paperboard, and Converting Mills. The primary output of the industry is paper and paperboard; pulp may be considered an intermediate good, and converted products secondary manufactures.

The Conference Board survey examined pulp, paper, and paperboard mills only, as this covered the primary aspects of the industry. The American Paper Institute also limits its coverage to this area.

The definitions of the three industries in the 1972 Standard Industrial Classification are as follows:

Pulp Mills, SIC 2611, are establishments primarily engaged in manufacturing pulp from wood or from other materials such as rags, linters, waste paper, and straw. Pulp mills, combined with paper mills or paperboard mills, and not separately reported, are classified with the latter, respectively.

Paper Mills, SIC 2621, are establishments primarily engaged in manufacturing paper (except building paper—2661) from wood pulp and other fibers; they may also manufacture converted paper products.

Paperboard Mills, SIC 2631, are establishments primarily engaged in manufacturing paperboard, and they may also manufacture converted paperboard products.

Many of the firms surveyed also produce lumber and wood products. These operations are omitted from this analysis.

The basic production process may be summarized as follows. Paper-making starts with pulp wood. The original log is de-barked, with the bark frequently being collected and used as a fuel. In the past, a layer of wood was removed along with the bark. However, improved de-barking techniques have been developed that remove little or no wood. Further, techniques have been developed to remove the wood content from materials de-barked by the older methods, for use as a raw material in pulping. These factors are reducing the amount of energy that can be derived from de-barking by-products by reducing the amount of waste per log.

Next, the log is reduced to chips by a mechanical chipper using electric drive. In chemical pulping (75% of 1971 pulping output), the chips are mixed with chemicals and then cooked in a digester under controlled pressure, temperature, liquor composition, and time. After the pulp is cooked to remove the lignin components, the mixture undergoes a second state of processing wherein the liquor (chemical solution containing the lignin compounds) is removed, the condition of the cellulose fiber is developed, and the mixture is cleaned and in some cases bleached. The waste fluid, or "black" liquor, is a significant source of energy in pulp and paper. It should be noted, however, that the net energy gain is less than the inherent BTU content of the black liquor, as partial evaporation is required before use as a fuel. (There is yet another by-product used as fuel by the industry, namely, hogged wood. The definition of this term varies among firms. It can mean either purchased or self-generated wood waste.)

In mechanical pulping (25% of the 1971 pulping output), force instead of heat is used to obtain the necessary fiber state, either by grinding or explosive decompression (defibrating). Mechanical pulping wastes less raw material and potentially produces fewer effluent solids than the chemical processes. But chemical pulping produces a better grade of paper and is less energy intensive. In addition, it permits the recovery of chemicals for fuel use and re-use. For these latter reasons, chemical pulping is and will remain the favored method. (Semi-chemical pulping, about two-fifths of mechanical pulping, employs both mechanical and chemical action.)

Once pulp is produced, it may be moved to a paper machine in the case of an integrated mill, or may be dried and shipped in the case of a pure pulp mill. Drying is accomplished in most cases by steam.

In an integrated mill, the mixture of cellulose and water, with whatever additions the resulting paper requires, are passed through a "head box" onto a moving screen. Here, much of the water is drained off. In some mills, this hot (relatively clean, or "white") water is discarded, but there is a growing practice in the design of new mills to clean and re-use this water. The advantages are two-fold. (1) less heat is required to bring the water up to the necessary temperature in new liquor, and (2) discharge of hot water is substantially lowered, reducing thermal pollution. The thickened mixture (furnish) then goes into a long series of multiple rollers that press the fibers into a sheet and are heated to dry the product. Superheated steam is the source of heat in most cases, although radiant heating elements fueled by natural gas are not uncommon. In addition to steam or dry heat for drying, the paper machines require considerable energy input for electric drive.

Machinery to produce paper or paperboard is similar in basic operation; however, the thicker the product, the greater the energy required for drying, per unit of area.

Summary

The intent of this pilot study was to develop and test a methodology for intensive study of the patterns and trends of energy consumption in manufacturing industries. The hypothesized method was the construction of a series of matrices, one for energy-consumption data and one for output data. These would be used to calculate a matrix containing energy-output coefficients. The data would be collected through a mail survey, filled out by mill-level personnel.

Returns from the survey show the energy-product ratios of the sample mills decline with increasing mill size, except for a bulge in the 200-349.9 thousand tons group. This is because integrated mills, which have the highest energy-product ratios, are usually large (but not the largest). In effect, the energy-product ratio declines, jumps to a higher level for the large combined mills, then continues to decline with increasing mill size.

Integrated mills account for the major portion of industry energy consumption, 63.1% of the total; and production, 59.6% of the total. They have the highest energy-product ratios because their energy consumption for pulp production is included in their energy totals, while their pulp output is not included in final output tonnage figures. Much confusion arises from trying to study energy use in such complex product flows by means of a BTU per pound measure. In hindsight, a BTU per dollar of value added measure would have been much better.

Respondents to the survey predicted no major changes in the structure of the industry's energy consumption and production between 1971 and 1975. Moreover, they expected no significant decline in the energy-product ratio.

The prospect of continued rises in energy prices, however, would seem to dictate a substantial rate of decline in the energy-product ratio, in contrast with the expectations of the respondents. It is not clear whether the respondents failed to foresee the extent of these price rises, or whether they expected pollution-control requirements to negate possible energy savings. Nevertheless, it is most likely that energy price increases will be the dominant factor of the two in the industry through 1975.

On the basis of the survey findings and other sources, the following projections have been made. Final output, that is, paper and paperboard production, is expected to reach 58.894 million tons by 1975, and 72.346 million tons by 1980. This is an average annual growth rate of 4.2% from 1971 to 1980.

The energy-product ratio is expected to decline slowly at first, reaching 19,903 BTUs per pound by 1975, or a 2.0% annual decline from 1971 to 1975. From 1975 to 1980, a faster decline is expected, at a 4.0% average annual rate. The ratio should reach 16,228 BTUs per pound by 1980. This would result in a total energy consumption (captive plus purchased) by the industry of 2,354 trillion BTUs by 1975, and 2,348 trillion BTUs in 1980.

SECTION II.   METHODOLOGICAL CONSIDERATIONS

Data Collection
Because this industry is far less concentrated than aluminum, we had to sample a far larger number of firms; and we were able to develop face-to-face contact with only a much smaller proportion.

It was our good fortune to obtain the advice and assistance of the American Paper Institute (API), especially Dr. Ronald Slinn and Mr. Jeffrey Duke.

There are some 750 pulp, paper, paperboard, or integrated mills in the U.S. On the basis of capacity data available in Lockwood's Directory, we chose a random sample of 250 mills. We imposed the constraint that no one company would be asked to provide data for more than six of its mills. This constraint became effective in only two firms, and a total of three excess mills were removed from the sample.

A check indicated that the sample accounted for approximately one-third of U.S. capacity. In terms of whether the mills were pure pulp (i.e., engaged in the manufacture and sale of what the industry terms "market" pulp), pure paperboard, or integrated (including pulp, paper, or paperboard operations), pure pulp mills were slightly over-represented.

A sample questionnaire was designed with the assistance of the API. (See Appendix.)

The questionnaires were grouped according to the company owning the mills, and were sent to the president of each firm with a covering letter. Simultaneously, the API took our list of companies included in its membership and sent a letter urging them to cooperate.

Of the 250 questionnaires mailed out, 125 were returned with data. Of these, 28 had to be discarded for various reasons. The most important reason was that the respondent had given partial data and was unable, when contacted in a follow-up phone call, to provide more information. Another frequent reason was that mill data were anomalous, and contacts revealed that there was usually an obvious reason: for example, manufacture of other products was involved, and data could not be separated for pulp and paper. This left 8 pulp, 23 paper, 25 paperboard and 41 integrated mills in the sample.

The useable questionnaires accounted for about 20% of capacity and for 25.4% of 1971 output of paper and paperboard. It should be noted that while the total of 97 mills in the sample came to about 13% of the total number of mills in the industry, the sample mills accounted for roughly 20% of capacity and for 25% of 1971 output of paper and paperboard. This indicates that larger mills were over-represented in the useable survey returns. It should also be noted that 1971 was an adverse year for the industry, and one in which it experienced much unused capacity.

Many errors were found in the useable questionnaires. In some 25% of these returns, misplaced decimals appeared in the output data. In each return we checked output against capacity published in Lockwood's, and where errors appeared, we corrected them. Similar errors appeared in the fuel data with alarming frequency. To weed these out, we imposed a range of 100-50,000 BTU/lb. of output. Where the data fell outside this range we usually found that where thousands of barrels, (10^9) cu. feet, etc., should have been entered, barrels or (10^6) cu. feet, for example, had actually been entered. We had also asked for percentage changes in fuel and electricity use from 1971-1975, and for the physical amounts of fuel used in those years. In virtually half of the cases, the percentage change derived from the submitted physical data bore no relationship to the percentage figure that was entered. In such cases, we used the physical data and ignored the percentages.

While the questionnaire was relatively long, and did ask some complex questions, the poor quality of response was not confined to The Conference Board sample. Most respondents also sent copies of their 1967 and 1971 submissions to the Census Bureau. Roughly 20% of these appeared to carry significant errors and omissions.

The second phase of our plan was the interviewing, with an additional set of questions, of personnel at the divisional or corporate level in a limited number of firms. This involved broader queries, requiring more speculative answers, aimed generally at gathering expectations about the future. These interviews were primarily conducted with the firms in the industry that had demonstrated a high level of energy awareness. (See Appendix for Corporate Interview Questionnaire.)

Conceptual Findings

Before presenting the data compiled from the survey, a discussion of the methodology's strengths and weaknesses, as revealed by an analysis of the survey's end product, is in order.

The intent of the pilot studies was to develop and test a methodology for intensive study of the patterns and trends of energy consumption in narrowly defined manufacturing industries.

The method was the construction of a series of matrices, for each year examined, with the cells embodying detailed energy data. A set of matrices would be constructed for each year: one with the elements E_{ij}, defined as the total quantity of energy consumed from the ith fuel by the jth process in that year; and one with the elements Q_{ij}, defined as the total quantity of output derived from the ith fuel and the jth process in that year. A matrix of coefficients would then be estimated with the elements C_{ij}, defined as the energy used from the ith fuel in moving one unit of output through the jth process.

Change in the coefficients C_{ij} over time could be interpreted as changes in energy use arising from changes in technology, relative prices, company practices, etc. The study of the possible future trends in these factors could, in turn, be used to project the coefficient C_{ij}. This projected coefficient, when combined with projections of total output, would provide estimations of future energy consumption levels and patterns. These matrices are illustrated, in a very simplified manner, in Figure 32-1.

In Figure 32-1, energy E_{11} shows that 180 million BTUs were derived from coal for use in pulp processes. Production Q_{11} shows that three

(Hypothetical data)

Eij—Energy (million BTUs)

i \ j	1) Pulp Process	2) Paper Process	3) Paperboard Process
1 Coal	180	140	110
2 Oil	496	1,152	560
3 Gas	180	140	330

Qij—Production (short tons)

i \ j	1) Pulp Process	2) Paper Process	3) Paperboard Process
1 Coal	3	2	2
2 Oil	8	16	10
3 Gas	3	2	6

Cij—Coefficients (million BTUs per ton)

i \ j	1) Pulp Process	2) Paper Process	3) Paperboard Process
1 Coal	60	70	55
2 Oil	62	72	56
3 Gas	60	70	55

Figure 32-1. Illustrative Matrices for Integrated Mill.

short tons of pulp output was processed using coal as a fuel. Coefficient C_{11} shows that 60 million BTUs are consumed when coal is utilized to move one ton of output through pulp processing.

Further, the hypothesis was that the necessary historic data to construct such matrices could be obtained at the mill level by means of a mail survey. After initial study of the industry, it was found that a great number of fuels and production processes were in use. To provide complete understanding of the industry, extremely large matrices would have had to have been constructed. These would have had the following fuel rows (i subscripts): electricity, purchased steam, coal, distillate fuel oil, residual fuel oil, gas except liquid petroleum gas, liquid petroleum gas, gasoline, hogged wood and bark, spent liquors, other. And the following is but a partial listing of the necessary columns of processes (j subscripts): electric or steam generation; barking; groundwood, steamed, disc, defibrated, sulfite, soda, sulfate, or alkali pulping; screening; bleaching; engine, tub, or suface paper sizing; Fourdrinier or cylinder paper forming; water removal, finishing; etc. Energy and output data would have to be provided for every cell of this matrix by the mill personnel.

In addition, it was found that the paper industry is characterized by very complex flows of energy and product. (See Figures 32-2 and 32-3). To over-simplify somewhat, a pulp or paper mill feeds fuels, including coal, oil, gas, or such by-products as bark, wood waste, and spent liquors, into boilers to generate steam, some of which is passed through a turbine to generate electricity. The steam may then be recycled for use in paper drying or pulping. Because of such flows of captive and recycled energy, a proliferation of energy accounting methods among the mills exists, primarily in financial terms.

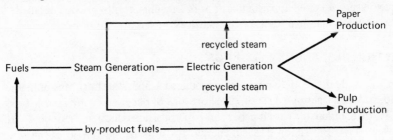

Figure 32-2. Energy Flows in Pulp and Paper Production.

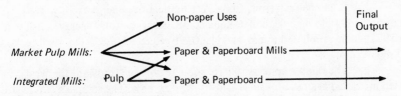

Figure 32-3. Product Flows in Pulp and Paper Production.

BTU accounting, which would greatly improve understanding of energy flows, is just beginning to be utilized by the industry. This method entails measuring in BTUs, and accounting for: (1) the total energy content of fuels entering the mill; (2) the amounts of energy fed into, consumed by, and passed on from every stage of production.

Output flows are only slightly less complex. Pulp production by integrated mills is an intermediate good. Market pulp is the output of its specific industry, but is also an intermediate good for the total paper industry. Yet energy consumed in pulp production is included in the respective industry totals. (It was later found that energy accounting among pulp, paper, or paperboard output in mills was not closely followed in general.) Therefore, integrated mills have higher energy consumption per ton than do non-integrated paper or paperboard mills, because of the former's inclusion of pulp-energy consumption. This complexity, arising from intermediate product flows, illustrated the weakness in using energy per unit of weight processed as a measure of energy use. In hindsight, energy used per dollar of value added would have been better.

Last, there are a great number of products in the industry—45 paper and 27 paperboard products are listed in the SIC codebook. Energy use varies significantly among the different types of paper.

Thus, the pilot studies were in a sense feasibility studies. For the paper industry, it was apparent that the amount of data needed to complete the maximum desirable matrices could not be provided. Therefore, to limit the questionnaire to a reasonable level, it was decided to concentrate on the energy matrix. All fuels were included in the questionnaire, and the processes were aggregated into their major categories. However, because of the errors in the survey responses cited above and lack of or unwillingness to provide detailed data, only the marginal totals of the matrices proved useful for analysis.

SECTION III.   SURVEY FINDINGS

In 1971, the sample mills produced 1,365,700 short tons of market pulp, and manufactured 12,680,700 short tons of paper and paperboard—or 25.4% of the industry's total paper and paperboard production. In doing so, they consumed 541.34 trillion BTUs of energy. The unweighted average of the energy product ratios of each of the individual plants came to 20,126 BTUs per pound.

It can be seen from Table 32-1 that captive energy from waste materials and pulping by-products equaled 38.3% of the total energy consumed in 1971, while purchased steam, and electricity equaled 17.3% and fossil fuels 44.4% of total.

The sample appears to have some regional bias toward the West, when measured against Bureau of Census regional data. The sample's coverage ratios (sample as a per cent of Census data) for paper and paperboard

Table 32-1.   Per Cent Distribution of Fuel Use, Sample Mills, 1971

	Converted Energy	*Fossil Fuels*	*Waste & By-products*
Purchased electricity	13.8%		
Purchased steam	3.5		
Coal		10.9%	
Distillate fuel oil		0.5	
Residual fuel oil		12.1	
Gas, except l.p.g.		19.4	
L.P.G.		1.8	
Hogged wood and bark			6.9%
Black liquors			31.4

Source: The Conference Board.

production from region to region are: Northeast, 25.0%; North Central, 28.2%; South, 27.5%; West 34.1%.

Integrated mills are concentrated in the South and West. As these include energy consumption for intermediate pulp production, their energy consumed per ton of final product is necessarily higher than non-integrated mills; and the South and West have correspondingly higher energy-product ratios. In addition, these and other mills in the South and West tend to be newer and larger, explaining these areas' higher share of output and energy consumption. A summary of regional data from the survey is shown in Table 32-2.

Expansion of the sample data to obtain an estimate of total energy use in 1971 was done on a regional, rather than on a national, basis. Mill size, mill type, and other characteristics tend to coalesce along regional lines, creating strong regional variations in the industry. This consideration looms important when it is recalled that large mills were over-represented in the useable survey returns and when it is noted that the West was over-represented. When the unweighted average energy-product ratios for each region are multiplied by total

Table 32-2.   Sample Mills Data, by Region, 1971

	Northeast	*North Central*	*South*	*West*
Production (thousand short tons) ...	2,188.5	2,586.5	6,891.8	2,379.7
Energy consumption (trillion BTUs)	50.40	93.96	294.45	102.53
Energy-product ratio ..... (BTU per lb.)	16,177	16,506	24,359	25,070

Note: Energy-product ratios are unweighted averages of the ratios for the establishments in each region.
Source: The Conference Board.

product on a regional basis, estimates of aggregate energy use by region are derived. Aggregate national energy use by the industry, obtained by summing the regional aggregates, was an estimated 2,156 trillion BTUs in 1971. The derivation and the regional totals are shown in Table 32-3.

As can be seen in Table 32-4, and as might be expected, market pulp, paper, and paperboard production, and energy consumption rise with mill size, except for the very largest mills of which there are only a few. The energy-product ratio, however, declines with increasing mill size, except for the 200-349.9 thousand tons group. This is because integrated mills, which have the highest energy-product ratios, are usually large. In effect, the energy-product ratio declines with the increasing size of non-integrated mills, jumps to a higher level for the large combined mills, and then resumes declining.

In the discussion of energy consumption by mill type, one should note that pulp mills producing "market pulp," SIC 2611, differ in energy use

Table 32-3.   Estimated Total Energy Consumption, by Region, 1971

	Northeast	*North Central*	*South*	*West*	*Total*
Industry production (thousand short tons)	8,754	9,188	25,028	6,988	49,958
Sample energy-product ratio (BTU per lb.)	16,177	16,506	24,359	25,070	a
Industry energy consumption (trillion BTUs)	283.2	303.3	1,219.3	350.4	2,156.2
Industry energy consumption (per cent of total) . . .	13.1%	14.1%	56.5%	16.3%	100.0%

[a]Not applicable
Sources: Bureau of the Census, *Current Industrial Reports,* M26A(71)-13; Table 32-2; The
Conference Board.

Table 32-4.   Sample Mill Data, by Mill Size, 1971

	Annual Output in Thousands of Tons				
	0-49.9	*50-99.9*	*100-199.9*	*200-349.9*	*350-999.9*
Production (1,000 short tons) . . .	691.7	1,316.0	3,306.7	4,504.9	4,227.1
Energy consumption (trillion BTUs)	26.86	51.52	110.36	221.64	130.95
Energy-product ratio (BTUs per lb.)	21,662	18,572	16,866	24,578	16,605

Note: Energy-product ratios are unweighted averages of the ratios for the establishments in
each size category.
Source: The Conference Board.

from integrated pulp mills, because market pulp must be dried. This difference is greatest in heat energy, with little difference being evident in electricity usage. For the market pulp mills, heat per pound of pulp produced lies in the range of 5,000 to 25,000 BTUs. The breadth of these ranges—a feature appearing throughout the study of pulp and paper—arises from a number of factors, each of which has wide variation: the age of capital equipment; the efficiency of furnaces and boilers; the type of wood used; the pulping process; and the grade of product. It is notable that these mills obtain 48.6% of their energy from wastes generated by the pulping process; and another 11.4% of their energy from hogged wood and bark.

Non-integrated paper and paperboard mills utilize virtually no waste products as an energy source. Most wastes having an energy content arise in the logging and pulping states of production. Non-integrated paper and board mills not only do not produce pulp, but also they tend to be market-located rather than resource-located. Unlike the pulp mills discussed above or the integrated mills discussed below, the paper and board mills in this sample show a much higher incidence of location in or near urban areas, and a much lower incidence of location in the timber-producing areas of the South or Northwest.

As can be seen in Table 32-5, integrated mills account for the major portion of the industry, 63.1% of the total energy consumption and 59.6% of total production among the sample mills. These mills produce more than one of the three SIC code products, but most are integrated with pulp production. Under SIC coding, these mills are grouped under their primary product. Because of their importance, they have been grouped separately here. As discussed above in Conceptual Findings, pulp production is an intermediate good for these mills. Because energy consumption for pulp production is included in these mills' total, and pulp tonnage is not, they have a much higher energy-product ratio than the non-integrated mills. It is known from other sources that these mills tend to be newer and larger and are usually located in the South or Northwest near their raw materials.

Table 32-5.   Sample Mill Data, by Mill Type, 1971

| | SIC code of product | | | |
	2611	*2621*	*2631*	*Integrated*
Production (1,000 short tons)	1,365.7	1,484.8	2,828.3	8,367.7
Energy consumption (trillion BTUs)	57.60	46.73	95.33	341.68
Energy-product ratio .... (BTUs per lb.)	18,802	18,873	13,916	24,875

Note: Energy-product ratios are unweighted averages of the ratios for the establishments in each SIC code category.

Source: The Conference Board.

It would be interesting to examine the relative energy intensiveness of pulp, paper, and paperboard production as it differs between integrated and nonintegrated mills. Unfortunately, the quality of responses did not allow a reliable breakdown of energy consumption data into the phases of integrated production.

The complexities of comparing energy use per unit of output between different types of mills are, perhaps, reflected in a comparison of energy-product ratios per pound and per dollar of value added. For example, Table 32-6 shows mills classified as SIC 2631 to be least energy-intensive on the poundage basis and most energy-intensive on the value-added basis. It is doubtful that the difference in years used as observations accounts for the substantial difference in pattern.

The mere measurement of total energy consumed by the industry presents problems. As a result, energy consumption for pulp, paper, and paperboard mills compiled by different sources differ (see Table 32-7); and reconciliation can be difficult because of problems in comparing definitions.

Our inspection of the census forms (MA. 100-1971) returned with the questionnaires revealed a large number of errors. The API sample, covering 85% of paper and paperboard capacity, was much larger than the Conference Board's. However, the API questionnaire was the simplest of the three. Although the Conference Board survey sought more disaggregated data, we accept the API measure of total energy consumption as the standard.

Finally, the questionnaire sought estimates by the mill respondents of 1975 levels of production and energy consumption. Their estimates contained serious contradictions and proved too unreliable to justify presentation.

Table 32-6.   Energy Intensiveness Indexes

	2611	*2621*	*2631*
Per lb. basis, 1971	100.0	100.4	74.0
Per value added basis, 1967	100.0	87.3	107.7

Sources: Bureau of the Census, The Conference Board.

Table 32-7.   Estimates of Total Energy Consumed by the Paper Industry, 1971

	American Paper Institute	*Bureau of the Census*	*The Conference Board*
Trillion BTUs (gross energy)	2,402	1,968	2,156

SECTION IV.   PROJECTIONS TO 1980

Paper is a basic material for the entire economy. It has held a constant share of GNP historically, so its growth has moved with the GNP growth rate. Paper industry output was projected using the INFORUM model and other sources. The result is an expected annual average growth rate of 4.2% from 1971 to 1980. This would result in a level of production of 58,894,000 short tons of paper and paperboard in 1975, and 72,346,000 short tons in 1980.

In recent years, environmental regulation has created a need to redesign or refurbish plant and equipment in the industry to prevent air and water pollution. In addition, the industry has had a large proportion of plant and equipment in need of replacement due to age or obsolescence. These needs have absorbed much of the available capital. Now a further need for repair and replacement, in order to realize energy savings, has been added.

Capital expenditures by the industry have been rising since the end of the 1969-1970 recession, from $1.18 billion in second quarter 1971 to $2.00 billion in the third quarter of 1973.[2] A large portion of these expenditures has gone for plant and equipment replacement or modernization, instead of for net additions:[3] 61% in 1971, 70% in 1972, 65% in 1973, with 70% expected through 1976. The effects of this replacement and modernization effort will begin to be fully felt by 1975. Therefore, from 1971 to 1975, the energy-product ratio will probably decline slowly at a 2.0% average annual rate, reaching 19,903 BTUs per pound by 1975. Thereafter, capital expenditures will probably be more oriented towards totally new plant and equipment that can be designed to effect greater energy savings than can renovations. A rising proportion of such new plant and equipment in the industry should cause the energy-product ratio to decline faster between 1975 and 1980, at a 4.0% average annual rate. The energy-product ratio would then reach 16,228 BTUs per pound by 1980.

Table 32-8.   Energy Utilization in the Paper Industry, 1971-1980

	1971	*1975*	*1980*
Paper and paperboard production (thousand short tons)	49,958	58,894	72,346
Energy consumption (trillion BTUs)	2,156	2,354	2,348
Energy-product ratio (BTUs per lb.)	21,578	19,903	16,228

Note: Output is projected to increase at an average annual rate of 4.2%. The energy-product ratio is projected to decline at an annual rate of 2.0% between 1971 and 1975, and 4.0% between 1975 and 1980. The energy-product ratio for 1971 is calculated by dividing total energy consumption by total production.

Sources: Bureau of the Census, INFORUM; Table 32-3; The Conference Board.

At the above levels for output and energy-product ratios, the industry is projected to consume a total (captive plus purchased) of 2,354 trillion BTUs of energy in 1975, and 2,348 trillion BTUs in 1980.

Notes

[1] Jeffrey M. Duke, *Patterns of Fuel and Energy Consumption in the U.S. Pulp and Paper Industry* (New York: American Paper Institute, 1973), Appendix I.

[2] Department of Commerce, Bureau of Economic Analysis.

[3] McGraw-Hill, 25th & 26th *Annual Survey of Business' Plans for New Plant and Equipment*, Table II.

SECTION V. APPENDIX

ENERGY DEMAND SURVEY: PULP & PAPER
Establishment Questionnaire

Company name _____

Establishment name _____

Location _____

Name & title of person completing this form _____

Questions may be directed to M. Elliott-Jones, The Conference Board, 845 Third Avenue, New York, N.Y. 10022. 212–759-0900. Please return by April 15th, 1973, at the latest.

1.A Please enclose with this form a copy of U.S. Bureau of the Census, Annual Survey of Manufactures, Form No. MA 100 for year 1971 that your plant submitted to Census during 1972.

1.B Please enclose a copy of U.S. Bureau of the Census, Census of Manufactures, MC form for the year 1967 that your plant submitted to Census during 1968.

1.C Please check the appropriate boxes below for *1971* operations.

The establishment produces:

Pulp SIC 261 .... ☐

Paper SIC 262 .... ☐

Board SIC 263 .... ☐

Converted products (other SIC 26) .... ☐

Primary pulping process (if applicable)

Dissolving Pulp .... ☐

Sulfite (paper grade) .... ☐

Sulfate (paper grade) .... ☐

Groundwood .... ☐

Semi-chemical .... ☐

Other .... ☐

(continued)

2. PURCHASED AND GENERATED POWER IN THE ESTABLISHMENT:

| | 1971 (actual) | | | | 1975 (expected) | | |
	PURCHASED	GENERATED fossil	hydro	TOTAL	PURCHASED	GENERATED fossil	hydro	TOTAL
		thousand KWh				thousand KWh		
ELECTRICITY								
		million lb hr				million lb hr		
STEAM								

3. PRODUCTION 1971 AND EXPECTED CHANGE 1971-1975 AND 1971-1980

Please indicate actual production in 1971. Also, please indicate future plans, plans under consideration, or expectations of output levels of the establishment; assume normal full-capacity operating level including additions for 1975 and 1980. For 1980, best estimates are acceptable. Please ignore changes in product mix unless a major change is contemplated — for example, from groundwood to semichemical pulping — in which case, divide the category into two parts and use the extra row.

| 1971 PRODUCTION | PRODUCT | PLANNED OR EXPECTED INCREASE (DECREASE) IN TONNAGE PRODUCTION* | |
		1971-1975	1971-1980
Thous. short tons		(Per Cent)	
	SIC 261 Pulp		
	SIC 262 Paper		
	SIC 263 Paperboard		
	Converted paper (Other SIC 26)		
	TOTAL OUTPUT ALL SIC 26		

*For example, if pulp output in 1975 is expected to be one third higher than in 1971, enter +33%. If one third lower, enter −33%. If the same, enter 0.0%.

4. ENERGY USAGE CHANGES AND CAUSES OF CHANGE—1971-1975

In question No. 3 you have indicated a 1971 output level, and expected growth of output to 1975. We would now like to explore the change in fuel use related to this growth. Please enter the percentage increase over 1971 to 1975 in total use of the fuel named in the row, which will be required to produce the growth in output shown in No. 3. We shall use fuel data from your 1971 MA 100 as a basis of this growth (see Question No. 1A). We are particularly interested in switching among energy sources. For each energy source presently used, or expected to be used in 1975, please indicate the principal cause (or causes) of increases or decreases, *relative to the growth of output*, expected in its use.

| Energy source | Expected change in use of the fuels named in the rows to produce the output shown in No. 3. Period 1971-1975 Increase / Decrease (Per Cent) | | CAUSES OF HIGHER OR LOWER GROWTH* Please indicate one or more with a √ mark | | | | | *If lower please enter the number of the fuel which will be used as a substitute** |
	Increase	Decrease	Shortage of the fuel	Price of the fuel	Plant & equipment Changes originating in Pollution abatement	Other modernization	Other (Specify)	
1. Electricity								
2. Steam								
3. Coal								
4. Distillate fuel oil								
5. Residual fuel oil								
6. Gas (except L.P.G.)								
7. L.P. Gas								
8. Gasoline								

(continued)

Energy source	Expected change in use of the fuels named in the rows to produce the output shown in No. 3. Period 1971-1975 (Per Cent)		CAUSES OF HIGHER OR LOWER GROWTH* Please indicate one or more with a √ mark		Plant & equipment Changes originating in			If lower please enter the number of the fuel which will be used as a substitute**
	Increase	Decrease	Shortage of the fuel	Price of the fuel	Pollution abatement	Other modernization	Other (Specify)	
9. Hogged wood fuel								
10. Other								
11. Bark, wood waste, etc.								
12. Spent liquors								
13. Other								

*Higher or lower than growth of output 1971-1975; see your entry for 1971-1975 in No. 3 bottom line. If the change in col. 1 is the *same* as in No. 3, no entry need appear under CAUSES.

**If lower due to fuel saving, where no substitute fuel use is expected, please enter the number 99.

Note: For definitions of fuels, see the Census of Manufactures form MA 100 for 1971 mentioned in 1A, page 1.

5. PATTERNS OF ENERGY USAGE—1971

Please indicate the use of fuel in the establishment during 1971 for the processes named. Process groups may be combined if necessary, but we would appreciate even "guesstimates" of the use by each process. Estimates based on rated horsepower of machinery are acceptable. Please avoid double counting in any one row. The total usage column should be consistent with data on your Census 1971 form MA 100 requested on p. 1.

| | | | Pulping | | Paper making | | All cranes | | | |
Energy Use Energy Source	Electric generation	Steam generation	Recovery furnace	Other	Paper	Paper-board	vehicles, etc.	All other	Total usage	Units
1. Electricity										Thousand KWh
2. Steam										Million lb hr
3. Coal										Thousand short tons
4. Distillate fuel oil										Thousand 42 gal. bbl.
5. Residual fuel oil										Thousand 42 gal. bbl.
6. Gas (except L.P.G.)										Billion cu. ft. (10^9)
7. L.P. Gas										Thousand gallons
8. Gasoline										Thousand 42 gal. bbl.
9. Hogged fuel										Thousand short tons
10. Other										
11. Bark, wood waste, etc.										Thousand short tons
12. Spent liquors										Thousand tons solids
13. Other										

Manufactured Purchased fuels

Note: If steam is used for paper and then reused for pulping, please indicate here: temperature at input to paper machinery _____ °C and at input to pulping _____ °C. If steam is also run through a turbine to generate electricity, please indicate temperature at turbine input _____ °C.

(continued)

6. PATTERNS OF ENERGY USAGE—PROSPECTIVE 1975.

If you expect changes in plant and equipment by 1975 which will change your fuel use patterns, please fill in the appropriate boxes of this Table.

The structure of this Table is identical to No. 5 but applies to 1975. If for example in 1971, 50% of your gas usage was for generating electricity and 50% for generating steam, and by 1975 you expect to have switched to purchasing all your electricity and will use gas only for steam, you would enter 100% of your expected 1975 gas usage in the 2nd column of the 6th row of this table. If you expect no change in your *pattern* of use of any one fuel (that is, the percentage distribution along a row as shown in Table 5) please write "SAME" in the corresponding row of this table.

Energy use Source	Electric generation	Steam generation	Pulping Recovery Furnace	Other	Paper making Paper	Paper board	All cranes vehicles, etc.	All other	Total usage	Units
1. Electricity										Thousand KWh
2. Steam										Million lb hr
3. Coal										Thousand short tons
4. Distillate fuel oil										Thousand 42 gal. bbl
5. Residual fuel oil										Thousand 42 gal. bbl
6. Gas (except L.P.G.)										Billion cu. ft. (10⁹)
7. L.P. Gas										Thousand gallons
8. Gasoline										Thousand 42 gal. bbl
9. Hogged wood fuel										Thousand short tons
10. Other										

11. Bark, wood
waste, etc.   Thousand short tons

12 Spent
liquors   Thousand tons solids

13. Other

Manufactured Purchased fuels

In the following please answer yes or no.

7. Do you now have _____ : do you expect _____ interruptable gas supplies? Does interruptable gas raise your operating costs _____ ?

8. Do you now have _____ ; do you expect _____ interruptable electricity supplies? Does interruptable electricity raise your operating costs _____ ?

ENERGY DEMAND SURVEY: PULP-PAPER
Corporate Questionnaire.

This questionnaire is designed to serve as a basis for our interview, as well as a vehicle for gathering information. We would appreciate your efforts in providing these data for your firm's pulp, paper, and paperboard operations (defined as SIC 261, 262, & 263). If you prefer, you may make separate copies of questions 2, 3, and 4 and present data for each of your mills; the added detail would be useful for our analysis. Please make every effort to provide data consistent with one another throughout the questionnaire.

If questions arise, please call collect: Michael F. Elliott-Jones, The Conference Board, 845 Third Avenue, New York, 10022. Phone 212 759-0900.

Company _____ Location _____

(continued)

1. PURCHASED FUEL PRICES: HISTORICAL & EXPECTED RATES OF CHANGE

Please indicate your firm's general expectations about rates of increase in fuel price. These may be based on formal studies, or on opinions generally held by management. Include increases that stem from all sources: market conditions, import prices, regulatory agency actions, etc.

Data on the rates of fuel price increase that you have experienced during the decade 1962-1971 would also be useful.

NOTE: In the last line, please fill in your expectations for the rate of increase in the overall price level. The 1962-1971 figure entered is the rate of change in the GNP deflator. If you use another indicator or basis, please note it below.

| | Average Annual Rate of Price Change (Percent) | | |
	Experienced 1962-1971	Expected or Anticipated 1971-1975 1975-1980	Fuels Not Used 1975-1980
1. Electricity			
2. Steam			
3. Coal			
4. Distillate fuel oil			
5. Residual oil			
6. Gas (except LPG)			
7. L P Gas			
8. Gasoline			
9. Hogged wood fuel			
10. Other			
General price level			

COMMENTS:

2. ENERGY USE PATTERNS AND SUPPLY CONDITIONS

In this question, we wish to explore patterns of fuel and power use in your pulp, paper, and paperboard operations. In col. A, please indicate the energy sources which your operations used in 1971. Please use cols. B and C to offer some idea of the changes you expect by 1975 and 1980. Col. D asks for purchase practices; cols. E through G ask for your 1971 experience with, and your expectations about interruptions and shortages. NOTE: Please interpret "interruption" and "shortage" as being conditions which have some effect on your cost of production, and/or scheduling of operations—for example, a slowdown in production; a shift to a standby fuel; etc.

Please avoid double counting in cols. A–C. Restrict information in ROWS 1 and 2 to *purchased* electricity and steam. If you generate your own steam, and/or electricity, see question 4, below.

IMPORTANT Please base percentage distribution down cols. A–C on some general physical measure such as BTUs, OR, barrels of fuel oil equivalents, etc. DO NOT BASE ON DOLLAR DATA BECAUSE PRICES DO NOT REFLECT ENERGY CONTENTS.

	ENERGY USAGE PATTERNS				*SUPPLY CONDITIONS*	
	Dependency on energy sources	Expected dependency on energy sources		Percentage of fuel bought under contract	Percentage subject to inter-ruption/shortage	Percentage likely to be subject to shortage or interruption
Fuel not used	*percentage of total energy requirements in*			*in*	*in*	*in*
( )	*(A) 1971*	*(B) 1975*	*(C) 1980*	*(D) 1971*	*(E) 1971*	*(F) 1975 (G) 1980*
1. Electricity						
2. Steam						
3. Coal						
4. Distillate oil						
5. Residual oil						

(continued)

	Fuel not used ( )	ENERGY USAGE PATTERNS			Percentage of fuel bought under contract in (D) 1971	SUPPLY CONDITIONS		
		Dependency on energy sources (A) 1971	Expected dependency on energy sources percentage of total energy requirements in (B) 1975	(C) 1980		Percentage subject to interruption/shortage in (E) 1971	Percentage likely to be subject to shortage or interruption in (F) 1975	(G) 1980
6. Gas (except LPG)								
7. L P Gas								
8. Gasoline								
9. Hogged wood fuel								
10. Other								
Total purchased								
11. Bark, wood waste, etc.								
12. Spent liquors								
Grand total		100%	100%	100%				

3. IMPACT OF MODERNIZATION AND ENVIRONMENTAL CONTROLS ON FUEL USAGE 1971-1980

This question explores changes in your pulp, paper, and paperboard capacity, and energy used per unit of output produced. Our purposes are best illustrated by an example.

Say for instance, you expect to have 10% of your 1980 pulping capacity in a new mill, and 60% in substantially modernized mills (30% expected to remain essentially unchanged). Enter 70% in col. (A) beside PULP. Continuing along the STEAM-HEAT row in the PULP sector of this question:

For illustration, say that in 1971, on the average throughout your mills; 20,000 BTUs were required in STEAM and HEAT to produce one pound of pulp. Enter 20 in col. (C). Say, further, that in the unchanged 30% of your capacity, you expect programs to economize on fuel use, and minor modifications to *reduce* this 20,000 BTUs input by 5% by the year 1980. Enter −5% in col. (D). (Note: Use minus sign for reduction.) On the other hand, economizing programs, plus major changes in modernized mills, and in the design of new mills may be expected to result in a net 10% reduction from the 1971 figure of 20,000 BTUs. Enter −10% in col. (E). Within the above changes, there may be *increases* in energy use caused by installation of evaporators, etc. (in the electricity rows, increases caused by fans, scrubbers, etc.) If you determine that in all pulp capacity, environmental programs will raise your energy use by, say, 1000 BTUs in STEAM and HEAT per pound of pulp produced, then enter +5% in col. (F). (Note: use plus sign for increases.)

A similar procedure should be followed for the ELECTRICITY row in PULP, and each row following.

Percentage of the firm's expected 1980 capacity classified as new or modernized compared with 1971 capacity (A)	Products	Energy use measure		Expected Percentage Change by 1980 in energy per unit produced by		
		Definition[1] (B)	Average 1971 (C)	Old capacity only, resulting from all causes (D)	New or modernized capacity, resulting from all causes (E)	All capacity, resulting specifically from environmental program causes (F)
	Pulp	thous BTUs in STEAM or HEAT per lb pulp produced				
		thous KWh in ELECTRICITY per lb pulp produced[2]				
		thous BTUs in STEAM or HEAT per lb paper & board produced				

(continued)

| Percentage of the firm's expected 1980 capacity classified as new or modernized compared with 1971 capacity (A) | Energy use measure | | Expected Percentage Change by 1980 in energy per unit produced by | | |
	Definition¹ (B)	Average 1971 (C)	Old capacity only, resulting from all causes (D)	New or modernized capacity, resulting from all causes (E)	All capacity, resulting specifically from environmental program causes (F)
Products					
Paper & Board	thous KWh in ELECTRICITY per lb paper & board produced				
Steam*	thous BTUs per lb of steam produced				
Electricity*	thous BTUs per KWh electricity produced				

* Internally generated steam and electricity only.

¹ Measure energy use on the basis of gross input. For example, electricity may be measured on the basis of the 10-11,000 BTUs required to generate a kilowat hour, OR, on the basis of the 3412 BTUs theoretically recoverable from a KWh. Please use the convention illustrated in the former. (This convention is that used by Bureau of Mines in "Gross Energy Consumption" data.)

² Include recovery furnace fuel here.